Human Accomplishment

Human Accomplishment

The Pursuit of Excellence
in the Arts and Sciences,
800 B.C. to 1950

CHARLES MURRAY

HarperCollins*Publishers*

FIRST EDITION

Design and composition by Robert Bull Design

Library of Congress Cataloging-in-Publication Data

Murray, Charles A.
Human accomplishment: the pursuit of excellence in the arts and sciences, 800 B.C.
to 1950 / Charles Murray.
p. cm.
Includes bibliographical references and index.
ISBN: 0-06-019247-X
1. Gifted persons—Case studies. 2. Genius—Case studies. 3. Civilization—History.
4. History—Psychological aspects. I. Title.

BF416.A1M87 2003   2003047820
908'.7'9—dc21

03 04 05 06 07 ❖ /RRD 10 9 8 7 6 5 4 3 2 1

To

Irwin Stelzer, Charles Krauthammer, and Harlan Crow

It turns out I had brothers after all

CONTENTS

Acknowledgments *ix*
A Note on Presentation *xiii*
Introduction *xv*

PART ONE
A Sense of Accomplishment 1

1. A Sense of Time 3
2. A Sense of Mystery 13
3. A Sense of Place 25
4. A Sense of Wonder 53

PART TWO
Identifying the People and Events That Matter 57

5. Excellence and Its Identification 59
6. The Lotka Curve 87
7. The People Who Matter I: Significant Figures 107
8. The People Who Matter II: The Giants 119
9. The Events That Matter I: Significant Events 155
10. The Events That Matter II: Meta-Inventions 209

PART THREE
Patterns and Trajectories 245

11. Coming to Terms with the Role of Modern Europe 247
12. . . . and of Dead White Males 265
13. Concentrations of European and American Accomplishment 295
14. Taking Population into Account: The Accomplishment Rate 309
15. Explanations I: Peace and Prosperity 331
16. Explanations II: Models, Elite Cities, and Freedom of Action 353
17. What's Left to Explain? 379

PART FOUR

On the Origins and Decline of Accomplishment   **383**

18. The Aristotelian Principle   385
19. Sources of Energy: Purpose and Autonomy   391
20. Sources of Content: The Organizing Structure
and Transcendental Goods   409
21. Is Accomplishment Declining?   427
22. Summation   449

APPENDICES   459

1. Statistics for People Who Are Sure They Can't Learn Statistics   461
2. Construction of the Inventories and the Eminence Index   475
3. Inventory Sources   491
4. Geographic and Population Data   505
5. The Roster of the Significant Figures   513

Notes   *589*
Bibliography   *625*
Index   *639*

ACKNOWLEDGMENTS

Human Accomplishment consumed my professional life from the fall of 1997 to the end of 2002, almost to the exclusion of the research on social policy that is my stock in trade. Christopher DeMuth, president of the American Enterprise Institute (AEI), where I am a fellow, gave me his unreserved support throughout this long project, as did my colleagues and the Institute's trustees. AEI is a wonderful home for intellectual inquiry.

In the literature on historiometric analysis of greatness and achievement, one name dominates: Dean Keith Simonton, whose works fill a shelf in my library. He generously shared his expertise with an outsider coming into his domain and provided invaluable guidance. If you want to know more about almost any topic in this book, go to the list of Simonton references in the bibliography.

At the outset of the project, Michael Novak predicted in his gentle way that I would find Christianity's role in Western human accomplishment to be pivotal. I privately doubted him (it seemed to me that the Greeks had set the stage without Christianity), but he opened my mind to possibilities that came to fruition in material you will find in Part 4—the most important, but only one, of Michael's many contributions to the book.

As I worked my way through the quantitative analyses in Part 3, I turned first to Douglas Hibbs, a friend since he was on my dissertation committee 30 years ago. Others who responded to my many requests for consultation on technical matters were AEI colleagues Kevin Hassett, Nicholas Eberstadt, John Lott, and Brent Mast, plus anonymous others who provided help at second-hand as my queries were circulated.

Christopher DeMuth, Richard Posner, and Joan Kennedy Taylor undertook the daunting task of reading the entire draft, providing strategic comments along with line-by-line editorial advice.

My topic required that I deal with disparate technical subjects. Kevin Grau, Miles Hoffman, and Roger Kimball were especially unstinting in their response to queries about issues involving the histories of science, music, and aesthetics respectively. I also gratefully acknowledge the review of many others who had expertises I lack: Munawar Anees, Eileen Blumenthal, Harlan Crow, John Derbyshire, Henry Harpending, Masaaki Harada, Gertrude Himmelfarb, Ralph Holloway, Irving Kristol, Charles Krauthammer, Marvin Kruger, James Lilley, Elizabeth Lurie, Richard McNally, Steven Reiss, Samuel Schulman, Irwin Stelzer, Scott Tanona, Steven and Kazuko Tripp, Arthur Waldron, Benjamin Wong, José Zalaquett, Kate Zhou, and others who prefer to remain anonymous.

The responsibility for mistakes that remain are mine, with this emphasis: Almost all of the people I just named did not see the full manuscript, but isolated pages of draft. None saw the final manuscript that went to press. That a name appears in the paragraphs above does not imply that person's seal of approval on anything.

I enjoy everything about the kind of research that *Human Accomplishment* entailed, so I did as much as I could myself. But there was too much to do alone, so I enlisted help along the way. Thanks go to AEI research assistants and interns who took on tasks at one time or another over the years: Hans Allhoff, Bion Bliss, Masaaki Harada, Daniel Mindus, Todd Ostroske, Sara Russo, Julian Sanchez, and Sharon Utz.

The publishing business with which I have interacted for almost 20 years has been filled all along with nothing but engaging, able people who had the best interest of each book at heart. Not every writer has this experience, I am told. That it has been mine is because my agent, Amanda Urban, has made it so. It is high time that I acknowledge how important she has been to my professional life. For this book, Amanda arranged matters so that I should have the pleasure of being edited by Hugh van Dusen, whom I didn't meet face-to-face for the first four years, after we had long since developed an epistolary friendship in the best Victorian tradition. In John Yohalem, I had a copy editor of formidable erudition who spotted obscure historical errors as fast as syntactical ones. Bob Bull coped with the book's many design challenges and its meddlesome author with equal measures of skill and patience.

Catherine Bly Cox is the other editor of *Human Accomplishment*, as she has been of everything I have published since 1982. I doubt whether there is a page of text in the book that has not been improved by her red pen. But she was also my wife throughout this most difficult project. Her role in getting me through it was of a kind for which thanks are both inadequate and superfluous.

Charles Murray
Burkittsville
3 August 2003

A NOTE ON PRESENTATION

Human Accomplishment uses several devices to organize an unwieldy body of material. Boxed text is scattered throughout the book for excursions that I think are worth including but can be skipped. Brackets around an endnote number indicate that the note contains additional detail. The appendices are reserved for full-scale discussion of methods and for the presentation of data too bulky to fit in the text.

I have adopted two conventions for labeling centuries and years to minimize the clutter in a text filled with dates. One is to refer to a century by its number followed by a capital C, so that, for example, *the eighteenth century* becomes *18C*. The second is to dispense with BC and AD or their more recent replacements BCE and CE. The putative year of Christ's birth has become the world's cross-cultural base year for a dating system, even in countries that still use another base year in their own calendars, so I will treat it as such and be done with it. Thus 300 AD becomes simply 300 and 300 BC becomes −300. One other convention involving dates should be kept in mind: A span of time designated (for example) "1400–1600" should be read as "1400 to the outset of 1600," not "1400 through 1600." Thus the two periods 1400–1600 and 1600–1800 do not overlap.

On matters involving alternative spellings of names, their order (e.g., "Leonardo da Vinci" or "da Vinci, Leonardo"), birth dates, death dates, or *fluorit* dates, I used the consensus version whenever one existed and otherwise followed the source I judged to be most authoritative.

Chinese names, places, and phrases are usually transliterated using the Pinyin system. For Chinese historical figures and places that are well known in the West by labels the Chinese themselves do not use, I have used the version least likely to cause confusion to Western readers—e.g., Confucius instead of Kongfuzi and Yangtze River instead of Chang Jiang River.

Regarding the thorny problem of singular third-person pronouns, I continue a quixotic campaign that is now 20 years old. My position is that constructions such as "his or her" are cumbersome and that restricting sentences to plural pronouns is silly. The reasonable solution is for the author, or the principal author, to use his or her sex as the basis for all third-person singular pronouns unless there is an obvious reason not to, and I hereafter hew to that principle in *Human Accomplishment*.

INTRODUCTION

At irregular times and in scattered settings, human beings have achieved great things. They have discovered truths about the workings of the physical world, invented wondrous devices, combined sounds and colors in ways that touch our deepest emotions, and arranged words in ways that illuminate the mysteries of the human condition. *Human Accomplishment* is about those great things, falling in the domains known as the arts and sciences, and the people who did them.

In choosing to focus on these categories of great things, I have in mind the metaphor of the résumé. What, I ask, can *Homo sapiens* brag about—not as individuals, but as a species? In keeping with the metaphor, I ignore the kinds of achievements that personal résumés ignore. Our job applications do not include much about whether we are caring individuals; so also, this book has nothing about whether we are a caring species. Military accomplishment is out—putting "Defeated Hitler" on the human résumé is too much like putting "Beat my drug habit" on a personal one. I also omit governance and commerce—mostly for technical reasons, but also remaining true to the metaphor. In their effect on the individual's freedom to pursue happiness, the creation of prosperous and free societies is the greatest of all achievements by humans on behalf of other humans. But as an accomplishment of the species, those achievements are akin to paying the rent and putting food on the table, freeing *Homo sapiens* to reach the heights within reach of the human mind and spirit—heights that are most visibly attained in the arts and sciences.

The first purpose of this book is to assemble and describe inventories of human accomplishment, a task that implies the book's first thesis: *the dimensions and content of human accomplishment can be apprehended as facts.* It is more than a matter of opinion that Rembrandt was a greater artist than, say, Edward Hopper, or Dante a greater poet than Carl Sandburg. The same is true at a higher level of aggregation: Assessing the comparative contributions of the Greeks and the Aztecs to human progress is not a choice between equally valid constructions of reality.

Apprehending the facts of human accomplishment does require judgment, which implies a corollary to the thesis. *Judgment is separable from opinion in matters of artistic and scientific excellence.* It is possible to distinguish the important from the trivial, the fine from the coarse, the credible from the meretricious, and the elegant from the vulgar. Doing so is not a simple matter, and no single observer is infallible, but a realm of objective knowledge about excellence exists. That knowledge can be tapped systematically and arranged as data that meet scientific standards of reliability and validity.

From this view of excellence in human endeavors flows the following claim: I have assembled inventories that contain the people and events most important to the story of human accomplishment in the arts and sciences from −800 to 1950. In Part 2, I will quickly amend that claim with qualifications and demurrers, but not ones that compromise its core meaning.

The bulk of the material in this book uses those inventories to describe who, what, when, and where. Who are the people that must be part of the story when historians set out to describe the history of the arts and sciences? Among those who must be part of the story, which ones are pivotal and why? How has human accomplishment been distributed across the centuries? Around the world? Within Europe and the United States? What distinguishes great accomplishment from lesser achievements? Such questions are informed by many kinds of sources. Chronologies of events and biographical dictionaries provide the raw material for reconstructing the pageant of human accomplishment. Histories provide a linear account and analysis of how it has unfolded over time. The primary contribution of this book, I hope, will be to help see the pageant whole, making it possible to compare accomplishment across domains, eras, and geography.

In the latter chapters, I take up the question of *why*. What distinguishes the eras and places in which human accomplishment has flourished from those eras and places where it has languished? In Part 3, I explore the mechanics of the process. What are the roles of the basic economic, political, and demographic factors? To what extent are streams of accomplishment, once started, self-reinforcing? These questions lend themselves to quantitative analyses using well-established techniques. In Part 4, I ask what starts those streams of accomplishment in the first place—a harder question, with answers that are more exploratory. My short answer is that the human capital for great accomplishment and the underlying human attraction to excellence are always with us, but environments for eliciting great accomplishment are not. Some of the hallmarks of environments that foster and shape great accomplishment can be identified. In the final chapter, I use those hallmarks to assess the prospects for human accomplishment in our own time.

TWO TOPICS THAT ARE NOT PART OF THE BOOK

Let me specify two topics that could easily be part of an account of human accomplishment but that are not part of this one.

Human Accomplishment is not about why civilizations rise and fall. Over the years, distinguished scholars in a line from Oswald Spengler through Arnold Toynbee to Jared Diamond have set out to explain why some parts of the world never developed advanced civilizations, why classical China was unable to adapt to modernity while classical Japan could, or why the West rose to worldwide dominance in the middle of the second millennium. These are important questions, and some of the material in this book informs them, but they are not the ones I ask. Sometimes the trajectory of a civilization tracks with its accomplishments in the arts and sciences; sometimes it does not. In this book, I want to describe the ways in which the characteristics of civilizations help us to understand their accomplishments, not why those civilizations came about or why they declined.

Human Accomplishment is not about the psychological nature of genius and creativity. This topic too has been the subject of a large literature adorned by the recent work of scholars such as Mihaly Csikszentmihalyi, Howard Gardner, and Dean Simonton, to name three from whom I have benefited. In this book I focus on how the realization of genius and creative potential has varied across times and places.

It should be clear by now that I am engaged in an enterprise that begins with a certain view of the world—a subtext, as it is called these days. Now is a good time to declare that subtext explicitly.

To celebrate human accomplishment is to embrace a heroic view of mankind and its destiny. I am joining with the view expressed once in these words:

> What varieties has man found out in buildings, attires, husbandry, navigation, sculpture, and painting! . . . What millions of inventions has he [in] arms, engines, stratagems, and the like! What thousands of medicines for the health, . . . of eloquent phrases to delight, of verses for pleasure, of musical inventions and instruments! . . . How large is the capacity of man, if we should dwell upon particulars!

My ally here is not some Victorian triumphalist talking about the glories of the Industrial Revolution, but Augustine of Hippo, writing in *City of God* in the first decades of 5C as the Roman Empire was collapsing. His enthusiasm prefigures the Idea of Progress that during the Enlightenment became the linchpin of intellectual discourse about history: Societies and technologies are not just changing, but changing for the better.

From the outset of the Enlightenment until 1914, that view accumulated so much evidence that the idea of progress seemed self evident. Mankind seemed to be progressing not just economically and technologically, but as a civilized and moral species. World War I shattered that assumption. Then came the Hitlerian, Stalinist, and Maoist atrocities over the next fifty years, making many wonder whether mankind might actually be degenerating.

The disillusionment following the World Wars has since given rise to a broader intellectual rejection of the idea of progress. The idea of the Noble Savage, another fancy of the Enlightenment, has reemerged in our own time. It has become fashionable to decry modern technology. Multiculturalism, as that word is now understood, urges us to accept all cultures as equally praiseworthy. Who is to say that the achievements of Europe, China, India, Japan, or Arabia are "better" than those of Polynesia, Africa, or the Amazon? Embedded in this mindset is hostility to the idea that discriminating judgments are appropriate in assessing art and literature, or that hierarchies of value exist— hostility as well to the idea that objective truth exists.

The contrasting perspective of *Human Accomplishment*—an empirically appropriate perspective, I hope to persuade you—is this:

Humility is an appropriate starting point. We human beings are in many ways a sorry lot, prone to every manner of vanity and error. The human march forward has been filled with wrong turns, backsliding, and horrible crimes. But taken in its grand sweep, it has indeed been a march forward. On every dimension, the last half-dozen centuries in particular have brought sensational improvement which, with qualifications, continues to this day.

A useful way of thinking about this issue is to ask yourself a question: Can you think of any earlier moment in history in which you would prefer to live your life? One's initial reaction may be to answer yes. The thought of living in Renaissance Florence or Samuel Johnson's London or Paris in *La Belle Époque* is seductive. But then comes the catch: In whatever era you choose, your station in life will be determined by lottery, according to the distribution of well-being at that time—which means that in Renaissance Florence you are probably going to be poor, work hard at a menial job, and find an early grave. But I doubt whether I need go to such lengths to make the point. Let me ask the question another way: Would you be willing to live your life at any time before the invention of antibiotics?

When it comes to wondering whether the human race has progressed in matters of daily life, I admit that I have a hard time taking the negative seriously. I am happy to engage in discussion with those who accept that technology and affluence are a net plus, but who worry about their troubling side effects. Spare me, however, the sensitive souls who deplore technological advance and economic growth over their cell phones on their way to the airport. Do technology and economic growth create problems? Certainly. But as Maurice Chevalier said about the disadvantages of growing old, consider the alternative.

I will hedge my optimism when it comes to the arts, but only marginally. It is hard to make a case that the literature, art, and music of today come close to the best work of earlier ages, let alone signify progress. On the other hand, if you chose to live in Renaissance Florence you would not be able to enjoy Cézanne and Picasso. In Johnson's London, you would not be able to listen to Beethoven and Brahms. In *La Belle Époque*, you would not be able to read Joyce or Faulkner. To live in today's world is not only to have access to all the best that has come before, but also to have a breadth and ease of access that is incomparably greater than that enjoyed even by our parents, let alone earlier generations. And if what passes for high culture in today's world seems sterile and self-indulgent, have you noticed the extraordinary level of talent reflected in the products of today's popular culture? I believe that the potential for the creation of great art is out there in abundance.

Driving this optimism about both the arts and the sciences is my faith in human impulses that I believe are so embedded in the makeup of *Homo sapiens* that no historical circumstances can permanently deflect them. Some of these aspects of human nature, discussed in Part 4, are more arguable than others. But as we embark, let me propose two that I think almost everyone can agree upon, impulses so broad and so deep that one or the other seems to embrace almost every specific accomplishment.

The first is the abiding impulse of human beings to understand, to seek out the inner truth of things. We never succeed all at once, and often the increments are so small and so infrequent that even the appearance of progress is hard to detect. But, as individuals, we are able to discover many small truths. As a species, as time goes on, we begin to converge on Truth in some of its large and final forms.

The other impulse is *Homo sapiens'* abiding attraction to beauty. Some of the earliest artifacts of the species evince the impulse to create something that has no purpose but to be pleasing to the human eye or ear, to our sense of taste or touch, to our internal sense of what is beautiful. A lucky few of us are able to create beauty; all of us have some corner in our souls that yearns for it. Many of the most enduring human accomplishments have been, simply, things of beauty.

Truth and beauty. Keats heard the Grecian urn telling him that they are one and the same—

> *Beauty is truth, truth beauty—that is all*
> *Ye know on earth, and all ye need to know.*

Keats's romanticism still seems apt. I am struck by the number of scientists who come to the same equation, seeing in nature and the universe not only truths about how things work but also the beauty embedded in those truths. We needn't push the thought too far—some truths are unlovely, and some beauty has only the most tenuous relationship to any truth. But in the realm of human accomplishment, truth and beauty are foci: twin ends toward which the human spirit inclines. *Human Accomplishment* describes what we have achieved, provides some tools for thinking about how it has been done, and celebrates our continuing common quest.

PART ONE

A SENSE
OF
ACCOMPLISHMENT

T he goal of this book is to view the pageant of human accomplishment whole. Many of the chapters skip across centuries and countries. The discussion shifts from one science to another, from the sciences to the arts, from the arts to philosophy. The analysis is long on numbers and graphs about achievements that should be the stuff of tales told beside the fire. A sense of that stuff is essential if the numbers and graphs are to be kept in context, and conveying that sense is the purpose of Part 1.

Chapter 1 parses the span of time to be covered.

Chapter 2 sets the scene as we pick up the story in −800.

Chapter 3 describes three concrete but very different settings in which human accomplishment has unfolded.

Chapter 4 tries to evoke the wonder of the accomplishments that serve as observations and variables in the databases.

ONE

A SENSE OF TIME

Before human accomplishment could begin, we had first of all to become human. It took a long time. Bipedality came first, somewhere in the vicinity of five million years ago. After bipedality, about two and a half million years passed before the animal that walked on two legs learned to make crude tools. The taming of fire required another one and a half million years.

Even then, after these unimaginably long spans of time, the creature was still *Homo erectus*, of formidable talents compared to every other animal but not yet recognizably human. With his beetled visage and lumbering gait, *Homo erectus* did not look human. More to the point, he did not think like a human. *Homo erectus* had a cranial capacity averaging only two-thirds of ours, and his mind was inhumanly slow.

The animal that the paleo-anthropologists call *Homo sapiens* and that we identify as human appeared about 200,000 years ago.[1] It is sometime after that point that human accomplishment begins. But when? Shall we mark the beginning at the moment when a human first spoke a word? Drew an image? Sang a song? Choosing a precise moment is, of course, as subjective as trying to specify exactly when human beings stopped being *Homo erectus* and started being *Homo sapiens*. But if one were forced to mark the dawn of human accomplishment, the year −8000 has much to recommend it.

AS IT WAS IN THE BEGINNING

In its topography and climate, the world in −8000 was much the world we know today. The last major glaciation of the Pleistocene had been receding for centuries, and Europe was no snowier than it would be in modern times. The Rhine, Seine, and Danube already rolled past countryside that we would recognize today, and the Alps, though 10,000 years newer and a few meters less eroded, would have looked the same to our eyes. In the Americas, the southern tip of the remaining great glacier was already north of Lake Superior, and the geology of what would become the United States had been determined. Rockies and Appalachians, Mohave Desert and Mississippi valley and Manhattan Island—all would have looked familiar. A few landmarks were different then. The Sahara was verdant, and the white cliffs of Dover overlooked a river valley linking England with the European mainland. But a time traveler from 21C would have had to fly over the surface of the Earth for many days to discover these occasional surprises.

. Nor would a visitor from the future have been surprised by the flora and fauna. The forest on Manhattan was oak and elm and chestnut, inhabited by chipmunks and robins and crows. The world still contained a few lonely mastodons and saber-tooth tigers, but almost all of the animals you would have found were familiar, even if some were found in unaccustomed places— bison in Ohio, wolves in Germany, lions in Greece.

The most striking difference to a modern observer visiting −8000 would have been the scarcity of humans. People lived just about everywhere, from the farthest southern reaches of today's Chile to the Norse tundra, but they would have been hard to find, living in small and isolated bands. They had to be scattered, because the human animal is a carnivore by preference, and large carnivores surviving off the land require a large range—about 5,000 acres per person, in the case of carnivore *Homo sapiens*. Depending on local conditions, a band of just 25 hunter-gatherers could require more than a thousand square miles.[2] The world of −8000 probably supported fewer than 4 million human beings, roughly the population of contemporary Kentucky.[3]

What kind of people were they? In the important ways, just like us. That doesn't mean that people of −8000 perceived the world as we do, but the differences were caused by cultural and educational gulfs, not smaller brain size. All of us had our counterparts in the world of −8000—people as clever, handsome, aesthetically alert, and industrious as any of us, with senses of humor as witty or ribald.[4] Humans of −8000 were so like us that one of their infants raised in 21C would be indistinguishable from his playmates.

The humans of −8000 had already accomplished much. Fire had been not just tamed, but manipulated, adapted for uses ranging from lamps to the oxidation of pigments.[5] Stone tools were sophisticated, including finely crafted hammers and axes, and spears and arrows with razor edges. The technology for acquiring and working the materials for such objects had evolved remarkably by −8000. There is evidence of underground mining of chert, a quartz used for spearheads and arrowheads, as early as −35,000.

By −8000, humans already had fully developed languages, the most advanced of which expressed ideas and emotions with precision. A few of them apparently had begun to work fibers into textiles. They knew how to grind seeds to make flour. The first tentative efforts to work copper had already occurred. And the human spirit was manifesting itself. Burial of the dead, drawings, sculptures, the conscious use of color, concepts of gods and cosmic mysteries were all part of human cultures scattered around the earth in −8000.

These were large accomplishments, and already set *Homo sapiens* apart from other living creatures. And yet most of the world's population in −8000 lived a daily life that in its physical dimensions was only marginally different from that of the animals they hunted. Humans had learned to find shelter from the cold and wet, but nothing we would find much more comfortable than the dens used by other animals. They had tools for hunting and gathering, but food nonetheless had to be obtained continually, by tracking and killing game or by finding wild vegetables and fruits. It was not always an exhausting life. When food was plentiful, Paleolithic man actually had a considerable amount of leisure time. But the tiny surpluses humans accumulated by smoking or salting their meat were stopgaps for emergencies, not surcease from the endless quest to find enough to eat. Their weapons gave them only a fighting chance against their predators, not security. Humans could keep warm in cold weather, up to a point, but otherwise had to take the environment as they found it. Those lucky enough to survive the first year of life—about a quarter did not—were likely to be physically decrepit in their thirties and dead in their forties.

Most of the accomplishments I have listed were not new as of −8000. The emergence of *Homo sapiens* in his present form, using fire and shelters and spoken language and simple tools, is dated to somewhere around −40,000, which amounts to a distance from −8000 three times as great as our own distance from −8000. And yet if we were to be whisked from our vantage point in −8000 back to −40,000 and the only thing we had to go on was the state of the human beings we observed, anyone but a sophisticated student of prehistoric life would have a difficult time telling one of those years from another.

The year −8000 is our point of reference because it is at about that time, in one particular part of the world, that these generalizations about primitivism and stasis start to break down.[6] As I write, the first place this break is known to have occurred lies in today's Near East, a few hundred miles south of Ankara.[7] In the ensuing Neolithic period, goats and dogs were domesticated, a radical step forward. Shelters became sturdier and more spacious, built of sun-dried mud brick. Embryonic forms of accounting emerged, in which things were not only counted but also recorded. Why? Apparently because some form of commerce had come into being. Religious observances became more elaborate, requiring temples and paraphernalia.

IN TECHNICAL TERMS

The year I have chosen to illustrate the beginning of human accomplishment, −8000, is the accepted beginning of the Neolithic period in the Middle East. The pre-agricultural world I have been describing is a combination of Upper Paleolithic (40,000 to 10,500 years ago) and Mesolithic, a period which began 10,500 years ago and persisted in parts of the Eurasian continent until as late as −3000.[8]

Above all, it is around −8000 when something truly revolutionary occurred: People began to understand that the seeds of food plants could be collected and then deliberately put into the ground at a selected place. The plants could be tended and eventually harvested. Not only could the produce be eaten, some could be preserved and thereby accumulated. Animals could be kept in one place, bred, and used as a continually available source of meat and milk.

Not all of the consequences of this revolution were good. Agriculture can require more labor than hunting and gathering—leisure time probably decreased for the average male who was now an agriculturalist rather than a hunter. Evidence from prehistoric skeletons suggests that life expectancy may also have decreased after the introduction of agriculture. Domesticated animals brought with them diseases such as beriberi, rickets, diphtheria, and perhaps leprosy. Milk alone can transmit some 30 distinct diseases. Nor did the Neolithic revolution trigger anything resembling a sudden surge in progress. It took two more millennia before the barest beginnings of a genuine civilization can be discerned. Vast areas of the world did not participate in even this much progress for still more millennia.

But despite the problems and despite the glacial pace of change, a decisive turning point was reached in −8000. Agriculture requires that humans cease being nomads and put down roots in one place. The tasks of harvesting and storing food spur technological innovation. Riverine agriculture, the only option in the arid lands where the Neolithic revolution began, requires irrigation. Irrigation requires technological innovation and complex forms of social organization. Most of all: To control the food supply is to free up human resources for other activities. Specialization of labor expands, and with it new opportunities for mankind to explore its potential. The beginning of agriculture in about −8000 opens the way for all the rest of human accomplishment, the topic of this book.

DEMARCATING 10,000 YEARS

The chapters to come will deal primarily with the last 2,800 years of human history, with successively more detailed attention given to the last 1,000 years and then to the last 600. The differences in the density of accomplishment over time warrant this treatment, but it also introduces a distortion. Just as Saul Steinberg's famous map of America for *The New Yorker* equated the distance from the East River to the Hudson with the distance from the Hudson to Los Angeles, it is easy when looking back to lump everything beyond a few centuries into an undifferentiated *long ago*. It is better if we can avoid that distortion, for part of understanding the story of human accomplishment is understanding its context, and an important dimension of that context is time.

The first task then is to try to acquire a sense of time: to grasp the *how long* that separates the actors and events in the pageant from one another—Aristotle from Newton, Newton from Einstein, the first tunnel under the Euphrates from the first tunnel under the Thames. If we continue to take −8000 as a rough starting point, we have a span of 10,000 years to hold in our heads. The measuring rod I will use for this exercise is a four-century packet of time that I hereby designate a *unit*, and the device for making a unit meaningful will be the events that fill it.

By "events that fill it" I mean a counterpart to the landmarks on a map that enable us to maintain an intuitive grasp of geographic distance, or at least earth-size distances. You may not know the mileage from Shanghai to New York or even from London to Paris, may never have traversed those routes, but built into the experience of most of us is a sense of *how far* those distances are. We have that sense because we have grown up with a visual image of the globe, and the space on that globe is filled in our mind's eye with the continents and oceans that give a context to *how far*.

To understand how long ago something occurred requires us to fill time with events, just as the globe is filled with oceans and continents. In our own lives, this is easy. We may say that time has flown, that 20 years seem to have passed by in an instant, but we are easily able to set straight our internal sense of how long ago something occurred by thinking about intervening events. Time in one's own life is kept from collapsing into an undifferentiated lump by the events that fill it.

We use the same technique to keep a sense of time about modern history. It is commonplace for older adults to have an intuitive sense of how long ago events throughout 20C occurred—our memory fills 20C with events. How long ago was the Korean War? The year was 1950, but it is not simple subtraction of 1950 from the current year that tells us how long ago it was. An American of a certain age is likely to recall Eisenhower's election, then perhaps Sputnik, or Nikita Khrushchev banging his shoe on the table at the UN. Then follow the assassination of John F. Kennedy, the Vietnam War, the first lunar landing, Watergate, the Iran hostage crisis, the Gulf War, and 11 September 2001, all filling up the space between 1950 and today and thereby configuring our sense of how long ago the Korean War occurred.

The First Unit. As we move back even just 100 years from 20C to 19C, distortions begin to set in. The period from, say, 1812 to the Civil War is an undifferentiated lump for many Americans who don't enjoy history. But two centuries is still manageable, because most people can use a sense of their own national history to grasp how long it was. If one isn't able to think of exactly what happened from 1812 to 1861, most Americans are nonetheless likely to know in at least a vague sort of way that the nation expanded westward and engaged in a debate over slavery.

Move back another 200 years from 1800 to 1600. As of 1600, American history hasn't really begun. The only resident Europeans north of Mexico are a handful of Spanish in Florida and a handful of French fur traders on the St. Lawrence River. In Rome, the Renaissance has drawn to a close. Elizabeth I is on the English throne. *Julius Caesar* and *As You Like It* are the current attractions at the newly opened Globe Theatre.

Already, it is hard to hold a sense of elapsed years in one's head—the two centuries from 1600 to 1800 seem blurrier than the two centuries from 1800 to 2000. For many of us, naming even a dozen events that occurred between 1600 and 1800 requires some thought. But we are still not completely bereft of anchor points. Louis XIV, Charles II, Cromwell, the Restoration, Frederick the Great, Isaac Newton, Peter the Great, the settlement of the American colonies, the Revolutions in America and France—each of us will recall different specifics, but enough big events loom through the mist to give some sense of the length of 1600 to 1800. It stretches most of us to the limit, but the combined four centuries from 1600 to 2000 thus remain a comprehensible period of time—the 400 years during which the world we know was mostly built. This constitutes the first unit, and with it we will measure our way back to −8000 and see if we can hold a sense of 10,000 years in our heads.

Two Units. Two units back from 2000, one unit back from Shakespeare, take us to 1200 and a Europe working its way free from the intellectual desolation of the Dark Ages. Venice is the commercial capital of a Europe that is being introduced to the mathematical concept of zero recently imported from the Arabs (who in turn had borrowed zero from the Indians). Siena and Oxford Universities have been founded in the last few decades. A campanile recently built in Pisa is tilting alarmingly. Halfway across the world, the Chinese are near the apogee of more than a thousand years of development, with a culture that makes Europe look primitive. In England, Richard the Lion-heart reigns and dies, and stories begin to be told about a man named Robin Hood.

Consider how our sense of time has already collapsed. Unless you really know your history, the England of Robin Hood is likely to be part of a generalized image of castles and kings jumbled into a picture of an old England that also includes Shakespeare. Yet as many years separate Richard the Lion-heart from Shakespeare as separate Shakespeare from us.

Three Units. One more unit takes us back to 800. Charlemagne is crowned head of the western Roman Empire on Christmas Day. Japan's seat of government has just been moved to Kyoto, where it will remain for almost 1,100 years. Within the last decade, the Norse have conducted their first raids on the British Isles, beginning a century of terror that will spread from the British Isles to parts of Northern and Eastern Europe. As many years separate the first Viking raids from Robin Hood as separate Shakespeare from us.

Four Units. Another unit takes us to the year 400 and a Roman Empire nearing its death throes. Among the other events attendant to the fall of the

Empire, Roman military forces are preparing to leave Britain. If medieval England is to many of us an undifferentiated lump of time, our loss of perspective on Roman Britain is far greater. Most of us remember that Britain was a sort of frontier outpost for the Romans. And yet, as the Roman legions evacuate Britain in 407, Britain has been ruled from Rome almost 150 years longer than today's United States has been in existence. Roman Britain as of 407 has ancient and prominent families, with lineages going back for a dozen generations—every generation of which spoke Latin. Some of them live in magnificent villas that are older in 407 than many of the venerable stately homes of today's Britain.

Five Units. One more unit brings us to the year one. Jesus of Nazareth is about seven years old, perhaps learning the rudiments of carpentry. It is less than half a century since Julius Caesar was assassinated. Virgil is only a few years dead and Ovid is alive, scandalizing Roman society with *Ars Amatoria.* China institutes formal civil service examinations as a requirement for holding public office.

Six Units. One unit back from the birth of Jesus takes us to −400. It marks a special point for the people of the West, the earliest moment from which we can yet see unbroken links reaching to our present day. In the year −400, Socrates still meets with his students in the Athenian *agora.* In a few centuries—mostly, in a few decades—immediately before and after −400, the city-state of Athens lays down the foundations of Western art, literature, music, philosophy, mathematics, medicine, and science.

Seven Units. If −400 is the frontier of the West's direct link with its past, −800 is its last outpost. Only three remnants of that world, albeit glorious ones, will still be an important part of our culture today: The *Iliad* and the *Odyssey* are already being recited, though they have yet to be written down, and parts of the Old Testament are already inscribed. With these exceptions, we are in an alien world as of −800. We are also in a world that is increasingly barren of remembered events. By −800, it is getting difficult even for a specialist to fill up the years with events, to talk with confidence about what happened in −600 versus −700.

Eight Units. Another unit takes us to −1200, where only a handful of landmarks can be discerned—and no wonder. The world of −1200 is as remote from the Roman Empire as we are from Charlemagne. The Trojan War occurs sometime around −1200, but it is fought between small Mediterranean fiefdoms, hardly more than glorified tribes. There are no topless towers of Ilium, just a small walled town on the Anatolian plain. The great civilization in −1200 is Egypt, which is in the middle of the sequence of pharaohs named Ramses—one of whom, Ramses II, is the pharaoh of Exodus.

We are only eight units back, but remembered events have by now all but ceased to exist. The Egyptologist knows the dates for the markers of a pharaoh's reign and can reconstruct some aspects of society, government, and the economy from the archaeological record, inscriptions, and the occasional papyrus, but when it comes to describing intellectual, artistic, and technological accomplishments, scholars are required to talk about fragments of evidence from which they try to infer the whole. We now use the word *circa* to describe a range sometimes measured in decades, even centuries.

Twelve Units. Recorded events are so sparse that I will forgo moving back just a single unit. Instead, we leapfrog back four more units—1,600 years, the length of time that separates us from the fall of Rome. This brings us to −2800. Egypt is the dominant civilization in −2800 as it was in −1200 (a breathtaking fact when one stops to think about it), but in −2800 it is a civilization in full flower, not in decay. In fact, Egypt in −2800 is on the verge of becoming technologically more advanced than the Egypt of four units hence.

It goes without saying that the intervening 1,600 years have been filled with events that we cannot recover. One of the first literary documents in the world's library comes from this era, a pharaoh's instructions to his son. That we have this papyrus is a freak of preservation, but it is a reminder that fathers are giving instructions to sons during these intervening 1,600 years, just as mothers are giving birth, marriages are being celebrated, and deaths are being mourned. Families rise to fortune, become a local aristocracy for generations, and then fall into obscurity—a cycle repeated many times over within those four units. Local heroes perform deeds so heroic that people sing their praises for centuries—deeds that, by −1200, have been forgotten for centuries. Individual humans experience life as intensely in those 16 centuries as we do. But if one asks after the events with which we can fill out our conception of those centuries, there is little to offer except the barest records of wars won and lost and dynasties rising and falling.

Twenty-five units. Only a few other way stations remain to guide us along the path back to −8000. Sumer got its start earlier than Egypt, although trying to assign a date to the time when Sumer stopped being a collection of villages and started being a civilization is difficult. Some take that point back as far as −6000, others put it 2,000 years later. Just knowing that the differences can be so great indicates how trackless the plain has become. So I will bring the exercise to an end. At our last outpost, we were at −2800.

Contemplate how far we had come from 2000 to −2800. Twelve units alto-gether—twelve times the distance that separates us from Shakespeare. Get as firm a grasp as you can on that 4,800-year package. Tack on 200 years. Then double it. *Double* that immense span of time—and we have arrived at −8000.

* * *

It is not possible to hold 10,000 years in one's head for long, but to have done it for even a few minutes will serve two useful purposes as we proceed.

Understanding that 10,000 years is actually a very long time is an anti-dote to the tendency to think of human civilization as a figurative nanosec-ond relative to the history of human evolution, the history of the earth, or the history of the universe. Those perspectives are valid for their purposes, but it is also true that we are part of a pageant that stretches back a very long time indeed in human terms, brief as it may be in the time scale of the cosmos.

Understanding how long 10,000 years really is also serves as an antidote to the all-eras-are-equal mindset. Just one unit out of the 25—a mere 400 years—got us back to Shakespeare. We of 21C are the beneficiaries of recent centuries that have been spectacularly unlike any others.

TWO

A SENSE OF MYSTERY

−8000 to −800

The rest of *Human Accomplishment* is restricted to events after −800, when the written historical record begins to match the archaeological record in sufficient detail to make a fine-grained reconstruction of the achievements possible. The purpose of this chapter is to give you the broad lay of the land during the preceding seven millennia.

The accumulated record leaves us with two contrasting states of affairs. If we confine ourselves to the end of the period, from around −1000 to −800, we are on reasonably secure ground. Archaeologists have reconstructed a picture of the state of human accomplishment as of −800 that still needs to be amended now and then (I will give you an example of one such amendment presently), but is unlikely to require a sweeping restatement. Alongside the secure story of −800 are some authentic mysteries about technology and knowledge in the millennia prior to −800 which, were they to be resolved, could radically change our understanding of human history.

ACCOMPLISHMENT AS OF −800

The table on page 15 condenses the accomplishments we know to have occurred at least somewhere in the world as of −800 or earlier. They are grouped under the three basic headings of science, art, and applied knowledge, the last of which embraces technology, medicine, commerce, and governance. Note that the table shows the highest level of known human accomplishment as of −800. Few of these accomplishments were known to more than a fraction of the human population at that time. Even something as elemental as the wheel was apparently known only on the Eurasian land mass and in North Africa. Agriculture had become sophisticated in parts of the Mediterranean and China, but elsewhere remained primitive or altogether unknown.

Much of the technology listed in the table on the facing page had been around for a few thousand years by the time of −800. Another area in which a high degree of sophistication had been achieved long before −800 was governance. The administrative systems used to rule Egypt and China had hallmarks of modern hierarchical, geographically extended, specialized bureaucracies. Legal codes were sophisticated, including distinctions between the civil and criminal realms.

Several of the categories have the word "indeterminate" in the line that is supposed to contain the leading accomplishments. For some of these, we have reason to believe that accomplishment was already substantial. This is especially true for the arts. We know that literature, music, and dance existed prior to −800, but can only estimate their level of development. The record is more extensive for visual art, but the surviving works antedating −800 are a fraction of the whole.

The absence of progress is most striking in the sciences. The ancients knew the movements of the stars and planets and they could perform complicated arithmetic, but, as far as we know, they had virtually no knowledge of chemistry, the earth sciences, or physics. What they thought they knew about the physiology of the human body was mostly wrong.

THE DECLINE OF ACCOMPLISHMENT

We of the West know that the state of human existence can go both ways, down as well as up, because we witnessed it in our own civilization. The Dark Ages following the fall of Rome saw Europe sink back to technologies that were far more primitive than those used during the preceding millennium. The philosophical and literary foundations of Western civilization were forgotten for centuries. Many works were lost irretrievably.

The same thing happened in the more distant past. The two greatest civilizations that predate −800, the Sumerian and Egyptian, passed their technological and artistic peaks long before our story begins, in about −1700 and −2300 respectively.[1] Among the other civilizations that predate −800, the Indic civilization reached its peak circa −2200, the Minoan circa −1500, the

THE STATE OF HUMAN ACCOMPLISHMENT AS OF –800

Practical Knowledge

Means of acquiring food Animal husbandry, a variety of grain and fruit crops, apiculture. The fishing net, plow, sickle, seed drill, hoe. Irrigation, paddy cultivation.

Measurement The scale, sundial, measures of length, calendar.

Information Alphabets, pictographic script, record-keeping, counting boards.

Construction Stone buildings, walled cities, monumental structures, the arch, water storage and distribution, drainage, city planning.

Tools The bow drill, windlass, composite bow, rope, simple pulley, abrasives, lens, mirror, knife, ax, saw, scissors, various weapons.

Materials Leather, glass, iron, copper, silver, zinc, lead, boron, tin, mercury, bronze, papyrus, pottery, linen, silk, cotton. The loom, knitting, smelting, metal casting, quarrying, mining.

Recreation Recreational hunting. Racing. Board games.

Controlled energy Coal, natural gas. Chimney furnace.

Appliances Sanitary facilities, fireplace, furniture, mirror, dishes, cooking utensils.

Transportation Canoes, rafts, framed boats, the sail, the anchor, pack animals. The highway, bridge, tunnel, canal. The sledge, cart, chariot, skis.

Medicine Opiates, herbal pharmaceuticals, basic surgery, medical training.

Governance Separation of secular from religious leadership, separation of military and civil powers, complex administrative systems, hierarchical structures, laws, sworn testimony, proportional punishment, redress for civil charges. Surveying, mapping.

Commerce Long-distance trading, sale of goods and services, money.

Production Specialization of labor, cottage industries.

The Sciences

Earth sciences Indeterminate.

Astronomy Systematic stellar and planetary observations, knowledge of solar and lunar cycles, obliquity of the ecliptic, first approximation of planetary movements, astronomically-based calendars.

Mathematics Numerals, positional notation, arithmetic, rudimentary algebra and geometry, mathematical permutations. Incomplete use of zero. First math textbook.

Biology Indeterminate.

Chemistry Introduction of the concept of elements.

Physics Indeterminate.

Philosophy & religion Monotheism. Codified moral precepts. Complex religious practices.

The Arts

Visual arts Sculpture, painting, mosaics, architecture.

Music Existed, but of indeterminate development.

Literature Epics. Poetry. Probably some form of drama.

Dance Existed, but of indeterminate development.

Decoration Pigments, red and blue dyes, jewelry, cosmetics, decorative clothing.

Hittite circa −1300, and the Syriac (the Levantine civilization encompassing the Phoenicians, Israelites, and Philistines) circa −1000.[2]

By −800, the Sumerian, Minoan, Hittite, Syriac, and Indic civilizations had either disappeared or no longer warranted the word *civilization*. The two Western civilizations still worthy of the name were in disorder and decay. Mesopotamia was temporarily ruled by the Assyrians, the latest victor in wars that had torn the region for centuries. In Egypt, the Libyans ruled over an empire that had fragmented into several parts, fending off a local Cushite state pushing into Upper Egypt. Technologically and artistically, Egypt was a shell of its former self. Of all the great civilizations, only the Chinese remained on an upward trajectory in −800.

The period from −8000 to −800 cannot be seen as a time in which human accomplishment slowly accumulated, reaching a critical mass that led to the subsequent takeoff. It is more accurately seen as a time of slow accumulation for the first 4,000 years, then a period in which great advances in human accomplishment took place at rates ranging from gradual (Sumer) to stunningly fast (Egypt), and then a downward slide everywhere but in China, which was still in an early stage of development. Or to put it another way, the world's leading technological, artistic, and economic societies in −800 were not nearly as advanced as Egypt had been 1,500 years earlier.

PUZZLES

The problem with the standard archaeological account of human accomplishment from −8000 to −800 is not that the picture is incomplete (which is inevitable), but that the data available to us leave so many puzzles.

The Antikythera Mechanism as a case in point. It postdates −800 by several centuries, but the lesson generalizes.[3] The Antikythera Mechanism is a bronze device about the size of a brick. It was recovered in 1901 from the wreck of a trading vessel that had sunk near the southern tip of Greece sometime around −65. Upon examination, archaeologists were startled to discover imprints of gears in the corroded metal. So began a half-century of speculation about what purpose the device might have served.

Finally, in 1959, science historian Derek de Solla Price figured it out: the Antikythera Mechanism was a mechanical device for calculating the positions of the sun and moon. A few years later, improvements in archaeological technology led to gamma radiographs of the Mechanism, revealing 22 gears in four layers, capable of simulating several major solar and lunar cycles, including the 19-year Metonic cycle that brings the phases of the moon back to the same calendar date. What made this latter feat especially astonishing was not just that the Mechanism could reproduce the 235 lunations[4] in the Metonic cycle, but that it used a differential gear to do so. Until then, it was thought that the differential gear had been invented in 1575.

I begin with the Antikythera Mechanism because it is at once so comprehensible and so rich in implications. The Mechanism itself is no more than a sophisticated mechanical device for replicating astronomical findings, but "no more" is already quite a lot. The existence of this one artifact tells us that a hitherto unsuspected technology existed as of −1C that may well have included many such mechanisms. But what might they have been? We have no idea. The Antikythera Mechanism is one of the rare examples of mechanical devices to survive—understandably, since mechanical devices made of metal will by their nature hardly ever survive the centuries.

Nor can we make judgments about how extensive the technology might have been based on the written record, for the written records that survive comprise the barest fragment of the corpus of work that existed. The great library at Alexandria burned within about 20 years of the time that the ship carrying the Antikythera Mechanism sank, destroying some 400,000 manuscripts, and its successor burned a few centuries thereafter.[5] How many engineering textbooks were among the 400,000 manuscripts destroyed in the first fire? The 200,000 manuscripts destroyed in the second fire? Again, we have no idea. We know only that the technology of the era was more extensive than the archaeological record can reconstruct.

This leaves us with two kinds of mystery about the peaks of human accomplishment prior to −800: the unexplained but explicable, and the potentially revolutionary.

Known Unknowns

Known unknowns is a phrase used by engineers to refer to aspects of a problem that remain unsolved but that don't require any new breakthroughs for their solution. The science is already understood. I use *known unknowns* to refer to accomplishments that unquestionably occurred prior to −800 but that require additional knowledge before we can explain exactly how they were done. For example, the lidless coffer believed to be Khufu's sarcophagus in the Great Pyramid is carved from one piece of granite. How does one go about hollow-ing out a block of granite seven and a half feet long and about three and a half feet wide and deep? Flinders Petrie, the famous Egyptologist and a founder of modern archaeology, determined that it was done with tubular blades used to drill a circular groove deep into the granite. The cores were then broken away and, core by core, the interior space was created. Because bronze is the only metal known to have been available to the Egyptians at that time (about −2500), Petrie reasoned that the blades must have been inset with jeweled cutting points—probably diamond, if they were to cut the unusually hard type of granite used in the sarcophagus.[6]

Petrie recovered some of these cores and was able to examine the spirals made by the cutting blade. "On the granite core No. 7," he wrote, "the spiral of the cut sinks one inch in the circumference of six inches, a rate of plough-ing out which is astonishing." Astonishing indeed. Granite core No. 7 was cut with a four-inch drill, which means that it had a circumference of about 13 inches. Petrie's wording implies that the drill was cutting an inch into the rock in roughly half a turn. Petrie inferred from his findings that somehow the Egyptians must have placed a load of "at least a ton or two" on the drills.[7]

Petrie's explanation is plausible given the artifact he saw before him, but to say that such a drill was used leaves us without any clear idea of how the Egyptians managed to do it—especially because, as Petrie himself noted, Egypt is not known to have possessed diamonds at that time. Nor have any examples of jeweled saws or drills survived. Egyptologist Mark Lehner argues that a copper drill could have done the job, with an abrasive slurry of water, gypsum, and quartz sand doing the actual cutting, but, he acknowledges, the Egyptians' ability to cut stone as hard as granite and basalt "remains one of the truly perplexing questions of pyramid-age masonry."[8] We know that the deed was done, but to do it required not just a single technical feat but an inte-grated body of technology in mining and the working of extremely hard minerals; the fabrication of drills that integrated different materials; and means of applying extremely high pressure to the drills. None of these accomplishments is specifically mentioned in the table of human accomplish-ment by −800 because they are all inferred. We have no direct information about the specific tools and techniques that were invented.

The most famous illustration of the known-unknowns problem is the Great Pyramid at Giza. It was built; there is no doubting that. But how? In asking that question, I am not raising any of the wild and wonderful theories that have been advanced about the Great Pyramid. The Great Pyramid poses genuine mysteries without them.

Consider first the most readily verifiable of all the Great Pyramid's aspects, its physical shape and placement. The alignment of the Great Pyramid with the cardinal points of the compass is nearly perfect, with an average error for each face of less than .02 percent. The difference between the longest and shortest sides is an inch and three-quarters, in a structure the length of two and a half football fields made of large stone blocks. The base is level to within slightly less than inch.[9] This betokens precision surveying of a high order. Such precision is not obtained by taking a few sightings of the direction of the sun at the spring and fall equinox or by crude measuring rods. Whatever surveying procedures the Egyptians had, they were capable of minute calibration.

Once the measurements had been obtained, there remained the problem of making good on them in the construction phase, just one of the problems that the pyramid builders overcame. The Great Pyramid is built of approximately 2.3 million blocks, most of them weighing about 2.6 tons. It was originally covered with an additional 115,000 polished casing stones, each weighing about ten tons. Maneuvering blocks of that size without modern equipment can be done with enough manpower, but assembling them into a structure 480 feet high requires some sort of lifting mechanism. Herodotus tells us that levers were used, but gives us no sense of their nature. The only mechanism that we know was available to the Egyptians was ramps.[10] But the ramp theories that have been proposed all involve practical difficulties that leave no one solution with a clear advantage.[11] Some have argued that the difficulties are so great and would have involved so much material and weight that none of the ramp solutions is satisfactory.[12]

The solution to these mysteries need not be exotic. One engineer has suggested that the most energy-efficient way to raise the blocks to the upper courses of the pyramid was just to drag them up, perhaps aided by a simple pulley system.[13] Mark Lehner, who built a small pyramid with the help of a stone mason using tools known to be available to the Egyptians, concluded that "it was abundantly clear that [the Egyptians'] expertise was not the result of some mysterious technology or mysterious sophistication, but of generations of practice and experiment."[14] But while we are able to imagine ways in which the Egyptians might have done it, we still have no way of knowing exactly which of those ways were used, or whether they might have had some other approach altogether.

Other known unknowns are associated with Egyptian technology, but these should make the point. We can be confident that the earlier

THE WALLS AT SACSAYHUAMAN

The pyramids at Giza are only the most famous examples of the ancient human impulse to wrestle huge rocks from point *A* to point *B* and then assemble them into structures. Up to a certain weight of rock, these constructions do not require a high level of engineering sophistication. Abundant manpower plus some basic knowledge of ropes and levers suffice. But how does one use manpower to maneuver and assemble much heavier blocks? Egyptian structures pose some interesting problems in this regard, but at least with Egypt we are dealing with a society known to possess sophisticated technology. The walls at Sacsayhuaman, just outside the Inca city of Cuzco in Peru, are more baffling. They are built of about 1,000 stone blocks, expertly dressed in polygonal forms and assembled as if they were pieces of a jigsaw puzzle. The Spanish invaders who first saw the wall marveled at the precision of its assembly. "They are so well fitted together that you could not slip the point of a knife between two of them," wrote Spanish explorer Garcilaso de la Vega of the blocks, ". . . which are more like pieces of a mountain than building stones."[15] Many of the blocks are in the 200-ton range. The weight of the largest is approximately 355 tons.[16] The Incas, to whom the walls of Sacsayhuaman are attributed, did not even have the wheel. It has been a daunting task to find a plausible scheme for moving a 355-ton stone from the quarry to the site of the wall, dressing it as a polygonal form, and then hoisting and fitting it perfectly with other polygonal forms, with the technology known to be available to the Incas, though efforts have been made.[17] It would be a challenge to move such an object even with today's technology.

table offers a reasonably good profile of the state of human accomplishment in −800. It is far off the mark as a profile of all that human beings had ever accomplished before −800.

A Renegade Paradigm

The parsimonious explanation for the known unknowns is that their existence implies lost technology that could be made to fit within the parameters of the established model of ancient history. But these and other anomalies are sufficiently strange to have made people wonder whether something more exotic is involved. The result has been an array of theories ranging from ancient visitors from other planets to lost civilizations of miraculous powers. These theories have usually been addressed in books written by authors so ardently partisan that it is easy to find ways in which they have exaggerated, made mysteries out of matters that could have simple explanations, seized upon coincidence, and selectively ignored evidence that does not fit their favored explanations.

Barely discernible behind the swirling New Age smoke is a glimpse of something that may be fire. That possibility has attracted a handful of scientists, still a renegade minority, who are trying to investigate systematically the hypothesis that a lost human civilization predated the Egyptian and Sumerian civilizations. As to when that civilization existed, where, how advanced it was, why there are so few traces of it—the answers to all these questions remain so speculative that I will not even outline them. But the record with which these renegade scientists are working contains some data so challenging that they are correct in saying, "If this is true, then the accepted model of ancient history cannot be true." I briefly describe two of the puzzles that fit this category, each of which is based on a different type of evidence.

Evidence for historical origins of the monomyth. It is commonly understood that something like the story of Noah and the flood is part of the mythology of cultures around the globe. It is less widely realized that the unity of the world's myths goes far beyond such basic similarities. So elaborate and intertwined are the mythic traditions in places as disparate as Mayan Central America, Viking Scandinavia, and Pharaonic Egypt, that it has for some decades been widely accepted among specialists in the field that a single mythic tradition, what Joseph Campbell named the *monomyth*, underlies all the known discrete mythic traditions.[18]

Once we grant the existence of the monomyth, we have a choice between two broad explanations: Either the human psyche is such that cultures everywhere produce extraordinarily similar myths (the view propounded by psychoanalyst Carl Jung and comparative-religion scholar Mircea Eliade, and accepted as well by Campbell), or the myths had a common historic origin. The problem with a common historic origin is that it requires us to posit a means by which the myths were shared across continents, and the standard paradigm of ancient history does not allow for that.

In 1969, science historians Giorgio de Santillana of M.I.T. and Hertha von Dechend of Frankfurt's Goethe-Universität came down on the historical side of the debate with a book entitled *Hamlet's Mill: An Essay on Myth and the Frame of Time*.[19] At its center is the proposition that the world's mythologies were drawn from a common historical source with a common body of astronomical knowledge that included knowledge of precession of the equinox.

The precession of the equinox is an astronomical phenomenon caused by the earth's wobble (the earth spins like a top that has lost a little speed). One of the results of the wobble is that, seen from the earth's surface, the constellation against which the sun rises at the spring and fall equinoxes changes over time. At the beginning of 21C, the sun at equinox rises in front of the constellation Pisces—but only for another century or so, because, as the song says, we are at the dawning of the Age of Aquarius.

A complete cycle through all twelve constellations of the zodiac takes 25,920 years, with each "age" lasting 2,160 years. Thus the first salient fact about the precession of the equinox is that it cannot be discovered without accurate star records over a significant period of time. It takes 72 years for the constellations to move one degree of arc—about as far along the horizon as the width of your forefinger held out at arm's length. The standard histories hold that the Greek astronomer Hipparchus discovered precession of the equinox in about –134 by comparing his star charts with ones that had been prepared a century and a half earlier.

De Santillana and von Dechend were not especially concerned with trying to date the original discovery of precession, mentioning almost in passing that the most likely date is about –5000, nor did they try to assign it to a lost civilization.[20] Their concern was to establish their basic contention about the historical-astronomical nature of the monomyth. But, like it or not, to demonstrate that precession was known millennia before Hipparchus and that this knowledge was disseminated throughout the world—both of which are minimal implications of *Hamlet's Mill*—already means that the standard paradigm is in disarray. I will not try to summarize the evidence in *Hamlet's Mill*, but it should be emphasized that the book is not the work of sensationalists, but of exceptionally erudite scholars of the world's mythic traditions.

Hamlet's Mill is only one source of evidence that the advocates of an early and advanced lost civilization present on behalf of the hypothesis that precession was known much earlier than Hipparchus. Some of the archaeological evidence, which includes purported astronomical and mathematical features of the design of the great ancient monuments around the world, is intriguing. But in trying to evaluate it, we are once again confronted with advocates who appear to be torturing the data until they confess. The limited point here is that the core scholarly work on the monomyth as it relates to knowledge of precession of the equinox poses challenges to the standard paradigm that justify investigation.

Dating the age of the Sphinx. The Great Sphinx of Giza is customarily dated to circa −2500 and the reign of Khafre, which followed the reign of Khufu and the construction of the Great Pyramid. In 1991, questions about the accuracy of that dating led to a geological examination of the weathering of the limestone from which the Sphinx was carved. Geologist Robert Schoch of Boston University, a mainstream academic with no prior connection to Egypt or to controversies about ancient history, concluded that the body of the Sphinx was eroded by water, not by sand. If true, this finding made the conventional date of −2500 impossible. Egypt in general and the Giza plateau in particular were arid then and have remained arid since.

But Egypt has not always been dry. At the end of the most recent Ice Age, Egypt began to enjoy a moist climate called the Nabtian Pluvial. For thousands of years, the land that we know as a bone-dry desert was a green savannah. The Nabtian Pluvial lasted until around −3000, when the desiccation of Egypt began.[21] So it was indeed possible that the Sphinx was eroded by water runoff if the construction of the Sphinx had occurred early enough. Subsequent study in collaboration with seismologist Thomas Dobecki provided triangulating information. The rump of the Sphinx had been carved more recently than the rest of the body, it was determined, and collateral evidence strongly suggested that the more recent work had indeed been done in −25C. A comparison of the depth of weathering in the newer and older portions led Schoch and Dobecki to conclude that the minimum date for the carving of the older portion was in the region of −7000 to −5000, with an open-ended possibility that it was older still.[22]

Schoch and Dobecki presented their findings at the 1991 annual meeting of the Geological Society of America. This was followed by a presentation of competing papers under the aegis of the American Association for the Advancement of Science in February 1992.[23] A variety of objections to the geological findings were raised, with alternative theories involving fast-eroding limestone, failure to take remaining precipitation into account (it still rained in Egypt after the Nabtian Pluvial, though infrequently), and confusion of differential erosion with changes in rock strata.[24] In each case, Schoch had a technical response and found some independent support.[25]

Meanwhile, the Egyptologists have remained unconvinced. Their position is that the archaeological reconstruction of Egypt's ancient past is rich and systematic. A chain of evidence gives them good reason to conclude that they understand the evolution of Egyptian society in the pre-dynastic period. A civilization capable of building the Sphinx in −5000 or earlier would have left an archaeological trace. It did not. The geological evidence must be wrong.

The continuing debate is taking a new tack as I write, with Schoch arguing that other monuments in the Giza area exhibit water-weathering features, suggesting that the archaeological traces of an earlier dynasty exist.[26] How the debate will turn out is anybody's guess; the arguments involve arcane issues in two fields, geology and Egyptology, that outsiders cannot assess independently.

A SALUTARY CAUTION

How far had human accomplishment advanced by −800? By this time I hope you will understand the reasons for being circumspect about the answer. It is possible that the renegades are right, and that ancient human prehistory may have to be rewritten from scratch. I have no idea what the odds are, but the history of science is replete with other renegades who were ridiculed and eventually triumphed. In living memory, the theory of plate tectonics went from a far-fetched, widely derided hypothesis to the consensus explanation. So did the theory that a collision between earth and an asteroid wiped out the dinosaurs. An open mind is prudent in these matters.

However the story prior to −800 comes to be told, I will now retreat to our more confident understanding of human accomplishment as we cross that dividing line. Virtually nothing of the art, literature, music, tech-nology, mathematics, medicine, and science of −800 is now part of our everyday world. It was during the centuries beginning with −800 that our heritage in all of these fields began to accumulate, and it is to that story which I now turn.

THREE

A SENSE OF PLACE

This chapter tries to convey a sense of what it was like to live in the midst of three very different configurations of human accomplishment. The sites and times have been chosen to prefigure themes that will surface later in the book. For Western readers, Antonine Rome takes us close to our cultural roots in ancient Greece. It also serves as an example of a culture of great power and high technology that is short on artistic and intellectual creativity. The Chinese city of Hangzhou in the Song Dynasty serves as a window into an advanced civilization that developed apart from that of the West. It is also an example of the merits and defects of stability in a culture. Samuel Johnson's London is close enough to our time to be recognizable but startlingly less advanced in some ways than Hangzhou. London in 18C also serves as a reference point for later questions about what has made the last 600 years so different from all the rest.

Another objective of this chapter is to break loose from the condescension toward the past that has become fashionable in recent years. The phrase "dead white males" represents one form of that condescension. A more troubling aspect of it is the presumption of moral superiority that too often causes us to look down on just about anyone who lived more than a few decades ago. But we can step outside that impulse at least momentarily. Obviously—as soon as we stop to think about it—our descendants will find our own moral sensibility on issues such as class, race, and gender as flawed as we find the moral sensibility of our ancestors, and our descendants will also be just as inappropriately confident of their superior perspective as we are of ours. By the same token, we can look back on the accomplishments of the past understanding that we are unlikely to have a grasp of right and wrong more nuanced than that of Aristotle or Confucius—or, for that matter, to have a sense of a life well lived superior to that of Aristotle's sandal-maker or Confucius's cook.

ANTONINE ROME, 138–180

"In the second century of the Christian era the empire of Rome comprehended the fairest portion of the earth and the most civilized portion of mankind."[1] So Gibbon begins his epic, *The Decline and Fall of the Roman Empire*, describing the apogee of Rome under Antoninus Pius and Marcus Aurelius.

A Roman citizen lucky enough to be free and possessed of a little money lived a life that in many ways remains competitive with any to follow. If he wished to study history, he could read Thucydides, Herodotus, or Plutarch. If he wished to study philosophy, he had before him, in more complete form than we do, the works of Plato and Aristotle. If he wished for literature or drama, he had available to him *The Iliad*, *The Odyssey*, *The Oresteia*, the *Oedipus* plays, *Antigone*, *Electra*, *Medea*, *Lysistrata*, *The Aeneid*, and more.

Our Roman citizen had easy access to these works. Rome under the Antonines boasted over 25 public libraries, with books that could be checked out for reading at home.[2] The affluent bought rather than borrowed—easy enough, since booksellers abounded—and bought in profusion. No house of any pretensions, Seneca wrote, lacked "its library with shelves of rare cedar wood and ivory from floor to ceiling."[3]

The Roman connoisseur of painting and sculpture lived in a world that already possessed works that today are among the most prized items in Europe's greatest art museums—*Nike of Samothrace*, the *Laocoön* group, *Venus de Milo*, the Elgin marbles. As in the case of literature, the pieces that survive are only a fragment of the fine art that the Roman citizen of 2C could enjoy. Pausanias, a travel writer of that era, wrote a ten-volume tourist guide to Greece, which among other things contained the equivalent of today's "must see" lists of the best art. Of dozens of works he singles out, we have only a handful. Or consider the most famous Greek sculptor, Phidias. We have originals in the form of the Elgin marbles, copies of a few of his statues, and nothing at all of what the ancients considered to be his masterpiece, the statue of Zeus at Olympia. The Greek statuary that we still find so compelling today consists largely of what the ancient world considered its second-tier work.

We know even less about the paintings of antiquity. The mural painter Polygnotus was widely considered to be Phidias's equal in genius, but nothing survives to our day. Pliny the Elder, writing in 1C, tells us that the Greek painter Zeuxis depicted some grapes with such success that the birds flew up to them, and that Zeuxis's contemporary Parrhasius depicted a linen curtain with such truth that Zeuxis asked for it to be drawn aside. We have none of their work.[4] Petronius writes in the *Satyricon* that ". . . when I came upon the work of Apelles [Alexander's court painter] . . . I actually worshipped it. For the outlines of the figures gave a rendering of natural appearances with such subtlety that you might believe even their souls had been painted."[5] For Pliny, Apelles "surpassed all those who were born before him and all those who came later."[6] Nothing of his work survives.

Everything we know about the painting of antiquity comes from a comparative handful of works from the Roman era, mostly copies, many of which survived only because they were preserved under the volcanic ash that buried Pompeii—and Pompeii was only a provincial town. Trying to judge the glories of Greek painting from these remnants is impossible. Furthermore, we know that Roman critics at the time of the Antonines were unanimous in thinking that the art of their day had deteriorated.[7] But at least the Romans were enthusiastic consumers. The famous *Medici Venus* that now resides in the Uffizi gallery in Florence is merely a copy, the best of the 33 Roman copies of the Greek original that still survive.[8] We can only guess at how many copies existed in the time of the Antonines.

Rome had not only access to great literature and art but to advanced technology. Our Roman citizen traveled beyond Rome on highways built on raised causeways and packed in layers of stones, gravel, and concrete. They were self-draining, wide enough for two of the largest wagons to pass without difficulty, with smooth surfaces (sometimes stone, sometimes metalled). Like today's interstate highways, they tunneled through hills, spanned marshes on viaducts, maintained an easy grade, and typically stretched for miles between curves. Posthouses with fresh horses were maintained all along the roads, enabling military and administrative communications to cover more than 100 miles per day.[9] These highways crisscrossed the empire—a distance, from the far northwest corner in England to the far southeast corner in Jerusalem, of more than 3,700 miles. Or, if our Roman citizen traveled by sea, he could sail from Ostia, conveniently located a mere 16 miles from downtown Rome—not because there was a natural harbor in Ostia, but because Roman engineers had built an artificial one.[10]

The Romans built structures on a colossal scale. The Coliseum, seating

50,000 people, the largest amphitheatre built anywhere in the world until 20C, is the most famous but not the most spectacular. A candidate for that title might be the Baths of Caracalla, built a few decades after the death of Marcus Aurelius, covering 270,000 square feet, about half again as large as the ground area of the U.S. Capitol building. The main block was about as high as the nave of St. Paul's Cathedral in London.[11] It was built of marble and decorated with gold, ivory and rare woods, containing not only baths and a *calidarium*, much like our modern sauna, but also gardens, libraries, gymnasia, and recreation centers. These lavish facilities were open to all free citizens, including women and children, for a trivial fee.

Amidst these evidences of advanced technology were strange lacunae. At the baths, for example, one followed a good sweat in the *calidarium* by having one's skin scraped with a *strigil* made of bone or wood. Why scrape? Why not a thorough soap and rinse? Because the Romans had neglected to invent soap. What makes this omission so striking is the other ways in which the ancient Romans' lives were just like ours. In ancient Rome, people lived in apartment buildings, followed professional sports, went out for a drink at the local bars, picked up a quick bite from a fast-food restaurant, whistled popular songs.[12] They hunched over board games in public parks, had household pets, went to the theatre, carried on extensive correspondence, ran complex business enterprises.[13] Men went to barbershops and women went to hairdressers. The wealthy of Rome dressed for dinner, escaped from the noise of the city to their beach homes, and collected fine wine (the vintage of −121 was so famous that bottles of it were still being hoarded two centuries later).[14]

But Rome had no soap. And so it is with dozens of other aspects of Roman life which were nothing whatsoever like our own. Take medical care, for example. Some kinds of medical facilities were extensive. Every chartered city maintained a corps of physicians who worked in complexes that were typically well-designed and spacious.[15] Most slave-owning homes included a slave physician and an infirmary in which sick slaves could be tended. Rome's water supply was abundant and sanitary. An elaborate sewage system carried off waste water, and Rome maintained public latrines, with marble seats (some of them heated in winter), flushed by a stream of running water.[16] Private physicians abounded, and the fashionable ones made a good living— 600,000 sesterces in one instance that has come down to us, equivalent to a six-figure-dollar income today. Physicians made house calls, and had a vast array of medications. An able Roman surgeon had a set of instruments as good as any that would be available until the French Revolution (200 different kinds of surgical instruments have been found at Pompeii[17]), and he was able to conduct a number of sophisticated operations with them—repairs of hernia and fistula, removal of gall stones and abscesses, and plastic surgery for removing the brands of slaves who had become freedmen. The Roman physician could set fractures and amputate limbs as professionally as any physician until 20C. The obstetrics of the time included podalic version, turning the fetus in the uterus, a life-saving technique that was forgotten for a thousand years after the Roman Empire fell.

However: The same Rome had no public hospitals and threw its garbage in the street. The pristine water from the mountains flowed through lead pipes, slowly poisoning the population. The surgeon had no anesthesia and no knowledge of antiseptic practice. The clinical descriptions of disease were reasonably accurate, but the etiology of those diseases was conjecture, almost always wrong. The understanding of human anatomy and physiology was fragmentary. So while Galen, whose work would be considered definitive until the Renaissance, understood that blood ebbed and flowed, he did not understand that it circulated. Erasistratus correctly noted the difference between sensory and motor nerves, but thought they were hollow tubes carrying liquid. And so it was with most knowledge of the human physiology: a few half-truths alongside a mountain of error.

The inventory of medicines consisted of a few useful items—the juice of mandragora and atropin, drugs for dulling pain, for example. But the rest of the Roman physician's vast *materia medica* consisted of varieties of snake oil. In the office of that physician I mentioned with an annual income of 600,000 sesterces were chests with titles such as "Eye-salve tried by Florus on Antonia, wife of Drusus, after other doctors had nearly blinded her"; "Drug from Berytus for watery eyes. Instantaneous"; and "Remedy for scab. Tested successfully by Pamphilius during the great scab epidemic." The ingredients in these ointments and medicines might be hyena skin, dried centipedes, or a variety of mammalian excretions. Thus one Roman was led to observe sourly that "Diaulus has been a surgeon and is now an undertaker. At last he's begun to be useful to the sick in the only way that he's able."[18]

We cannot reconstruct life expectancy with precision, but the available data are grim. The experience of a few famous families, who presumably had access to state-of-the-art medical care, shows high infant mortality, and the fragmentary data about common folk are even worse—of 164 surviving epitaphs of Jews in Rome, for example, 40 percent are of children below the age of 10.[19] Nor was adulthood safe. Appendicitis, strep throat, or an infected scratch could easily be fatal in Antonine Rome.

Roman ignorance about human physiology and the nature of disease extended to the rest of the sciences. The Greeks had made some progress. Five centuries earlier, Parmenides had suggested that matter can be neither created nor destroyed, and Leucippus and Democritus had enunciated theories of atomism. Archimedes had understood the principles of the lever and of buoyancy. Strato had suggested that falling bodies accelerate and Strabo had suggested that volcanos make mountains. Anaximander had proposed something resembling an evolutionary hypothesis. But these and other accomplishments in the hard sciences were the merest glimmerings of an understanding of the way the physical world works. And it is only hindsight that lets us select these truths, or half-truths, from among the host of things the Romans believed that were completely wrong.

Even when the results looked right, Roman science was usually wrong. During the first decade after Antoninus Pius came to power, Claudius Ptolemy completed the *Almagest* and thereby brought ancient astronomy to its summit. His mathematical elaboration of a geocentric system predicted planetary motion with great accuracy, and it remained in use for more than a thousand years. But this elegant construction, in spite of its great predictive power, was wholly wrong about how the solar system actually works.

Perhaps stranger to our sensibility than the Romans' lack of scientific knowledge was their lack of curiosity. The Roman code, widely honored from the Republic through the Antonines, demanded that the Roman gentleman engage in public service, that he embody vigor and industriousness, that he shun *lexus* (self-indulgence) and *inertia* (idleness). But Romans despised learning for learning's sake. A Roman gentleman might study philosophy so that he could learn how to live properly, die with dignity, and be stoically indifferent to the vagaries of fortune. But to study philosophy merely for the sake of knowledge was unseemly—a kind of *inertia*.[20]

Architecture was the one art to which a Roman gentleman might properly apply himself. It involved science and aesthetics, but to a clear and present purpose. Otherwise, Romans disdained artists as much as they disdained scholars. As some earlier quotations from Petronius and Pliny indicated, Romans of the upper class often loved the art itself. They shared with our own time the rites and sensibilities of connoisseurship. Ancient Rome had art critics, historians, and collectors who spent vast sums on their Great Masters. But Lucian, writing in the Antonine era, observes matter-of-factly that a sculptor was without prestige, "no more than a workman, doing hard physical labor . . . obscure, earning a small wage, a man of low esteem, classed as worthless by public opinion, neither courted by friends, feared by enemies, nor envied by fellow citizens."[21] Even more startling are the words of Plutarch about Phidias, whose artistic works were regarded by the ancients with the awe that we accord Michelangelo's: "No gifted young man upon seeing the Zeus of Phidias at Olympia ever wanted to be Phidias. For it does not necessarily follow that, if a work is delightful because of its gracefulness, the man who made it is worthy of our serious regard."[22]

That the Romans could so reverently admire a work of art and so scorn the person who created it is perhaps part of the reason that the Romans left us so little of their own creation in the arts and sciences. There are the exceptions of Virgil, Horace, Cicero, and Ovid, plus a sprinkling of other fine Roman writers, the Stoics in philosophy, and a few major scientific achievements across the Mediterranean in Alexandria. But taken as whole, the Roman world throughout its history, whether republic or empire, was a near intellectual void when it came to the arts and sciences—"peopled by a race of pygmies" in Gibbon's contemptuous words.[23] Scientific, philosophic, and artistic progress did not come to an end when Rome fell, but, without much exaggeration, when Rome rose.

In matters of religion, Antonine Rome was boundlessly cynical. The authorities kept the temples of the Roman gods in immaculate condition, and each of the many deities' festival days were attended with the prescribed rites. But hardly any Romans actually believed that the gods were gods, any more than they believed that the dead emperors became gods. If one looks for a Roman true faith, astrology is a better candidate. People of every rank, including emperors, hung on the readings of the stars, and the top astrologers had both celebrity and political power. Oracles were taken seriously as well, along with magic.

Real religious devotion in Antonine Rome was concentrated among the cults that had been coming and going for centuries—the cults of Isis, Cybele, and the various mystery sects, for example. Two of the cults had gravitas—the worship of Mithras, imported from Persia, and Christianity—but at the time of the Antonines, both were still exceptions to the larger religious environment of Rome which was, not to mince words, spiritually and theologically vacuous.

Roman shortcomings in the arts, sciences, and religion were matched by a history of governance that can charitably be described as spotty. On the positive side, the Romans were exceptional administrators. They could dispatch Roman governors to distant territories, create efficient bureaucracies, and speed directives and resources across the empire. To their credit, Romans usually ruled with restraint. They could be ruthless in suppressing uprisings, as we know from the story of the Jews and Masada, but they had a deserved reputation for accommodating local customs and institutions while maintaining firm political control. We may also admire Roman law, developed over the course of centuries into a body of jurisprudence that would be used to restore the rule of law in Northern Europe after the Dark Ages.

But efficiency in administration and sophistication in law is not the same as possessing an advanced or just political system. Rome was a functioning republic for some three centuries, about a century longer than the United States has yet survived as a republic, but it was aristocratic, with voting rights limited to a small portion of the population. The Roman republic was also a slave state on such a scale that Gibbon estimated that the number of slaves may have outnumbered the free inhabitants of the Roman world. A proposal that slaves should wear a distinctive garment was rejected, Gibbon notes dryly, because "it was justly apprehended that there might be some danger in acquainting [the slaves] with their own numbers."[24] Nor was Roman slavery kindly. Roman masters might dispose of the lives of their slaves at will, and were not reluctant to use that power. We know, for example, that the size of the slave force in the palace of a Roman noble family could number about four hundred souls. The reason we know that number is that the Roman archives record an instance in which the master in such a palace was murdered, and the household slaves were executed for failing to prevent his murder—all four hundred of them.[25]

Apart from slavery, Roman politics were brutal and primitive even in the heyday of the Republic. By the time Caesar ended the Republic in −45, it had become cutthroat. Caesar himself died at a meeting of the Senate, killed by senators. Pompey and Cicero died violent deaths at the hands of their political rivals. After the fall of the Republic, the cruelties of Nero and Caligula were so egregious that they have become legend. These were just the most obvious examples of a broader streak of violence in polite circles of Roman life. By the time of the Antonines, the largest single category of medication in the Roman pharmacy was said to be antitoxins.

HANGZHOU DURING THE SONG DYNASTY, 960–1279

To many Westerners, classical China is a collage of images dimly recalled from films and childhood books: terraced rice paddies, the obedient son bowing to his father, women with bound feet, barefoot coolies pulling rickshaws, teeming masses. The image is wonderfully exotic—China has fascinated the West since the days of Marco Polo—but also evokes a country both quaint and backward.

Classical China was neither. A sophisticated culture when Rome was still an obscure city-state on the Italian peninsula, classical China's accomplishments are impressive not only relative to the barbarity of the Western Dark Ages, but impressive by any standard. The example of Yongle's maritime expeditions will make the point.

Yongle, the second emperor of the Ming Dynasty, wished to incorporate the states of South and Southeast Asia into the Chinese tribute system that China used to maintain trade and diplomatic relations with the states on its periphery. Until Yongle came to the throne, China had relied on land routes. Yongle decided to send China to sea. He directed that maritime expeditions be carried out — a total of seven over almost three decades —commanded by a court eunuch named Zheng He.

Zheng He's fleet set sail at the beginning of the same century that would end with Columbus's first trip to the New World. Since Columbus's voyage is rightly considered a huge step in the West and technologically on the cutting edge of what the West was able to do, it is instructive to contemplate what Zheng He's feat entailed. Columbus successfully negotiated a round trip from the Western Mediterranean to the Caribbean, conducted with three vessels that were little more than large boats (the flagship *Santa Maria* is thought to have been only about 85 feet long) and a company numbering 90 men and boys. Total elapsed time of the expedition, including time ashore, was a little more than seven months.

The first of Zheng He's voyages, begun 90 years before Columbus left harbor, went to Java and Sumatra, then passed through the Straits of Malacca and on to Ceylon and India before returning. Zheng He covered about the same total distance as Columbus, but with 62 ships instead of 3. The last of the seven expeditions, in 1433–1435, involved 317 ships crewed by 27,750 men.[26] The largest of these vessels was 444 feet long, about the length of a large modern destroyer, with four decks and watertight bulkheads. The *smallest* of the 317 ships was about twice the length of Columbus's flagship. The final Chinese expedition traveled from China down to Java, west to Arabia, and then down the east coast of Africa before turning for home. Total time at sea was more than two years.

To put a fleet of 317 ships and 28,000 men to sea for two years would be a major undertaking for a modern nation. It bespeaks formidable technological, industrial, and administrative capacity. Imperial China did it at the beginning of 15C. To judge China by its standing in 19C and 20C is as misleading as to judge the Roman Empire by its condition in 6C and 7C.

For a portrait of China in all its imperial grandeur, the Ming Dynasty (1368–1644) that sponsored Zheng He's voyages would be a good place to remain. But the apogee of Chinese culture as a whole is more often taken to be the Song Dynasty (960–1279), "glorious in art as in poetry and philosophy, the period which for Asia stands in history as the Periclean age in Europe," as one historian put it.[27] Our point of departure is Hangzhou, the capital of Song China, the city Marco Polo called Kinsay.

Hangzhou became the capital by happenstance. In 1127, it was still a minor provincial city, midway between the Yangtze and the trading ports of the southeast China coast, chosen as a refuge by an emperor fleeing nomad barbarians. He chose a beautiful place. To the west was a large artificial lake (constructed more than 500 years earlier—a reminder of the staggering span of Chinese continuity), backed by the graceful curve of low-lying mountains. To the east, upon a spreading plain, ". . . there sparkle, like fishes' scales, the bright-colored tiles of a thousand roofs," one visitor wrote. "One would say it was landscape composed by a painter." [28]

Sparkle was an apt word. Hangzhou, like other Chinese cities, was unimaginably clean by Western standards of that time. The crenellated walls of the old city, also built some 500 years earlier, 30 feet high and 10 feet thick, were freshly whitewashed every month. The streets were cleaned frequently. Each year, the canals that crisscrossed the city were dredged and cleaned. The homes of the rich had cesspools. The poor collected their night soil in buckets that were carried off each day to central collection points. Hangzhou's standards for hygiene wouldn't be approached in Europe until late in 19C, and then only in the most advanced cities.

This advanced municipal administration was carried out in a metropolis that dwarfed any city in the West. After the fall of Rome, Europe had become a rural landscape dotted with market towns. Even as late as 12C, the populations of Paris and London numbered no more than a few tens of thousands each—we cannot know exactly, because the concept of official statistics lay far in the future. The city-states of northern Italy were growing, but even the largest of them had not reached the 100,000 mark at the end of 12C. Hangzhou in 12C numbered over a million people. How do we know? Because China had for some centuries been conducting regular censuses, listing the names and ages of every member of every family, their exact location, and, if they were farmers, the size of their cultivated holding.

Hangzhou had extremes of wealth and poverty. Parts of the city were traversed by wide, well-drained avenues of smoothed stone, and the houses of the wealthy stood on ample, walled plots. In other parts, the streets were narrow and crooked, with multi-story houses crowded on each side where half a dozen people might live in a single small room. Increased urbanization also led to overcrowding, homelessness, and pauperization of the city's unemployed who had become disconnected from their families remaining in the countryside. Hangzhou responded in various ways. Food warehouses supported by special taxes were set aside for the indigent. Private charities specialized in caring for orphans and old people, burying paupers, and providing schooling for indigent children.[29] As in the case of Rome before and London later, commendable responses to need coexisted side by side with accepted practices that today are felonies. One of the reasons that orphanages were required was that infants were commonly abandoned on the streets by parents who could afford no more children—so commonly that the practice was banned in 1138, though with only partial success.[30]

Whether the lives of the impoverished were conspicuously better or worse in Hangzhou than in ancient Rome or Georgian London is hard to say from our distant vantage point. But for persons outside that extreme group, at least some of Hangzhou's public amenities were available to all. Where Rome had its public baths, so did Hangzhou—three thousand of them, according to Marco Polo, who observed that the people of Hangzhou "are very cleanly in their persons."[31] He was even more impressed with the public facilities on the lake:

> In the middle of the Lake there are two Islands, on each of which stands a palatial edifice with an incredibly large number of rooms and separate pavilions. And when anyone desired to hold a marriage feast, or to give a big banquet, it used to be done at one of these palaces. And everything would be found there ready to order, such as dishes, napkins and tablecloths and whatever else was needful. These furnishings were acquired and maintained at common expense by the citizens in these palaces constructed by them for this purpose. Sometimes there would be at these palaces a hundred different parties. . . and yet all would find good accommodation in the different apartments and pavilions, and that in so well ordered a manner that one party was never in the way of another.[32]

A detail, trivial in itself, may give a sense of the administrative detail that went into the governance of Hangzhou: the balustrades along the canals. Some time after Hangzhou began to grow, it was noticed that every year a number of people, commonly revelers after a night on the town, were falling into the canals and sometimes drowning. One of the governors of the city directed that balustrades be built all along the banks of the canals, with gates provided at convenient points for embarkation.

One may get a sense of the scope of Hangzhou's administrative capability from statistics. In the 13 months from October 1268 to November 1269, for example, we know from the surviving records that a project to renovate the bridges of Hangzhou was carried out, involving 117 bridges within the ramparts and another 230 in the suburbs. Half of them were rebuilt from scratch, and the other half repaired. Low bridges were heightened and narrow ones widened. This was just one routine municipal project, routinely reported.

In addition to its public facilities, Hangzhou numbered hundreds of tea-houses, restaurants, theatres, and hotels. In the West, the concept of sumptuous dining and lodging outside the private home took an oddly long time to develop—taverns serving meals had existed since ancient times, but the first luxury restaurant didn't open until 1782.[33] It wasn't until 19C that European travelers could begin to count on finding decent public accommodations. In Hangzhou of 12C, one could get cheap-but-good noodles, meat pies, or oysters from small shops, as one does in today's East Asia. Those with more money to spend could choose a tea-house in a garden landscaped with dwarf pines and hung with brightly colored lanterns, or they could dine in one of the large restaurants hung with works of celebrated painters and calligraphers and set with fine porcelain. If it were a hot summer day, the diner might want to choose among the refreshing iced drinks—or iced foods, for that matter—that were widely available. In medieval Europe of 12C, the food of the rich still consisted largely of slabs of flesh of one kind or another, heavily spiced to hide signs of rot. In the restaurants of Hangzhou, one contemporary wrote, "Hundreds of orders are given on all sides: this person wants something hot, another something cold, a third something tepid, a fourth something chilled; one wants cooked food, another raw, another chooses roasted, another grilled."[34] The variety of Chinese food was as broad then as it is today, and the people of Hangzhou could get just about any kind they wanted—not just their own cuisine, but the cuisines of distant provinces as well. As today, the Chinese delighted in the restaurant that served one special dish. There was the sweet soya soup at the Mixed-Wares Market, the fish soup of Mother Song outside the Cash-Reserve Gate, and pig cooked in ashes at the Longevity-and-Compassion Palace. Fifteen major markets dotted Hangzhou, each large enough to handle thousands of sellers and buyers at one time. The specialization was staggering, with more than 200 shops selling nothing but varieties of salted fish.

The market in food was just one aspect of an economy that employed many elements of modern commerce. Paper money had appeared in 9C in the form of bills of exchange ("flying money") to pay for goods purchased from distant areas. Then private bankers began issuing certificates of deposit that could be cashed for a three percent service charge. In 1023, one of the most famous of these banks was acquired by the government and the certificates of deposit were converted to the first government-backed paper money. The abacus, a primitive version of which had existed as early as −400, had reached its final design by the Song, enabling arithmetic calculation faster than any mechanical device until well into 20C.

China's was a national economy, as goods moved along a road system that rivaled the Romans' and an even more extensive water system. Tens of thousands of ships traveled the coastal sea-routes, the Yellow and Yangtze rivers, and a vast system of internal canals and improved waterways. Documents from the Song describe 10 types of sea-going vessels, 21 types of functionally specific vessels (for example, floating restaurants, passenger boats, ferries, manure boats), 20 vessels categorized by structure (including man-powered paddle-wheel boats), and 35 types of craft grouped by the river system they traveled or by port of origin.[35]

Oils, sugar, silk, lacquer ware, porcelain, iron and copper goods, rice, and timber were routinely shipped throughout the nation. We know, for example, that a Daoist temple constructed in Kaifeng in north central China in 11C was constructed of pinewood brought from Gansu and Shanxi, cedar from Shanxi, catalpa wood, camphor-tree wood and oak from Hunan and Jiangxi, zelkova wood from Hunan and Zhejiang, cryptomeria from Hunan, and several other woods from Hubei and Shanxi.[36] Agriculture was already specialized by the Song, with an economy that supported tea plantations, silk cultivation, cattle ranching, and fish farming.

Specialization had also reached into industrial processes. China did much more than merely invent paper, for example. By the Song Dynasty, the paper industry was turning out papers for dozens of uses—elegant, heavy stock for formal correspondence, light-weight, inexpensive paper for everyday use, and specialized papers suitable for painting, money, printing, wrapping, lanterns—and for the toilet as well. The magnitude of paper production was immense. Just one city in Hunan contributed 1.8 million sheets to the government annually in lieu of taxes.[37] Or there is the case of iron production. Song China in 11C seems to have produced as much iron as would be produced in all of Europe in 1700, and the real price of iron fell to levels that would not be seen in Europe until the turn of 19C.[38]

Specialization in agriculture and industry demanded correspondingly sophisticated economic organization. China during the Song had already developed a system of brokers that mediated between local and central markets. *Wholesale* and *retail* were concepts thoroughly understood in Song China. So were contracts, interest, joint stock ventures, distributorships, franchises, warehousing, and commissions. Song China had professional managers, running businesses owned by others not related by blood. Money managers existed in Song China, investing funds on behalf of clients.[39]

But what of the world of the sciences? The answer is maddeningly incomprehensible to a Westerner. It is as if the Chinese periodically dipped into the world of science and effortlessly pulled out a few gems, then ignored them. Some of these Chinese discoveries have become the stuff of conventional wisdom — gunpowder and paper being the most famous. But the recountings by Westerners give these discoveries the flavor of accidents, as if the Chinese stumbled onto something and then didn't know what to do with it.

Unsystematic the discoveries may have been, but there was nothing accidental about them. Rather, they represent sheer cognitive ingenuity of a remarkable order. When next you read the cliché that East Asians are intelligent but lack creative flair, consider, for example, Chinese mathematics. China had no Euclid, no body of mathematical logic that started from first premises. Nonetheless, by the middle of 3C the Chinese already knew the value of π to five decimal places; by the end of 5C, they knew it lay between 3.1415926 and 3.1415927 (the best the West had done was four decimal places).[40] By the middle of 7C, Chinese mathematicians had methods for dealing with indeterminate equations, arithmetical and geometric progressions, and the computation of otherwise immeasurable distance through a form of trigonometry. Chinese mathematicians of the Song Dynasty knew how to extract fourth roots, deal with equations containing powers up to the tenth, and had anticipated a method for obtaining approximate solutions to numerical equations that would not be developed in the West until 1819. None of these accomplishments was produced from a theoretical system, but through the creativity of individual scholars.

By the time of the Song, Chinese astronomy could call on a thousand years of observations of sunspots.[41] The armillary had been fully developed for 900 years in China, as had planetaria. Centuries before the Song, the Chinese had identified the precession of the equinox and knew that the year is not exactly 365.25 days. During the Song itself, Chinese astronomers correctly demonstrated the causes of solar and lunar eclipses. But again there was no theory, no Ptolemaic characterization of the universe. The Chinese simply discovered certain things. Shen Gua, writing in 1086, outlined the principles of erosion, uplift, and sedimentation that are the foundation of earth science, principles that would not be developed in the West for centuries, but his book, *Dream Pool Essays*, sits alone, an anomaly.

Chinese medicine, unlike Chinese science, was backed by abundant theory, but that theory is so alien to the Western understanding of physiology and pharmacology that Western scientists even today are only beginning to understand the degree to which Chinese medicine is coordinate with modern science.[42] It worked, however, for a wide range of ailments. If you were going to be ill in 12C and were given a choice of living in Europe or China, there is no question about the right decision. Western medicine in 12C had forgotten most of what had been known by the Greeks and Romans. Chinese physicians of 12C could alleviate pain more effectively than Westerners had ever been able to do—acupuncture is a Chinese medical technique that Western physicians have learned to take seriously—and could treat their patients effectively for a wide variety of serious diseases.

The vibrant Song economy and its eclectic scientific achievements coexisted with an intellectual and aesthetic high culture. Like the upper classes of Rome, the upper classes of Song China drew on an artistic her-itage that stretched centuries into the past, including access to a vast body of work that is lost to us today. Unlike Rome, Song China did not live passively off that heritage. The canons of Chinese art that stretched back to the Han a thousand years earlier are thought by many to have reached their peak in the Song. It was an art that is still accessible to the modern eye. In many ways, Chinese art of the Song—spare of line, secular, often impressionistic—speaks directly to today's artistic sensibility.

Art was cherished. "The delight [the Chinese] take in decoration, in painting and in architecture, leads them to spend in this way sums of money that would astonish you," wrote Marco Polo. Nor was this passion limited to the rich. Li Qingzhao, a famous woman poet of the Song, recalled how her husband, De Fu, would take advantage of every break from his university studies to pawn his clothing for a bit of cash and go to Xiang Guo Temple in search of old prints. He would buy some fruit along with his newly acquired treasures to bring home.

We would enjoy examining what he had bought while munching fruit together. Two years later, when he got a post in the government, he started to make as complete as possible a collection of rubbings or prints from bronze or stone inscriptions and other ancient scripts. When a print was not available, he would have a copy made and thus our collection of famous calligraphy and antiques began. Once a man tried to sell us Xu Xi's painting of "Peony" for 200,000 cash, and De Fu asked permission to take it home and keep it for a few days and consider. We found no means to buy it and reluctantly returned it to the owner. De Fu and I were upset about it for days.[43]

Huge private and public collections were established and detailed art catalogs published. Provenance was taken seriously, with connoisseurs in various schools of painting, bronze, porcelain, and the other visual arts providing professional advice to the collector. And the leading artists? Not disdained craftsmen as in Rome, but admired during their lives and occasionally becoming near-mythic cultural icons in death.

If art was a high pleasure, literature was a necessity. Chinese cultural life intertwined poetry, philosophy, essays, and narratives into the political life of the nation. A cultivated person was not only expected to be well versed in the classics, he (or she) was also expected to be a skilled writer, especially of poetry. A Chinese tradition of *belles-lettres* grew up during the Tang and Song Dynasties that transcended even the high importance that had been attached to scholarship in earlier dynasties. Aesthetics were only part of the importance of literature, however. Knowing Chinese literature was also a way to achieve high rank, via the Chinese examination system.

By the time of the Song, the examination system was already centuries old. Of the several categories of examination, the least important, leading only to low positions, were the tests in law and mathematics. The test in the Confucian classics was more prestigious and led to more powerful posts. The most prestigious of all awards was the *jin shi*, the "presented scholar" degree, based not just on the classics relating to philosophy and governance but on the whole of Chinese literature.

Selecting officials on the basis of their mastery of literature and philosophy had several advantages. It ensured that most Chinese bureaucrats were smart—the examinations had the effect of screening for IQ as well as the ability to memorize. Another advantage of the examination system was its emphasis on merit over family background, engaging the loyalties of the lower classes by making it possible for a man of humble birth to pass the *jin shi* and become a mandarin. Still a third advantage was that the examination system co-opted the intellectual classes, who in other societies were often critics of the established order. Intellectuals in traditional China had a ready avenue to power.

Above all, the examination system ensured that throughout the country, voluntarily, each generation of the most talented people in China steeped themselves in the core cultural values of the empire. From a pragmatic standpoint, this was a good thing for preserving cultural continuity. But it was also a good thing because those core cultural values constituted such a remarkable legacy in themselves, amalgamating properties that in the West would be divided into religion and civic culture.

In matters purely religious, China was a mirror image of Rome. In Rome, just about everyone formally acknowledged the Roman gods and hardly anyone believed in them. In China, none of the three major belief systems—Confucianism, Daoism, Buddhism—even specified the existence of a god, and the two with temples and priests (Daoism and Buddhism) were followed by small proportions of the Song population. And yet the typical Chinese propitiated the spirits with the punctility of true believers. If the values that we call *Chinese* did not have as strong a religious component as those of Hindu, Judaic, Christian, and Islamic cultures, they were nonetheless promulgated and, more importantly, lived. Marco Polo, arriving from 13C Europe, described the operational effect of this historically unique cultural/religious synthesis in daily life:

> The natives of the city [Hangzhou] are men of peaceful character, both from education and from the example of their kings, whose disposition was the same. They know nothing of handling arms and keep none in their houses. You hear of no feuds or noisy quarrels or dissensions of any kind among them. Both in their commercial dealings and in their manufactures they are thoroughly honest and truthful, and there is such a degree of good will and neighborly attachment among both men and women that one would take the people who live in the same street to be all one family.[44]

Chinese social life was not as uniformly peaceful as Marco Polo describes, but he was not far off the mark. Classical Chinese culture powerfully fostered an amicable, law-abiding, stable social life, and the reason is no mystery. These issues, not epistemology or metaphysics, were the topics that most deeply occupied Chinese philosophers. Westerners label this tradition Confucian, but by the end of its development it incorporated, like a series of Chinese boxes, glosses upon glosses of ancient texts that go back to at least −8C and perhaps as far as −10C.

At the core of the Confucian ethic was the quality called *ren*, the supreme virtue in man—a quality that combines elements of goodness, benevolence, and love. This ethic was most essential for those with the most power: "He who is magnanimous wins the multitude," Confucius taught. "He who is diligent attains his objective, and he who is kind can get service from the people."[45] Indeed, to be a gentleman—another key concept in Confucian thought—required one above all to embody *ren*. And lest one think that a gentleman could get by with mouthing the proper platitudes, Confucius added, "The gentleman first practices what he preaches and then preaches what he practices."[46]

The Chinese way of governance was an organic whole. Once set in motion, it was not a system that depended on a multitude of laws and punishments. The punishments that existed could be harsh—the death of a thousand cuts is another of those tidbits of Chinese lore that have fascinated Westerners—but China was not a country governed by fear. One of the defining Confucian tenets is this, from the *Analects*: "Lead the people by laws and regulate them by penalties, and the people will try to keep out of jail, but will have no sense of shame. Lead the people by virtue and restrain them by the rules of decorum, and the people will have a sense of shame, and moreover will become good."[47]

By the time of the Song Dynasty, Confucianism had governed Chinese life for more than a thousand years. Then in 12C came Zhu Xi, who systematized Confucianism, gave it metaphysics, and, in concert with other eminent exegetes of the Song, produced neo-Confucianism, revitalizing this uniquely comprehensive system for structuring a harmonious society. It would serve as China's cultural bedrock into 20C.

SAMUEL JOHNSON'S LONDON, 1737–1784

At two o'clock on an August afternoon in 1768, the bark *Endeavor* put to sea from Plymouth under the command of second lieutenant James Cook, then just thirty-nine years old. Cook's orders were to sail southwest down the Atlantic, double Cape Horn, and then make for Tahiti, a one-way voyage of some 13,000 miles. The motive behind this expensive, lengthy, and dangerous trip was not trade. No diplomatic services were to be rendered, nor, for that matter, did Cook have messages to convey to anyone at his destination. The purpose of *Endeavor*'s voyage was to observe an astronomical phenomenon known as the transit of Venus.[48]

A transit of Venus occurs when Venus as observed from Earth crosses the face of the Sun. The transits occur in pairs, separated by eight years, with each pair of transits separated by more than a century. There were no transits of Venus in 20C, for example. A century prior to Cook's departure, English astronomer Edmond Halley had realized that the transit of Venus offers a unique opportunity to measure precisely the distance from the earth to the sun, by taking advantage of the phenomenon known as *parallax*—the differences in the apparent position of a heavenly body depending on the observer's location. If the magnitude of the apparent displacement is known, the application of basic trigonometry will yield the desired result. But to get the data, people had to be waiting in place at widely dispersed points on the globe when the auspicious day arrived, hence the trip to Tahiti.

In a request for the government's support of the expedition, the British Royal Society had pointed out that everybody else was going to do it and it would be humiliating for Britain to hang back, because

> . . . the British nation has been justly celebrated in the learned world, for their knowledge of astronomy, in which they are inferior to no nation upon earth, ancient or modern; and it would cast dishonour upon them should they neglect to have correct observations made of this important phenome-non. . . .[49]

And so the British government decided to send a vessel halfway around the world, hoping for clear skies on the appointed day.

Once the decision had been taken, the Admiralty decided to tack on another task. After completing his astronomical observations, Cook was to proceed southward, seeking out *Terra Australis Incognita*, the continent that had long been thought to be somewhere at the bottom of the world, coun-terbalancing the land masses of the northern hemisphere. Upon discovering it, he was to take care to describe the land, its features and soils, and collect samples of its "beasts, birds, fishes and minerals, seeds of trees, fruits and grains."[50] The naturalist who would assist him in this endeavor was one Joseph Banks, 22 years old, a wealthy amateur educated at Harrow, Eton, and Oxford, who was paying £10,000—on the order of a million dollars in today's money—for the privilege of cramming his six-foot-four-inch frame into a cabin six feet long and running a fair risk of dying over the next two years.

Few episodes better capture the spirit of intellectual life in 18C Europe. A passion to *know* was everywhere—to catalog and classify; to order; to probe into the how and the why of things; to take the world apart and see what made it tick. It was a small change in some ways—humans had been curious since they became human—but by Cook's time humans had found a way to continually satisfy that curiosity. They had discovered how to accumulate knowledge.

* * *

The rage to learn, understand, and then shape the world had its manifestations all over the Island. Perhaps Britain's most portentous accomplishment during the 1760s occurred in Scotland, in a room that Glasgow University had given over to the use of a young instrument-maker named James Watt. Some years earlier, Watt had been asked to repair a working model of the steam engine, a balky, inefficient, and unreliable device. By the end of the 1760s, Watt had created the engine that would power the Industrial Revolution.

The implementation of that revolution was concentrated not around London, but in a small region of central England, bounded on the west by Shropshire's Coalbrookdale, where Abraham Darby had first smelted iron with coal in 1709; on the south by Birmingham, where mechanized cotton-spinning began in the 1740s; on the east by Derby, where the world's first recognizable factory opened in 1721; and on the north by Preston, where in 1732 Richard Arkwright, inventor and entrepreneur of the cotton textile industry, was born. But for all the activity elsewhere, the indisputable center of English creative life and to an important degree the center of Western civilization—Paris was its only competitor—was London. "When a man is tired of London he is tired of life," Samuel Johnson famously wrote, and never did the city merit the accolade more than during Johnson's years there.

When he arrived in 1737, London was huge by the standards of the time, even though it was still smaller than Hangzhou in 12C. The population of London was approaching 700,000, making it more than twice as large as any city in Europe except Paris.[51] Within the confines of Great Britain, no other city even came close. Cities like Birmingham and Manchester had fewer than 30,000 inhabitants, and Oxford had only about 8,000.[52]

Londoners were crammed into an area that is a fraction of the city we know today. Since the time of Elizabeth, the Crown had tried to restrict new construction. Occasionally new areas were built from scratch, as after the Great Fire of 1666, but within a few decades property owners had subdivided the buildings, adding new entrances, and surreptitiously filling up courtyards and back gardens with new structures. London became a rabbit-warren of buildings crisscrossed by tiny lanes—as of 1732, London counted 5,099 streets and alleys.[53] Open country began at Hyde Park.[54]

The London Johnson knew was the London that Hogarth painted—muddy, unpaved, with open sewers and a stinking Thames, lavish wealth facing desperate poverty in an intimacy that we can scarcely imagine today. "Here lives a Personage of high Distinction," wrote one observer, "next door a Butcher with his stinking Shambles! A Tallow-Chandler shall front my Lord's nice Venetian window; and two or three brawny naked Curriers in their Pits shall face a fine lady in her back Closet."[55] Fishmongers, theatres, silversmiths, brickworks, brothels, hospitals, docks, chophouses, factories, churches, gardens, grocers, palaces, tenements—all were jammed together on the twisting streets. In the slums, a gin shop could be found in one of every four dwellings, advertising "Drunk for a penny, dead-drunk for twopence."[56] The crowds of pedestrians mingled every level of English society—"rambling, riding, rolling, rushing, jostling, mixing, bouncing, cracking and crashing in one vile ferment of stupidity and corruption," complained Smollett's Squire Bramble.[57]

The noise was deafening and the stench prodigious. London had no municipal program for collecting waste, no street-cleaners. Policing was like Antonine Rome—nearly nonexistent. Until 1750, the City of London had been patrolled by some 1,000 night watchmen who had become a national joke—drunken and ineffectual, the "charlies" of derisive abuse. In 1750, Henry Fielding hired some thief-takers who later evolved into the Bow Street Runners, rudimentary police patrols. But for practical purposes a citizen of London who ventured out of doors after dark should be prepared to fend for himself. Hangzhou of seven centuries earlier had been cleaner and safer.

The transportation system of Georgian Britain had yet to catch up with the one enjoyed by Roman Britons 17 centuries earlier. By the 1780s, the Newcastle & London Post Coach was advertising a service that would leave Newcastle at four in the morning and get the passenger into London after 39 hours of continual travel, breaking only for meals, jouncing along rutted roads at six miles an hour—phenomenally fast by previous standards.[58] But a Roman Briton making the same journey routinely did it in the same elapsed time, on a much smoother road, with a full night's sleep at a comfortable way station to break the journey.

The British of 18C knew immeasurably more than the Romans about the physics and mechanics of heat, but if you were looking for creature comforts, the villa of a wealthy Roman Briton with its central heating and good plumbing would have been a more comfortable place to live than the palaces built by Georgian aristocrats. And if you caught a chill during the winter damp, good luck. Bleeding was still the treatment of choice for a wide variety of ailments, germ theory was a century in the future, and hygiene was unheard of. A new wife of 18C had to enter upon childbearing knowing that she must expect to lose half of her babies before they reached adolescence and face odds of about one in 20 of dying in each childbirth herself. All in all, if you were going to get sick, you were better off in Song Hangzhou, and perhaps even in Antonine Rome, than in Johnson's London.

British physicians and their continental counterparts had made progress in preventing people from getting sick. One of the first controlled studies in the history of medicine established in 1747 that scurvy could be prevented by the juice of citrus fruits and thereby transformed the health of sailors on long voyages. Western medicine was finally becoming a science of precisely described symptoms and diseases, even if physicians still couldn't cure many of them.

Despite the bad hygiene and filthy streets, public health was improving, mainly because plagues were slowly disappearing. The word *plague* evokes the Black Death of mid-14C, but plagues had been a continuing fact of life. The single city of Besançon reported plague 40 times between 1439 and 1640.[59] London suffered too. As late as 1667, Sir William Petty still had reason to expect about five plagues in the next century:

> London within ye bills hath 696 thousand people in 108 thousand houses. In pestilential yeares, which are one in twenty, there dye one sixth of ye people in ye plague and one fifth of all diseases. The people which ye next plague of London will sweep away will be probably 120 thousand.[60]

But Sir William was wrong. Exactly why is still unclear, but the plague disappeared from Western Europe after an outbreak in Marseilles in 1720. Infectious diseases remained a problem—pandemics of typhus and influenza swept most of Europe in the late 1730s and early 1740s, and influenza struck London in 1782—but the scale of mortality diminished. Other infectious diseases, known today only by their descriptions in obsolete medical books, disappeared altogether. Smallpox had been a killer rivaling the plague—a medical text of 1775 estimated that it still affected 95 of every 100 people, and killed 1 in 7.[61] But in 1717 Mary Montagu published a treatise on the Turkish use of pus to inoculate against smallpox. Only four years later, Cotton Mather and Zabdiel Boylston used primitive statistical methods to demonstrate its effectiveness in Boston. By 1796, when Edward Jenner developed a safe method of inoculation using the cowpox virus, inroads against smallpox had already been made in the upper classes and vaccination was becoming widespread throughout Europe. Little by little, the power of disease to destroy was being circumscribed. Epidemics in 19C would continue to carry off tens of thousands of people at a time, but in the last half of 18C, Europe saw the end of the days when whole societies were routinely crippled by outbreaks of disease.

Famines subsided along with the plague. It is hard to realize today, but famine was a common European phenomenon through 18C. France, for example, among the richest of the European countries, experienced 13 general famines in 16C, 11 in 17C, and 16 in 18C, plus hundreds of local famines that affected a single town or region. The explanation for the famines was simple. The yields from cereal grains were low and the capacity to store reserves primitive. Two bad harvests in a row, and people starved. It was during 18C that technological progress in agriculture began to break the grip of that brutal arithmetic.

The most striking constant across imperial Rome, Song Hangzhou, and Georgian London was a widespread passion for the arts. An inventory conducted in 1785 tells us that 650 individual businesses in London made their money through books, from writing to printing to engraving to sales.[62] When the newly established Royal Academy opened an exhibition of paintings in the spring of 1780, it drew 61,381 persons by the end of the year —roughly 1 in every 12 Londoners in that one season alone, from a population that was overwhelmingly poor and illiterate.[63] Crowds swarmed to the two licensed dramatic companies of the era, Drury Lane and Covent Garden, packing theatres that by the end of the century had been built and rebuilt so that each accommodated 3,000 people at a time.[64] London's first professional concert series began in the 1760s, and by 1771 had led to a dedicated concert auditorium at the Pantheon on Oxford Street—"the most elegant structure in Europe, if not on the globe" in the mind of one observer—and then in 1775 to a 900-seat auditorium in Hanover Square and Oxford Street.[65]

Whether they were attending the theatre, a concert, or an exhibition at the Royal Academy, or buying a book at the local bookseller, Londoners in 18C had available to them a range of work that the citizens of neither imperial Rome nor classical China could approach. And yet the major artistic genres were in curiously different phases, and the public's attitude toward their practitioners was mixed. Some fine painters were at work in 18C, among them Britain's own Reynolds, Gainsborough, and Hogarth. But the prevailing British attitude toward these living artists, like the Romans toward theirs, was scathing—to the influential art critic Anthony Ashley Cooper, contemporary British painters were "illiterate, vulgar and scarce sober."[66] History has treated the targets of Cooper's scorn more respectfully, but the world of art was still absorbing the extraordinary outpouring of great art during the Renaissance, and the output of 18C could not compete. Drama had a similar problem. Despite a few luminaries such as Congreve, Goldsmith, and Sheridan, the legacy of the Elizabethan era was so daunting that it still cast a long shadow over playwrights of 18C. In contrast, fiction and poetry were blossoming. Fielding and Richardson were turning out the earliest examples of the genre that would peak in 19C, the domestic novel, and late 18C would see the first work of the great Romantic poets.

If you sought a golden age in 18C, the place to look was music. Johnson's London consisted of a half-century that saw parts or all of the careers of Mozart, J. S. Bach, Haydn, and Handel. Any one of them would have made the era musically distinguished. To have all four, plus Gluck, Rameau, Telemann, Pergolesi, Domenico Scarlatti, and Stamitz at the same time, plus Couperin and Vivaldi in the early decades of the century and Beethoven showing his emerging genius at the end of it, makes 18C the most densely packed century of realized musical genius in history. London did not contribute people to this constellation of stars—it had not produced a major composer since Henry Purcell in 17C—but it provided enthusiastic patrons. When Joseph Haydn was brought to London late in the century, he was astonished and overwhelmed by the British passion for music—"his presence seems to have awakened such a degree of enthusiasm in the audience, as to almost amount to a frenzy," wrote another musician.[67] In a sign of things to come, the British backed their enthusiasm for the arts with cash. Haydn cleared £350 for one concert in 1791 and £800 for another in 1794 —liberating sums for a composer who had felt himself little more than a glorified servant in the continental courts.

Densely packed is the right descriptor for Johnson's intellectual London writ large. The city was jammed with men of immense accomplishment, sometimes resident, sometimes visitors, and they knew each other across disciplines and professions in a way that rarely happens today. In Johnson's London, this intellectual cross-fertilization was reified in The Club, which formed in the winter of 1763–1764. It was nothing like the imposing institutions that became the famous London clubs of 19C, just a group of men getting together every Monday night at the Turk's Head in Gerrard Street.

But those men included statesmen James Fox and William Wyndham, linguist Sir William Jones, naturalist Sir Joseph Banks, painter Sir Joshua Reynolds, dramatists Oliver Goldsmith and Richard Brinsley Sheridan, actor David Garrick, Bishop Percy, historian Edward Gibbon, Johnson himself, and two men who together were to provide the intellectual templates for the Whigs and the Tories of British politics for the next century, Adam Smith and Edmund Burke. Other eras have had their roundtables and salons, but in 18C London they were peopled by men who would change the intellectual shape of the West, for Samuel Johnson's London was above all the London of the Enlightenment.

By the 1750s the Enlightenment had become the continent's child as well, but it had been Britain's baby. Isaac Newton's revelation in *Principia Mathematica* (1687) that the universe is rational, obeying fixed and predictable laws, had changed the way that people perceived the universe. God was no longer the interfering, jealous God of the Old Testament nor the loving personal God of the New, but God the Clockmaker, setting the universe on a course governed forever after by mathematically perfect immutable laws. If only mortals had enough data, they could predict everything that happened, and the tool whereby they could do this in a clocklike universe was reason. Reason, sweet and infallible, should be brought to bear on hoary traditions that governed the pursuit of knowledge, relationships between the sexes and the social classes, standards of art and music, and the exercise of political power.

In 1690, three years after Newton published *Principia*, John Locke, an English physician and friend of Newton's, published two short works that fit perfectly with this emerging new world view. The first to appear was *Essay Concerning Human Understanding*, proclaiming the doctrine of *tabula rasa*: Humans came into the world as blank pages upon which experience writes —a doctrine perfect for a world in which reason rules, perfect for a world beginning to think that all things are possible. Human nature was not immutable, nor was human history required to move in cycles. By applying reason not only to institutions but to the socialization of the young, humans could be improved along with their institutions. History henceforth could take on a direction, and that direction was progress.

A few months later, Locke's *Second Treatise of Government* was published, averring that government is the servant of men, not the other way around, and that men come into the world possessing natural rights to their own bodies (and therefore to their labor) that governments can legitimately circumscribe in limited ways. We in the United States think of Locke as an intellectual inspiration of the American Founders, which he was. But his more immediate role in English life was to put in philosophical terms the movement toward liberty that had swept England during its Glorious Revolution and was to provide the foundation for the reforms that continued throughout 18C.

By the late 1720s, England's combination of economic prosperity, social stability, and civil liberties had no equivalent anywhere on the continent. The young Voltaire, forced by circumstances to live in England (he had been exiled for inappropriately challenging a nobleman to a duel), was entranced. After returning to France, he wrote *Letters on the English*, praising their virtues. The book was a sensation in French intellectual circles. Before *Letters on the English*, according to report, there were but two Newtonians in all of Paris; now, Parisian thinkers learned English, translated English works, and borrowed from English fashion.[68] Voltaire followed up with essays on Newton and Locke, taking the Enlightenment to Paris, where it evolved in its own way, producing some decades later a Revolution very different from England's Glorious one.

The *philosophes* of the Enlightenment, whether French, English, or Scottish, included only a few actual philosophers. As a group they were more like a meeting of The Club, thinkers from many fields who had a common interest in starting with first principles, with human liberty heading the list. The *philosophes*, in Peter Gay's words, sought "freedom from arbitrary power, freedom of speech, freedom of trade, freedom to realize one's talents, freedom of aesthetic response, freedom, in a word, of moral man to make his way in the world."[69]

Some, like Rousseau, would be the inspiration for artistic and literary movements that continue to this day. Another, the University of Glasgow's Adam Smith, would lay out an economic theory so influential that it would be as powerful a force for economic growth in 19C as James Watt's steam engine would be for industrial growth. Published in 1776, *Wealth of Nations* introduced three elementary principles that now are seen as common sense, but which were at the time revolutionary. It was Smith who taught the world that a voluntary exchange benefits both parties—trade is not a zero-sum game in which one person wins while another loses, but win-win. It was Smith who taught governments that the trick to becoming rich is competitive advantage—don't try to subsidize the production of goods that others can produce better or cheaper. It was Smith who invoked the metaphor of the Invisible Hand to explain why a person whose only motive is to make money will be led to produce goods that other people need, of the right quality, at prices they can afford, if only that person is constrained to compete with others who are also trying to make money. Beyond these specifics, Smith changed forever the age-old assumption that wealth is a limited pie over which governments and men fight to get the biggest piece. Wealth can grow without limits—that was perhaps Smith's most revolutionary idea of all.

Growth, accumulating knowledge, change—Johnson's Britain was in a ceaseless, restless state of becoming. In the decades when Johnson was in London, the visible results were still limited. When Johnson died in 1784, London was not physically much different from the way it had looked when he arrived in 1737. The city was still lit by candles, people still traveled no faster than a galloping horse, and they communicated no more rapidly than a message could be conveyed on horseback. The middle class had grown during Johnson's decades but was still a thin layer sandwiched between manual laborers below and the landowning gentry above. Women had few more rights in 1784 than they had enjoyed in 1737. Even among men, the right to vote in 1784 was still restricted to a minority. Poverty and illiteracy were rampant. On a long list of measures, a comparative ranking of Rome, Hangzhou, and London at their respective observation points would show London lagging. What London had that the other two cities did not was dynamism. In 18C, the intellectual change was already kaleidoscopic. In a few decades, every other kind of change would become kaleidoscopic as well.

FOUR

A SENSE OF WONDER

And so we approach the point where the good stories end and the numbers begin. I hope that the preceding chapters have helped set the contexts that lie behind the numbers and at least temporarily fend off the parochialisms of present time and present place that so easily seduce us.

The other purpose of this stage-setting has been to remind you that the tables and statistics in the rest of the book stand for the remarkable achievements of flesh-and-blood human beings. To that end, it is important as we proceed to keep in mind two other blind spots.

The first of these blind spots is the tendency to forget how problems looked to the people who had to solve them. One reads a history of geology and smiles at the wrongheadedness of the Neptunist theory of the evolution of the earth. People seriously thought that rocks were precipitated from a heavily saturated fluid that once covered the globe? One reads a history of chemistry and smiles at the idea of phlogiston. People seriously thought that combustion is explained by an "oily earth" hidden within materials that burn? We identify with Hutton and Lavoisier, the ones who came up with the right answers.

But it was not at all obvious to the scientists who first wrestled with these problems, and it would not have been obvious to us. And so this antidote: The next time you find yourself driving through a rural landscape, look at the surrounding terrain, forget everything you've ever learned about geology, and then imagine you've been told you must determine how that landscape was created—how rivers and mountains and rocks came to be. Or the next time you light a candle, look at the flame, forget everything you've ever learned about chemistry, and imagine trying to explain the mechanism of fire.

Start with the assumption that you must learn it all from scratch, and the difficulty of the challenge that faced our forebears becomes real.

The second blind spot is the tendency to confuse that which has been achieved with that which must inevitably have been achieved. It is easy to assume that someone like Aristotle was not so much brilliant as fortunate in being born when he was. A number of basic truths were going to be figured out early in mankind's intellectual history, and Aristotle gave voice to some of them first. If he hadn't, someone else soon would have. But is that really true? Take as an example the discovery of formal logic in which Aristotle played such a crucial role. Nobody had discovered logic (that we know of) in the civilizations of the preceding five millennia. Thinkers in the non-Western world had another two millennia after Aristotle to discover formal logic independently, but they didn't. Were we in the West "bound" to discover logic because of some underlying aspect of Western culture? Maybe, but what we know for certain is that the invention of logic occurred in only one time and one place, that it was done by a handful of individuals, and that it changed the history of the world. Saying that a few ancient Greeks merely got there first isn't adequate acknowledgment of their leap of imagination and intellect.

The same complacency about the legacy we have inherited applies to works of art. Because *A Winter's Tale*, *The Night Watch*, and Beethoven's Fifth Symphony exist, it is easy to take their existence for granted. It is more accurate to think of each as a priceless gift. If Beethoven had died at 35, as Mozart did, we would have no Fifth Symphony—or Sixth, Seventh, Eighth, or Ninth symphonies, for that matter. If Michelangelo had died at 35, we would have no *Moses*, no *Last Judgment*, none of Michelangelo's architecture, and would be stranded with just a few tantalizing portions of the ceiling of the Sistine Chapel. Or we can go the other direction, and try to imagine what treasures we would have been given if Mozart had *not* died at 35, Schubert at 31, Keats and Pergolesi at 26, Masaccio at 27. It is nowhere written that works of genius have to be created, that something in the air will bring forth another Mozart if the first one falls. One may acknowledge the undoubted role of the cultural context in fostering or inhibiting great art, but still recall that it is not enough that the environment be favorable. Somebody must actually do the deed.

Another thought experiment. This time, imagine that the responsibility for doing the deed has fallen to you. When next you stand before a work of representational art in an art museum—not necessarily a great work by a great name, but one merely good enough to warrant a place in a respectable museum—put aside the theoretical artistic reasons for admiring it and focus just on its technique—its control of light and shadow, use of color, rendering of physical objects. Then imagine someone handing you a brush and a canvas and saying, "Here, you try it." Or when next you listen to a work in the classical repertory, imagine that you had to create a structure of coherent, beautiful sounds. To imagine being given such tasks is, for most of us, to force upon ourselves a recognition of how far they are beyond our own powers.

THE ART WE THINK WE CAN CREATE

We can all hum a made-up tune or sketch a picture of sorts, but few of us think we might be able to compose great music or paint great pictures. Writing is different. Every educated adult can write, and many, with reason, think they write pretty well. It thus crosses the minds of many that they could write good fiction if only they put their minds to it.

This offers a direct way of testing out my "Here, you try it" thought experiment. There is no better way to appreciate the difficulty of creating even minimally adequate art, let alone great art, than trying to write a paragraph of fiction. A daunting gulf separates the stringing together of words into good sentences from the creation of stories and characters that speak to people across time and cultures.

In the chapters to come, I will refer to human accomplishment in truckload lots. Great accomplishments will be discussed as outcomes of large historical and cultural influences. The painstaking work of a lifetime may be treated as one line in a database. These are standard operating procedures for exploring the kinds of questions I ask of the data. But before embarking on those discussions, it is well to begin by recalling that the achievements we will be analyzing have been, literally, wonderful.

PART TWO

IDENTIFYING THE PEOPLE AND EVENTS THAT MATTER

P art 2 presents the inventories of people and events essential to the story of human accomplishment.

The topic is human excellence, not mere fame. Chapter 5 opens by considering the nature of excellence in the arts and sciences and then presents the methods used to compile inventories of significant figures in the arts and sciences.

Chapter 6 presents the Lotka curve, the mathematical manifestation of a fact that reappears whenever the eminence of artists and of scientists is studied: a surprisingly small number of people loom over all the rest.

Chapter 7 presents the inventories of significant figures, describing what kinds of contributors make the cut.

Chapter 8 focuses on the giants, the handful of figures who have dominated their fields.

Chapter 9 turns from people to events, discussing the ways in which identifying significant events poses different problems for the arts versus the sciences. It includes a compilation of the most important events in the sciences.

Chapter 10 shifts to another kind of event—not discrete discoveries, inventions, or works of art, but 14 meta-inventions that expanded the cognitive repertoire of Homo sapiens.

EXCELLENCE AND
ITS IDENTIFICATION

In any list of the people and events preeminent in the history of human accomplishment, some names and events are certain to be mentioned more than others. But what are we measuring when we end up with names like Beethoven and Shakespeare and Einstein at the top of the list? Why are $E=mc^2$ and the Sistine Chapel and *The Divine Comedy* sure to be part of our inventory whereas other formulae and paintings and poems are not? Is the decisive factor their fame? Arbitrary decisions of keepers of the Canon? Authentic superiority?

The safe answer is *fame*, a value-neutral word that requires no explanation of why the Sistine Chapel keeps popping up whenever people write about art. It just does, and the fact it does means that it is famous. The safe answer is also close to my own operational answer throughout the rest of the book, as I use *eminence* to characterize people and *importance* to characterize events; words with meanings that overlap with *fame*.

But if fame were at the core of what I really meant, the exercise would not be worth my time to conduct nor yours to read. Who cares who the most famous artists are, if their fame signifies nothing more substantive than celebrity? Let it be understood from the outset that I do not consider eminence and importance to be slightly glorified measures of fame, but more than that. They are reflections of *excellence* in human accomplishment. The Sistine Chapel keeps popping up because it is home to one of the greatest works of art ever to come from a human hand and mind.

In whose opinion? Who is to say that some paintings are fine art and others are not? That some poems are greater than others? That some music is classical and other music is pop? That the achievements of some scientists are central and others are peripheral? In a world where *judgmental* has become an insult, who is to judge?

We have a long and winding road to travel in this chapter. First, I will describe what I define as excellence in the sciences and arts respectively. Next comes a description of my reasons for concluding that standard historiometric methods do a pretty good job of identifying excellence in the terms I have set. Then comes an overview of the procedures used to compile the inventories of accomplishment based on these methods. The chapter concludes with short answers to basic questions about the validity of the inventories.

EXCELLENCE IN SCIENTIFIC ACCOMPLISHMENT

Scientific is a word I will use throughout the rest of the book as a label for referring to the individual hard sciences (astronomy, biology, chemistry, the earth sciences, and physics) plus mathematics, medicine, and technology. In all of these human endeavors, the meaning of excellence is intimately connected with the discovery or application of objective truth about how the world or universe works.

A Workaday Definition of Truth

By *truth*, I mean nothing more abstruse than William James's pragmatic view that truth ". . . is a property of certain of our ideas. It means their 'agreement,' as falsity means their disagreement, with 'reality.'" How are we to deal with those words that James puts in quotes, "agreement" and "reality"? Again, pragmatically: "True ideas are those that we can assimilate, validate, corroborate, and verify. False ideas are those we cannot."[1] *Truth* as I am using the term similarly refers to knowledge that meets standard scientific criteria. A falsifiable hypothesis that has so far resisted falsification is a candidate for a truth. The more extensive the failed efforts to falsify it, the better the candidate. If a phenomenon can be replicated at will, science has made progress in understanding the truth of the dynamics of that phenomenon. Perfect, unvarying replicability suggests that a truth has been identified. Accurate prediction in non-experimental situations is another indicator of truth. Perfectly accurate prediction suggests that a law of nature has been identified.

In the hard sciences and mathematics, excellence involves the *discovery* of truth. In technology and medicine, excellence involves the *application* of truth to produce desired results. Philosophy, related to science (remember that scientists used to be called natural philosophers), is a poor cousin in this regard—falsifiability, replicability, and prediction in matters of metaphysics, ethics, and epistemology have yet to give us ways of comparing the truth content of the work of Plato and Kant in the same way we can compare the truth content of the work of Ptolemy and Copernicus. But philosophy at its best is engaged in the same enterprise, the search for truth, even if the markers of success are less clear.

When I say that my use of the word *truth* is uncomplicated, I do not mean that it is unambiguous. Truth in scientific endeavors is a moving target, constantly subject to amendment or outright refutation. The edifice of scientific accomplishment can be seen as a process of convergence, sometimes with major deviations and backslidings, on that final Truth with a capital T that we may reasonably think will forever be incompletely known to us. But to say that the current state of knowledge represents only our best approximation of truth is not to say that truth doesn't exist.

And so in three paragraphs I define my use of *truth*, a word that has been the subject of countless philosophical meditations and, in recent decades, of relentless academic attack. But adding another few dozen pages, or few hundred, to flesh out those three paragraphs would accomplish nothing. *Truth* in scientific endeavors has a workaday meaning that is broadly accepted, and it satisfies me. My attitude is not unlike Samuel Johnson's when James Boswell claimed that Bishop Berkeley's argument that matter does not exist independently of the perceiver could not be refuted. "I refute it *thus*," Johnson replied, kicking a large stone.[2] In the question of whether science deals in truth, my stone is our behavior in everyday life, where the same people who tell us there is no such thing as objective truth get on airplanes without a second thought. If the pilot is not in possession of a truth when he pulls back the stick, what other word might we use?

Does Importance Equal Excellence in Scientific Accomplishment?

In an ideal world, I would devise a measure that ordered scientific accomplishments according to the importance of the scientific truths that they discovered or the extent to which they established a framework within which scientific knowledge could be accumulated. At the top of the list would be such events as the discoveries of the fundamental laws of physics, the devel-

opment of the great taxonomic systems, or the discoveries of basic physio-
logical truths about living organisms.

In reality, historians of science use a variety of criteria for deciding how
much attention to give specific events, and some of those criteria confuse the
issue. Copernicus's heliocentric model of the universe is an example. It was
an authentically important contribution to scientific truth and deserves a high
spot on its own merits, but it also was a pivotal event in Renaissance Europe
with political, religious, and cultural repercussions that transcended its scientific importance. A score based on the amount of attention given to it in the
history books is in that sense "too high" because it is based in part on things
that have nothing to do with the scientific discovery in itself.

I return to this issue in Chapters 8 and 9. I will observe for the moment
that, the occasional problem case aside, the correspondence between *importance* defined by the historians' allocation of attention to events and *excellence*
as I am defining the term is close. You will have a chance to judge for yourself when you examine the leading scientists and events in the inventories
to come.

EXCELLENCE IN THE ARTS

Now we enter onto more contentious ground. The new proposition on the
table is that accomplishment in the arts is susceptible to judgments of intrinsic worth—excellence. Since I have identified scientific excellence with
truth, it is tempting to identify artistic excellence with beauty. But artistic
quality can be high or low in respect of dimensions for which the word *beauty*
narrowly defined is inadequate. Let me substitute the phrase *high aesthetic
quality* for what I have in mind by excellence in the arts. The question then
becomes whether *high aesthetic quality* has any objective meaning.

Just as it is one thing to say that the truth is hard to determine and
another to claim that truth does not exist, so is it one thing to say that
aesthetic standards are elusive and another to assert that such standards do not
exist. It is not a problem much thought about in our day. *Chacun à son goût*
has won out, and many people are not even aware that the argument has
another side. But countless generations preceding our own have grappled
with the problem of aesthetic judgment and standards. They discerned relationships that should inform our understandings today.

It is unnecessary to align the argument of this book with any particular school of aesthetics. My objective is a limited one: to communicate why I think that identifying excellence in the arts is possible. To that end I adopt a minimalist approach consistent with many schools. It draws most directly from a few basic observations by David Hume.

Expertise and Aesthetic Judgment

In 1757, Hume wrote an essay entitled "Of the Standard of Taste." It opens with a statement of the problem that, style aside, could have come from the pen of a multiculturalist today:

> The great variety of Taste . . . that prevails in the world is too obvious not to have fallen under every one's observation. Men of the most confined knowledge are able to remark a difference of taste in the narrow circle of their acquaintance. . . . But those who can enlarge their view to contemplate distant nations and remote ages are still more surprised at the great inconsistence and contrariety. We are apt to call *barbarous* whatever departs widely from our own taste and apprehension; but soon find the epithet of reproach retorted on us. And the highest arrogance and self-conceit is at last startled, on observing an equal assurance on all sides, and scruples, amidst such a contest of sentiment, to pronounce positively in its own favour.[3]

Hume understood as clearly as we do that cultural chauvinism is a potential problem. Yet it is obvious in everyday life, as Hume continues, that some works seem to endure across time and cultures. "The same Homer who pleased at Athens and Rome two thousand years ago, is still admired at Paris and at London," he writes.[4] Hume might observe today that the Handel of his own era is still admired at Tokyo and New Delhi.

Are the enduring works *better* than the ones that fade? If so, are fallible human beings able to say what it is that makes them better? When we are talking about works of similar quality, saying that one is better than another is difficult indeed. But at the extremes, the pedestrian versus the first rate, the reality of difference in quality is more than a matter of opinion. One person may assert with complete sincerity that a nude painted on black velvet is more beautiful to him than Titian's *Venus of Urbino*, but that is not the same as saying that the two are of equal aesthetic quality.

Hume tackles this issue by distinguishing between two aspects of taste, sentiment and judgment. "All sentiment is right," Hume writes, because "no sentiment represents what is really in the object."[5] *Sentiment* is a matter of perception. When it comes to sentiment, we may not argue with the admirer of nudes on black velvet. *Judgment* is a different matter, Hume says. It refers to the attempt to make true statements about the object being contemplated.

Nature has decided the relationship between certain rules of composition and the enduring attraction that they possess, Hume continues. He does not know why the rules of composition are as they are. He rejects the views of earlier thinkers that the rules can be deduced *a priori*. He makes the simpler assertion, one that the neurophysiologists are beginning to document, that human beings inherently find certain qualities attractive and others unattractive. So whereas perceptions of beauty and deformity are themselves sentiments, not qualities in the object itself, and men's opinions of the beauty or deformity of a particular object may vary widely, "it must be allowed that there are certain qualities in objects which are fitted by nature to produce those particular feelings."[6] These are the qualities that inhere to objects, and to which judgment may be applied.

THE GENETIC ROOTS OF AESTHETIC RESPONSES

Within a matter of years, we will understand a great deal about the biological origins of Hume's "qualities in objects which are fitted by nature." Progress has already been made in the fields of evolutionary psychology and neuroscience. Increased genetic knowledge will feed the findings of both. The note gives some accessible sources.[7] So far, a fair generalization about the findings is that they accord with traditional understandings of beauty. Humans are adaptable up to a point—some of the music of Mozart and Beethoven was initially considered dissonant and painful to listen to—but only up to a point. Schoenberg's hope that in time his music would be hummed in the streets seems doomed to disappointment.

People have differing capacities for discerning those qualities—that is Hume's next assertion, and the next stumbling block for someone reading Hume in 21C. Is it true that some people are better able to judge the objective quality of a work of art, or a novel, or a musical composition, than others are? To make sure everyone understands where he stands on this question, let me leave Hume for a moment and break down the assertion into smaller steps.

The first, most elementary proposition is that *people vary in their knowledge of any given field.* That much seems beyond dispute.

The next assertion is that *the nature of a person's appreciation of a thing or event varies with the level of knowledge that a person brings to it.* All of us can easily think of a range of subjects in which our own level of knowledge varies from ignorant to expert. If you know a lot about baseball, for example, you and an ignorant friend who accompanies you to the ballpark are watching different games when there is one out, runners on first and third, and the batter is ahead in the count.[8] The things you are thinking about and looking for as the pitcher delivers the next pitch never cross your ignorant companion's mind. Is your friend as excited by the game as you? Having as much fun? Maybe or maybe not, but that's not the point. Your appreciation of what is happening is *objectively* greater. You are better able to apprehend an underlying reality inhering in the object, and it has nothing to do with your sentiments.

Hobbies provide more examples. If you are a gardener, what you see when you visit Sissinghurst Castle is different from what a non-gardener sees. Your judgment of the quality of the garden has an element of the objective that goes beyond sentiments about how pretty the flowers are. If you are a stamp collector, the reasons you value a particular stamp involve aspects of it that someone who isn't a stamp collector overlooks. If you are an oenophile, your judgment of the quality of a wine has an element of the objective that goes beyond sentiments of how good it tastes. Expertise changes the quality of the experience, and also introduces an element of the objective.

I use the word *objective* gingerly. I am not defending the existence of a set of objective rules that experts know and amateurs don't (in the arts, anyway). The element of the objective I have in mind involves only components of the expert's assessment of a work of art, not the overall response to it, which inextricably mixes judgment and sentiment. The degree of objectivity varies from expertise to expertise and varies on topics within the expertise. I am willing to grant all sorts of caveats, but hold to a statistical understanding of *objective*: given a large number of expert opinions about a dozen specific qualities of a work of art, we will not see a random set of responses, but ones that cluster around a central tendency.

This leaves plenty of room for disputes among experts. Baseball fans, gardeners, stamp collectors, and oenophiles argue furiously about all sorts of things within their fields of expertise. But even these arguments are informed by common understandings that transcend sentiments. In aesthetics, Kant labeled this quality *disinterestedness* and held it to be an essential aspect of any aesthetic judgment. Judgments influenced by one's personal gratification in an object " . . . can lay no claim at all to a universally valid delight," he wrote. "Taste that requires an added element of *charm* and *emotion* for its delight, not to speak of adopting this as the measure of its approval, has not yet emerged from barbarism."[9]

Can human beings attain this kind of detachment, or are they kidding themselves when they profess to be making statements about art, or literature—or gardens or wines or stamps—that are independent of their emotional response? Everyday experience tells us that disinterestedness is not only possible but common. Knowledgeable people in every field routinely admire achievements that are not to their own taste and rate people who are not their personal favorites above people who are. The baseball fan admires the technical excellence of a notoriously boorish player. The gardener who doesn't care for topiary admires a well-executed example. The wine critic who gets more personal pleasure out of burgundy gives a higher rating to a bottle of rhône that is a better realization of its type.[10]

I take from such observations my third proposition, that *the relationship of expertise to judgment forms a basis for treating excellence in the arts as a measurable trait.* This is obviously the most controversial of the three assertions and does not lend itself to incontrovertible proof. An explicit statement of the position will at least let us know where we may disagree at the end.

I am talking about an indirect measure of excellence, not a measure of the thing itself. Physicists study subatomic particles not by examining them directly, but by the tracks they leave. The crowd's roar tells an experienced football fan whether the pass was complete or incomplete, a short gain or a long one. I deal with artistic excellence and the judgments of experts in analogous ways: If we measure the attention they give to different objects of their expertise, we can infer something about what they think of them.

The logic is that, by and large, the reason people who know a lot about a subject prefer A to B is because A is better than B—*better* in a sense that is intrinsic to the nature of the excellence in the field in question. Those who know the most about music devote so much attention to Bach because understanding Bach calls upon every bit of fine discrimination and knowledge that the expert can bring to the table. The prolonged study of Bach does not become boring, because Bach keeps presenting new facets for examination. A lesser composer does not pose the same challenges. His mysteries can be deciphered more quickly. He does not reward study as Bach does. Or to go back to my original example, the person who knows a lot about art can look at Titian's *Venus of Urbino* for a long time and the looking alone—not the social context of Titian's era, not the meaning of the female nude in the construction of gender, not what sort of person Titian was, but *just the looking*—absorbs the full attention of the art expert. Titian offers a lot to look at—to contemplate—for someone who knows about art. That same knowledgeable person cannot contemplate the nude painted on black velvet. He can think about its social context. He can think about the meaning of the female nude in the construction of gender. He can wonder about what sort of person the artist was. But there's not much to get out of the looking.

The argument is that people who know the most about an artistic field are drawn to certain works. The qualities that draw their attention are those that offer the biggest payoff in the aesthetics of the art, and this payoff is based on qualities distinct from subjective sentiments.

YOUR OPINION OF EXPERTISE IN YOUR OWN FIELD OF EXPERTISE

Experts are in bad odor these days. In courtrooms, expert witnesses flatly contradict each other. In the media, experts analyze the news in ways that reflect Hume's concept of sentiment rather than his concept of judgment. But away from the spotlight, expertise still has a meaning that virtually all readers can understand for themselves because virtually all of you can call upon something in your life on which you are an expert.

Now ask yourself whether you share this common tendency: On topics about which we know little, we are dismissive of the importance of expertise ("I don't know much about art, but I know what I like"). On topics about which we know a great deal, we are dismissive of amateur opinions. The difference between these two reactions is that one has an empirical basis and the other doesn't. On topics about which we know little, we by definition have no way of knowing that expertise is unimportant. On topics about which we know a lot, we have concrete reasons for concluding that amateur observations are either wrong or boringly obvious.

Caveats need to be added to that statement. Of course some experts are driven by contemporary intellectual fashion and devote their time to topics for reasons having nothing to do with aesthetic excellence. Of course some people who claim to be experts are faking it. Of course some people get into a field not because they find its subject matter fascinating, but because of other interests that they then impose upon the field. The list of ways in which the judgments of any particular expert, or self-proclaimed expert, can be wrongheaded is long indeed. But that brings us back to Hume and his observations about safety in numbers. We cannot know that any particular expert in a field is making an accurate judgment about a particular object at a particular time. His opinion may be clouded by anything from his sentiment to a bout of dyspepsia. But we are saved from these occasional lapses by the consensus that emerges across critics and across time. Each individual critic is reflecting in some way the underlying qualities that inhere in a work, independently of sentiment, and the experts' combined judgments cancel out the sentiments, which are likely to be what a statistician would call random noise.[11]

In discussing such arguments with friends and colleagues, I have found that their responses seem to depend on how comfortable they are with statistical distributions. To some, the idea that even one person with discerning taste can dislike Bach (which happens to be true of one widely-read critic) points to insuperable difficulties. To others, outliers are a fact of life—there's always the odd case in every large sample—and the existence of a reliable consensus is the important thing. I side with the latter. To summarize the position of this book regarding the arts: Excellence in the arts is defined in terms of high aesthetic quality. The combined evaluations of experts can provide a usable measure of high aesthetic quality.

The Impossibility of Being Nonjudgmental

To accept the position I just laid out requires one to adopt considerable humility about the arts in which one is not expert. While I am free not to enjoy the music of Richard Wagner, it is silly for me to try to argue that Richard Wagner does not deserve his standing as one of the greatest composers. That's a matter of judgment and I'm not competent to judge (Mark Twain said that "Wagner's music is better than it sounds," which seems about right to me[12]). Surrendering that independent judgment is irksome, and gets more so as one's knowledge approaches the fringes of expertise. I know more about literature than I know about music, and I nonetheless do not enjoy the later novels of Henry James that are most highly regarded by the experts. But my wife is an expert on Henry James and over the years I have had to accept that I don't know what I'm talking about.

In dealing with such situations, Hume's distinction between sentiment and judgment is invaluable. One is not required to surrender one's opinions, but merely to acknowledge their nature. I am not able to *argue* that the later Henry James does not write well; all I can do is *assert* that his later style is not to my taste—an assertion that is true and valid within its limits. The cliché "I don't know much about art, but I know what I like" is in this sense a precise and admirable preface to whatever comment comes next.

Another bothersome implication of the position I have laid out is that I must have an answer to a charge that goes something like this:

> *If you think that we should take the word of experts about what's good and bad, are you prepared to accept that John Cage and Andy Warhol belong up there with Brahms and Titian? That melody and harmony are boring and outdated? That representational art is boring and outdated? That the concept of beauty is meaningless? That's what one school of experts is saying these days.*

The direct answer to that objection is that I am choosing one type of expertise and rejecting another, allying myself with the classic aesthetic tradition and rejecting the alternative tradition that sprang up in 20C. A capsule history of aesthetics may help explain why I make that choice.

Human history is replete with forgotten knowledge of the kind I invoked in Chapter 2, but we identify such losses with ancient history. Other kinds of knowledge have been forgotten more recently than that. In the case of aesthetics, we have witnessed almost total amnesia overtake the West in just the last century.

Perhaps the word itself is partly to blame. *Aesthetics* was coined around 1750 by an obscure German philosopher named Alexander Baumgarten, who got it from the Greek word *aesthesis* (perception). By the time Kant wrote the most influential of all works on aesthetics, *The Critique of Judgment* (1790), the word was used synonymously with the judgment of beauty. The word *aesthete* followed, which to many readers may call to mind Bernard Berenson or John Ruskin, fussy men who seemed to be obsessed with "taste." In fact, even though the word *aesthetics* itself is new, inquiries into beauty and the judgment of beauty have been an important topic of inquiry for more than 2,300 years. The results of these centuries of work were various and contentious, in the same way that writings about epistemology and ethics have been various and contentious—at odds in some respects, but also bound together by a certain common understanding of the nature of the topic. In the case of aesthetics, this common understanding was that works of art are subject to judgment. Some works are better than others, not just as a matter of opinion, but according to underlying standards of excellence.

In the West, systematic inquiry into the nature of beauty postdated the appearance of the arts by some thousands of years, skipping the Mesopotamian and Egyptian civilizations.[13] It had entered the Chinese intellectual dialogue by the time of Confucius and appeared in Greece during the age of Plato.[14] In India, aesthetic inquiry was taking form by 5C.[15] Once established, aesthetics became a topic that attracted the attention of most of the great philosophers. In the West, these included Aristotle, Augustine, Hume, Kant, Schiller, and Hegel. In China, the study of aesthetics was intertwined with social and political thought, the subject of a scholarly tradition at least as elaborate as anything in the Western tradition.

Then, over the course of 20C, aesthetics disappeared—not just "encountered opposition" or "lost influence," but, for practical purposes, vanished from intellectual discourse. Many scholars have recounted how the classic conception of aesthetics came to take such a beating during 20C.[16] I will give only the sketchiest outline here.

The revolution began in the first half of 20C with influential new voices, especially those of Benedetto Croce and John Dewey.[17] Their message as it percolated to the wider world (their actual writings were more nuanced) was that objective standards of beauty are absurd, that we must rescue art from the stuffy confines of museums and concert halls, and that what counts is the artist's obligation to vent his creative impulse, to express himself, to challenge the onlooker. If we the audience don't understand what the artist is saying, that's our problem, not his.

At about the same time that classic aesthetic standards were being challenged, another influential movement got underway. It was embodied in the title of one of its pioneering works, *The Meaning of Meaning*, by C. K. Ogden and I. A. Richards (1923).[18] Out of this inquiry came semiotics—the study of the ways in which words, concepts, and arguments are, beneath their superficial meanings, functioning as signs of something else. Semiotics launched us on the path to the postmodernism that now dominates the academic study of literature, art, music, politics, and sociology. It uses "social construction" as a catch-all explanation of human differences and institutions, mocks the idea that an objective truth exists, and has given rise to the everything-is-equally-valid-in-its-own-context relativism.

In aesthetics, the legacy of postmodernism has been a wholesale rejection of the idea that there is anything worth talking about. People foolishly used to think that objective aesthetic judgments were possible, this attitude holds, but in 20C we realized that objective aesthetic statements are impossible because they are culturally bound. Today's mindset incorporates a heedlessness that would have dismayed Dewey, Croce, Ogden, and Richards.

Today, few postmodernists bother to refute classic aesthetic thinking or even concede an obligation to be conversant with it.

So when I acknowledge that I am picking which experts I choose to defer to, it is not quite as arbitrary as saying that I prefer a particular school that was fashionable in a particular time and place. Rather, I am allying myself with a view of the nature of aesthetic inquiry that can without strain encompass everyone from Aristotle and Confucius to Hume, Kant, and beyond—a long, broad, and distinguished tradition indeed. I am rejecting a postmodernist alternative of recent origin that within a few decades of its founding had become so politicized that its original merits were lost.

In saying this, I should acknowledge that I find it impossible to take postmodernism seriously. Harold Bloom, referring to the postmodernist critique of Shakespeare, captures what is, to me, its essential silliness:

> [T]he procedure is to begin with a political stance all your own, far out and away from Shakespeare's plays, and then to locate some marginal bit of English Renaissance social history that seems to sustain your stance. Social fragment in hand, you move in from outside upon the poor play, and find some connection, however established, between your supposed social fact and Shakespeare's words. It would cheer me to be persuaded that I am parodying the operations of the professors and directors of what I call "Resentment"—those critics who value theory over the literature itself—but I have given a plain account of the going thing, whether in the classroom or on the stage.[19]

Readers who want to investigate more detailed reasons for my dismissiveness may consult the titles in the note.[20] Here, I put it as an assertion: If the criteria for the choice are rootedness in human experience, seriousness of purpose, and intellectual depth, choosing the classic aesthetic tradition over postmodernism is not a close call.

This brings us to a broader issue than postmodernism narrowly defined. Despite postmodernism's influence in academia, the number of dogmatic postmodernists in the wider population is small, and I doubt if many readers are among them. The widespread attitude these days is an extreme reluctance to be "judgmental" in any arena, an ethos that has spread across questions of morality, religion, politics, and the arts.

My first objection to this stance is that being nonjudgmental is internally contradictory and an impossibility. Return to the extreme cases: If you refuse to accept that there are *any* objective differences, expressible as continua from negative to positive, between the nude painted on black velvet and Titian's *Venus of Urbino*, between a Harlequin romance and *Pride and Prej-*

udice, between *How Much Is That Doggy in the Window* and *Eine Kleine Nacht-musik*, you are not standing above the fray, refusing to be judgmental. It is a judgment on the grandest of all scales to say that *How Much Is That Doggy in the Window* is, in terms of its quality as a musical composition, indiscriminable from *Eine Kleine Nachtmusik*. And if you really believe it, you have also made a sweeping judgment about the capacity of the human mind to assess information.

The impossibility of being nonjudgmental does not go away as the differences in quality become smaller. The nature of the judgments merely changes. When we are comparing *Venus of Urbino* with a Rembrandt self-portrait, we immediately understand that no objective dimension enables us to say that one work is better than the other. But there remain dimensions on which the two paintings differ, and those dimensions lend themselves to comparisons in which one work may be found superior to the other. One may choose to examine those differences or not, but one does not have the option of saying that no differences exist.

Nor does one have the option of saying that differences exist but that one will not judge them. To notice a difference is to have an opinion about it—unless one refuses to think. And that is my ultimate objection to the nonjudgmental frame of mind. We can refuse to voice our opinions, our judgments, but we cannot keep from *having* them unless we refuse to think about what is before our eyes. To refuse to think is to reject that which makes a human life human. In saying that excellence in the arts is defined in terms of high aesthetic quality, I do not mean to trivialize the complications of determining high aesthetic quality. I do insist that to deny the existence of such a thing as high aesthetic quality is to take the lazy way out.

THE OPERATIONAL MEASURES OF EXCELLENCE

This discussion of the meaning of excellence has raised all sorts of issues that do not lend themselves to hard and fast conclusions. When we turn instead to a framework for operationalizing the definitions I have proposed, we find firmer ground. Whether consistency of judgment across critics reflects what Hume thinks it does—genuine excellence—or whether it merely reflects jointly held sentiments is debatable. But whether the consistency itself exists is an empirical question that can be settled definitively.

The quest to measure the gradations of greatness goes back to 1869 and the publication of Francis Galton's *Hereditary Genius*, an early document in the field that would become known as historiometry.[21] Galton was the first to hypothesize, and then support with data, that reputation is a useful measure of a person's importance. "By reputation," he wrote, "I mean the opinion of contemporaries revised by posterity—the favorable result of a critical analysis of each man's character, by many biographers."[22] He obtained his classifications by examining a biographical dictionary and various sources of obituaries.

Galton and his immediate successors were self-critical about their results.[23] Did a subject's reputation rest on his accomplishments or his social standing? Were the accomplishments the direct result of the ability of the subject, or was he merely in the right place at the right time? These problems of interpretation were real, but as time went on, it became apparent that they were tractable.[24] Once adjustments had been made, the major reference works and histories were found to have two roles in determining *eminence*— the descriptor that soon replaced Galton's original word, "reputation."

First, these works could be used to identify the population of people who were worthy of study. The founding document of historiometry, Adolphe Quetelet's 1835 study of productivity and age among dramatists, was based on plays included in French and English theatrical repertories.[25] Others have based their populations on everyone who merited at least one column in an encyclopedia,[26] everyone who was the subject of a biography in a public library,[27] or everyone who was included in at least one of three biographical dictionaries.[28]

Second, these reference works and histories could be used to calibrate eminence within the population of qualified people. The gradations were based on the amount of space devoted to different figures—space measured, for example, in terms of the number of pages of a book in which a person is mentioned, or the number of columns devoted to an entry in a biographical dictionary. J. McKeen Cattell was the first to gradate eminence in this way a full century ago, using six major biographical dictionaries from Britain, the United States, France, and Germany. Cattell discarded everyone who did not appear in at least two of his sources and measured the space allotted to the remaining sample. He then took the top 1,000 and ranked them in order, adding a "probable error" to indicate how much confidence could be attached to the ranking.[29] The scholars who have followed in Cattell's wake have used a profusion of specific procedures to measure eminence, but all of them come down to the same rationale: When people knowledgeable in their fields attempt to write balanced and comprehensive accounts of who did what, they tend to allocate space according to the importance of the person they are talking about.

To see how this procedure works in practice, a specific example may help. Our topic, we shall say, is Western art. The first source that comes to hand is a staple of undergraduate art courses, *Art Through the Ages*, still commonly referred to as "Gardner" after Helen Gardner, its original author. In the sixth edition (1975), Michelangelo has the highest total of page references and examples of works devoted to him, more than twice the number devoted to either Picasso or Donatello, tied for number two. Then comes a tie among Giotto, Delacroix, and Bernini, followed by a tie among Leonardo, Rembrandt, and Dürer, and then still another tie between van Eyck and Raphael.[30] The list provides a nice illustration of what *statistical tendency* means. There are a few surprises—does Delacroix really belong in the top 11 in the history of Western art? Some famous names are missing from this top 11. But the tendency for important artists to get the most space is evident.

After examining the index of Gardner's *Art Through the Ages*, we turn to the index of another major history, H. W. Janson's *History of Art*.[31] In the fifth edition (1997), Michelangelo is once again on top. Then, in order, come Picasso, Leonardo, and Donatello. Raphael and van Eyck are tied for fifth, followed by Dürer, Titian, and then a tie among Giotto, Bernini, and Masaccio.

Notice both the similarities and differences between this list of the top 11 and the one from Gardner. The most striking point is that 9 names were on both lists. Notice also how using just 2 sources already begins to correct for the deficiencies of either. Delacroix, who seemed to have too much space devoted to him in Gardner, has yet to appear in Janson's list. If we combine the 2 sources, Delacroix's rating will be knocked down considerably. Janson's top 10 has Titian and Masaccio, important painters who did not make Gardner's top 10. Their scores will go up in a combined list.

For our third list, we leave the English and the single-volume history, and instead use the 12-volume *Lexikon der Kunst* (1990), edited by Wolf Stadler and compiled with the assistance of an international board of contributors. Picasso barely edges out Michelangelo for the most page citations, followed in order by Rembrandt, Dürer, then the quartet of Bernini, Leonardo, Raphael, and Velazquez (tied), and next Titian and Rubens (tied). Eight of Stadler's top 10 are on one of the other two lists. Six artists—

Michelangelo, Picasso, Leonardo, Dürer, Raphael, and Bernini—are on all three lists.

These shared judgments at the top of the list of artists go deeper into the ranks. A total of 184 painters and sculptors were mentioned in all three sources. The correlation coefficients for the ratings obtained from the sources are .85 for Gardner and Janson, .75 for Janson and Stadler, and .76 for Gardner and Stadler. It is such high correlations among histories of the same field, not the anecdotal evidence I have just presented, that has led to the extensive use of such measures of eminence in the technical literature. To summarize what the source of that correlation is, and the position that underlies the rest of this book:

The high correlations among sources are a natural consequence of the attempt by knowledgeable critics, devoted to their subject, to give the most attention to the most important people. Because different critics are tapping into a common understanding of importance in their field, they make similar choices. Various factors go into the estimate of importance, but they are in turn substantially associated with excellence. The same rationale applies to events: Attention has been accorded to events in accordance with authors' estimates of their importance, and that importance is substantially associated with excellence.

WHAT IS A CORRELATION COEFFICIENT?

A correlation coefficient is a number ranging from −1 to +1 that mathematically expresses the degree to which one phenomenon is linked to another. Height and weight, for example, have a positive correlation (the taller, the heavier, usually). A positive correlation is one that falls between 0 and +1, with +1 being a perfectly linear relationship. A negative correlation falls between 0 and −1, with −1 representing a perfectly linear inverse relationship. A correlation of 0 means no linear relationship whatsoever. Correlations in excess of ±.7, as in the correlations among Gardner, Janson, and Stadler, are high for most topics in the social sciences. A more general discussion of correlation and statistics is given in Appendix 1.

THE INVENTORIES: AN OVERVIEW

Armed with this framework for investigating the eminence of people and the importance of events, I assembled databases of people and events into what I hereafter call *inventories* of human accomplishment. What follows is the bare minimum needed to understand how the concepts discussed in the foregoing pages are used for the inventories. I have reserved most of the technical detail for Appendix 2.

Delimiting Accomplishment

What qualifies as a human accomplishment? To think about such a question is to think about how we evaluate ourselves as individuals and as a species. What is important? What is not?

In the Introduction, I invoked the image of a résumé of the human species. Let me return to that metaphor, because it has shaped the choice of topics to include and exclude. Its utility lies in the meaning of the word *résumé*—not a report card, diary, or chronology, but evidence of a person's capacities. A résumé of the species demonstrates our capacities as a species.

Because it is a résumé of the species, its emphasis is the original discovery, the invention, the unique creation. Sometimes this can naturally be associated with an individual; sometimes not. It is possible to put the composer of the *Kreutzer* sonata in the music inventory—there is just one such person—but it is not possible to assign a person to the accomplishment of the species known as "learned to play beautiful music with the violin." The great violinists who have performed the *Kreutzer* sonata are not part of the inventory.

One other thing about a résumé: it makes no pretense at balance. Neither do the inventories. They are intended to represent our species at its best.

The Categories of Accomplishment

The inventories may be broadly categorized under the familiar phrase "the arts and sciences," but in practice I created separate databases in twelve domains: literature, visual arts (limited to sculpture and painting), music, astronomy, biology, chemistry, earth sciences, physics, mathematics, medicine, technology, and philosophy.

THE OMITTED CATEGORIES OF ACCOMPLISHMENT

The two great categories of human accomplishment that I have omitted from the inventories are commerce and governance. After reviewing histories and chronologies of those fields, my judgment was that while it was possible to compile inventories of people and events, the compilations were unlikely to have either the face validity or the statistical reliability of the inventories for the arts and sciences. The process whereby commerce and governance have developed is too dissimilar from the process in the arts and sciences.

I ignore some specific categories within the arts. I obtained data on architects in the course of assembling the inventory for the visual arts, but the treatment of architecture varied widely from source to source. When all the data were assembled I decided that combining architects with painters and sculptors would not add much (great architectural accomplishment went roughly in tandem, in both timing and geography, with great accomplishment in painting and sculpture) and ran the risks of combining apples and oranges. The visual arts inventory also omits such categories as jewelry, cabinetry, and decoration. Dance could not be treated as a separate category except within the last few centuries at most, and even then the documentation for dance is of a different order from the documentation for the other arts.

The social sciences are omitted. The sources I reviewed were inconsistent in the level of detail they devoted to the social sciences, and the scholarship devoted exclusively to the history of the social sciences does not yet permit the kind of multiple-source compilation that was possible for the hard sciences, medicine, mathematics, and technology. Anthropology, technically classified under earth sciences and therefore one of the hard sciences, was also omitted, partly because of uneven treatment in the sources and partly because anthropology as it evolved in 20C moved away from physical anthropology and toward topics that share more with sociology than with the hard sciences.

Each of the eight inventories involving scientific endeavors have separate inventories for persons and events. Coverage in all of the scientific inventories is worldwide.

The arts and philosophy have inventories based only on persons, not works, for reasons discussed in Chapter 9. Worldwide coverage is not feasible in the arts and philosophy inventories, because all sources, no matter how broad their scope, demonstrated some degree of skew toward the tradition in which they were written. Philosophy was broken into separate inventories for China, India, and the West. Literature was broken into separate inventories for the Arab world, China, India, Japan, and the West. The visual arts were broken into separate inventories for China, Japan, and the West. A single music inventory was prepared, limited to the West.

The decision about which geographic areas to cover was based on pragmatic judgments. The first question was how extensive the work was in a given field. Thus a separate philosophy inventory was not prepared for Japan because so much of Japanese philosophy derives from Chinese sources. A separate philosophy inventory was not prepared for the Arab world because so much of Arabic philosophic writing consists of commentaries on the Greeks. The second question, applied specifically to the arts, was whether work was attributed. The reasons for requiring that an artistic tradition be based on named artists arise from technical issues that make inventories of artistic works more problematic than inventories of artists. These issues are discussed at length in Chapter 9. Thus a separate visual arts inventory was not prepared for India because so much of Indian art is anonymous. The Chinese art inventory is restricted to painting, because so much of Chinese sculpture was the work of anonymous craftsmen. Music inventories were not compiled for any tradition except the West, because only the West has a substantial tradition of composed pieces by named composers. Lest enthusiasts for one of the omitted traditions feel slighted, I will put the point in italics: *That an inventory does not exist for an artistic tradition of anonymous art is not a commentary on the quality of the art, but on the technical problems associated with compiling inventories based on works of art rather than artists.* In Chapter 11, the discussion of European dominance explicitly considers the issue of anonymous artistic traditions (see page 260).

The Unweighted Measure of Eminence: Significant Figures

Eminence will be our proxy measure for excellence in persons, using multiple sources. Earlier, I gave the example of the correlation among three art history sources. Now leap ahead to the point at which I have assembled data from many sources, each with its useful but imperfect distribution of the attention it devotes to the different figures in the story it tells. The details of what happens next in the creation of the inventories are described in detail in Appendix 2. Here, you need to be familiar with the meaning of two terms that will be used throughout the remainder of this book: *significant figures* and *index scores.*

A *significant figure* is defined as anyone who is mentioned in at least 50 percent of the qualified sources for a given inventory, with *qualified source* being one that meets certain criteria of comprehensiveness in covering the topic in question. In effect, this is an unweighted measure of eminence—a binary, yes/no measure that says nothing about how much attention a person got in these sources, but merely says that at least half of the sources for this field mentioned him.

The Weighted Measure of Eminence: Index Scores

The second term you will be seeing frequently is *index scores.* In simplest terms, it measures how the significant figures stack up against one another. It provides a weighted measure.

The computation of index scores varied from inventory to inventory. The general principle was to use all the information available, which varied by inventory and source—for example, the number of index page references, column inches of text, number of plates of artistic works—collected, combined, and converted to a metric that is common to all of the inventories.

The common raw score across inventories represents in effect the average percentage of material devoted to a given person. For example, the raw score of Chopin is 1.06, meaning (ignoring technical caveats) that, in the 16 sources used for the Western music inventory, Chopin averaged 1.06 percent of the attention distributed among all the significant figures in the music inventory.

These raw scores varied widely in their range and from inventory to inventory. In the Western art inventory, for example, the highest raw index score was only 2.2 percent (Michelangelo) compared to a whopping 17.4 percent top score in the Chinese philosophy inventory (Confucius). To facilitate comparisons across inventories, I converted the raw scores in the various inventories into a common scale in which the lowest score and highest scores are always 1 and 100 respectively, and the distribution in between matches the distribution of the raw index scores. In other words, it is a linear transformation, and the shape of the raw and transformed distributions are precisely the same. These are the index scores.

SHORT ANSWERS TO BASIC QUESTIONS

When describing these inventories to friends and colleagues during the years I was preparing them, I found that a few questions always came up immediately. The full answers to them take considerable space, and are to be found in the various chapters where they are most relevant and in the technical appendices. Because it is likely that these questions are already in your mind, it may be helpful to give brief answers now.

How valid and reliable are these measures of eminence and importance?

There are two ways of assessing whether the scores I present are meaningful. The simplest is to ask whether the results possess *face validity*. Face validity in this instance means that the rank order produced by these measures looks reasonable to a knowledgeable observer, so that one's reaction is, "That's about what I would expect." Whether the inventories fit that description is up to you to decide.

The second way of assessing the measures is by examining their *statistical reliability*. A statistically reliable index is one that is stable, meaning that the scores continue to look pretty much the same for any large subset of the sources. "Pretty much the same" translates technically into the statement that if you were to split the sources for any given inventory into two groups, prepare separate measures from each half, then correlate the two sets of measures, then repeat that process for every permutation of split halves, the average correlation coefficient would be high. For the inventories used in *Human Accomplishment*, the reliability coefficients are at or above .9 for 13 of the 20, with a median of .93. These are extremely high reliabilities for social science indexes in general, but are typical of the reliability of indexes of eminence.[32]

Aside from their importance in assessing the scores within each inventory, these high reliabilities give reason to believe that the results from this set of sources will be similar to the results from any other similar set of sources. Insofar as the sources used to prepare the inventories qualify as comprehensive and balanced, the high reliabilities of the indexes presented here are evidence that the estimates of eminence are reflections of the state of expert opinion (in the classic tradition), as of the last half of 20C.[33]

So far I have been talking about the reliability and validity of the index scores. A separate issue is whether the people and events chosen for inclusion in the inventory would be the same no matter who chose them. The 50-percent criterion was chosen specifically because tests of the sources indicated that it produced stable samples, with *stability* in the choice of persons and events being analogous to *reliability* in the calculation of scores. As discussed more fully in Chapter 7: If you were to go out and assemble a dozen histories, biographical dictionaries, and encyclopedias of music and prepare your own inventory, using comparable procedures, you would end up with a population of composers that would be roughly the same in size and would include all the major figures and a high proportion of the minor figures that are in my inventory. Do not misunderstand: my population of significant figures is not a uniquely correct set. Your inventory might contain dozens of marginally significant people who were mentioned in 55 percent of your sources but only 45 percent of mine, and vice versa. But the distribution of your set of orphans and my set of orphans over time and geography would be similar. The statistical profiles of the two inventories would be effectively indistinguishable.

How much are these estimates of eminence a matter of current fashion?

"Reflections of the state of expert opinion as of the last half of 20C" raises the next question. To what extent are we taking a snapshot of expert opinion at an arbitrary point in time that is mostly a matter of fashion and may be quite different a hundred years from now?

For assessing recent people and events, this objection has force. Will string theory and punctuated equilibrium turn out to be major scientific discoveries? Insights that are not quite right but eventually inspire the right answer? Major goofs? Will Andy Warhol and Thomas Pynchon be seen as significant figures in art and literature or will they soon be forgotten?

The principal way I have dealt with this problem is to assume that answers to such questions are little better than guesses, and to avoid such guesses by cutting off the inventories at 1950. This cutoff date means that I have excluded people and events in the scientific inventories that will be of major historic importance, but there is plenty of material for analyzing human accomplishment in the sciences without the events of the last 50 years. In the arts, it is not clear that cutting off the inventories at 1950 involves the loss of much material at all. No doubt some art, music, and literature created from 1950 to the present will survive, but it is hard to imagine that the last half-century will be seen as producing an abundance of timeless work.

Does fashion remain a problem for assessing events and people before 1950? The answer depends on the inventory. For inventories dealing with the sciences, technology, mathematics, and medicine, fashionability seems to be only a minor problem. Given the pace of contemporary science, 50 years of reexamination and replication of findings is a long time for a false finding to survive.

Fashion poses more of a threat in the arts. By cutting off the inventory at 1950, I have reduced one aspect of the problem, the problem of delayed recognition. The starving painter in his garret, creating masterpieces that will be appreciated only after his death, is a cultural cliché, but we have had more than 50 years now to identify those previously ignored artists, composers, and writers. It seems unlikely that many geniuses are still left languishing—the putatively ignored geniuses of the past were seldom ignored for more than a few decades.

For both the arts and the sciences, 50 years is not long enough to deal with the other aspect of the problem, which involves what has been variously called the *discount effect* or (Dean Simonton's phrase) *epochcentric bias*.[34] As Oswald Spengler put it, "The 19th century A.D. seems to us infinitely fuller and more important than, say, the 19th century B.C.; but the moon, too, seems to us bigger than Jupiter or Saturn,"[35] and the result is that recent work gets more attention than it will turn out to deserve in the long run.

Sometimes recent work gets disproportionate attention because it is more accessible in its language or sensibility than a text of a few centuries earlier. Sometimes it is seen as more relevant to the concerns of contemporary audiences. Whatever the reasons, it has been established that the attention devoted to an historical event decays as its date moves deeper into the past for reasons that have nothing to do with its intrinsic importance.[36] The cutoff date of 1950 avoids the worst of the potential epochcentric bias, but how much might remain? I am not sure. If at the end of the book I were in the position of arguing that the most recent century has also seen the highest rates of accomplishment, the uncertainty would be problematic. That is not where the story comes out, however, so whatever epochcentric bias remains actually gives a margin of error for the argument I will be making, that the density of accomplishment has declined (see Chapter 21).

What about problems of fashion that might go back much further than 1900? Even the greatest names, including Shakespeare and Bach, have experienced ups and downs in reputation. Presumably such vagaries of fashion will mean that inventories in 25C will show a somewhat different set of rankings from the inventories I present at the beginning of 21C. But the ups and downs are often overstated. Johann Sebastian Bach is a case in point. Bach was underestimated in the first century after his death, but he was by no means obscure. He was admired and studied by Mozart. Beethoven was deeply influenced by Bach, whom he called the "immortal god of harmony."[37] Even the most adamant 18C partisans of progressive music (the critics who provided us with dismissive quotes about Bach) usually acknowledged his greatness in their less strident writings.[38] He would have ranked lower in an inventory of musical accomplishment prepared in 1800 than he does today, but he would have been a major figure even then. By 1900 he would have been about as near the top as he is now.

The method of constructing the inventories also offers some protection against fads. It protects against sudden infatuations (Jane Austen's sudden surge in popularity in the 1980s and 1990s, for example) by using resources that were prepared over several decades, and it protects against parochial fads (it was only Anglophone countries that joined in the Austen fad) by using sources written in several different countries and languages.

A third protection lies in the wider pool of critical judgment in today's world than in earlier centuries. In Bach's case, one reason his reputation took time to develop was the physical inaccessibility of his work. Those who didn't happen to be attending church services in a certain part of Germany on certain Sundays never heard much of Bach's *oeuvre*. As late as the 1940s, music historian Paul Lang could write of Bach's work, "How tightly the scholar's room is still closed, how inaccessible to the millions of music lovers," lamenting that "The large concert hall, the only place where we encounter Bach's music, is not his rightful element."[39] A decade later, with the invention of the long-playing record, that barrier began to shrink. Similarly, the accessibility of high-quality color reproductions of art has increased dramatically in the last half-century. Today's appraisal of pre-20C artists may still suffer some element of modishness, but it is based on widespread availability of all the relevant work. This helps to damp the amplitude of swings in fashion.

In sum, the expert opinion that lies behind the inventories does indeed represent the view of late 20C, and it will not be immutable, but there is no reason to think that fashion has deformed the broad patterns that form the basis for the discussion.

What about Eurocentrism, sexism, racism, chauvinism, and elitism?

The inventories are dominated by the accomplishments of white males. This raises issues of bias that are a familiar part of today's intellectual landscape. When it comes to the inventories used for *Human Accomplishment*, one may predict that each of the specific allegations of bias will be a variation on a theme that goes something like this:

> *Our understanding of every field of human accomplishment has been confined and biased by its own canon: the novels, plays, poems, paintings, sculptures, symphonies, sonatas, and operas that the intellectual establishment has designated as great. This designation of greatness is artificial, a function of the mindset of the members of the establishment rather than of objective criteria of excellence (objective criteria that cannot exist). Even in science and technology, our view of human accomplishment is distorted by preconceptions of what is important. Once the canon in any given field has been established, it takes on a life of its own. Of course the sources used to compile the inventories show correlations in their allocations of space. They are all copying from one another, buying into the same narrow definition of what is good and bad.*

As this general view is disentangled—deconstructed?—into its component allegations, it becomes possible to examine the degree to which it makes sense. The components that loom largest are Eurocentrism, sexism, racism, national chauvinism, and elitism. What follows are short summaries of how the allegations appear to relate to the inventories, once again presented with the understanding that there is more to come.

Eurocentrism. The question of Eurocentrism gets a chapter of its own (Chapter 11). For now, these summary points: For the philosophy and arts inventories, I have mooted most aspects of Eurocentrism by creating separate inventories for non-European traditions. For example, the inventory of Chinese artists is not in competition with Western artists. When assessing the inventory, the only way that Eurocentrism could be a problem is if Western writers on Chinese art have a systematically different perspective than Chinese writers on Chinese art, and this was not the case. Similar comments apply to the other inventories drawn from non-European traditions. By creating separate inventories for the Arab world, China, India, and Japan, while creating a combined inventory for all of the West, I also introduced a systematic inflation of the number of non-Western significant figures, a point which I discuss at length in Chapter 11.

Eurocentrism is a potential problem for the scientific inventories, each of which is a worldwide compilation of persons and events. The view I brought to these inventories is that, ultimately, each deals with universal truths. Chinese and Western painting may not be comparable, but Chinese and Western science are. The Pythagorean Theorem may be named for a Greek, but a right triangle has the same relationship between its sides and hypotenuse everywhere. A bamboo bridge over a Chinese canal and a stone bridge over a Dutch canal both carry their loads because of the same laws of physics.

When it comes to the period from −800 onward, the period for which I shall be analyzing the inventories, historians of science have done excellent work in reconstructing who discovered what. Nor is there much residual disagreement among historians of science from different cultures—no Chinese or Indian texts claim a significant set of scientific or mathematical discoveries that are not acknowledged as well by Western experts on those subjects. Since the act of discovery—being first—is the requisite for getting into an inventory, this reduces the number of uncertainties to a small set.[40] I have been unable to find evidence that inventories of scientific, mathematical, technological, or medical accomplishment drawn from reputable sources in any non-Western culture would look much different from the inventories we will be working with.

Chauvinism. National chauvinism within the West remains a problem. Works purporting to cover all of the Western world are skewed toward the nationality of the author. For example, British art historians tend to give more space to Constable and Turner than Italian art historians do, and French historians of philosophy tend to include French thinkers that hardly anyone else mentions.

An examination of these tendencies reveals that the effect of chauvinistic tendencies is minor to begin with and eliminated if the sources come from a mix of nations. Therefore the inventories for the West (visual arts, music, literature, and philosophy) employ sources that have been balanced among the major European nations (Britain, France, Germany, Italy, and Spain) plus the United States and a scattering of other nations (Japan, Argentina, Denmark). A number of the compilations are also the product of multinational teams.

Examination revealed that the effect of chauvinistic tendencies for most of the inventories were minor to begin with and eliminated by using sources from a mix of nations. The exception was literature. A German can listen to a work by Vivaldi as easily as he can listen to one by Bach, and an Englishman can look at a painting by Monet as easily as one by Constable. The same cannot be said of literature, because of the language barrier. German historians of literature give disproportionate attention to German and Austrian authors, English historians to English and American authors, and so on. The selection of significant figures and computation of their index scores were therefore based exclusively on sources *not* written in the language of the author in question (e.g., Thackeray's selection as a significant figure and his index score are based exclusively on sources not written in English).

Sexism. This sensitive topic also gets most of a chapter to itself (Chapter 12). If one is to approach that material dispassionately, it is important to distinguish between two questions. Has sexism been a barrier to accomplishment among women? Yes, without doubt. But that barrier is not the subject of this book. The question relevant to our purposes is whether significant accomplishments by women have gone unrecognized in the inventories. To that question, the answer seems to be just as clearly "no." The last 30 years have seen a cottage industry in books on achievement by women and a proliferation of courses in universities on women's accomplishment. The vast majority of the sources used to compile the inventories have not only had access to this scholarship, they have been prepared in an era when pressure to include people other than males has been intense.

Racism. The comments about sexism apply equally to racism. Non-whites living in Europe and the United States through 1950 suffered severe discrimination, which helps explain their small numbers in the inventories. But there is no evidence that important non-white contributors to the arts and sciences during that period are ignored in the sources used to prepare the inventories. The bias in sources written during the last few decades is in the direction of over-emphasizing, not neglecting, the contributions of non-whites.

Elitism. Is a book on human accomplishment inherently elitist? With regard to social background, education, IQ, wealth, or influence: No. With regard to excellence: Yes.

SIX

THE LOTKA CURVE

I t is a fact that takes some getting used to, but the evidence for it is overwhelming: When you assemble the human résumé, only a few thousand people stand apart from the rest. Among them, the people who are indispensable to the story of human accomplishment number in the hundreds. Among those hundreds, a handful stand conspicuously above everyone else. This chapter lays out the empirical phenomenon driving this conclusion, the Lotka curve. The next chapter describes what "a few thousand," "hundreds," and "handful" mean in terms of the members of the specific inventories.

THE "THIS CAN'T BE RIGHT" DISTRIBUTION OF EMINENCE

To see just how strange the distribution of eminence is, it is useful to take a moment to think about how talents are distributed in humans. They usually take the form of a normal distribution, also known as the bell curve. It looks like this:

On almost any human trait, most people are bunched in the middle, with the number of people who are either talented or untalented diminishing rapidly as one approaches the extremes. This is true of the talents for which we

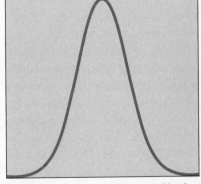

No talent   Highest possible talent

have formal measures, such as intelligence, but it also seems to be true of any trait that affects success in life. Industriousness? A few people are really lazy and a few are compulsive 18-hour-a-day workers, but most people are somewhere in between. The same may be said of charm, enthusiasm, intensity, punctuality, and just about any other personality characteristic you can name.

Now suppose that we are talking about artistic talent and the 479 artists who made it into the Western visual arts inventory we will be using for the rest of the book. Obviously, they are all somewhere on the right-hand side of the bell curve. Since we are talking about only 479 people out of all the people who have lived since −800, it seems fair to assume that they are far out on that tail. In other words, the distribution of artistic talent in the visual arts inventory is not a bell curve, but looks more like this:

Technically, what you are looking at is the portion of a bell curve from three standard deviations on out (for more about standard deviations and the normal distribution, see Appendix 1), but the precise segment of the curve

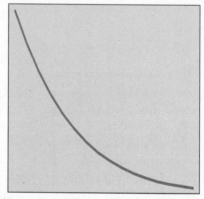

Extraordinary talent   Highest possible talent

isn't important. The point is that all of those 479 artists are presumably very, very talented compared to the rest of the population and are somewhere out on the relatively flat portion of the normal curve. At the same time, common sense tells us that artistic talent isn't the only thing that determines the excellence of artists. It is not necessarily true that the eminence of the artists will track precisely with their artistic talent, nor is it even necessarily true that the excellence of the artists (were we able to measure that quality directly) would track precisely with artistic talent, nor that all the people with the most artistic talent ever realize that talent. All we know for sure is that those 479 bring a narrower range of ability to the table than does the population at large. The most plausible guess is that the range is actually extremely narrow, with almost all of the difference among the eminence of artists being attributable to something other than simple talent.

What then do we expect the distribution of eminence to be? We know that at least one person will have a score of 100 and another will have a score of 1—that much is ensured by the way the index scores are calculated.[1] But even though someone such as Michelangelo has to have a score of 100, that still leaves plenty of artists such as Rembrandt, Giotto, Monet, Cézanne, Goya, Rubens, Titian, Picasso, van Gogh, Dürer, Raphael, and a few dozen others, who get a great deal of space in art histories and are bound to have high scores.

But the history of art is not written in ways that correspond to this reasonable expectation. When the computer spits out the distribution of index scores for the Western art inventory, it looks like the following figure.

The "this can't be right" distribution of index scores
in the Western art inventory

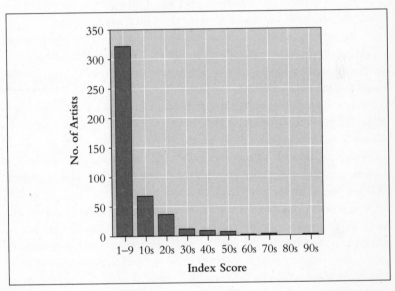

Note: Index scores are limited to Western artists who were active from 1200 to 1950.

Fully 71 percent of the 479 significant figures in the Western art inventory have scores in the first decile.[2] Only 4 artists have scores of 60 or higher, and one of those (the 100-point score) was obligatory. The upper half of my 100-point scale is nearly unpopulated.

When confronted with radical results that look suspicious, one strategy is to see what happens when a different kind of measure is used. The index scores are based on the amount of space that artists get, combining measures of the total amount of text devoted to them and the number of plates showing their work. What happens if we tighten up on the requirement for getting into the inventory, getting rid of minor artists who might be cluttering up the lower end of the index scores, and use a more egalitarian measure that cuts down the advantage of the most famous? To get rid of the minor figures, I restrict the sample to artists who had at least one picture or sculpture shown as a plate in the sources. To make the measure more egalitarian, I switch from the total amount of space given to an artist to a simple count of the number of *different* paintings or sculptures represented in those plates— Michelangelo no longer gets credit for all the different times that a plate of the Sistine Chapel is shown. The Sistine Chapel counts the same as a Grandma Moses painting.

It would seem that the result should at least dampen to some degree the skew in the distribution of index scores. But it doesn't. On the contrary, it makes matters worse, as illustrated in the chart on the facing page.

Fifty-four percent of the artists who had at least one work to their credit in all the sources combined had *only* one work. The shape of the distribution continued to show a highly skewed distribution—even more skewed than the original one.

Other attempts to straighten out this skew and produce a scale in which scores are more evenly spread across the range also fail. Try as one might, it is impossible to produce a measure that plausibly represents the attention given to different artists and that also shows anything except a highly skewed distribution. Something is going on with the distribution of eminence among Western artists that has to be confronted and explained.

If it had affected only the Western art inventory, I would have put this story in a box or an endnote. But I have presented a typical case, not an exception. The same shape is found in the other inventories. It is not limited just to this book or just to measures of eminence. Scholars investigating analogous phenomena have been finding these radically skewed distributions for 80 years.

ALFRED LOTKA'S DISCOVERY

The first person to put numbers to this phenomenon was a Hungarian-born American demographer named Alfred James Lotka. In the mid-1920s, he set out to quantify the contributions of scientists to the scientific literature by counting the number of articles they had published, using the indexes of *Chemical Abstracts* and *Auerbach's Geschichtstafeln der Physik* for his data.[3] Lotka's first discovery was that about 60 percent of all the authors represented in his database had published just a single article. The other was that the number of

Substituting a supposedly more egalitarian measure
makes the distribution even more skewed

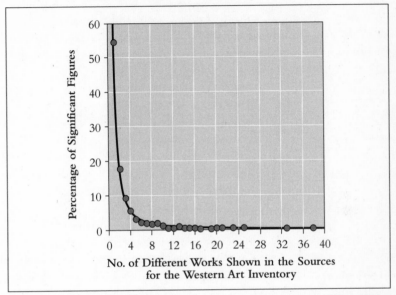

Note: Index scores are limited to Western artists who were active from 1200 to 1950.

scientists who had published greater numbers of articles plunged drastically in a hyperbolic curve of the type shown on page 92.

The mathematics of the curve are given in the note.[4] What the mathematics come down to is an equation saying that in most cases the percentage of persons with one article will be in the region of 60 percent of all the people who write any article. Although the equation is sometimes called Lotka's law, it really isn't a law, because it does not give an a priori way to predict the values for a given distribution. Apart from that, subsequent work has demonstrated that the specific distributions of productivity are too varied to settle on .6 as a reliable estimate for the proportion of persons who will have just one article.[5] But if we discard the notion of a law and stick with the more basic idea of a hyperbolic curve of the type shown in the preceding figure, it is appropriate to call his discovery the Lotka curve.

Others have since proposed different ways of specifying the mathematics of the curve. Science historian Derek de Solla Price suggested Price's Law, whereby half of all contributions to a given field are produced by the square root of the number of contributors.[6] The accuracy of Price's Law appears to

Lotka's curve describing the relationship between the scientific
literature and the contributors to it

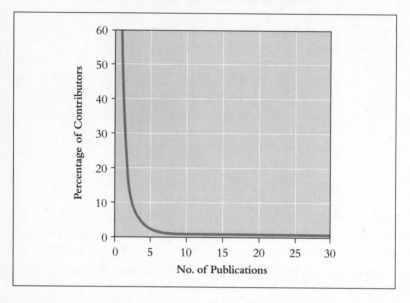

depend on the number of contributors—it tends to become less valid as the
number of contributors to a field grows larger—and on how tightly the
universe of contributions is defined.[7] Psychologist Colin Martindale has
argued that an equation developed by George Yule for an unrelated purpose
best describes the distribution of eminence.[8] But these are uncertainties about
the precise mathematical formulation of the relationship. There is no active
disagreement in the literature about the general form of the empirical distribution. Whether we are talking about the arts or the sciences, the distribution
of any known aggregate measure of human accomplishment by individuals
looks like the Lotka curve. In the words of Dean Simonton, so much
evidence has accumulated that this general pattern may by now be said to
represent an "undeniable law of historiometry."[9]

WHY NOT A BELL CURVE?

But why? As I noted when I began the discussion, human talents are not
skewed in this way; they form normal distributions. Why should measures of

accomplishment and eminence be so distributed? A number of theories have been advanced.[10]

The natural first impulse was to think that the Lotka curve really just represents the right-hand tail of a bell curve. Psychologist Wayne Dennis, examining the productivity of American psychologists in the early 1950s, was the first to advance this explanation in print.[11] But Herbert Simon quickly responded with a mathematical demonstration that Dennis's data were too extreme to be part of the right tail of a normal distribution.[12] You can see the sense of Simon's argument for yourself by comparing the Lotka curve on page 88 with the right-hand side of the bell curve I showed on page 92. The right-hand tail of the bell curve is not nearly as skewed as the Lotka curve. Something else must be at work.

The earliest and most commonsensical explanation for the "something else" is that the source of great accomplishment is multidimensional—it does not appear just because a person is highly intelligent or highly creative or highly anything else. Several traits have to appear in combination. The pioneer of this view was British polymath Francis Galton in the late 1800s. Even though he had been instrumental in creating the modern concept of intelligence, Galton argued that intelligence alone was not enough to explain genius. Rather, he appealed to "the concrete triple event, of ability combined with zeal and with capacity for hard labour."[13] Ninety years later, William Shockley specified how the individual components of human accomplishment, normally distributed, can in combination produce the type of hyperbolic distribution—highly skewed right, with an elongated tail—exemplified by the Lotka curve.[14]

A second explanation calls upon what S. K. Merton has called "the Matthew effect,"[15] referring to Matthew 25:29: "Unto every one that hath shall be given, and he shall have abundance: but from him that hath not shall be taken away even that which he hath." Simplified, the argument, labeled *accumulative advantage*, goes like this:

Imagine a hundred young scientists, each submitting a paper for publication to his field's premier journal. Assume that all of the papers are equally good. The space in the premier journal is scarce, and only one of the papers is accepted. The lucky young scientist whose paper is chosen now has several advantages working in his favor. His confidence goes up, making it easier to write the next article. The fact that he has been published in a prestigious journal makes placing the next article easier. The likelihood that he enters the tenure track at a top university increases, and winning that tenured position makes it easier for him to conduct high-quality research and to get his subsequent articles placed. Meanwhile, those who were rejected suffer setbacks that are mirror images of the advantages enjoyed by the lucky one. Those who were successful the first time are more likely to write more articles and to get them published; those who were unsuccessful are less likely to write more articles and less likely to get them placed.[16] Over the long run, and with large samples of scientists, the result will be a Lotka curve of publications. Success breeds success; failure breeds failure—such is the underlying logic of accumulative advantage. Like the multiple-factor theories, it corresponds to real-world examples that most people have encountered.

Dean Simonton has developed a third approach, called the *chance-configuration theory*, that is at once the most ambitious and the most complex of the current explanations.[17] It seeks not just to explain the skewed distribution of intellectual productivity across samples of scientists and artists, but also to model the fundamental creative process at work. Simonton has elaborated and modified the chance-configuration theory over two decades, and it includes mathematical specifications that would take us far afield. Put colloquially, Simonton envisions a world in which each creative individual starts his career with a large stock of creative raw materials such as research hypotheses or artistic ideas or musical themes. These raw materials lend themselves to a huge number of combinations. Out of all the combinations that a creative person could create from his stock of raw materials, he has time to develop only a comparative handful. He concentrates on those that seem to have the most potential. This results in a series of finished products that are presented to the world, sometimes successfully and sometimes not. The ratio of hits to misses can be low, as low as 1 to 100, but the hits can still be sufficient to make him famous (Galton's "capacity for hard labour" coming into play).[18] Simonton is able to explain a variety of phenomena about productivity and career trajectories with the chance-configuration model. The relevant point for our purposes is that the number of successful combinations is not normally distributed. The precise degree of exponential growth depends on specific assumptions that I will not go into, but the growth is explosive under a wide range of assumptions and reproduces the Lotka curve.

FAME OR EXCELLENCE?

Mathematically, there is no problem explaining why the distribution of eminence forms a Lotka curve. Any of the above explanations suffices. But when it comes to the substantive question—why do the scores of a few people soar so far above the rest?—one obvious possibility has yet to be mentioned: The Lotka curve is explained by differences in excellence. Shakespeare gets more attention than everyone else because Shakespeare wrote better than everyone else.

There are reasons to resist that explanation, if only because the skew in the Lotka curve is so extreme. As Colin Martindale asked in his analysis of literary fame, how is one to interpret the datum that Shakespeare has 9,118 books written about him while Marlowe has just 205? That Shakespeare was 44 times better than Marlowe?[19]

The Lotka Curve and Face Validity

The first and simplest way to think about whether the Lotka curve captures fame or excellence is to examine the names of the people at the top and ask whether they belong there. The technical term for this way of looking at the problem is *face validity*, meaning, "On the face of it, these results make sense." We will be discussing the people at the top of the index scores at length in Chapter 8, but you can quickly check out the face validity of the index scores by looking at the table on page 96 with lists of the five top-ranking persons in each inventory.

A case could be made for some people who did not crack the top five, but just about everyone who did make it is there for a reason that easily corresponds to real excellence in his field. One way of confirming this is to go to basic sources in each field and look at the qualitative discussions of these people. Virtually without exception, the discussion will have some phrase in it that says, in one form or another, that experts consider this person to be among the best who ever lived. For many of the names, you will not need to go that far, because you are already familiar with their reputations. The names speak for themselves.

The face validity test has a troubling circularity about it, however. The Lotka curve puts a handful of people out at the right-hand edge. They turn out to be the people whom we already know about because they are so famous. And while it may be true that the history books talk about them as being the best, not just the most famous, we still lack an objective measuring stick for being sure that we are not looking at celebrity, or the effects of an established canon, or some other artificial reason for their eminence that contaminates the value of the index scores as measures of excellence.

In an odd way, the radical skew of the curve that everyone has found when examining eminence makes it easier, not harder, to explore whether

THE TOP FIVES

Astronomy	Biology	Chemistry	Earth Sciences
Galileo	Charles Darwin	Antoine Lavoisier	Charles Lyell
Johannes Kepler	Aristotle	Jöns Berzelius	James Hutton
William Herschel	Jean-Baptiste Lamarck	Carl Scheele	William Smith
Pierre-Simon	Georges Cuvier	Joseph Priestley	Agricola
de Laplace	Thomas Hunt Morgan	Humphrey Davy	Abraham Werner
Nicolas Copernicus			

Physics	Mathematics	Medicine	Technology
Isaac Newton	Leonhard Euler	Louis Pasteur	Thomas Edison
Albert Einstein	Isaac Newton	Robert Koch	James Watt
Ernest Rutherford	Carl Gauss	Hippocrates	Leonardo da Vinci
Michael Faraday	Euclid	Galen	Christiaan Huygens
Galileo	Pierre-Simon	Paracelsus	Archimedes
	de Laplace		

Chinese Art	Chinese Literature	Chinese Philosophy	Arabic Literature
Gu Kaizhi	Du Fu	Confucius	al-Mutanabbi
Zhao Mengfu	Li Bo	Laozi	Abu Nuwas
Wu Daozi	Bo Juyi	Zhu Xi	al-Ma'arri
Mu Yuan	Su Dongpo	Mencius	Imru' al-Qays
Dong Qichan	Han Yu	Zhuangzi	Abu Tammam

Japanese Art	Japanese Literature	Indian Literature	Indian Philosophy
Toyo Sesshu	Matsuo Basho	Kalidasa	Sankara
Tawaraya Sotatsu	Chikamatsu	Vyasa	Nagarjuna
Ogata Korin	Monzaemon	Valmiki	Ramanuja
Hasegawa Tohaku	Murasaki Shikibu	Asvaghosa	Buddha
Kano Eitoku	Ihara Saikaku	Bhartrhari	Madhva
	Mori Ogai		

Western Art	Western Literature	Western Music	Western Philosophy
Michelangelo	William Shakespeare	Ludwig van	Aristotle
Pablo Picasso	Johann von Goethe	Beethoven	Plato
Raphael	Dante Alighieri	Wolfgang Amadeus	Immanuel Kant
Leonardo da Vinci	Virgil	Mozart	Rene Descartes
Titian	Homer	Johann Sebastian	Georg Hegel
		Bach	
		Richard Wagner	
		Franz Joseph Hadyn	

we are observing a measure of fame or of accomplishment. In the preceding chapter, I described my reasons for thinking that excellence underlies the measures of eminence I am using. That explanation was necessarily qualitative. Now we have before us a concrete, highly distinctive mathematical shape to use for making a prediction: *If the Lotka curve reflects excellence, not just fame, it will also be found when we turn to fields that have objective measures of excellence.*

The World of Sports as a Source of Clear-Cut Cases

It is surprising and a little depressing to realize how few fields of human endeavor have objective measures of excellence. Measures of *success* are abundant. Money income can be a useful measure of success among persons within certain occupations. Number of elections won can be a useful measure of success for politicians. But linking success with excellence is tricky. The businessmen with the largest income packages, the writers with the biggest book sales, and the composers with the biggest album sales are not necessarily the people whom their peers judge to be the best businessmen, writers, or composers. A congressman who is reelected twenty times is a more successful politician than the one who gets beaten after one term, but the accumulative advantage of incumbency contributes to that success. Even measures of success are subject to complications. Mortality rates for physicians can be misleading for a surgeon who deliberately takes on the most difficult cases.

One of the rare fields of human endeavor in which an objective measure of excellence is available is sports. The best source of measures within sports involves games where individuals compete alone (e.g., golf and tennis) or achievements in team sports that do not depend on the cooperation of teammates (e.g., batting average in baseball). Within this subset, the most unambiguous measures of excellence come from sports in which the result is determined by an objective process rather than by judges (diving or gymnastics). I will use professional golf as my extended example, and then briefly present parallel results from other sports.

The Professional Golf Association (PGA) compiles individual statistics on the component skills that go into the game of golf, enabling a comparison between those component skills and overall excellence. The figure on the next page shows four of these component skills for card-carrying members of the male tour: driving distance, percentage of fairways hit, percentage of greens reached in the regulation number of strokes, and average number of putts per round. The dots represent the actual data. The line in each figure represents the mathematically perfect bell curve for these data.[20]

You will seldom find a closer match with a bell curve in real-world data than you see in those four examples. What makes the distributions especially striking is that they are produced by a tiny sliver from the far right-hand tail of the distribution of all male golfers. Nobody who becomes a regular on the PGA tour is a "poor" putter or striker of the ball, if the reference group is everyone who plays these games. And yet even the men within that elite group fall into a normal distribution on the component skills of golf.[21]

Now we turn to an undisputed measure of excellence in golf: tournament victories.[22] For the sample, I wanted to define a set of golfers who had completed their careers and had demonstrated that they were capable of playing at a high level on the pro tour. I settled upon all golfers who had made the cut (survived to the last two rounds) of the men's PGA Championship at least once from 1970 to 1989, and who had completed their careers by the end of 2001. A total of 361 golfers met these criteria. How many tournaments had they won?

The component skills of golf form bell curves even among professionals

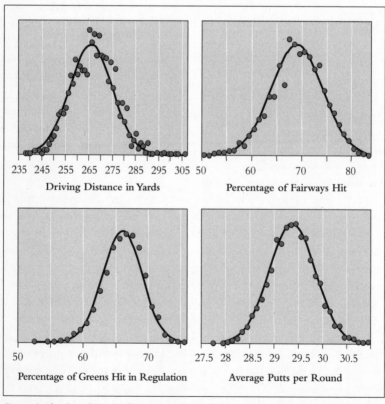

Source: Author's analysis, Professional Golf Association statistics for exempt PGA players, 1991–2000.

The most decisive finding is that, among this elite group of golfers, 53 percent failed to win even a single tournament during the entire course of their careers. If you want evidence that winning a golf tournament is difficult, here it is. More than half of this highly selected set of professional golfers couldn't do it in years of trying.

Now we turn to the 47 percent who did achieve at least one victory. The figure below shows the distribution of number of victories.

A hyperbolic curve appears instead of the bell curve that described the component skills. Notice, however, that the percentage with a single victory is only 26 percent, not close to the concentration with a single entry (in the region of 60 percent) that inspired Lotka, Price, and the others to examine the extreme skew of accomplishment. The steepness of the decline is also accentuated by the high maximum, which goes all the way out to 71.

When the measure is tournament victories, the bell curve is replaced by a Lotka curve, but one of comparatively modest skew

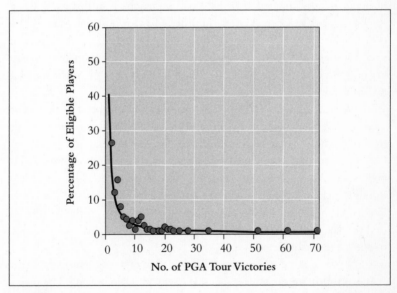

"Eligible players" consists of all players who were under the age of 45 as of 1970, had made the cut of the men's PGA Championship at least once from 1970 to 1989, who had retired or passed the age of 45 by the end of the 2001 season, and had won at least one tournament in the course of their careers.

Source: Author's analysis, PGA and career statistics obtained from the PGA and ESPN web sites.

The skew is still pronounced. Of the minority who won any tournaments, almost all won only 1, 2, or 3. A handful of players won between 3 and 25 tournaments. Only 4 players won more than 30. At the far right-hand tail of the graph are Arnold Palmer, with 61 PGA victories, and Jack Nicklaus, who won 71.

Now let us ratchet the bar several notches higher. We have already seen how hard it is for a professional to win even one tournament, but it remains true that a majority of players who win one golf tournament go on to win another, suggesting that some accumulative advantage is at work. But any golf fan could give you another explanation: In most PGA tour events, only some of the top players participate. The figure on page 99 doesn't tell us what happens when all the top players are present and all of them are highly motivated to win. To examine that situation, we focus on the ultimate measure of excellence in professional golf, the Majors—the U.S. Open, British Open, PGA, and Masters.

Once again I limit the sample of players to men who had completed their careers as of the end of 2001,[23] but the requirement that really slashes the population is that the player had to have won at least one Major in the course of his career. The sample of Majors includes all U.S. and British Opens since 1900, and all PGA and Masters championships since those tournaments began (1916 and 1934 respectively). The figure opposite shows the distribution of victories.

We are back to a curve in which close to 60 percent of all the people who achieved one accomplishment achieved only one. In assessing the figure's implications, it is important to remember the sample. We are no longer talking just about professional golfers, or even about professional golfers who have proved they can win a tournament, but about the elite of the elite, men who had the nerve and skill to win a tournament that all of the best players in the world wanted desperately to win. And yet the distribution of these data is about as skewed as the distribution of the ability of academics to publish journal articles.

Are we looking at fame or excellence? One of the satisfying simplicities of sports is that we can answer that question without agonizing. The men at the right-hand tail are not where they are because of social constructions that artificially designate them as the best. No keepers of the golf canon awarded Jack Nicklaus his 71 PGA tour victories or his 18 professional Majors. The champions sit where they are because they were the best at what they did.

The phenomenon I have described for professional golfers in the 1970s through 1980s fits the champions of golf in other eras. It also applies to other competitions. I have investigated four examples—running, baseball, tennis, and chess—in some detail. In each of these cases, the component skills show normal distributions. Season batting averages in baseball are normally distributed. So is the speed of first serve in tennis, the distribution of running times in marathons, and ELO rating (produced by a mechanistic process) in chess, along with all of the other component skills I was able to explore.

Converting the component skills into major achievements is the trick in these sports as it is in golf. The figure on the next page shows a measure of excellence in each of those sports: combined number of wins in the Boston and New York marathons for running, number of batting championships for baseball, number of Grand Slam titles for tennis, and points in world championship matches for chess. Once again, as in the case of golf, the bell curve disappears and the Lotka curve reemerges when measures of component skills are replaced by measures of overall excellence.

**As the measure of excellence becomes
more demanding, the Lotka curve becomes more extreme**

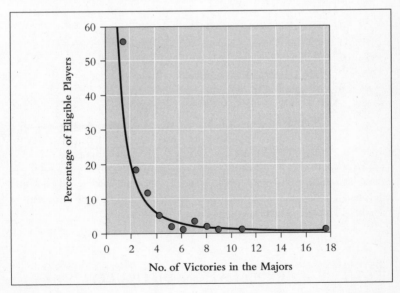

"Eligible players" consists of all players who had retired or passed the age of 45 by the end of the 2001 season and had won at least one Major in the course of their careers.

Source: Author's analysis, Statistics for the U.S. Open, British Open, PGA Championship, and Masters Tournament as given on their respective web sites.

Four other examples of measures of competitive excellence
that produce Lotka curves

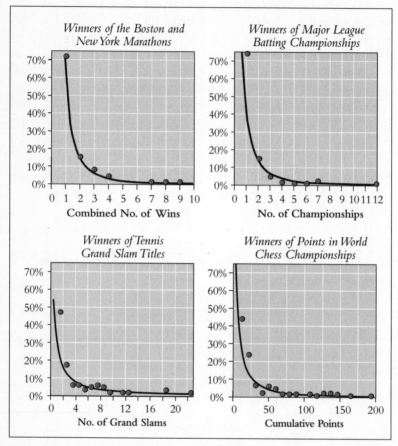

Sources: The official web sites for Major League Baseball and the four tennis grand slam
tournaments; a web site of marathon information (marathonguide.com) and a web site
with data on world chess championships (mark-weeks.com/chess).

AN EXPLANATION: DIFFICULTY

As we consider whether the Lotka curves in the arts and sciences reflect fame
or excellence, the rule of parsimony comes into play: If direct measures of
excellence in sports show the same distribution as indirect measures of excel-

lence in the other fields, the least complicated explanation is that we are observing the same phenomenon in both cases.

The patterns in the sports examples also suggest why excellence is hyperbolically distributed.[24] The harder the task, the more likely that the modal number of such accomplishments among the people who try to achieve it will be zero and the next most common number will be one. The harder the task, the steeper will be the reduction in each incremental number of successes. It is in the nature of difficulty. Of course hardly any professional golfer wins even one of the Majors. It's too hard.

In parallel, the reason that the component skills tend to be distributed in bell curves is that the easier the task, the more likely that almost anybody will be able to do it many times. We may visualize this simple explanation in terms of a continuum. Suppose that we array tasks from the easiest to the hardest in any given field. At the "easiest" end lies something so simple that everyone can do it almost every time. If we observe multiple repetitions in a sample of people working in this field, we will observe a hyperbolic curve, but the mirror image of the ones we have been looking at so far, skewed to the right instead of to the left. The number of people with many misses will be vanishingly small and those with 100 percent successes will be high. *As the difficulty of the task increases, the curve will first become less skewed to the right, then become a normal curve, and, as the task continues to become harder, will shift toward the left-skewed shape of a Lotka curve.*

The Difficulty Explanation Applied to Golf

All of this conforms to experiences that should resonate with just about anybody who has pushed himself to take harder and harder courses in school, who has tried to climb a corporate ladder, or who has taken a passionate interest in some difficult hobby. But to spell it out in terms of our continuing example of golf: Any professional golfer will have one-putt greens and hit the fairway with towering drives, typically many times in every round. For a professional golfer, these are easy accomplishments. But to be near the lead on Sunday morning means that you have strung together an unusually large number of those one-putt greens, drives in the fairway, and a half-dozen other individually easy accomplishments over the course of the three successive rounds that begin the tournament. This is not so easy. Now, on Sunday, the opportunity to win the tournament is within reach. The individually simple tasks must be done under increased psychological pressure that makes the breath come shorter and the hands shake as you line up the putt. The number of people who are good enough to have survived the first three days to put themselves in that position is small; the number who can play well on Sunday under those conditions is smaller still. And now suppose it is not just any Sunday in any tournament, but instead that you are on the tee of the Road Hole at St. Andrews in the British Open with a one-stroke lead. The number of people who can deal with that situation even a single time has dwindled to a few handfuls in every generation. To do such things repeatedly is given to a handful of golfers per century. Hence Lotka curves.

We need not ignore the logic of the accumulative advantage argument, which stresses the importance of the initial achievement. In the golf world as in other sports, it is a cliché that winning the first championship is harder than winning the second, and the reason for the cliché has to do with self-confidence. But some people can take that first victory and build upon it while others cannot—this is one of the psychological strengths of champions that is just as much a part of their makeup as fast reflexes or dazzling hand-eye coordination. It was a commonplace among professional golfers that other players in Jack Nicklaus's generation could come up with more sensational shots than he could. The others just couldn't win as well as Nicklaus could. It is also a cliché in sports that great champions acquire an awe factor that works in their favor. As chess champion Bobby Fischer wryly observed, he never played an opponent who was at his best. But every great champion acquires that additional advantage by winning in the first place. The complex of qualities that constitute genius transcends any simple catalog of skills.

Incremental differences in sports also give us a way to think about what qualitative superiority does and doesn't mean. A few pages ago, I mentioned Colin Martindale's finding that 44 times as many books have been written about Shakespeare as about Marlowe, and his plausible doubt that Shakespeare is 44 times better than Marlowe. The analogies with sports help to recast the meaning of such disparities. Ted Williams won six American League batting titles while Lou Gehrig won just one—a ratio of six to one. The meaning of that comparison is not that Williams was six times as good a hitter as Gehrig (Williams's lifetime batting average was only four points higher than Gehrig's). Rather, it is a measure that explains why Ted Williams is always in the conversation when baseball fans argue about who was the greatest hitter of all time and Lou Gehrig is not. The measures that produce Lotka curves not only discriminate the excellent from the mediocre, but the unparalleled from the merely excellent.

Why Difficulty Is Also the Most Plausible Explanation
for Lotka Curves in the Arts and Sciences

It is easier to acknowledge the dominance of a few people in athletics, where measures of winning and losing are woven into the nature of the enterprise, than it is in the arts and sciences. But the same logic transfers. Let us return for a moment to the finding that initially inspired Lotka: 60 percent of the people who publish scientific articles publish just one. Could this be changed if editorial boards of journals were fairer, or if we encouraged the people who dropped out after the first article to write another?

To some extent, yes, for the accomplishment in question is not one of the hardest ones. If a $100,000 fee were offered for second published article, a great many people could find it in themselves to come up with a second one that would be published by some journal. If we kept offering another $100,000 for each additional article, we could eventually produce something resembling a bell curve, even if it remained a highly skewed one.

Suppose instead that the accomplishment in question is getting an article into *Nature*, one of the premier scientific journals, and a $100,000 fee is offered for publishing a second article in *Nature*. Now "trying harder" becomes noticeably less effective. Nor do the arguments about accumulative advantage sound convincing. It is all very well to have greater confidence, or to have gotten a better academic position, but confidence and tenure don't help much in coming up with another research finding that will win the stiff competition for space in *Nature*. To publish that second *Nature* article you need more than incentive. You must also be exceedingly good at what you do.

In this light, consider the difficulty of getting into the inventories compiled for this book. Now your assignment is to do something that historians of your field will consider worth mentioning a century from now. Just putting it in words brings home how difficult a task you have been given. Judging from past experience, hardly anyone who is an intellectual celebrity today will merit a sidelong glance a century from now. How many readers under the age of 50 recognize the names of Mortimer Adler or Walter Lippmann? Each was as famous in the first half of 20C as Carl Sagan or George F. Will has been more recently, but contemporary fame is no help in making the history books. If, a century after you are dead, you still have a single picture hanging in a museum, a single composition still being played by the world's orchestras, or a single scientific finding still being cited in the technical journals, you will have put yourself in a tiny company. No wonder the most common frequency of such feats even in that elite group is just one.

These remarks by no means dispose of the argument about whether we are looking at fame or excellence. But the data on Lotka curves in fields where the only explanation is excellence gets us past an important hurdle. Many of the discussions of Lotka curves in the literature to date have sought explanations that do not call on real superiority as an explanation for why some people produce more than others. They advance instead some variation on a theme in which some people luck out. The explanation can be simpler. Some people are authentically the best at what they do. There is no meaning in the statement that Shakespeare was 44 times better than Marlowe. There is meaning in the statement that, as good a playwright as Marlowe was, Shakespeare was hugely greater. The large difference separating the index scores of Marlowe and Shakespeare reflects the clarity of that verdict.

SEVEN

THE PEOPLE
WHO MATTER I:
SIGNIFICANT FIGURES

In recounting human accomplishment in the arts, sciences, and philosophy for the last 2,800 years, who are the people without whom the story is incomplete?

The discussion of the Lotka curve provided part of the answer: The index scores give us a way of identifying the giants in every field who stand out conspicuously from all the rest. They are the topic of Chapter 8. But before getting to them, what about the rest, those who may not loom quite so large but who qualify as individuals "without whom the story is incomplete"? This chapter describes who they are and how they have been chosen.

The task is to establish a criterion for deciding whether a person is in or out. When Alfred Lotka discovered the Lotka curve, he had already selected a subset of the population of scientists in which he was interested, chemists who had published at least one article. That criterion constitutes a clear bright line distinguishing his subset from the total population of chemists. The subset of golfers who win at least one tour tournament is separated by a clear bright line from the total population of professional golfers. No equivalent line separates "the people without whom the story is incomplete" from the rest. I tackle this task first by establishing the outer boundaries of that potential population, then looking for a reasonable way to define the inner circle.

ESTABLISHING THE OUTER BOUNDARIES
OF THE POPULATION

Establishing the outer boundaries of the population is easy. Modern scholars have helpfully produced large and comprehensive biographical dictionaries with the avowed purpose of containing everyone who is worth mentioning in their particular field. For the sciences, an international consortium of scholars has been laboring for more than four decades on the *Dictionary of Scientific Biography*, now up to 18 volumes.[1] In philosophy, we have the *Encyclopédie Philosophique Universelle*,[2] only two volumes, but fat ones. For Western art, we may turn to the 17-volume *Enciclopedia Universale dell'Arte* compiled by the Istituto per la Collaborazione Culturale. At least one such encyclopedic reference work is among the sources for every inventory.

The entries in an encyclopedic source typically number in the thousands. The problem is that a large proportion of those people do not come close to any reasonable definition of "people without whom the story is incomplete." To see this, consider the case of music. In all, the music inventory combines information from 16 sources. Here is a sampling of the people who are mentioned by one, but no more than one, of those 16. To approximate randomness, I have chosen the first such person mentioned for the first five letters of the alphabet:

- *Jeno Ádám, 1896–1982.* Hungarian composer, conductor, and educator, known chiefly for his role in the reform of Hungarian musical education.
- *Valentin Babst, 16C.* Mentioned in 16C sources in a discussion of the vernacular religious songs for congregational singing.
- *Vinzenzo Calestani, 1589–c. 1617.* Taught music to the wealthy Mastiani family and published a collection of pieces for one and two voices with continuo.
- *Innocentius Dammonis, 16C.* Mentioned in 16C sources as a composer represented in a collection of polyphonic laudi that Petrucci brought out in 1508.
- *Piotr Elert, d.c. 1685.* Mentioned in 17C sources as a composer of one of the operas composed by members of the Royal Chapel at Warsaw at the command of Wladyslaw IV of Poland.

Accomplished as these people surely were, they are not crucial to the development of Western music. Readers who worry that important contributors have slipped through the net may rest easy. Undiscovered geniuses undoubtedly exist in the sense that people who could have been great scientists or artists or philosophers never got the chance to realize their potential, but the idea that undiscovered scientists or artists or philosophers who actually contributed important works have failed to get consideration does not square with the mind-numbing level of detail included in contemporary reference works.

NARROWING THE FIELD

We need a way to narrow the field. Large, well-regarded general histories of a field are the natural tool for doing that—natural, because the historian's task is to sift through the mass of historical material represented by the encyclopedic sources, winnowing out the marginal and retaining the significant.

Suppose (staying with music as our example) we take as our first approximation of "people without whom the story is incomplete" those who are included in three major histories of music. We begin with Donald Grout's magisterial *History of Western Music* (5th ed., 1996), weighing in at a hefty 862 pages.[3] It contains at least a mention of 512 different composers.[4] Then we turn to Lucien Rebatet's *Une Histoire de la Musique* (1969), a French history of music almost 600 pages long.[5] Rebatet mentions 643 composers. Then we move on to Germany and examine *Weltgeschichte der Musik* (1976), written by six authors headed by Kurt Honolka. It is 640 pages long and mentions 653 composers.

So we have three major histories of the same topic covering the same period of time. Whom do they consider essential to an account of Western music? The Venn diagram at the right (drawn only approximately to scale) shows the number of composers that were shared, and not shared, among them.

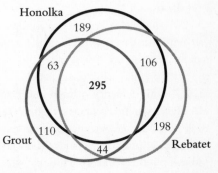

In all, the three sources mentioned 1,005 unique composers—a large number, but fewer than half those mentioned in *The Harvard Biographical Dictionary of Music* (1996). Histories are far more selective than the encyclopedic sources. On the other hand, 497 of the composers—half of them—

were mentioned in just one of the three volumes. It is clear that each author did his own homework and made decisions about whom to include that were not shared by the other two, a desirable characteristic when trying to assemble independent judgments of experts.

Since our purpose is to focus on the people without whom the story is incomplete, the element in the Venn diagram that attracts the most interest is that inner circle with the number 295, denoting the composers that all three sources saw fit to include. The logic is that if three major sources, each of which exhibits considerable independence in its preparation, all mentioned a person, that person probably did something significant.

Now imagine that we continue to add a fourth source, then a fifth, and so on. With each additional source, the total number of composers who are mentioned by at least somebody grows or at least holds steady, and the number who are mentioned by everybody shrinks. But another thing happens as we add more sources: the twin curves formed by the composers mentioned by somebody and the composers mentioned by everybody begin to flatten. The actual curves produced by the 12 most comprehensive sources used for the Western music inventory are shown on the facing page, starting with the most comprehensive source and working down.

What you see in that figure is typical of all the inventories. The black dot at the far left represents the most comprehensive source of the 12, the *Harvard Biographical Dictionary of Music* (1996), containing entries for 2,242 composers.[6] Even though the other encyclopedic sources were individually extensive, they added only 236 more names. By the fifth source, the total number of names was within two persons of the maximum it would reach after the twelfth.

Meanwhile, the number of composers so central to the story of Western music that *every* writer on the subject has to include them dropped rapidly after the first few sources and never completely leveled off through the first 12 sources. But it did flatten out substantially around the six-source mark. In this tendency of both lines to reach asymptotes lies a strategy for identifying significant figures: require that a significant figure be mentioned by at least a certain percentage of the sources.

A criterion that demands that a person be mentioned in every source is too severe—that defines the indispensable, not the merely excellent. A criterion that asks only that a person be mentioned in any source at all is too lax—the encyclopedic sources include too many obviously marginal figures. Along the continuum from a single source to 100 percent of the sources, where should we draw the line?

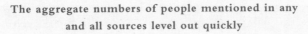

The aggregate numbers of people mentioned in any
and all sources level out quickly

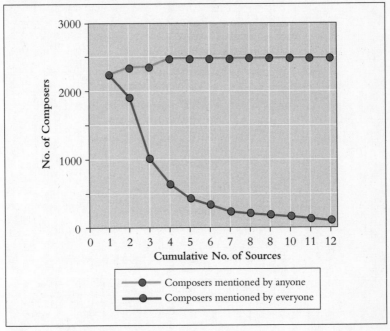

Note: Sources are entered in descending order of their number of composers.

SELECTING THE SIGNIFICANT

Inevitably, any cutoff point has an element of the arbitrary. My choice was to draw the line at 50 percent. Everyone who is mentioned in at least 50 percent of the qualified sources is designated a *significant figure* and enters the samples for analysis in the rest of the book. The technical considerations behind the choice of 50 percent are discussed in Appendix 2, but they come down to a search for a balance between the competing goals of large sample size and high sample stability.

The virtues of a large sample size are obvious. The larger the samples, the greater the analytic leverage in discerning patterns in the data and in testing whether those patterns are real or illusory. The importance of sample stability is to ensure that the results of the analysis are not sensitive to the sources I happened to choose. I originally intended to include everyone who was mentioned in at least 20 percent of the sources. This more relaxed cutoff

FAUX LOTKA

Do not confuse the falling line in the figure on page 111 with a Lotka curve. It isn't, partly for mathematical reasons but most importantly because Lotka curves cannot be made to appear or disappear depending on the choice of sources. Lotka curves represent the way difficult accomplishment is distributed, no matter how one slices the data and no matter what sources are used. In contrast, the falling line is highly sensitive to choice of sources. For example, I could make that line drop shallowly if I confined all of my sources to encyclopedic ones that include thousands of composers, or I could make it fall more steeply if I were to combine just one encyclopedic source with histories listing only a few hundred composers per history.

The one thing I cannot do with the falling line, no matter what sources I use, is force it to converge on zero. As long as the sources represent major, comprehensive histories of Western music, several dozen figures will be mentioned in every source. This does raise an issue, however. If I were to include, say, a 100-page pocket history of music that discussed only a handful of major composers, I could artificially minimize that number. It is thus important to define a floor of comprehensiveness for the histories that were used to select significant figures. The floor that was selected is discussed in Appendix 2. To illustrate its effect: In the case of the music inventory, any source had to include a minimum of 283 composers who had been mentioned by a second source as well.

rule would have produced a larger sample (about double). But as an empirical matter, the price of that larger sample would have been a set of significant figures that could change drastically with fairly minor changes in the mix of sources (see Appendix 2 for documentation on this and the subsequent statements about sample stability). This does not necessarily mean that the alternative samples would have produced different results in the analyses that form the later chapters of the book, but it was a danger to worry about. Setting the cutoff point at 50 percent produced samples that are demonstrably insensitive to changes in the configuration of sources, as long as one observes a few basic guidelines in selecting the sources.

The 50 percent criterion produces a sample of 4,002, broken down by inventory as shown in the table below.

THE SIGNIFICANT FIGURES

Inventory	Number
The Sciences	
Astronomy	124
Biology	193
Chemistry	204
Earth Sciences	85
Physics	218
Mathematics	191
Medicine	160
Technology	239
Not classifiable	28
Philosophy	
China	39
India	45
The West	155
Visual Arts	
China	111
Japan	81
The West	479
Literature	
Arab World	82
China	83
India	43
Japan	85
The West	835
Music (*Western*)	522
Total	**4,002**

These 4,002 are, for operational purposes, the people who matter—*operationally*, because obviously this precise set of people would not be identified if one were to replicate the research. Throughout the rest of the book, the frequently-used phrase *significant figures* will refer to this specific set of people. A complete list of all of them is given in Appendix 5 along with national origin, index score, and the year in which each person turned 40 (or died, whichever came first).

BROTHERS, LEGENDS, AND POLYMATHS

Nine of the 4,002 are not individuals at all, but relatives whose work was so intertwined that to put them into the inventory as individuals would be double counting. The nine entries in question are those for the Vivarini family, the Le Nain brothers, and the Limbourg brothers (Western art), the Grimm brothers and Goncourt brothers (Western literature), and four pairs of brothers in technology: the Lumières, who made major advances in cinematography; the Biros, who invented the ballpoint pen; the Montgolfiers, who began manned balloon flights; and, of course, the Wrights, inventors of the airplane.

At least one of the 4,002 and perhaps as many as four didn't exist at all. The one who certainly didn't exist is Nicolas Bourbaki, the pseudonym used by a group of French mathematicians. The three questionable ones are the epic poets Homer (*Iliad* and *Odyssey*), Vyasa (*Mahabharata*), and Valmiki (*Ramayana*). As for that other notorious dispute about authorship, I will use the name William Shakespeare to stand for whoever wrote the works of Shakespeare—somebody wrote them—and let others worry about who he really was.

The roster of significant figures consists of 3,869 unique individuals. The difference between 4,002 and 3,869 is explained by people who were in two, three, or four different inventories. In all, 116 people qualified in more than one inventory. This does not mean that we have 116 genuine polymaths, in the sense of people whose expertise spanned disparate fields. Many of the people who qualified in more than one inventory (42 percent of them) were people who show up in related scientific inventories (e.g., biology and medicine, physics and mathematics). Another third consists of people who qualified in philosophy and literature, or philosophy and a scientific inventory—not surprising, since until a few centuries ago the distinctions among philosophy, science, and literature were blurred.

If we restrict *polymath* to mean people who made major contributions that called for conspicuously different knowledges and skills, the best candidate—no surprise here—is Leonardo da Vinci, who qualified for the art, biology, physics, and technology inventories. Aristotle is the other authentic polymath, though he technically qualified for just the biology and philosophy inventories. This artificially restricts the recognition of Aristotle's exceptionally broad range of contributions—for example, his contributions that fall under philosophy include seminal contributions to aesthetics, political

theory, and logic, entirely apart from his contributions to ethics and epistemology. Others worthy of mention are René Descartes, who is part of the
philosophy, mathematics, biology, and physics inventories; and Jean-Jacques
Rousseau, with substantial contributions to both literature and philosophy
plus minor contributions to music.

These various considerations mean that it is difficult to refer to the total
number of people in the inventories—shall we count the brothers separately?
Count the probable legends? Count unique names or total appearances? I will
stick with 4,002 as a convenient way of referring to the total number of
significant figures, with the understanding that it is a convenience.

WHAT SEPARATES THE SIGNIFICANT
FROM THE NON-SIGNIFICANT?

The shortcoming of the 50 percent rule is that it does not provide a clear
bright line. No qualitative difference separates the people just below the
cutoff from those just above. Whereas it is easy to argue the qualitative superiority of those at the top, it is not possible to do so for the significant figures
who barely qualified versus the non-significant figures who fell just short.

Consider some Americans close to the cutoff line in the arts. Clifford
Odets and Willa Cather qualify as significant figures in Western literature
while Maxwell Anderson and Pearl Buck (despite her Nobel Prize) do not.
Duke Ellington and Jerome Kern qualify in Western music while Cole Porter
and Richard Rodgers do not. George Bellows and Thomas Hart Benton
qualify in Western art while Frederic Church and Frederic Remington do
not. In each of these instances, those who qualified and those who failed did
so by narrow margins. I cannot imagine an objective case to be made for the
superiority of the names that qualified, and I can easily imagine those names
switching places if I were to add or subtract a few sources.

But let's not go too far. Those who failed to qualify by larger margins
typically have résumés that are qualitatively inferior to the résumés of those
who made the cut. And when famous names that failed by a large margin
catch our eye, they can inspire a useful sense of perspective about artists and
scientists who may loom large to us but not so large to the wider world.
For example, Dorothy Parker and James Thurber are names that American
readers will recognize. Each has been the subject of dissertations, learned articles, biographies, and at least one movie dealing with their lives and work.

But they are mentioned in fewer than 20 percent of reference works and histories of literature written by people other than Americans. Is this just because Americans aren't sufficiently appreciated by the rest of the world? Is Europe too snooty to give credit to vibrant American voices? But Europe has had no trouble noticing American voices such as John Steinbeck, Mark Twain, John Dos Passos, Theodore Dreiser, and Ernest Hemingway in 100 percent of the sources. Eighty or 90 percent of such sources found room for Upton Sinclair, Thomas Wolfe, Bret Harte, Sinclair Lewis, and Jack London. It is well to consider the possibility that with whatever fondness we may reread Dorothy Parker and James Thurber, the story of Western literature is effectively complete without them.

I have gone out of my way to pick the best known of those who were are not part of the sample. They are rare. Besides sample stability, the 50 percent rule has a virtue that became evident only as I explored the work of the people who had been omitted: It cut out people who had no business being in the inventory. For every borderline case, dozens of others clearly did not belong in the inventory because they were not engaged in the same kind of enterprise as the people who qualified. Many of those mentioned in a quarter or a third of the sources achieved their reputations as teachers, educators, popularizers, or performers, not as research scientists, composers, painters, sculptors, or writers. A lesser standard, such as the 20 percent rule I had initially contemplated, runs serious dangers of changing the nature of the pool to one heavily loaded with people who, though distinguished, did not make the creative contributions that constitute our topic.

The best way to think about the set of significant figures is that it includes 100 percent of everyone who has to be part of the story of their respective fields; nearly 100 percent of everyone who even comes close to that standard; and some very large sample of everyone else who is authentically *significant* in the qualitative sense of that word. I will close by giving you a concrete illustration of how deep into the ranks the inventory of significant figures dips. On the facing page are the five people at the bottom of the list of significant figures in each of the scientific inventories and each of the Western inventories (i.e., those with the five lowest index scores). How many of them can you identify?

None is a household name. Three of the names are, in effect, ringers—the Davy is Edmund, not the famous Humphrey; the von Mises is Richard, not his famous brother Ludwig; and the Strutt is Robert, not his famous father, John. Everyone is likely to recognize a few of the others, but, despite

THE FIVE BOTTOM-RANKING PEOPLE IN THE SCIENTIFIC
AND WESTERN ARTS INVENTORIES

Western Art	*Western Literature*	*Western Music*
Francesco Solimena	Johann Hebel	Thomas Simpson
François Clouet	Bernard Mandeville	John Hothby
Adriaen de Vries	Alfred Mombert	Marbrianus Orto
Il Sodoma	Dubose Heyward	Joannes Gallus
Bertram of Minden	Joseph Roth	Mattheus le Maistre

Western Philosophy	*Astronomy*	*Biology*
Ralph Cudworth	Anders Celsius	Jules Bordet
Roscellinus	Thomas Wright	Albert Szent-Györgi
William of Champeaux	John Plaskett	Alexandre Yersin
Alexander of Hales	John Michell	Vincent du Vigneaud
Antiphon of Athens	Nevil Maskelyne	Benjamin Duggar

Chemistry	*Earth Sciences*	*Mathematics*
Otto Unverdorben	John Tuzo Wilson	Emil Artin
Henri Deville	John Wesley Powell	William Clifford
Edmund Davy	Vagn Ekman	Leonard Dickson
Pierre-Joseph Macquer	William Ferrel	Joseph Wedderburn
William Cullen	C.H.D. Buys-Ballot	Richard von Mises

Medicine	*Physics*	*Technology*
Charles Huggins	Jordanus de Nemore	William Nicholson
William Gorgas	Homi Bhabha	Girolamo Cardano
Valerius Cordus	Ernst Chladni	William Crookes
George Crile	Robert Strutt	H. Duhamel du Monceau
Simon Flexner	Bernard Lyot	Charles Steinmetz

the requirement that all had to be mentioned in at least 50 percent of the qualifying sources to gain their place, even experts are unlikely to know offhand anything except the name and a few elementary facts about most of the names at the bottom. Setting the cutoff at 50 percent includes almost everyone who is famous and large numbers of the obscure.

EIGHT

THE PEOPLE
WHO MATTER II:
THE GIANTS

Any plausible measure of eminence ends up identifying a few people who are widely separated from the rest. *Giant* was the word Johannes Brahms chose to express this phenomenon as seen from the inside. Brahms was an active composer by the age of 20 and had achieved international acclaim in his early thirties, yet he did not publish his first symphony until he was 44 years old. Ordinarily briskly efficient, Brahms had been fussing with it for more than 20 years. Why the procrastination? Because someone had written nine symphonies a few decades earlier and set an appalling standard. "You have no idea," Brahms told his friends, "how it feels for someone like me to hear behind him the tramp of a giant like Beethoven."[1] That image, invoked by a man who in others' eyes was a giant himself, is as good a way as any of thinking about the men who are alone on the tail of the Lotka curve.

THE TOP TWENTIES

On the pages that follow I show separate lists of the people with the top 20 index scores in each of the inventories. The purpose of the lists is to show how the top-ranked people in each inventory compare with one other. Including 20 means that we have gone beyond the giants to the merely great in every field, but the inclusiveness helps set the scores of the people at the top in context.

In evaluating these lists, misinterpretations can be avoided by remembering three points. The first is that *specific ranks and index scores can stimulate interesting discussion, but they are not analytically important.* It is entertaining to see who comes out in what place—that's why lists of the top 10 or top 100 are so popular, and why I have shown you how the top 20 come out. But few of these orderings are etched in stone. It is hard to imagine any set of sources dislodging Michelangelo, Confucius, or Shakespeare from their first-place rankings, but just about everyone else could easily rise or fall several places if the set of sources were altered. High statistical reliability for the index as a whole does not mean that orderings of specific individuals remain the same across subsets of sources. Nor does it make any difference whether they do. The dynamics we will be examining in the rest of the book depend on groups, statistical tendencies, and patterns, not on whether Debussy should have been lower than eighth in the Western music inventory or whether Berlioz belongs precisely at twelfth.

The appropriate way to look at the rankings is as if they were bicyclists in the Tour de France, who are counted as having the same time if they cross the day's finish line in the same group. Figures with index scores in the same vicinity should be counted as having the same score. A qualitative reading of the 16 sources used to create the music index reveals that Debussy and Berlioz both belong among the most important figures in Western music, and that's where their index scores put them. That same qualitative reading of those sources reveals that no historian of music puts them anywhere near Beethoven, Mozart, and Bach—and the index scores appropriately show a considerable gap between Debussy and Berlioz and the peak. The value of the indexes is not that they identify the precise ranks of people at the top, but that they broadly order large numbers of figures.

The second key point is that *index scores are not comparable across invento-ries.* Consider the inventories for Western and Chinese art. Four Chinese artists have inventory scores of 80 or higher, compared to a single Western artist. This does not mean that Chinese art produced four great artists while the West produced but one. It tells us only that, in the evaluations of Western art, one man stands out further from the rest than in the evaluations of Chinese art. It could be that the West had a hundred painters greater than any in China (assuming that such judgments were possible), or vice versa. A given inventory tells us only how the prominent figures are distributed within that inventory, not across inventories.

This leads to the third key point, that *the index scores measure the frog rela-tive to the size of the pond,* and the sizes of the ponds vary substantially. It so happens that the available sources permit me to treat all the countries of the West as a cultural whole, comparing philosophic and artistic figures across the countries that comprise the West, and there is analytic advantage in doing so. The available sources do not permit me to compare (with any confidence) philosophic and artistic figures across even China and Japan and India, let alone to include the West in the comparison, and so each of those countries has a separate inventory. In other words, the Western pond for the philosophy and arts inventories is bigger than the ponds for China, India, and Japan (an important point that will return in another context. See page 250). To take a specific example, Ibsen is not even shown in the figure for the top 20 in Western literature, because he came in 24th. But he had to compete with everyone in Western literature, whereas Basho had to compete only with everyone in Japanese literature to attain his first-place standing. If I had shown instead a graph for the top Norwegian writers, Ibsen would have been the unrivaled number one, towering over number two (Bjørnstjerne Bjørnson, 131st in the Western literature inventory). It would be nice to have some common measuring rod for comparing the sizes of the ponds, but none of the quantitative possibilities I have been able to test have proved satisfactory in the end. The best we can do is treat each inventory for what it is, and then talk about which people within that inventory have gotten the most attention. The concluding chart in the set for the scientific inventories (see page 130) offers a concrete example of this point. It shows the top 20 for the combined inventories of the hard sciences, mathematics, and medicine. The sciences have worldwide coverage and in that sense constitute a single pond. But within the sciences, different fields get different levels of attention, with physics receiving the most and the earth sciences the least. No one from technology or the earth sciences makes the top 20 on the combined index. Far from it—Thomas Edison, top-ranked in technology, ranks only 50th in the combined index. Charles Lyell, top-ranked in earth sciences, ranks 58th.

Enough caveats. Here are the charts of the top 20 philosophers, artists, and scientific figures by inventory. I have coded the scores by shades to make it easy to move from one list to another and get a quick sense of how the distribution of giants and near-giants varies across the inventories. Black denotes those with scores of 90 and above, dark blue those with scores of 70–90, progressively lighter blue for scores of 50–70 and 20–50, and white for scores below 20.

ASTRONOMY

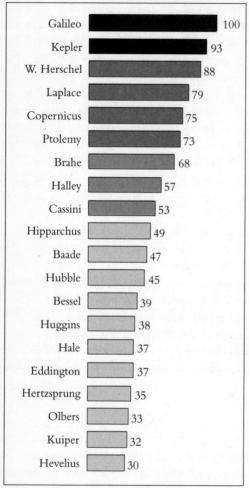

Significant figures: 124
Index reliability: .92

Galileo's first-place position (based exclusively on his achievements in astronomy) is easy to understand. As the first person to use a telescope to study the night sky, he made a long list of basic discoveries about the moon, sun, and planets. Does it make sense that a figure as famous as Copernicus ranks fifth while a figure as obscure as William Herschel is third? I use this question to illustrate a major theme in the text ("System Builders Versus Brick Layers," see page 147). That discussion should convey what an extraordinary range of accomplishments Herschel amassed, despite his obscurity among the general public.

Other than Herschel, the person who to a layman may seem high on the list is Pierre-Simon Laplace. His place rests on his role as a seminal figure in the application of mathematics to the problems of celestial motion plus his development of the nebular hypothesis to explain the formation of stars and a prescient prediction of the existence of black holes.

Astronomy is notable for having two native-born Americans among the top 20 (the technology index is the only other one): Edwin Hubble, ranked twelfth, determined that Andromeda is a galaxy, revolutionizing our understanding of the universe's size, and demonstrated Hubble's Law, confirming that the universe is expanding. George Ellery Hale, fifteenth, is most famous for his role in developing the large telescopes at Mount Wilson and Palomar, but he also invented the spectro-heliograph and discovered that sunspots are subject to an electromagnetic field.

BIOLOGY

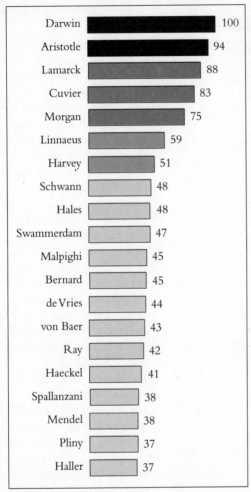

Darwin	100
Aristotle	94
Lamarck	88
Cuvier	83
Morgan	75
Linnaeus	59
Harvey	51
Schwann	48
Hales	48
Swammerdam	47
Malpighi	45
Bernard	45
de Vries	44
von Baer	43
Ray	42
Haeckel	41
Spallanzani	38
Mendel	38
Pliny	37
Haller	37

Significant figures: 193
Index reliability: .88

Biology is such a sprawling discipline that the top 20 represent different types of accomplishment including, among others, botany, zoology, evolution, genetics, and physiology. Note that some top biologists (Pasteur is the most famous example) are missing, because their major accomplishments are associated with the etiology and treatment of disease. They show up in the medicine inventory.

The roles of the top two figures, Darwin and Aristotle, are widely known. Lamarck is a lesser known figure identified with Lamarckism, a mistaken theory of evolution. But his *Système des Animaux sans Vertèbres* founded modern invertebrate zoology, the three-volume *Flore Française* classified the wild plants of France, and his work on evolution, while ultimately proved wrong, was pivotal in stimulating others' thinking about evolution. He also introduced the very term *biology*. Georges Cuvier, another figure not well known to the general public, founded comparative anatomy as a discipline and made major contributions to both biological classification and morphology in general.

For Americans, the biology inventory is noteworthy because it includes a native-born American among the top five, the only American to climb so high in the hard sciences. His name is Thomas Hunt Morgan, whose seminal work in the first three decades of 20C established much of our knowledge of genes and chromosomes in the era preceding electron microscopy and the discovery of the structure of DNA.

CHEMISTRY

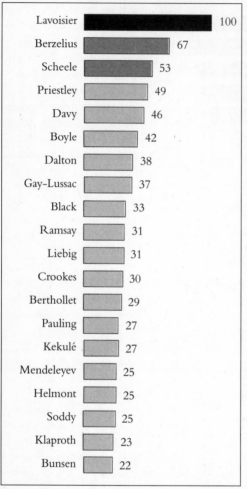

Lavoisier	100
Berzelius	67
Scheele	53
Priestley	49
Davy	46
Boyle	42
Dalton	38
Gay-Lussac	37
Black	33
Ramsay	31
Liebig	31
Crookes	30
Berthollet	29
Pauling	27
Kekulé	27
Mendeleyev	25
Helmont	25
Soddy	25
Klaproth	23
Bunsen	22

Significant figures: 204
Index reliability: .93

That Lavoisier is in first place without close competition should be no surprise. Lavoisier had major accomplishments in theory (*Traité Élémentaire de Chemie* stated the law of conservation of matter and is generally accepted as the founding text of quantitative chemistry), experimentation (he deciphered the process of combustion, found that diamond consists of carbon, and discovered the composition of air), and practice (he developed the first list of known elements and established a system of chemical nomenclature).

The ordering of those who follow Lavoisier reflects a peculiarity of the chemistry inventory. Chronologies of events in chemistry consistently include the discovery of each element as an event. This is understandable—each element is a building block from which much else may follow, and the discovery of each new element was a genuinely significant event. But it also happens that a few chemists, especially Berzelius, Scheele, and Davy, were on hand just as some of the basic techniques for isolating elements became available (e.g., electrolysis). They each discovered several elements using these powerful new techniques, thereby accumulating large scores from the chronology sources. All of them belong in the top rank of chemists, but their scores are somewhat inflated by their luck in timing—always a factor in determining who discovers what, but especially so in their cases.

EARTH SCIENCES

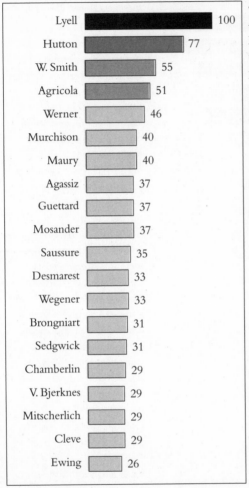

Name	Value
Lyell	100
Hutton	77
W. Smith	55
Agricola	51
Werner	46
Murchison	40
Maury	40
Agassiz	37
Guettard	37
Mosander	37
Saussure	35
Desmarest	33
Wegener	33
Brongniart	31
Sedgwick	31
Chamberlin	29
V. Bjerknes	29
Mitscherlich	29
Cleve	29
Ewing	26

Significant figures: 85
Index reliability: .81

Earth sciences, an umbrella term for geology, oceanography, and aeronomy, produced the least reliable of the inventories. One reason is that the science sources gave less attention to the earth sciences than to any of the other scientific categories. As the material devoted to a field decreases, the influence of idiosyncrasies in the sources tends to increase, and one of the side effects is lower reliability, although .81 is still respectable.

The relative positions of the top two figures, Charles Lyell followed by James Hutton, is qualitatively arguable. Hutton's original monograph, "Concerning the System of the Earth," published in 1785, followed by his full-scale treatment ten years later in *Theory of the Earth, with Proofs and Illustrations*, introduced the uniformitarian view of earth's development, displacing earlier and incorrect theories, and founded geology as an organized field of study. This seminal contribution could be argued to justify giving him pride of place over Lyell, who came along two generations later. But if Hutton began geology as an organized field of study, Lyell's three-volume *The Principles of Geology* (1830) could be said to have founded modern geology itself, establishing that geological formations are created over millions of years and setting a new time frame not only for the earth sciences but for collateral disciplines. Add to that Lyell's other major contributions, and his first-place rank is plausible.

PHYSICS

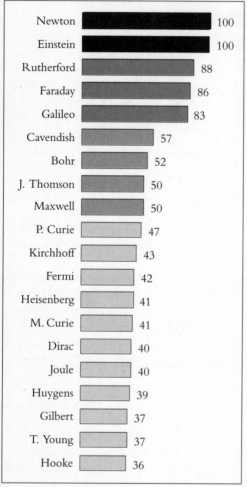

Newton	100
Einstein	100
Rutherford	88
Faraday	86
Galileo	83
Cavendish	57
Bohr	52
J. Thomson	50
Maxwell	50
P. Curie	47
Kirchhoff	43
Fermi	42
Heisenberg	41
M. Curie	41
Dirac	40
Joule	40
Huygens	39
Gilbert	37
T. Young	37
Hooke	36

Significant figures: 218
Index reliability: .95

Isaac Newton and Albert Einstein are separated by a hair. Newton had, at the fourth decimal place, the higher raw score, but Einstein got more space in 9 out of the 15 sources. A tie is fitting. Galileo's high rank (based exclusively on his accomplishments in physics, as is Newton's) will also surprise no one.

Ernest Rutherford, ranked third, discovered two types of uranium radiation, alpha and beta rays; discovered the nucleus of the atom, leading to an understanding of the true structure of the atom; invented the alpha-particle counter; used atomic bombardment to alter atomic nuclei, constituting the first controlled nuclear reaction; discovered the proton; and demonstrated that uranium and thorium break down into a series of radioactive intermediate elements. These were just his major accomplishments.

Michael Faraday, ranked fourth, was a protean figure and as famous in England as Edison and Bell would later become in the United States. Again limiting the list to just major accomplishments, it was Faraday who discovered that a changing magnetic force can generate electricity (the basis of electrical generators), discovered that electrical forces can produce motion (the basis of electric motors), and worked out the basic laws governing chemical reactions when an electric current is passed through a solution.

MATHEMATICS

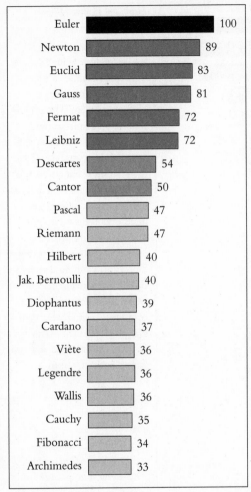

Euler	100
Newton	89
Euclid	83
Gauss	81
Fermat	72
Leibniz	72
Descartes	54
Cantor	50
Pascal	47
Riemann	47
Hilbert	40
Jak. Bernoulli	40
Diophantus	39
Cardano	37
Viète	36
Legendre	36
Wallis	36
Cauchy	35
Fibonacci	34
Archimedes	33

Significant figures: 191
Index reliability: .93

Historians of mathematics form no consensus about who is the greatest mathematician. The ordering in this inventory could easily be shifted by tweaking the rules for combining the sources. Everyone agrees that the top-ranked mathematician, Leonhard Euler, belongs somewhere close to the top, but his score is partly a function of his immense productivity. His published work is enough to fill more than ninety volumes.

If the criterion for the rankings were pure mathematical genius, many would put Carl Gauss in first place. Unlike Euler, Gauss was reluctant to publish, and it appears from his notebooks that a number of major discoveries credited to others were discovered first by him but never revealed.

If the criterion were fame, Newton would win. His second-place finish is based exclusively on his accomplishments in mathematics, excluding his contributions in physics and optics.

If the criterion were influence, Euclid would probably come in first. He is an example of how fame and influence can be won by a brilliant synthesis of the work of others. In his *Elements*, Euclid contributed some new theorems of his own, but his major achievement was to combine the scattered but extensive geometric knowledge of his day, refining and organizing the whole into a book that became the West's standard geometry text for more than two thousand years.

MEDICINE

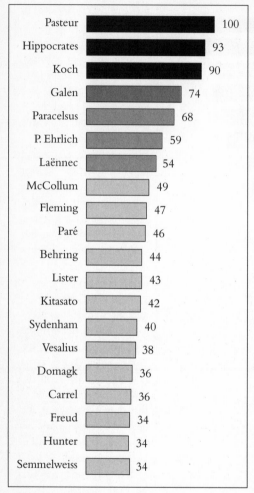

Pasteur	100
Hippocrates	93
Koch	90
Galen	74
Paracelsus	68
P. Ehrlich	59
Laënnec	54
McCollum	49
Fleming	47
Paré	46
Behring	44
Lister	43
Kitasato	42
Sydenham	40
Vesalius	38
Domagk	36
Carrel	36
Freud	34
Hunter	34
Semmelweiss	34

Significant figures: 160
Index reliability: .87

Deciding whether specific achievements belong in the medicine inventory or the biology inventory was a chronic problem. The general rule to was to classify an accomplishment under medicine only if it was related to the identification, etiology, or treatment of disease. Thus, for example, the discovery of microorganisms is classified under biology, while the discovery that a microorganism causes a certain disease is classified under medicine. Using this rule, Louis Pasteur is an unsurprising winner of first place. Readers will also be familiar with Hippocrates and Galen, both of whom were founders of medicine as a profession while being wrong in most of their medical pronouncements.

Robert Koch, who was active in the last quarter of 19C, is not a household name as Pasteur is, but he deserves to be. He isolated the bacilli that cause tuberculosis, cholera, and anthrax respectively and transformed the study of infectious diseases. He introduced important public health practices and steam sterilization of medical instruments. "Koch's postulates" are still used as a guide for research into the causes of infectious diseases.

Freud shows up because of his contributions to the clinical description of mental illnesses and his introduction of the use of cocaine as an anesthetic, both of which were classified under medicine. His writings on psychoanalysis were classified under psychology and are not part of his index score for this inventory.

TECHNOLOGY

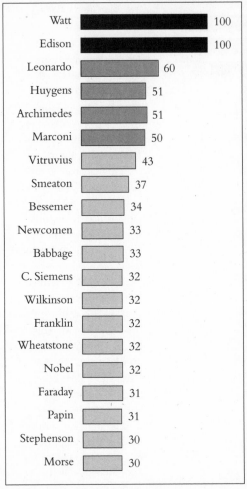

Watt	100
Edison	100
Leonardo	60
Huygens	51
Archimedes	51
Marconi	50
Vitruvius	43
Smeaton	37
Bessemer	34
Newcomen	33
Babbage	33
C. Siemens	32
Wilkinson	32
Franklin	32
Wheatstone	32
Nobel	32
Faraday	31
Papin	31
Stephenson	30
Morse	30

Significant figures: 239
Index reliability: .84

Thomas Edison, at the end of 19C an icon who rivaled presidents in fame and esteem, is the only American who is at the top of any index. I show him effectively tied with James Watt, rounding up his actual index score of 99.4. Their accomplishments have different profiles. Edison invented many things while Watt fundamentally changed the capability of one very big thing, the steam engine.

Far behind Edison and Watt are Leonardo da Vinci, Christiaan Huygens, Archimedes, and Marconi. Leonardo attracts the attention of historians of technology for his brilliant ideas, far ahead of his time. But his mind ran ahead of his ability to implement. Christiaan Huygens is one of the great polymaths of history. In addition to his landmark accomplishments in astronomy, mathematics, and physics (none of which affect his score in the technology index), he improved optical glasses and invented the first pendulum escapement and the first hairspring for the balance wheel of a clock, fundamentally improving timekeeping. Archimedes shows up in the technology inventory primarily for his invention of the screw pump, the discovery of the principle of the lever, and his development of the pulley. Marconi, like many of the people who follow him in the top 20—Smeaton, Siemens, Newcomen, Nobel, Morse, Papin, and Stephenson—is known for one major invention, in his case the wireless transmission of sound.

COMBINED SCIENCES

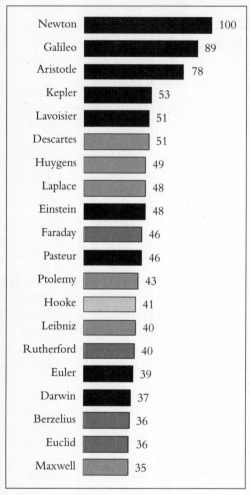

Significant figures: 1,445
Index reliability: .94

This graph shows what happens when everyone from the separate hard science inventories plus mathematics, medicine, and technology is thrown into the same pond. The color coding retains the values each person attained in his own specialty, as shown in the preceding graphs, to indicate how increasing the size of the pond and combining accomplishments across fields changes the relative attention devoted to these eminent people.

The list may be seen as the triumph of the poly-maths. Only five out the 20—Lavoisier, Einstein, Rutherford, Berzelius, and Euclid—can be said to have remained within a single field. In the cases of Aristo-tle, Descartes, and Leibniz, this ordering doesn't even represent their full poly-mathic sweep—none of them gets any credit here for his philosophic writings.

The graph is also notable for those who are missing. No one from the earth sciences made it into the top 20 on the combined rankings, while only Huygens made it from the technology inventory—but largely because of his major contributions to physics. Meanwhile, eight out the 20 were also in the top 20 in the physics inventory, indicating how dominant that discipline was through 1950. Since then, one may speculate, biology has made major inroads on that dominance via its transforming discoveries in genetics and neuroscience.

CHINESE PHILOSOPHY

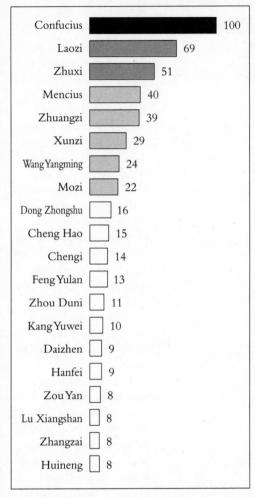

Confucius	100
Laozi	69
Zhuxi	51
Mencius	40
Zhuangzi	39
Xunzi	29
Wang Yangming	24
Mozi	22
Dong Zhongshu	16
Cheng Hao	15
Chengi	14
Feng Yulan	13
Zhou Duni	11
Kang Yuwei	10
Daizhen	9
Hanfei	9
Zou Yan	8
Lu Xiangshan	8
Zhangzai	8
Huineng	8

Significant figures: 39
Index reliability: .96

Despite the wide gap that separates Confucius from Laozi, the graph actually understates the real dominance of Confucianism in Chinese thought. In addition to Confucius himself, the third- and fourth-ranked philosophers, Zhu Xi and Mencius, were exegetes of Confucius.

It may come as a surprise to some that Zhu Xi outranked Mencius, who is better known to the Western public, but this ordering is consistent across all the philosophy sources, both those written by Chinese and those written by foreigners. Mencius played a crucial role in making Confucianism the state philosophy in –4C, but Zhu Xi receives still more attention, by substantial margins, for his reinvigoration of Confucianism in 12C. For that matter, it was Zhu Xi who was responsible for making Mencius as well known as he is today, by including Mencius's work as part of "The Four Books" that became the central texts for both primary education and the civil service examinations.

The Chinese philosophy index continues all the way to 1950 because, unlike Chinese art and literature, there is no break between the philosophy of classical China and the philosophy of post-classical China.

INDIAN PHILOSOPHY

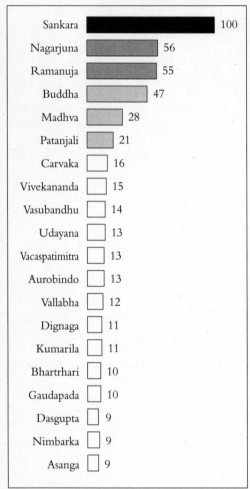

Sankara 100
Nagarjuna 56
Ramanuja 55
Buddha 47
Madhva 28
Patanjali 21
Carvaka 16
Vivekananda 15
Vasubandhu 14
Udayana 13
Vacaspatimitra 13
Aurobindo 13
Vallabha 12
Dignaga 11
Kumarila 11
Bhartrhari 10
Gaudapada 10
Dasgupta 9
Nimbarka 9
Asanga 9

Significant figures: 45
Index reliability: .93

A curiosity of the Indian philosophy index is that it does not include the author of the most important single work in Indian philosophy, and indeed the first work that historians of philosophy call philosophy: the *Upanishads*, the last component of the *Veda*, the founding document of Hinduism. A collection of 108 discourses, the *Upanishads* was transmitted orally for an indeterminate period. We have some of the names of the individual authors, but none of them has a sufficiently central role to qualify for major credit, let alone to take credit for authorship of the work as a whole.

The named philosopher who dominates the index even more decisively than Confucius dominated the Chinese philosophy index is Sankara, who added metaphysics and system to the haphazard insights of the *Upanishads*, became the leading exponent of the Advaita Vedanta school of philosophy, and whose thought still forms the mainstream of modern Hinduism.

After Sankara, lagging far behind, are Nagarjuna, who founded Mahayana Buddhism, and Ramanuja, second only to Sankara in Vedanta thought, who tried to pull Hinduism toward an appreciation of the phenomenal world and the knowledge it can provide us. Why does Buddha languish in fourth place? Because, despite his place alongside Abraham, Jesus, and Muhammad as founders of the world's great religions, Buddhism has always been secondary to Hinduism in India, both as philosophy (which is the basis for Buddha's inclusion here) and as a religion.

WESTERN PHILOSOPHY

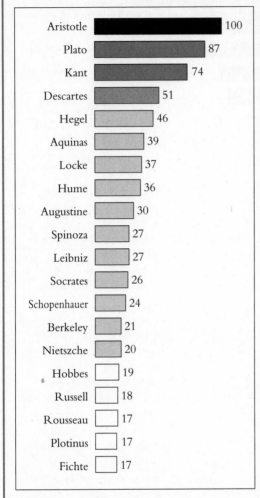

Aristotle	100
Plato	87
Kant	74
Descartes	51
Hegel	46
Aquinas	39
Locke	37
Hume	36
Augustine	30
Spinoza	27
Leibniz	27
Socrates	26
Schopenhauer	24
Berkeley	21
Nietzsche	20
Hobbes	19
Russell	18
Rousseau	17
Plotinus	17
Fichte	17

Significant figures: 155
Index reliability: .96

Western philosophy, like Chinese and Indian philosophy, is dominated by a handful of figures. Only 15 Western philosophers had index scores of 20 or higher, and only 4 of those 16 had index scores over 50. Aristotle and Plato are separated by a large enough gap to warrant treating their scores as different, with the continuing warning not to make too much of it.

What separates the Western and Asian philosophy inventories is represented by Kant, standing in third place. In China, the great figures after Confucius and Laozi were their exegetes and reinterpreters. The same was true in India of the great figures after the *Upanishads* and Buddha—even Sankara was an interpreter of an existing tradition. The West followed that pattern through 17C, with all the great figures drawing substantially from the Platonic or Aristotelian traditions. But then came Kant, whose contributions amounted to an expansion of philosophic thought after the founders that is unique among the three great philosophic traditions. He was followed by the innovative and influential 19C contributions of Hegel, Schopenhauer, and Nietzsche.

Some anomalies: If Bertrand Russell's score seems high, the explanation lies in his triple role as a philosopher, logician, and a historian of philosophy. Political thinkers were treated as secondary figures in some of the sources, which affected the scores of Locke, Hobbes, and Rousseau as well as familiar names not part of the top 20 (e.g., Cicero and Machiavelli).

WESTERN MUSIC

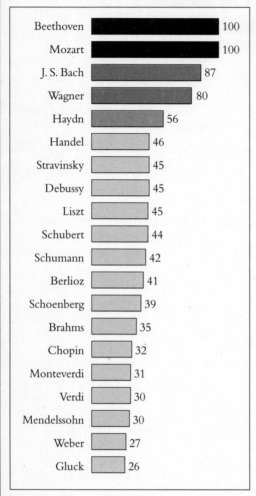

Beethoven — 100
Mozart — 100
J. S. Bach — 87
Wagner — 80
Haydn — 56
Handel — 46
Stravinsky — 45
Debussy — 45
Liszt — 45
Schubert — 44
Schumann — 42
Berlioz — 41
Schoenberg — 39
Brahms — 35
Chopin — 32
Monteverdi — 31
Verdi — 30
Mendelssohn — 30
Weber — 27
Gluck — 26

Significant figures: 523
Index reliability: .97

One reason that the Western music inventory has 16 sources, even though a highly reliable index had been reached with 10, was to see whether the neck-and-neck scores of Beethoven and Mozart might separate. They did not. I show them as tied with scores of 100. Strictly speaking, their scores were not identical. But the difference was both trivial and ambiguous. Ten of the 16 sources gave more space to Beethoven than to Mozart. The sum of the scores from all 16 sources put Beethoven on top. But when I discarded the high and low scores for computing the index scores—a standard precaution against giving undue influence to an aberrant source—Mozart slipped into the lead by the slimmest of margins. Showing both men as tied at 100 seemed the reasonable choice. I have put Beethoven on top in the chart because a qualitative reading of the sources indicates that, though the authors admire Mozart unreservedly, Beethoven is impossible to put second to anyone.

Casual fans of concert music, asked to guess the top four, usually include Mozart, Beethoven, and Bach, but are likely to guess Haydn or Brahms as the fourth. Few think of Wagner. In contrast, a professional violist whom I asked to guess said Beethoven and Mozart were number one and two ("of course") and then asked matter-of-factly, "Who came in third, Bach or Wagner?" His reaction reflects Wagner's high standing among experts, consistent with his index score.

CHINESE PAINTING

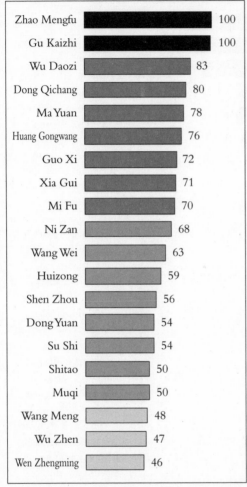

Zhao Mengfu	100
Gu Kaizhi	100
Wu Daozi	83
Dong Qichang	80
Ma Yuan	78
Huang Gongwang	76
Guo Xi	72
Xia Gui	71
Mi Fu	70
Ni Zan	68
Wang Wei	63
Huizong	59
Shen Zhou	56
Dong Yuan	54
Su Shi	54
Shitao	50
Muqi	50
Wang Meng	48
Wu Zhen	47
Wen Zhengming	46

Significant figures: 111
Index reliability: .91

Only painting had a consistent tradition of named artists in China. The inventory thus ignores distinguished Chinese traditions in sculpture and ceramics.

Gu Kaizhi's index score was 98.9, but he was ranked above Zhao Mengfu in a majority of the sources; hence the tie. But interpreting these scores is problematic. Gu Kaizhi (fl. 4C) and the third-ranked artist, Wu Daoxi (fl. 8C), have no surviving works of certain authenticity. The early critics after Gu Kaizhi's death differed in their evaluations of his work, with some of them unimpressed. He did not attain his semi-legendary reputation until the Tang Dynasty, four hundred years later—as if Michelangelo had not been recognized as more than merely very good until 20C. This reliance on secondary accounts leads to a large degree of uncertainty about who belongs where.

Significant figures are identified throughout the range from −800 to 1950, but index scores are computed only for artists through the end of 18C, as the Qing dynasty spiraled downhill. As in India, important creative cultural activity effectively shut down during an interval between the collapse of the traditional civilization and its reformulation in 20C, and many of the sources plainly treated modern artists with separate criteria.

JAPANESE ART

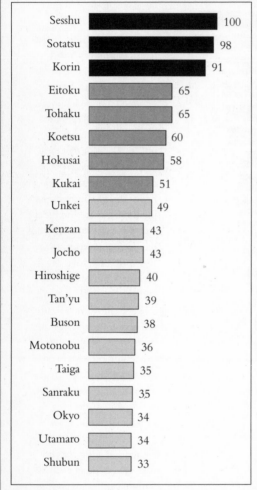

Artist	Score
Sesshu	100
Sotatsu	98
Korin	91
Eitoku	65
Tohaku	65
Koetsu	60
Hokusai	58
Kukai	51
Unkei	49
Kenzan	43
Jocho	43
Hiroshige	40
Tan'yu	39
Buson	38
Motonobu	36
Taiga	35
Sanraku	35
Okyo	34
Utamaro	34
Shubun	33

Significant figures: 81
Index reliability: .93

Japan has no counterparts to China's Gu Kaizhi or Greece's Zeuxis, artists of legendary genius for whom no works survive. Provenance is often a problem in assigning works to the top-ranking Japanese artists, but enough solidly attributable examples exist for modern art historians to assess their achievements directly.

The top three appear in chronological order. Sesshu was active in the last half of 15C. A Zen monk, he is considered the greatest master of the monochrome ink style, though he used color to great effect late in his career. Sotatsu followed in the early 17C, founder of the *Rimpa* school that in turn affected Japanese painting though its successive phases. Korin, the second great master of the *Rimpa* school, was active in early 18C. He was the brother of Ogata Kenzan, often considered to be Japan's greatest potter and himself tenth in the top 20.

An oddity in the index, and another reminder that specific ranks are not to be confused with holy writ, is the discrepancy between the index scores of Sotatsu (98) and Koetsu (60). They are closely linked in their work and were founders of the same school. If the criterion is all-around artistic accomplishment in calligraphy, pottery, and design as well as painting, Koetsu is sometimes given priority over Sotatsu. But the qualitative descriptions of their art at its best suggest that Sotatsu is a step beyond Koetsu. Perhaps the difference in their index scores is commensurate with that qualitative difference.

WESTERN ART

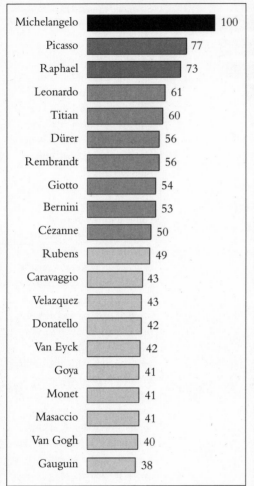

Michelangelo	100
Picasso	77
Raphael	73
Leonardo	61
Titian	60
Dürer	56
Rembrandt	56
Giotto	54
Bernini	53
Cézanne	50
Rubens	49
Caravaggio	43
Velazquez	43
Donatello	42
Van Eyck	42
Goya	41
Monet	41
Masaccio	41
Van Gogh	40
Gauguin	38

Significant figures: 479
Index reliability: .95

Significant figures in Western art were identified from ancient Greece onward, but index scores were assigned only to figures who postdated 1200. In Western art histories, the space devoted to the Greek masters known only by reputation or from scattered copies is a fraction of the space given over to the post-1200 masters, and the reason has nothing to do with their relative merit. Rather, the experts have little material to go on, and are correspondingly brief.

Michelangelo's dominance obscures an important fact about the Western art inventory: A large number of artists of the first rank get close to equal treatment. For example, if we recomputed the index scores after deleting Michelangelo, all of the top 20 would have index scores of 50 or higher. Only Picasso and Raphael would stand apart from the rest, with the scores thereafter forming such a gradual slope that no adjacent pair of scores are significantly different. But subtracting Michelangelo from Western art is something that can be done only by a computer.

The presence of Picasso in second place will surprise and perhaps outrage some readers. The amount of space accorded to him reflects not just the high regard in which his art is held, but also his seminal role in several phases of the break with classicism that occurred in late 19C and early 20C.

ARABIC LITERATURE

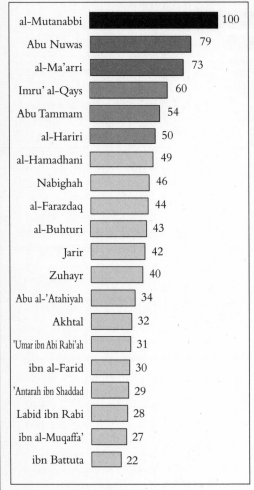

al-Mutanabbi	100
Abu Nuwas	79
al-Ma'arri	73
Imru' al-Qays	60
Abu Tammam	54
al-Hariri	50
al-Hamadhani	49
Nabighah	46
al-Farazdaq	44
al-Buhturi	43
Jarir	42
Zuhayr	40
Abu al-'Atahiyah	34
Akhtal	32
'Umar ibn Abi Rabi'ah	31
ibn al-Farid	30
'Antarah ibn Shaddad	29
Labid ibn Rabi	28
ibn al-Muqaffa'	27
ibn Battuta	22

Significant figures: 82
Index reliability: .88

The roster of significant figures include those who wrote in either Arabic or Persian, and includes persons writing through 1950. The index scores are limited to persons writing in Arabic prior to 19C—in effect, Islamic literature.

Islamic literature operated under two theological constraints. Drama was considered to be a representational art and forbidden. Realistic fiction was considered to be a form of lying, and also forbidden. The poetry that came to play such a large part in Arabic literature thus was pushed in the direction of poetry and panegyrics that are ornate, elliptical, and given to fantastical uses of the language that are said to be not only untranslatable but to draw from an Arabic sensibility that it is difficult for anyone not Arabic to appreciate.

Al-Mutanabbi's wide margin over everyone else is consistent with the qualitative descriptions of his work. The first line in any entry about him is likely to say outright that he is the best classic Arabic poet of all time. Abu Nawas is in second place, though his racy poetry is frowned upon by orthodox Muslims. He seems to have taken to heart his famous line "Accumulate as many sins as you can," making him a vivid contrast to the third-ranked Arabic writer, also a poet, al-Ma'arri, who led an abstemious, secluded life.

CHINESE LITERATURE

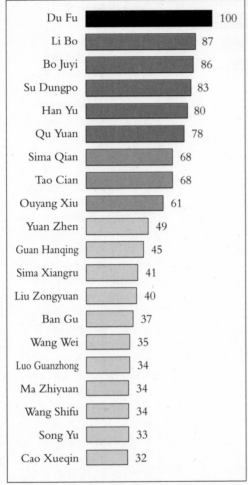

Du Fu	100
Li Bo	87
Bo Juyi	86
Su Dungpo	83
Han Yu	80
Qu Yuan	78
Sima Qian	68
Tao Cian	68
Ouyang Xiu	61
Yuan Zhen	49
Guan Hanqing	45
Sima Xiangru	41
Liu Zongyuan	40
Ban Gu	37
Wang Wei	35
Luo Guanzhong	34
Ma Zhiyuan	34
Wang Shifu	34
Song Yu	33
Cao Xueqin	32

Significant figures: 83
Index reliability: .89

The ordering in the Chinese literature index changes drastically depending on whether one chooses to consider the philosophical classics as literature. If they were to be included, then Confucius, Laozi, and Mencius would rank first, sixth, and seventh in Chinese literature. There are good arguments for including them. The Chinese philosophic classics transcend philosophy. But Confucius is so extraordinarily dominant in Chinese thought (if he is included, Du Fu's score is a mere 42) that including him reduces everyone else to also-rans, which does not reflect the special stature of China's greatest writers outside of philosophy. So the top 20 shown in the graph exclude philosophers and critics while including poets, dramatists, fiction writers, historians, and essayists.

Du Fu is barely known in the West. He is not only ranked first here but, according to those who are in a position to evaluate such things, was one of the greatest poets ever, anywhere. The problem for Western readers is that the aesthetic nuances and layers of meaning in great Chinese poetry cannot be retained in even the best translations.

Significant figures are included through 1950 in the Chinese literature inventory, but index scores are computed only for authors who flourished before the end of 18C, for the same reasons described for the Chinese art inventory.

INDIAN LITERATURE

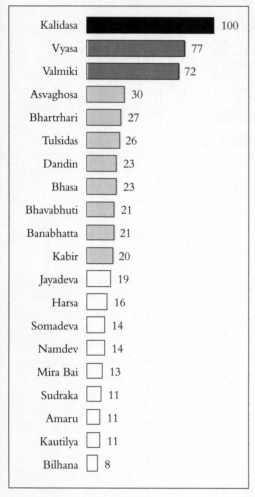

Significant figures: 43

Index reliability: .91

The Indian literature inventory is overwhelmingly dominated by just three figures: Kalidasa, the great poet and dramatist, and Valmiki and Vyasa, the putative authors of the *Ramayana* and *Mahabharata* respectively. The fourth- and fifth-ranked authors, the poet Asvaghosa and the romancier/critic Dandin, have index scores of just 26. No other inventory drops off so sharply, so quickly. The Indian literature inventory is also odd in that two of the top three authors are semi-legendary figures whose historical reality is even more questionable than Homer's. Finally, it is unique in that the era of great writing ends so early. Kalidasa is the most recent of the big three in Indian literature, and he lived (with the usual caveats surrounding Indian dates) in 5C. It should be emphasized that these comments refer to the body of formal work. The Hindu tradition of fables is one of the richest in the world, but little of it is associated with specific authors.

As in the cases of Chinese art and literature, significant figures are identified throughout the range from −800 to 1950, but the index scores for the Indian literature inventory stop at figures who wrote through 17C, before the Mughal empire began the decline that ended in the subjugation of the subcontinent by the British over the next century. The Indian literary tradition revived in late 19C. It quickly reached the heights with Rabindranath Tagore, who won the Nobel Prize in 1913.

JAPANESE LITERATURE

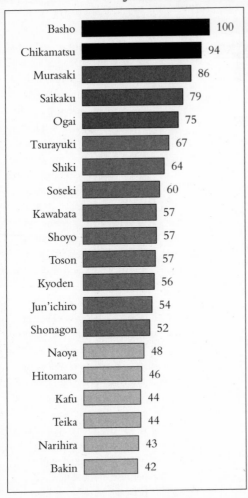

Basho	100
Chikamatsu	94
Murasaki	86
Saikaku	79
Ogai	75
Tsurayuki	67
Shiki	64
Soseki	60
Kawabata	57
Shoyo	57
Toson	57
Kyoden	56
Jun'ichiro	54
Shonagon	52
Naoya	48
Hitomaro	46
Kafu	44
Teika	44
Narihira	43
Bakin	42

Significant figures: 85
Index reliability: .86

The Japanese literature inventory is characterized by a large number of writers who receive substantial attention rather than by a few dominant figures. The variety in the first four rankings is of interest: Basho (1644–1694), by consensus Japan's greatest poet and the master of *haiku*; Chikamatsu (1653–1725), by consensus Japan's greatest dramatist, writing mostly for the *bunraku* (puppet theatre); Murasaki Shikibu (c. 978–1014), author of *The Tale of Genji*, by consensus Japan's greatest work of literature (and the highest ranking woman in any of the inventories); and Saikaku (1642–1693), writer of brilliant erotic tales and famous for his speed-writing of *haikai*, humorous linked-verse poems that were the source of *haiku*. He is said to have written 23,500 *haikai* in one twenty-four hour period, a rate of more than 16 per minute (a story that is hard to believe).

Unlike China and India, Japan did not experience a substantial gap between the end of the old order and the emergence of the new, a transition which in Japan took just a few decades at the end of 19C. Both the Japanese art and literature inventories continue from the earliest figures through to 1950.

WESTERN LITERATURE

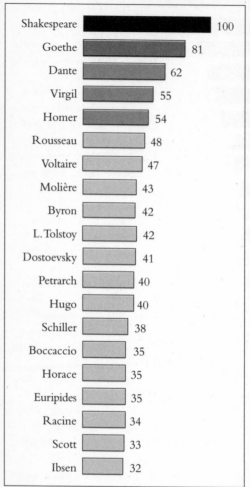

Shakespeare	100
Goethe	81
Dante	62
Virgil	55
Homer	54
Rousseau	48
Voltaire	47
Molière	43
Byron	42
L. Tolstoy	42
Dostoevsky	41
Petrarch	40
Hugo	40
Schiller	38
Boccaccio	35
Horace	35
Euripides	35
Racine	34
Scott	33
Ibsen	32

Significant figures: 835
Index reliability: .95

The first five places are hard to argue with. Shakespeare, Goethe, Dante, Virgil, and Homer are giants in Western literature by anyone's standards. Shakespeare stands noticeably apart even from the other four. Of all the giants in all the fields, Shakespeare is the one who seems to leave historians stretching for some way to convey his awesome impact not just on literature but on the modern West.

After the top five, one can expect to hear cries of indignation. What is Rousseau doing in sixth place? Voltaire in seventh? Byron in ninth? Scott in nineteenth?

In the cases of Rousseau and Voltaire, the ratings partly reflect their combined fiction and nonfiction. But even when I recomputed indexes based exclusively on fictional work, they ranked high, because of the difference between histories of literature and of the other arts. Historians of music and the visual arts discuss composers and artists almost exclusively in terms of their place in their artistic worlds. Histories of literature spend more space on the influence of authors, including authors of fiction, on social and political movements—the Enlightenment in the case of Rousseau and Voltaire, the Romantic movement in the case of Byron and Scott. This tendency contaminates the Western literature index as a representation of purely literary excellence, but it appropriately reflects the way in which Western literature has been intertwined with politics and society.

The handful with the plain black bars is a select list indeed. With apologies to very great names who fell just short, consider those in black, denoting index scores of 90 and above:

Astronomy	Galileo and Kepler
Biology	Darwin and Aristotle
Chemistry	Lavoisier
Earth sciences	Lyell
Physics	Newton and Einstein
Mathematics	Euler
Medicine	Pasteur, Hippocrates, and Koch
Technology	Edison and Watt
Combined scientific	Newton
Chinese philosophy	Confucius
Indian philosophy	Sankara
Western philosophy	Aristotle
Western music	Beethoven and Mozart
Chinese painting	Gu Kaizhi and Zhao Mengfu
Japanese painting	Sesshu, Sotatsu, and Korin
Western art	Michelangelo
Arabic literature	al-Mutanabbi
Chinese literature	Du Fu
Indian literature	Kalidasa
Japanese literature	Basho and Chikamatsu Monzaemon
Western literature	Shakespeare

What can we make of these 30 people? All are male. Among the 14 in the scientific inventories, which have worldwide coverage, all but one are from Europe (Edison is the lone exception). Two people qualified for their black bar in 2 indexes: Aristotle in biology and Western philosophy, and Newton in physics and the combined science index.[2]

Of the 30, just 3 (Confucius, Hippocrates, and Aristotle) lived prior to Christ and just 6 (Gu Kaizhi, Kalidasa, Du Fu, Sankara, al-Mutanabbi, and Zhao Mengfu) lived in the first 1,400 years after Christ. Eighteen of the remaining 21 who came after 1400 were concentrated in the three centuries from 1600–1900.

These tidbits mark issues (e.g., Why Europe? Why no women?) that we will take up in due course, but the most obvious question is,

WHY THEM?

When we have painters as great as Raphael, Leonardo, Titian, Dürer, Picasso, and a few dozen other huge figures, what is it about Michelangelo that has led historians of Western art to pay the most attention to him? Why Aristotle instead of Locke or Descartes? Why Einstein instead of Bohr or Maxwell?

Philosophy: Defining a Culture

The three philosophy inventories offer the most straightforward answer: The men at the top—Confucius, Sankara, and Aristotle—are where they are because each, in some important sense, defined what it meant to be Chinese, Indian, or Western. Confucian ethics, aesthetics, and principles of statecraft became China's de facto state religion in −3C and remained so for another two thousand years. As the man who shaped the Advaita Vedanta school of Hinduism, Sankara has pervasively shaped Indian thought down to the present day.

In the West, there is more ambiguity. Plato preceded Aristotle, Aristotelian thought owes extensively to Plato, and it was, after all, Plato rather than Aristotle of whom Alfred North Whitehead famously said that all of Western philosophy is his footnote. And yet in the end Aristotle has had the more profound effect on Western culture. Some of Plato's final conclusions, especially regarding the role of the state, are totalitarian. In contrast, Aristotle's understandings of virtue, the nature of a civilized polity, happiness, and human nature have not only survived but have become so integral a part of Western culture that to be a European or American and hold mainstream values on these issues is to be an Aristotelian.

The Arts: "How Can a Human Being Have Done That?"

The greatest figures in the arts play a less defining role. Subtract Confucius, Sankara, and Aristotle, and each of the three civilizations in which they lived would be profoundly changed. Subtract Michelangelo, Shakespeare, Beethoven, Du Fu, Kalidasa, and the other artists in our group of giants, and the effect might be hard to notice. The great art museums of the world would still be open for business, all but a handful with exactly the same inventory that they have now. The world's libraries would still be filled with great literature. The world's musicians would still have plenty of great music to play.

The world would be the poorer for not having the works of the giants in the arts, but none created a genre that wouldn't exist otherwise. They stand at the peaks for a reason that is at once more elemental and more mysterious: In their best work, the giants transcend the excellent and rise to a level of achievement that is, to the rest of us, inexplicable. The quality that sets them apart from the rest can be labeled by the reaction their masterpieces evoke among experts and laymen alike— *"How can a human being have done that?"* Here, for example, is art historian Ernst Gombrich, ordinarily a man of measured words, writing about Michelangelo's ceiling of the Sistine Chapel:

> It is very difficult for any ordinary mortal to imagine how it could be possible for one human being to achieve what Michelangelo achieved in four years of lonely work on the scaffolding of the papal chapel. The mere physical exertion of painting this huge fresco . . . is fantastic enough. . . . But the physical performance of one man covering this vast space is as nothing compared to the intellectual and artistic achievement. The wealth of ever-new inventions, the unfailing mastery of execution in every detail, and, above all, the grandeur of the visions which Michelangelo revealed to those who came after him, have given mankind a quite new idea of the power of genius.[3]

In part, Gombrich is reacting to aspects of Michelangelo's composition and technique that are to be judged by classical aesthetic standards for painting. It takes some expertise to understand why the Sistine Chapel is so great by those standards. On another level, Gombrich joins amateur observers in recognizing that something otherworldly has been accomplished. What Michelangelo did with brush and paint and a two-dimensional surface confounds our sense of what is possible with these tools. It is hard to imagine how a human being could have done it. And he was a better sculptor than painter.

In the case of Shakespeare, the world long ago exhausted its superlatives. "The more one reads and ponders the plays of Shakespeare, the more one realizes that the accurate stance toward them is one of awe," writes Harold Bloom. "The plays remain the outward limit of human achievement: aesthetically, cognitively, in certain ways morally, even spiritually. They abide beyond the end of the mind's reach; we cannot catch up to them."[4] But one does not have to ponder them for years, one does not have to be a scholar— that's one of the marvels of Shakespeare. Some readers may have memories similar to mine: Forced to read Shakespeare as a class assignment in secondary school, I was determined not to be impressed. Then, ineluctably, I could not help seeing the *stuff* in those words—the puns and allusions, the layers of meaning, the way that a few of his lines transformed a stage character into a complex human personality. Sooner or later, the question forces itself upon anyone who reads Shakespeare and pays attention: "How can a human being have written this?"

Other artists beside Michelangelo and other writers besides Shakespeare can prompt the how-is-that-possible reaction in their best work, but it is not much disputed that each occupies the pinnacle in his field. As we turn to classical music, there will be fierce argument about whether Wolfgang Amadeus Mozart or Ludwig van Beethoven is primus inter pares (and a fierce minority backing Bach). Each has a case to be made in his behalf. There is the legendary prodigy, Mozart, who started composing when he was six, could write out one score while he was thinking about another, could turn out a masterpiece in an afternoon; who left behind an *oeuvre* huge in quantity, with matchless works in every musical genre, and, most frustrating to posterity, was still getting better when he died at thirty-five. Beethoven's body of work is smaller than Mozart's, but he, more than Mozart, burst the bounds of what had been seen as possible. "There is still no department of music that does not owe him its very soul," wrote music historian Paul Lang, who speaks of Beethoven's "unique position in the world of music—even in the whole history of civilization."[5]

I will not try to adjudicate technical or aesthetic disputes about who was the greater of these two giants, but I cannot leave Beethoven without mentioning his deafness, a touchstone for thinking about the mysteries of genius. Beethoven began to experience hearing problems in 1796, while still in his twenties. The affliction progressed slowly and relaxed its hold on him occasionally, but he had lost most of his hearing by 1806 and by 1817 he was for practical purposes deaf.[6]

Beethoven was tormented by his growing inability to hear, understandably. But was it a misfortune from our selfish point of view as the beneficiaries of his genius? Certainly his deafness contributed to a single-minded focus on composing rather than performing (he was a brilliant pianist), encouraging more compositions than we would have had otherwise. It is also commonly accepted in discussions of Beethoven's music that his deafness was a source of creativity—"in some indefinable sense necessary (or at least useful) to the fulfillment of his creative quest," as biographer Maynard Solomon put it.[7] Thus the first mystery to dwell upon, the possibility that only this devastating personal loss to Beethoven the man made it possible for him to become the Beethoven of the later symphonies, the seminal late string quartets, and *Missa Solemnis*.

The second mystery is for us amateurs. Professional musicians, among whom the capacity to "hear" by looking at a score is not uncommon, see nothing strange in Beethoven's continuing to compose after he could no longer hear music. Beethoven himself told a pupil never to compose with a piano in the room, lest he be tempted to use it.[8] But knowing these things only gives us another way of apprehending the gulf that separates Beethoven from the rest of us. For amateurs, the idea of being able to hear an unfamiliar melodic line by reading a score is already impressive. Musicians who have the capacity to hear complex works in their heads—not just the melodic line, but the chords and the counterpoint and the way the timbre of the different instruments interact—are already operating on a plane that the rest of us find hard to comprehend. To be able to *compose* complex works in one's head is a quantum leap beyond that. For Beethoven to have been enclosed in a silent world for years, and then to have composed the Ninth Symphony. . . .

Most Westerners have difficulty taking works from cultures as alien as traditional China, Japan, and India, and responding to them as to works from their own culture. This difficulty is compounded in the case of literature by the barrier of translation. But critics in other cultures talk about their artistic giants in the same way we talk about ours: How can a human have done this? Sometimes the amazement can reach across cultures. Goethe read Kalidasa's play *Shakuntala* and was enraptured, later writing of it in his own poetry, "Wouldst thou the Earth and Heaven itself in one sole name combine? I name thee, O Shakuntala! And all at once is said."[9]

Awe is a response reserved for those at the very top. Reading the sources used to make up the indexes, one can find warmly worded critical praise for the works of artists deep into the lists of significant figures. But critics who wish to be taken seriously choose their words carefully, and the ordinary vocabulary of praise suffices for nearly everyone. It is only for the rarest artists that ordinary words fail.

The Sciences: System Builders Versus Brick Layers

Great achievement in the sciences differs from great achievement in the arts. The artist creates something unique. Boccaccio's *Decameron* cannot be written twice, and Velazquez's *Las Meninas* cannot be painted twice. It makes no difference how many hundreds of outstanding books and paintings come afterwards. Boccaccio and Velazquez each created a work of timeless beauty, and their eminence is secure as long as mankind values great books and paintings. The relative eminence of the great artists may also be said to be reasonably fair, after enough time has elapsed to dampen the swings of fashion. We may not yet have a firm grip on who the great artists and composers of the last fifty years will prove to be (if any), but when considering earlier periods, we have no reason to think that painters who were as great as Velazquez or writers as great as Boccaccio are still being ignored.

A scientist's eminence is more ambiguous. The scientist is engaged in an intellectual Easter egg hunt. The pretty eggs are hidden about the playing field in the form of undiscovered truths about how the physical universe works. Somebody is bound to find any given egg sooner or later, denying any scientist the joy of accomplishing something that would not have occurred otherwise. Nobody had to paint *Las Meninas*. But in a world in which the scientific method has taken hold, somebody has to discover the chemical composition of water and somebody eventually has to discover $E=mc^2$. This state of affairs creates two sorts of unfairness that pervade the assignment of scientific eminence.

The first is the harsh rule that serves as a powerful engine for scientific progress: The winner is the one who grabs the egg first, not the one who sees it first. Almost everyone has heard of Alexander Graham Bell. Almost no one has heard of Elisha Gray. Bell and Gray independently invented similar devices for transmitting speech over electric wires, but Elisha Gray submitted his application for a patent two hours later than did Alexander Graham Bell.

Examples of such unfairness stud the history of science. The case of Darwin involves one of the central scientific events of all time, the publication of the theory of evolution by natural selection. Darwin had become an evolutionist in 1837, shortly after returning from his famous voyage in the *Beagle,* and formulated the principle of natural selection by the end of 1838. But although he prepared enough written material in the form of correspondence and notebooks to establish his priority when the necessity arose, he postponed publication for 20 years. He was finally impelled to action in 1858 when he learned that an obscure naturalist of humble origins named Alfred Russel Wallace was about to publish his own version of the theory of evolution. As Darwin wrote to Lyell after seeing Wallace's paper, "I never saw a more striking coincidence; if Wallace had my manuscript sketch written out in 1842, he could not have made a better short abstract! . . . so all my originality, whatever it may amount to, will be smashed."[10] Darwin wrote to Wallace explaining the situation. In a classic display of Victorian gentlemanliness, Wallace suggested they present their papers jointly, acknowledged Darwin's priority, and never complained.

The magnitude of Darwin's achievement remains huge. Far more than simply state the principle of evolution by natural selection, he grappled with its complexities in a series of major works. Darwin's insights have survived the test of time with less revisionism than the ideas of others who created similar sensations in their own lifetimes (Freud being the obvious example). But even had Darwin been run over by a hackney cab upon stepping off the *Beagle* in 1837, we have every reason to think that the theory of evolution by natural selection would have been presented to the world circa 1858—and Alfred Russel Wallace would be one of the most famous names in the history of biology.

The second unfairness involves the frequent discrepancy between a scientific discovery's importance and the difficulty of discovering it. A great artistic work involves a considerable degree of effort. Not every artist has to paint over his head for four years as Michelangelo did under the ceiling of the Sistine Chapel, and an artist may stumble across a good idea that smacks more of luck than of genius, but every great artistic work has been accomplished by the conscious exercise of talent, will, and labor.

In contrast, the effort that goes into scientific discoveries can span the range from titanic intellectual struggles lasting for years to a lucky accident. Furthermore, the discovery by luck can be a landmark in the history of the field. Alexander Fleming owes his fame to his failure to cover the petri dishes in which he was growing staphylococcus cultures when he left work one day in 1928. Because they were left uncovered, a spore of mold was able to enter one of the dishes and begin to grow. Of all the spores that might have grown, this one was a spore of *Penicillium notatum*. Fleming deserves credit for noticing the next day that the invading mold was surrounded by a ring of dead and dying staphylococcus microbes, which led him to isolate the mold and note that it produces a substance that destroys bacteria. But Fleming's knowledge of chemistry wasn't up to the next step, isolating this mysterious substance. If we had had to depend on Fleming's work alone, we still wouldn't have the antibiotic known as penicillin.

From an objective standpoint, Fleming was engaged in research of a kind that has been a staple of chemistry and its offshoots since chemistry was invented: discover a new substance, determine its properties, and isolate it. If his work were graded purely as biochemistry practice, Fleming might get an *A* for noticing the subtly anomalous phenomenon, a *B* or *C* for determining its properties, and an *F* for isolating it. It isn't that Fleming was incompetent—he was trained as a bacteriologist, not a biochemist—but had the mold been any ordinary substance, Fleming's discovery would have been seen as an incomplete piece of work at best. It so happened that Fleming had stumbled upon the mold that would lead to one of the most important medicines in the history of medicine, and so he became Sir Alexander Fleming, Nobel Laureate.

The differences between great achievement in the arts and in the sciences lend themselves to a generalization: In the arts, eminence arises from genius manifested in a body of work. In the sciences, eminence arises from the importance of the discovery, which may or may not be the result of genius. The generalization is unfair to the scientists of genius who have wrested one solution after another from the tangled puzzles they took on. But it has enough validity to play havoc with the ratings at the top of some of the specific science inventories. For example, I could easily have produced an inventory of astronomers that put Copernicus in first place, and another that put him in thirty-eighth place. Two alternative math indexes could have put Euclid in first place or thirteenth. Two different biology indexes could have put Aristotle in first place or twenty-sixth. The difference depends on how one chooses to value two different kinds of scientific contribution that I label *brick laying* and *system building*.

The case of Copernicus and William Herschel illustrates the general problem of measuring eminence in the sciences. Copernicus is one of the most famous names in the history of science. It was Copernicus who in 1543 finally published *De Revolutionibus Orbium Coelestium* (he had formulated the hypothesis decades earlier), leading to general acceptance that the earth revolves around the sun and not the other way around. With that acceptance came consequences that transcended astronomy and marked a fundamental change in the way that Western man saw the world. The single accomplishment of Copernicus was about as big as accomplishments get. On the other hand, he produced just that one.[11]

William Herschel is not just less famous but positively obscure to anyone not an astronomer. An oboist by training, he emigrated from Germany to England in 1757 at the age of 19. After 15 years of making his living as a music teacher and conductor of a military band, he devoted himself full time to his avocation, astronomy. What did Herschel accomplish? He discovered Uranus, the first new planet to be discovered since prehistory. He discovered four satellites of Saturn and Uranus. He discovered the Martian ice cap. By determining the proper motion of 13 stars, he discovered that the sun and solar system are moving through space relative to the stars. He discovered the existence of binary stars, and eventually cataloged 711 of them. He discovered planetary nebulae, shells of gas surrounding certain stars. He prepared the first catalog of clusters and nebulae. His book *On the Construction of the Heavens* was the first quantitative analysis of the shape of the

Milky Way. Herschel was among the first to argue that the Milky Way is only a small part of the universe. He discovered that the highest temperature in the sun's spectrum is a spot beyond red that has no color at all—infrared radiation. Late in his career, he theorized that stars originate in nebulae. That is a partial list of what William Herschel, erstwhile oboist, known to few outside his field, contributed to astronomy.

With a single theory, Copernicus built a system that fundamentally altered not only astronomy but Western civilization. Herschel laid bricks—many bricks, soundly made, constituting a major part of the foundation for modern astronomy. Whom shall we place above whom in a ranking of astronomers, Herschel or Copernicus? It is an arbitrary choice. All I can do is be explicit about what choices have been made.

The sources used to build the index consist broadly of two kinds: narrative histories that tend to give more space to the system builders (I include the biographical dictionaries in this category), and chronologies of events that tend to give more space to the brick layers. Each type of source is true to its mission. Even a multi-volume history of science can legitimately sum up William Herschel's contributions in a paragraph no longer than the one I used. A shorter history could get away with a single sentence such as, "In the late 1700s, British astronomer William Herschel made a series of major astronomical discoveries," without shirking its responsibility to the reader. That same history cannot responsibly give less than several paragraphs to the ramifications of the Copernican Revolution. Any index of eminence based on historical sources will put Copernicus far above William Herschel. In contrast, a chronology of important events in astronomy can reasonably sum up Copernicus's contribution in a single item, whereas it must include several items for Herschel. An index based on chronologies of events will put Herschel far above Copernicus.

Since the two types of sources will imply different eminence, how are they to be reconciled? The solution I have used is the simplest I could think of: *The index scores for the scientific inventories combine the data from both the histories and chronologies so that the two types of data have equal weight.* I would like to tell you that this decision has a theoretical rationale, but it doesn't, at least no more than this: Each kind of accomplishment is important. Each kind of accomplishment can exaggerate a scientist's contribution in its own way. Lacking any reason to favor one over the other, I give them equal weight.

To show you how this decision played out in practice, I computed two separate indexes, one based exclusively on histories and biographical dictionaries, and the other based exclusively on chronologies of events. The figure below shows how these scores differed for the three top-ranked people on the aggregate index.

Two types of scientific evidence as measured by two types of sources

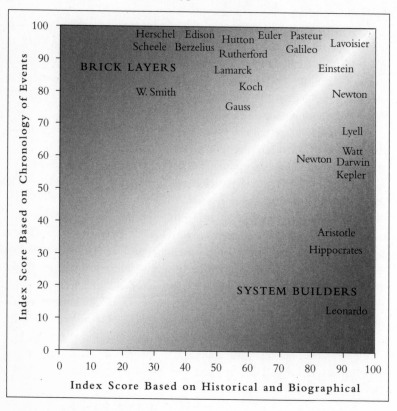

The people in the light portion of the graph represent those who got reasonably balanced scores from both types of sources. The farther out into the shaded area, the more imbalanced the score. The most conspicuous outliers in the System Builders quadrant are Leonardo da Vinci (technology), Hippocrates (medicine), and Aristotle (biology), all of whom owed their high aggregate index scores primarily to their places in the history books. Of these three, Hippocrates and Aristotle are classic system builders—each had a profound effect upon his respective discipline for the next millennium and a half, but neither contributed many bricks that survive in today's medicine and biology. Leonardo is *sui generis*. Histories of technology spend a great deal of time discussing the ways in which Leonardo anticipated technologies far ahead of anyone else. But the list of Leonardo's *successful* inventions is short, none of those few was especially important, and so he is barely mentioned in the chronologies.

The most conspicuous outliers in the Brick Layers quadrant are William Herschel (astronomy), Carl Scheele and Jöns Jacob Berzelius (chemistry), William Smith (earth sciences), and Thomas Edison (technology), all of whom owed their high aggregate index score to their impressive numbers of important discrete achievements[12] All are archetypal brick layers. None of them contributed a major theoretical framework.

So the answer to "Why Them?" with regard to the giants of science is not a simple one. In a few instances (e.g., Aristotle, Hippocrates), individuals made such immense contributions to system building that they are given precedence over people who contributed far more of enduring substance to their field. In a few other instances (e.g., Herschel, Scheele, Berzelius, Smith), men made such profuse specific contributions to the foundations that they pushed ahead of others who are more famous in the history books. But the exceptions should not obscure the rule: Typically, the giants contributed importantly both to the great theoretical issues of their eras and to laying bricks on the growing structures of their disciplines.

· · ·

As people, the giants resist classification. Some fit the caricature of the mad artist, others were colorless and plodding. Some were good family men and loyal friends, others self-absorbed egomaniacs. Some were deeply religious, others atheists; some were stoic, others whiners; some were humorless; a few could have been stand-up comics. Some were mostly lucky to have been at the right place at the right time. But far more of them operated at a level that cannot be comprehended by the rest of us—more poignantly, cannot be comprehended even by their colleagues. I began the chapter with Brahms sighing over the looming presence of Beethoven. I close it with the observation of the eminent Polish mathematician, Mark Kac, discussing the Indian mathematician Ramanujan.

An ordinary genius is a fellow that you and I would be just as good as, if we were only many times better. There is no mystery as to how his mind works.

Once we understand what he has done, we feel certain that we, too, could have done it. It is different with the magicians. They are, to use mathematical jargon, in the orthogonal complement of where we are and the working of their minds is for all intents and purposes incomprehensible. Even after we understand what they have done, the process by which they have done it is completely dark.[13]

As we consider such magicians, hero worship is not required, nor indifference to their personal failings. But it is important to acknowledge their unique stature. They show us the outer limits of what *Homo sapiens* can do.

THE EVENTS
THAT MATTER I:
SIGNIFICANT EVENTS

Through the 1950s, an iconic list of the most important human accomplishments was part of American popular culture. The message was sometimes conveyed by a piece on highbrow literature or longhair music—"highbrow" and "longhair" being adjectives that have since left the language—in magazines like *Colliers*, *Look*, or *Life*. The list was also in the air in more diffuse ways. If Bob Hope had a skit involving a work of art, he was likely to use the *Mona Lisa*. If the intellectual character in a movie was reading a book, it was likely to be *War and Peace*. One way or another, it came to be widely accepted that the *Mona Lisa* was the greatest painting, *War and Peace* the greatest novel, *Venus de Milo* the greatest sculpture, *Hamlet* the greatest play, and Beethoven's Fifth Symphony the greatest musical work. Fire, the wheel, gunpowder, and the printing press were the most important inventions. In the sciences, there were the five revolutions: Copernican, Newtonian, Darwinian, Freudian, and Einsteinian.

Icons did not fare well in the 1960s. In the arts, the concept of greatness was falling out of intellectual fashion. In science, Thomas Kuhn's *The Structure of Scientific Revolutions* (1962) told us we should substitute *paradigm* for *truth* if we wished to understand how science works. In technology, the boring old list of Most Important Inventions gave way to more inventive alternatives. In the same year that *The Structure of Scientific Revolutions* appeared, historian Lynn White's *Medieval Technology and Social Change* caught the imagination of many readers by arguing that the really important invention for understanding the course of Western history was nothing as obvious as gunpowder or the printing press, but the stirrup. Before the stirrup, a rider who tried to use a lance against an enemy would be knocked off the back of his own horse by the impact. With his feet planted in stirrups, he could brace himself. Thus the couched lance came into being and with it the military tactic known as shock warfare, which enabled a small force of mounted men to defeat a large force of foot soldiers. France's Charles Martel had recognized this, White wrote, and as a result developed not only shock cavalry but also a new class of landed vassals, the *chevaliers*, to be a reliable source of manpower. Out of this new military elite rose feudalism. "Few inventions have been so simple as the stirrup, but few have had so catalytic an influence on history," White concluded.[1]

Arguments of the same genre have been made for the pivotal importance of the invention of hay, horseshoes, the horse collar, the machine-made screw, the cultivation of legumes, the eraser, board games, distillation, reading glasses, the rudder, the interrogative sentence, aspirin, the mirror, waterworks, chairs, and stairs.[2] Some of these nominations have been tongue in cheek, but many of them followed the stirrup model, describing a single, seemingly innocuous change in technology that produced a cascade of momentous results. The invention of hay, for example, is another idea from Lynn White: Until hay was invented, horses could not be maintained throughout the winter, limiting civilization to warm climates. The invention of hay allowed civilization to develop in Northern Europe.

This approach was taken to its extreme by science writer James Burke in a series of BBC television documentaries entitled *Connections*, later converted to a book.[3] Burke liked to link one discovery to another until he ended in a place no one could have predicted. Thus a chapter that begins with Arabic astrology in 9C ends with the development of the modern production line. Another that begins with the development of the Dutch *fluytschip* in 17C ends with the invention of polyvinyl chloride. This is an entertaining way to present the history of science, but it is a variety of just-so story—post hoc, ergo propter hoc. It does not take much reflection to think of ways to link the development of the Dutch *fluytschip* with dozens of subsequent events besides polyvinyl chloride, and to think of ways that the invention of polyvinyl chloride could be linked with dozens of other antecedent events. Tracing any one path among the thousands of nodes in this network can provide an illuminating story, but it cannot easily claim to be a causal story. Even when the chain of events is short, there is a basic logical limitation: Yes, hay (or horse collars or machine-made screws) were authentically important, but they are at best only necessary, not sufficient, conditions for the consequences that followed.

Sometimes the ingenious insight is plain wrong. In the case of the stirrup, a pair of articles published in 1970 in the *English Historical Review* and

Studies in Medieval and Renaissance History called into question whether the battles White discussed had been much affected by mounted shock tactics, whether the armies had stirrups, and whether the Franks had fought on horseback at all. White's book remains a useful discussion of the importance of technology in understanding medieval institutions, but the stirrup thesis has fallen on hard times.[4]

It is easier to make a case for the old standbys. The effects of Gutenberg's printing press on European civilization were direct and momentous. So were the effects of the publication of Darwin's *On the Origin of Species*. But beyond these most obvious choices, how are we to decide which are the events in the arts and sciences that must be part of the human résumé? I classify accomplishments under two headings: *significant events*, the subject of this chapter; and *meta-inventions*, the subject of the next.

SIGNIFICANT EVENTS IN THE SCIENTIFIC INVENTORIES

The challenge of compiling inventories of important events throughout history has inspired a number of bulky chronologies. The first was Werner Stein's *Kulturfahrplan*, published in 1946. It included separate rosters of events for history and politics, literature and theatre, religion and philosophy, the visual arts, music, science and technology, and daily life. The book has sold millions of copies in its various editions, including an updated and expanded English version by Bernard Grun, *The Timetables of History* (1991).

Other chronologies that focused specifically on science and technology have produced inventories of events that are both more detailed and more precise than those in the all-purpose chronologies. Some of these are works of devoted scholarship that took years to assemble; all are based on wide coverage of histories of the various scientific disciplines and attempt to be inclusive, covering not only the most important events but second- and third-tier events as well. The inventory for *Human Accomplishment* was created by combining the events in nine such chronologies, augmented by other chronologies devoted to a specific discipline, all listed in Appendix 3.

In general, assembling data on events is similar to assembling data on people. Just as different but overlapping people were represented in the histories and biographical dictionaries (see page 109), the chronologies included different but overlapping events. For example, 3,399 events from *The Timetables of Science* (1988) were entered into the science and technology inventory.

Of these, 703 were not mentioned in any of the other sources. Of the 2,474 events entered from *Science and Technology Firsts* (1997), 642 were unique to that source, as were 361 of the 2,673 events from *The Wilson Chronology of Science and Technology* (1997) and 577 of the 2,162 events from *Breakthroughs: A Chronology of Great Achievements in Science and Mathematics* (1986).

The compilers' different choices of events once again produce a situation in which the number of items that get attention from multiple sources plunges rapidly, as shown in the figure below.

Extremely small proportions of scientific events are so important that everyone feels compelled to include them

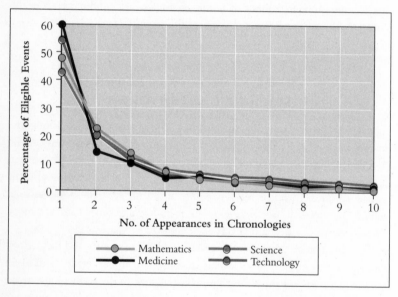

The general shape is familiar from the discussion of Lotka curves (though technically it is not a Lotka curve, for the same reasons discussed in the box on page 112). In all, the database for scientific events contained 8,759 unique events. Of these, only 1,560—about one out of five—were mentioned in at least 50 percent of the sources. These 1,560 will be called *significant events.*

The Different Uses of Significant Events
and Significant Figures

The labels and definitions for significant figures and significant events are parallel, but the inventories of people and events have different uses. For analyzing geographic patterns and trajectories of science over time, the inventory of people is statistically more useful and will play the lead role in the quantitative analyses.[5] But for getting a panoramic sense of what happened, the list of names is useless, because few of the names after the top fifty or so are ones that a non-specialist has heard of. Consider Joseph-Marie Jacquard, for example—not a name of intrinsic interest. But Jacquard's invention, the use of punch cards to enable a loom to create patterns in woven cloth, represents the first non-alphabetic means of storing information. His invention represents the same method that would be used for the first generation of electromechanical calculators and still later the first generations of programmable computers. That accomplishment is of great intrinsic interest. So are virtually all of the 8,759 events in the scientific inventories.

The Roster of Central Events

The problem is making the long list of events digestible. A narrative summary is hopeless. It would of necessity focus on the famous landmarks—Gutenberg's printing press, the Wright brothers' first flight, and the Curies' discovery of radium—whereas the virtue of the roster of significant events is that it puts famous landmarks in the context of events that preceded and followed. But if a summary doesn't work, neither does an unadorned listing of even the 1,560 significant events (let alone the 8,759 total events), which would be too long to ask readers to read. My compromise has been to select a subset of events that I have labeled *central events*. Its core is the 369 events that are mentioned all of the sources—the events that were indispensable to the story—augmented by selected events that were mentioned in all but one of the sources and that I judged essential to flesh out the chronology.[6] The subjective choices this forced were often on the margin. I am prepared to defend all of my inclusions but am less confident about my exclusion of others that were near misses.

I have altered the wording of a few events to reflect their broader sense. For example, the aspect of Lavoisier's *Traité Élémentaire de Chemie* mentioned in every source is that it contained the first statement of the law of conservation of matter. But *Traité Élémentaire de Chemie* is also, in a broader sense, the founding document of quantitative chemistry, and I make note of that. Conversely, I let some events stand in for others. For example, the best known and most thorough statement of James Hutton's uniformitarian theory of the earth's evolution is his *Theory of the Earth, With Proofs and Illustrations*, published in 1795. But the first statement of the theory came ten years earlier, in an essay entitled "Concerning the System of the Earth," and that is the work that was most commonly mentioned in the chronologies. Since the purpose of the list is to focus on the substance of the events, not their provenance, I did not bother to add the better known title to the description of the event. You may also assume that the events associated with major advances in such large topics as genetics and atomic structure have important subsidiary events that did not make the list but are included in the larger inventory.

Even this comparatively short list is long enough that many readers will reasonably prefer to pick and choose among topics. To that end, I have split the events into separate lists for astronomy, biology, chemistry, earth sciences, physics, mathematics, medicine, and technology. Some capsule observations about the events in the different scientific fields:

In astronomy, important work occurred before the Christian era, but almost exclusively in classification and enumeration. The ancient astronomers prepared accurate star catalogs and star maps, timed the solstices, discovered precession of the equinox, and, by the end of 2C, had prepared a system that accurately predicted the movements of the planets. In some respects, astronomy progressed farther and faster than biology, chemistry, the earth sciences, or physics. In another respect, understanding the inner workings of things, astronomy was the slowest of all those disciplines. It wasn't until 1918 that astronomers knew even the size of our own galaxy, not until 1923 that they knew for certain that the Milky Way was just one galaxy of many, not until 1929 that they knew the universe was expanding, not until 1948 that the Big Bang theory of the universe's history was stated, and not until the 1960s that it became accepted.

Biology, chemistry, and the earth sciences follow a broadly similar pattern. A handful of key advances occurred in the pre-Christian era, usually around –4C, followed by little in the next 1,500 years, and then an accelerating rate of change that steepened sharply in 18C. This sudden rise in the number of central events coincides in all three cases with major breakthroughs in understanding the inner workings of things.

Physics presents another profile. Biology has plants and animals, astronomy has celestial bodies, chemistry has elements and minerals and compounds, geology has landforms, all of which lend themselves to enumeration and classification even in the absence of theory. Physics, by its nature, must be more centrally theory. While the lack of valid theory did not prevent the other hard sciences from accumulating substantial bodies of information early on, physics didn't really get started until the advent of experimentation and the mathematization of physical phenomena during the Renaissance. When physics finally took off, it did so rapidly and with transforming impact. Newton's discovery of the laws of gravity and motion had a profound effect on Europe's view of the universe and man's place in it, rivaled only by Copernicus's overthrow of the geocentric solar system.

The profile of events in mathematics is distinctive on two counts. First, mathematics made major substantive progress early. The rosters for other disciplines have a few events involving landmarks in the development of theory prior to 11C, but they are usually ones that qualify primarily because they were brave and imaginative forays into the unknown, not because they were right. Mathematics has a dozen theoretical advances before 11C, and they represent a solid base of knowledge that still undergirds today's mathematics. Furthermore, this progress is not confined to classical Greece. What we call Arabic numerals, along with that crucial conceptual leap called *zero*, evolved during the first post-Christian millennium and were fully realized by the end of 8C. Indian and Arab mathematicians also made substantial progress in algebra during the last half of the first millennium, at a time when little progress was being made in the other sciences. Second, and uniquely among all the scientific inventories, a graph of the raw number of significant events in mathematics does not continue to rise into 20C. The greatest burst of mathematical progress occurred in 17C–19C, and was already tailing off by the latter part of 19C.

In some respects, medicine looks like biology, chemistry, and the earth sciences, with some progress early on, a long period in which little happened, and a steep rise in events during 18C. But while medicine made considerable progress in preventative medicine, public health, and antisepsis before 20C, it is not clear that a trip to the doctor did much good, on average, until sometime into the 1920s or 1930s. "On average" is the key phrase. For centuries, physicians had helped some people recover from some ailments and injuries, but many encounters with physicians were wholly ineffective and a large number were harmful. The tipping point at which the practice of medicine became an unambiguous net plus for the patient occurred about the same time as the great cosmological discoveries in astronomy, with antibiotics being the decisive breakthrough.

The technology inventory is unique because so much occurred before the inventories even begin. By −800, a large array of key advances in the construction of large structures, road building, irrigation, transportation, and the maintenance of large cities had already been part of the repertoire of human civilizations, in some cases for thousands of years, and therefore do not appear in the roster of central events.

This ends the preliminaries. I invite you to explore the rosters on your own, with strategies tailored to your particular interests. In reading the tables, note that the country represents the place where the work was done, not where the person came from. The date often represents only one of several that might be used (e.g., when an effort began, when the report of the work was published, etc.). The older the event, the less reliance you can place on the precise accuracy of the year. Dates for events before 1000 are usually approximate.

As an aid to scanning the lists, I have put in boldface the events that are commonly treated as special even among this small set of landmarks. These usually involve discoveries that represent not merely the uncovering of a new species or compound, but discoveries that contain an answer to a causal or structural issue central to the field. In other cases, they represent a turning point because they had such a decisive effect on subsequent work (e.g., Ptolemy's *Almagest*). These choices were subjective, and should not be treated as anything other than a visual aid for organizing an otherwise featureless plain.

CENTRAL EVENTS IN ASTRONOMY

Year	Country	Event
−500	Greece	Pythagoras of Samos discovers that the morning and the evening star are the same.
−165	China	Chinese astronomers describe sunspots.
−134	Alexandria	Hipparchus invents a system of magnitude for measuring the brightness of stars, still the basis of the modern system.
−134	Alexandria	Hipparchus prepares the first accurate, systematic star catalog and sky map.
−130	Alexandria	Hipparchus calculates the first reasonably accurate estimate of the distance to the moon.
140	**Alexandria**	**Ptolemy's *Almagest* constructs a model of a geocentric solar system that accurately predicts the movements of the planets.**
1514	**Poland**	**Nicolaus Copernicus's *Commentariolus* is the first statement of the heliocentric theory. It culminates in the publication of *De Revolutionibus Orbium Coelestium* in 1543.**
1572	**Denmark**	**Tycho Brahe records the first European observation of a supernova, discrediting the Aristotelian system of a fixed sphere of stars.**
1604	Germany	Johannes Kepler observes a second nova, confirming Brahe's discovery.
1608	**Netherlands**	**Hans Lippershey and Zacharias Jansen independently invent a crude telescope.**
1609	Germany	Johannes Kepler's *Astronomia Nova* contains the first statement of Kepler's first two laws of planetary motion.
1609	**Italy**	**Galileo conducts the first telescopic observations of the night sky, transforming the nature of astronomical investigation.**
1609	Italy	Galileo constructs the first working telescope, 9× magnification initially, improved to 30× by the end of the year.
1610	**Italy**	**Galileo discovers four moons of Jupiter and infers that the earth is not the center of all motion.** (Simon Marius makes a disputed claim to the same discovery.)
1611	Italy Germany	Galileo, Christoph Scheiner, and Girolamo Fabrici independently demonstrate that sunspots are part of the sun and revolve with it.
1612	Germany	Simon Marius publishes the first systematic description of the Andromeda Nebula.
1631	France	Pierre Gassendi describes the transit of Mercury.

Year	Country	Event
1655	Netherlands	Christiaan Huygens discovers the rings of Saturn. He also discovers the first moon of Saturn, Titan, another in a series of discoveries of planetary satellites, asteroids, and other celestial bodies that continues to the present. Several of these discoveries are cited in all of the sources and are included separately in the full inventory, but only a few of special significance are included in this roster.
1668	England	Isaac Newton invents the first working reflecting telescope.
1705	England	Edmond Halley's *A Synopsis of the Astronomy of Comets* includes calculation of the orbits of comets and the first prediction of a comet's return.
1718	England	Edmond Halley discovers stellar motion (proper movement of stars).
1755	Germany	Immanuel Kant's *Allgemeine Naturgeschichte und Theorie Des Himmels* hypothesizes that the solar system is part of a huge, lens-shaped collection of stars, that other such "island universes" exist, and proposes a theory of the evolution of the universe in which particles conglomerated to form heavenly bodies.
1761	Russia	Mikhail Lomonosov infers the existence of a Venusian atmosphere.
1781	England	William Herschel discovers Uranus.
1782	England	John Goodricke is the first to observe an eclipsing variable star.
1785	England	William Herschel's *On the Construction of the Heavens* is the first quantitative analysis of the Milky Way's shape.
1794	Germany	Ernst Chladni and Heinrich Olbers defend the extraterrestrial origin of meteorites and offer a scientific explanation of them.
1802	Germany	Heinrich Olbers argues that asteroids are fragments of an exploded planet.
1803	France	Jean-Baptiste Biot discovers empirical verification of meteorites as extraterrestial objects.
1814	**Germany**	**Joseph von Fraunhofer discovers that spectral lines observed in light reflected from the planets are shared, while light from stars contains differing lines, leading to the development of astronomical spectroscopy.**
1838	Scotland Germany	Thomas Henderson and Friedrich Bessel are the first to measure a star's heliocentric parallax, permitting an estimate of stellar distance.
1843	Germany	Samuel Schwabe discovers the sunspot cycle, founding the modern study of solar physics.
1844	Germany	Friedrich Bessel infers an unseen "dark companion" star of Sirius, the first known binary star.

Year	Country	Event
1845	Ireland	William Parsons discovers spiral nebulae.
1846	England France Germany	John Couch and Urbain le Verrier predict the existence and orbit of Neptune, which is then observed by Johann Galle.
1859	Germany	Gustav Kirchhoff and Robert Bunsen conduct the first analysis of the chemical composition of the stars, the first step in understanding the evolution of the stars.
1905	Denmark	Ejnar Hertzsprung defines a scale for color and stellar luminosity, used to establish stellar magnitudes.
1908	USA	George Hale discovers that sunspots exhibit the Zeeman effect, implying that they are subject to an electromagnetic field.
1912	USA	Henrietta Leavitt devises a method for determining the luminosity of a Cepheid variable from its period, thereby enabling a determination of its distance and measurement of other extragalactic distances.
1914	USA	Henry Russell's "Relations Between the Spectra and Other Characteristics of the Stars" develops a theory of stellar evolution.
1918	**USA**	**Harlow Shapley determines the center of the galaxy, providing a correct picture of our own galaxy plus the first accurate estimate of its size.**
1920	USA	Albert Michelson calculates the first measurement of stellar diameter, for the star Betelgeuse.
1924	**USA**	**Edwin Hubble determines that Andromeda is a galaxy, revolutionizing the understanding of the universe's size and structure.**
1927	Belgium	Georges Lemaître introduces the idea of the cosmic egg, the forerunner of the Big Bang theory.
1929	**USA**	**Edwin Hubble discovers Hubble's Law, introducing the concept of an expanding universe.**
1930	France	Bernard Lyot invents the coronagraph, permitting extended observations of the sun's coronal atmosphere.
1930	Germany	Bernhard Schmidt invents the Schmidt camera and telescope, permitting wide-angle views with little distortion.
1930	USA	Clyde Tombaugh discovers Pluto based on analysis of the perturbations in the orbits of the outer planets caused by an unknown body.
1932	**USA**	**Karl Jansky detects radio waves from space, founding radio astronomy.**
1934	Switzerland USA	Fred Zwicky and Walter Baade predict the existence of neutron stars.

Year	Country	Event
1934	Switzerland USA	Fritz Zwicky and Walter Baade discover the difference between novae and supernovae.
1937	USA	Grote Reber invents the radio telescope.
1938	Germany USA	Hans Bethe and Carl Weizsacker present a detailed case for nuclear fusion as the source of a star's energy.
1942	USA	Grote Reber prepares the first radio map of the universe, locating individual radio sources.
1944	Germany	Carl Weizsacker formulates the planetesimal hypothesis to explain the origin of the solar system.
1948	USA	George Gamow and Ralph Asher develop the Big Bang theory, employing Hans Bethe's results from thermonuclear reactions.
1949	USA	Fred Whipple discovers the "dirty snowball" composition of comets.

CENTRAL EVENTS IN BIOLOGY

Year	Country	Event
−500	Greece	Alcmaeon conducts dissections on animals, and perhaps on a human cadaver, for scientific purposes.
−350	**Greece**	**Aristotle creates a classification system for animals and plants, founding biological taxonomy.**
−320	Greece	Theophrastus's *Enquiry into Plants and Causes of Plants* founds botany.
−310	Greece	Praxagoras discovers the difference between veins and arteries.
−280	Alexandria	Herophilus's improvements in dissection and vivisection produce more detailed knowledge of the functions of internal organs, nerves, and the brain, founding scientific anatomy.
77	Italy	The 37 volumes of Pliny the Elder's *Historia Naturalis* summarizes the natural world as seen by the ancients.
180	**Greece**	**Galen dissects animals, demonstrating a variety of physiological processes and founding experimental physiology.**
1543	**Italy**	**Andreas Vesalius writes *De Humani Corporis Fabrica*, a more scientifically exact anatomy text based on dissection that supplants Galen.**
1553	Italy	Early attempts to describe blood circulation culminate in Realdo Colombo's discovery that blood passes from the lung into the pulmonary vein.
1555	France	Pierre Belon identifies similarities in skeletons across animals (homologies), specifically birds and humans.
1583	Italy	Andrea Cesalpino's *De Plantis*, the first scientific textbook on theoretical botany, introduces a major early system of plant classification.
1628	**England**	**William Harvey's *Exercitatio Anatomica de Motu Cordis et Sanguinis in Animalibus* describes the heart as a pump and accurately describes the nature of blood circulation.**
1653	Sweden	Olof Rudbeck discovers the lymphatic system, demonstrating its existence in a dog.
1658	Netherlands	Jan Swammerdam discovers red corpuscles.
1660	Italy	Marcello Malpighi discovers capillaries linking the arterial and venous circulation in the lungs.
1665	England	Robert Hooke's *Micrographia* includes the first description of cells and coins the term *cell*.
1669	England	Richard Lower describes the structure of the heart and its muscular properties, along with the observation that blood changes color in the lungs.

Year	Country	Event
1676	**Netherlands**	**Antoni van Leeuwenhoek discovers microorganisms.**
1677	Netherlands	Antoni van Leeuwenhoek confirms the existence of sperm and speculates that they are the source of reproduction.
1682	England	Nehemiah Grew's *Anatomy of Plants* includes the discovery and description of plant sexuality.
1683	Netherlands	Antoni van Leeuwenhoek discovers bacteria.
1686	England	John Ray's *Historia Plantarum* presents the first modern plant classification and introduces the idea of species as a unit of taxonomy.
1727	England	Stephen Hales's *Vegetable Statics* describes the nature of sap flow and plant nourishment.
1733	England	Stephen Hales's *Haemastaticks* describes the first quantitative estimate of blood pressure and fundamental characteristics of blood circulation.
1735	**Sweden**	**Carolus Linnaeus's *Systema Naturae* uses systematic principles for defining the genera and species of organisms. A later edition (1749) develops binomial nomenclature for classifying plants and animals.**
1779	Netherlands	Jan Ingenhousz describes photosynthesis.
1800	Germany France	Karl Burdach, Jean-Baptiste de Lamarck, and Gottfried Treviranus introduce the term *biology*.
1801	France	Jean-Baptiste de Lamarck's *Système des Animaux sans Vertèbres* founds modern invertebrate zoology.
1809	France	Jean-Baptiste de Lamarck's *Philosophie Zoologique* includes a clear statement of organic evolution but wrongly theorizes that acquired traits can be inherited.
1818	France	Marie Bichat's *Traité des Membranes en General* founds histology.
1827	Germany	Karl von Baer discovers the mammalian ovum.
1828	Germany	Karl von Baer's *Über die Entwickelungsgeschichte der Thiere* founds modern comparative embryology.
1831	Scotland	Robert Brown discovers that the cell nucleus is a general feature of all plant cells.
1837	France	René Dutrochet demonstrates that photosynthesis requires chlorophyll.
1838	**Germany**	**Theodor Schwann's *Mikroskopische Untersuchungen* and Hubert Schleiden's *Beitroge zur Phytogenesis* argue that cells are the fundamental organic units and develop in the same basic way, founding modern cell theory.**
1858	Germany	Rudolph Virchow's *Die Cellularpathologie* founds cellular pathology.

Year	Country	Event
1859	**England**	**Charles Darwin's *On the Origin of Species* introduces the theory of evolution through the mechanism of natural selection, independently developed by Alfred Wallace.**
1861	France	Pierre-Paul Broca introduces the theory of localization of the brain's speech center, with differing hemispheres containing the center for right- and left-handed individuals.
1865	Germany	Julius von Sachs discovers that chlorophyll is the key compound that turns carbon dioxide and water into starch while releasing water.
1866	**Austria**	**Johann Mendel's "Experiments in Plant Hybridization," founds the study of genetics, though the paper goes unnoticed for decades.**
1869	England	Francis Galton's *Hereditary Genius* applies Darwin's theory of evolution to man's mental inheritance, arguing that individual talents are genetically transmitted.
1882	Germany	Walther Flemming delineates the sequence of nuclear division, mitosis.
1883	England	Francis Galton introduces eugenics as a theory and a term.
1884	Germany	Hans Gram introduces bacterial staining, later an important tool in developing anti-bacterial agents.
1889	Spain Italy	Camillo Golgi and Santiago Ramon y Cajal describe the cellular structure of the brain and spinal cord, validating neuron theory.
1892	Netherlands Russia	Martinus Beijerinck and Dmitri Ivanovsky discover that a filtrable virus is the causative agent of tobacco mosaic infection, the first identification of a virus.
1900	Austria	Karl Landsteiner discovers blood types.
1900	Germany Austria Netherlands	Karl Correns, Erich Tschermak, and Hugo de Vries independently rediscover patterns of heredity found by Mendel and apply them to Darwin's theory of evolution.
1901	Netherlands	Hugo de Vries's *Mutation Theory* applies mutations to evolution (and acknowledges Mendel's priority).
1902	England	William Bayliss and Ernest Starling discover secretin, the first hormone, and its role as a chemical messenger.
1907	USA	Ross Harrison achieves the first tissue culture, demonstrating the development of nerve fibers from neural tissue.
1909	Denmark	Wilhelm Johannsen introduces the word *gene* for the unit of inheritance and distinguishes between genotype and phenotype, backed with experimental evidence.
1910	USA	Thomas Morgan discovers sex-linked characteristics.

Year	Country	Event
1911	USA	Thomas Morgan and Alfred Sturtevant prepare the first chromosome map, showing five sex-linked genes in the fruit fly.
1915	England France	Felix d'Hérelle and Frederick Twort independently discover bacteriophages.
1915	USA	Thomas Morgan, Alfred Sturtevant, Hermann Muller, and Calvin Bridges propose that chromosomes contain genes that determine heredity.
1926	USA	Thomas Morgan discovers that mutant characteristics in fruit flies are connected to paired Mendelian genes, which are joined to chromosomes.
1927	USA	Hermann Muller discovers that X-rays produce mutations.
1929	Germany	Johannes Berger invents electroencephalography, measuring brain waves in humans and opening up the study of neurophysiology.
1935	USA	Wendell Stanley crystallizes the tobacco mosaic virus, demonstrating that crystallization is not a dividing line between life and non-life.
1937	England	Hans Krebs discovers the Krebs Cycle of citric acids and its role in metabolism.
1944	England	Dorothy Hodgkin, Barbara Low, and C. W. Bunn discover the structure of penicillin.
1944	USA	Oswald Avery, Colin MacLeod, and Maclyn McCarty discover that DNA is the genetic material in cells.
1948	USA	John Enders, Frederick Robbins, and Thomas Weller develop a method to culture viruses.

CENTRAL EVENTS IN CHEMISTRY

Year	Country	Event
–440	Greece	Democritus and Leucippus hypothesize that matter is composed of atoms.
750	Arab World	Jabir ibn Hayyan prepares acetic acid, the first pure acid.
900	Arab World	First production of concentrated alcohol, by distilling wine.
1300	Germany	False Geber describes the preparation of sulphuric acid.
1597	Germany	Libavius's *Alchemia* is the first chemistry textbook, with detailed descriptions of many chemical methods.
1624	Belgium	Jan van Helmont recognizes that more than one air-like substance exists and coins the term *gas* to describe any compressible fluid.
1661	**England**	**Robert Boyle's *Skeptical Chymist* separates chemistry from medicine and alchemy; defines elements and chemical analysis.**
1662	**England**	**Robert Boyle states Boyle's Law, that the volume occupied by a fixed mass of gas in a container is inversely proportional to the pressure it exerts.**
1674	Germany	Hennig Brand discovers phosphorus, a.n. 15, the first element known to have been discovered by a specific person, and the first element not known in any earlier form.
1735	Sweden	Georg Brandt discovers cobalt, a.n. 27, the first discovery of a metal not known to the ancients.
1751	Sweden	Axel Cronstedt discovers nickel, a.n. 28, the first metal since iron found to be subject to magnetic attraction.
1755	**Scotland**	**Joseph Black identifies "fixed air" (carbon dioxide), the first application of quantitative analysis to chemical reactions.**
1766	England	Henry Cavendish discovers "inflammable air" (hydrogen, a.n. 1).
1772	France	Antoine Lavoisier discovers that air is absorbed during combustion.
1772	France	Antoine Lavoisier discovers that diamond consists of carbon.
1772	Scotland England Sweden	Daniel Rutherford, Carl Scheele, Joseph Priestley, and Henry Cavendish independently discover "mephitic air" (nitrogen, a.n. 7).
1773	England Sweden	Joseph Priestley and Carl Scheele independently discover "respirable air" (oxygen, a.n. 8).
1774–1925		The discovery of the rest of naturally occurring elements becomes a central quest of chemists for the next century and a half. Most of these discoveries qualify as central events and are included separately in the full inventory, but only the elements of special significance are included here.

Year	Country	Event
1775	**France**	**Antoine Lavoisier accurately describes combustion, discrediting phlogiston theory.**
1779	France	Antoine Lavoisier discovers that the gas identified by Joseph Priestley and Carl Scheele is responsible for combustion. He names it oxygen.
1784	England	Henry Cavendish discovers the chemical composition of water.
1785	France	Claude Berthollet determines the composition of ammonia.
1789	**France**	**Antoine Lavoisier's *Traité Élémentaire de Chemie*, a founding document in quantitative chemistry, states the law of conservation of matter.**
1797	France	Joseph Proust proposes his law of definite proportions, followed by experimental evidence obtained in 1799.
1800	England	William Nicholson and Anthony Carlisle discover that an electric current can bring about a chemical reaction (electrolysis), founding electro-chemistry.
1801	France	Rene Haüy's four-volume *Traité de Minéralogie* founds crystallography.
1803	England	John Dalton publishes the modern statement of atomic theory and introduces the concept of atomic weight.
1803	France	Claude Berthollet's *Essai de Statique Chemique* lays the foundation for understanding chemical reactions and is a step toward the law of mass action.
1805	Germany France	Friedrich Sertürner isolates morphine from laudanum, initiating the study of alkaloids.
1806	France	Louis Vauquelin isolates asparagine, first of the amino acids.
1811	Italy	Amadeo Avogadro hypothesizes that all gases at the same volume, pressure, and temperature are made up of the same number of particles.
1813	Sweden	Jöns Berzelius develops the foundation of universal chemical notation.
1814	**Germany**	**Joseph von Fraunhofer discovers that the relative positions of spectral lines is constant, forming the basis for modern spectroscopy.**
1815	France	Joseph Gay-Lussac identifies the first organic radical (cyanogen, the cyano group).
1817	France	Joseph Caventou and Pierre Pelletier isolate chlorophyll.
1820	Germany	Joseph von Fraunhofer invents the diffraction grating for studying spectra.

Year	Country	Event
1823	England	Michael Faraday produces the first laboratory temperatures below 0° F., enabling liquefaction of gases, a founding event in cryogenics.
1825	England	Michael Faraday discovers and isolates benzene.
1828	**Germany**	**Friedrich Wöhler prepares the organic compound urea from inorganic compounds, the first synthesis of an organic substance, founding organic chemistry.**
1831	Scotland	Thomas Graham discovers Graham's Law, that the ratio of the speeds at which two different gases diffuse is inverse to the ratio of the square roots of the gas densities, a founding event in physical chemistry.
1836	Germany	Theodore Schwann isolates pepsin, the first animal enzyme.
1836	Sweden	Jöns Berzelius discovers a common force among catalytic reactions and introduces the terms *catalysis* and *catalytic force*.
1840	Germany	Christian Schönbein discovers ozone.
1846	France	Louis Pasteur discovers crystal asymmetry.
1852	England	Edward Frankland describes the phenomenon that later became known as valence.
1858	**Germany**	**Friedrich Kekulé establishes two major facts of organic chemistry: carbon has a valence of four and carbon atoms can chemically combine with one another.**
1858	Scotland Germany	Archibald Couper and Friedrich Kekulé develop a system for showing organic molecular structure graphically.
1859	Germany	Gustav Kirchhoff and Robert Bunsen discover that each element is associated with characteristic spectral lines.
1859	Scotland Austria	James Maxwell develops the first extensive mathematical kinetic theory of gases, later augmented in collaboration with Ludwig Boltzmann.
1860	Italy	Stanislao Cannizzaro introduces a reliable method of calculating atomic weights, leading to acceptance of Avogadro's Hypothesis and opening the way to classification of the elements.
1863	England	John Newland's Law of Octaves stimulates work on the table of elements.
1863	Norway	Cato Guldberg and Peter Waage discover the law of mass action, regarding the relationship of speed, heat, and concentration in chemical reactions.
1865	Germany	Friedrich Kekulé discovers the structure of the benzene ring, enabling the solution many problems of molecular structure.

Year	Country	Event
1868	England France	Pierre Janssen and Joseph Lockyer discover helium, a.n. 2, based on spectral analysis rather than a physical specimen.
1869	Ireland	Thomas Andrews identifies the critical temperature for liquifying gases.
1869	**Russia**	**Dimitri Mendeleyev publishes a periodic table of the elements, including the prediction of undiscovered elements.**
1873	Netherlands	Johannes van der Waals provides a molecular explanation for the critical temperature above which gas can exist only as a gas.
1874	Netherlands France	Jacobus Van't Hoff and Joseph Le Bel independently discover that the four bonding directions of the carbon atom point to the four vertices of a regular tetrahedron, founding stereochemistry.
1877	France Switzerland	Louis Cailletet and Raoul Pictet independently liquefy oxygen, nitrogen, and carbon dioxide, the first liquefaction of gases.
1879	USA Germany	Ira Remsen and Constantin Fahlberg synthesize saccharin.
1884	Germany	Emil Fischer discovers purines, which turn out to be an important part of nucleic acids, which in turn prove to be the key molecules of living tissues.
1884	Sweden	Svante Arrhenius introduces the theory of ionic dissociation.
1885	Switzerland	Johann Balmer develops a formula for the wavelengths at which hydrogen atoms radiate light.
1886	France	Ferdinand Moissan isolates fluorine, a.n. 9, after 75 years of effort by others.
1895	Scotland Sweden	William Ramsay and Per Teodor Cleve independently discover helium on earth.
1898	Scotland	James Dewar invents a method of producing liquid hydrogen in quantity.
1901	USA	Jokichi Takamine and John Abel independently isolate adrenaline, the first pure hormone.
1904	England	Frederic Kipping discovers silicones.
1905	Germany	Richard Willstätter discovers the structure of chlorophyll.
1906	Russia	Mikhail Tsvet invents chromatography for studying dyes, eventually applied to complex chemical mixtures generally.
1926	USA	James Sumner prepares the first crystallized enzyme, urease.
1927	England USA	Clinton Davisson and George Thomson independently create large nickel crystals that exhibit X-ray diffraction, confirming Louis de Broglie's theory of matter waves.

Year	Country	Event
1931	USA	Harold Urey discovers deuterium, heavy hydrogen.
1933	England Switzerland	Walter Haworth and Tadeus Reichstein synthesize vitamin C.
1934	France	Irène and Frédéric Joliot-Curie develop the first artificial isotope, a radioactive form of phosphorus.
1937	USA France	Emilio Segrè and Carlo Perrier prepare technetium, a.n. 43, the first artificial element.
1938	Switzerland	Albert Hofmann and Arthur Stoll synthesize LSD, later (1943) recognized as a hallucinogen.
1944	England	Archer Martin and Richard Synge invent paper chromatography, a faster form of chromatography that requires only a few drops of the substance being analyzed.
1949	England	Derek Barton describes the conformation of a steroidal molecule having several six-membered carbon rings, changing the way organic chemists view molecules.

CENTRAL EVENTS IN THE EARTH SCIENCES

Year	Country	Event
−520	Greece	Pythagoras of Samos argues that the earth is spherical.
−300	Greece	Pytheas of Massilia describes the ocean tides and their relationship to the moon.
−240	Alexandria	Eratosthenes calculates values for the circumference and diameter of the earth accurate to within about 15 percent of the true values.
1546	**Germany**	**Agricola's *De Natura Fossilium* classifies minerals, founding mineralogy. The term fossil is introduced for anything dug from the ground.**
1544	Germany England	Georg Hartman discovers magnetic "dip," or inclination, rediscovered in 1576 by Robert Norman.
1568	Belgium	Mercator invents the Mercator projection for maps.
1668	England	Robert Hooke proposes that fossils can be used as a source of information about the earth's history.
1669	Denmark	Nicolaus Steno diagrams six levels of stratification, arguing that shifts in earth's strata caused the formation of mountains.
1669	Denmark	Nicolaus Steno identifies fossils as ancient creatures.
1671	France	Jean Picard's *Mesure de la Terre* gives an estimate of the size of the earth accurate to within about 90 feet.
1680	England	Robert Boyle develops the silver nitrate test for sea water, founding chemical oceanography.
1725	Italy	Luigi Marsigli's *Histoire Physique de la Mer* is the first treatise on oceanography, discussing topography, circulation, ocean plants and animals, along with many measurements.
1746	**France**	**Jean-Étienne Guettard prepares the first true geological maps, showing rocks and minerals arranged in bands.**
1752	France	Jean-Étienne Guettard identifies heat as the causative factor of change in the earth's landforms.
1756	Germany	Johann Lehmann's *Versuch einer Geschichte von Flötz-Gebürgen* describes earth's crust as a structured sequence of strata.
1760	England	John Michell writes "Essay on the Causes and Phenomena of Earthquakes," beginning the systematic study of seismology.
1770	USA	Benjamin Franklin prepares the first scientific chart of the Gulf Stream.
1779	Switzerland	Horace Saussure writes *Voyage dans les Alpes*, describing his geological, meteorological, and botanical studies, and coining the term *geology*.

Year	Country	Event
1785	**Scotland**	**James Hutton's "Concerning the System of the Earth" is the first statement of the uniformitarian view of earth's development.**
1798	England	James Hall demonstrates that lavas can be fused into glass, explaining otherwise puzzling geologic formations and founding experimental geology.
1799	England	William Smith discovers ways in which fossils can be used to identify correspondences between strata in different regions.
1811	**France**	**Georges Cuvier's and Alexandre Brongniart's maps of formations in the Paris region establish the basic principles of paleontological stratigraphy.**
1812	France	Georges Cuvier's *Recherches sur les Ossemens Fossiles* systematically analyzes and classifies extinct forms of life, founding vertebrate paleontology.
1812	France	Georges Cuvier's *Recherches sur les Ossemens Fossiles* introduces catastrophism as an explanation for extinctions.
1815	**England**	**William Smith prepares the first geologic map showing relationships on a large scale, including England, Wales, and part of Scotland.**
1830	**England**	**Charles Lyell's *Principles of Geology* argues that geological formations are created over millions of years, creating a new time frame for other disciplines as well and founding modern geology.**
1835	France	Gaspard de Coriolis discovers the Coriolis effect, the deflection of a moving body caused by the earth's rotation.
1837	**USA**	**Louis Agassiz's "Discourse at Neuchâtel" is the first presentation of the Ice Age theory.**
1838	Scotland	Roderick Murchison describes the Silurian System, establishing the sequence of early Paleozoic rocks.
1842	England	Richard Owen coins the word *dinosaur* and describes two new genera.
1847	USA	Matthew Maury publishes the first extensive oceanographic and weather charts.
1855	USA	Matthew Maury writes *Physical Geography of the Sea*, the first textbook of oceanography.
1866	France	Gabriel Daubrée presents his theory that the earth has a nickel-iron core.
1880	England	John Milne invents the first precise seismograph, founding modern seismology.

Year	Country	Event
1883	USA	Edward Cope's *The Vertebrata of the Tertiary Formations of the West* reports the discovery of the first complete remains of dinosaurs of the Cretaceous.
1902	England USA	Oliver Heaviside and Arthur Kennelly independently predict the existence of a layer in the atmosphere that permits long-distance radio transmission, confirmed in 1924 by Edward Appleton.
1902	France	Léon Teisserenc de Bort describes the atmosphere as divided into the troposphere and stratosphere.
1909	Croatia	Andrija Mohorovicic discovers the Mohorovicic discontinuity in the earth's crust that separates the outermost crust from a more rigid layer.
1913	France	Charles Fabry discovers ozone in the upper atmosphere and demonstrates that it filters out solar ultraviolet radiation.
1914	USA	Beno Gutenberg discovers the Gutenberg Discontinuity in the earth's structure, separating a liquid core from a solid mantle.
1915	**Germany**	**Alfred Wegener's *Die Entstehung der Kontinente und Ozeane* presents evidence for a primordial continent, Pangaea, and subsequent continental drift.**
1920	Norway	Jakob and Vilhelm Bjerknes describe air masses and fronts, and their use in weather prediction.
1924	England	Edward Appleton discovers the ionosphere.
1924	South Africa	Raymond Dart discovers Australopithecus and categorizes it as a hominid, neither human nor ape.
1930	USA	Charles Beebe's first bathysphere reaches a depth of 417 meters, allowing the first direct access to the ocean depths.
1931	Switzerland	Auguste Piccard and Paul Kipfer use a high altitude balloon to reach the stratosphere.
1935	USA	Charles Richter invents the Richter scale for measuring the magnitude of earthquakes.

CENTRAL EVENTS IN PHYSICS

Year	Country	Event
−260	Greece	Archimedes discovers the principle of the lever.
−260	**Greece**	**Archimedes discovers the principle of buoyancy, leading to the concept of specific gravity.**
1025	Arabia	Alhazen's *Opticae Thesaurus* discusses the properties of lenses, the nature of refraction and reflection, and correctly states that the object seen is the source of light rays.
1269	France	Peter Peregrinus's *Epistola de Magnete* identifies magnetic poles, also representing an early, unsophisticated use of the experimental method.
1583	Italy	Galileo discovers that a pendulum's period of oscillation is independent of its amplitude.
1583	Netherlands	Simon Stevin introduces the theory of static equilibrium, founding hydrostatics.
1586	Netherlands	Simon Stevin presents evidence that falling bodies fall at the same rate.
1589	**Italy**	**Galileo's tests of falling bodies represent a landmark use of experimental data.**
1592	Italy	Galileo invents the thermometer (precisely, barothermometer).
1600	**England**	**William Gilbert's *De Magnete, Magnetisque Corporibus, et de Magno Magnete Tellure* describes the magnetic properties of the earth and founds the scientific study of electricity.**
1604	**Italy**	**Galileo discovers that a free-falling body increases its distance as the square of the time, a pioneering mathematization of a physical phenomenon.**
1609	Netherlands	Zacharias Jansen and Hans Lippershey invent the compound microscope.
1621	Netherlands	Willebrord Snell discovers Snell's Law for computing the refraction of light, later discovered independently by Descartes.
1638	**Italy**	**Galileo's *Discoursi e Dimostrazioni Matematiche, Intorno à Due Nuove Scienze* founds modern mechanics.**
1643	Italy	Evangelista Torricelli invents the barometer in the process of discovering air pressure.
1643	Italy	Evangelista Torricelli creates the first (near) vacuum known to science.
1645	Germany	Otto von Guericke discovers that, in a vacuum, sound does not travel, fire is extinguished, and animals stop breathing.
1648	France	Blaise Pascal states Pascal's principle, that pressure on an enclosed fluid is transmitted without reduction throughout the fluid, founding hydraulics.

Year	Country	Event
1650	Germany	Otto Von Guericke demonstrates the force of air pressure, using teams of horses to try to pull apart metal hemispheres held together by a partial vacuum.
1665	England	Robert Hooke's *Micrographia* introduces the first major challenge to the concept of light as a stream of particles, arguing instead that light is a vibration.
1665	Italy	Francesco Grimaldi gives the first major account of light diffraction and interference.
1669	Denmark	Erasmus Bartholin describes double refraction, the apparent doubling of images when seen through a crystal.
1670	Netherlands	Christiaan Huygens develops a wave theory of light, published in 1690.
1672	England	Isaac Newton describes the light spectrum, and discovers that white light is made from a mixture of colors.
1675	France	Ole Rømer deduces that light has a speed and calculates an approximation of it (put at 141,000 miles per second).
1687	**England**	**Isaac Newton's *Philosophiae Naturalis Principia Mathematica* states the law of universal gravitation.**
1687	**England**	**Isaac Newton's *Principia* states the laws of motion.**
1687	England	Isaac Newton's *Principia* predicts that the shape of the earth is nonspherical, based on the finding that gravity at Cayenne is less than that at Paris.
1701	France	Joseph Sauveur describes the production of tones by the vibration of strings and coins the word *acoustic*.
1704	England	Isaac Newton's *Opticks: A Treatise of the Reflections, Refractions, Inflections, and Colours of Light* discusses optical phenomena, including the suggestion that light is particulate in nature.
1714	Netherlands	Daniel Fahrenheit invents the Fahrenheit scale.
1714	Netherlands	Daniel Fahrenheit invents the mercury thermometer, the first accurate thermometer.
1728	England	James Bradley discovers the aberration of starlight, leading to a better measure of the speed of light and providing evidence for a heliocentric solar system.
1733	France	Charles DuFay discovers that there are two types of static electric charges and that like charges repel each other while unlike charges attract, linking electricity to magnetism.
1738	**Switzerland**	**Daniel Bernoulli's *Hydrodynamica* states Bernoulli's Principle and founds the mathematical study of fluid flow and the kinetic theory of gases.**
1742	Sweden	Anders Celsius invents the Celsius scale.

Year	Country	Event
1745	Germany Netherlands	Ewald von Kleist and Pieter van Musschenbroek independently invent a practical device for storing an electric charge, the Leyden jar.
1748	France	Jean Nollet discovers osmosis, the passage of a solution through a semi-permeable membrane separating two solutions with different concentrations.
1752	USA	Benjamin Franklin discovers that lightning is a form of electricity.
1762	Scotland	Joseph Black develops the concept of latent heat, the quantity of heat absorbed or released when a substance changes its physical phase at constant temperature.
1787	France	Jacques Charles demonstrates that different gases expand by the same amount for a given rise in temperature, known both as Charles's law and Gay-Lussac's law (Joseph Gay-Lussac is the first to publish, in 1802. The relationship was first stated a century earlier by Guillaume Amontons, then forgotten).
1798	England	Henry Cavendish and Nevil Maskelyne measure the gravitational constant, leading to an accurate estimate of the mass of the earth.
1798	Germany	Benjamin Thompson (Count Rumford) demonstrates that heat is a form of motion (energy) rather than a substance.
1800	England	William Herschel discovers infrared radiation, and that invisible light beyond the red produces the most heat.
1801	England	Thomas Young uses diffraction and interference patterns to demonstrate that light has wavelike characteristics.
1801	Germany	Johann Ritter discovers ultraviolet light.
1808	France	Étienne Malus discovers the polarization of light.
1815	France	Jean Biot discovers that the plane of polarized light is twisted in different directions by different organic liquids.
1818	France	Augustin Fresnel's *Mémoire sur la Diffraction de la Lumière* demonstrates the ability of a transverse wave theory of light to account for a variety of optical phenomena, converting many scientists to a wave theory.
1820	Denmark	Hans Ørsted invents the ammeter.
1820	**Denmark**	**Hans Ørsted demonstrates that electricity and magnetism are related, jointly (with Ampère) founding the science of electrodynamics.**
1820	Germany	Johann Schweigger invents the needle galvanometer, later essential for the telegraph.
1821	**England**	**Michael Faraday's "On Some New Electromagnetic Motions" reports his discovery that electrical forces can produce motion and describes the principle of the electric motor.**

Year	Country	Event
1822	France	Jean Fourier's *Théorie Analytique de la Chaleur* applies Fourier's theorem to the study of heat flow, an influential application of mathematics to physical phenomena.
1822	Germany	Thomas Seebeck discovers that two different metals will generate electricity if their points of juncture are maintained at different temperatures, the Seebeck effect, and demonstrates thermoelectricity.
1823	England	William Sturgeon invents the electromagnet.
1824	France	Nicolas Carnot's *Réflexions sur la Puissance Motrice du Feu* is the first scientific analysis of steam engine efficiency, founding thermodynamics.
1827	**France**	**Andre Ampère publishes Ampere's Law, a mathematical expression of Ørsted's relationship between magnetism and electricity.**
1827	Germany	Georg Ohm publishes Ohm's Law, that an electrical current is equal to the ratio of the voltage to the resistance, a founding event in electrical engineering.
1827	Scotland	Robert Brown discovers continuous random movement of microscopic solid particles when suspended in a fluid, later known as Brownian motion.
1829	Scotland	William Nicol invents the Nicol prism for measuring the degree of twist in a plane of polarized lead, founding polarimetry.
1829	USA	Joseph Henry uses insulated wire to create an electromagnet able to lift a ton of iron.
1831	**England USA**	**Michael Faraday and Joseph Henry independently discover that a changing magnetic force can generate electricity, the phenomenon of electromagnetic induction.**
1832	England	Michael Faraday discovers the basic laws of electrolysis that govern the production of a chemical reaction by passing electric current through a liquid or solution.
1834	France	Jean Peltier discovers the Peltier effect, that a current flowing across a junction of two dissimilar metals causes heat to be absorbed or freed, depending on the direction in which the current is flowing.
1839	France	Alexandre Becquerel discovers the photovoltaic effect, whereby light can be used to induce chemical reactions that produce an electric current.
1842	Germany	Christian Doppler discovers the Doppler effect, that the frequency of waves emitted by a moving source changes when the source moves relative to the observer.

Year	Country	Event
1842	Germany	Julius von Mayer and Carl Mohr develop early formulations of the concept of conservation of energy.
1843	England	James Joule discovers Joule's first law, describing the heat produced when an electric current flows through resistance for a given time.
1847	**Germany**	**Hermann von Helmholtz states the law of conservation of energy, the first law of thermodynamics: in an isolated system, the total amount of energy does not change.**
1848	Scotland	William Thomson (Baron Kelvin) defines absolute zero and proposes the Kelvin scale.
1849	France	Armand-Hippolyte-Louis Fizeau and Jean-Bernard-Léon Foucault determine the speed of light to within less than one percent error.
1850	England	George Stokes discovers the terminal velocity of objects falling through viscous liquid.
1850	Germany	Rudolf Clausius discovers the second law of thermodynamics, that the disorder of a closed system increases with time.
1851	France	Jean-Bernard-Léon Foucault demonstrates the rotation of the earth with the Foucault pendulum.
1852	England	James Joule and William Thomson discover the Joule-Thomson effect, which later permits liquefaction of some permanent gases.
1855	Germany England	Johann Geissler invents Geissler tubes, producing a better vacuum. As improved by William Crookes, the tubes produce cathode rays, leading to discovery of the electron.
1865	**Scotland**	**James Maxwell's "A Dynamical Theory of the Electromagnetic Field" presents Maxwell's equations describing the behavior of electric and magnetic fields and proposes that light is electromagnetic in character, constituting the first theoretical unification of physical phenomena.**
1873	Scotland	James Maxwell's *A Treatise on Electricity and Magnetism* elaborates the mathematical model of electromagnetic waves, predicting such phenomena as radio waves and pressure caused by light rays.
1875	England	William Crookes invents the radiometer, thereby providing support for the kinetic theory of gases.
1876	Germany	Eugen Goldstein discovers cathode rays, streams of fluorescence flowing from the negatively charged electrode in an evacuated tube.
1876	USA	Josiah Gibbs publishes the first of a series of papers applying thermodynamics to chemical change, defining the concepts of free energy, chemical potential, equilibrium between phases of matter, and the phase rule, thereby establishing general principles of physical chemistry.

Year	Country	Event
1879	Austria	Josef Stefan discovers Stefan's Law, that the radiation of a body is proportional to the fourth power of its absolute temperature.
1879	USA	Edwin Hall discovers the Hall effect, enabling a method of measuring the strength of strong magnetic fields in small spaces.
1880	France	Pierre and Jacques Curie discover that ultrasonic vibrations are produced by piezoelectricity.
1883	USA	Thomas Edison discovers the Edison effect, later a major factor in the invention of the vacuum tube.
1886	**Germany**	**Heinrich Hertz produces radio waves in the laboratory, confirming Maxwell's electromagnetic theory and laying the basis for radio, television, and radar.**
1887	**USA**	**Albert Michelson and Edward Morley fail to confirm the existence of ether and demonstrate that the speed of light is a constant, raising questions about the adequacy of classical physics.**
1888	Germany	Eugen Goldstein discovers canal rays, from cathode rays.
1892	Ireland	George Fitzgerald hypothesizes the Fitzgerald contraction, that distance contracts with speed, accounting for the results of the Michelson-Morley experiment.
1892	Russia	Konstantin Tsiolkovsky begins theoretical work on rocket propulsion and space flight.
1892	Scotland	James Dewar invents the Dewar flask.
1895	Germany	Wilhelm Röntgen discovers X-rays.
1895	Netherlands	Hendrik Antoon Lorentz extends Fitzgerald's work, hypothesizing that mass also increases with velocity, leading to the conclusion that the speed of light is a universal maximum.
1895	Scotland	Charles Wilson invents the cloud chamber, which later becomes an indispensable tool in the study of atomic particles.
1896	France	Antoine Becquerel discovers spontaneous radioactivity.
1896	Netherlands	Pieter Zeeman discovers the splitting of lines in a spectrum when the spectrum's source is exposed to a magnetic field, the Zeeman effect, later used to study the fine details of atomic structure.
1897	**England**	**J. J. Thomson discovers the first subatomic particle, the electron.**
1897	**France**	**Marie and Pierre Curie demonstrate that uranium radiation is an atomic phenomenon, not a molecular phenomenon, and coin the word *radioactivity*.**
1899	England	Ernest Rutherford discovers two types of uranium radiation, alpha rays (massive and positively charged) and beta rays (lighter and negatively charged).

Year	Country	Event
1900	France	Antoine-Henri Becquerel demonstrates that the process of radioactivity consists partly of particles identical to the electron.
1900	**Germany**	**Max Planck discovers Planck's Law of black body radiation, introducing Planck's constant and the concept that energy is radiated in discrete packets called quanta, founding quantum physics.**
1902	England	Ernest Rutherford and Frederick Soddy demonstrate that uranium and thorium break down into a series of radioactive intermediate elements.
1904	England	J. J. Thomson proposes the "plum-pudding" model of the atom in which electrons are embedded in a sphere of positive electricity.
1905	**Switzerland**	**Albert Einstein's "Zur Elektrodynamik bewegter Körpen" introduces the special theory of relativity.**
1905	Switzerland	Albert Einstein shows that the assumption that light is quantized can explain the photoelectric effect.
1905	**Switzerland**	**Albert Einstein deduces as a consequence of the special theory of relativity that the mass of a body is a measure of its energy content, expressed as $E=mc^2$.**
1905	Switzerland	Albert Einstein explains Brownian motion mathematically, the most convincing evidence to date for the existence of molecules and atoms, and proposes a method to deduce the size of molecules and atoms.
1906	Germany	Hermann Nernst states the third law of thermodynamics, that all bodies at absolute zero would have the same entropy, though absolute zero cannot be perfectly attained.
1908	England	Ernest Rutherford and Johannes Geiger invent an alpha-particle counter.
1908	France	Jean Perrin calculates atomic size from Brownian motion.
1911	**England**	**Ernest Rutherford, using experimental results from Ernst Marsden and Johannes Geiger, proposes the concept of the atomic nucleus, leading to the deduction of the true nature of the atom.**
1911	**Netherlands**	**Heike Kamerlingh-Onnes discovers superconductivity, the disappearance of electrical resistance in certain substances as they approach absolute zero.**
1911	USA	Victor Hess discovers the phenomenon later called cosmic rays.
1912	Germany	Max von Laue develops X-ray diffraction using crystals, founding X-ray crystallography.
1913	Denmark	Niels Bohr applies quantum theory to the structure of the atom, describing electron orbits and electron excitation and de-excitation.

Year	Country	Event
1913	England	Frederick Soddy and Kasimir Fajans discover isotopes, leading to the radioactive displacement law.
1913	USA	Robert Millikan completes experiments determining the charge of an electron, leading to the conclusion that the electron is the fundamental unit of electricity.
1914	England	Henry Moseley introduces the concept of atomic number, the amount of positive charge on the nucleus, for classifying atoms.
1914	England	Ernest Rutherford discovers the proton.
1916	**Germany**	**Albert Einstein's general theory of relativity describes space as a curved field modified locally by the existence of mass, replacing Newtonian ideas which invoke a force of gravity, and derives the basic equations for the exchange of energy between matter and radiation.**
1919	England	Francis Aston invents the mass spectrograph to measure the mass of atoms.
1919	England	Francis Aston discovers isotopes in non-radioactive elements and states the whole-number rule.
1919	England	Ernest Rutherford uses atomic bombardment to alter atomic nuclei, transforming one element into another and constituting the first nuclear reaction.
1923	France	Louis de Broglie states that every particle should have an associated matter wave whose wavelength is inversely related to the particle's momentum, providing an explanation for the wave-particle duality of light.
1923	USA	Arthur Compton discovers the Compton effect, whereby the wavelength of X-rays and gamma rays increases following collisions with electrons.
1925	Germany	Wolfgang Pauli develops the exclusion principle, stating that in a given atom no two electrons can have the identical set of four quantum numbers.
1926	Austria	Erwin Schrödinger develops the mathematics of wave mechanics, including the Schrödinger wave equation.
1927	England	Paul Dirac's relativistically invariant form of the wave equation of the electron unifies aspects of quantum mechanics and relativity theory.
1927	Germany	Werner Heisenberg's "On the Intuitive Content of Quantum Kinematics and Mechanics" introduces the uncertainty principle.
1928	Denmark	Niels Bohr's "The Philosophical Foundations of Quantum Theory" introduces the principle of complementarity, arguing that different but complementary models may be needed to explain the full range of atomic and subatomic phenomena.

Year	Country	Event
1930	England	Paul Dirac predicts the existence of antimatter.
1930	USA	Nils Edlefsen and Ernest Lawrence invent the cyclotron, an instrument used to produce directed beams of charged particles that transforms research into fine nuclear structure.
1931	Switzerland	Wolfgang Pauli predicts the existence of the particle later named the neutrino.
1932	England	James Chadwick discovers the neutron.
1932	England	John Cockroft achieves a nuclear reaction by splitting the atomic nucleus.
1932	USA	Robert Millikan and Carl Anderson discover the positron, the first antiparticle.
1933	Germany	Ernst Ruska and Reinhold Ruedenberg invent an electron microscope that is more powerful than a conventional light microscope.
1934	Russia	Pavel Cherenkov, Ilya Frank, and Igor Tamm discover and interpret the Cherenkov effect, the wave of light produced by particles apparently moving faster than the speed of light in a medium other than a vacuum.
1934	USA	Enrico Fermi achieves the first nuclear fission reaction.
1935	Japan	Hideki Yukawa predicts the existence of mesons as fundamental carriers of the nuclear force field.
1938	Germany	Otto Hahn and Friedrich Strassman split an atomic nucleus into two parts by bombarding uranium-235 with neutrons.
1940	USA	Martin Kamen discovers carbon-14, the most useful of all the radioactive tracers.
1942	**USA**	**Enrico Fermi, Walter Zinn, and Herbert Anderson achieve the first sustained nuclear reaction.**
1943	USA Japan	Richard Feynman, Julian Schwinger, and Sin-Itiro Tomonaga independently work out the equations of quantum electrodynamics governing the behavior of electrons and electromagnetic reactions generally.
1945	Russia USA	Edwin McMillan and Vladimir Veksler independently invent the synchrotron.
1947	England	Dennis Gabor develops the basic concept of holography, which must wait on the laser for implementation.
1948	**USA**	**John Bardeen, Walter Brattain, and William Shockley discover the transistor effect.**

CENTRAL EVENTS IN MATHEMATICS

Year	Country	Event
−600	**Greece**	**Thales founds abstract geometry and deductive mathematics with the "Thales Proposition" (triangles over the diameter of a circle are right-angled), the oldest theorem of occidental mathematics.**
−520	Greece	The Pythagorean theorem appears, allegedly proved by Pythagoras.
−420	Greece	Hippias of Elis discovers the quadratix, the first known curve that cannot be constructed with a straightedge and compass.
−350	Greece	Menaechmus makes the first known attempt to investigate the geometry of the cone.
−300	**Alexandria**	**Euclid's *Elements* synthesizes and systematizes knowledge of geometry.**
−260	Greece	Archimedes calculates the first known value for π.
−250	Greece	Conon of Samos discovers the curve known as the spiral of Archimedes.
−232	Greece	Apollonius of Perga's *Conicorum* presents a systematic treatment of the principles of conics, introducing the terms *parabola*, *ellipse*, and *hyperbola*.
50	Greece	Hero of Alexandria discovers the formula for expressing the area of a triangle in terms of its sides.
98	Greece	Menelaus gives the first definition of a spherical triangle and theorems on congruence of spherical triangles, founding spherical trigonometry.
250	**Greece**	**Diophantus discovers solutions to certain equations, known as Diophantine equations, that represent the beginnings of algebra.**
490	China	Zu Chongzhi calculates that π lies between 3.1415926 and 3.1415927, by far the most accurate estimate of π to that time.
500	India	Aryabhatiya summarizes Indian mathematical knowledge.
700	India	Over the course of 8C, a full and consistent use of zero develops.
810	**Persia**	**Al-Khwarizmi's *Hisab al-Jabr W'al-Musqabalah* gives methods for solving all equations of the first and second degree with positive roots, synthesizes Babylonian with Greek methods, and is the origin of the word *algebra*.**
870	Persia	Thabit ibn Qurra translates Greek mathematical texts into Arabic. His translations will become the major source for European knowledge of Greek mathematics.
1100	Persia	Omar Khayyàm is the first to solve some cubic equations.
1120	England	Adelhard of Bath translates an Arabic version of Euclid's *Elements* into Latin, introducing Euclid to Europe.

Year	Country	Event
1202	Italy	Leonardo Fibonacci's *Liber Abaci* awakens Europe to the advantages of Arabic numerals and computation.
1350	France	Nicole Oresme anticipates coordinate geometry with a plot of time against velocities.
1360	France	Nicole Oresme introduces fractional exponents.
1464	Germany	Regiomontus's *De Triangulis Omnimodus* is the first systematic European work on trigonometry as a subject divorced from astronomy.
1491	Italy	Filippo Calandri publishes an account of the modern method of long division.
1494	Italy	Luca Pacioli's *Summa de Arithmetica* presents an overview of mathematics handed down from the Middle Ages, becoming one of the most influential mathematics books of its time. It is also the first book to discuss double-entry bookkeeping.
1525	Austria	Christoff Rudolff's *Die Coss* introduces the square root symbol and introduces decimal fractions.
1535	Italy	Tartaglia discovers a general method for solving cubic equations.
1545	Italy	Girolamo Cardano's *Ars Magna* is the first book of modern mathematics.
1551	Germany	Rheticus prepares tables of standard trigonometric functions, defining trigonometric functions for the first time as ratios of the sides of a right triangle rather than defining them relative to the arcs of circles.
1557	Wales	Robert Recorde introduces an elongated version of the equal sign into mathematics, and introduces the plus and minus signs into English.
1572	Italy	Rafael Bombelli introduces the first consistent theory of imaginary numbers.
1580	France	François Viète introduces a precise analytic definition of π.
1585	Netherlands	Simon Stevin's *De Thiende* presents a systematic account of how to use decimal fractions.
1591	France	François Viète introduces the systematic use of algebraic symbols.
1613	Italy	Pietro Cataldi develops methods of working with continued fractions.
1614	**Scotland**	**John Napier's *Mirifici Logarithmorum Canonis Descriptio* introduces logarithms.**
1631	England	William Oughtred's *Clavis Mathematicae* summarizes the status of arithmetic and algebra, employing extensive mathematical symbolism.

Year	Country	Event
1635	Italy	Francesco Cavalieri's *Geometria Indivisibilibus Continuorum* expounds a method of using "indivisibles" that foreshadows integral calculus.
1637	France	Pierre de Fermat states his Last Theorem.
1637	**Netherlands**	**René Descartes' "La Géométrie," an appendix to *Discours de la Méthode*, founds analytic geometry.**
1637	Netherlands	René Descartes' "La Géométrie" introduces exponents and square root signs.
1638	France	Pierre de Fermat achieves major progress toward differential calculus, determining maxima and minima by procedures used today.
1640	**France**	**Pierre de Fermat founds number theory through his work on the properties of whole numbers.**
1648	France	Girard Desargues's *Manière Universelle de Mr. Desargues pour Pratiquer la Perspective* contains Desargues's theorem, founding projective geometry.
1654	**France**	**Pierre de Fermat and Blaise Pascal found probability theory with methods for judging the likelihood of outcomes in games of dice.**
1654	France	Blaise Pascal's "Traite du Triangle Arithmétique" analyzes the properties of the arithmetical triangle.
1655	England	John Wallis's *Arithmetica Infinitorium* introduces concepts of limit and negative and fractional exponents, along with the symbol for infinity.
1657	Netherlands	Christiaan Huygens introduces the concept of mathematical expectation into probability theory.
1662	England	John Graunt's *Natural and Political Observations Made upon the Bills of Mortality* is the first significant use of vital statistics.
1668	Belgium	Nicolus Mercator calculates the area under a curve, using analytical geometry.
1668	Scotland	James Gregory introduces a precursor of the fundamental theorem of calculus, expressed geometrically.
1669	**England Germany**	**Isaac Newton's *De Analysi per Aequationes Numero Terminorum Infinitas* presents the first systematic account of the calculus, independently developed by Gottfried Leibniz.**
1670	England	Isaac Barrow discovers a method of tangents essentially equivalent to those used in differential calculus.
1676	England	Isaac Newton formally states the binomial theorem.
1685	England	John Wallis introduces the first graphical representation of complex numbers.

Year	Country	Event
1687	**England**	**Isaac Newton's** *Philosophiae Naturalis Principia Mathematica* **appears, representing the origin of modern applied mathematics.**
1693	England	Edmond Halley prepares the first detailed mortality tables.
1704	England	Isaac Newton's *Enumberatio Linearum Tertii Ordinis* describes the properties of cubic curves.
1713	Switzerland	Jakob Bernoulli's *Ars Conjectandi* contains Bernoulli's theorem, that any degree of statistical accuracy can be obtained by sufficiently increasing the observations, thereby also representing the first application of calculus to probability theory.
1715	England	Brook Taylor's *Methodus Incrementorum Directa et Inversa* introduces the calculus of finite differences.
1718	England	Abraham de Moivre's *Doctrine of Chances* is the first systematic treatise on probability theory.
1720	Scotland	Colin Maclaurin's *Geometrica Organica* describes the general properties of planar curves.
1731	France	Alexis Clairaut's *Recherches sur les Courbes à Double Courbure* is a pioneering study of the differential geometry of space curves.
1733	Italy	Girolamo Saccheri's *Euclides ab Omni Naevo Vindicatus* inadvertently lays the foundation for non-Euclidean geometry.
1770	France	Johann Lambert demonstrates that both π and π^2 are irrational.
1795	Germany	Carl Gauss proves the law of quadratic reciprocity.
1796	Germany	Carl Gauss discovers a method for constructing a heptadecagon with compass and straightedge and demonstrates that an equilateral heptagon could not be constructed the same way, constituting the only notable advance in classic geometry since ancient Greece.
1797	Norway	Caspar Wessel introduces the first geometric representation of complex numbers employing the x-axis as the axis of reals and the y-axis as the axis of imaginaries.
1799	France	Gaspard Monge introduces advances in projecting three-dimensional objects onto two-dimensional planes, founding descriptive geometry.
1799	Germany	Carl Gauss presents a new and rigorous proof of the fundamental theorem of algebra.
1801	**Germany**	**Carl Gauss's** *Disquisitiones Arithmeticae* **expands number theory to embrace algebra, analysis, and geometry.**
1803	France	Lazare Carnot's *Géométrie de Position* revives and extends projective geometry.
1807	France	Jean Fourier introduces Fourier's theorem and the beginnings of Fourier analysis.

Year	Country	Event
1810	France	Joseph Gergonne's *Annales de Mathématiques Pures et Appliqués* is one of the first periodicals devoted to mathematics and becomes highly influential.
1812	France	Pierre Laplace's *Théorie Analytique des Probabilités* introduces the Laplace transform and expands the power of probability theory.
1813	France	Siméon Poisson derives the Poisson distribution.
1817	Czechoslovakia	Bernardus Bolzano develops calculus using a continuous function, dispensing with infinitesimals.
1822	France	Fourier's *Théorie Analytique de la Chaleur* gives a full presentation of Fourier's dimensional analysis, using mass, time, and length as fundamental dimensions that must be expressed in consistent units.
1822	France	Jean Poncelet's *Traité des Propriétés Projectives des Figures* serves as a foundation of modern geometry.
1823	Hungary	János Bolyai develops the first consistent system of non-Euclidean geometry, but publication is delayed until 1832.
1824	Norway	Niels Abel proves the impossibility of a general solution for quintic equations.
1825	France	Adrien Legendre's *Traité des Fonctions Elliptiques et des Intégrales Eulériennes* presents a systematic account of his theory of elliptic integrals.
1825	France	Jean Poncelet and Joseph Gergonne develop the first clear expression of the principle of duality in geometry.
1825	Norway	Niels Abel creates elliptic functions and discovers their double periodicity.
1829	**Russia**	**Nikolai Lobachevsky introduces hyperbolic geometry, replacing Euclid's parallel postulate and founding one of the most important systems of non-Euclidean geometry.**
1830	**France**	**Évariste Galois develops group theory, critical later for quantum mechanics.**
1843	Ireland	William Hamilton introduces quaternions (algebra with hyper-complex numbers).
1844	Germany	Hermann Grassmann's theory of "extended magnitude" generalizes quaternions, creating an algebra of vectors.
1847	**England**	**George Boole's *The Mathematical Analysis of Logic* introduces Boolean algebra, systematically applying algebraic operations to logic.**
1851	Germany	Bernhard Riemann introduces topological considerations into the study of complex functions and lays the basis for Riemann surfaces.

Year	Country	Event
1854	Germany	Bernhard Riemann's *Über die Hypothesen Welche der Geometrie zu Grunde Liegen* introduces a new non-Euclidean geometry and accelerates the acceptance and potential utility of non-Euclidean geometries.
1857	England	Arthur Cayley introduces the algebra of matrices.
1872	Germany	Felix Klein's "Erlanger Programm" calls for geometry to be based on groups of transformations.
1872	Germany	Richard Dedekind introduces theory that any rational or irrational number can be defined in terms of rationals.
1873	France	August Hermite proves that *e* is transcendental.
1874	**Germany**	**Georg Cantor's first formal publication on set theory founds the field.**
1881	USA	Josiah Gibbs's *Elements of Vector Analysis* introduces a system of vectors in three dimensions.
1882	Germany	Carl Lindemann proves that π is transcendental.
1883	Germany	Georg Cantor introduces transfinite set theory.
1884	Sweden	Sonya Kovalevskaya demonstrates that certain kinds of Abelian integrals can be expressed in terms of simpler elliptic integrals.
1895	**France**	**Henri Poincaré's *Analysis Situs* effectively founds topology** (although a few theorems of topology had already been proved).
1899	Germany	David Hilbert's *Grundlagen der Geometrie* establishes the basic axiomatic-formalist approach to systematizing mathematics, initiated by compactly deriving a formal axiomatic model for Euclid's geometry.
1902	France	Henri Lebesgue introduces a new theory for integrating discontinuous functions.
1906	France	Maurice Fréchet introduces a geometry of abstract spaces and the concepts of separability and completeness.
1910	England	Bertrand Russell's and Alfred Whitehead's *Principia Mathematica* represents the best, though flawed, attempt to establish mathematics as branch of logic.
1931	Austria	Kurt Gödel demonstrates that any formal system strong enough to include the laws of arithmetic is either incomplete or inconsistent.
1934	Russia	Aleksander Gelfond and T. Schneider demonstrate that an irrational power of an algebraic number other than zero or one is transcendental.
1936	England	Alan Turing's "On Computable Numbers" develops the hypothetical Turing machine as a method of determining what kinds of mathematical results can be proved.

CENTRAL EVENTS IN MEDICINE

Year	Country	Event
−400	**Greece**	**Hippocrates and his followers develop the empirical study of disease, distancing medicine from religion.**
20	Rome	Celsus's *De Medicina* is one of earliest medical texts and is used for centuries.
70	Rome	Dioscorides's *De Materia Medica*, covering 600 plants and 1,000 drugs, is the first systematic pharmacopoeia.
180	Greece	Galen writes medical texts that are treated as authoritative for the next 13 centuries.
1320	France	Henry of Mondeville's *Chirurgia* advocates use of sutures, cleansing of wounds, limitation of supperation, and wine dressing for wounds.
1530	**Germany**	**Paracelsus pioneers the application of chemistry to physiology, pathology, and the treatment of disease.**
1538	Italy	Girolamo Fracastero's *De Contagione et Contagiosis Morbis* is the first explanation of the spread of infectious disease that invokes analogues of microbes or germs as a cause.
1545	France	Ambroise Paré's *Méthode de Traicter les Plaies* discourages the practice of cauterizing wounds and introduces ligature for stopping arterial bleeding.
1665	England	Richard Lower attempts the first blood transfusion, between dogs.
1710	France	Dominique Anel invents the suction syringe for surgical purposes.
1736	England	Claudius Aymand conducts the first successful appendectomy.
1747	Scotland	James Lind uses a controlled dietary study to establish that citrus causes scurvy.
1761	Austria	Leopold Auenbrugger introduces the use of percussion for medical diagnosis.
1775	England	William Withering discovers digitalis.
1776	England	Matthew Dobson proves that the sweetness of diabetics' urine is caused by the presence of sugar.
1784	USA	Benjamin Franklin invents bifocal lenses.
1796	**England**	**Edward Jenner systematizes vaccination for smallpox, founding immunology.**
1800	England	Humphrey Davy explores the physiological properties of nitrous oxide and recommends its use as an anesthetic.
1801	France	Philippe Pinel's *Traité Médico-Philosophique sur l'Alienation Mentale ou la Manie* is an early and influential empirical study of mental illness.
1816	France	René Laënnec invents the stethoscope.

Year	Country	Event
1831	Germany France USA	Justis von Liebig, Eugene Soubeiran, and, later, Samuel Guthrie, independently prepare chloroform.
1846	**USA**	**William Morton popularizes the use of ether through a demonstration at Massachusetts General Hospital.**
1847	Germany USA	Ignaz Semmelweiss and the elder Oliver Wendell Holmes independently argue that puerperal fever is a contagious disease caused by attending physicians.
1849	England	John Snow uses epidemiological data to demonstrate that cholera is spread by contaminated water.
1849	England	Thomas Addison describes the disease of the adrenal glands known as Addison's disease.
1851	Germany	Hermann Helmholtz invents the ophthalmoscope.
1853	Scotland France	Alexander Wood and Charles Pravaz invent the hypodermic syringe.
1854	England	Florence Nightingale founds modern nursing practice.
1856	**France**	**Louis Pasteur invents pasteurization.**
1862	**France**	**Louis Pasteur gains acceptance for the germ theory of disease, transforming the course of medical research and practice.**
1863	France	Casimir Davaine discovers the microorganism that causes anthrax, the first linkage of a disease with a specific microorganism.
1863	Germany	Johann Baeyer discovers barbituric acid, the first barbiturate.
1865	**England**	**Joseph Lister introduces phenol as a disinfectant in surgery, reducing the death rate from 45 to 15 percent.**
1865	France	Claude Bernard's *Introduction à l'Etude de la Médecine Expérimental* is instrumental in establishing medicine as a science with observation, hypothesis, and experimentation.
1874	USA	Andrew Still discovers that dislocations of the vertebrae are a source of disease, founding osteopathy.
1876	Germany	Robert Koch demonstrates that bacilli are the cause of anthrax.
1881	**France**	**Louis Pasteur invents anthrax inoculation, the first effective treatment of an infectious disease with an antibacterial vaccine.**
1881	Austria	Christian Billroth successfully excises a cancerous pylorus, beginning intestinal surgery; sometimes said to be the beginning of the modern era of surgery.
1881	Germany	Robert Koch introduces steam sterilization.
1881	**USA**	**William Halsted conducts the first known human blood transfusion.**

Year	Country	Event
1882	Germany	Robert Koch isolates the tubercle bacillus.
1884	Austria	Sigmund Freud and Carl Koller use cocaine as a local anesthetic.
1884	England	Rickman Godlee surgically removes a brain tumor.
1884	Germany	Edwin Klebs and Friedrich Löffler isolate the bacterium for diphtheria and identify it as the causative agent.
1885	France	Louis Pasteur invents a rabies vaccine.
1887	France	Augustus Waller records the electrical activity of the heart, founding electrocardiology.
1890	Germany	Emil von Behring develops the first antitoxin, for tetanus.
1891	Germany Japan France	Emil von Behring, Kitasato Shibasaburo, and Émile Roux develop an antitoxin for diphtheria.
1893	USA	Daniel Williams conducts the first successful heart surgery on a human.
1896	Germany	Hermann Strauss introduces X-rays for diagnostic purposes.
1896	Germany	Ludwig Rehn successfully sutures a wound in a human heart.
1896	Italy	Scipione Riva-Rocci invents the mercury sphygmomanometer, the precursor of modern version.
1896	Netherlands	Christiaan Eijkman discovers that beriberi is caused by a dietary deficiency.
1897	England	Ronald Ross discovers the malaria parasite in the anopheles mosquito.
1899	Sweden	Tage Sjogren achieves the first proven cure of a patient by X-ray treatment.
1901	Netherlands	Gerrit Grijns discovers that the cause of beriberi is removal of an essential nutrient in polished rice.
1902	USA	Alexis Carrel introduces suturing for blood vessels.
1903	Netherlands	Willem Einthoven invents the forerunner of the electrocardiogram.
1904	Germany	Alfred Einhorn invents Novocaine.
1905	Germany	Fritz Schaudinn and Erich Hoffmann discover the spirocheta pallida, the cause of syphilis.
1906	**England**	**Frederick Hopkins discovers that food contains ingredients essential to life that are not proteins or carbohydrates, leading to the discovery of vitamins.**
1909	**Germany Japan**	**Paul Ehrlich and Sahachiro Hata discover salvarsan, an effective treatment for syphilis, founding modern chemotherapy.**
1910	USA	Frank Woodbury introduces iodine as a disinfectant for wounds.
1911	USA	Russell Hibbs conducts a successful spinal fusion operation.

Year	Country	Event
1913	USA	Elmer McCollum and Marguerite Davis discover and isolate vitamin A.
1915	Japan	K. Yamagiwa and K. Ichikawa identify the first carcinogen by exposing rabbits to coal tar.
1916	USA	Jay McLean discovers the anti-coagulant heparin.
1920	USA	Harvey Cushing and W. T. Bowie introduce cauterization of blood vessels in surgery.
1921	Canada	Frederick Banting, Charles Best, and James Collip invent a method for isolating insulin and injecting it in patients.
1921	USA	Elmer McCollum and Edward Mellanby discover an antiricketic substance in cod liver oil and name it vitamin D.
1926	USA	George Minot and William Murphy successfully treat pernicious anemia with liver.
1928	**England**	**Alexander Fleming discovers penicillin, the first antibiotic.**
1928	USA	George Papanicolaou invents the pap test for diagnosing uterine cancer.
1929	USA	Philip Drinker, Louis Shaw, and Alexis Carrel invent an artificial respirator (the iron lung).
1932	Germany	Gerhard Domagk discovers that prontosil has antibacterial properties.
1934	USA	John and Mary Gibbon invent a heart-lung machine.
1938	England	Philip Wiles conducts a total artificial hip replacement, using stainless steel.
1939	England	Howard Florey and Ernst Chain isolate the antibacterial agent in penicillin mold.
1939	USA	Karl Landsteiner, Philip Levine, and Alexander Weiner discover the connection between the RH factor and pathology in newborns.
1941	USA Germany	André Cournand, Werner Forssmann, and Dickinson Richards introduce cardiac catheterization.
1943	USA	Selman Waksman, William Feldman, and Corwin Hinshaw discover streptomycin, the first antibiotic effective in treating tuberculosis.
1943	USA	Willem Kolff invents the dialysis machine.
1944	USA	Alfred Blalock, Helen Taussig, Vivien Thomas, and Edgar Sanford conduct the first "blue baby" operation, correcting the blood supply to the lungs of an infant.
1945	USA	John Frisch and Francis Bull initiate the fluoridation of water.
1948	USA	Benjamin Duggar and Albert Dornbush discover the tetracycline group of antibiotics.
1950	USA	Richard Lawler conducts a successful kidney transplant between two live humans.

CENTRAL EVENTS IN TECHNOLOGY

Year	Country	Event
−400	China Egypt	First known use of the abacus.
−270	Greece	Sostrates builds the first known lighthouse, the Pharos of Alexandria.
−245	Levant	First known glass blowing.
−200	Asia Minor	First known use of parchment.
1	China	Chinese engineers invent the sternpost rudder, enabling efficient steering of large vessels.
100	China	First known use of paper for writing (earlier versions had been used for packing and other purposes).
250	China	First gunpowder (date uncertain).
300	China	First known use of stirrups.
984	China	Chinese engineers invent locks for canals.
1045	China	Bi Sheng invents movable type, reinvented by Gutenberg in Germany, 1440.
1502	Germany	Peter Henlein invents the mainspring in a pocket watch (and invents the pocket watch itself).
1556	Germany	Georgius Agricola's *De re Metallica* is for centuries the best text on mining.
1589	England	William Lee invents the stocking frame, the basis for all subsequent knitting and lace-making machines.
1603	England	Hugh Platt discovers coke, essential to steel production.
1622	England	William Oughtred invents the slide rule by repositioning Gunter's scales.
1642	France	Blaise Pascal invents a calculating machine, the Pascaline, that can handle up to nine-digit numbers.
1656	Netherlands	Christiaan Huygens invents the pendulum escapement and thereby invents the pendulum clock.
1679	France	Denis Papin invents the pressure cooker.
1690	France	Denis Papin invents the atmospheric engine, pioneering many design principles of the steam engine.
1693	Germany	Gottfried von Leibniz invents an improved calculator for multiplication and division.
1698	England	Thomas Savery invents the Miner's Friend, a practical atmospheric steam engine without a piston.
1699	England	Jethro Tull invents the modern seed drill.
1709	England	Abraham Darby successfully uses coke in iron smelting.

Year	Country	Event
1712	England	Thomas Newcomen uses steam to push a piston.
1731	England	John Hadley invents the reflecting octant, precursor of the modern sextant, which follows in 1757.
1733	England	John Kay invents flying shuttle, an important step toward automatic weaving.
1740	England	Benjamin Huntsman develops the crucible method for making homogeneous steel (Sheffield steel), with high tensile strength.
1742	USA	Benjamin Franklin invents the Franklin stove, a major improvement in heating efficiency.
1750	USA	Benjamin Franklin invents the lightning rod.
1764	England	James Hargreaves invents the spinning jenny, which does the work of 30 spinning wheels.
1764	**Scotland**	**James Watt invents the condenser, employing latent heat to improve the efficiency of the steam engine, the first of several improvements that create the modern steam engine.**
1765	**England**	**John Harrison completes 40 years of refinement of an accurate ship's chronometer, enabling the determination of longitude and revolutionizing navigational techniques.**
1769	**England**	**Richard Arkwright invents the water frame, a waterwheel-driven device that powers multiple spinning machines and a foundation of the modern factory system.**
1770	England	Richard Arkwright, Samuel Need, and Jedediah Strutt open a water-driven mill at Cromford, the start of the factory system.
1776	England	John Wilkinson invents the first precision boring machine, essential for the manufacture of cylinders for steam engines.
1779	England	Abraham Darby III and John Wilkinson build an all-iron bridge at Coalbrookdale.
1781	Scotland	James Watt invents a governor for a steam engine and uses a sun-and-planet gear to use a steam engine to drive a wheel.
1782	Scotland England	James Watt and Jonathan Hornblower invent a double-acting steam engine in which steam is admitted alternatively on both sides of the piston.
1783	France	L. S. Lenormand, Jean Blanchard, and André Gernerin invent the first parachute capable of carrying a human.
1783	France	The Montgolfier brothers conduct the first manned flight of a hot air balloon.
1785	France	Claude Berthollet invents chemical bleach (chlorine and potash).
1785	USA	Oliver Evans invents an elevator to move grain, automating the process and requiring only two workers.

Year	Country	Event
1787	USA	John Fitch invents a working steamboat.
1793	USA	Eli Whitney invents the cotton gin, revolutionizing the economics of cotton production.
1795	France	Nicolas Appert discovers that food can be preserved by heating, leading to the invention of canned food.
1796	Bohemia	Aloys Senefelder invents lithography.
1800	**Italy**	**Alessandro Volta invents the voltaic cell, the first battery.**
1804	England	Richard Trevithick uses a steam locomotive on rails to pull iron from an ironworks to the Glamorgan canal.
1805	France	Joseph-Marie Jacquard invents punch cards to create patterns with the Jacquard loom, the first nonalphabetic means of storing information.
1807	**USA**	**Robert Fulton builds the first commercially successful steamboat.**
1814	**England**	**George Stephenson invents a practical steam locomotive.**
1815	**Scotland**	**John McAdam invents the modern paved road.**
1820	USA Scotland	Cyrus McCormick, Obed Hussey, and Patrick Bell invent independent versions of the mechanical reaper in the course of the decade.
1822	France	Joseph Niépce creates the first permanent photograph.
1824	England	Joseph Aspdin invents Portland cement.
1825	England	Stephenson begins the first rail service using a steam locomotive.
1831	**England**	**Michael Faraday invents the electric generator.**
1831	**USA**	**Joseph Henry invents a practical electric motor.**
1833	England	Charles Babbage designs an "analytic engine," programmed by punch cards, that is the conceptual origin of the computer.
1835	USA	Samuel Colt invents the Colt revolver.
1836	England	John Daniell invents the Daniell cell, the first modern battery.
1830	**USA England**	**William Cooke, Charles Wheatstone, and Samuel Morse independently invent the telegraph in the course of the decade.**
1839	England	William Grove invents the fuel cell, producing electricity by combining hydrogen and oxygen.
1839	**France**	**Louis Daguerre invents the camera and plates that make photography practical.**
1839	Scotland	Kirkpatrick Macmillan invents the first true bicycle.
1839	USA	Charles Goodyear invents vulcanization, revolutionizing the utility of rubber.

Year	Country	Event
1841	England	William Fox-Talbot invents a photographic negative that permits unlimited paper positives.
1842	**England**	**John Lawes invents the first chemical fertilizer.**
1843	England	Isambard Brunel builds a propeller-driven, iron, transatlantic liner.
1843	England	John Lawes founds the Rothamsted Experimental Station for improving agricultural production, introducing rigorous experimental procedures and field trials.
1844	USA	Samuel Morse creates the first functioning telegraph line, from Washington to Baltimore.
1845	Germany	Christian Schönbein invents nitrocellulose, or gun cotton.
1846	USA	Elias Howe invents a two-thread, lock-stitch sewing machine.
1847	Italy	Ascanio Sobrero prepares nitroglycerine.
1851	USA	Isaac Singer invents an improved sewing machine with treadle and lock stitch.
1852	France	Henri Giffard conducts the first successful flight of a powered airship (a steam powered dirigible).
1852	France	Jean Foucault invents a gyroscope that can be used as a substitute for a magnetic compass.
1852	USA	Elisha Otis invents the safety elevator.
1853	England	Abraham Gesner and James Young invent kerosene.
1853	England	George Cayley invents a glider that accomplishes the first unpowered, manned flight in a heavier-than-air vehicle.
1854	France Germany	Robert Bunsen and Henri St.-Claire Deville develop an electrolytic process for obtaining metallic aluminum from sodium aluminum chloride.
1856	England USA	Henry Bessemer and William Kelly invent the Bessemer process for manufacturing steel.
1856	England	William Perkin invents a synthetic dye (mauve), founding the synthetic organic chemical industry.
1859	France	Gaston Planté invents the rechargeable storage battery.
1859	USA	Edwin Drake drills the first successful oil well, in Titusville, Pennsylvania.
1859	USA	George Pullman invents the sleeping car.
1860	**France**	**Jean Lenoir invents a practical internal combustion engine.**
1861	France	Eugene Meyer and Pierre Michaux invent the chain-driven bicycle.
1865	England	Alexander Parkes creates laboratory samples of celluloid.
1865	USA	Linus Yale invents the pin-tumbler cylinder lock.

Year	Country	Event
1866	**Sweden**	**Alfred Nobel invents dynamite.**
1866	USA	Cyrus Field lays the first successful transatlantic telegraph cable.
1867	France	Georges Leclanché invents the forerunner of an easily manufactured dry cell battery.
1867	USA	Carlos Glidden and Christopher Sholes invent the first commercially practical typewriter.
1868	USA	George Westinghouse invents an automatic air brake for railroad cars.
1869	Belgium	Zénobe Gramme and Ernst Siemens develop and manufacture a DC dynamo.
1869	France	Ferdinand de Lesseps supervises the design and construction of the Suez Canal.
1869	**USA**	**John Hyatt invents a commercially successful plastic (celluloid).**
1876	Germany	Nikolaus Otto invents the four-stroke cycle basic to modern combustion engines.
1876	**USA**	**Alexander Bell and Elisha Gray independently invent the telephone.**
1877	**USA**	**Thomas Edison invents the phonograph.**
1878	**England USA**	**Thomas Edison and Joseph Swan independently invent the carbon filament incandescent bulb.**
1880	USA	Herman Hollerith invents the first workable electromechanical calculator, used to automate tabulation of the 1890 U.S. Census.
1883	France	Louis de Chardonnet invents the first synthetic fabric, rayon.
1883	USA	Nikola Tesla invents a motor using alternating current.
1884	England	Charles Parsons invents a successful steam turbine.
1884	USA	Lewis Waterman invents the free-flowing fountain pen.
1884	USA	Ottmar Mergenthaler invents the linotype machine.
1885	Germany	Carl Benz invents the first true automobile.
1885	USA	William Stanley invents a transformer for shifting voltage and amperage.
1886	France USA	Charles Hall and Paul Héroult invent an inexpensive method for extracting aluminum.
1887	Scotland	John Dunlop invents the pneumatic rubber tire.
1888	USA	George Eastman invents the Kodak camera.
1889	England	Frederick Abel and James Dewar invent cordite, leading to smokeless gunpowder.
1889	**USA**	**Thomas Edison invents the motion picture camera.**
1891	USA	Edward Acheson invents carborundum, the first industrial abrasive.
1892	Germany	Rudolf Diesel invents the diesel engine.

Year	Country	Event
1900	Germany	Ferdinand Zeppelin begins the first airline, using rigid airships.
1901	**Italy**	**Guglielmo Marconi broadcasts radio waves from England to Newfoundland.**
1903	**USA**	**The Wright brothers' airplane achieves the first successful powered flight by a heavier-than-air machine.**
1904	USA	John Fleming invents the rectifier, the first radio tube.
1906	USA	Lee De Forest invents the amplifier vacuum tube.
1908	**Germany**	**Fritz Haber invents a process, later perfected by Carl Bosch, for mass production of nitrates, which in turn permits mass production of fertilizers (and explosives).**
1908	**USA**	**Henry Ford invents the assembly line.**
1909	USA Scotland	Leo Baekeland and James Swinburne independently invent a thermosetting plastic.
1911	Switzerland	Jacques Brandenberge invents cellophane.
1911	USA Germany	Elmer Sperry and Hermann Anschutz-Kämpfer independently invent the gyrocompass.
1911	USA	Charles Kettering invents an electric starter for cars.
1912	Germany	Friedrich Bergius invents a process to produce gasoline from coal hydrogenation.
1914	USA	The Panama Canal is completed.
1917	USA	Clarence Birdseye and Charles Seabrook invent a technique for quick-freezing foods, founding the frozen food industry.
1918	**USA**	**Edwin Armstrong invents the superheterodyne receiver, making home radio receivers possible.**
1921	USA	Thomas Midgley, Jr., invents tetraethyl lead, an anti-knock compound for gasoline.
1923	**USA**	**Vladimir Zworykin invents the iconoscope, the precursor of the television tube.**
1926	**USA**	**Robert Goddard invents the liquid-fuel rocket.**
1926	USA	Samuel Warner introduces a motion picture system that integrates sound into the film.
1927	USA	Charles Lindbergh pilots the first nonstop flight from the United States to continental Europe.
1929	Germany	Fritz Pfleumer invents magnetic recording of sound.
1929	USA	Edwin Armstrong invents frequency modulation (FM), a method of transmitting radio waves without static; perfected in 1933.
1930	**England**	**Frank Whittle invents the jet engine.**
1930	USA	Thomas Midgley, Jr., discovers freon, the refrigerant.

Year	Country	Event
1930	USA	Vannevar Bush invents a machine capable of solving differential equations.
1931	USA	Wallace Carothers invents nylon.
1932	USA	Edwin Land invents a synthetic substance that will polarize light, leading to the first synthetic light-polarizing film.
1935	Scotland	Robert Watson-Watt invents a way to display radio wave information on a cathode ray tube, enabling the development of radar.
1936	USA Germany	Igor Sikorsky and Heinrich Foch independently invent a successful helicopter.
1938	USA	Roy Plunkett invents Teflon.
1938	USA	The Biro brothers invent the first workable ballpoint pen.
1939	Germany	Hans Ohain designs the first successful jet plane.
1939	**Switzerland**	**Paul Müller discovers the insecticidal properties of DDT.**
1940	USA	George Stibitz invents the Complex Number Calculator, the first machine to service more than one terminal and to be used via a remote location.
1943	France	Jacques Cousteau and Émile Gagnan invent the aqualung.
1943	USA	Martin Whitaker and Eugene Wigner lead the construction of the first operational nuclear reactor.
1945	England	Arthur Clarke conceptualizes the use of satellites for global communication.
1946	**USA**	**ENIAC, the first entirely electronic computer, developed by John Eckert, John Mauchly, Arthur Burks, and John von Neumann, becomes fully operational.**
1946	**USA**	**Arthur Burks, John von Neumann, and Herman Goldstine's "Preliminary Discussion of the Logical Design of an Electronic Computing Instrument" provides the conceptual foundation for computer development in the coming decades.**
1947	USA	Charles Yeager pilots the first supersonic flight.
1947	USA	Edwin Land, Howard Rogers, and William McCune invent the Polaroid camera.
1948	**USA**	**John Bardeen, Walter Houser, and William Shockley invent the transistor.**
1948	USA	Peter Goldmark invents the long-playing record.
1950	England	Alan Turing creates the Turing test, establishing a criterion for judging artificial intelligence.

SIGNIFICANT EVENTS IN THE ARTS

This is the place where you might reasonably expect to find a list of the 500 or perhaps 5,000 most famous works of art, music, and literature, using the same methods I employed to identify the most eminent artists, composers, and authors. But I have no such lists to offer.

The nature of great accomplishment in the arts is fundamentally different from great accomplishment in the sciences. The distinction goes back to a point I made in the discussion of great people in the arts and sciences (see page 144): In the arts, eminence arises from genius manifested in a body of work, whereas eminence in the sciences arises from the importance of the discovery, which may or may not be the result of genius. The practical result is that the techniques that work for measuring the eminence of artists do not work for measuring the importance of specific artistic creations, nor do the techniques that work for identifying the most important events in the sciences work for identifying the most important events in the arts.

Suppose, for example, we count the number of times a given work of art appears as a plate in nine major histories of Western art, taking as our hypothesis that the pictures that appear the most often will also be the most important ones. The hypothesis quickly falls apart. We start with the only three works of art that were shown in all nine art histories: Michelangelo's ceiling of the Sistine Chapel, Leonardo's *Last Supper*, and Bernini's sculpture *Ecstasy of St. Theresa*.[7] The first two are plausibly among the most important works of Western art, but it is odd to see *Ecstasy of St. Theresa* in their company. A great work, but plausibly in the top three?

Then we come to the works that appear in eight out of the nine art histories. They were Velazquez's *Las Meninas*, one or another of the pages of the Limbourg brothers' illuminations for *Les Très Riches Heures du Duc de Berry*, Ghiberti's *Gates of Paradise* on the north baptistery door of the Florence cathedral, Edvard Munch's *Scream*, and Theodore Gericault's *Raft of the Medusa*. All are important works, and at least two, *Las Meninas* and *Gates of Paradise*, attract extravagant praise in many art histories. The others are among the finest representatives of a movement or genre—but that's why they are shown so often, not because anyone thought they belonged at the very apex of artistic greatness. Thus the first and obvious difference between a list of art works and the index of artists: Whatever quibbles one might have with the precise ordering of a list of great artists in the Western art inventory, all the people who are near the top belong somewhere near the top. The same cannot be said of all the works of art that are near the top. The ordering of Western artists has high face validity, whereas the ordering of works of Western art does not.

These results could be improved through a close textual analysis of all the sources. One could give extra weight to text that had adjectives such as "pivotal," "momentous," or "seminal" attached, for example. But even though it may well be possible to produce a statistically satisfactory catalog of the most important works of art, a deeper problem ought to keep us from making too much of it. The reason goes to this fundamental substantive difference between artistic and scientific accomplishment, a difference that no amount of methodological fine tuning can circumvent:

In recounting the history of science, events can rarely be substituted for one another. The historian of science may choose which events he thinks merit inclusion, but he cannot choose among three or four different versions of the same event. Even in the case of simultaneous independent discoveries, such as the development of the calculus, the stories of Leibniz and Newton are each about the same step forward. In contrast, the historian of the arts has many choices, because there are so many more great works than great artists. For example, Rembrandt is represented by 29 different paintings in the nine sources used to compile specific works of art, but only one of those paintings, *Night Watch*, is shown in even a bare majority of those sources. Twenty-one of the 29 works are shown in a single source. Rembrandt's greatness can be demonstrated by many combinations of works.

The same distinction applies to the portrayal of genres. An art historian has no choice about whether to give substantial attention to French Impressionism. It is too important to ignore. He does not have the option of discussing French Impressionism without mentioning Cézanne, Manet, Monet, Renoir, and van Gogh. But he can use dozens of paintings as exemplars of Impressionism. To be specific, the nine art sources contain 97 different paintings by the five Impressionists I just mentioned, but only four of those 97 are shown in even a majority of the sources. Neither Cézanne nor van Gogh has a single painting that is shown in more than four of the nine sources. Both Cézanne and van Gogh produced paintings regarded as among the greatest of that era, but they produced so many that any given pair of histories is unlikely to have chosen the same ones.

A multitude of choices is not the only barrier to measuring the stature of a given work. Any attempt to compile a catalog also runs into the confusion between *great* and *significant*. The Impressionist work with the most frequent appearance in art histories is Seurat's *Un Dimanche Après-Midi à l'Île de la Grande Jatte*, shown in seven sources. It is widely considered to be

Seurat's masterpiece, but it stands out in part because it was a big fish in a small pond—Pointillism was a fashion of brief duration relative to the broader development of modern art. The less important the genre, the more likely that a few of the best works will stand out.

Similarly, great literary and musical works can get lost in the crowd. In a comprehensive history of literature, Shakespeare is a sure bet to be allotted more space than any other single author, but the amount of attention given to any one of his plays may have little to do with its stature. If the historian spends several paragraphs on *King Lear*, he is less likely to give a detailed account of *Macbeth*. All histories of music discuss Beethoven's contribution to the symphonic form, but the choices among his nine symphonies vary widely across histories and are not necessarily based on the symphonies that the historian thinks are the best. Paul Lang's *Music in Western Civilization* spends many pages on Beethoven and the symphony but comparatively little on the famous Fifth Symphony. And yet among the brief comments is this one: "The Fifth Symphony does not require discussion; it will remain *the* symphony, the consummate example of symphonic logic."[8] Clearly, it would be a bad idea to try to rank Beethoven's symphonies based on the space that Lang devotes to them.

Finally, there is the question of shifting popularity. Dean Simonton has used the same dataset to demonstrate both that an underlying consistency of aesthetic judgment exists and that the popularity of specific works is subject to shifts in fashion.[9] But complementary studies consistently demonstrate that the reputations of complete bodies of work by creative individuals are stable.[10] Simonton offers as a specific case in point Handel, whose operas fell out of favor for a time. "Yet his oratorios, concerti grossi, orchestral suites, and other masterpieces kept him from falling from the highest ranks until his operas enjoyed a substantial revival in the present century."[11]

So while it would be great fun if I could give you lists of the top paintings or novels, I cannot, nor can I give you any other means by which you can compare *War and Peace*'s place in the pantheon of novels with that of *Middlemarch*, or see exactly how far down the list Pachelbel's *Canon* stands with the experts. The building block of the sciences is the discovery. The building block of the arts is the artist.

THE EVENTS THAT MATTER II: META-INVENTIONS

I n 1884 an Anglican clergyman named Edwin Abbott published *Flatland*, a little book that remains in print today, in which his narrator describes a world consisting of just two dimensions, complete with social classes, religion, and family life. The narrator himself is of the middle class, a Square. The dramatic climax of the book occurs when a three-dimensional object, a Sphere, visits Flatland and takes the narrator into the world of Space. "I looked, and, behold, a new world!" exclaims the Square, able to look *down* for first time.[1] A dimension that had been inconceivable moments earlier had become part of his mental repertoire.

This chapter is about rare points in the history of human accomplishment when similar reconceptualizations occurred in the arts and sciences. Over spans of time ranging from a few decades in some cases to a few centuries in others, the dimensionality of a domain in the arts and sciences changed, opening up new realms of potential accomplishment. I call this handful of accomplishments *meta-inventions*.

By meta-invention, I mean the introduction of a new cognitive tool for dealing with the world around us. *Cognitive* tool, not *physical* tool. The essence of a meta-invention resides within the human brain. A cognitive tool is one that, once known, can be forgotten (recall Chapter 2), but not stolen or physically lost. It is necessary to know some form of technology to reproduce a physical tool that has been taken away. It is not necessary to know any technology to retain a cognitive tool—it is necessary only to remember it.

But if a meta-invention is in the mind, everything new that develops in the mind is not necessarily a meta-invention. Here, explicitly, are the criteria I have applied:

- The essence of a meta-invention is an idea, not a thing.

- A meta-invention is literally an invention—a creation that occurred in one or more human societies but not in all of them.

- A meta-invention does not have a single application, but rather enables humans to do a class of new things.

- A meta-invention is followed by transforming changes in practice and achievement.

The printing press does not qualify as a meta-invention, nor the wheel, nor hay. Each had enormous consequences and each was the product of human intellect, but none was a cognitive tool. At the other extreme is a set of cognitive tools that were not inventions in any meaningful sense of that word. Human language is an example. Language is the cognitive tool sine qua non, but it occurred in every human tribe at its earliest known level of development. It is better classified as an inevitable outcome of the human brain than as something humans could invent or fail to invent.[2]

Diffuse cultural attributes are not meta-inventions. As examples, consider Western individualism and Chinese Daoism. The importance of the complex of beliefs that we call Western individualism is surely on a par with any other cultural development in history. Individualism is often argued to have been a decisive factor in the ascendancy of Western civilization, a position with which I agree and expound upon in Chapter 19. But individualism is a phenomenon with roots that sprawl across the Greek, Judaic, and Christian traditions. It manifested itself in different ways across different parts of the West in the same era and within any given country of the West across time. Similarly, Daoism, while technically denoting a specific literature identified with Laozi and Zhuangzi, labels a Chinese world view that permitted traditions of art, poetry, governance, and medicine that could not conceivably have occurred in the West—but, like Western individualism, it is grounded in such diffuse sources that to call it an *invention* stretches the meaning of that word too far. In searching for meta-inventions I am looking for more isolated, discrete cognitive tools.

So much for what a meta-invention is not. The archetypal example of what does qualify as a meta-invention is the invention of written language. It occurred over centuries, so it cannot be called discrete in terms of time. But it was definitely an invention, something that a few cultures managed to devise and the rest did not. Independent inventions of writing are believed to have occurred in only four places (or even fewer; controversy continues about whether the latter three were truly independent): Sumer between −3500 and −2800, Egypt a little later, China before −1300, and Mexico before −600.[3] Writing is definitely a cognitive tool, the intellectual insight that it is possible to encode information not just as pictures or isolated symbols, but in a systematic fashion that permits an unlimited amount of information to be preserved. Every one of the alphabets and logograms that have been used to write the world's languages amounts to a different manifestation of this one supremely important cognitive tool.

With that understanding of how I am defining the term, let me propose 14 meta-inventions that occurred after −800. Six are in the arts, three in philosophy, three in mathematics, and two in the sciences:

- Artistic realism
- Linear perspective
- Artistic abstraction
- Polyphony
- Drama
- The novel
- Meditation
- Logic
- Ethics
- Arabic numerals
- The mathematical proof
- The calibration of uncertainty
- The secular observation of nature
- The scientific method

Are these *the* meta-inventions since −800, exactly 14 in number? That claim is too ambitious. The borders of a meta-invention are fuzzy, and drawing boxes around a single meta-invention is sometimes arbitrary—the single meta-invention called *scientific method* in my list could easily be broken into half a dozen separate ones. I will describe the thinking behind my choices as I go along, noting some borderline cases that barely missed the cut. The note discusses some others.[4]

META-INVENTIONS IN THE ARTS

The first candidates for meta-inventions in the arts are the inventions of the arts themselves—the invention of pictorial and sculpted images, of linked musical sounds, of the tale. But besides predating our beginning point of −800, their very universality, like the universality of language, stretches the concept of invention past the breaking point. Visual art, music, and the story seem to be part of the human repertoire everywhere.

The next possibility is to treat the invention of new movements and genres as meta-inventions—the invention of haiku, or the symphony, or the landscape, for example. The problem here is deciding where to stop. Each of these examples seems too small. They were important new forms of artistic expression and involved significant innovations, but none was a landmark change in what human beings were able to do with words, music, or paint. In a meta-invention in the arts, I seek the handful of innovations in artistic vocabulary and syntax that transformed the possibilities.

The Invention of Artistic Realism. Greece, circa −500.[5]

For the first three and a half millennia or so after the beginning of Sumer, the world's visual arts in every civilization followed a similar course. Conventions developed for portraying people and scenes, and the conventions became rules that each succeeding generation observed rigidly. The conventions did not have much to do with conveying the visual reality of the thing being portrayed. An ancient Egyptian artist did not try to show the person that was before his eyes, but what he knew belonged to that person. The face is in profile, but the eye looks like an eye seen from the front. The top half of the body is as seen from the front, showing the chest and both arms, yet the lower half is seen in profile, showing both legs and feet in the way that it is easiest to draw.

These conventions for portraying a person were not followed so unvaryingly because Egyptian artists were not capable of anything else, but because that's the way art was done. A good artist's job was to execute the conventions in the most craftsmanlike way that he could. A break in that rigid tradition occurred in −14C, when the pharaoh Akhenaton encouraged innovation of many kinds, including artistic. The famous bust of his queen, Nefertiti, shows a woman who was unmistakably a flesh and blood person. A statue of Akhenaton himself shows a man with a bit of a pot belly and a dreamy expression, also definitely a real person. Some of the paintings surviving from his reign show people standing in informal poses that were intended to represent the way that people really stand. But the flare of artistic innovation did not survive Ahkenaton.

A thousand years passed before Greek artists renewed the effort to reproduce what people saw before their eyes in everyday life. The beginnings were humble. "It was a tremendous moment in the history of art," writes Ernst Gombrich, "when, perhaps a little before 500 B.C., artists dared for the first time in all history to paint a foot as seen from the front. In all the thousands of Egyptian and Assyrian works which have come down to us, nothing of that kind had ever happened."[6] Gombrich was referring to the discovery of foreshortening, ways of distorting the painted image or carved relief so that the result appears to the viewer as it would in real life. In the case of the foot, on a vase signed by Euthymedes, the artist shows us the front of the five toes, which the human eye immediately recognizes as a foot seen from in front. The revolution occurred in sculpture in the same era. The people portrayed in statues began to stand in natural ways, with more weight on one foot than another, the hips no longer in line, the axis of the body no longer a straight line. Knees began to look like real knees and smiles like real smiles.

The invention of artistic realism is one of the cleanest examples of the meta-invention as a cognitive tool. The realization of the invention required more than a century of experiments and mistakes and improvements until classical Greek sculpture and, we are told, painting, reached the heights of realism, but the initial invention was simple and wholly in the brain: Pay attention to what you see in front of you, not what the rules of art tell you to do, and try to figure out how to translate what you see into your medium in a fully realistic way.

The Invention of Linear Perspective. Italy, circa 1413.

We do not know how close Greek painters came to the portraying the illusion of three dimensions on a two-dimensional surface. In addition to foreshortening, they developed ways of shading light to correspond to the way in which the human eye perceived light across distance. Agatharcus of Samos, writing in −5C, described techniques that suggest some aspects of what we know today as linear perspective. The Greeks made enough progress to cause Plato to grumble about the falsity of paintings that showed two men of different size just because they stood at different distances from the painter. Only vase paintings and a few frescoes survive, however, and the Roman examples are not thought to represent the best work.

Since the illusion of depth on a two-dimensional canvas had been achieved to some degree, it is an exaggeration to call the development of linear perspective in 15C a completely new invention. But when something has been as forgotten as perspective had been forgotten, and when the new version is qualitatively so much better than the old one appears to have been, and when the new version has momentous consequences, the invention of linear perspective in 15C qualifies as a meta-invention in its own right.

Some of the technical characteristics of linear perspective were under-stood in the late medieval era. The ceiling in Giotto's *Confirmation of the Rule of St. Francis*, circa 1325, is based on a point of convergence so close to math-ematically correct that it seems unlikely to have been produced just by Giotto's artistic judgment.[7] Some of the paintings of Duccio and Lorenzetti dating from 14C indicate a growing facility at handling depth. But the inven-tion of linear perspective as a systematic set of principles took its giant leap forward at a much more specific date and with a more clearly identified inventor than most meta-inventions. The man was Filippo Brunelleschi and the date, less clear, was probably 1412 or 1413.[8]

Brunelleschi is known to history as one of the most influential archi-tects of all time. The famous dome of the cathedral of Florence is his work. His principles of proportion and design were to shape the appearance of European cities through 19C. Probably his needs as an architect prompted his interest in perspective—a realistic three-dimensional rendering of an unbuilt building is a useful thing for an architect to be able to draw—but we do not know exactly how he managed to take the vague knowledge of perspective then circulating and put it to such exact use. Perhaps he extrapolated from medieval surveying techniques, or he adapted the geometry of the existing optical science, or he adapted the projective mapping techniques known since Ptolemy. Competing stories are told.

What we do know is the dramatic way in which Brunelleschi demon-strated his discovery to the world, with a mirror-image painting of the baptis-tery of the Florence cathedral, a mirror, and a peep-hole device. He invited his Florentine friends to come to the piazza, sat them at the appropriate point, and had them look through the peephole first at a reflection of the painting in the mirror and then at the actual baptistery. According to a contemporary account, the accuracy of Brunelleschi's perspective was so great that the view of the real baptistery could scarcely be distinguished from the reflection of the painted view shown in the mirror.

If the demonstration in the piazza occurred by 1413, as recently uncovered evidence indicates, it took more than a decade for the discovery of linear perspective to make its way into the wider world of painting via Masaccio's fresco of the Trinity, which may still be seen on a wall of the church of Santa Maria Novella in Florence. It took another decade for Leon Battista Alberti, another of the great Renaissance architects, to write *Della Pittura* (dedicated to Brunelleschi), laying out both the mathematics of perspective and devices for artists to use in applying perspective to their own work. Within a few decades, every major artist was painting in perspective. The theory of perspective developed as well, along with technical apparatus—artists were employing screens and grids by the end of 15C, and later began using the *camera obscura*, to produce ever more precise representations of three-dimensional objects. But these were elaborations on the core invention of Brunelleschi, a method for creating, in Alberti's words, "an open window through which the subject to be painted is seen," and then reproducing that subject with a fidelity hitherto unimagined.[9]

The new stance of the painter toward his subject had consequences that transcended art and went to the essence of the Renaissance's new attitude toward man's place in the world and the cosmos. It also fundamentally changed the status of painting itself. Painters were no longer merely craftsmen, but partook of the same acquisition of truth that was the business of the sciences—or natural philosophy, as science was known in 15C. "The science of perspective, by making painters into philosophers, had created an eighth liberal art," in the words of historian Daniel Boorstin, "and as the interpreter of the divine order in the visible universe the artist acquired the dignity of the scientist."[10] But apart from all of these second-order and third-order outcomes was the fundamental change in two-dimensional art. It had acquired a third.

The Invention of Abstraction. France, last half of 19C.

The third meta-invention in the visual arts consisted, in a sense, of discarding the first two. By mid-19C, all the problems of conveying a precise rendering of a scene had been solved. Many of the famous still life paintings that have come down to us from the interim centuries are bravura displays of the artist's virtuosity. Thus we have in a famous Willem Kalf still life—expressed in two dimensions, using nothing but oil paints—simulacra of a rough-woven figured tablecloth, its fringe, a cooked lobster, bread, lemon peel, the meat of the lemon, the steel of the knife blade used to peel the lemon, a polished hunting horn, silver chasing, polished silver, an engraved crystal goblet half filled with white wine, a clear crystal goblet half filled with white wine, a linen napkin, and the stone table—each surface and texture and color rendered with stunningly lifelike realism.

Then, in the second quarter of 19C, came photography. Probably artists would have searched out new problems to solve anyway, but the invention of a technology that promised to capture the literal truth of a scene offered a clear and present incentive for art to head off in new directions.

I do not use the word *abstraction* to stand for a particular school that developed thereafter, but for a generalized change in the way that painters approached their canvases. Nor do I suggest that the retreat from literalism in art was new. Deliberate distortions of reality had always been a part of art, both East and West. Sometimes it was subtle; sometimes, as in the work of El Greco, dramatically obvious. By the first half of 19C, departures from literalness had spread. A picture such as J. M. W. Turner's *Steamer in a Snowstorm*, painted in 1842, would look at home in a gallery of modern art—and in fact is displayed at London's Tate Gallery rather than at the classically oriented National Gallery. But a step remained, to offer an alternative to the underlying idea of the painting as a window on the world. If one person is to be singled out as the one who took that step, it should be Édouard Manet (1832–1883). The painting is *not* a window on the world, Manet announced. It consists of patches of color on a two-dimensional surface. You don't look *through* a painting but *at* it. Manet proclaimed further that "realism" does not consist of a Kalf-like fidelity to the way things look when they are minutely inspected. When people observe a scene in real life, they perceive it as a whole, focusing on some objects and not on others; seeing motion, with all its blurriness, rather than movement frozen in time; seeing light and shapes rather than specific clouds and shadows.

In the decades that followed, a succession of schools—Impressionism, Post-Impression, Fauvism, Expressionism, Cubism, Surrealism—developed theories as far removed from Manet as Manet had been from Alberti. The idea of the artist as a Bohemian outsider came out of this revolution, as did the contempt that artists would develop for the public, an obsession with self-expression and iconoclasm, and the rejection of classical standards of beauty as an objective of art. Abstraction is a meta-invention that has much to answer for. But in its first flush and at its best, it produced works from 1850 to our cutoff point of 1950 that have so far survived the test of time as judged by the opinions of experts, prices in the auction room, and popularity in the museums.

The Invention of Polyphony. Central France, 11C–13C.

When thinking about meta-inventions in music, five candidates come to mind, each of sweeping importance: musical scales, musical notation, the diatonic scale, polyphony, and tonal harmony. I judge the first three and the fifth, to be near misses. The invention of musical scales looks promising, but music antedated the invention of scales, just as painting antedated the invention of artistic realism, and it is hard to tell to what degree musical forms actually expanded after the definition of formal scales. The invention of musical notation enabled a musical tradition to build upon the work of the past, but musical notation is in one sense a specific manifestation of the invention of writing. Also, as in the case of scales, it is not clear that musical notation is sufficient unto itself. It is a *necessary* condition for the expansion and development of musical expression (India's lack of an adequate system of notation is a case in point[11]), but having a system of notation apparently did not lead to radically changed music in either ancient Greece or China.

The third candidate for a meta-invention is the discovery of the connection between mathematical ratios and musical intervals attributed to Pythagoras in the West and later independently discovered by the Chinese.[12] These formed the basis for the scales that became the building blocks of the music of the West. But whether Pythagoras gave us a cognitive tool for thinking about music that is qualitatively different from the cognitive tool represented by other scales is doubtful. There is also the historical fact that the invention of the diatonic scale did not, as far as we know, in and of itself enable people to compose music that was markedly different from the music they had been composing before. Finally, there is the quite specifically physical aspect of notes, vibrating at certain frequencies. All in all, I put the Pythagorean scale on the borderline but tipping toward the wheel or printing press variety of invention rather than meta-invention.

The fourth candidate for a meta-invention, the invention of polyphony, is unequivocally the real thing. Just as linear perspective added depth to the length and breadth of a painting, polyphony added, metaphorically, a vertical dimension to the horizontal line of melody.

We cannot be sure that polyphony was not developed by the Greeks. We know from Plato and Aristotle that music was considered to be a force that shaped character, ethical behavior, and society itself. To have achieved that role, Greek music must have been considerably more powerful than a few simple melodies. But as far as can be determined from the evidence, every previous musical tradition, Greek or otherwise, consisted of horizontal linkages of notes placed one after the other, forming melodies. The melody might have a rhythmic accompaniment. Many instruments might be involved in playing the melody. But the music had a single, linear melodic line. Polyphony was the first expression of the idea that notes could be stacked on top of one another, creating musical lines that went different directions at the same time.

Technically, polyphony has a narrow meaning. It is music in which simultaneous voice or instrumental parts are in two or more melodic lines, each of which can stand alone. Exactly where and when polyphony began is uncertain.[13] The Welsh apparently sang in different parts very early, and so did the Danes. It may well be that other folk cultures had local musical traditions that used simultaneous melodic lines. But the main sequence for the development of polyphony came through the Catholic monasteries, especially the great monastery of St. Martial in Limoges, in central France, via an evolution of the method of singing prayers called *organum*. Originally consisting of a few tones not even resembling a melody, *organa* grew gradually more complex. We know that by 11C two-part *organa* were being sung in Winchester, England. By 12C, *organa* were being sung in which the lower voice served as the principal melody while the upper, solo voice sang phrases of varying length against it. The end of 12C and the beginning of 13C saw the advent of named composers of polyphonic music, Léonin and Pérotin. The music grew more complex and sophisticated. Secular versions of polyphony began to develop, as the troubadours adapted polyphony to their popular melodies. The motet—a polyphonic, unaccompanied choral composition—began to flourish, soon adding a third part and sometimes being sung in French rather than Latin.

The process that had begun with the invention of polyphony would continue for centuries. If one were looking for the most dazzling immediate effects of a musical invention, the most promising candidate would not be the original invention of polyphony, but the development of modern tonal (major-minor) harmony that began in the Renaissance and reached its full expression in the Baroque. It is tonal harmony that made possible the music from the Baroque, Classical, and Romantic eras, and that fills most of today's concert programs. But tonal harmony falls in the category of a great invention that builds on a more fundamental expansion of the human cognitive repertoire—in this instance, the idea that music has a vertical dimension as well as a horizontal one. Notes can be stacked. Melodies can be stacked. Once that idea was in the air, all else became possible.

The Invention of Drama. Greece, in the century following −534, and India, date unknown.

Identifying the source of meta-inventions in literature is difficult because so many of them have roots in prehistory. Literature itself, in the sense of making up stories and consciously imposing structure on them, is a meta-invention, but no one knows when or where it began. We must assume that story-telling came early, as one of man's first amusements around the fire at night. The invention of fiction, meaning stories with characters that are neither historical nor taken from established mythology, is another meta-invention that almost certainly predates −800.[14] What we do know for certain is that literature as a meta-invention was already in a highly developed form by the time of the *Ramayana* and *Mahabharata* in India and the *Iliad* and *Odyssey* in the West, all of which had appeared in written form by −4C and had been recited long before that.

The invention of the performer and the audience is also immeasurably old. Archaeologists have uncovered spaces that seem to have served as theatres for large audiences in the earliest civilizations of East Asia, Europe, and the Americas. We do not know exactly how and when these evolved from rituals in which the members of the audience were also participants to performances in which the audience became purely spectators.

The invention of drama is a separate meta-invention, postdating −800, with a known history. If we trust a rhetorician named Themistius, the crucial event took place in −534, when a poet named Thespis—the source of the word *thespian*—created a character that stood apart from the Greek chorus which until then had been a unitary voice telling the story. This individual engaged in a dialogue with the chorus and, stunning departure that it was, pretended to be someone he was not. He was called the Answerer, which in ancient Greek was Hypocrites, the source of *hypocrite* and *hypocrisy*.

The development of the dramatic role once again added a new dimension to an existing art, putting new obligations on both the performer and the spectator. The performer must pretend to be another person. The spectator must ignore all the imperfections of the pretense that, acknowledged, would spoil the effect. If both performer and spectator did their respective jobs, the resulting collaboration was nothing less than the ability to observe events outside one's own life.

Drama went from a standing start to historic peaks within a century. The chorus was reduced to about a dozen people and its role as narrator was slashed, with multiple individual roles carrying the burden of the drama. Stages evolved, incorporating multiple entrances, painted scenery, and scene changes. Actors were masked and costumed to fit their parts. And what a stunning outpouring of plays this infant genre got to work with—the tragedies of Aeschylus, Sophocles, and Euripides, and the comedies of Aristophanes.

A similar evolution must have taken place in India. It is known that the tradition of public recitations of epic poetry goes back several centuries before the Christian era. By the time of the great Indian poet and playwright Kalidasa, circa 5C, the dramatic form was well established. Beyond that little can be said about the timing or nature of the Indian invention of drama, or whether Alexander's invasion of the western edge of the Indian subcontinent in −4C conveyed any information about Greek drama to India.

The Invention of the Novel. Europe from 1500, culminating in England, 1740–1749.

Other genres of literature—the lyric poem, nonfiction essay, historical narrative and analysis, memoir, biography, and philosophical dialogue among them—have been highly developed for more than 2,000 years. Changes in technology have played a major role in the way that drama has been staged, with the invention of the motion picture creating an altogether new form of drama. But these changes, while they expanded the forms of expression of poetry and drama respectively, did not radically alter the literary experience. The exception, and the sole meta-invention in literature since the invention of drama, is the novel.

If by *novel* we mean simply a fictional prose narrative of substantial length, then we have had novels for 2,000 years as well, with Petronius' *Satyricon* and Apuleius' *Golden Ass* being the most highly regarded examples surviving from ancient Rome. The first great novel is often said to be *The Tale of Genji*, written by a lady of the Japanese court, Murasaki Shikibu, circa 1010. But *novel* is technically used to name something more than a long fictional prose narrative, and it is in that more specific sense that I use the word here.

In Lionel Trilling's words, the novel is "a perpetual quest for reality, the field of its research being always the social world, the material of its analysis being always manners as the indication of the direction of man's soul."[15] The essential characteristic of the novel in this more specific sense, that it constitutes a simulacrum of real life, sets it apart from the genres that went before.

WHY NOT FILM?

The mention of film raises an obvious question: Why not include motion pictures as a form of drama, and therefore as part of the literature inventory?

In assembling the inventory of authors, I entered data on screenwriters whenever a source mentioned them. But biographical dictionaries of literature did not include film directors, who are typically more truly the artistic creators of films than the screenwriters, and literature histories that have comprehensive coverage of drama seldom cover film.

That left the option of creating a separate inventory for film, an attractive solution if *Human Accomplishment* were being written a hundred years from now. But when the cutoff date for the inventories is set at 1950, only 23 years after the first talking picture, creating a separate inventory for film seemed premature.

Not completely apart—that's why the *Satyricon* and *Tale of Genji* are called novels by some critics—but substantially so.

Jacques Barzun dates the first novel to 1500 and the appearance of the anonymous *La Vida de Lazarillo de Tormes*.[16] *Lazarillo*'s hero is an orphan who becomes a servant, not a nobleman. The book depicts society matter-of-factly, neither idealizing nor satirizing it. Its characters are just that—characters, with complex strengths and weaknesses, virtues and vices.

Lazarillo was followed a century later by Cervantes' *Don Quixote*, widely seen as the first great Western novel, but still a transitional work, integrating large dollops of allegory, philosophy, and the fantastical alongside its rich portrayal of character and social scene. Madame de Lafayette's *La Princesse de Clèves* (1678) was another precursor. But it was not until Samuel Richardson's *Pamela* in 1740 and, a decade later, Henry Fielding's *Tom Jones*, that the novel reached the form as we know it today, and opened an outpouring of work in 19C that would transform literature throughout the West.

Nothing quite like the novel developed in China, Japan, or India until late 19C, when it was adapted from the Western model. China and Japan (though not India) had produced works that portrayed common people and gave detailed descriptions of social life. A famous anonymous Chinese work,

Jin Pingmei, not only portrayed the details of everyday life in 16C China but contained such detailed accounts of sexual practices that early translators felt compelled to render them in Latin. However, elements of the supernatural remained woven into Chinese fiction through the end of 19C, and the plots were more episodic than in the Western form—characteristics that are true even of the work often labeled the greatest Chinese novel, Cao Zhan's *Dream of the Red Chamber*. In Japan, the *Tale of Genji* was followed in 17C by a writer ranked second only to Murasaki Shikibu, Ihara Saikaku, who wrote two immensely popular books, *The Life of an Amorous Man* and *Five Women Who Loved Love*, that could be called novels in a loose sense. But while Saikaku sparked a brief flurry of imitators, Japanese literary energy at that time was directed toward poetry and drama. Perhaps the best evidence that the Western novel never really had a counterpart in China, Japan, and India before their contact with the West comes from the commentary of Chinese, Japanese, and Indian intellectuals *after* contact with the West. In each case, it was recognized that the Western novel was something unlike anything in their own tradition.

The emergence of the novel is important for many reasons, but the most salient is the way in which the novel added a new dimension not just for creating beauty, but for seeking out truths. Writers since Homer had been trying to get at the truth of the human condition in its psychological dimensions, and the greatest writers succeeded spectacularly well even in ancient times. But there was hardly anything at all in the fictional literatures of the world about humans as social creatures. The novel made that inquiry possible, and in so doing made literature a partner with the social and behavioral sciences in understanding how humans and human societies work.

META-INVENTIONS IN PHILOSOPHY

The first surviving written records of philosophic thinking postdate the first civilizations. Sumer and Egypt must have had wise men who were famous for teachings that today we would call philosophy, but their work is lost. We have religious texts and ethical homilies from those civilizations, but no systematic inquiries into the nature of knowledge, human existence, and the cosmos—the stuff of philosophy.

The last quarter of −6C saw the opening of a two-century burst of philosophic work across the Eurasian land mass, dating roughly from −520 to −320, in which human beings thought through some large proportion of all the great philosophic issues—not in primitive forms that were later discarded, but as profound philosophic systems.

Both of India's dominating traditions were founded at the outset of this two-century seminal period—Hinduism with the assembly of the *Upanishads* sometime in −6C, and Buddhism with Buddha a century later. In some of the same decades when Buddha was teaching his disciples, so was Confucius in China. In Greece, the earliest thinkers to take up philosophic topics, Thales and Anaximander, were at work in the early part of −6C, followed by Pythagoras at its close.

The period around −350 saw the creation of China's second important tradition, Daoism, the founding documents being the brief, elegant *Dao-de Jing*, attributed to the shadowy figure of Laozi, and the eponymous work of Zhuangzi. At about the same time, Mencius elaborated and systematized Confucianism, laying the foundation for its eventual dominance.

In Greece, the contribution to philosophy during the seminal period is so compressed in time and place that it constitutes one of the enduring mysteries of human accomplishment. The time is a single century from −420 to −320. The place is a single city, Athens, so ravaged by the Peloponnesian War and by plague that the population of free men at Socrates' death in −399

WHAT IS PHILOSOPHY?

"Philosophy asks the simple question, 'What is it all about?'" Alfred North Whitehead once observed, and that is the definition adopted here.[17] Philosophy is an inquiry into the true nature of things, be it the true nature of the universe or the human soul or a table. It overlaps with religion but is distinct from it. Philosophy is "something intermediate between theology and science," in the words of Bertrand Russell,[18] seeking truths about great metaphysical and ethical questions as does religion, but, like science, appealing to the mind instead of faith. This definition permits a number of Western theologians (e.g., Thomas Aquinas) and Buddhist thinkers (e.g., Nagarjuna) to be classified as philosophers. Buddha himself did not invoke a divine being as part of his teachings, and he too qualifies here as a philosopher. The teachings of Jesus and Muhammad seem qualitatively different in this regard, containing philosophical elements but ones that are subordinate to their religious message, and they are not part of the philosophy inventory.

may have fallen as low as 21,000.[19] In that time and place, in successive teacher-student relationships, came Socrates, Plato, and Aristotle, each of whom constitutes one of the great figures of Western intellectual history.

The profusion of great work in China, India, and Greece in those few centuries shaped their respective civilizations in ways so pervasive that their role has become invisible. Hardly anyone in the West thinks of himself as an Aristotelian, for example, even though Western ways of conceptualizing virtue, happiness, the beautiful, and logic still trace back to Aristotle's teachings. Comparatively few Chinese still think of themselves as Confucians, even though the values they act upon in daily life may reflect Confucius's teachings. The great thinkers of the world from −6C to −4C established the frames of reference with which we still approach the world we live in. Cutting across their contributions to metaphysics, epistemology, aesthetics, and ethics were two new cognitive tools that qualify as my opening nominations for meta-inventions in philosophy, one from India and another from Greece. They are also strangely related. In the realm of cognitive tools, they are mirror images, *yin* and *yang*, matter and anti-matter, polar opposites: the inventions of meditation and of logic.

The Invention of Meditation. India, culminating circa −200.

Shortly after *Homo sapiens* developed consciousness, he must also have become aware of one of the curious aspects of consciousness, its chaotic substrate. However lucid the conversation we may be holding, or however intently we think we are concentrating on the task before us, a little self-examination quickly shows that, flowing along just below the surface of the coherent line of thought, is a string of flighty, unpredictable, apparently uncontrollable other thoughts, irrelevant to what we're supposed to be thinking about. Try to walk for a hundred yards, for example, while thinking about nothing but the act of walking. Untrained people can seldom get beyond the first few steps without finding that their attention has already wandered.

In this simple observation about the nature of human consciousness lies a challenge that was taken up sometime in the course of Hinduism's long development: focus the mind so that the tumble of extraneous thoughts is slowed, then stilled altogether. The practice that developed, which we know as meditation, is of unknown antiquity. It was certainly already in use when the *Upanishads* were put into writing circa −6C. An archaic form may be inferred from the *Rig Veda*, which takes the practice back at least to −1200. If recent arguments that the *Rig Veda* dates to the Indus-Sarasvati civilization hold up, then we must think in terms of an additional millennium or two during which some form of meditation was practiced. I have dated the culmination of the development of meditation to −2C because that is the most popular dating for the life of Patanjali, the Hindu sage who is seen as the progenitor of classical Yoga, an advanced system of meditation.

Since its initial development in India, forms of meditation have become part of most religions and of a wide range of secular schools as well. In the West, despite the importance of forms of meditation in Catholicism and some Protestant Christian churches, the word *meditation* has become identified with some of the flamboyant sects that attracted publicity in the 1960s and 1970s. In some circles, meditation is seen as part of Asian mysticism, not a cognitive tool. This is one instance in which Eurocentrism is a genuine problem. The nature of meditation is coordinate with ways of perceiving the world that are distinctively Asian. But to say that the cognitive tool called meditation is peculiarly useful to Asians is like saying that logic—my next meta-invention—is useful only to Europeans. Meditation and logic found homes in different parts of the world, but meditation, like logic, is a flexible, powerful extension of human cognitive capacity.

The Invention of Logic. Athens, −4C.

At about the same time that meditation reached an advanced form in India, the West was inventing the mode of thought that would be as influential in shaping and embodying the course of Western history as meditation was in shaping and embodying the course of Asian history. Parmenides had begun the process in −5C. Instead of merely stating his vision of epistemology (he was disputing Heraclitus), he presented an argument on its behalf. He tried to reason, struggling to understand what was real and what was illusory by means of abstract ratiocination. Medieval legends to the contrary, Parmenides did not invent logic, but he was trying to make use of dimly apprehended principles that would eventually become logic.

Others, notably the Sophists and Zeno of Elea with his famous paradoxes, flirted at the edges of logic, extending the kind of reasoning used by Parmenides into more sophisticated (note the root of that word) forms. Plato added structure to their work, distinguishing affirmation from negation and suggesting that the reasoning of the Socratic dialogue could be a generalizable method for reaching the truth. But it was left to the Promethean mind of Aristotle to discover the basic principles of logic and to establish a discipline that has continued to develop to this day.

Aristotle's works on logic are known collectively as the *Organon*, which translates as *tool* or *instrument*, reflecting Aristotle's awareness that logic represented not a science unto itself, but a resource that could be brought to every aspect of man's exploration of the nature of the world around him and the nature of reality itself. It is from Aristotle that we receive the vocabulary of logic: the syllogism, the types of logical fallacy, the elements of deductive reasoning, and a long list of terms for analyzing propositions. Underlying all the specifics was a radical expansion of the way humans could think about what was true and not true. Being held to the rules of logic is what ultimately enables us to move beyond the child's "'Tis so, 'Tis not" level of dispute. It forces discipline upon our thinking and, at least sometimes, provides a way to save ourselves from our prejudices. In the sciences, Aristotle's invention of logic turned out to be a mixed blessing. Its power was so great that the importance of logic overrode empiricism for centuries. But when the balance was restored, logic once again stood as one of empiricism's strongest allies; together, they produced the scientific revolution.

The Invention of Ethics. China, India, and Greece, −520 to −320.

A number of other achievements of philosophy might be nominated as meta-inventions, starting with the invention of the philosophical outlook itself. The invention of empiricism is still another obvious candidate, which I will instead fold into the discussion of meta-inventions in science. The effects of Judaic monotheism, especially as modified by Christianity, were so pervasive that it is tempting to treat it as a meta-invention, inappropriate as the word "invention" may be. But I will confine myself to just one more meta-invention in philosophy: ethics conceived independently of religion.

It may seem an odd thing to assert that ethics began only a few centuries before the Christian era. Definitions of right behavior go back as far as the advent of civilization and in recent times have been found by anthropologists to exist among every known human tribe. Even the most ancient codes of right behavior could be elaborate, with the books of the Torah offering a readily available example. But, at least as far as anything in the surviving record tells us, the codes were constructed as expressions of the will of gods or rulers. This is not to say that they were irrational. The aspects of law that dealt with justice reveal concepts of fairness and proportionality that we recognize in our own legal codes, with the Mosaic Law of the Old Testament again providing a window into early ways of dealing with complex cases. But until about –5C, we have nothing that puts the question of right behavior in the following fashion: *Here we are, human beings, living a relatively short span of years in the company of other human beings. What is the underlying nature of a human life? How should this underlying nature lead us to comport ourselves, both for our own private happiness and to create harmonious and happy communities?* It was the first attempt to answer such questions independently of religion that I call the invention of ethics.

Two issues regarding the invention of ethics need to be separated. One involves the merits of the different systems, which I will not try to assess. The practical reality is that people who adhere to the teachings of Confucius's *Analects,* Aristotle's *Nicomachean Ethics,* or Buddhism's *Tipitaka* will behave in generous, compassionate, and civil ways that each of those ethical systems would describe as virtuous. I wish to emphasize another issue: The new cognitive tool was the idea that right behavior *could* be thought about, and *must* be thought about, by trying to understand the meaning of virtue independently of gods and kings. The consequences would cascade down the centuries.

Chief among these consequences was the development of political theory. Before the invention of ethics, kings might be individually good or bad and just or unjust, but thinkers had no template against which to think about whether the political system was good or bad. The essence of political thought about systems requires one to ask of any given set of rules or laws, Good for *what*? The proximate answer is that a system must be good for the human beings who live under that system.

When it comes to specific issues, knowing just the immediate outcomes of a policy seems to make it easy enough to decide whether a given policy is good or bad. Does the trash collection policy result in trash being collected or not? Does transportation policy result in the trains running on time? But as we generalize from the specifics of collecting trash and running trains to more general questions of deciding what laws are appropriate, how leaders should be chosen, and what powers they should be given, we are forced back to a deeper question: what does it mean for a system to be good for human beings? What is it that human beings *are,* in their fundamental nature? What does it mean to live a fulfilling human life? What are the limits and potentialities of human beings as social creatures? It is the answers to those questions that ultimately form that missing template against which to assess how a political system corresponds to the nature of man, and then for assessing the degree to which a political system is good or bad. It was the invention of the idea of ethics that enabled this process to begin.

The relationship is most obvious in China, where the dominating topics of Confucianism were man as a social being and the nature of a rightly ordered society, but the links between Aristotle's ethics and subsequent political theory are no less rich. I would argue that the development of liberal democracy itself is intimately linked with the invention of ethics—and enter the *Federalist Papers* as my first exhibit.

META-INVENTIONS IN MATHEMATICS

Number systems themselves might seem to be the prototype of the meta-invention in mathematics, but they are almost as universal as language. Egypt, Sumer, India, China, and, later but independently, the Maya had number systems. Credit for the first fully developed number system goes to the Egyptians, circa −3500, who had a system with a base of 10 and separate pictographs for each power of 10 up to 10 million. A closer approximation to a meta-invention in the centuries before −800 is the invention of positional notation, which occurred sometime in the vicinity of −2400 in Sumer.

After −800, an indefinite number of mathematical achievements could meet the criteria I set out for meta-inventions, because every invention in mathematics is the invention of a cognitive tool. Take, for example, the invention of non-Euclidean geometries by Bolyai and Lobachevsky in the 1820s. What could be more clearly a new dimension than the invention of a wholly new geometric system? But of course the invention of calculus in the late 1600s by Newton and Leibniz also was a new cognitive tool with far-reaching applications. And then there was the invention of Boolean algebra in the 1840s, applying algebra to logic. But if the question is which developments in mathematics opened up completely new ways of thinking mathematically, three developments seem to this non-mathematician to be qualitatively different from the rest.

The Invention of the Mathematical Proof. Greece, circa −585.

The mathematicians of Sumer, Egypt, China, and India achieved great things by using informal rules and principles. The Chinese and Indians went the furthest. It appears that the Chinese understood the properties of the Pythagorean triangle a thousand years before Pythagoras. In about −300, the *Juizhang Suanshu* laid out the solutions to more than 200 problems on engineering, surveying, right triangles, and calculation. In 3C, the

META-INVENTIONS IN GOVERNMENT AND COMMERCE

Mentioning politics may remind you that I omitted government and commerce from the inventories of human accomplishment. What might the meta-inventions be for those arenas? I can at least list some likely candidates.

In commerce, the basics occurred prior to –800. Agriculture was founded through the invention of the *cultivated crop*, which derives from a cognitive tool: seeds can be planted, not just harvested. It dates to roughly –8000. Conceptually, the *domestication of animals* is quite similar, and can be treated as a conglomerate meta-invention. The idea of *division of labor*, the necessary if not sufficient condition for the existence of an economy, could be even older, dating back to flint-knappers and other specialists within Paleolithic hunter-gatherer tribes. A more recent meta-invention, attributable primarily to Adam Smith, is the concept that *a voluntary, informed exchange always benefits both parties*: commerce is not a zero-sum game.

The inventions of *money* and *credit* date back to the earliest records from Sumer. The invention of *paper money*, conceptually distinct from the invention of money, is more recent, 9C, in China. The idea of *accounting*—not any particular method, but the concept of keeping track of inflows and outflows of money—is a good candidate for a meta-invention in commerce. So is the idea of *managing risk*, though it is largely a product of a meta-invention in mathematics, probability theory. The invention of *mass production* is even more recent, dating from the last half of 18C.

In government, what one considers to be a meta-invention depends in part on what one considers the proper role of government to be. In this, I am at one end of the spectrum, believing that government has extremely limited legitimate functions, and so my list of meta-inventions is shorter than others would devise. A natural first candidate is the invention of *law*, but law in the simplest sense of rules governing a group may be akin to speech: Something that arises naturally as part of human groups, however primitive. I will leave it to someone more qualified to specify the landmark conceptual changes in the law that fit the meaning of meta-invention. One of those changes in the concept of law that spills over into meta-inventions in government involves the idea that *government is contractual*, with provisions that bind both the governors and the governed. The idea that *the purpose of government is to serve the governed* qualifies as a meta-invention, as does the concept that *government derives from the consent of the governed*. I would also nominate the concept of natural rights, identified most closely with John Locke in late 17C, as a meta-invention, while others would nominate the ideas that gave rise to the welfare state. At this point, one person's meta-invention is another's meta-mistake, and I will desist from further nominations.

Chinese developed a method of approximation that foreshadowed what is known in the West as Horner's method, named for the Westerner who developed it 1,700 years later. The *Brahma-sphuta-siddhanta*, written by the Hindu mathematician Brahmagupta early in 7C—the same book through which the Arabs became familiar with Arabic numerals—contained discussions of second-degree indeterminate equations, permutations and combinations, and cyclic quadrilaterals.

But the unsystematic inventive genius of individuals could take mathematics only so far. Mathematics as we know it today has a unique structure among the domains of human accomplishment. We may speak metaphorically of Michelangelo's work resting on a foundation laid by the Greeks, or of Newton standing on the shoulders of the giants who had gone before. In mathematics, the structure into which any new contribution fits is more literal. Any given bit of mathematical knowledge within a given field can be related to every other bit within that field by means of specific steps. Sometimes the relationship can be discerned only by tracing all the way down the structure to the axioms of the system, and then heading up on a different path, but the relationship always exists, and is always completely specifiable.

The raw material of that structure is the mathematical proof: rigorous logic leading to a valid conclusion from a minimal set of axioms. It seems to have been a Greek invention—nothing like it has been found in earlier traditions—but assigning more specific credit is hazardous. The earliest specific proof is attributed to Thales, the man often called the first scientist, and a man credited with feats that, if all true, would make him as protean in his accomplishments as Aristotle. He came from Miletus, an ancient city in Asia Minor, and he lived from around −624 to −547. His first mathematical proof—he is said to have produced five in all—was that the diameter divides a circle into two equal parts. The result is in itself trivial. The meta-invention it exemplifies is that mathematical relationships have a structure that can be spelled out, and that the spelling-out can lead to knowledge that can be built upon. If you know A for certain, then you can rigorously prove that other implications, such as B, must also be true. You can use B to prove C. By the time you are proving F and G and H, you are discovering mathematical truths that are not as perceptible by direct inspection. By the time you reach the Zs, you are in the realm of mathematical truths that not even the most gifted mathematical improviser could find.

Thales's proofs were flawed by the standards of a later age, but were good enough that they started a line of Greek mathematicians who, by the time of Euclid, had laid the foundations of geometry. In the process, the repertoire of mathematical logic had also expanded. Thales used deduction, but Euclid's *Elements* also contained indirect proofs, or proof by *reductio ad absurdum*, establishing the truth of a statement by proving that the contradiction of it is wrong. Other forms of mathematical logic were recognized early, but were not formally described until later—the first use of the term "inductive proof" did not occur until Augustus de Morgan's work in 1838.

The nature of the mathematical proof is related to Aristotelian logic, but mathematical logic predates Aristotelian logic in time and, it may be argued, transcends it in power. Aristotelian logic must be conjoined with empirical investigation if it is to be applied to questions of real-world phenomena—a lesson that took some 1,500 years to learn—but mathematical logic erected the vast structure of modern mathematics with nothing but its own internal rigor. Mathematics has been invaluable to investigations of the real world, though the real world need be of no interest to mathematicians.

The Invention of Arabic Numerals, Including Zero.
India, no later than 8C.

That the number system we call *Arabic* has been adopted the world over is testimony to how indispensable it became to mathematics once it was known. But reaching the full set of ten symbols took a long time and went through many cultures.

The most crucial of the numbers is zero, and competition for the credit of inventing it has been intense. The ambiguous reality seems to be that though the Egyptians, Babylonians, Greeks, and Indians all had symbols they occasionally used to represent zero at dates ranging from thousands to hundreds of years before Christ, in none of those cases did zero take a full and consistent place in the number system. This failure is especially mystifying in the case of the Greeks. Archimedes famously managed to represent a number greater than the number of grains of sand in a space the size of the universe with nary a zero. "How could he have missed it?" complained Carl Gauss.[20]

The next landmark comes in 662, when the bishop Severus Sebokht in Syria wrote that the Hindus had developed methods of computation surpassing anything the Greeks had done. But then the bishop says that the Hindus used nine symbols to achieve this wonder, which suggests that zero still had not fully come into its own. Seventy years later, during the reign of the Arabian caliph al-Mansur, the *Brahma-sphuta-siddhanta* was translated into Arabic and the Arabs took possession of the full ten-numeral set. The great Arabic mathematician al-Khwarizmi wrote up a full description of the system in about 810 in *Hisab al-jabr w'al-musqabalah*. Thus, within decades of its debut outside India, zero was used in the same work that gave the world algebra (and the word itself—sound out the title), the first example of the transforming effect that Arabic numbers would have on the development of mathematics.

The Calibration of Uncertainty. Europe, 1565–1657.

An intuitive sense of the notions underlying probability has probably characterized winning gamblers since gambling was invented. The Greeks had a word for probability, *eikos*, with the modern meaning of "to be expected with some degree of certainty," and Aristotle came close to putting quantities to it when he wrote in *De Caelo* that ". . . to repeat the same throw ten thousand times with the dice would be impossible, whereas to make it once or twice is comparatively easy."[21] But against this limited qualitative understanding that some things were more probable than others was acute awareness of chance in the affairs of humans, uncontrollable and unfathomable.

The intuitions of gamblers began to find their way into mathematics in 1494, when a Franciscan monk named Luca Paccioli posed what came to be known as the "problem of the points," drawing from a gambling game called *balla*. "A and B are playing a fair game of *balla*," he stipulated. "They agree to continue until one has won six rounds. The game actually stops when A has won five and B three. How should the stakes be divided?"[22] The first approach to answering the question was given about fifty years later by Girolamo Cardano, a Renaissance polymath and a self-confessed chronic gambler, but was not published until 1663.

The credit for inventing probability theory goes to Blaise Pascal and Pierre de Fermat, who in the course of a correspondence in the 1650s solved the problem of the points by means of what has become known as Pascal's Triangle, a way of laying out the number of ways in which a particular event can occur. Armed with Pascal's Triangle, it is possible to determine the proportion that any one, or any combination, of those events represents of the total.

Christiaan Huygens put the capstone on basic probability theory with "De Ratioiniis in Ludo Aleae" ("Of Reasoning with Random Lots") in 1657. He presented a sequence of 15 propositions and established the crucial concept of mathematical expectation, as in his third proposition: If the number of chances leading to *a* is *p*, and the number of chances leading to *b* is *q*, and all chances are equally likely, then the expectation is valued at

PRECURSORS

Pascal's Triangle had been foreshadowed 350 years earlier by Chinese mathematician Zhu Shijie's "Precious Mirror of the Four Elements," yet another example of the way the Chinese originated, but did not follow up, inventions, discoveries, and insights that later became key elements in the development of Western science and technology.

The credit for the first known quantification of possible outcomes goes to the Talmud, which denies the right of a man to divorce his wife without penalty for adultery that occurred before marriage. The Talmud argues that the authorities face a double doubt: that the premarital loss of virginity was due to another man (a yes/no possibility) and that it was voluntary on the bride's part (another yes/no possibility). Only one in four of the scenarios leading to the deflowered bride justifies a divorce without penalty, the Talmud correctly concludes.[23]

$$\frac{pa + qb}{p + q}.$$

Pascal's work had gone further than Huygens's in some respects, but Huygens's clear structure for laying out probability theory made his work the one that was read, cited, and translated in the years that followed.[24]

The discovery that uncertainty could be calibrated fundamentally changed human capacity to acquire and manage knowledge. In science, it led not only to the edifice of statistical analysis that is indispensable in all the hard sciences, the social sciences, engineering, and industrial processes of all sorts, but to the unraveling of mysteries that could be understood only in terms of probabilities—quantum theory is one example. In economics, the ability to analyze reality not just in terms of yes or no, but as precise numbers in between, enabled the management of risk that in turn makes possible modern economies.

META-INVENTIONS IN SCIENCE

I offer just two meta-inventions in science. The first is the invention of the secular observation of nature. The second is the invention of the scientific method—a meta-invention that consists of several components that could as easily be treated as meta-inventions on their own.

The Invention of the Secular Observation of Nature.
Greece and China, circa −600.

Human beings have always had a practical side that enabled them to put aside worries about the gods and their whims long enough to deal with the reality of the world around them. The distances that technology could advance with this amount of practicality were great. But as far as the record enables historians to judge such things, humans in prehistory and down through the Egyptian civilization saw nature and its forces as beyond inquiry, inherently unknowable. The gods disposed.

Sometime around −6C, a new idea began to emerge: Nature and its forces could be observed and understood. *The secular observation of nature* is no more exotic than that—and no less revolutionary. Human beings could look at sunrises, storms, the flowering of plants, and the death of parents independently of whatever they might believe about gods. They could record their observations and think about why these phenomena came about.

In the West, the invention of secular observation is attributed to Thales of Miletus, whose early mathematical proofs I have already mentioned. The specific accomplishments attributed to Thales, keeping in mind that none of his actual writings survive, include the first geological observation (the effects of streams on erosion of land), the first systematic description of magnetism, and the discovery of triboelectrification. But the overarching accomplishment of Thales, or the group of innovators whose work came to be associated with his name, was to realize that such phenomena were susceptible to human observation. Thales was soon followed by Leucippus, in the middle of −5C, who argued that all events have natural causes, and by Hippocrates at the beginning of −4C, who undertook the first systematic empirical observation of medical phenomena.

The Chinese independently adopted an empirical approach to nature early. Bone records indicate that systematic meteorological records of precipitation and winds were being kept as early as −13C, but apparently for purposes of divination rather than weather forecasting.[25] Accurate astronomical observations of planetary movements, sunspots, and eclipses also date deep into Chinese history, but again primarily for purposes of divination. Without trying to assign precedence, it may at least be said that by the time

Thales was at work in Greece, the Chinese had also developed a secular, observational approach that was used to understand the nature of the world around them. By −4C, for example, the Chinese had already deduced the water cycle of rain and evaporation.

The difference between Greece and China was that the development of secular observation of nature in Europe slowed after a few centuries, was more or less stagnant (with a few exceptions) during the Roman Empire, and then retrogressed for centuries, while in China progress continued without a break. It was not until well into the Renaissance that Europe caught up and passed China, and the mechanism for doing that was not simple observation, but the last of the meta-inventions I will nominate, the invention of the scientific method.

The Invention of the Scientific Method. Europe, 1589–1687.

I have not tried to organize the meta-inventions in order of importance because they are too obviously incomparable. However, it is hard to avoid the conclusion that the invention of the scientific method is primus inter pares, in this sense: in combination with mathematics, the scientific method has given us the world we live in today. The other meta-inventions enriched human life, but recall the descriptions of life in Antonine Rome and Song China in Chapter 3, and all the ways in which, at least for the affluent, daily life resembled our own. Now think of the ways in which today's daily life does *not* resemble life in Antonine Rome and Song China. Almost all of them owe their existence to the invention of the scientific method.

A near miss: Chinese experimentalism in the first millennium. The boundary between the scientific method and any other sort of empirical investigation blurs as the thoroughness of ordinary empirical investigation increases. In the case of the Chinese, empirical investigation had become so sophisticated by the Song Dynasty that it lacked only a few refinements to qualify as science. For example, a Chinese text written in 340 describes a practice among orange growers in the southern provinces. At a certain time of year they would go to the market where they could purchase bags containing a variety of ant that ate the mites that damaged the orange trees.[26] This practice cannot be ascribed to the kind of trial and error that might lead a primitive tribe to discover useful herbal remedies. It required an understanding of the damage that certain mites did to oranges, an understanding of the feeding habits of different kinds of ants, and a clear sense of causation. It is hard to imagine how that understanding could have developed without some form of natural experiment being observed as well. In any case, we are seeing the result of systematic investigation, by persons unknown, that produced complex, empirically valid understandings of causation in nature.

The capacity to develop causal explanations from observational data extended as well to scholarly fields. In the year 1070, Chinese scholar Shen Gua wrote:

> Now I myself have noticed that Yendang Shan is different from other mountains. All its lofty peaks are precipitous, abrupt, sharp and strange; its huge cliffs, 300 meters high, are different from what one finds in other places. . . . Considering the reasons for these shapes, I think that (for centuries) the mountain torrents have rushed down, carrying away all sand and earth, thus leaving the hard rocks standing alone.[27]

Shen Gua then goes on to describe the process of sedimentation and infers that "in this way the substance of the whole continent must have been laid down." As Joseph Needham, the translator of these passages, dryly observes, "Thus in the eleventh century Shen Gua fully understood those conceptions which, when stated by James Hutton in 1802, were to be the foundation of modern geology."[28] If what Shen Gua was doing was not science, it was a first cousin.

The Chinese also came close to the scientific stance in their attitude toward the acquisition of knowledge as a cumulative, disinterested enterprise. Even as the Confucian and Daoist traditions appealed to a lost Golden Age, Chinese scholars just as consistently argued that old ideas must give way to new ones when new observations point the way. When Liu Jo sought authorization for a new geodetic survey of a meridian arc, he wrote to his emperor:

> Thus, the heavens and the earth will not be able to conceal their form, and the celestial bodies will be obliged to yield up to us their measurements. We shall excel the glorious sages of old, and resolve our remaining doubts about the universe. We beg Your Majesty not to give credence to the worn-out theories of former times and not to use them.[29]

The contrast with the unquestioning reverence of medieval scholars for Aristotle and Ptolemy could hardly be sharper. As it happened, the then-emperor did not grant Liu Jo's request, but a subsequent one did. The meridian arc survey was 2,500 kilometers long—another evidence of the seriousness with which the Chinese took the accumulation of knowledge.

The Chinese never completed the scientific project. They brought a consistently pragmatic curiosity to their inquiries and achieved extraordinary insight in individual cases, but they never developed the framework that would enable the accumulation of scientific knowledge.[30]

The real thing: The advent of the scientific method in post-medieval Europe. The historiography on the scientific method is as large as its importance warrants, and it should be understood that I am skipping over a host of complications and nuances.[31] For example, I date the invention of the method within just 98 years, from 1589 (the publication of Galileo's *De Motu*) to 1687 (the publication of Newton's *Principia*). I could as easily have started around 1200, making the total time for the invention of the scientific method considerably longer than the period from *Principia* to today.

That the basic ideas were in the air for so long without being developed suggests how complex and mind-stretching the change was. Indeed, a major continuing issue in the history of science is the degree to which it is appropriate to talk of a scientific method as a body of principles and practice that has clear, bright lines distinguishing it from science practiced by other means. It is not a debate that I am about to adjudicate here. In claiming the scientific method as a meta-invention, or a collection of synergistic meta-inventions, I am associating myself with the position that, incremental as the process may have been, a fundamental change occurred in post-medieval Europe in the way human beings went about accumulating and verifying knowledge. The common-sense understanding of the phrase *scientific method* labels the aggregate of those changes. I use the phrase to embrace the concepts of hypothesis, falsification, and parsimony; the techniques of the experimental method; the application of mathematics to natural phenomena; and a system of intellectual copyright and dissemination.

Hypothesis and experiment. Roger Bacon (c. 1214–1292) is the most famous early proponent of experimentation, but he was augmenting the work of a man who deserves more credit than he usually gets, Robert Grosseteste (c. 1168–1253). Grosseteste is best known to the history of science for his work in optics, and especially for his innovative, if failed, attempt to determine a quantitative law of refraction. It is less often noted that Grosseteste had preceded his work on optics with commentaries on the *Physics* and *Posterior Analytics* of Aristotle that anticipated the basics of the scientific method. Investigations must begin with observed facts, he wrote—a major departure from medieval Scholasticism's devotion to deduction as the way to truth— and then attempt to determine what caused those observed facts. In an even greater leap of imagination, he argued that the causes should be resolved into their component elements and then used to derive a set of expectations that would enable the investigator to reconstruct the phenomena. In effect, Grosseteste had invented the hypothesis, even though the word itself would not enter the English language in its scientific usage until 17C. If experience did not match expectations, then the expectations needed to be rethought, Grosseteste also pointed out—a simple thing to our minds, but in fact the first, inexact statement of the principle of falsification. The investigator can never prove beyond doubt that any hypothesis *is* true (the unobserved exception could always be lurking just around the corner), but a hypothesis can be framed so that it is possible to prove that it is *not* true. As a theoretical issue, the principle of falsification remains contentious.[32] As a practical tool for forcing people to frame their research so that they can be proved wrong, it has immense value.

Parsimony. Around 1320, almost a century after Grosseteste's work, an English Franciscan named William of Ockham, a disputatious man who so irritated the faculty at Oxford that he was never formally awarded his degree, expanded on an idea that had recently been expressed by a Dominican monk, Durandus of Saint-Pourçain.[33] "*Pluralitas non est ponenda sine necessitate,*" Ockham wrote, usually (though not literally) translated as "Entities are not to be multiplied beyond necessity."[34] He invoked this principle so vigorously, and used it to pare away so many opposing theories, that it became known as Ockham's Razor. Today it is known more commonly as the principle of parsimony. Given two theories that explain the known facts, use the simpler until you find reason not to.

On its face, Ockham's Razor may not seem attractive. Complicated explanations are sometimes true. Pick up any social science journal, and you will come away with the impression that complicated explanations are even to be preferred. But the hard sciences work to sterner standards than the social sciences, and Ockham's Razor has served them well. Given any complex body of observations, Ockham's Razor pushes the scientist to find the simplest explanation—like the principle of falsification, imposing a discipline on the researcher that has acted as a useful prod for getting at the underlying truth of things. Even when complications have forced reevaluations of simple models—the discovery of subatomic particles is a case in point—the parsimony principle has served a useful function because simple models are good for revealing anomalies. Commonly, the simpler of two explanations has proved to be the right one.

The invention of controlled data. When the scientists of the Renaissance used the word *experiment*, they commonly meant "putting something to the test" by observing nature. A crucial innovation occurred in 16C with the recognition that phenomena that occurred "naturally" were not essentially different from those that occurred under controlled conditions. The natural philosopher could create controlled situations in which the desired phenomena could be produced and studied at will, and the knowledge he acquired would transfer to naturally occurring events as well.

Galileo's account of his tests of falling bodies in *De Motu*, 1589, is the generally accepted watershed. Others had written on falling bodies before him, and others—notably William Gilbert of *De Magnete*—had used procedures that today we recognize as controlled experimentation. But Galileo reported his experiments with a level of detail and meticulousness that set a standard for natural philosophers thereafter. He had not observed naturally falling bodies, but had constructed situations in which falling bodies could be observed repeatedly, under consistent conditions.

DID GALILEO MAKE UP HIS DATA?

In *De Motu*, Galileo reported that the lighter body falls faster at the beginning, then the heavier body catches up and arrives at the ground slightly before the lighter one. Since this should not be true of the objects that Galileo used, a wooden sphere and an iron one, if they are released simultaneously, it has been inferred that Galileo was either a poor observer or making up his data. But in replications of Galileo's procedure, it has been found that when a light wooden sphere and a heavy iron one are dropped by hand, the lighter wooden sphere does start out its journey a bit ahead—a natural, if misleading, consequence of the need to clutch the heavier iron ball more firmly than the wooden one. This causes the iron ball to be released slightly after the wooden ball even though the experimenter has the impression that he is opening his hands at the same time. Then, because of the differential effects of air resistance on objects of different weight, the iron ball catches up with and passes the wooden ball, just as Galileo reported. There is a satisfying irony in this finding. The modern critics of Galileo were making the same mistake that the ancients made, criticizing results on the basis of what "must be true" rather than going out and doing the work to find out what *is* true.[35]

Scientists' control over their data reached another landmark—and one recognized as such by contemporaries, not just by historians—when Robert Boyle invented an effective air pump in 1657. Almost a decade earlier, Blaise Pascal had inveigled his brother-in-law into carrying an early version of the barometer to the summit of Mont Puy-de-Dôme, proving that the level of mercury rises as altitude increases, and verifying a theory of air pressure that had been evolving for several years. Boyle's apparatus did not require people to climb mountains. Boyle could simulate an atmosphere with progressively thinner air, showing what would have happened if Pascal's brother-in-law had carried the barometer to the summit of Mont Blanc or, for that matter, to a height greater than any mountain on earth.

As time went on, the scientific techniques for structuring the circumstances under which data are observed would add layers of sophistication. Shortly after Boyle began his experiments with the air pump, Francesco Redi decided to test whether maggots were, as generally believed, spontaneously generated by rotting meat. He put one piece of meat on a plate in the open, another on a plate covered by gauze, and discovered that only the exposed piece of meat developed maggots. It was powerful evidence against the theory of spontaneous generation—and also the first known use of a controlled comparison.

By 20C, the scientist's apparatus for simulating nature had gone from Robert Boyle's air pump to machines costing billions of dollars that reproduce the inner workings of stars. Redi's primitive comparison of two plates of meat had evolved into the sophisticated array of techniques for single-blind and double-blind experiments that are a mainstay of research in fields from pharmaceuticals to psychology. The simple yes/no conclusions of experiments in 17C have given way to alternative systems of statistical analysis that deal exclusively in probabilities. But at the origin of it all remains this fundamental cognitive tool: the idea that the observation of natural processes can be manipulated and controlled.

Primary versus secondary qualities. In 1623, Galileo's *The Assayer* laid out a distinction that is a classic example of the cognitive tool—a purely intellectual construct that affects the mindset that scientists take to their investigations. The Aristotelian dogma held that the *matter* out of which something was made (e.g., the marble of a statue) is secondary and the *form* is primary. Galileo looked at things the other way around. The smell of a rose or the sweetness of a peach is its secondary quality, the impression that the rose or the peach makes upon us. The *primary* qualities are those elemental aspects of a thing that create the secondary qualities we experience.

From one perspective, one may ask, What's the difference? Historian Alan Gabbey observes that "previously, opium sent you to sleep because it had a particular dormitive quality: now it sent you to sleep because it had a particular corpuscular micro-structure that acted on your physio-logical structures in such a way that it sent you to sleep."[36] Both views were circular. Practically speaking, however, the difference in viewpoint was profound. Aristotle's perspective confronted the scientist with a massy, opaque, undifferentiated "dormitive quality" of which little could be said. Galileo's perspective tempted the curious onward, promising the chance to understand what that "particular corpuscular micro-structure" might be.

The mathematical structure of nature. Western thinkers from Pythagoras onward had seen mathematics as intimately linked with truths about the universe. Plato himself declared that "the world was God's epistle written to mankind" and that "it was written in mathematical letters." Mathematics were used successfully for a variety of applications, such as predicting the movements of the planets and measuring the circumference of the earth. Archimedes proved mathematically the relationship between the force that needed to be applied to a lever and the distances of the effort and the load from the fulcrum of the lever. But these and a few other precursors notwithstanding, it was left to Galileo to take the decisive step in demonstrating that mathematics was the language of nature, and a language that could be deciphered. Realizing that he couldn't get sufficiently accurate measurements when he dropped objects from a height, Galileo switched to inclined planes down which the balls rolled slowly enough to measure their progress. In his discovery, in 1604, that a systematic relationship exists between the distance traveled and the square of the time lay the first mathematization of a complex physical phenomenon.

The rest of 17C saw a continuing dispute among scientists about the extent to which mathematics should be relied upon, for an underlying tension beset the new enthusiasm for observation and the search for mathematical laws. To say that a physical phenomenon would always, undeviatingly conform to a precise mathematical expression smacked of the overweening dicta that had brought Aristotelian physics to a dead end. Even Boyle, the discoverer of another early mathematization of physical phenomena, adamantly refused to claim that Boyle's Law was a law, preferring to stick to the language of probability. It took Isaac Newton, working at the end of 17C and the beginning of 18C, to silence the doubters. Newton not only discovered a variety of laws that could be expressed mathematically and not only demonstrated that these could be used to predict the outcomes of new experiments with great precision, but he confidently proclaimed that he had in fact discovered *laws*. From Newton onward, the scientific enterprise was to be not just a search for accurate observation and correct understanding of proximate causes, but a search for the underlying mathematical order of things, and a trust in mathematical reasoning as a way of proceeding to new knowledge about the physical world.

Disseminating findings and assigning credit. In nominating the scientific method as the greatest of all the meta-inventions, I am celebrating the method, not the men, and do not mean to imply that scientists are by nature more objective or honest than anyone else. One of the chief merits of the scientific method is that it gives frail humans a system offering them some protection from themselves and permitting knowledge, steadily converging on Truth, to be accumulated from generation to generation. It is appropriate, then, that the final element in this complex meta-invention is one that caters specifically to human frailty, the system for disseminating findings and assigning credit.

Girolamo Cardano, the polymath gambler who figured in the story of probability theory, fortuitously established the first part of the system, the first-to-publish principle. In 1545, he included in his *Ars Magna* a method of solving the cubic equation of the form $x^3+qx^2=r$, a problem that had been vexing mathematicians for centuries. But the method was not his own. It had been worked out by Niccolò Tartaglia who, following the custom of the time, had treated his discovery as a great secret and divulged it only after swearing Cardano to silence. The publication of *Ars Magna* infuriated Tartaglia, and he said so without restraint when he published his own version of the method a year later. But Cardano's perfidy established a new way of doing scientific business. The old road to public esteem was to know something no one else knew and to exploit private knowledge as a sort of franchise. After Cardano, the road to esteem was to discover something no one else knew and to tell everyone as soon as possible, so that you got the credit. It was a rule unnecessary for a world of disinterested scholars, but perfect for a world of jealous and ambitious competitors. It ensured that any new bit of information found by one competitor was made immediately available for the others to build upon and encouraged the correction of error by proving the other fellow wrong.

The second part of the system for disseminating findings was the invention of the scientific report. The problem it solved is exemplified by a famous story from the early days of science, when a professor from Padua denied that Jupiter could have moons, and then refused Galileo's invitation to look through Galileo's telescope to see for himself. Today, the story is told as an example of irrational refusal to confront the truth. At the time, his position was understandable. Galileo's telescope was primitive, looking at the night sky through it required training that the professor from Padua had not acquired, and seeing could not confidently result in believing. When Galileo did assemble disinterested fellow scholars to look through his telescope, they often did not see the moons, and those who saw something could not be sure what that something was.

Other problems arose even when the phenomenon itself could be more unequivocally demonstrated. How was Robert Boyle to communicate his findings about the relationship of the height of a mercury column to the evacuation of air from his air pump? He could assemble witnesses to his experiments and encourage others to replicate his experiment by making public the details of his apparatus. But both methods had their limitations— the number of witnesses in the former case, and the difficulty of reproducing the apparatus in the latter. The solution, in Steven Shapin's phrase, was to make "virtual witnesses" of the readers of Boyle's written reports, by providing such a detailed account of everything that was done, including problems and ambiguities in the results, that the verisimilitude of the account was apparent. Replication remained an option, but Boyle's solution engendered a set of standards—perhaps a culture is a better word—for the write-up of scientific findings that enabled scientists to read the work of another and trust the account enough to base their own work upon it, without having to replicate everything. Violation of that trust became the mortal sin of science, carrying with it professional destruction. So began a scientific tradition that has evolved into the elaborate system of technical articles and responses, the journals and proceedings, the letters and research notes that we know today.

· · ·

So ends my list of 14 cognitive tools created by the mind of man, each of which transformed a domain of human accomplishment. Perhaps others belong as well, but these convey the magnitude of the impact that discrete human accomplishments can have on the world. They also bring us back to a theme I raised in Chapter 4: These inventions did not have to happen. One may argue that all of them would eventually have occurred, given the nature of human intelligence and a long enough period of time. But human intelligence equivalent to our own existed for thousands of years before any of the 14 appeared, and some of them appeared in one civilization without occurring to thinkers in other civilizations.

Pondering these 14 also provokes the question: How many more cognitive tools are still out there, waiting to be discovered? The most recent of the 14 (the invention of abstraction in the visual arts) is only 150 years in the past. It would be imprudent to assume that none are left to discover, if we have the imagination to do so.

Finally, it may have been noticed that the list is not especially multicultural. Two of the 14—meditation and the world's current number system—were invented in India. China and India were independent partners with the Greeks in inventing a third, ethics. China was an independent partner of the Greeks in inventing a fourth, the secular observation of nature. India got shared credit for drama, and I pointed out when appropriate—mostly in discussing the novel and the development of the scientific method—the contributions of non-Western cultures. But that leaves the West importantly or wholly responsible for 12 of the 14 meta-inventions—an imbalance that raises questions about the geography and trajectory of human accomplishment, the topic to which we now turn.

PART THREE

PATTERNS AND TRAJECTORIES

P art 3 provides a wide array of material, much of it technical, preparatory to talking about why great human accomplishment arises and why it declines.

The inventories are overwhelmingly European and male, raising questions of Eurocentrism and sexism. Chapter 11 argues that Europe's unique place does not admit of much empirical ambiguity. Chapter 12 makes the same case for males and incorporates the remarkable story of the Ashkenazi Jews.

Even within Europe, the level of accomplishment has varied. A few countries, and a few regions within countries, have produced the bulk of the significant figures. Chapter 13 shows how the significant figures have been distributed across the landscapes of Europe and the United States during different eras. Chapter 14 turns to the rate of accomplishment after taking the size of the population into account, showing how the rate rose and fell for different inventories across the centuries and across the world.

Chapters 15 and 16 explore some basic potential explanations of the patterns and trajectories: the roles of peace and prosperity, governance, demographics, and the ways in which streams of accomplishment are self-reinforcing. Chapter 17 describes what is still left unexplained.

COMING TO TERMS WITH THE ROLE OF MODERN EUROPE

The purpose of Part 3 is to describe the trajectories and patterns of human accomplishment as they have played out over the centuries since −800 and around the world. Yet the material in these chapters keeps returning to a time and place where the globe's accomplishment has been concentrated: Europe during the period from 1400 to 1950.

For some readers, that concentration of accomplishment is a fact requiring no further proof; for others, it is a discredited Western conceit requiring no further consideration. But for those at neither extreme, let me describe in some detail the problem that confronts anyone who tries to write about human accomplishment around the world and across the centuries without devoting an overwhelming proportion of the analysis to Europe since 1400.

I begin with the simplest aggregation across time and geography. Combined, the inventories from around the world have a total of 4,002 significant figures. If those 4,002 are divided into three groups consisting of people from Europe, people from the rest of the West (the Americas and Antipodes), and people from everywhere else, how are they distributed over the period from −800 to 1950?[1]

The story line implied by the graph on the following page is that not much happened from −800 until the middle of 15C, that really intense levels of accomplishment didn't begin until a few centuries ago (fully half of all the significant figures do not make their appearance until 1800 or after), and that from the middle of 15C to the beginning of 20C, almost everything came from Europe. As late as the 1890s, 81 percent of the newly entering significant figures were European. The proportion contributed from anywhere but Europe never rose above 40 percent through the 1940s.

The alternative story line is the Eurocentric hypothesis: *When Western-*

The distribution of the significant figures across time and place

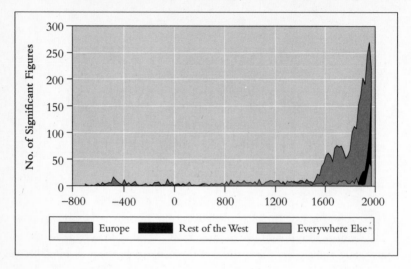

ers set out to survey history they conveniently find that most of that history was made by people like themselves. Sometimes their parochialism is fostered by the existence of a canon, as they rely on standards of what constitutes fine art, music, and literature that marginalize non-Western traditions. Sometimes their parochialism is a function of ignorance, as European historians are oblivious to scientific and technological achievements from other parts of the world. In either case, the result is a skewed vision that looks like the one shown in the preceding graph. It does not reflect European dominance, however, but Eurocentric bias.

The strategies for testing the Eurocentric hypothesis are somewhat different for the arts inventories and the scientific inventories, and are presented separately.

TESTING FOR EUROCENTRISM IN THE ARTS INVENTORIES

The first possibility is that the graphic above would change drastically if it had been limited to the arts. Lumping all the inventories together gives undue influence to the sciences, goes this line of argument, which accounts for some disproportionate amount of the skyrocketing European role in the last five centuries. This possibility is easily checked by breaking out data for just the arts inventories and replicating the graph, as shown opposite.[2]

DOES TAKING EMINENCE INTO ACCOUNT
MAKE A DIFFERENCE?

The most obvious objection to the story told by the graph on page 248 is that a head count of significant figures is a wrong-headed way to think about the distribution of accomplishment. The reason for studying Greek philosophy is not that 32 significant figures in Western philosophy come from ancient Greece, but that 2 of those 32 are Plato and Aristotle. European literature of 19C is not important because it produced 293 significant figures, but because the 293 include writers of the stature of Tolstoy, Hugo, Keats, and Heine.

True enough; but as history has worked out, the ages rich in giants have also been rich in near-giants and the rest of the significant figures who make up the inventory. This point is demonstrated on an inventory-by-inventory basis in the graphs of Chapter 14, which consistently show the close correspondence of measures based on counts of significant figures and on summed index scores. Similarly, when the figure above is replicated using summed index scores instead of a head count, its main theme—the dominance of the West and of the period after 1400—is unchanged.

The European role is effectively unchanged when the significant figures are limited to the arts

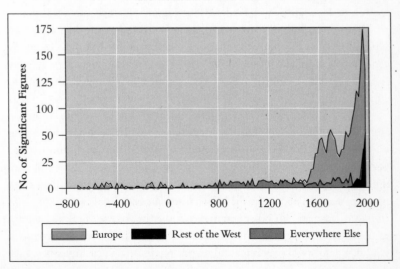

No. of Significant Figures

Europe   Rest of the West   Everywhere Else

The contributions of "everywhere else" are indeed concentrated in the arts, and many of these contributions came in the centuries from 400 to 1200, when Europe was quiescent, but these amount to little in comparison to the surge of accomplishment in the arts in Europe after 1400. The overwhelming role of Europe and of the last five centuries is not changed when only the arts inventories are at issue.

The graph on the previous page serves a useful purpose, however, because it establishes the *upper* limit of non-European significant figures in the arts. Recall I compiled separate inventories in the arts for India, China, Japan, and the Arab world, while compiling a single inventory in each of the arts for all of the West. My reason was that no source in the arts, however comprehensive, can be assumed to use the same sieve to filter the material from every tradition. A worldwide history of art written by a German or American may include chapters on non-Western art, but if those chapters amount to 40 pages out of a 500-page book, one may reasonably worry that equal weight has not been accorded to West and non-West.

By preparing separate inventories, I also ensured that the graph of significant figures in the arts systematically exaggerates the number of non-Western figures relative to the West, because the non-Western figures had to compete for recognition only within their individual countries, whereas Western figures had to compete with everyone else in the West.

To see how this inflationary effect works, suppose that I had compiled the inventory of American artists using only histories of American art. The roster of significant figures would unquestionably have included Charles Wilson Peale, Grant Wood, Frederic Remington, George Catlin, and Frederic Church. Each almost always gets space—often pages of space and a few illustrative plates to boot—in American histories of art. And yet not one of those artists is in the inventory of *Western* art, which was compiled from sources that range over the whole body of art coming out of Europe, the Americas, and the Antipodes.

The inflationary effect of using sources devoted to a single country is large. Twenty-seven U.S.-born artists survived the 50 percent criterion for selecting significant figures and entered the Western art inventory. If I had been preparing an art inventory just for the United States, the number of significant figures would have been in the region of 90—more than three times as many as appear in the Western inventory.[3] I did not try to make additional estimates for other countries or other inventories, but even a quick scan of the data suggests that the inflationary effect for American artists is typical. Eighty-two Swedish authors were mentioned by at least one of the

Western literature sources (none of which was written by a Swede), but only 16 qualified as significant figures. For Hungary, the comparable figures were 61 total authors and just 5 significant figures. For Poland, 95 and 13. The smallest of these ratios is over 5:1. If we make the highly plausible assumption that any Swedish writer mentioned in a general history of Western literature will be mentioned by at least 50 percent of the histories of Swedish literature, and likewise for any other country, the implication is that the 3:1 inflationary effect observed in the test using American art is typical, perhaps on the conservative side.

So far, I have been talking about what would happen to the estimate of Western significant figures if we had sources devoted specifically to the smaller nations. If the same recalculation were applied to Britain, France, and Germany, hundreds of figures would be added to the arts inventories. For example, the sources used for the literature inventory contained mentions of 781 British writers, of whom 149 qualified as significant figures; 465 French writers, of whom 156 qualified as significant figures; and 315 German writers, of whom 105 qualified as significant figures. Even if inventories based on sources devoted exclusively to each country only doubled the number qualifying as significant figures, a minimal expectation, the Western total would be increased by half from those three countries alone.

Drawing a more precise estimate is unnecessary for this minimal conclusion: the dominance of Europe in the arts as shown in the preceding figure would be greater under any recalculation that applied the rules for assembling the Arabic, Chinese, Indian, and Japanese inventories to the individual European nations.[4]

TESTING FOR EUROCENTRISM
IN THE SCIENTIFIC INVENTORIES

The graph for the scientific inventories, combining the hard sciences, mathematics, medicine, and technology, is shown on page 252.

The overall dominance of Europe remains, but with three differences. The category of "everywhere else" virtually disappears, the action is even more concentrated in the most recent centuries, and the category of "rest of the West" plays a more important role—but still not equaling Europe's contribution until the last decade in the graph. The chart on the bottom of page 252 shows the breakdown across continents, using two different measures: number of significant figures, and number of significant events.

Significant figures in the scientific inventories
across time and place

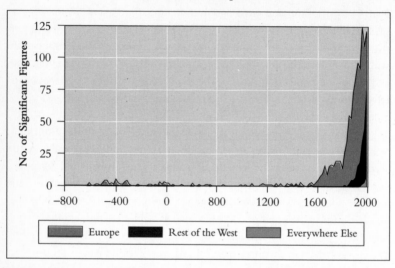

Whether measured in people or events, 97 percent
of accomplishment in the scientific inventories occurred
in Europe and North America

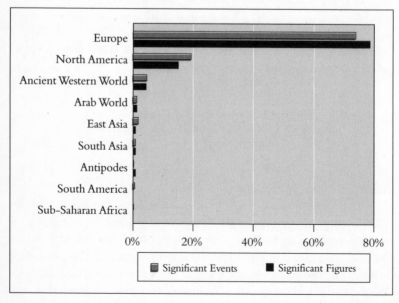

Europe continues to dominate, with an aggregate of 78 percent of the events and 82 percent of the significant figures. Unlike the arts, however, somewhere other than Europe (North America) plays a significant role.

Are these Eurocentric numbers? In science as in the arts, I write at a moment in history when readers come to this text exposed to claims that the European contribution is overrated. Here is the essence of the new historical perspective as stated by historian Nathan Sivin:

> The historical discoveries of the last generation have left no basis for the old myths that the ancestry of modern science is exclusively European and that before modern times no other civilization was able to do science except under European influence. We have gradually come to understand that scientific traditions differing from the European tradition in fundamental respects—from techniques, to institutional settings, to views of nature and man's relation to it—existed in the Islamic world, India, and China, and in smaller civilizations as well. It has become clear that these traditions and the tradition of the Occident, far from being separate streams, have interacted more or less continuously from their beginnings until they were replaced by local versions of the modern science that they have all helped to form.[5]

And here is the essence of the countervailing view as stated by David Landes in response to the passage from Sivin:

> This is the new myth, put forward as a given. Like other myths, it aims to shape the truth to higher ends, to form opinion in some other cause. In this instance, the myth is true in pointing out that modern science, in the course of its development, took up knowledge discovered by other civilizations; and that it absorbed and combined such knowledge and know-how with European findings. The myth is wrong, however, in implying a continuing symmetrical interaction among diverse civilizations.
>
> In the beginning, when China and others were ahead, almost all the transmission went one way, from the outside to Europe. That was Europe's great virtue: unlike China, Europe was a learner. . . . Later on, of course, the story was different: Once Europe had invented modern science, the current flowed back, though not without resistance. Here too, the myth misleads by implying a kind of equal, undifferentiated contribution to the common treasure. The vast bulk of modern science was of Europe's making. . . . Not only did non-Western science contribute just about nothing (though there was more there than Europeans knew) but at that point it was incapable of participating, so far had it fallen behind or taken the wrong turning. This was no common stream.[6]

Rhetoric Versus Reality

This may seem to be one of those conflicts between experts that a layman cannot assess independently, but it's not. On the contrary, it can be easy to reach an independent judgment about allegations of Eurocentrism if one borrows a technique from literary criticism and subjects the allegation to close textual scrutiny. Sivin's language *evokes* the image of an exaggerated European contribution without ever *specifying* that it is exaggerated. It is standard practice. Let me give you other two examples where we have the opportunity to compare the evocation with the evidence actually presented. Exhibit A is the publicity copy on the back cover of the softcover edition of Arnold Pacey's *Technology in World Civilization* (1991):

> Most general histories of technology are Eurocentrist, focusing on a main line of Western technology that stretches from the Greeks through the computer. In this very different book, Arnold Pacey takes a global view . . . portray[ing] the process as a complex dialectic by which inventions borrowed from one culture are adopted to suit another.

Exhibit B is the publicity copy on the back cover of the softcover edition of *Science and Technology in World History* (1999) by James McClellan and Harold Dorn:

> Without neglecting important figures of Western science such as Newton and Einstein, the authors demonstrate the great achievements of non-Western cultures. They remind us that scientific traditions took root in China, India, and Central and South America, as well as in a series of Near Eastern empires.

Lest we fail to get the point, the publishers add a blurb from a professor at Stanford, who tells us that "Professors McClellan and Dorn have written a survey that does not present the historical development of science simply as a Western phenomenon but as the result of wide-ranging human curiosity about nature and attempts to harness its powers in order to serve human needs."

Shall we expect that these two books challenge my assertion of a few pages ago that 97 percent of accomplishment in the scientific inventories occurred in Europe and North America? No—not if you ignore the tone of the quotations and instead focus on what they do not say. No one is saying that the books reveal a new distribution of scientific accomplishment. All that the book jackets claim as a statement of fact (and all that Sivin claimed as a statement of fact) is that scientific and technological activity has occurred outside Europe. Which of course it has.

If you then turn to the text between the covers, you will discover that Pacey's *Technology in World Civilization* is a fascinating, wide-ranging account of the dialogue through which the recipients of new technology do not apply it passively, but adapt it to their particular situation.[7] Gunpowder is the most famous example, invented in China but inspiring a radically different set of "responsive inventions" (Pacey's phrase) when Europe got hold of it. With this interaction between technology and culture as his topic, Pacey does indeed spend more time on non-European civilizations than would a historian of who invented what, where, when. For example, he has a chapter on railroad empires, with 18 pages of material on how railroads developed in Russia, Japan, China, and India. But who invented the railroad engine? Tracks? Trains? The infrastructure of complex railroads? All this occurred in England.

Similarly, McClellan and Dorn's *Science and Technology in World History* presents material on non-European societies. But McClellan and Dorn are also trying to present the substance of what crucial things happened where, done by whom. The 10 people with the most index entries are, in order, Aristotle, Newton, Copernicus, Galileo, Darwin, Ptolemy, Kepler, Descartes, Euclid, and Archimedes—a wholly conventional roster of stars. Of the scientific figures mentioned in McClellan and Dorn's index, 97 percent come from Europe and the United States—precisely the same percentage as yielded by the *Human Accomplishment* inventory.

There is nothing wrong with McClellan and Dorn's ordering of the top 10 or with their percentage of European and American scientists, just as there is nothing wrong with the historiography of either *Science and Technology in World History* or of *Technology in World Civilization*. On the contrary, both books are consistent with the sources used to compile the inventories for *Human Accomplishment*.[8] The contrast between the packaging for the books and their actual texts is emblematic of our times. The packaging evokes the way that intellectual fashion says things should be. The facts reflect the way things really are.

Terra Cognita

The reason that any responsible history of science and technology will end up with these numbers is that historians of science and technology are all working with the same database, vast as it may be, and the data in it are, for the period we are exploring, reasonably complete. Gaps still exist, but none of them is large enough to do more than tweak the details of the large-scale portrait of what happened where.

Herein lies a difference between the layman and the specialist. Is the average European or American often unaware of the technological sophistication reached by non-European cultures? No doubt about it, and in this sense the charge of Eurocentrism is often appropriate. But what really matters is whether the people who have been writing accounts of science and technology in the last half-century are aware of the non-European record—and they are. The works of the great Arabic scholar-scientists of a millennium ago formed the basis for the take-off of European science (which is why so many Arab scholars are known by Latinized names). The great works of Indian mathematics have long since been translated and incorporated into the history of mathematics, just as the works of Chinese naturalists and astronomers have been translated and incorporated into the narratives of those fields.

Over the course of 20C, the body of knowledge about non-Western science and technology grew exponentially. Thus, while Pacey's book draws together a body of material inaccessible to the average reader, almost all of that material, including treatises on such things as "The geographical extent of the use of bark fabrics," "Terrestrial and meteoritic nickel in Indonesian kris," and "The plant world of the sixteenth and seventeenth century lowland Maya," is in English—fragments of a huge scholarly mosaic.[9]

In recognizing how thoroughly non-European science and technology have been explored, let's also give credit where credit is due: By and large, it has not been Asian or Arabic scholars, fighting for recognition against European indifference, who are responsible for piecing together the record of accomplishment by non-European cultures, but Europeans themselves. Imperialists they may have been, but one of the by-products of that imperialism was a large cadre of Continental, British, and later American scholars, fascinated by the exotic civilizations of Arabia and East Asia, who set about uncovering evidence of their accomplishments that inheritors of those civilizations had themselves neglected. Joseph Needham's seven-volume history of Chinese science and technology is a case in point.[10] Another is George Sarton's *Introduction to the History of Science*, in five large volumes published from 1927–1948, all of which is devoted to science before the end of 14C, with the bulk of it devoted to the period when preeminence in science was to be found in the Arab world, India, and China.

Triangulation

Another way of thinking about Eurocentrism is to ask whether, within the sources used to compile the science and technology inventories, we can find the fingerprints of bias. The strategy uses this logic: Non-European contributions may be no secret, but they are also unevenly included in European accounts of science. Within the sources used to compile the inventories, some sources are going to be more inclusive of non-European contributions than others. If Eurocentrism is a problem, then the better the source, the greater the inclusion of non-Europeans.

The test of this hypothesis is to compare a source that is unimpeachably authoritative with the results from the less comprehensive histories and chronologies. Such a source exists in the form of the *Dictionary of Scientific Biography* (*DoSB*), sponsored by the American Council of Learned Societies, now up to 17 large volumes plus an eighteenth for the index. It is designed to be a definitive source in the hard sciences and mathematics (it is not intended to be definitive for medicine and technology, and I exclude those categories from this analysis). The *DoSB*'s editorial staff includes experts in Arabic, Indian, and East Asian science drawn from universities around the world. Consistent criteria are applied to the choice of who does and does not gain admittance.

What makes the *DoSB* even better for our purposes is that the core 14 volumes first appeared in 1970 and the last two supplemental volumes were issued in 1990, giving the editors two decades to hear about omissions—decades in which such sources were under intense scrutiny for omissions of women, non-whites, and non-Europeans. It seems reasonable to conclude that the *DoSB* in its present form has been as thoroughly cleansed of Eurocentric bias as it is possible for a source to be.

Using the *DoSB* as the yardstick, I prepared two rosters of scientists and mathematicians. One consists of everyone who appears in the *DoSB*. The other roster consists of everyone who would have been part of *Human Accomplishment*'s database of scientists and mathematicians if the *DoSB* had not been one of my sources. The chart on page 258 shows how the geographical distributions of the rosters compiled by these two different methods compare.

The geographic distributions produced by the two rosters are effectively the same. Eighty-one percent of the set in the *DoSB* comes from Europe compared to 76 percent in the *Human Accomplishment* set, numbers that rise to 94 and 91 percent respectively when the United States and Canada are included.[11]

A comparison of the scientists identified
by the *Dictionary of Scientific Biography* and those identified
by the rest of the sources

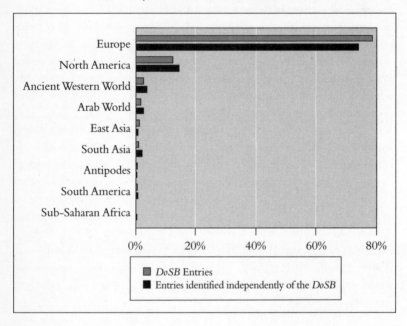

Is this merely evidence that the *DoSB* is as Eurocentric as any other source? Perhaps, but at this point the ball is in the other court. On the face of it, the *DoSB* has been as carefully assembled as any scholarly endeavor of its kind ever has been. It is incumbent on those who continue to allege Eurocentrism to specify the names and contributions of the large numbers of important Asian and Arabic scientists and mathematicians who have been left out, or to explain why some thousands of the European entries don't belong.

A CHALLENGE

My contention is that there is no significant body of ignored non-European accomplishment out there for the historical period represented by −800 to 1950. Let me make this point in the form of a challenge that embraces the inventories for both the arts and the sciences.

For the sciences, we have a specific target to shoot at, the 97 percent figure that defines the proportion of scientific accomplishment I assign to Europe and North America. The challenge is to augment the list of non-European people and events in such a way that it will meaningfully alter the 97 percent figure.

There are two provisos. The first is that the new events must consist of discoveries, inventions, and other forms of "firsts." No fair adding the first Indian suspension bridge to a catalog of Indian technology if suspension bridges were already in use elsewhere.[12]

The other proviso is that the rules for inclusion of a person or event must be applied evenly. If you augment the inventory of non-European accomplishment by going to Joseph Needham's seven-volume account of Chinese science and technology, you must also augment the inventory of European accomplishment by going to comparably detailed histories specifically dealing with German science (for example)—in other words, no fair using the naked eye to search for European accomplishments and a microscope to search for non-European ones.

If one observes these two constraints, here is what will be found: If the definition of "significant event" or "significant person" is relaxed to permit a dozen new non-European entries, hundreds of new entries will qualify for the European list, and the relative proportions assigned to Europe and non-Europe will not change. They may become even more extreme, because the reservoir of non-trivial European accomplishment that did not get into the inventory is so immense.

For the arts, we have no equivalently hard target. Seventy-four percent of the significant figures in the visual arts and literature come from the West, and we already know that the methodology used to identify significant figures in the arts substantially inflates the non-Western numbers. In music, the lack of a tradition of named composers in non-Western civilizations means that the Western total of 522 significant figures has no real competition at all. How might the non-Western numbers be augmented in the arts? What if we were to discard artists as the unit of analysis, and substitute artistic works? What if we were to broaden the definition of artistic objects?

If we limit ourselves to attributed works, the substitution of artistic works in favor of the artist will have no effect, or work in the West's favor. The authors, composers, painters, and sculptors of the post-1400 West were, as a rule, prodigiously productive. Compare the body of work by Shakespeare or Goethe with that of Li Bo or Murasaki; that of Michelangelo or Picasso with that of Sesshu or Zhao Mengfu; and so on down the list from the giants to the merely excellent. At every level, the average number of major works per artist is as large for the West as for the non-West.

Shall we consider lost works? Some of the most highly regarded Chinese artists have no surviving works at all, and the music that Confucius considered so important to Chinese culture is lost altogether. But as noted in Chapter 3, the West similarly had painters such as Zeuxis, Polygnotus, and Apelles, seen by their contemporaries as artistic equals to the sculptor Phidias. None of their paintings survives, nor does any work of their lesser contemporaries. None of the Western music that Plato and Aristotle considered to be so important to Greek culture survives. Even in literature, the masterpieces the West retains from ancient days are probably outnumbered by the ones we have lost. We know that Sophocles wrote at least 123 plays, of which only 7 survive in their entirety. Aeschylus wrote about 90 plays, of which we have 7. Euripides wrote at least 92 plays, of which we have have only 19. One of the greatest of Euripides's surviving works, *The Trojan Women*, won only second prize in a contemporary competition. We know nothing about the play that came in first. Inserting a correction for lost work will not redress the imbalance between West and non-West.

Adding anonymous works won't help. In literature, many non-Western cultures have traditions of authorless folklore—but so does Europe, starting with the Greek myths and continuing for another two thousand years, adding Norse sagas, the stories of Camelot, Central European fairy tales, the poetry of anonymous French troubadours. . . . The list could go on for every European language. In the visual arts, countries such as India and Persia have important bodies of unattributed painting and sculpture—but so do the countries of Europe, embracing virtually all the sculpture, painting, and mosaics from the fall of the Roman Empire through the Middle Ages.

Demonstrating that the non-European role in the arts has been underestimated by the presentation here can be done only by expanding the definition of artistic accomplishment to include other forms of art that exist in East Asia, South and Southeast Asia, Africa, and pre-Columbian America. Once again, however, comes the proviso: the rules for including new works must be applied evenly to Western and non-Western cultures.

Shall we add architecture, a category omitted from the visual arts inventory? There are temples in Asia and Central America that certainly belong in any list of great architectural accomplishment. But the entire roster of such architectural landmarks from outside Europe will be exceeded by ones in late medieval and Renaissance Europe alone, before even getting started on European architectural accomplishment since then. Shall we introduce the decorative arts and crafts into the inventory of art works? Whatever gems of fine artisanship are introduced from Asia, Africa, and the Americas are going to be matched in quality and overwhelmed in number by the flood that will enter the inventory from Europe. Putting aside everything else, consider just the volume of fine artisanship in stone masonry, stained glass, tapestry, and painted decoration from European churches and cathedrals.

Shall we treat functional objects—gracefully designed eating utensils, baskets, warriors' shields, fabrics—from non-European cultures as works of arts? We will have to include centuries of European production of beautiful things, from medieval armor and drinking goblets to Cellini's golden saltcellar to Parisian *haute-couture* to Barcelona chairs—an endless variety of categories of beautifully designed practical objects, with distinctive traditions coming out of every European country.

Shall we add popular music to the definition of accomplishment in music? Every European country has a rich tradition of popular music, often comprising separate folk traditions for vocal and instrumental music, and separate traditions for different regions, separate traditions for different eras.

Hence the proposition: Whatever mechanism one uses to try to augment the non-European contribution in both the arts and sciences will backfire if the same selection rules are applied to Europe.

CODICIL: THE MOVING FINGER WRITES

I have gone to considerable lengths to document facts about the geographic and chronological distributions of human accomplishment that are controversial because of intellectual fashion, not because the facts are ambiguous. Now is a good time to introduce some cautions when interpreting those distributions.

The first caution is directed to those of us in the United States. Americans often use *West* interchangeably with *Europe*, but one lesson of the data in this chapter is how presumptuous that is. In his landmark *Configurations of Culture Growth* (1944), written during the 1930s, A. L. Kroeber observed in passing that "it is curious how little science of highest quality America has produced"—a startling claim to Americans who have become accustomed to American scientific dominance since 1950.[13] But Kroeber was right. Compared to Europe, the American contribution was still small then. In the arts, a large dose of American humility is in order. Much as we may love

Twain, Whitman, Whistler, and Copland, they are easily lost in the ocean of the European *oeuvre*. What we are pleased to call Western civilization has been in fact European civilization until the last half century.

The other caution is not to carry the numbers too far. The period prior to 1400 may have had comparatively few significant figures, but it was rich in giants. The figure opposite recasts the initial graph, combining all significant figures across all inventories and all countries, superimposing the names of some of the top-ranked figures from the indexes that antedate 1400. The names appear roughly over the date to which they apply.

The names over the low-lying columns from −800 to 1400 are protean figures in the history of the world's civilizations—and I have included only a sampling of the best known of the 690 significant figures who fall between −800 and 1400. But we may document the point more systematically. For example, 226 people had index scores of 40 or higher—a mere 6 percent of the 4,002 significant figures. But of that elite 6 percent, almost half (48 percent) appeared prior to 1400. To some degree, this reflects the use of separate inventories for China, India, and Japan, which guaranteed that a number of top-scoring figures would appear before the modern era, but the broad point holds.

Furthermore, much of that genius came from outside Europe. No Western philosophers have had greater impact on their cultures than Confucius and Buddha had on theirs. Those who are in a position to make such judgments describe the great poets of China as among the greatest anywhere, not just the greatest of China. A fine Japanese rock garden or ceremonial tea bowl reflects an aesthetic sensibility as subtle as humans have ever known.

If we are to consider science and technology, this would be a good time to go back to the account of Zheng He's fleet of 317 ships and 27,750 men in 15C (page 33), to be reminded of just how grand Chinese technological and administrative capacity could be, or to reread the account of life in Hangzhou (pages 34–37), to be reminded of the sophistication of Chinese urban life when Europe was mired in the Dark Ages, or to examine the account of experimentalism in Chinese science before 1400 (pages 235–37).

A third caution is to remember that we are beginning only at −800. Return to Chapter 2 and reconsider all that humans had accomplished before then. Then think of all the civilizations that arose independently of Europe, before and after −800, and consider how many of them rose to similar technological levels—on different schedules, but ending up with a common package of tools and techniques that enabled them to build large structures and road networks, put together the interlocking systems that enable cities to

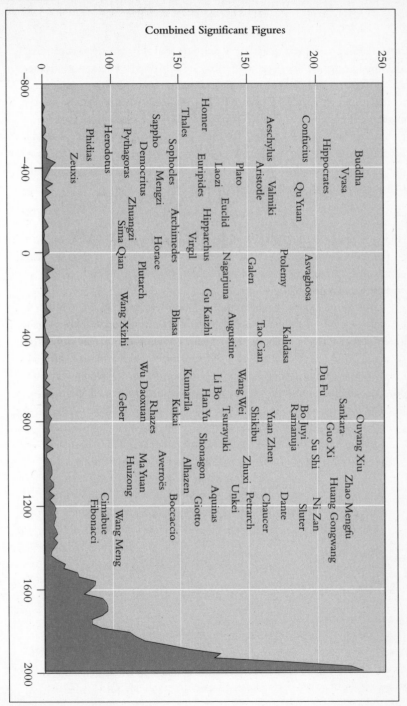

An antidote to "not much happened before 1400"

exist, develop complex agricultural practices and distribution mechanisms, and conduct commerce. The technology inventory encourages misinterpretation insofar as it lists each of these accomplishments just once, assigning it to the place where it first occurred. The potential for misinterpretation is augmented because many of the inventions involved in this basic package of technology antedate −800 and therefore do not enter the analysis at all. Evidence scattered from Angkor Wat to Machu Picchu attests to the ability of human beings throughout the globe, not confined to the leading civilizations, to achieve amazing technological feats.

*   *   *

And yet, and yet. . . . Modern Europe has overwhelmingly dominated accomplishment in both the arts and sciences. The estimates of the European contribution are robust. They cannot, in any way I have been able to devise, be attenuated more than fractionally.

As I write, it appears that Europe's run is over. In another few hundred years, books will probably be exploring the reasons why some completely different part of the world became the locus of great human accomplishment. Now is a good time to stand back in admiration. What the human species is today it owes in astonishing degree to what was accomplished in just half a dozen centuries by the peoples of one small portion of the northwestern Eurasian land mass.

... AND OF DEAD WHITE MALES

Not only does Europe dominate the narrative of human accomplishment, so does the minority that has become known in recent years as dead white males. In this chapter, as for the European role in the preceding chapter, I document the reasons for concluding that the inventories fairly represent the role played by people who were not males and not white.

The evidence for that conclusion is simplified because the inventories stop in 1950, when women and ethnic minorities residing in Western countries had yet to acquire full access to the institutions of the arts and sciences. The story that stands out does not involve women, Asians, or Africans, but another minority that had suffered centuries of legal and social discrimination: the Ashkenazi Jews. The rapid pace at which they entered the inventories as soon as the barriers were even partially lifted is astonishing.

Why women have played so disproportionately small a role and Jews have played so disproportionately large a role in the arts and sciences have both been the subject of intense and acrimonious debates over the last few decades, ones that I am not about to resolve. An overview of the competing explanations concludes the chapter.

WOMEN

On the wall of Columbia University's mathematics library hang four large portraits of famous mathematicians: Carl Gauss, Henri Poincaré, Emmy Noether, and Sonya Kovalevskaya.[1] They are of somewhat different stature. In the mathematics inventory for this book, Gauss ranks fourth and Poincaré

26th. Noether ranks 94th and Kovalevskaya 113th. The 2:2 split between the sexes is also at odds with the split in the mathematics inventory, which is 187:4.

The motives behind Columbia's choice of portraits are understandable, but it is important not to conflate aspirations with history. Just as only two percent of the mathematics significant figures were women, two percent of all the significant figures were women—88 out of the 4,002 persons in the inventories. They are split among the inventories as shown in the table below.

WOMEN AMONG THE SIGNIFICANT FIGURES

Inventory	No. of women	Percentage of total significant figures
The Sciences	24	1.7
Astronomy	5	4.0
Biology	4	2.1
Chemistry	1	0.5
Earth Sciences	0*	0
Physics	6	3.1
Mathematics	4	2.5
Medicine	4	1.8
Technology	0	0
Chinese Philosophy	0	0
Indian Philosophy	0	0
Western Philosophy	0	0
Arabic Literature	1	1.2
Chinese Literature	3	3.6
Indian Literature	2	4.7
Japanese Literature	7	8.2
Western Literature	37	4.4
Chinese Art	1	0.9
Japanese Art	0	0
Western Art	12	2.5
Western Music	1	0.2
Total	**88**	**2.2**

*The earth sciences inventory did not include anthropology, which was classified instead as a social science and therefore was not among the inventories for analysis. Among the 130 anthropologists identified in any of the science sources, four were women, or 3.0 percent.

The earliest woman to appear in the inventories is the Greek poet, Sappho of Lesbos, in –6C. A thousand years later comes the next woman, the natural philosopher Hypatia of Alexandria, who lived from about 370 to 415. Another 13 women appear between Hypatia and 1600, but all of them are confined to just one domain, literature. The first woman to qualify as a significant figure in the visual arts is Wen Shu (1595–1634) of Ming China. The first woman to qualify in any of the scientific inventories after Hypatia is astronomer Caroline Herschel (1750–1848), sister and colleague of William Herschel. The first and only woman in the music inventory is French composer Germaine Tailleferre (1892–1983). No woman qualified as a significant figure in any of the philosophy inventories.

The dearth of women in the inventories until 19C and 20C reflects near-total exclusion, by law and social pressure, from the possibility of participating. But the legal emancipation of women, which began in 19C at about the same time as Jewish emancipation, took even longer to complete. In some European countries, women did not get the legal right to engage in certain professions until early 20C. The figure on page 268 shows the percentage of significant figures who were women for each half-century from 1800 to 1950, limiting the figures for the arts to the Western inventories.

The most conspicuous increase over the three half-centuries is found in the scientific inventories, where the number of women went from 1 to 2 to 19. Clearly, something happened to increase the access of women to scientific professions in the first half of 20C. Literature also saw an increase in female significant figures in raw numbers, but no increase as a percentage. During the most recent half century we are examining, 1900–1950, women still constituted only 5 percent of significant figures in the hard sciences, 3 percent in mathematics, 7 percent in medicine, and none in technology. In the combined arts inventories, women constituted 5 percent of the significant figures—a figure that was virtually identical if the numbers are split into the Western versus non-Western arts inventories.

Women have even smaller representation among the highest index scores. The figure on page 269 shows this visually by superimposing the placement of the index scores of all the top-ranked women on a Lotka curve based on a composite of all the index scores in all the inventories.

Murasaki Shikibu, the author of *Tale of Genji*, with the third-highest index score in Japanese literature, is the lone woman at the far right-hand side of the Lotka curve. Marie Curie, who won Nobel Prizes in both chemistry and physics, is the only other woman who has an index score higher

The varied record of female significant figures from 1800 to 1950

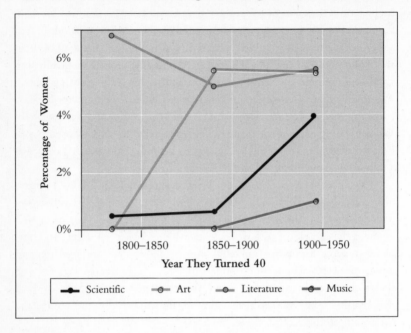

than 18. The likelihood that a woman significant figure will have an index score higher than 60 is less than half (47 percent) of the probability for significant figures as a whole. A woman significant figure's likelihood of reaching the 20–60-point range is only about a third (36 percent) of the probability for significant figures as a whole. In short, inventories in the arts and sciences, based on multiple sources, almost all of them written in the last few decades, producing highly reliable indexes, tell us that women constitute only a little more than 2 percent of all the significant figures, fewer than 5 percent of the significant figures in the first half of 20C, and that even the top-ranked women are, with the rarest exceptions, well back in the pack of the distributions in their fields. Are these fair characterizations of the role of women in human accomplishment in the arts and sciences through 1950?

The Dictionary of Scientific Biography *as a Benchmark in the Sciences*

In the sciences, the *Dictionary of Scientific Biography* (*DoSB*) once again offers a useful benchmark (the same reasons that make the *DoSB* an exemplary source for non-Europeans also makes it an exemplary source for women),

The Location of the Top-Ranked Woman in Each Inventory
on the Lotka Curve

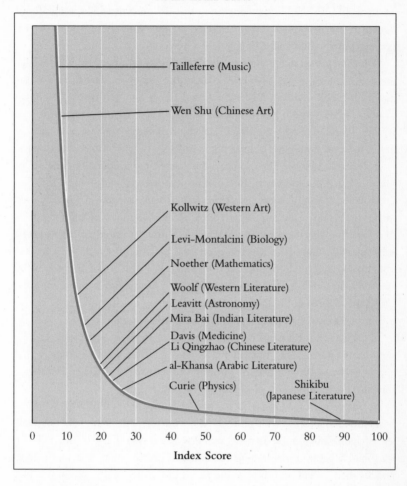

and we are again able to set up a test of this logic: Sources differ in their coverage of women's contribution to the sciences. The definition of significant figures is based on consensus (being mentioned in at least half of the sources). What if we ignore consensus among sources of varying comprehensiveness, and focus on one superior source in which we have special confidence? If significant figures in the hard sciences and mathematics had been defined as everyone included in the *DoSB*, would we find a different story than the one told by the dozen-plus sources actually used to compile each inventory?

In such a case, the proportion of women significant figures in the sciences would have dropped by more than half. Relying exclusively on the *DoSB* would have led to the conclusion that 0.7 percent of all the significant figures in mathematics and the hard sciences were women, instead of the 1.9 percent actually designated.[2]

Is there a way that the roster of women significant figures could be augmented by another way of thinking about the use of the *DoSB*? For example, if the *DoSB* is as good I have claimed, let us assume that every woman in the *DoSB* should be considered a significant figure—otherwise, she wouldn't have survived the *DoSB*'s selection process—and we will include her in the inventory even if she is not mentioned in half of the other sources.

But this strategy fails. To see why, consider the concrete example of Helen Dean King, an American biologist who lived from 1869 to 1955. She developed the King colony, part of the Wister stock of white rats widely used for research, and made important contributions in understanding the effects of inbreeding and the mechanism of sex selection. In other words, she had a substantial, distinguished career in genetics. The *DoSB* not only included her but also spent 6.4 columns on her biography, well over twice as much as the average length of 2.5 columns—and yet Helen Dean King is not among the significant figures in the biology inventory, having failed to meet the criterion of mentions in 50 percent of the qualifying sources.

On the merits of her career, there's no reason why she shouldn't be a significant figure. Many men in the biology inventory have narratives that appear to be less impressive, or no more impressive, than King's. We therefore add her to the roster of significant figures in biology.

But then we ask: What about the *male* biologists in the *DoSB* who had biographies as long as or longer than King's but who, like King, did not qualify as significant figures? It turns out that there were sixty of them. These sixty had biographies averaging 8.7 columns. Six of them had biographies greater than 12 columns long. One had a biography of 19 columns. When one reads through those biographies, it becomes clear that they made scientific contributions at least as distinguished as King's. Fair's fair. If the rule for significant figures says that King belongs, then so should at least those sixty other biologists who hadn't made the cut under the original criterion. It is the same problem I discussed when trying to augment the non-European contribution (see page 259): If the selection rules used to augment the number of women are applied to men as well, the proportion of women will remain effectively unchanged, even drop, because the pool of mistakenly omitted men is at least as large as the pool of mistakenly omitted women. As it stands, *Human Accomplishment*'s inventory of biologists has 4 women and 189 men, or 2.1 percent women. If we were to take *DoSB* as the sole source, the roster of biologists would consist of 12 women and 1,218 men, or 1.0 percent women, half the proportion in the actual inventory. If we stick with *Human Accomplishment*'s inventory but go back to *DoSB* and add its women to it *but also add all the men with equal or higher scores who were also excluded from the significant figures,* the percentage in the inventory would drop to 2.0 percent. There is no way to drive up the percentage of women in these inventories without positing that every source, including the *DoSB,* is massively biased against women.

The Women Who Were Left Out

Despite the material in the preceding discussion, an everyday reason exists for continuing to think that such a massive bias exists: One may go into any large bookstore and find an entire section devoted to women's studies, including compendia of women scientists, artists, composers, and authors. Any one of these volumes will have far more women in its field of specialty than in the corresponding inventory for *Human Accomplishment.* The continuing problem applies here: The selection rules for a book on women scientists (or Irish-American scientists, Jewish scientists, black scientists, or any group selected on the basis of their group membership) are different than the selection rules based on their importance to the history of science. But I can be more specific about the nature of the populations in such books. If you go to such a section of a major bookstore, pick up one of the books about women in science, and start scanning the entries, here is an example of what you will find:

1. Women with significant scientific accomplishments but whose work postdates 1950.

2. Educators who taught science (e.g., Abella, Laura Bassi, Dorotea Bocchi, Margaret Bryan).

3. Pioneers, the first women to get a degree in a given field, go into a given profession, etc. (e.g., Florence Bascom, Rachel Bodley).

4. Translators and popularizers of scientific works (e.g., Maria Ardinghelli, Florence Bailey, Aphra Behn, Ada Byron).

5. Women, usually amateurs, who collected data that were used by scientists (e.g., Isabella Bishop).

6. Activists in women's rights and social reform whose profession was in medicine or the sciences (e.g., Elizabeth Anderson, Elizabeth Blackwell).

7. Wives, sisters, and children of famous male scientists (e.g., Elizabeth Agassiz, Sarah Banks, Giuseppa Barbapiccola, Sophia Brahe, Mary Buckland) who had some involvement in the work of the famous males.

8. Women with accomplishments ancillary to science though not involving scientific discoveries (e.g., Agamede, Agnodike, Aglaonike, Arete of Cyrene, Aspasia, Axiothea of Phlius, Juliana Barnes, Marie Biheron, Marie Boivin).

9. Women who were directly engaged in scientific professions and conducted substantial original research (e.g. Mary Anning, Herthe Ayrton, Mary Blagg, Alice Boring, Mary Brandegee, Elizabeth Britton, Elizabeth Brown) but are not included in *Human Accomplishment*'s roster of significant figures.

10. Scientists who qualified as significant figures (e.g., Maria Agnesi).

The specific names are drawn from Marilyn Ogilvie's *Women in Science: Antiquity through the Nineteenth Century* (1988). The names represent all of Ogilvie's entries under the letters *A* and *B*. Among them, we have 1 woman who qualified as a significant figure (category 10), 7 women whose careers would at least make them eligible for consideration (category 9), and 27 women in the other 8 categories who had interesting and important careers, but not ones that would ordinarily lead them to be part of a history of science or mathematics. In the case of the 7 women in category 9 who were potentially eligible, we face a diluted example of the Helen King example. None achieved anything comparable in importance to King's accomplishments in genetics. One of them, Herthe Ayrton, is included in *DoSB*, and trying to add her to the inventory poses the same problem as posed in the King case: Ayrton was a physicist. Among physicists included in the *DoSB*, 120 people who also did not qualify as significant figures have biographies as long as or longer than Ayrton's. Of those 120, 119 are men.

Generalizing from the Case of the Sciences

Similar procedures could be applied to the arts inventories, but none of the sources used for the inventories have as much face validity as a comprehensive source as the *DoSB*. The exercises already conducted for the sciences point to a few large realities. One is that the representation of women is so small that even fairly large errors in under-representation wouldn't make much difference. Let us say for the sake of argument that the sources used for the inventories were so biased against women that they left out half of the women who should have been included. In that case, the inventories should consist of 95.6 percent men instead of 97.8 percent men—a distinction without a difference. The broad historical patterns in these data are not going to be changed even by implausible errors, let alone plausible ones.

Since 1950

With all the changes that have taken place in the standing of women over the course of 20C, how much increase in the proportion of women could we expect from a roster of significant figures that covered all of 20C? Based on the most obvious indicator of distinguished achievement, the Nobel Prizes, little seems to have changed. The table below shows the number of Nobel Prizes awarded to women from 1901 to 1950 expressed as a percentage of all prizes awarded, compared to those awarded from 1951 to 2000.

PERCENTAGE OF WOMEN NOBEL PRIZE
WINNERS IN LITERATURE AND THE
SCIENCES DURING THE TWO HALVES OF 20C

Prize	1901–1950	1951–2000
Sciences total	2%	2%
Chemistry	4%	1%
Medicine	2%	4%
Physics	2%	1%
Literature	11%	8%
Total	**4%**	**3%**

Note: The prizes for economics (awarded only since 1969) and peace are in fields not included in the inventories. Women won 3 and 7 peace prizes in the two halves of the century respectively. No woman had won a prize in economics through 2002.

Source: Nobel Prize web site

In the first and second halves of the century respectively, women won four and seven prizes in the sciences, and five and four prizes in literature. In percentage terms, their proportion decreased marginally.

The record for the Nobels may be augmented with raw data used to compile the inventories for *Human Accomplishment*. Although the inventories for full-scale analysis were cut off at 1950, entry into the raw databases often was not. The specifics are given in the note.[3] The augmented database consists of a list of *all* persons mentioned in any source, including those who turned 40 after 1950. These data cannot be used to infer much about changes in the importance of women to accomplishment (though presumably a correlation exists), but they at least give us a fix on the change in *participation* of women in various fields. The figure below uses these raw entries for Western art, literature, and music, and for the combined scientific fields.[4] The timeline runs in two-decade periods, from 1870–1890 to 1970–1990, based on the year in which the people in the inventories turned 40.

The trendlines for raw mentions of women from 1870 to 1990

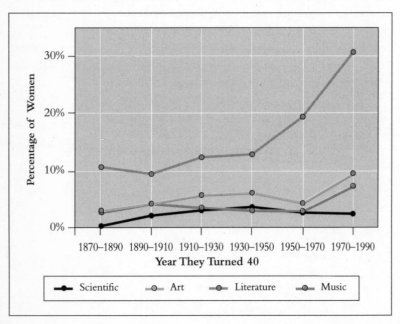

In the field where women historically have been most prominent, literature, the last half of 20C saw a steady and substantial increase in participation, with women amounting to more than 30 percent of all entries in a recent encyclopedic source. For the visual arts and music, participation by women was effectively flat from 1870 until 1970, with an uptick in the 1970–1990 period. No upward trend is found for the combined scientific inventories.

THE JEWS

Jews make their first appearance in the annals of the arts and sciences during the centuries when the Middle East and Moorish Spain were at their cultural peak. When science historian George Sarton set out to enumerate the top scientists across the world, including East Asia, South Asia, the Arab world, and Christian Europe, from 1150 to 1300, he came up with 626 names, of whom 95 were Jews—15 percent of the total, produced by a group that at the time represented about half of 1 percent of the world's population that was in a position to produce scientists.[5] But few of those 626 are important enough in the broader sweep of scientific history to warrant a mention in histories that are less tightly focused. Of the 11 Jews who qualified as significant figures in the inventories prior to 19C, only 2 are still familiar to the general public, Montaigne and Spinoza, and neither of them was a typical Jew of his time. Montaigne's mother came from a wealthy Spanish/Portuguese Jewish family, but Montaigne himself was a lifelong Catholic. Spinoza was excommunicated by his Dutch Jewish community for his unorthodox views.

Five of the 9 other Jews who appear in the inventories before 1800 were also part of the philosophy inventory. They were Philo Judaeus from ancient Roman Alexandria, Solomon ibn Gabirol (Avicebron) and Maimonides from Moorish Spain, and Moses Mendelssohn and Johann Herder from 18C Germany. In all of those 26 centuries, the roster of Western significant figures includes not one Jewish artist, scientist, physician, or inventor, and just two writers (Fernando Rojas and Hans Sachs), one composer (Salamone Rossi), and one mathematician (Paul Guldin).

This sparse representation in European arts and sciences through the beginning of 19C reflects Jews' near-total exclusion from the arts and sciences. Jews were not merely discouraged from entering universities and the professions, they were often forbidden by law from doing so. Socially, they were despised. "Underlying everything," writes historian David Vital, "was the central fact that under the old regime no Jew was, or could be, a member of civil society. No matter how learned or wealthy or contingently influential he might be within or without Jewry itself, a Jew was held to belong to a moral and, of course, theological category inferior to that of the meanest peasant."[6] I will not try to establish a hierarchy of victimhood among Jews, women, and other minorities, but an uncomplicated point needs emphasis: Until the end of 18C throughout Europe, and well into 19C in most parts of Europe, Jews lived under a regime of legally restricted rights and socially sanctioned discrimination as severe as that borne by any population not held in chattel slavery.

In a practical sense, legal equality for Jews first occurred in the newly formed United States, where Jews were given full rights under federal law, though full protection at the state level had to wait upon the equal protection clause of the Fourteenth Amendment in 1868.[7] France and the Netherlands emancipated their Jewish populations in the 1790s. Throughout the first half of 19C, the rest of Western and Central Europe evolved toward more tolerant policies without actually granting full legal equality. In England, Jews faced comparatively few legal restrictions after mid-18C, though it was not until the Promissory Oaths Act of 1871 that the last remnants of discriminatory law were revoked. The revolutions of 1848 saw civil rights granted (though not necessarily enforced) in most of Austro-Hungary and Germany. Bismarck completed the emancipation of Prussian Jews in 1869. Emancipation of Italian Jews began in the Piedmont in 1848 and ended in 1870 in Rome. Switzerland granted emancipation in 1866.

In Russia, which in 19C also meant Poland, events moved the other way. The assassination of Alexander II in 1881 intensified long-standing Russian anti-Semitism. What had before been occasional acts of violence became the *pogroms.* The Russian state reinforced popular hostility toward Jews with the supposedly temporary May Laws of 1882—laws that were unofficially said to have the goal of forcing one-third of Russian Jews to emigrate, one-third to convert, and one-third to starve. They succeeded in the first of these aims, prompting a great exodus of Russian and Polish Jews heading mostly to the United States.

This history provides us with a nice example of what social scientists call an interrupted time series. Until nearly 1800, Jews are excluded. Then, over about 70 years, the legal exclusions are lifted and the social exclusion eases. What happens? "The suddenness with which Jews began to appear . . . is nothing short of astounding," writes historian Raphael Patai. "It seemed as if a huge reservoir of Jewish talent, hitherto dammed up behind the wall of Talmudic learning, were suddenly released to spill over into all fields of

Gentile cultural activity."[8] During the four decades from 1830 to 1870, when the first Jews to live in emancipation (or at least to live under less rigorously enforced suppression) reach their forties, 16 Jewish significant figures appear. In the next four decades, from 1870 to 1910, when all non-Russian Jews are living in societies that offer equal legal protections if not social equality, that number jumps to 40. During the next four decades until 1950—including the years of the Third Reich and the Holocaust—the number of Jewish significant figures almost triples, to 114. The figure below shows how these numbers work out as percentages of all significant figures for the three half-centuries from 1800 to 1950.

The sudden emergence of Jewish significant figures,
1800–1950

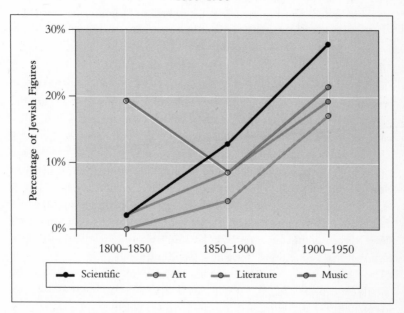

I do not show the results for philosophy because the Jewish proportion becomes so high in 1900–1950, when Jews represented 6 out of the 18 significant figures in philosophy (33 percent), that it distorts the other trend-lines. The results shown in the graph above are already impressive enough without philosophy, as Jewish representation rises steeply in all the inventories but music, where it had begun at a high rate even in 1800–1850.

The Magnitude of Disproportional Jewish Representation in the Inventories

These numbers quantify a familiar observation about Jewish achievement. Here is Lord Ashley, the future seventh Earl of Shaftesbury, speaking in the House of Commons in December 1847, as Her Majesty's government debated whether to amend the oath required of members of the Commons so that non-Christians could honorably swear to it:

> The Jews were a people of very powerful intellect [the minutes record Ashley as saying], of cultivated minds. . . . [Lord Ashley] was speaking not of the old Jews in their palmy days, but of the Jews oppressed and despised in their days of dispersion. Even thus, their literature embraced every subject of science and learning, of secular and religious knowledge. . . . The Jews presented . . . in our day, in proportion to their numbers, a far larger list of men of genius and learning than could be exhibited by any Gentile country. Music, poetry, medicine, astronomy, occupied their attention, and in all they were more than a match for their competitors.[9]

Lord Ashley's comments were made in 1847, when Jews had barely begun to reappear on the world stage as leading figures within the arts and sciences. Within another few decades, scholars were undertaking statistical analysis to estimate the degree of disproportional Jewish representation in the arts and sciences, the issue to which I now turn.[10]

To get a sense of the density of accomplishment these numbers represent, I will focus on 1870 onward, after legal emancipation had been achieved throughout Central and Western Europe. Only from this latter period can we draw a roughly accurate sense of the magnitude and patterns of Jewish accomplishment—"roughly," because Jews were still subject to pervasive social and educational discrimination even after 1870.

The next step is to compare the number of significant figures that would be expected on the basis of Jewish representation in the population. As of 1900, the best estimate is that the Jewish population of Europe and the United States (where all of the Jewish significant figures were born or worked) represented about 2.1 percent of the population. As of 1940, the best estimate is 2.2 percent.[11] I will take 2.2 percent as my working figure for the period throughout 1870 to 1950. It is important to note that if I had added in the population for the rest of the Americas, where Jews had immigrated in far lower numbers, this percentage would have been much smaller. The following are conservative estimates of disproportional Jewish representation in the inventories.

The simplest approach to estimating the Jewish contribution is to take the entire number of significant figures from Europe and the United States in the Western inventories of 1870–1950, ask what number of these we would expect to be Jewish given their 2.2 percent representation in the population, and compare the two numbers. The table below shows the results.

Disproportional Representation of Jews by Inventory of 1870–1950

Inventory	Expected significant figures*	Actual significant figures	Ratio of actual to expected significant figures
Combined scientific inventories	14.5	94	6:1
Astronomy	1.0	1	1:1
Biology	2.3	18	8:1
Chemistry	2.4	13	6:1
Earth Sciences	0.8	2	3:1
Physics	3.0	26	9:1
Mathematics	1.1	13	12:1
Medicine	1.8	14	8:1
Technology	2.1	7	3:1
Visual Arts	3.1	16	5:1
Literature	6.8	26	4:1
Music	3.1	14	5:1
Philosophy	0.6	8	14:1

*Total number of significant figures times .022.

In every case except astronomy, Jews are disproportionately represented. The period 1870–1950 saw the addition of 1,277 significant figures to the Western inventories. If the Jews had produced significant figures strictly in accordance with their representation in the population, about 28 of those 1,277 should have been Jewish. The actual number was at least 158 (data on ethnicity were not available for many of the less prominent significant figures, and some Jews have doubtless been missed).[12] The disproportional representation since 1870 has been most pronounced in philosophy, where Jews have outperformed their expected contribution by 14:1, followed by mathematics (12:1) and physics (9:1).[13]

Jewish Disproportional Representation Within Countries

A possible artifact comes to mind: Jews were either growing up in or immigrating to countries such as France, Germany, Britain, and the United States, all of which were producing disproportionate numbers of significant figures during the period 1870–1950 even without counting the Jewish contribution. The apparent disproportional representation of Jews merely reflects their participation in these active countries.

This hypothesis may be tested by breaking down the figures according to the country where significant figures achieved the bulk of their careers and comparing the number of significant figures produced by Jews and Gentiles. The period is still 1870–1950. The computation of significant figures per million is based on an average of the populations in 1900 and 1940, once again having the effect of skewing the figures to minimize the Jewish contribution, for reasons explained in the note.[14] The table below shows the results for the six countries with the most significant figures for 1870–1950.

Disproportional Representation of Jews by Country, 1870–1950

Work country*	Total Jewish significant figures	Total Gentile significant figures	Ratio of Jewish to Gentile significant figures after controlling for population†
Austro-Hungary	21	50	7:1
Britain	8	170	8:1
France	18	185	19:1
Germany	40	155	22:1
Russia	9	63	4:1
USA	48	261	5:1

*Work country refers to the nation where a significant figure spent the most important part of his career.

† The numerator is Jewish significant figures per million Jewish population. The denominator is Gentile significant figures per million Gentile population.

In each instance, the hypothesis that Jewish accomplishment is explained by the activity in the countries where they worked fails. France's and Germany's high ratios of 19:1 and 22:1 respectively, much higher than in Britain and the United States, are intriguing. Immigration of people who had made their reputation in Russia and then emigrated to Germany or France in mid-career is not a factor—the work country for such persons is classified as Russia. Immigration of children from Eastern Europe is not a factor. Germany lost more to Jewish emigration than it gained from immigration (it had a net loss of 7 significant figures from 1870–1950), while France had a net gain of just 5. The United States was the big winner from immigration, with a net gain of 26 during that period.

The parsimonious explanation for the high ratios in France and Germany is that those countries provided favorable environments in which Jews could rise. This is hard to believe of Germany when one thinks of Hitler and the Third Reich. But throughout 19C and through World War I, Germany was a success story of growing Jewish opportunity and assimilation into German high culture.[15]

Another intriguing aspect of the table is the story for Russia. Russia drove out a large portion of its Jewish population. It persecuted the ones who remained, through legal restrictions and virulent anti-Semitism. After the Revolution, Stalin killed substantial numbers of the most able elements of the remaining Jewish population. Socially, anti-Semitism remained a fact of Soviet life as it had been a fact of Czarist life. And despite all that, Jews are disproportionately represented among Russian significant figures from 1870–1950 by a ratio of 4:1.

In closing, a caution: Jewish disproportional representation should not be confused with Jewish domination. Even in Germany, Jews amounted to only 40 out of 195 significant figures who appeared from 1870–1950, 21 percent of the total. The point of this exercise is to document the extreme density of the Jewish contribution relative to the size of the Jewish population.

Since 1950

As in the case of women, it seems inarguable that education and occupations were more open to Jews in the last half of 20C than they had been in the first half of 20C (even without considering the Third Reich). The expectation is that Jewish accomplishment would continue to increase—and so, judging from one readily available indicator, it has. The table on page 282 replicates the story for Nobel Prizes shown earlier for women.

In raw numbers, Jews won 29 prizes in the sciences and literature in

Percentage of Jewish Nobel Prize Winners in Literature
and the Sciences During the Two Halves of 20C[16]

Prize	1901–1950	1951–2000
Sciences total	17%	29%
Chemistry	12%	22%
Medicine	22%	32%
Physics	15%	32%
Literature	4%	15%
Total	**14%**	**29%**

Note: The prizes for economics (awarded only since 1969) and
peace are in fields not included in the inventories. Jews won 2
and 7 peace prizes in the two halves of the century, and won 18
of the 46 economics prizes (39 percent) through 2000.

Sources: See note 16.

the first half of the century, 14 percent of the total awarded, and 96 in the
second half, 29 percent of the total awarded—more than a tripling of
numbers and almost a doubling of the percentage.[17] As one would expect,
this was accompanied by greatly increased ratios, but trying to estimate those
ratios produces ludicrous results. During the second half of 20C, the Nobel
Committee explicitly tried to expand its frame of reference to include the
entire world, awarding prizes to people from several Asian, African, and
Latin American countries. But Jews as of the last quarter of 20C represented less than half of one percent of the world's population. If one expresses the Jewish population as a proportion of the developed world's population,
using 1 percent as the estimate, then the ratios for 1951–2000 range from
a minimum of 15:1 to a maximum of 35:1. Instead, the table opposite
shows the ratios if we continue to use 2.2 percent as the basis for the calculation. This no longer produces merely conservative estimates, but radically
understated ones.

In the sciences and literature, Jews were disproportionately represented
during 1901–1950 by a ratio of 6:1. During 1951–2000, that ratio doubled,
to 12:1, rising substantially in every prize category, even when calculated by
a method that understates the per capita Jewish contribution by several-fold.
This trend is consistent with the hypothesis that Jewish accomplishment up
to 1950 was still being held back relative to its potential.[18]

Ratio of Actual to Expected Jewish Nobel Prize Winners in
Literature and the Sciences During the Two Halves of 20C

Prize	1901–1950	1951–2000
Sciences total	8:1	13:1
Chemistry	5:1	10:1
Medicine	10:1	14:1
Physics	7:1	14:1
Literature	2:1	7:1
Total	**6:1**	**12:1**

Note: Expected winners are estimated by multiplying the total
number of winners times .022. The ratio represents actual winners divided by expected winners.

Sources: See note 16.

RECENT TRENDS FOR NON-WHITES, MALE AND OTHERWISE

The story for non-whites living in their native countries was described in
Chapter 11 when I compared the contributions from Europe, the rest of the
West, and everywhere else. But that discussion did not look at recent trends,
nor did it take into account the contributions of ethnically non-white significant figures who did their work in Europe or the United States. The
question arises: If we focus on ethnicity instead of nationality, how does the
picture change?

When we restrict the inquiry to significant figures and the cutoff date
of 1950, hardly anything changes. Four ethnically African writers and one
African composer appear in the roster of significant figures, but otherwise all
the significant figures in literature, music, and the visual arts from non-
European backgrounds were already treated in Chapter 11.[19] Some changes
may be observed when we turn to the evidence that includes people who
were active after 1950. As before, I begin with the Nobel Prizes.

As the figure at the top of page 284 shows, the trend is definitely up in
both prize categories, but the proportions remain small even in the second
half of 20C.

Again following the example used for women and Jews, I now turn to
the complete roster of people mentioned even once in any source, including
those after 1950 (see the figure at the bottom of page 284). We are limited
to people in the scientific inventories, because the arts inventories were prepared separately for some non-European nations.

PERCENTAGE OF ETHNICALLY NON-EUROPEAN NOBEL PRIZE WINNERS DURING THE FIRST AND SECOND HALVES OF 20C

Ethnicity	Science Prizes*		Literature Prize	
	1901–1950	1951–2000	1901–1950	1951–2000
African	—	—	—	4%
Arabic	—	1%	—	2%
Chinese	—	2%	—	2%
Indian	1%	1%	2%	—
Japanese	1%	2%	—	4%
Total	**2%**	**6%**	**2%**	**12%**

*Chemistry, Medicine, Physics.

The Japanese have been on an upward trend. The Chinese increased in the second half of 20C. Africans and Indians have remained at a lower level.[20] Only two Arabic persons are mentioned. In interpreting these numbers, recall that living persons were not included in the *DoSB*, which means

The trendlines in the combined scientific inventories for raw mentions of ethnically non-European persons from 1830 to post-1950

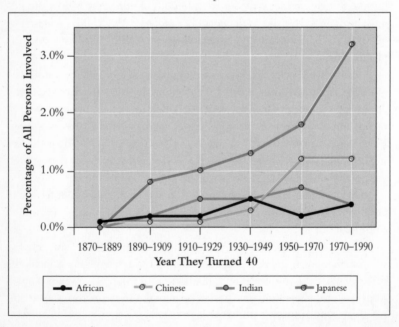

that some eminent scientists from these ethnic groups whose contributions came in the last half of 20C were omitted.

To summarize: recent trends suggest that the proportional contributions of non-whites are likely to increase in the years to come, even if adding ethnicity to the analysis does not change the picture prior to 1950.

DO WE HAVE ANY IDEA WHY?

Explanations of the disproportionately high representation of Jews and low representation of women in the inventories can be biological or environmental. We are not required to choose from just one bin. Biological and environmental explanations can both play a role, separately or interacting in such complex ways that the line between the roles of biology and environment blurs.

As I set out to discuss the possibilities, a peculiarity of this historical moment should be kept in mind: Almost all of the current evidence regarding the causes of group differences is circumstantial and inconclusive. The debate will not have to depend on circumstantial evidence much longer, however. Within a few decades, we will know a great deal about the genetic differences among groups. Not all of the controversy will go away, but the room for argument will narrow substantially. It therefore seems pointless to use historical patterns of accomplishment to try to anticipate what these genetic findings will be. I am reminded of a colleague who received his Ph.D. in the late 1950s for a factor analysis that had taken him more than a year to complete with his protractor and hand calculator. In the same week that he submitted the thesis, he reproduced all that painstaking effort on the university's brand-new computer in the course of an afternoon. In retrospect, he would have been much better off choosing another topic. So too with any attempt to defend a particular causal theory underlying gender and ethnic differences in human accomplishment as of the opening of 21C. Here, I confine myself to a synopsis of current thinking about causes, without trying to be exhaustive or conclusive.

Women

Why, despite the removal of the legal obstacles, do women continue to show up in such small numbers in rosters of accomplishment? The account of Jewish accomplishment adds an implicit stinger to this question: If the Jews could rise to the top so rapidly once legal obstacles were removed, why couldn't women?

Environmental causes. Part of the answer is that the nature of the obstacles facing Jews and women differed. Winning the legal battle could not have nearly the liberating effect for women that it had for Jewish males. A Jewish male trying to take advantage of his newly won legal rights was acting as males had always been expected to act, but in new venues. A woman trying to take advantage of her newly won legal rights by entering a profession had to be prepared to make three new sacrifices. First, she had to accept being an oddball, which, depending on her situation, could mean being the object of curiosity, ridicule, scorn, or sometimes hatred, and not just from strangers (as was the case with anti-Semitism) but from her own community and even family. Second, she had to confront the reality that to pursue a career would automatically reduce the likelihood of marriage (the number of men willing to marry a career woman was then limited) and would increase the likelihood that any marriage she did enter would be strained if she continued her career. Third, even if she found herself in a good marriage, she had to confront another reality: Pursuing a career at full throttle, as first-rank accomplishment demands, is at odds with being a full-time mother. In practice, pursuing a career at full throttle often meant forgoing motherhood altogether.

These sacrifices did not go away when the legal battle was won. Professors in scientific and engineering faculties continued to tell young women that they shouldn't be taking up men's places in their classes. Employers continued to prefer men over women, pay them more, and promote them higher. Men as a group continued to feel threatened by intelligence and independence in the women they might be considering for wives. Husbands continued to discourage wives from pursuing careers that would compete with their own. It is hard to measure trendlines for such behaviors, but anecdotal evidence indicates they were not much less prevalent in 1950 than they had been earlier. The conflict between career and motherhood had not even lessened.

On these grounds alone, it is not surprising to see that legal emancipation failed to produce the same profusion of significant figures among women that it produced among Jewish males, and not surprising to see that progress even after 1950 has been slow. The only causes that need to be invoked are environmental ones that no one doubts have been real. The remaining question is whether they are underwritten by other more basic differences between men and women. I will offer two scenarios, one focus-

HOMOSEXUALITY AND HUMAN ACCOMPLISHMENT

Thinking about the possible biological correlates of human accomplishment raises the question of homosexuality. In our own era, the disproportionate representation of homosexuals in the arts is taken for granted, though specific magnitudes are hard to come by. For the period −800 to 1950, the significant figures claimed as homosexuals in a recent book, *The Gay 100*, include Socrates, St. Augustine, Michelangelo, Leonardo da Vinci, William Shakespeare, Piotr Tchaikovsky, Lord Byron, and Francis Bacon, in addition to significant figures of more recent years, such as Oscar Wilde and Walt Whitman, whose homosexuality is indisputable.[21]

The relationship of homosexuality to accomplishment in the arts and its possible biological roots are fascinating topics, but ones that I will leave for others. The difficulties in identifying homosexuality in significant figures are too great. Many of the claims now being made about homosexuals of the past, such as Shakespeare, are dubious. On the other side, it must be assumed that some significant figures were so effectively closeted that they are not part of even the most inclusive lists. I conclude that any historiometric estimates of the representation of homosexuals among the significant figures are so uncertain as to be useless.

ing on the role of motherhood and the other drawing more broadly from the socio-biological perspective.

Women and Motherhood. Exceptions exist, but, as a rule, the experience of pregnancy and birth appears to be a more profoundly life-altering experience for women than becoming a father is for men. So closely is giving birth linked to the fundamental human goal of giving meaning to one's life that it has been argued that, ultimately, it is not so much that motherhood keeps women from doing great things outside the home as it is men's inability to give birth that forces them to look for substitutes.

Motherhood affects women's achievement through several mechanisms. The central importance of motherhood means that many women do not want to jeopardize the opportunity to become a mother. Single-minded devotion to a profession involves such a risk. Recall that the mean age at which peak accomplishments occur, following years of preparation, has been about 40. The years crucial to realizing great achievements have been precisely those years during which women are sexually most attractive, best able to find mates, and best able to bear children.

Among women who have already become mothers, the possibilities for accomplishment in the arts and sciences shrink. The problem here is not one that can be changed with better child-care arrangements. Rather, it is argued, the emotional distractions of parenthood are far greater for most mothers than for most fathers. However equally the physical burdens of child care are divided, the woman is likely to spend much more of the rest of her time thinking about the child's needs than the man does.

We could still be talking about environmental causes—the generalizations I have just offered are true about the world in which we live, it may be said, but only because males and females are socialized differently. But the empirical record casts this explanation into doubt. I will not try to review that literature here, but instead give you an encyclopedic source in the note and make this assertion about the pattern of findings it reveals: Don't count on socialization being the answer.[22] The state of knowledge already suggests that, as groups, men and women have fundamentally different relationships to parenthood that are parsimoniously explained by genetics.

Even if the differences are inborn, this counter argument can be posed: Yes, motherhood may be more consuming for women than for men, but as opportunities open up for women in the arts and sciences, those who are most able to make great contributions are also the most likely to forgo motherhood. Thus the disparity between men and women will narrow anyway.

Time will tell what the relative numbers of such singly focused women might be. The point to remember here is that we are not talking merely about motherhood versus career or about juggling jobs and children. When we discuss accomplishments at the level of the people in the inventories, we are commonly talking about perfectionist, monomaniacal devotion to a calling. That calls for a much more ruthless tradeoff than the ones ordinarily required by a job and children. We should not be surprised or dismayed to find that motherhood tempers the all-consuming obsession that great accomplishment in the arts and sciences often requires.

The Raw Materials for Great Accomplishment. The most ambitious and controversial explanation for the disparity between accomplishment among men and women is based on biological differences in the types of human capital that go into great accomplishment.

The empirical observation at the core of this view is that in human societies around the world, men have without exception routinely held the top positions in hierarchies and dominated the high-status roles. *Without exception* is a strong statement, but the documentation for this aspect of the argument is persuasive. In 1970, sociologist Steven Goldberg published *The Inevitability of Patriarchy*, in which he asserted that these characteristics were universal. His book was met with a barrage of claims to the contrary, citing examples of societies and tribes in which men did not dominate the hierarchies and the high-status roles. In 1993, Goldberg published a new statement of his theory entitled *Why Men Rule*, in which he examined every supposed exception that had been cited in response to his first book. To my knowledge, no one is still trying to make a data-based case (although rhetorical claims continue) that Goldberg's claim of universality is wrong.

Using social construction to explain why human societies have been *universally* constructed according to these sex differences in role and attainment requires complicated arguments. Using biology to explain them requires simple ones. Parsimony suggests that at least part of the explanation must involve biological differences that give males an advantage in attaining those roles. Many of these differences are argued to cluster around male-female differences in aggressiveness, broadly defined. It could well be that the Sistine Chapel and the invention of the *blitzkrieg* both really come from the same cause: It is men who go to the extremes, compete ruthlessly, and, in whatever field they take up, are going to achieve the best and the worst. The word *testosterone* comes to mind as a causal factor.

One aspect of this male tendency toward extremes seems to apply to cognitive ability. Although the mean IQ of men and women is apparently the same, the variability of male IQ is higher—meaning that more men than women are to be found at both the high and low extremes of IQ. Conjoined with this is evidence that men's and women's cognitive repertoires are somewhat different.[23] Women tend to do better, for example, in a variety of verbal skills; men in a variety of mathematical and visual-spatial skills. The latter may explain a conundrum: Brain size is reliably correlated with IQ; men and women have different mean brain sizes; but men and women have similar overall IQ.[24] Some large portion of those extra brain cells in men may be devoted to three-dimensional processing, the largest and most consistently identified male cognitive advantage.

In any case, the male advantage in these areas, which has plausible evolutionary origins (see the following box), fits neatly with the observed patterns of human accomplishment in the inventories, whereby the male advantage corresponds to degree of abstraction involved in an art (literature

EVOLUTIONARY EXPLANATIONS

Cognitive tests consistently find that women are better at remembering the relative location of things within a known array of objects whereas men are better able to generate accurate representations of novel environments. Or to put it in terms of stereotypes that seem to have merit: Wives remember where the car keys are; guys read maps better than girls do. Why should this be?

The evolutionary psychologists point out that when *Homo sapiens* was evolving, the ability to mentally visualize how to get from point *A* to *B* and back again had major survival value, and so did the ability to identify food plants from within complex arrays of vegetation. Men did the hunting (fostered by other physical advantages of males) while women did the gathering. Their mental repertoires diverged corresponding to the skills that evolutionary pressure rewarded. Explaining the male advantage in rotating three-dimensional images in contemporary laboratory settings is even more direct: Being able to process the trajectory of objects in three dimensions is a terrific survival advantage if the rabbit is over there, you're over here, and you've got a rock in your hand.

being the least abstract and musical composition being the most abstract, with the visual arts in the middle). Women have been represented among the great writers since Sappho, whereas to this day there have been no women composers of the first rank and only a few second-rank ones, while the record of women in the visual arts is in between.

Within the sciences, the ordering from more to less abstract is not so clear cut—some tasks in astronomy, for example, are pure observation, cataloging, and description, while others call on the highest reaches of mathematical abstraction. But in scanning the roster of female significant figures in the sciences, the overwhelming majority made their reputations on achievements that were concrete rather than abstract, with the most famous of all women scientists, two-time Nobel winner Marie Curie, being an apt example.

In citing specific cases I risk confusing an exercise intended to illustrate with one intended to prove, and so I will desist. The existing circumstantial evidence is already strong enough to have persuaded me that disparities in accomplishment between the sexes are significantly grounded in biological differences, but nothing in this brief rehearsal of the arguments need sway readers who are confident that science will prove me wrong. I close the discussion of sex differences with the point that I made at the outset: All we need is a few decades' patience and we won't have to argue anymore.

The Jews

What explains the extraordinary level of accomplishment among the Ashkenazi Jews who came out of Central and Eastern Europe? Explanations of the causal dynamics vary, but they all start from one indisputable, consistent fact about traditional Jewish life: the extraordinarily high value attached to learning. Here is a senior official of Russian-controlled Poland writing of Polish Jews in 1818:

> Almost every one of their families hires a tutor to teach its children. . . . We [Gentiles] do not have more than 868 schools in towns and villages and 27,985 pupils in all. They probably have the same number of pupils because their entire population studies. Girls too can read, even the girls of the poorest families. Every family, be it in the most modest circumstances, buys books, because there will be at least ten books in every household. Most of those inhabiting the huts in [Gentile] villages have only recently heard of an alphabet book. . . .[25]

Devotion to learning has been a constant in Jewish life from time out of mind, and it is not surprising to see it associated with a high degree of realized intellectual ability. In the modern era, this intellectual ability has been measured with mental tests of various sorts, including IQ tests. Reports of the mean IQ of Ashkenazi Jews vary, but it is likely to be at least 107 on tests that are normed to have a mean of 100.[26] Note the specification of Ashkenazi Jews, the group that dominates Northern European and American Jewish populations, though I drop the specification in the rest of the discussion. The data for Oriental Jews do not show consistently elevated IQ means.[27]

Jews also have much larger proportions of people with extremely high IQs.[28] The famous Terman study of high-IQ children in the early 1920s found that 10.5 percent of California children with IQs of 135 or higher were Jewish. This percentage was found even with a definition that did not define any child as Jewish if he had even one non-Jewish *grand*parent, in an era when many Jewish families hid their ethnic identity, and in an era when many of those who did identify themselves as Jewish used Yiddish as the primary spoken language at home (the children were tested in English). Terman himself believed that the 10.5 percent estimate was a substantial underestimate of Jewish representation. In 1954, a psychologist took advantage of New York City's universal IQ-testing to identify all 28 children with measured IQs of 170 or higher. Twenty-four of them were Jews.[29]

These findings about IQ leave us with the chicken and egg problem still unresolved. Do Jews have high IQs because their culture encourages it, or does their culture value learning so highly because Jews are unusually good at learning? With admonishments to remember that we still do not know the answer, it is at least plausible that selection pressures have led to a higher Jewish IQ with some genetic basis. One cause of genetic difference could be the Diaspora and subsequent centuries of anti-Semitism, requiring the Jews to survive in alien and often hostile cultures. Those who survived and left behind offspring were statistically likely to be more resourceful than those who did not.[30] Another line of argument for a genetic basis is that status within traditional Jewish communities was closely linked with learning. The young rabbi was one of the most desirable marriage partners for young women, and also, given the intellectual demands of Talmudic study, probably had a high IQ. Others who were not rabbis but known to be learned were also desirable marriage partners. A culture in which the males with the highest IQs have the pick of the women is, over centuries, likely to become a population with a high mean IQ.

Any effects of cultural traits tending to select for high IQ would have been intensified in the case of the Ashkenazim by a genetic bottleneck that occurred about 500 years ago. As many as 1,500 Ashkenazi families may have lived in Europe as of 14C, but geneticists at Jerusalem's Hebrew University examining the DNA from large samples of Ashkenazi Jews conclude that many of these family lines subsequently died out and that far fewer, probably about 500, account for all of today's Ashkenazi Jews. They further believe that this subset was selected for better nutrition and lower infant mortality rates—which in turn suggests both greater wealth and greater ability than among the families who disappeared.[31]

IQ is by no means the only advantage that might explain the exceptional record of Jewish accomplishment. Jewish family units were strong through 1950, with few children growing up in broken homes and with close networks of grandparents, aunts, and uncles to step in when a parent died. The high expectations placed on Jewish children are the stuff of cultural cliché, as are the sacrifices that American immigrant Jewish parents made to ensure that their children received advanced educations. Once again, however, the chicken and egg problem remains to be resolved. Cultural values can certainly be fostered or undermined by environmental conditions. They also can be fostered or undermined by genetically grounded personality traits. The nature of the mix in the case of Ashkenazi Jews is still as unknown as it is in the case of sex differences, and as likely to become better understood within a few decades.

THIRTEEN

CONCENTRATIONS OF EUROPEAN AND AMERICAN ACCOMPLISHMENT

The main purpose of this and the following chapter is to provide some food for thought now and a great deal of raw material to which you can return later. In subsequent chapters, I make statements about trends and patterns of accomplishment as they relate to hypothesized causes. Some of those statements (Chapters 15 and 16) are founded on multivariate analyses; others, on qualitative interpretations of trends in European history. In preparing these narratives, I constantly returned to basic layouts of the raw data that helped me understand why the computer program was coming up with the coefficients it did, or whether my reading of history corresponded with where the significant figures came from and when. The plots in this chapter and the next give you the chance to do the same thing.

Both chapters have brief narratives describing a few key findings. I suggest you read the narrative, scan the graphics for whatever topics interest you, and then return to them when subsequent chapters raise questions that the graphics might answer.

THE EUROPEAN CORE

Despite its small size, common Christian heritage, and common racial heritage, a few places within Europe have been home to far more intense levels of human accomplishment than other places. This chapter describes what those places are for the different inventories at different points in Europe's history.

The concentration of European accomplishment from 1400–1950 is easy enough to sum up if you don't worry about complications: the numbers of significant figures from Britain, France, and Germany dwarf those from everywhere else except Italy. The chart below shows the distribution.

The big four, and everybody else

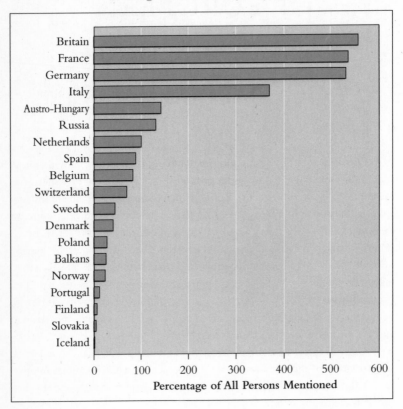

The big four alone account for 72 percent of all the significant figures from 1400–1950. Add in Russia and the Netherlands, and 80 percent of all significant figures are accounted for. But countries are bulky and their borders change. Saying that a certain number of significant figures came from Italy obscures the reality that most of them came from specific parts of Italy surrounding Florence and Venice. For that matter, Italy did not even exist as a unified nation-state until 19C. Neither did Germany. Britain encompasses four distinctive linguistic and cultural entities. During the period when

Russia accumulated its significant figures, it included within its borders parts or all of eight different countries on today's map. Even the French, who share a common language and have lived in a well-defined nation for several centuries, sprawl over a large and diverse geographic area. So let us put aside nations for a moment and consider how the map looks when more specific places of origin replace them. By *origin* I refer to the place where a significant figure spent the bulk of his childhood—usually, though not always, his place of birth.

To prepare the breakdowns that follow, I broke the map of Europe into 134 regions and 121 cities. Appendix 4 gives the details. Using those regions and cities rather than countries, let us reconsider the statement that Britain, France, Germany, Italy, Russia, and the Netherlands accounted for 80 percent of the European significant figures. If we ignore national borders and instead create the most compact polygon (in terms of land area) that encloses 80 percent of the places where the significant figures grew up, it forms the shape in the figure below, with borders defined by Naples, Marseilles, the western border of Dorset County in England, a point a few miles above Glasgow, the northern tip of Denmark, and a point a few miles east of the city that used to be Breslau in German Silesia (now Wroclaw in Poland).

The European Core

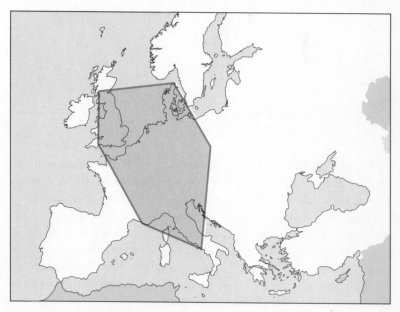

This new way of looking at the distribution of significant figures across Europe does not wholly contradict the dominating role of the big four shown in the chapter's initial chart, but it changes the emphases. All of the Netherlands is still in the new way of looking at Europe. *Parts* of Britain, France, Germany, and Italy are still in. Russia is out. Or you can think of it another way: 80 percent of all the European significant figures can be enclosed in an area that does *not* include Russia, Sweden, Norway, Finland, Spain, Portugal, the Balkans, Poland, Hungary, East and West Prussia, Ireland, Wales, most of Scotland, the lower quarter of Italy, and about a third of France.

The next graphic zooms in the focus, demonstrating how much a few regions dominate even within the European core.

Concentrations within the European Core

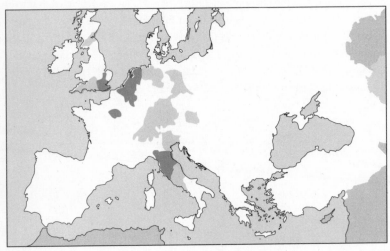

The colored regions in the European core (blue and black together) account for the origins—not where they went to work when they grew up, but where they were born and raised—of fully 50 percent of the total European significant figures. Just the five regions colored in black—Île de France, Southeast England, Tuscany, Belgium, and the Netherlands—account for 26 percent of the European total. The other 24 percent come from (in order of their contribution) Bavaria, Venetia, Southwest England, Switzerland, Lowland Scotland, Lower Saxony, Saxony, Baden-Württemberg, Northeast Austria, the Italian Papal States, and Brandenburg.

The figures above represent summaries. Now we turn to the distributions, significant figure by significant figure, that lead to them.

SCATTER PLOTS FOR THE EUROPEAN SIGNIFICANT FIGURES

The tides of history have raised and lowered the importance of the regions. Tuscany's appearance in the preceding figure is based almost entirely on significant figures who appeared prior to 1700, for example. We also know that the distribution of accomplishment over time consists of a steep, curving, upward trend in the last few centuries (page 248), which causes a problem in interpreting the concentrations in regions where most of the activity occurred late. It was much easier for a country to have 50 great scientists in 19C than it was in 14C. Somehow that nonlinear increase from 15C onward has to be taken into account.

For purposes of visual display I have divided modern European history into three segments: 1400–1600, 1600–1800, and 1800–1950. You may rightly doubt that such round numbers precisely denote the beginning of different eras, but the divisions have enough correspondence with the flow of accomplishment across history to make them interpretable.

The first period opens as Europe is recovering from the devastation of the Black Death in mid-14C and Italy is entering the Renaissance. In just a few years, Brunelleschi will discover the laws of linear perspective and European art will begin its historic explosion of creativity. By the mid-1400s, all of the arts and sciences are taking off, a process that is transformed by the contemporaneous introduction of the printing press. The remaining 150 years in this first era take us through the peak of the Renaissance and into its denouement after the Reformation begins in 1517.

At the beginning of the second era, 1600, the scientific method has evolved into a set of principles that are broadly understood and accepted—Galileo's *De Motu,* with its pioneering use of experimental data, had appeared just 11 years earlier, and Francis Bacon's *Advancement of Learning,* advocating the experimentation and observation he will bring to full expression in *Novum Organum,* is published in 1605. In the arts, the first years after 1600 witness the debut of Shakespeare's greatest works on the London stage. Carracci and Caravaggio have broken with Mannerism by 1600, opening the way to the Baroque in the visual arts. Monteverdi is about to write the operas that usher in the Baroque in music. In philosophy, the two centuries of 17C and 18C embrace the most productive period since classical Athens, opening with Hobbes and Descartes and ending in the aftermath of the Enlightenment. Science comes of age during these 200 years, with a succession of giants of whom Newton looms largest. By 1800, the technological framework for the Industrial Revolution is in place.

The third era, 1800–1950, the shortest of the three in time, is the most riotously active, taking us through the multiple scientific and technological leaps of 19C and the first half of 20C. All of the arts reach peaks of different sorts, and all evolve new genres that by the end of the period have separated them from their earlier foundations.

The sets of maps on the next three pages show the results for each of the eras. I have left a faint outline of borders to help organize the maps. They represent the contemporary boundaries of European countries with the exception of Germany and Poland. Germany's borders are shown as they existed at the outset of World War I, with formerly Prussian regions extending along the south coast of the Baltic, and the former Silesia forming a slice along the northern border of today's Czech Republic and Slovakia.[1] Prior to World War II, these areas produced many significant figures, all of whom were ethnically German.

Each dot represents the origin of an individual significant figure. How close are the dots located to the place of origin? About half of them are either on top of the specific city or town where the significant figure grew up (or as close as possible, in the case of a city such as London or Paris with too many dots for too little space). The other half of the dots are accurate to within the region of origin, and often accurate to within a portion of the region.[2]

To give you a way of comparing the density of concentration across the different eras and inventories, I have enclosed the smallest geographic area that can contain 25 percent of the significant figures, colored in the darker blue, and then enclosed the smallest additional areas that can contain the next 25 percent, colored in the lighter blue. In a few instances, the space containing the second 25 percent could have been chosen in more than one way, and readers who think they see an alternative that would be just as geographically compact may be right.

ORIGINS OF SIGNIFICANT FIGURES, 1400–1600

Art

Literature

Music

Science

ORIGINS OF SIGNIFICANT FIGURES, 1600–1800

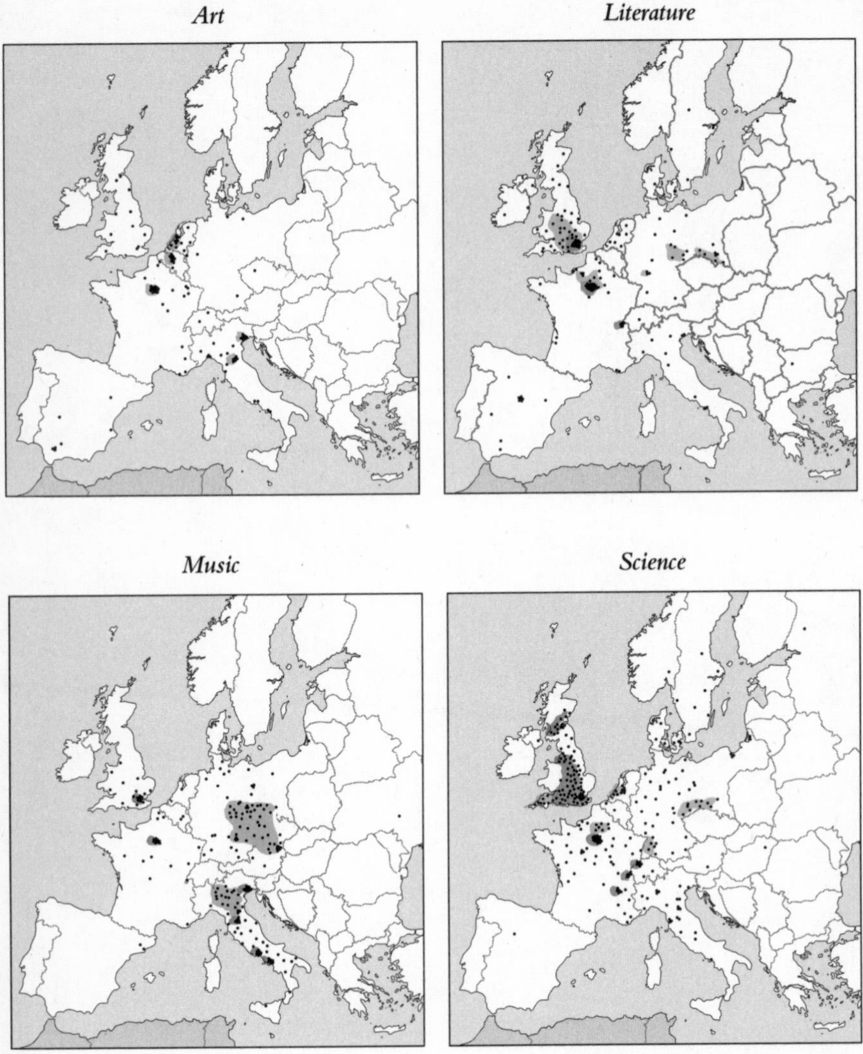

Art

Literature

Music

Science

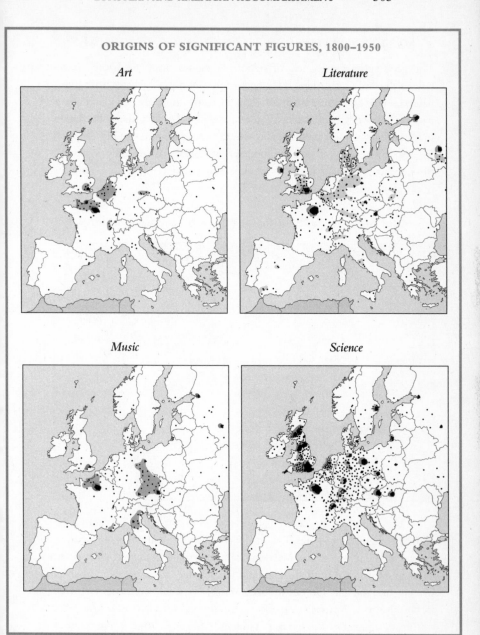

ORIGINS OF SIGNIFICANT FIGURES, 1800–1950

Art

Literature

Music

Science

SCATTER PLOTS FOR U.S. SIGNIFICANT FIGURES

The geographic distribution of significant figures from the United States reflects the rapidly changing settlement of the country. The East Coast dominates, inevitably, because hardly anyone lived anywhere else for much of the nation's history. If I could show you a map with America's significant figures in the last half century, it presumably would look much different from the first half of 20C, just because the population shifted so radically westward throughout 20C. With that in mind, the figure below is offered as a summary of the story from the founding to 1950.

Concentrations of Significant Figures in the United States

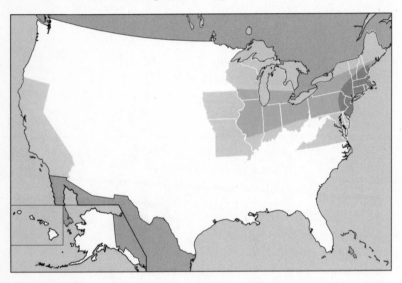

The states that are colored represent the origins of 90 percent of the American significant figures. The small dark blue slice running in an arc from Portland, Maine, to the southern tip of New Jersey encompasses the origins of about 50 percent of them. The light blue wedge encompasses another 25 percent, and the gray fills out the remaining 15 percent. Even after factoring in the history of American expansion, the primary concentration along the northeastern coast of the United States and the secondary concentration in the belt stretching to the Mississippi is striking.

An even more striking aspect of the map is the white space covering the American South. Although more lightly populated than the North, the

American South had a substantial population throughout American history. In 1850, for example, the white population in the South was 5.6 million, compared to 8.5 million in the Northeast. In 1900, the comparison was 12.1 million to 20.6 million. By 1950, the gap had almost closed—36.9 million compared to 37.4 million.[3] While it is understandable that the South did not have as many significant figures as the North, the magnitude of the difference goes far beyond population. The northeastern states of New England plus New York, Pennsylvania, and New Jersey had produced 184 significant figures by 1950, while the states that made up the Confederacy during the Civil War had produced 24, a ratio of more than 7:1.

The scatter plots on the following page show the way in which the American significant figures break down over the three half centuries from 1800–1950.

A POSTSCRIPT ON IMMIGRATION

Throughout this chapter, I have used the place of origin as the basis for the discussion. If instead I were to use the workplace of adult significant figures, how much would immigration change the picture?

The most visible change in the scatter plots would result from internal migration, not from movement between countries. Paris was the origin of 189 significant figures, already a large figure, but small compared to the 486 for which Paris was the workplace. For London, the comparable numbers are 113 and 295; for Berlin, they are 36 and 91. If the scatter plots had been based on the workplace, the concentration of dots around the great cities of Europe would have nearly denuded the rest of the map.

Migration from one country to another was by no means rare among the significant figures, however. They were a remarkably mobile lot. Twelve percent of them worked mainly in a country other than the one in which they were raised. This is not a recent phenomenon. The highest proportion of migration across countries, involving 14 percent of the significant figures, occurred from 1400–1600. Even 14 percent greatly underestimates the degree of "international" mobility, because it does not count movement from, for example, Milan to Florence or Cologne to Leipzig—in the Renaissance, tantamount to moving between countries.

Until 1800, this high level of international mobility had little effect on the net number of significant figures in a given country. All the countries in the European core gained about as many as they lost. In the third era,

ORIGINS OF SIGNIFICANT FIGURES FROM THE UNITED ST

1800–1850

1850–1900

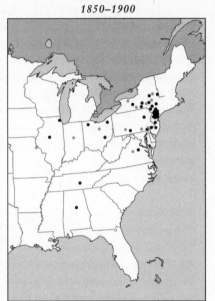

1900–1950

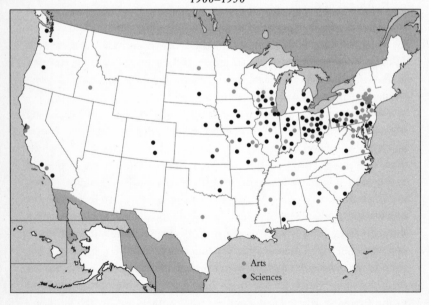

Arts
Sciences

1800–1950, a clear pattern did emerge. Europeans who would become significant figures moved north and west to realize their potential. Part of the movement from the east was caused by persecution. Seven Polish and Russian Jews who became significant figures emigrated westward during the long period of persecution in late 19C, and another two dozen fled central Europe after the Nazi rise to power.[4] But even after extracting this part of the story, the period from 1800–1950 saw the Balkan countries lose a net of nine. Germany lost a net of 15 (8 moved into Germany but 23 moved out, not counting the Nazi period), while Spain, Russia, Poland, and Italy each had a net loss of 5 and what is now the Czech Republic had a net loss of 4.[5]

Nearly all of the people who moved out of these countries on the periphery moved to just three places: Britain, northern France, and the United States. Britain did not end up with much of a net gain, because while 21 significant-figures-to-be moved into Britain, 16 Britons left for the New World. Only France and the United States had a substantial net gain: 31 for France and 37 for the United States.

France's net gain amounts to 8 percent of the significant figures who worked in France from 1800–1950, while America's amounted to 10 percent. If this seems small for the United States, where immigration has played such a large role in shaping the national character, remember how the number was calculated: It is restricted to people who grew up in a foreign country and then moved to the United States to conduct their most important work. Thus it excludes all the children of first-generation immigrants, all the immigrants who came here as infants or toddlers, and all the significant figures who came to the United States after their reputations were already established, as did many German and Austrian scientists and artists fleeing the Nazis. If we include all of those categories, then about 22 percent of all the American significant figures from 1800–1950 were either immigrants or the children of immigrants.

FOURTEEN

TAKING POPULATION INTO ACCOUNT: THE ACCOMPLISHMENT RATE

I t is no surprise that Britain has more significant figures than Belgium, or that France has more than Switzerland. They've got more people. The same explanation could apply to the steep, sweeping rise in human accomplishment that opened the presentation of patterns and trajectories in Chapter 11 (page 248). When we superimpose a line for the world's population this is the result:

Accomplishment and population both rose nonlinearly after 1400

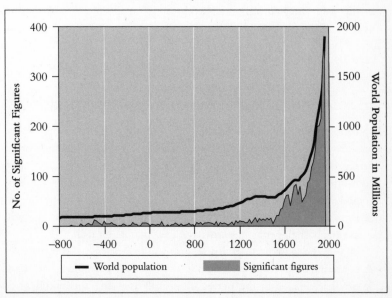

It is time to broach a topic that will be with us for the rest of the book, for it is central to understanding the intensity of human accomplishment within a given society: What happens when we take population into account?

The short answer is that taking population into account transforms the picture. Like the preceding chapter, this one sticks narrowly to presenting the evidence for what is and defers the discussion of why to later chapters.

THE GLOBAL NON-RELATIONSHIP OF POPULATION TO ACCOMPLISHMENT

Everything that follows about the relationship of population to accomplishment applies only to Europe and the United States. Elsewhere, the relationship is approximately zero. Take, for example, that tight relationship between population and the number of significant figures in the opening graphic. The correlation was almost perfect: +.98, to be exact. But it exists only because of the European surge of accomplishment since 1400, which coincided with the growth in world population. Suppose instead that I had calculated it for one slice in time—1900, let's say—entering the population and the number of scientific significant figures for each country in the world. That correlation works out to a trivial +.12.[1] For any moment in history, knowing how large the populations are within given geographic areas tells you little about whether you will find important work going on in the arts and sciences. Great human accomplishment has not come about just because the world accumulated enough people.

MEASURING THE RATE OF ACCOMPLISHMENT

Population can be "taken into account" in two ways. One is to enter population as a variable in a regression equation, a method that will be used subsequently. But the simpler and more familiar way is to calculate a ratio, using population as the denominator. The crime rate, unemployment rate, birth rate, and per capita earnings are familiar examples of such ratios. They are just one form of the widespread, everyday use of rates—miles per hour, calories per serving, bushels per acre, batting average, and interest rate.

Using the same method, I now give you the *unweighted accomplishment rate*, consisting of the number of significant figures per 10 million population. For example, France in the period 1850–1870 saw the appearance of 54 significant figures among a population that at the beginning of that period stood at about 35.7 million. The accomplishment rate is therefore 15.1.[2]

To get a sense of how the rate has varied over time, it is also useful to create a *weighted accomplishment rate* that incorporates information conveyed by the index scores. Instead of computing the rate by counting each significant figure equally, I add up the index scores and use them as the numerator. To continue with the example of France in 1850–70, the index scores of the 54 significant figures add up to 697. This use of summed index scores produces a weighted accomplishment rate of 195.2.

For the arts and philosophy inventories, these two measures of the accomplishment rate are the basis for tracking rises and declines across the centuries. The scientific inventories have counts of events as well as people, giving a third perspective: the number of significant events per 10 million. France from 1850–70 numbered 40 events in the scientific inventories combined, yielding an *event rate* of 11.2.

The pages that follow show timelines for each of the inventories.[3] The lines represent a moving average over three decades, meaning that each significant figure is counted for the decade in which he turned 40 plus the decade on either side.

Because I want to show how the alternative measures of the rate track with each other, I converted all the rates into what are known as *standard scores*. The computation and uses of standard scores are discussed in Appendix 1. To recapitulate, standard scores always have a mean of 0 and a standard deviation of 1. Except when noted, the scale in the timelines that follow runs from +3 to −3 standard deviations. Three standard deviations above or below a mean represents the top tenth of the top centile in a normal distribution. Because it is the shape of the moving average that conveys the important information, not the specific values (the specific values, like the mean, are sensitive to the choice of time span),[4] I have labeled the top and bottom of the scale simply "Very high" and "Very low."

THE SCIENTIFIC AND WESTERN INVENTORIES

I begin with the accomplishment rates for the Western inventories in art, literature, music, and philosophy, plus the inventories for scientific accomplishments. The timeline for the hard sciences combines astronomy, biology, chemistry, the earth sciences, and physics. Otherwise, a separate timeline is presented for each inventory.

THE HARD SCIENCES, 1400 TO 1950
(Astronomy, Biology, Chemistry, Earth Sciences, Physics)

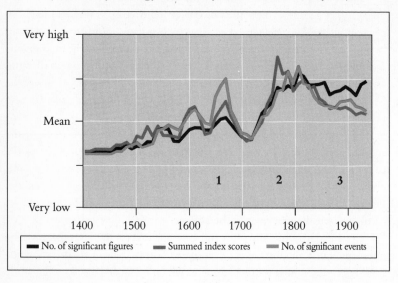

1. The first times that the production of significant figures in the hard sciences crept above the baseline are the two bumps around 1610 and 1680, and even then only for the summed index scores. Those small bumps represent periods that saw the publication of William Gilbert's *De Magnete*, the prime of Galileo's career, the invention of the telescope and microscope, and the introduction of Newtonian physics, among other accomplishments.

2. The last half of 18C and the first few decades of 19C were phenomenally productive, despite the French Revolution and the Napoleonic Wars. Each of the hard sciences experienced fundamental breakthroughs. In raw terms, the number of significant figures soared from 57 in the preceding hundred years to 220 in 1750–1850.

3. From the early 1800s onward, the summed index scores declined while the number of significant figures remained high. This could be seen as simply a reflection of a changing way of doing science, with teams replacing the lone hero, except that the number of significant events also declined during this period.

MATHEMATICS, 1400 TO 1950

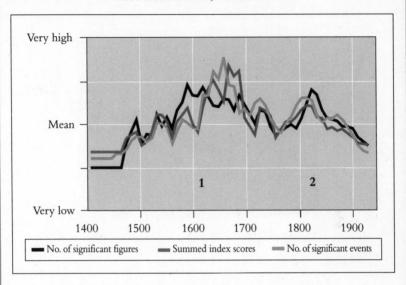

No. of significant figures   Summed index scores   No. of significant events

1   The golden age of mathematics occurred earlier than for any other scientific inventory, over the late 1500s to the end of the 1600s. A short list of the names explains why: Pascal, Fermat, Cavalieri, Descartes, Wallis, Huygens, Barrow, Leibniz, the first Bernoullis, and Newton, who discovered, among much else, logarithms, analytic geometry, probability theory, and the calculus.

2   A lesser but notable period of achievement in mathematics came in the early 1800s, led by Gauss but with a distinguished body of other mathematicians that included Abel, Cauchy, Galois, Lobachevsky, and Hamilton. After mid-19C, all the measures of accomplishment in mathematics, including those based on events, trailed off through the 1950 cutoff.

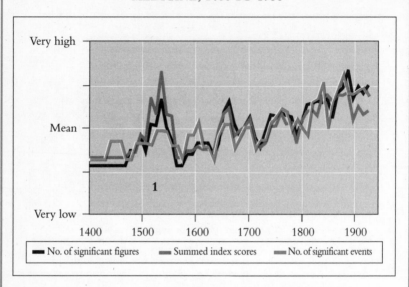

MEDICINE, 1400 TO 1950

- No. of significant figures
- Summed index scores
- No. of significant events

1 If we ignore the spike in the mid-1500s, the medicine inventory provides the most orderly of the trendlines: generally up, with only a few anomalies, from 1600 to the end of the observations. But there is that spike to consider. It consists of a flurry of activity led by Fracastoro, Paracelsus, Paré, and Vesalius that opened up lines of inquiry that would take a few more centuries to show their full potential for understanding and curing disease. The signal events were the publication of Paracelsus's *Die Kleine Chirurgia*, viewing the body as a chemical system subject to specific ailments; Fracastoro's *De Contagione et Contagiosis Morbis*, invoking microbes or germs as the cause of infectious disease; Paré's *Méthode de Traicter les Plaies*, introducing major advances in treatment of traumatic injuries; and Vesalius's *De Humani Corporis Fabrica*, the first scientifically exact anatomy text based on dissection.

TECHNOLOGY, 1400 TO 1950

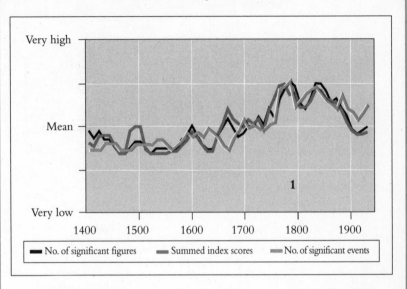

Very high

Mean

1

Very low

1400   1500   1600   1700   1800   1900

■ No. of significant figures   ■ Summed index scores   ■ No. of significant events

1 The story of technology is quiescence until the mid-1600s (that bump in
the summed index scores in 1500 is Leonardo da Vinci), then a general
increase to a high level in the late 1700s that for practical purposes continued into the second half of the 1800s. That period from about 1760 to
1880 ended before some key inventions like radio and the airplane, but
consider how much it encompassed: the practical steam engine that enabled
the industrial revolution, interchangeable parts, the technology of the
modern factory system, steel, the technology for creating large structures
made of iron, a host of key advances in industrial chemistry (including the
invention of the petroleum industry), the technology for modern agricultural production, the railroad, steamship, electric batteries, systems of artificial heating, artificial lighting (gas, then electric), the technology of
preserved foods, photography, the textile and garment industry, the telegraph (including transcontinental traffic), electric motors, electric trans-
formers, electric generators, refrigeration, vulcanization (revolutionizing the
uses of rubber), the invention of plastics, the internal combustion engine,
dynamite—and these are just the really important accomplishments. Much
may have changed because of technological advances since the late 1800s,
but what was done in the preceding century, from a much smaller base of
population and wealth, was vast.

WESTERN PHILOSOPHY, 1400 TO 1950

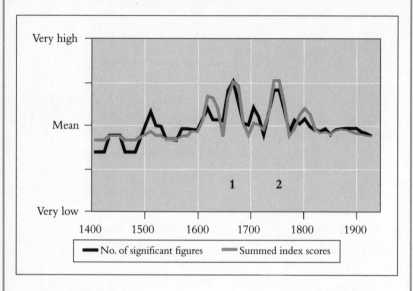

By starting at 1400, the graph misses the great age of classical philosophy, but there was no point in starting earlier. The spike in −4C is so dominant that everything after 1400 is flat—and no wonder. Take Socrates, Plato, and Aristotle, add major figures such as Heraclitus, Parmenides, Anaxagoras, Protagoras, Democritus, and Epicurus, then add the lesser but still signifi- cant figures, bunch most of them into a century and a half during −5C and −4C in a Europe that had a population somewhere around 20 million, and you have an accomplishment rate in European philosophy that will dwarf anything that comes after.

1 The last half of the 1600s provided the philosophical underpinnings of the Enlightenment. Descartes and Bacon had been precursors in the first half of the century. Then, clustered into a few decades, came Hobbes, Pascal, Leib- niz, Spinoza, and Locke.

2 The last two-thirds of the 1700s saw the culmination of the Enlightenment in Montesquieu, Helvetius, Hume, Rousseau, Diderot, and Voltaire and—so close in time that they form one spike in the graph—the philosophers who would set the stage for 19C, Moses Mendelssohn, Condorcet, Herder, Fichte, Bentham, and, towering over all, Kant.

WESTERN ART, 1400 TO 1950

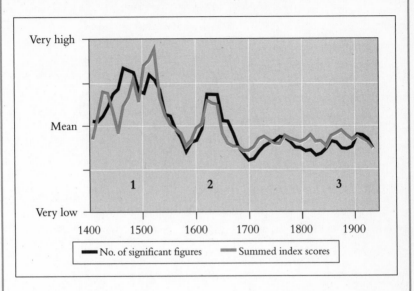

Very high

Mean

Very low

1400   1500   1600   1700   1800   1900

1   2   3

—— No. of significant figures   **——** Summed index scores

1. The mountain at the left of the plot is the Renaissance in graphic form. Occurring in 15C and the first decades of 16C when the European population was still low by later standards, it swamps everything that comes thereafter. But it would be a mistake to attach too much importance to the small population base. The raw number of significant figures and giants alike was high.

2. The next period in which both measures of accomplishment outstrip population is the first half of 17C. The Low Countries were the center of activity, with Rubens, Rembrandt, Hals, van Dyck, and (at the tail end) Vermeer as leading figures, but these decades also saw all or part of the careers of Caravaggio, Ribera, La Tour, Poussin, Bernini, Zurbaran, Lorrain, and Velazquez. As in the case of the Renaissance, the production of great art in this period was high in quantity as well as dense relative to the population.

3. I inserted this marker, toward the end of a monotonously below-baseline two centuries, because it sits directly beneath the flowering of Impressionism, Post-Impressionism, and the rest of the new genres that produced so many masterpieces in France and the rest of the Continent in the late 1800s. France as an individual country saw a noticeable bump during this period, but the graph here shows the West as a whole.

WESTERN LITERATURE, 1400 TO 1950

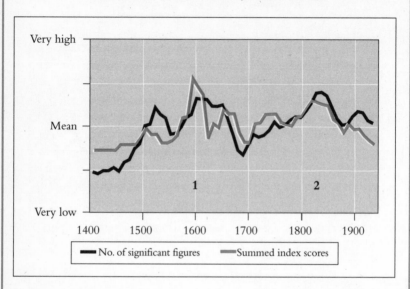

1 Dante was among the first to write in the vernacular, a century before the timeline opens in 1400, opening a long increase on both measures of the rate of accomplishment in literature. With a dip in the mid-1500s, this upward trend continued to the end of the 1500s and the age of Shakespeare, Cervantes, Spenser, Marlowe, Gongora y Argote, Lope de Vega, and Ben Jonson. After a dip in major figures came Corneille and Milton in the mid-1600s, marking the end of the first wave of literary accomplishment.

2 The second burst in the 1800s largely reflects the birth of the novel in the preceding century. Limiting the list to just the elite with index scores of 20 or higher who published from 1800–1880: Goethe, Hugo, Tolstoy, Dostoyevsky, Dickens, Flaubert, Stendhal, Turgenev, Scott, Gogol, Zola, Ibsen, and Balzac. Along with the novelists came a phalanx of important poets: Schiller (his last years), Byron, Poe, Pushkin, Baudelaire, Mallarmé, Whitman, Heine, Shelley, Keats, Verlaine, Hölderlin, and Wordsworth among them.

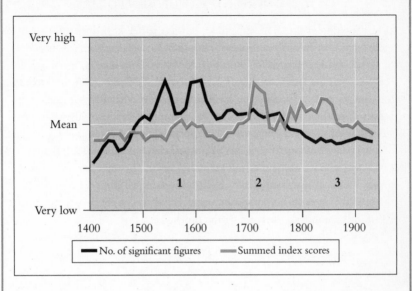

WESTERN MUSIC, 1400 TO 1950

Very high

Mean

Very low

1400   1500   1600   1700   1800   1900

1   2   3

▬▬ No. of significant figures   ▬▬ Summed index scores

1 For music, alone among all the inventories, the weighted and unweighted measures of accomplishment don't track. Disproportionately large numbers of significant figures appear from mid-16C through the first quarter of 17C, but the eminence of that large number lags substantially behind. Monteverdi is one of the few composers from that period whose name is still remembered and whose music is still part of the repertory. These were centuries when the groundwork for the forms and harmonic systems was being laid, but the mastery of them came later.

2 The number of still-familiar names begins to pick up at the end of the 1600s, but it is in the 1700s that Europe begins producing the giants who still figure so largely in the performed repertory. The conspicuous spike in 18C does not come where you might expect, at the end, but in the first third of the century when the leading figures were Scarlatti *père* and *fils*, Couperin, Vivaldi, Telemann, Rameau, and Handel. The three bumps that came later, representing Haydn, Mozart, and Beethoven (who didn't turn 40 until 1810), were comparatively lonely figures in their respective times.

3 For most of 19C, the pattern set in the ages of Haydn, Mozart, and Beethoven continued, with above-average production of the most eminent composers and below-average production of run-of-the-mill significant figures. At the end of 19C the trendline for the most eminent composers fell as well.

THE NON-EUROPEAN INVENTORIES

When looking at the graphs on the following pages, keep in mind that the plots for the non-European inventories are based on much smaller numbers of significant figures than the plots for the Western inventories. For example, the Western visual arts inventory has 479 significant figures compared to 111 for China and 81 for Japan. The smaller the number of figures, the greater the influence of small numbers. This creates a problem for the smallest inventories, especially Indian literature (43), Indian philosophy (45), and Chinese philosophy (39). Large swings can be produced by a few significant figures, as I will note again when discussing individual cases. The non-European inventories also encompass longer periods than the six and a half centuries used for the scientific inventories and Western arts inventories, another factor to be taken into account in interpreting the timelines.

ARABIC LITERATURE, 500 TO 1300

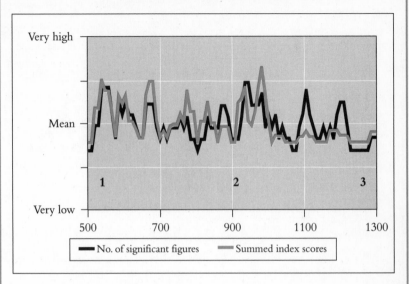

The graph portrays only literature written in Arabic, since index scores were not assigned to writers in other languages prevalent in the Arab world—none of the Persian writers are represented here, for example.

1 The first group represents the pre-Islamic writers in Arabic, led by Imru' al-Qays, inventor of the classic ode form *qasida*, who was considered by the Prophet Muhammad, among others, to be the greatest poet of pre-Islamic times.

2 This spike is dominated by a trio in early Islamic literature: al-Faraz-daq, Jarir, and al-Akhtal, ranked ninth, eleventh, and fourteenth respectively in the Arabic literature inventory. All were poets and wrote in similar styles, with Jarir and al-Farazdaq carrying on a 40-year battle of poems. al-Akhtal has the distinction of being a Christian Arabic poet.

3 The golden age of classic Arabic literature coincided with the golden age of Arabic culture in general. In literature, the peaks were reached in the century from 950 to 1050, which saw the first-ranked (by far) Arabic poet al-Mutanabbi and additional major writers al-Ma'arri, al-Hariri (a scholarly writer as well as poet), and al-Hamadhani, ranked third, sixth, and seventh respectively.

CHINESE PAINTING, 600 TO 1800

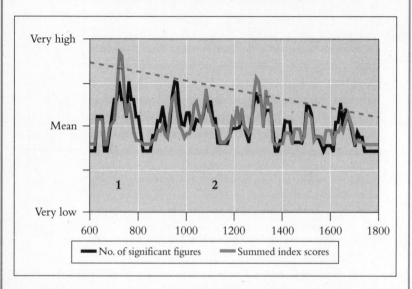

Chinese painting began centuries before the graph begins, but the surviving evidence is so fragmentary that the inventory cannot accurately reflect the number and eminence of those early painters.

1 The first great age of Chinese painting occurred during the Tang Dynasty, specifically during the hundred years that began with the reign of Emperor Minghuang in 712. It saw the careers of painters Wu Daozi, Zhang Xuan, and Han Gan (among others) and of Wang Wei, a poet, painter, musician, and scholar of near-mythic reputation.

2 The Song dynasty (960–1279) has three peaks corresponding roughly to the beginning, middle, and end (and the decades just after the end) of the dynasty. But because comparatively few people are involved in producing each peak, the period is better seen as a whole, as indeed it is seen in Chinese history, with the Song generally acknowledged to represent the apex of Chinese culture as a whole.

A striking feature of the accomplishment rate over the whole period is the way that the successive peaks diminish in elevation, shown by the gray broken line. It represents the best-fitting line for the peaks that occurred in 720, 950, 1080, 1290, 1500, and 1670.[5] I will leave it to specialists to argue about whether this visual metaphor corresponds to a diminishing vitality of Chinese art over these centuries.

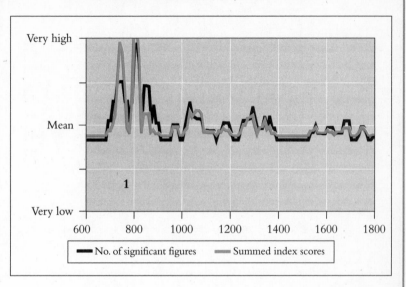

CHINESE LITERATURE, 600 TO 1800

Legend: No. of significant figures — Summed index scores

1 The Chinese golden age of literature coincided with its golden age in art, but with a much higher peak. Nothing thereafter came close. The same Tang century that saw so many fine painters was also the one in which the top two poets in all of Chinese history, Du Fu and Li Bo, made their appearance—not only as contemporaries but as drinking and traveling companions. They were far from the only great poets of that era. The highest peak of all, off the chart at 3.6 standard deviations in 800, does not include Du Fu and Li Bo (they are represented in the preceding peak), but a set of six poets who were ranked third, fifth, tenth, and thirteenth. In terms of raw numbers, the West has many periods in which it had more major literary figures, but it has nothing to compare with this extraordinarily dense cluster of so many of a culture's most revered poets.

CHINESE PHILOSOPHY, −600 TO 1200

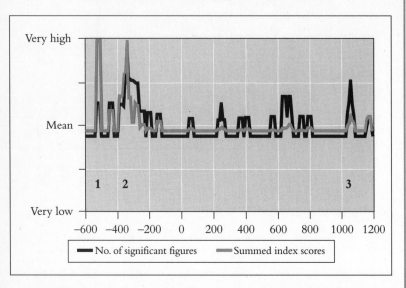

1 As in the West and India, great philosophy came very early. This peak, which stretches slightly off the scale (the score was +3.2 standard deviations) is owed to just two men, Confucius and Laozi. The date for Laozi is only an estimate, but the philosophic traditions associated with Confucius and Laozi both got their start within a narrow period of time.

2 While the original Confucian and Daoist texts go back to −6C, the consolidation of both traditions awaited their great initial exegetes, Mencius and Zhuangzi respectively, born within a few years of each other (circa −372 and −369).

3 The most important subsequent cluster of philosophic figures occurred in the latter part of the Song Dynasty, when several important neo-Confucianists appeared. They are spread out over a century and a half, beginning in the last half of 11C, when the population of China was about triple that of Confucius's China, so the rate jumped only modestly when the first set appeared and barely crept above the mean when Zhu Xi arrived at the end of 12C.

INDIAN LITERATURE, −500 TO 800

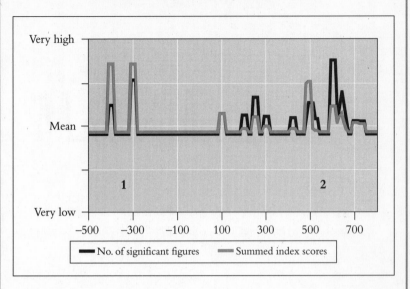

India's literature was produced in so many languages and so much of it developed anonymously—or has become anonymous over the course of centuries—that the inventory of significant figures does not capture nearly all of its bulk. On the other hand, if the issue is works that are still live elements of the Indian canon, then the graphic above, focusing on Sanskrit literature during its classical period, includes all the stars. For reasons noted elsewhere (page 135), index scores were not assigned to the major Indian novelists that emerged from mid-19C onward.

1 The two spikes represent the approximate dates of the two great epics of Sanskrit literature, the *Ramayana* and *Mahabharata*.

2 Don't pay much attention to the exact shape of the two spikes in 500 and 600; the birth and death dates of the constellation of important writers during this period are usually approximate. The giant here is Kalidasa, conventionally dated to about 500. The era also saw most notably the famous philologist Bhartrhari, the romancier Dandin, and Banabhatta, chronicler of the emperor Harsa.

INDIAN PHILOSOPHY, –600 TO 800

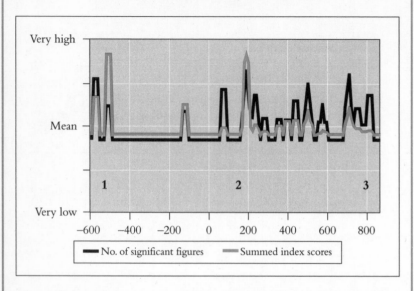

1 The number of significant figures in Indian philosophy is so small (45) that the spikes represent one major figure plus a few others. The first spike is based on Buddha, who was active around –500.

2 The bump in 1C clusters around Patanjali, the putative author of the *Yoga-sutras*, the four-volume systematization of Yogic thought, and of the *Mahab-hasya*, a classic commentary on the thought of Panini. Patanjali is variously dated somewhere between –2C and +5C;
I chose a middling date for him. The bump in 2C designates primarily Nagarjuna, the founder of the Madhvamika, the "Middle Path" school of Buddhism.

3 Sankara, the top-ranked philosopher in the Indian inventory, whose exposition of Advaita Vedanta school of Hinduism is still the source for much in contemporary Indian thought, is assigned his traditional dates of 788–820, though recent scholarship suggests that he may have been active 50 years earlier. It is best to think of the period 600–800, which saw a dozen other significant figures, as a generally fecund period for Indian philosophy.

JAPANESE ART, 1000 TO 1950

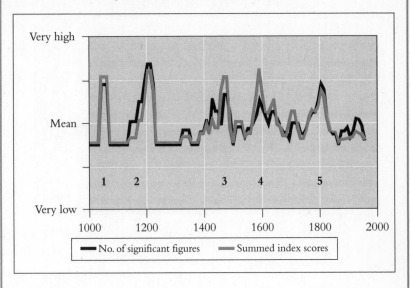

Very high

Mean

Very low

1000   1200   1400   1600   1800   2000

1   2   3   4   5

— No. of significant figures   — Summed index scores

1 Japan's population was still so small in 1000 that the bump in mid-11C is created by just two men, only one of whom, the sculptor Jocho, is a major figure.

2 The spike beginning in the late 1200s features the father-son pair of Kokei and Unkei, the latter considered to be one of Japan's greatest sculptors. Their realistic sculptures revived an earlier style that they carried to a new standard that dominated Japanese sculpture for centuries to come.

3 15C was a century of great painters in the monochrome ink style, beginning with Josetsu and culminating in the first-ranked Japanese figure in the visual arts inventory, Sesshu.

4 Another spike reflecting painting rather than sculpture, this one represents the Kano school, which employed both the monochrome ink style and bright, opaque colors. The leading figures during this period were Tohaku and Eitoku, tied for fourth in the inventory, followed by Koetsu (sixth) and culminating in Sotatsu (second).

5 Unaffected by the kind of hiatus in cultural production that affected China and India, Japan saw a proliferation of important new styles in the 1700s. One stream, still working primarily in monochrome and light color, was led by Ikeno Taiga and Yosa Buson. Another, led by Maruyama Okyo, incorporated aspects of Western realism into Japanese themes.

JAPANESE LITERATURE, 800 TO 1950

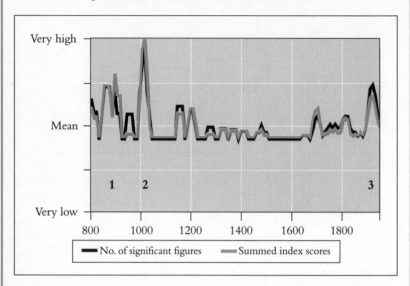

1 The first peak represents the work of the poets of the *Man'yoshu*, an anthology completed in the early 800s and then obscured for centuries, partly because of the prestige of Chinese literature and partly because its system of transcription became indecipherable. The second peak refers to the poets of the *Kokinshu*, another anthology, with Ki no Tsurayuki serving as compiler and one of its leading poets. The *Kokinshu*'s durable authority shaped Japanese poetry for centuries, even though the *Man'yoshu* is now widely considered to be the superior collection.

2 The spike at about 1000 reflects the work of a number of poets, but is primarily owed to the eminence of two women, the diarist Sei Shonagon and Murasaki Shikibu, author of *Tale of Genji*, sometimes argued to be the first novel and by consensus one of the masterpieces of world literature.

3 Japanese literature never had a prolonged quiescent period. Important writers dot the centuries between Murasaki and 20C, but none except possibly Fujiwara Teika (1162–1241) had the influence on subsequent writers that the early poets retained. The next great surge in Japanese literature occurred at the end of 19C, when Japanese literature, far from being disrupted by Westernization, was instead rejuvenated, producing major new novelists, poets, and literary critics.

POSTSCRIPT

The graphs have features of interest that I have tried to highlight through the text blocks accompanying each graph. Apart from the specifics, two broad themes emerge from these trajectories from such varied fields and places. One is the unsurprising finding that the accomplishment rate does indeed change drastically over time, including long falls from high peaks, and it is worth our while to try to understand why. The other concerns the Western inventories. That rise in accomplishment we see when a raw count of significant figures or events is used, as in the opening graphic for this chapter, disappears when we calculate a rate that has taken population into account. The story of the Western accomplishment rate in the last century before 1950 is one of decline if we take these plots seriously. Whether we should take them seriously is the subject of Chapter 21.

FIFTEEN

EXPLANATIONS I:
PEACE AND PROSPERITY

Seeking to explain the kinds of data that I have laid out in the last two chapters, the social sciences turn to a list of usual suspects. Economic conditions, political conditions, social conditions, and demographics each offer variables that are likely to be correlated to some degree with accomplishment in the arts and sciences. The task is to decide which combination of those variables does the best job of illuminating the underlying processes.

In this and the following chapter I use qualitative and quantitative arguments in tandem. The problem with the quantitative technique, multiple regression analysis, is that it requires extended technical explanation. You may reasonably ask whether you need to work through all that to understand the conclusions. The answer is no. The explanation of what is going on can be stated quickly and clearly. The quantitative analyses are valuable because they substantiate the conclusions. The material is too important to consign to an appendix—it is the quantitative analysis, not the narrative account, that makes the conclusions credible—but I begin this and the following chapter with self-contained non-technical discussion of the results, and you will be able to follow the subsequent chapters if you choose to skip the rest. For those prepared to make the investment, I have tried to make the quantitative portion of each chapter understandable to those who have no background in statistics.

• • •

The natural place to start searching for explanations of the patterns and trajectories of human accomplishment is with the *summa bona* of today's world, peace and prosperity. Besides being worthy goals in themselves, peace and prosperity might reasonably be expected to promote accomplishment.

War and civil unrest disrupt all sorts of human activities; why shouldn't the arts and sciences be among them? The role of prosperity is even more obvious. Starting around the time Europe discovered the New World, Europe's economies began a sustained, burgeoning expansion of wealth, unique in history, that continues to this day. During this same period, human accomplishment in the arts and sciences also flourished to a degree unique in history. A connection seems inescapable.

WAR AND CIVIL UNREST

Streams of human accomplishment have not typically been disrupted by war and civil unrest.

I begin the discussion of each topic with an italicized summary of the main finding. In this case, it represents a hypothesis that had to be rejected. The hypothesis—that war and civil unrest tend to disrupt streams of accomplishment—is simple and obvious. At the extremes of total chaos, it must be true. But we are looking for patterns, not worst cases. Total war is rare, and the effects of even total war can be brief—consider how few years it took Germany and Japan to recover from the devastation of World War II. Genuine civil chaos has been even rarer, typically brief and isolated to a few cities. The issue is not the effects of war and civil unrest at their worst, but whether war and civil unrest generally disrupt accomplishment.

The stories surrounding the most famous periods of great accomplishment suggest that the effects cannot be large. The first and most famous golden age of them all, in Athens from the repulse of Xerxes' invading fleet at the straits of Salamis in −479 to the death of Aristotle in −322, took place against a backdrop of civil and military strife. It began in the aftermath of a war, albeit a winning one. The First Peloponnesian War followed only 19 years later and lasted for 15 years. After a single decade of peace, the Great Peloponnesian War broke out. Thereafter followed 31 years of conflict that ended with Athens' abject surrender in −404. The Greek mainland descended into near chaos over the next few decades. Nowhere was the disruption of daily life greater than in Athens itself, ravaged by both war and a plague in −430 that killed a third of the population. And yet this century and a half of war and devastation embraces the Periclean Age. Skipping over the merely significant figures and listing just the major ones, those were the years that saw Aeschylus, Pindar, Parmenides, Anaxagoras, Sophocles, Herodotus, Protagoras, Euripides, Myron, Polykleitos, Lysippos, Phidias, Thucydides, Socrates, Democritus, Hippocrates, Polygnotus, Aristophanes, Zeuxis, Eudoxus, Praxiteles, Theophrastus, and, of course, Plato and Aristotle. Everyone in that list from Aristophanes to the end did his most important work in the darkest years of Athens' troubles and their aftermath.

Life in Renaissance Florence was not quite as harrowing as in Athens, but it was not tranquil. In the autumn of 1495, the Florentine Renaissance was about to enter its most sublime decades. Leonardo da Vinci, age 43, was beginning work on *The Last Supper*. Michelangelo, just turned 20, had already completed *Madonna of the Stairs* and was entering the period that would account for much of his finished sculpture. Raphael had turned 11 and was learning his craft from his father. Also that autumn, Florence had just ousted its ruler, was invaded by a French army under the command of Charles VIII, and was spared destruction only because it paid a large ransom. Florence would spend the next five years as a theocratic republic under the religious radical Savonarola, followed by his ouster and execution. The year 1495 is illustrative, not anomalous. Florence was in a chronic state of civil strife, invasion, or threat of invasion, during its greatest years.

The Dutch golden age in the last two-thirds of 17C gathered strength in the middle of the Thirty Years' War and ended in 1648 with its treaty with Spain. Only four years later, the first of three Anglo-Dutch wars broke out, ending in 1654 with the Netherlands' defeat. Rembrandt was 48 that year, Vermeer 22, Huygens 25. A decade later came the second Anglo-Dutch war, bloody but effectively a draw. Five years after that the French invaded and the Dutch were forced to breach the dikes to save Amsterdam from conquest. The third Anglo-Dutch war broke out the same year, ending in 1674. The Dutch golden age was not a peaceful one.

Of the most famous golden ages, only France's *La Belle Époque*, dated in various ways between 1870 to 1914, was a time of peace. Even in this case, France was on a downhill slide politically. Just as Athens' most intense period of great work began after defeat, Paris's *Belle Époque* began in the aftermath of France's humiliating capitulation in the Franco-Prussian war, and it continued during a period when France's international standing eroded.

To say that (with the French exception) golden ages were punctuated by war doesn't tell us much because almost every European age from 1400–1950, golden or not, was punctuated by war. Here are the major wars that occurred during those centuries involving Western Europe:

Hundred Years' War. England and France, 1337–1453.

Civil war within the Holy Roman Empire, 1400–1410.

Intermittent wars among Milan, Venice, and Florence, 1402–1454.

Hussite Wars, mostly within Bohemia, 1419–1436.

War of the Poles and Teutonic Knights (Prussia), 1454–1466.

War of the Roses, within England, 1455–1485.

War between Denmark and Norway, 1493–1497.

The Italian Wars, major Continental powers and Britain, 1494–1527.

War between Denmark and Sweden, 1506–1513.

French Wars of Religion, 1562–1598.

Dutch War of Independence, Spain and the Netherlands, 1567–1593.

Wars between Sweden and Poland, 1600–1611 and 1617–1629.

War between Sweden and Russia, 1613–1617. 1632–1634.

Thirty Years' War, the major Continental powers, 1618–1648.

English Civil War, 1642–1646, followed by periodic political turmoil until the Glorious Revolution of 1688.

War between Venice and Turkey, 1645–1670.

War between England and the Netherlands, 1652–1654, 1665–1667, 1672–1674.

First Northern War, Sweden and Poland, 1655–1660.

Franco-Allied War, France, the Netherlands, German principalities, 1672–1678.

War of the League of Augsburg, France, England, German principalities, 1688–1697.

Great Northern War, Sweden, Denmark, Russia, Poland, 1700–1721.

War of the Spanish Succession, most of the Continental powers and Britain, 1701–1714.

War of the Quadruple Alliance, France, Britain, Netherlands, Spain, 1718–1720.

War of the Polish Succession, German and Italian principalities, France, Spain, Poland, Russia, 1733–1738.

War of the Austrian Succession, the major European powers, 1740–1748.

War between Sweden and Russia, 1741–1743.

Seven Years' War, the major Continental powers and Britain, 1756–1763.

Russo-Austrian-Turkish War, 1787–1792.

War between Sweden and Russia, 1788–1790.

French Revolution, 1789–1792.

War of the First Coalition, the major Continental powers and Britain, 1792–1796.

Napoleonic Wars, the major Continental powers and Britain, 1796–1815.

Belgian War of Independence, Belgium and the Netherlands, 1830–1831.

The Revolutions of 1848, France, Austria, Italy, Bohemia, Hungary, and Germany, 1848–1849.

Crimean War, Britain, France, and Russia, 1853–1856.

War between France and Austria over Lombardy, 1859.

Wars of the Italian Reunification (*Risorgimento*), the Italian principalities, 1860–1870.

Schleswig-Holstein War, Austria, Prussia, Denmark, 1864.

Seven Weeks' War, Austria, Prussia, Italy, and Saxony, 1866.

Franco-Prussian War, 1870–1871.

World War I, 1914–1918.

World War II, 1939–1945.

The list, long as it is, represents only a portion of all the European conflicts from 1400 to 1950. It omits all the wars exclusively among countries in Eastern Europe and Russia, one-battle wars such as the British defeat of the Spanish Armada in 1588, conflicts involving the major European powers that occurred outside Europe (the American Revolution, for example), and the chronic Balkan wars pitting the Ottoman empire against Austria and Hungary. Some of the wars on the list lasted only a matter of weeks, but most of them were bloody and significant. Many of them involved armies and casualties of epic magnitude. The Thirty Years' War (1618–1648) cost an estimated eight million lives, of whom about seven million were civilians, and laid waste to large portions of Germany and Bohemia. Other obscure wars on the list involved multiple battles with casualties in the tens of thousands.

The chronicle of civil unrest is as long as the list of wars. In volume three of his four-volume study, *Social and Cultural Dynamics*, Pitirim Sorokin lists all the internal disturbances for the major European countries from ancient Greece through the early 1900s. For just the period after 1400, France has 79 separate internal disturbances, Germany and Austria share 43, and England has 66.[1]

It remains possible that the most severe wars and civil disorders could produce important effects on accomplishment that run-of-the-mill strife could not. The noticeable dip in the total number of significant figures in the

1600s (see graph on page 248) leads one to wonder whether the Thirty Years' War might have played a role, for example. A first look at accomplishment coming out of Germany during that period (when Germany lost about a third of its population) lends modest support to the hypothesis—the number of significant figures in the aftermath of the war, from 1650 to 1700, fell from 29 to 26. On the other hand, the number of German significant figures had increased from 12 in 1550–1600 to 29 in 1600–1650, the half-century that saw the actual fighting. This is typical of an ambiguous historical record that calls for multivariate analysis that can take several variables into account at the same time.

The results of that quantitative analysis in the second half of this chapter say that war and civil unrest did not play such a role, at least in Europe from 1400 to 1950. Given the narrative record I have just reviewed, the conclusion is not surprising. Peace cannot explain the trajectory of human accomplishment because there hasn't been enough peace for a good test. This doesn't mean that some degree of war and civil unrest are good for human accomplishment, just that they haven't consistently impeded it. *Consistently* is an important qualification here. It remains certainly true that accomplishment in the arts and sciences has suffered in specific cities during specific periods of the most intense conflict.

ECONOMIC WEALTH AND GROWTH

Accomplishment in the arts and sciences is facilitated by growing national wealth, both through the additional money that can support the arts and sciences and through indirect spillover effects of economic vitality on cultural vitality.

Human accomplishment in the arts and sciences first became possible because of wealth. Only with the accumulation of a surplus beyond the necessities of survival could human communities support a class of people who were engaged in work that did not directly contribute to food, shelter, clothing, and raising the next generation.

Logic suggests that this relationship between wealth and accomplishment could persist almost indefinitely. Expansion of wealth is accompanied by increases in the number of people who get the opportunity to identify and fulfill their talents, including talents in scholarship and the arts. Expansion of wealth is accompanied by increases in the number of jobs for such persons once they succeed in identifying their talents. Expansion of wealth is associated with demands for new technology, applications for new scientific findings, and growth in expenditures on concert tickets, books, an evening at the theatre, and pictures to hang on the wall. Expansion of wealth is associated with larger numbers of colleges and universities.

This doesn't mean that wealth alone causes accomplishment to occur. The case of the Italian Renaissance illustrates the general problem. Florence was booming when the Renaissance began. A class of rich merchants had emerged, and conspicuous consumption was in vogue. A link between that burgeoning wealth and the Renaissance seems incontestable. And yet as economic historians have accumulated data, that explanation has had to be revised, as Charles Mee describes:

> Historians have debated for more than a century the connection between economics and the artistic blossoming of the Renaissance. At first they thought the new capitalism produced unprecedented prosperity and, so, spare cash with which to commission art. Then it was discovered that Europe actually passed through a prolonged depression, and the economic determinists explained that during recession and inflation smart capital moves into art. Recently, detailed examination has revealed that the economies of some towns collapsed while those of others bloomed—and yet nearly all of them produced quantities of art.[2]

Florence's economic prosperity undoubtedly explains something—Florence could not have been the center of the Renaissance if it had remained a sleepy subsistence village instead of growing into a great financial center of Europe. But whether wealth was a direct cause of Florence's artistic accomplishments or whether the wealth and artistic accomplishments were both effects of some other cause is difficult to untangle.

Spain supplies the most intriguing connection between economics and accomplishment in the arts. In the decades after Columbus discovered the New World, Cortez conquered the Aztecs, and Pizarro conquered the Incas, Spain was flooded with gold and silver—on the order of 200 tons of gold and 18,000 tons of silver from 1500–1650.[3] It was a fortune of spectacular proportions, and it probably destroyed Spain as a major European power. It needn't have—the windfall could have been used for capital investment in agriculture and industry. But instead it was frittered away on war and luxury. Worse than merely wasted, Spain's temporary riches also inculcated in her people a reluctance to work that spread from the rich through the formerly industrious working class. "The love of luxury and the comforts of civilization have overcome them," wrote a Moroccan ambassador to Madrid in 1690–1691, long after the Spanish should have realized it was time to get back to work,

> . . . and you will rarely find one of this nation who engages in trade or travels abroad for commerce as do the other Christian nations. . . . Similarly the handicrafts practiced by the lower classes and common people are despised by the nation, which regards itself as superior to the other Christian nations. Most of those who practice these crafts in Spain are Frenchmen [who] flock to Spain to look for work . . . [and] in a short time make great fortunes.[4]

Spain used its treasure to invigorate the other European nations while losing its own momentum. By the mid-1600s, Spain had sunk into an economic torpor from which it would not fully recover through the middle of 20C.

Spain's record of significant figures in the arts and sciences parallels its economic roller coaster. Beginning half a century after the discovery of the New World came the artists: painters Zurbaran, Velazquez, and El Greco (an immigrant from Crete); writers Cervantes, Gongora y Argote, Lope de Vega, Quevedo y Vallegas, and Calderon de la Barca; and composer Cabezon. All of these men were major figures, accompanied by another 27 significant figures in the arts inventories. Then, just as abruptly as Spain had begun producing significant figures, it stopped. Between 1650 and 1850—during the same two centuries when Britain, France, and Germany were producing hundreds of significant figures and even Italy in its decline produced several dozen—Spain produced a single major figure (Goya) and 11 significant figures.

What is the connection between economics and human accomplishment in the case of Spain? One might argue that the riches encouraged its mini–golden age of writers and painters and its economic decline caused the subsequent dearth. But it is easier to argue that the misused wealth did nothing but harm. Spain was a major economic and cultural force in Europe before the discovery of the New World. Through 1650 Spain was simply continuing to participate, as it had before, in the general European creative era—its output even during its best years was not remarkable compared to the other major contributors. Windfall wealth didn't necessarily help Spain when it was pouring in, but it hurt Spain in the long run. Spain was, in Richard Tawney's memorable description, "like an heir endowed by the accident of an eccentric will," and was debilitated in the ways that great fortunes often debilitate unprepared heirs.[5]

A stronger case for the good effects of wealth is supplied by the Netherlands in 17C. A small country with few natural resources, controlled by Spain, threw off its foreign rulers and within a few years of the peace of 1609 became the most dynamic economy in Europe, "the image of Venice in the days when Venice was thriving," as a Venetian diplomat observed in 1618.[6] Dutch growth continued without a break for the rest of 17C. As in the case of Spain, the production of significant figures tracked almost perfectly with the riches, from only 6 significant figures in the last half of 16C to 46 during the course of 17C. The home-grown Dutch major figures of 17C include a roster of painters that only Florence at its height could match—Rubens, van Dyck, Hals, van Ruisdael, Vermeer, and Rembrandt. Spinoza in philosophy and Huygens in the sciences would have ornamented any country in any era. Descartes wasn't born in Holland, but he lived there during the prime of his career.

Unlike Spain, the Netherlands did not go into an economic funk, but growth slowed. From 18C onward, the Netherlands became just another European small-but-prosperous country. As in Spain, the production of great figures in the arts and sciences effectively came to a stop. Between Jan Swammerdam, who died in 1680, and Hugo de Vries, who began his career two centuries later, the Netherlands produced a solitary major figure (Daniel Fahrenheit, 1686–1736).

These case studies could be augmented, but the point can be summarized by looking at the correlation between national wealth and accomplishment. For the entire period from 1500 (when the available estimates of GDP begin) to 1950, the correlation of the number of significant figures with per capita GDP is .47—a substantial relationship.[7] The correlation with changes in GDP is smaller, .24, but statistically significant. Wealth and increases in wealth have a simple bivariate relationship with accomplishment.

The regression analyses demonstrate that these correlations persist after controlling for factors such as population and population density, but with an unexpected twist. Richer is better, but part of the effect comes from being richer *compared to other countries during the same time period*, not from being richer in an absolute sense. Specifically, countries that have more per capita gross domestic product (GDP) than others at a given point in time tend to produce more significant figures than their poorer competitors, particularly in the visual arts and the sciences. This finding could be interpreted as reflecting two separate causal routes. The direct route is that money is available to build universities and buy paintings. The indirect route is that a country's economic prosperity at any given time reflects a broad cultural and national vitality that goes beyond economics, and this greater vitality encourages accomplishment in the arts and sciences independent of monetary support.

• • •

This ends the non-technical half of the chapter. Some readers will prefer to go directly to Chapter 16. The rest of this chapter is for those who are curious about the details of the regression analyses.

A PRIMER ON REGRESSION ANALYSIS

Readers who are familiar with regression analysis may skip directly to the next section (page 346). Readers who are completely unfamiliar with statistics of any sort and have managed to get this far without reading Appendix 1, "Statistics for People Who Are Sure They Can't Learn Statistics," should consider reading it now.

The tool I employ in the subsequent analyses is *regression analysis*, the most widely used multivariate technique in the social sciences. The mathematics of regression analysis are complicated, but its purpose and structure are simple. You are faced with a phenomenon that you want to explain, the *dependent variable*. You have identified some conditions that might be causing this phenomenon, the *independent variables*. Regression analysis tells you how much each cause affects the phenomenon after taking all the other hypothesized causes into account, and how much confidence you can have that the results were not produced by chance.

It is the ability to take many variables into account simultaneously that makes regression analysis so valuable. Consider, for example, the problem of deciding whether war and civil unrest have effects on accomplishment. I could start by preparing a table of numbers on a country-by-country, war-by-war basis, as in the example I raised about German accomplishment in the years before and after the Thirty Years' War. But to calculate those numbers for every country and every period between every war would be inconclusive. We would observe some occasions when war seemed to depress the number of significant figures and others when it did not, but we would still have the problem of extracting a generalization from all those before/during/after comparisons. Furthermore, we know that the number of significant figures increased rapidly during the last two centuries. Somehow, the comparisons have to take into account the chronological point at which the comparisons are occurring.

The sensible initial goal—compare the number of significant figures coming out of times of peace and times of war—cries out for some method of taking a variety of variables into account at the same time and summarizing the magnitude and strength of the relationships. Regression analysis provides that method.

Interpreting the Results of a Regression Analysis

A regression analysis produces three numbers of immediate interest for our purposes: beta coefficients, *p* values, and expected values.[8]

Beta coefficients. A regression analysis produces a number, often called simply "the beta" after the Greek letter that is its conventional symbol, for each independent variable. The beta is a coefficient, meaning that it multiplies the value of the independent variable with which it is paired. Suppose you are trying to predict how tall your child will be. To help you make this prediction, you are given a database containing the mother's height, father's height, and the sex of the child for a large sample of other parents and their children. You put these data into a regression analysis in which the dependent variable is the child's height and the independent variables are mother's height, father's height, and the child's sex. If the beta for the variable called "father's height" is +.7, the regression results are saying that an extra inch of father's height is associated with an extra 7/10s of an inch of height in a child of a given sex and with a mother of a given height. *The beta tells you the estimated size of the net relationship between an independent variable and the dependent variable after taking all the other independent variables into account.*

p *values.* Each beta is associated with a number between 0 and 1 called a *p* value. The letter *p* stands for *probability* and expresses the statistical significance of the beta. Since "statistical significance" is widely misunderstood, some elaboration is in order.

A statistically significant relationship is not necessarily large in size. It is not necessarily important. To say that a relationship is statistically significant merely says that it is unlikely to have been produced by chance. The standard way of determining statistical significance is to assess the results against the assumption that the true size of a relationship is zero. A common threshold of statistical significance is called "the .05 level," meaning that if the true magnitude of beta were zero, a beta of the observed size could be expected to appear by chance five out of a hundred times. A beta that is significant at the .01 level is expected to appear by chance only once in a hundred times. When the level goes beyond a one-in-a-thousand chance, it is conventionally designated by .000, indicating that the actual p value can be expressed only with four or more decimal places.

If one is dealing with highly predictable phenomena in the hard sciences, statistical significance can be reached with a few dozen cases. But for the messier relationships that the social sciences take up, statistical significance is seldom found in small samples. Moreover—and this is a point to remember—even a relationship that is only trivially important will be statistically significant if the sample is large enough. To see this, consider the problem of deciding whether a coin is fair. You toss the coin 10 times and heads comes up 6 times. Intuitively, you know that this result doesn't mean anything. You throw the coin 10,000 times and it comes up heads 6,000 times. Intuitively, you know that something is wrong with that coin. You have intuited the difference between statistically insignificant and significant results. The probability that the difference is a result of chance has gone from very high in the first case to near zero in the second, even though the proportion of heads is the same in both cases.

Is it important to know whether a result is statistically significant? In the case of samples in the thousands, usually no, because almost anything will be statistically significant. In such cases, you will be focusing on the range within which you may safely assume that the value of the beta lies, not whether it is significantly different from zero. In the case of samples of a dozen or two, the answer is usually no again, because even important relationships (in a substantive sense) are unlikely to meet the threshold of statistical significance. The samples in the following analyses have several hundred observations, large enough to expect that substantively important relationships will reach statistical significance. In any case, the point to take away from this discussion is that *the level of statistical significance tells you the probability that the true value of beta is different from zero.*

Expected values. A regression analysis permits you to "predict" what value the dependent variable will take on for any particular set of circumstances. Go back to the example of predicting your child's height. Let's say you are 5 feet 10 inches, your spouse is 6 feet, and your child is female. Given the results of the regression equation, you can plug in the betas for each of those three variables and come up with the expected height of your own child. Whether you can have any confidence in this expected value depends on the explanatory power of the regression equation, but the expected value represents the best possible guess given the available data.

A Final Wrinkle: Dummy Variables

A few sentences ago I wrote that "you can plug in the betas for each of those three variables and come up with the expected height of your own child," but one of those three variables was the child's sex. How can a number be multiplied by sex? In Chapter 16, I analyze the role of political systems. How can a number be multiplied by a code of "democracy"?

The answer lies in the use of what are known as *dummy variables*. The computer doesn't see "female" or "male," "democracy" or "autocracy"; it sees a 1 or a 0. Let's say that in the prediction of your child's height we have arbitrarily assigned 1 to stand for female and 0 to stand for male, and the beta for sex is −2.4. "Plugging in the betas" means that you multiply −2.4 by 1 if your child is female, and multiply −2.4 by 0 if a male. If we hold parental heights constant, and rely on the results from this particular sample, these results say that the expected height of a female is 2.4 inches less than the expected height of a male.

Dummy variables can be used for categories that have more than two options. Suppose the analysis of political systems has four categories—democracy, autocracy, totalitarianism, and limited monarchy, let's say. Your analysis of four categories needs three dummy variables (just as the analysis of the two categories of sex needed just one dummy variable), because one category serves as a reference group.[9] You then code a 0/1 variable for each of the other categories.

· · ·

These are the bare essentials. The technical characteristics of the regression model used in the analyses that follow—it is known as a "negative binomial model"—and the reasons for choosing it are given in the note.[10] I periodically attach other notes to expand on some points in the text, but just the material above should let you make sense of the regression tables that follow.

BASICS OF THE PRESENTATION OF RESULTS

The Control Variables

Each of the analyses in this and the next chapter uses the same set of variables intended to extract the effects of potentially confounding variables.[11]

The population of the country. A basic assumption of the Poisson family of regression techniques, and one appropriate to these data, is that the phenomenon being examined can be expressed as an incidence rate. The observed number of events (the number of significant figures) represents that incidence rate multiplied by a measure of "exposure"—in our case, the population of the country. The population is incorporated into the regression analysis in its logged form, with its coefficient constrained to be one.[12]

Population density, expressed in the logged value of population (to the base *e*, as are all logged variables in the analyses) divided by geographic area.[13] I use population density as a way of taking the geographic size of a country into account. For example, France in 17C and 18C had one of the largest populations in Europe, but it was scattered over 210,000 square miles at a time of slow transportation and communication. The millions of people in western and southern France were for practical purposes cut off from the forces producing achievements in northeastern France. I use population density instead of directly entering a measure of geographic size because the correlation between population and density (.25) is much lower than the correlation between population and area (.70), which diminishes the likelihood of potential technical problems that go under the heading of multicollinearity.

A set of dummy variables representing time. The steep rise in accomplishment from 18C onward suggests that any variable we use to explain human accomplishment should take the chronological point in time into account. Following Dean Simonton's practice, I have aggregated the data into *generations*, with one generation consisting of a 20-year period—a length of time that corresponds to the typical length of the creative career.[14] Each significant figure is assigned to the generation that contains the year during which he turned 40 or died, whichever came first. I assign a dummy variable to each generation—a total of 28 dummy variables for the period from 1390–1410 to 1930–1950. The reason for using dummy variables rather than a single continuous variable is explained in note 10.

Two Approaches to the Dependent Variable

Many of the analyses use the total number of significant figures as the dependent variable. But the different inventories had very different numbers of significant figures in the database used for the quantitative analysis (Europe from 1390–1950): 1,325 scientists, 713 writers, 507 composers, 429 artists, and only 74 philosophers. The raw total is thus heavily loaded with scientists and writers. The raw total has a certain natural appropriateness. In terms of the daily life of a culture, it is reasonable that the total be tilted toward the scientists and away from the philosophers. Among the arts, the greater weight given to literature is commensurate with the role that literature played in the daily life of a culture compared to music and art prior to 1950. Any educated person with a middle class income could read the great writers and keep their books at hand. Until the advent of the phonograph and high-quality photographic reproduction, access to great music (at least, great music played well) and great art was limited to those with wealth or access to scarce cosmopolitan centers.

Nonetheless, it is prudent to see what happens when the imbalance is eliminated by transforming the raw numbers so that they all have equal weight—specifically, by multiplying the raw number in each two-decade period and each inventory by the weight that will produce a thousand significant figures for each inventory over the whole period from 1390–1410 to 1930–1950.[15] I have replicated all the reported analyses using these weighted numbers. The replications revealed few and minor differences.

The Choice to Analyze Sets of Independent Variables Separately

The presentations of regression results in this and the following chapter show separate analyses for each set of independent variables—one for the variables on war and civil unrest, another for the variables about the economy, and so forth. Why not follow the common practice of developing a model and presenting all of the independent variables in one equation? My reason involves the discrepancy between the theoretical capabilities of complex regression analyses and their practical limitations. When dealing with the kind of data reported here—counts of comparatively rare events, arranged by countries over periods of time—choices must be made about what regression model to use and how to implement it. Many of the choices involve judgments on which reasonable people might disagree. One way of coping with these uncertainties is to examine the results from a variety of perspectives, which is done in the analyses that follow. But a larger problem remains. Suppose, for example, that per capita GDP is important when entered along with the control variables, but ceases to have an important role when half a dozen other independent variables are added to the equation. If I were dealing with a database of normally distributed variables, taken from one point in time, with no lower bound to the value of the dependent variable, and a set of other independent variables that are all coded in natural metrics that directly measure the construct in question, then it might make sense to focus exclusively on the larger model and conclude that per capita GDP has no independent role. When dealing with a database that has none of those comforting simplicities, I prefer to look at independent variables separately and show you how they relate to the number of significant figures after the basic control variables are included. In an epilogue to Chapter 16, I combine the pieces into a single equation (page 376).

THE REGRESSION ANALYSES: WAR AND CIVIL UNREST

The variables for measuring war and civil strife use data from Pitirim Sorokin's *Social and Cultural Dynamics* mentioned a few pages ago. Volume III contains two long appendices detailing with wars in one and internal disturbances in the other, beginning in ancient Greece and carrying through the 1920s for European countries.[16] I used this material to produce separate measures for the cumulative severity of war and unrest experienced by a country over the course of each generation from 1400 to 1950, applying comparable standards to the years until 1950 not covered by Sorokin.[17] The measure of war is based on the size of the armies involved relative to the country's population, the number of fronts on which the war was fought, and the duration of the conflict over the course of the generation in question. The measure of unrest uses Sorokin's own index of the severity of internal disturbances, which was based on the social area of the disturbance (weighted by the size of the population centers involved), the intensity of the disturbance based on the amount of violence and the number of socioeconomic changes, and duration.[18] The distribution of measures for both war and unrest are severely skewed to the left, and are entered as logged values in the analysis.

The scales for these two variables have no natural meaning in themselves—they go from "no war" and "no unrest" during a generation to "extremely high." The top score on war goes to France from 1790–1810,

THE UNITED STATES RETURNS

In Chapter 13, the scatter plots for Europe and the United States had to be considered separately. Using regression analysis permits me to combine the European and American data. A main reason is the more detailed breakdown of time periods. Comparing a European country and the United States over the entire period from 1800–1950 is unrealistic—the United States went from a tiny, insignificant country to the most powerful nation on earth during those 150 years. Comparing two-decade periods reduces the unrealism, and adding the other basic control variables further reduces it to the point that combining the European and American data is feasible.

followed by Austro-Hungary in 1630–1650. At the top of the unrest scale is the Netherlands during its Great Revolution in 1570–1610, followed by Russia in 1430–1470 and Britain in 1630–1650.

War and unrest might affect the appearance of significant figures via two different routes. One involves interference in the ongoing work—the artist can't paint, the writer can't write—during a period of war or unrest. The other involves the effects of war or unrest on the children who have the potential to grow to be great artists or scientists. War and unrest could disrupt their education. It could also lead children to see the world as irrational and unpredictable, which would work against the development of personality traits that favor creativity.[19] If this hypothesis is true, then it is important to consider the effects of war and unrest during the period preceding the generation in question. The table on page 348 shows the results of a regression analysis employing the current values of war and unrest along with their values in the preceding generation, plus the standard control variables.

The main items of interest are the four lines that detail the variables we are using to characterize war and unrest. The short answer is that war and civil unrest have no relationship with significant figures worth worrying about in this model.

Might a relationship emerge if we looked at the same data from other perspectives? To check that possibility, a number of other analyses were conducted, standard procedure when working with multivariate analyses. The standard replications for every analysis used equally weighted inventories

WAR AND CIVIL UNREST AS PREDICTORS OF THE
NUMBER OF SIGNIFICANT FIGURES

Dependent variable: Total no. of significant figures in a generation
Observations: 427
Exposure: Country population

	Beta	p value	Percent change per SD*
Variables for characterizing war and unrest			
War index, current generation	+.004	.893	+1
War index, 1st preceding generation	−.036	.163	−7
Unrest index, current generation	−.012	.432	−3
Unrest index, 1st preceding generation	−.006	.700	−2
Control variables			
Population density (logged)	+.039	.696	+4
Time dummy variables (results not shown separately)			

Results are based on a random-effects negative binomial model.

* Percent change in the expected number of significant figures for a standard deviation increase in the independent variable on that line, holding all the other independent variables constant.

and the fixed-effects option. Neither produced results materially different from the random-effects results shown above. To give you a sense of the rest of the iceberg lying under the table that ends up being printed when a regression analysis is reported, the note lists some of the other alternatives that were tried.[20] The meager result of these efforts was the discovery that the number of significant figures in the visual arts had a statistically significant relationship with the war index in the first preceding generation. The effect was small, isolated, and not robust—probably meaningless, in other words.[21] Taken together, and in combination with the qualitative record, we emerge from this exercise with reason to have some confidence that war and civil unrest had no important consistent relationship to human accomplishment in this data set.[22]

WALKING THROUGH THE NUMBERS IN THE TABLE

Start with the problem of judging whether the size of the relationship is important for the war measure in the current generation (the first row). The sign of the beta is positive, which says that increases in the war index are associated with an increase in significant figures. The magnitude of the beta, +.004, looks small. In fact, it is impossible to tell whether it is small just by inspecting it, because the war variable is not measured in a metric that has a natural interpretation, such as inches or number of people, but you can tell how big it is by using the right-hand column, labeled "Percent change per SD." The entry for the first row is +1, which says that if the war index increases by one standard deviation, the increase in significant figures is 1 percent—not a big effect. The p value is .893, telling you that this variable is nowhere close to statistically significant.

This table happens to have no statistically significant variables. They will be easy to spot in subsequent tables because they will be in boldface and italics.

THE REGRESSION ANALYSES: ECONOMIC WEALTH AND GROWTH

Sophisticated measures of national economic activity such as gross domestic product (GDP) are of recent origin. Even some of the advanced European nations did not begin to produce such statistics until 20C. The measure of national economic wealth that I use is an estimate of GDP, but *estimate* is a word that needs to be kept in the forefront in this instance.

I combined several sources to reach the estimates of GDP that are used for the analysis that follows, as described in the note.[23] The net result of this effort is a database of generation-by-generation estimates of GDP from 1490–1510 to 1930–1950 for all the European countries except Poland and the Balkans, plus estimates for the United States and Canada from their foundings onward.

The primary variable for assessing the role of economics is logged *per capita GDP, in thousands of 1990 international dollars.*[24] The rationale for this variable is that the amount of wealth is positively related to human accomplishment—the richer, the better.[25] As in the case of war and unrest, I also prepared lagged values of both variables. The lagged variables provide information about the degree to which changes in economic wealth are related to the production of significant figures.

An alternative measure of economic wealth is a measure of *GDP relative to other economies in the same generation*. Specifically, it represents the standard score of a country's per capita GDP based on all the distribution of per capita GDP among the countries in a given generation (for an explanation of standard scores, see page 463).[26] The rationale is that wealth is relative. Renaissance Italy during its most prosperous years had far more discretionary income to be spent on paintings and architecture (for example) than is implied by comparing per capita income in constant dollars in Renaissance Florence versus the United States in 1940 (which is what the per capita GDP variable does).

The results of the analysis using contemporary per capita GDP and two lagged values produced the results shown in the table below.

ECONOMIC WEALTH AND GROWTH AS PREDICTORS OF THE NUMBER OF SIGNIFICANT FIGURES

Dependent variable: Total no. of significant figures in a generation
Observations: 308
Exposure: Country population

	Beta	*p* value	Percent change per SD*
Variables for characterizing war and unrest			
GDP per capita (in thousands of 1990 int'l dollars, logged)	**+.999**	**.000**	**+87**
GDP per capita, 1st preceding generation	−.069	.795	−4
Control variables			
Population density (logged)	+.105	.227	+12
Time dummy variables (results not shown separately)			

Bold italics indicate results statistically significant at or beyond the .05 level.

Results are based on a random-effects negative binomial model.

* Percent change in the expected number of significant figures for a standard deviation increase in the independent variable on that line, holding all the other independent variables constant.

Unlike the story for war and civil unrest, a large and statistically signif-icant relationship exists between wealth and the production of significant figures in the arts and sciences. These results say that when per capita wealth goes up by one standard deviation, the expected number of total significant figures goes up by 87 percent. Once that relationship is taken into account, the value of per capita GDP in the preceding generation has no important relationship with the total number of significant figures.

When I replicated the same analysis for each of the inventories sepa-rately, per capita GDP showed comparably strong relationships with the art, literature, and scientific inventories, but a smaller and statistically insignificant relationship with the number of significant figures in the music inventory.

The measure of relative wealth, comparing countries within a single generation, showed a substantial relationship with the total number of signif-icant figures (a standard deviation change was associated with a 38 percent increase, compared to the 87 percent increase for a comparable change in per capita GDP in constant dollars). When both variables are entered into the equation at the same time (along with the standard control variables), stan-dard deviation increases in per capita GDP and in relative wealth produce increases in the number of significant figures of 26 percent and 22 percent respectively. If we take that result literally, then the two types of effects are about equal. But the bivariate correlation between the absolute and relative measures of wealth was so high (.61), that these results are unstable. A more modest interpretation is that both the direct and indirect routes play substan-tial roles, with their exact relative proportions uncertain.

EXPLANATIONS II: MODELS, ELITE CITIES, AND FREEDOM OF ACTION

The three explanations of human accomplishment I consider in this chapter are not as obvious as peace and prosperity, but each has a strong rationale and an effect on accomplishment that emerges unmistakably in the multivariate analyses. As in Chapter 15, I begin with descriptive accounts of the three and then lay out the regression results.

MODELS

Streams of accomplishment become self-reinforcing as new artists and scientists build on the models before them.

The hypothesis is that the celebrity of people like Raphael and Faraday provides inspiration for aspiring young artists and scientists who grow up in their shadow. A related hypothesis is that success breeds success across fields—vitality in one aspect of the arts and sciences contributes to vitality in others.

The logic is similar to that which we have already encountered when discussing the Lotka curve, in the literature on cumulative advantage and the Matthew effect (page 93). But the idea that a stream of human accomplishment is sustained by emulation is far older than contemporary social science. In the later years of Tiberius's reign, a few years after the death of Jesus of Nazareth, a retired Roman soldier named Velleius Paterculus who had turned amateur historian stated the puzzle as well as anyone has since. "I cannot refrain from noting a subject which has often occupied my thoughts but has never been clearly reasoned out," he wrote. "For who can marvel sufficiently that the most distinguished minds in each branch of human achievement have happened to adopt the same form of effort, and to have fallen within the same narrow span of time."[1] It was true of tragedy, when Aeschylus, Sophocles, and Euripides appeared within a few decades of each other. It was true of the Greek geniuses of the Old Comedy and the New Comedy. It was most certainly true of the giants of philosophy, beginning with Socrates, who were "so crowded . . . into a brief epoch that there were no two worthy of mention who could not have seen each other." Velleius tentatively offered what seemed to him the most plausible explanation:

> Genius is fostered by emulation, and it is now envy, now admiration, which enkindles imitation, and, in the nature of things, that which is cultivated with the highest zeal advances to the highest perfection; but it is difficult to continue at the point of perfection, and naturally that which cannot advance must recede. And as in the beginning we are fired with the ambition to over-take those whom we regard as leaders, so when we have despaired of being able either to surpass or even to equal them, our zeal wanes with our hope; it ceases to follow what it cannot overtake, and abandoning the old field as though pre-empted, it seeks a new one.[2]

Nineteen hundred years after Velleius wrote, Alfred Kroeber, one of the founding fathers of anthropology, compiled his own inventories of signif-icant figures in *Configurations of Culture Growth* (1944), my source for the Velleius quotations. Writing in the 1930s, when statistical methods were nearly unknown in the social sciences, Kroeber invented *ad hoc* methods of assessing the quantitative existence of the florescences of artistic and scientific accomplishment that flare, then decline. To Kroeber, the florescences seemed to peak and then collapse for reasons similar in spirit, beneath Kroeber's anthropological jargon, to the ones seen by Velleius. If an artistic or scientific "high-value culture pattern," as Kroeber called it, does not run into conflict with something else in the culture, it will differentiate and expand through its own momentum. But even if it encounters no opposition from the culture, eventually it exhausts itself or develops strains that lead to "pattern rupture."

In the 1970s, Dean Simonton attacked the question anew with an arse-nal of quantitative techniques that his predecessors had lacked. His database consisted of about 5,000 creative persons and anonymous products in West-ern civilization from −700 to 1839, aggregated in two-decade generations. Using multivariate time-series analysis, he demonstrated that the strongest predictors of creativity in a current generation are the number of creative persons and products in the two preceding generations.[3] Switching from Western civilization to Chinese civilization, he subsequently found similar results in a time-series analysis of 10,000 Chinese creators, leaders, and celebrities stretching from −840 to 1979.[4] Simonton has supplemented these basic demonstrations of the relationship between creativity in adjacent generations with a number of articles elaborating the dynamics at work.[5] Simplifying, they are variations on the ways in which models inspire emulation and provide new creative material.

Because the inventories assembled for *Human Accomplishment* permit a replication of Simonton's analysis, there is no point in elaborating on the qualitative record. The quantitative analyses presented on page 366 show the same strong relationships between the preceding generations and the current one that Simonton found, and lesser but significant relationships between important figures in one field and the contemporary presence of important figures in other fields.

CRITICAL MASS: ELITE CITIES

Streams of accomplishment are fostered by the existence of cities that serve as centers of human capital and supply audiences and patrons for the arts and sciences.

Treating cities as a cause of human accomplishment may seem like treating restaurants as a cause of cooking. The causal relationship can be real, but it is also trivial because it is so obvious. Cities are where the facilities and audiences for the arts and sciences reside; of course artists and scientists disproportionately work in them. But in this section I am making a somewhat different and less obvious point: Cities are not only where the significant figures worked, but where they were born and raised.

Cities as Nurturers of Talent

The reason why so many significant figures grew up in cities could still be as simple as "That's where the people are." But cities dominate the production of significant figures even after taking population into account. The table on the next page shows a comparison between major European cities and their surrounding regions for the period from 1800–1950.[6] The pairs were chosen to be ones in which the city was large, where it was the only major city within its geographic region (see Appendix 4 for a list of the regions), and where the region as a whole had produced more than 25 significant figures. Details of the calculation are given in the endnote.[7]

ORIGINS OF SIGNIFICANT FIGURES: CITIES VERSUS THEIR SURROUNDING AREAS, 1800–1950

City / Comparison Area	Significant Figures per Million	
	City	Area
Austria: Vienna / Lower Austria	12	2
Belgium: Antwerp / Belgium	7	2
Belgium: Brussels / Belgium	5	2
Britain: Bristol / Southwest England	20	3
Britain: Dublin / Ireland	17	1
Britain: Edinburgh / Lowland Scotland	22	4
Britain: Glasgow / Lowland Scotland	6	4
Britain: Liverpool / Northwest England	5	1
Britain: London / Southeast England	6	5
Britain: Manchester /Northwest England	5	1
Czech Republic: Prague / Bohemia	14	1
Denmark: Copenhagen / Country	11	5
France: Paris / Country	24	2
Germany: Berlin / Brandenburg	5	2
Germany: Cologne / N. Rhine.-Westphalia	10	4
Germany: Hamburg / Lower Saxony	17	4
Germany: Königsberg / East Prussia	33	2
Germany: Munich / Bavaria	10	4
Germany: Stuttgart / Baden-Württemberg	91	3
Hungary: Budapest / Country	10	1
Italy: Rome / Country	4	1
Netherlands: Amsterdam / Country	5	2
Netherlands: Rotterdam / Country	4	2
Norway: Oslo / Country	20	5
Poland: Warsaw / Country	3	0.3
Russia: Moscow / Country	8	0.4
Russia: St. Petersburg / Country	8	0.4
Spain: Madrid / Country	7	1
Sweden: Stockholm / Country	25	2
Switzerland: Geneva / Country	123	2
Switzerland: Zurich / Country	17	2
Combined	**20**	**2**

The ratios for the different cities vary widely, from a low of 6:5 for London versus the rest of Southeast England to a high of 123:2 for Geneva versus the rest of Switzerland. The combined ratio for all of these cities is an unambiguous 20:2. The concentration of origins in the major cities is not a function of simple population, but of other features about urban areas.

In thinking about what those features might be, another salient point is that some cities have done much better than others. The table is restricted to cities in regions that produced at least 25 significant figures. But many cities at many periods of their history produced almost nothing. Thirteen cities were among the European top twenty in both 1800 and 1950. From largest to smallest as of 1950, they were London (at 8.3 million in 1950), Moscow, Berlin, St. Petersburg, Paris, Rome, Madrid, Vienna, Hamburg, Barcelona, Milan, Copenhagen, and Naples (at 1.0 million). Now go back and look at the maps showing the origins of the significant figures for the period 1800–1950 (page 303).[8] If you want to argue that large cities are centers of accomplishment, then London, Paris, Berlin, and Vienna make a powerful case for you. But Rome, Madrid, Hamburg, Barcelona, Milan, and Naples from 1800–1950 just as effectively make the case that large cities are not necessarily centers of accomplishment. Similar contrasts could be drawn throughout the history of modern Europe. The greatest centers of accomplishment in every era were among the largest cities in Europe, but some of the largest cities in every era produced little or no accomplishment.

Furthermore, the big four (Britain, France, Germany, and Italy) have exhibited strikingly different relationships between their cities and the origins of significant figures. The maps on the following page provide a close-up of the relationship between cities and the origins of total significant figures from each of four countries during its most dominant period: Italy during the Renaissance, France during the Baroque and Enlightenment, Britain during the Industrial Revolution, and Germany between the end of the Napoleonic Wars and World War I.

The stories for Italy and Britain are similar. Each country has several cities and the color is concentrated in or around them. But Italy's largest city during the Renaissance was Naples, and yet Naples, along with the rest of southern Italy, has almost no dots at all. Why not? A plausible explanation is that for practical purposes Naples and southern Italy were not part of what we think of as Renaissance Italy. They were controlled by the Spanish Hapsburgs and were politically and culturally separated from the rest of Italy. In contrast, Britain's largest city, London, was also the nation's capital politically, economically, and culturally. It also is the center of a mass of color.

FOUR MODELS OF HOW CITIES ARE RELATED TO THE ORIGINS OF SIGNIFICANT FIGURES

Italy During the Renaissance, 1400–1550

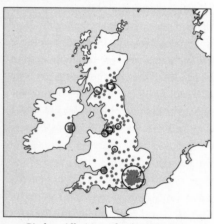

Circles: All cities of at least 25,000 people in 1500.

France During the Baroque and Enlightenment, 1600–1800

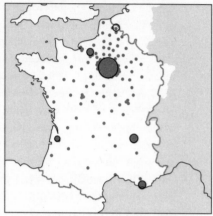

Circles: All cities of at least 40,000 people in 1700.

Britain During the Industrial and Romantic Revolutions, 1750–1850

Circles: All cities of at least 50,000 people in 1800.

Germany Between Waterloo and the Marne, 1815–1915

Circles: All cities of at least 60,000 people in 1850.

Note: All circles are sized proportionately to a common minimum of 25,000. minimum population sizes in each graph are chosen to provide roughly comparab thresholds for a community with the attributes of a city.

France shows a far different picture. No other country in Europe came close to France in centralization, not only of its government and of its urban population, but of its cultural resources. France had only six cities with populations greater than 40,000 people in 1700, with Paris dwarfing the other five. The south of France shows a modest number of significant figures separated from the rest, but otherwise the map resembles a pattern of iron filings scattered on a surface with a magnet where Paris sits.

Germany is also unique, but in the opposite way: No other country in Europe produced so many significant figures from such scattered places. I should note that the dispersion is not peculiar to 19C. If you review the maps for earlier periods (pages 301–302), you will find that Germany always drew its significant figures from scattered areas. For a world grown accustomed to thinking of Germany as the centralized military-industrial society of the two World Wars, it is easy to forget that until the last half of 19C, Germany was politically and culturally the most decentralized region of Europe. And yet cities are not irrelevant to the German story. Germany had 11 cities of 60,000 or more people in 1850 and several others not shown on the map that were close. Furthermore, Germany had another set of towns—Göttingen, Heidelberg, Tübingen, Halle, Jena, and Freiberg, among others—with concentrations of human capital in the form of Europe's finest universities. That leads us to the theme of the following discussion: Significant figures are associated not with just any sort of city, but a particular kind that I will call *elite cities* where a critical mass of talent can form.

Talent and Critical Mass

Why did some cities become the cradles of significant figures while others did not? Part of the answer depends not on the city itself but on the larger culture. *Accelerant*, a word used in connection with fires, seems appropriate in thinking about the role of cities. In a culture where the spark of creativity has been lit, the following are some of the combustible materials that elite cities possessed during the period from 1400–1950.[9]

Cities attracted human capital. As countries urbanized, some people in rural areas decided to pull up roots and move to the city, while others decided to stay put. On an individual level, these decisions were made for many reasons. Taken overall, the process tended to select for talent, ambition, industriousness, creativity, and spunk. Cities had a disproportionate amount of a nation's human capital, and the children who grew up there reflected that disproportion.

The disproportionate inborn talent that each new urban generation enjoyed was augmented by educational opportunities far better than those in the countryside. Primary education reached much larger proportions of urban children than rural children. Access to secondary and university education was greater. The facilities and staffing of urban schools were better.

Some cities provided more raw material than others for talented children to feed upon. In his analysis of Western civilization from ancient Greece to the first half of 19C, Dean Simonton discusses this raw material in terms of cultural diversity.[10] The literature on creative personalities consistently demonstrates the importance of relativism, complexity, diversity, and richness. Simonton notes that, historically, talented children who grew up in a rich, diverse cultural environment were more likely to develop than those who grew up in a culturally monolithic environment.[11]

Children who grew up in cities were also more likely to become artists and scientists just because there is a lot of art and science going on all about them. For the visual arts and music, the first determinant of whether a city had a lot going on was a large audience. Cities where thousands of people filled concert halls and patronized art galleries tended to be the cities where artists, composers, and musicians went to work. The secondary effect of an audience was that the presence of artists and composers in a city drew other artists and composers, which made the city still more attractive. At some points in history—Paris's domination of the art world from mid-19C until World War II is an example—a city became so conspicuously the center of activity that it acquired close to a monopoly.

Not all cities have audiences for art and music. The industrial cities of England grew large over the course of 19C, but the money in those cities mostly belonged to first-generation entrepreneurs who were too busy to go to concerts and bought their art through agents in London and Paris. Many were self-made men who scorned the arts as diversions of the idle aristocracy. The cities with large audiences for the arts were political and financial centers of power or intellectual centers.

With regard to the sciences, a city's combustible material consisted of facilities—libraries, laboratories, and colleagues. These are the properties of universities, and small university towns accordingly produced significant figures out of proportion to their populations. But urban centers could also fill that role. Some of the great cities of Europe were the homes of national libraries and research centers along with their local universities; others were not.

There is an element of circularity in this portrayal of elite cities when we are trying to explain where the significant figures worked—they went to work where the action was, and they were the cause of the action where they went to work. That circularity is a major part of the explanation for the self-reinforcing nature of streams of human accomplishment discussed in the preceding section. But, again, the circularity is diminished when we consider where the significant figures grew up rather than just where they worked. In the quantitative analysis, I look at both aspects, with the first set of regressions using the origins of significant figures as the dependent variable and the second set using their workplaces. In both cases, the powerful stimulus given to human accomplishment by elite cities—places such as London, Paris, Florence, Vienna, and Berlin—is borne out by the quantitative record. The largest effects are found for the variables recording the size of the largest city, whether a city was a political or financial center, and whether a city was home to a leading university.

FREEDOM OF ACTION

Streams of accomplishment are fostered by political regimes that give de facto freedom of action to their potential artists and scholars.

The final contributor to human accomplishment that I take up in this chapter is *freedom of action*. I mean by this phrase something related to, but not quite the same as, political freedom in the form of constitutionally guaranteed rights, limited government, and democratic rule. Political freedom technically defined fails to explain anything about accomplishment in the arts and sciences for the same reason that war and unrest fail. Just as most human accomplishment occurred in times of chronic warfare (because chronic warfare has been the historical norm), most human accomplishment occurred under regimes that had almost no guaranteed political freedoms (because guaranteed freedoms have not been the historical norm). Perhaps, given time, political freedom will prove to be a better environment for accomplishment than any other system, but if we are looking at the record until 1950, we have barely a century in which liberal democracy was widespread.

Republics have a longer history than liberal democracies, but the nature of a republic throughout history could be almost anything. A few were free and well-governed societies that fit the modern sense of *republic*—republican Netherlands, for example. Others, like republican Venice, were as authoritarian and occasionally repressive as an autocracy. The Florentine republic was on another dimension altogether—a paradox to political historian S. E. Finer: "the very fountainhead of the republican ideology and home of its most eloquent and influential publicists," but akin to the Wild West in its practice of government, with sporadic shootouts and unofficial oligarchs who ran the city behind the scenes. "The wonder is how the city managed to prosper," Finer continues, "for one is bound to suspect . . . that it did so despite and not because of its political institutions."[12]

The form of governance does have an important relationship with accomplishment if we focus on one extreme, the totalitarian state. The amount of experience the world has with totalitarian states is even more limited than our experience with liberal democracy, but the record is so one-sided that the conclusion seems warranted: Totalitarian states effectively quash human accomplishment in the arts and philosophy. They are only slightly less stifling in the sciences, and then because they create isolated enclaves within the totalitarian state that mimic to some degree the intellectual incentives and institutions of non-totalitarian states.

These judgments are based on the Soviet, Chinese Communist, and East European records through 20C. The inventories are of only limited use, because they end in 1950, when even those as young as 50 had grown up for at least their first 18 years in a non-Communist environment. It is still worth noting that as of 1950 the Soviet Union had produced no significant figures in the visual arts who had not made their reputations before the revolution. Only two composers (Kabalevsky and Shostakovich) were among the significant figures born in Russia who can be said to have made their reputations under the Soviet system. The significant figures among the writers who made their reputations after the Revolution do not have happy biographies. Isaak Babel was sent to the Gulag in the 1930s and died there. Valentin Katayev restricted himself to light humor or stories about children (who could be portrayed naturalistically, to a degree). Konstantine Fedin's one good novel was written in 1924, after which he parroted the Party line and helped prosecute writers who did not. Yuri Olesha was disgraced during the 1930s and rehabilitated only after Stalin died. Mikhail Sholokhov wrote his masterpiece, *Tikhy Don*, in his twenties and thereafter, writing under the eye of the Party, produced only hack work. Satirist Mikhail Zoshchenko was brought under strict scrutiny after 1930 and expelled in disgrace from the Union of Soviet Writers in 1946.[13]

The totalitarian states of 20C obsessively sought industrial and military strength, leading them to take special measures to nurture and reward scientific talent. But special privileges apparently did not compensate for the stifling effects of totalitarianism. The Soviet Union's record up to 1950 amounted to only 11 significant scientific figures who had made their reputations under Soviet rule, compared with 105 in the United States whose careers matured during the same period (1920–1950).

The common factor that distinguishes the totalitarian state from all other political systems is the condition that I have labeled *freedom of action.* If we ignore legal protections and focus instead on how much de facto freedom artists and scientists enjoyed, the monarchies from 1400–1950 could be as tolerant of heterodoxy and independent thought as contemporary democracies. This is not to say an autocracy such as France's in 17C and 18C was without its dark side but that its talented artists and scientists had considerable freedom of action. Molière was well advised not to write a savage satire about Louis XIV, and he lived in a world where the Catholic Church could prevent him from presenting *Tartuffe* for five years, but Molière did have the freedom of action to satirize many of the great and powerful while becoming one of the greatest comedic dramatists of all time.

Freedom of action in an autocracy or strong monarchy could be the result of liberties established by custom, or it could be the result of a tolerant ruler. In smaller autocracies, the limits of geographic scope also encouraged freedom of action. In 17C, for example, the area that would become Germany numbered 300 principalities, 51 independent cities, and nearly 2,000 counts or knights who possessed some territorial sovereignty. Even the largest German units such as Saxony existed in the midst of alternatives a few miles away. The alternatives might not be relevant to a peasant family tied to its small holding, but they were highly relevant to the young scholar or artist.

If monarchies are graded on the freedom of action they permitted, the striking under-representation of significant figures from Russia, the Balkans, and the Iberian peninsula (see the scatter-plot maps beginning on page 301) has a ready, if partial, explanation. Russia was a repressive, despotic autocracy in ways that France and the principalities of Central Europe were not. Property rights never developed in Russia, for example.[14] Until the late 1700s, Russia enforced obligatory service not just on the peasant but on the nobles. Secret police, use of the military for internal suppression of dissent, and indiscriminate use of imprisonment and exile to Siberia were tools of the Russian state long before the Bolsheviks perfected them. To the southeast, the Balkans were ruled for most of the period after 1400 by the Ottoman Empire. As one historian described Ottoman rule in the Balkans,

The Ottoman system took children forever from parents, discouraged family cares among its members through their most active years, allowed them no certain hold upon property, gave them no definite promise that their sons and daughters would profit by their success and sacrifice, raised and lowered them with no regard for ancestry or previous distinction, taught them a strange law, ethics and religion, and ever kept them conscious of a sword raised above their heads which might put an end at any moment to a brilliant career.[15]

That the Balkans did not produce great art and science under the Ottomans is no mystery.

At the other corner of Europe, Spain experienced a movement toward despotism that coincided with the economic windfall discussed in the previous chapter (page 337). Until Isabella and Ferdinand, the same monarchs who sponsored Columbus, Spain had been a poly-ethnic, poly-religious society. Then came the Inquisition, different in kind, scope, and duration from any of the Inquisitions elsewhere in Europe—different also in that it fell under the direct control of the crown, not the Church. It was used to suppress, torture, expel, and kill Jews, Moors, and Christian heretics, but also had open-ended authority that made it a tool of state power against whomever the crown identified as an enemy. And it went on for centuries, at different levels of repressiveness under different monarchs, until it was finally ended in the early 1800s. Spain was not as repressive as Russia or the Ottoman empire. But if one is looking for an explanation of Spain's persistent underachievement in the arts and sciences relative to its size, population, and wealth, its limited freedom of action must be taken into account along with the cultural dissipation that followed its windfall from the New World.

In the quantitative analyses, I convert these observations about the regimes in Europe to codings of de facto freedom of action that can be used in the multivariate analysis. The results are that countries with a history of despotism show sharply reduced levels of accomplishment. Parliamentary monarchies and liberal democracies were generally more productive than tolerant autocracies.

•   •   •

As in Chapter 15, the following sections describe the quantitative analyses that led to these conclusions. As in Chapter 15, you may proceed directly to the next chapter without much loss in substance.

THE REGRESSION ANALYSES: MODELS

The question to be explored is whether the rises and falls in human accomplishment are self-reinforcing processes that benefit from previous people working in the same field or from concurrent people working in other fields.

Lagged value of significant figures. Lagged variables are a standard tool for analyzing phenomena that stretch over time. In Chapter 15, I used the lagged value of the war and unrest indices to explore whether conditions in childhood might have a delayed effect on the emergence of significant figures. Lagged variables also have another use: to see whether the dependent variable is partly caused by the preceding value of the dependent variable. To see how lagged values are coded, consider this abbreviated mock-up of four observations in the visual arts inventory:[16]

Generation	Country	No. of significant figures	1st lagged no. of significant figures	2nd lagged no. of significant figures
1610–1630	Netherlands	4		
1630–1650	Netherlands	6	4	
1650–1670	Netherlands	8	6	4
1670–1690	Netherlands	3	8	6

In the above table, the lagged number of significant figures for the Netherlands in 1670–1690 is 8 if the lag is for one generation and 6 if the lag is for 2 generations. The results in the table below include values of lagged total significant figures for the two preceding generations—or more precisely, for reasons described in the note, rescaled logged values of those two variables.[17]

Significant figures working in the other domains. Another way of testing the effect of models on the production of significant figures in one inventory is to enter the number of significant figures being produced in the other inventories. For example, if the dependent variable is number of artists, the independent variables in such an analysis include the number of writers, composers, philosophers, and scientists in the same generation. This analysis is not available when the total number of significant figures is the dependent variable, but it can be applied to the analyses of the separate inventories.

The table on the following page shows the analysis of the lagged significant figures variable. I extend the lagged values back a full century so you can see how long the relationship persists.

THE FIVE PRECEDING GENERATIONS AS PREDICTORS OF THE NUMBER OF SIGNIFICANT FIGURES

Dependent variable: Total no. of significant figures in a generation
Observations: 352
Exposure: Country population

	Beta	*p* value	Percent change per SD*
No. of significant figures in the five preceding generations[†]			
First lag (0–20 years prior)	*+.368*	*.000*	*+87*
Second lag (20–40 years prior)	*+.121*	*.029*	*+23*
Third lag (40–60 years prior)	+.041	.397	+7
Fourth lag (60–80 years prior)	*+.099*	*.030*	*+18*
Fifth lag (80–100 years prior)	+.040	.334	+7
Control variables			
Population density (logged)	*−.512*	*.000*	*−41*
Time dummy variables (results not shown separately)			

Bold italics indicate results statistically significant at or beyond the .05 level.

Results are based on a random-effects negative binomial model.

* Percent change in the expected number of significant figures for a unit increase in X, holding all the other independent variables constant.

[†] Logged and rescaled for zero values. See note 17.

Through the first two periods, representing 40 years, the betas for the lagged variables show large, highly significant relationships to the number of significant figures in the current decade.[18] But decay in the magnitude of the effect is apparent. In the first lag, a standard deviation increase is associated with a 87 percent increase in the total number of significant figures. That increase drops to 23 percent for the second lag and is still lower thereafter. In subsequent analyses, I include just the first two lagged values. Some technical issues associated with the interpretation of time-series data and lagged variables are discussed in the note.[19]

Now we turn to the other way in which models could be important—models not in the same field but in different ones. Is it the case that artistic accomplishment is helped along if important work is also happening in the sciences? Are authors inspired by living in a milieu where composers are writing great works?

To obtain an answer to this question for a given inventory, I created variables which represented the total number of significant figures active in other inventories. For example, if the dependent variable is the number of significant figures in literature, the parallel independent variable is the number of significant figures in all fields other than literature.

ACTIVITY IN OTHER INVENTORIES AS A PREDICTOR OF THE NUMBER OF SIGNIFICANT FIGURES

Dependent variable: Total no. of significant figures in a given inventory
Independent variable shown: Total no. of significant figures in all the other inventories combined
Independent variables not shown: Population density, time dummy variables
Observations: 446

Exposure: Country population

	Beta	*p* value	Percent change per SD*
Results for the visual arts inventory	*+.029*	*.000*	*+44*
Results for the literature inventory	+.003	.411	+3
Results for the music inventory	*+.010*	*.011*	*+14*
Results for the combined scientific inventories	*+.016*	*.000*	*+12*

Bold italics indicate results statistically significant at or beyond the .05 level.
Results are based on a random-effects negative binomial model.

* Percent change in the expected number of significant figures for a standard deviation increase in the independent variable on that line, holding all the other independent variables constant.

The effects of activity in other fields are statistically significant and large for visual arts, and statistically significant but modest for music and the scientific inventories. Literature appears to have been unaffected by activity in other fields.

THE REGRESSION ANALYSES: ELITE CITIES

In all the multivariate analyses you have seen so far, the unit has been the country. To begin the exploration of the effects of cities, I use a database consisting of all cities in Europe and the United States that had a population of at least 30,000 sometime during 1400–1600, 50,000 in 1700, 100,000 in 1800, or 250,000 in 1900,[20] plus cities that were the political capital of a country but failed to meet the population criterion, or cities that had an elite university (see below) but failed to meet the population criterion. These procedures produced a set of 110 cities. I characterized each city for each half century from 1400–1950 on five dummy variables:

1. *Industrial.* A code of 1 was assigned to cities with economies that, during a given half-century, were heavily dependent on manufacturing and other industrial enterprises. The expectation for this variable is that industrial cities were not (absent other virtues) favorable places for producing significant figures.

2. *Entrepôt.* A code of 1 was assigned primarily to port cities, but also to few inland cities (e.g., Leipzig) that were hubs for trading. The expectation for this variable was that the cross-fertilization of information and goods associated with entrepôts facilitates the production of significant figures.

3. *Political or financial center.* A code of 1 was assigned to cities that were either capital cities of their countries or were centers of banking and investment. The expectation was that political and financial centers are cities with unusually high concentrations of educated and wealthy people, encouraging the production of significant figures.

4. *Elite university.* A code of 1 was assigned if the city had an elite university established no later than the preceding half century. In both Europe and the United States, a handful of universities have acquired elite status, widely known for their scholarship and serving as magnets for other cultural resources. Classification as an elite university was based on whether descriptions in basic reference sources used adjectives that indicated elite status. The universities that qualified as *elite* for some or all of the period since their founding were Cambridge, Oxford, the Sorbonne, Harvard, Yale, and the universities of Edinburgh, Vienna, Louvain, Berlin, Göttingen, Halle, Heidelberg, Leipzig, Tübingen, Bologna, Florence, Padua, Madrid, and Salamanca.[21]

5. *A non-elite university.* A code of 1 was assigned if the city had a university established no later than the preceding half century, but one that did not qualify as an elite university.

These variables, along with the population of the city and the country in which the city is located, were entered for each half century from 1400–1950. In this case, with both cities and countries acting as units, I employed a negative binomial regression in which countries were entered as dummy variables along with the time dummies, and the standard errors were adjusted for clustering on the city. The results are reported in the table below.

CITY PREDICTORS OF THE ORIGINS
OF SIGNIFICANT FIGURES

Dependent variable: Total no. of significant figures in a half century

Observations: 943

Exposure: City population

	Beta	*p* value	Percent increase if "yes"*
Variables for characterizing the city			
Industrial economy (yes/no)	+.183	.219	+20
Trading entrepôt (yes/no)	+.063	.550	+7
Political or financial center (yes/no)	+.493	.000	+64
Presence of an elite university (yes/no)	+1.044	.000	+184
Presence of only a non-elite university (yes/no)	−.212	.107	−19
Control variables			
Country dummy variables (results not shown separately)			
Time dummy variables (results not shown separately)			

Bold italics indicate results statistically significant at or beyond the .05 level.

Results are based on a negative binomial model.

* Percent change in the expected number of significant figures if a dummy variable is coded "yes," holding all the other independent variables constant.

Two characteristics of a city are systematically associated with the appearance of significant figures who grow up there: whether the city is a political or financial center, regardless of its population, and whether the city is the location of an elite university. The effect of these latter two variables is quite large. As the last column indicates, being a political or financial center increased the expected number of significant figures by 64 percent, holding everything else constant, while having an elite university increased that expected number by 184 percent.

A curiosity in the table is the negative effect associated with having just a non-elite university. This does not mean that the presence of such a university somehow discourages the appearance of significant figures. If the regression analysis is replicated without the elite university variable, then the presence of any university is associated with a positive, though small and statistically insignificant, increase in the number of significant figures.

These results were consistent with the analysis when it was replicated separately for each inventory. The notable exception involved the role of an industrial city in generating significant figures in the scientific inventories, which was large and statistically significant. The relationship makes sense—the industrial cities might not have had concert halls and art galleries, but they were centers of technological activity and often of scientific research as well.

On the basis of these results, it appears that the relevant variables are whether a city is a political or financial center, and whether it is the home of an elite university. The next step is to apply these findings to our usual database. I also include the size of the nation's largest city, to see if it might explain away (or attenuate) the role of the political and financial centers variable. The results of the regression are shown in the table below.

ELITE CITIES AS PREDICTORS OF THE NUMBER OF SIGNIFICANT FIGURES IN A COUNTRY

Dependent variable: Total no. of significant figures in a generation
Observations: 436
Exposure: Country population

	Beta	p value	Percent change per SD*
Variables characterizing a country's elite cities			
Population of the largest city (logged)	+.077	.281	+13
Number of political and financial centers	**+.291**	**.000**	**+49**
Number of cities with an elite university	**+.282**	**.000**	**+45**
Control variables			
Population density (logged)	−.188	.111	−18
Time dummy variables (results not shown separately)			

Bold italics indicate results statistically significant at or beyond the .05 level.

Results are based on a negative binomial model.

* Percent change in the expected number of significant figures if a dummy variable is coded "yes," holding all the other independent variables constant.

Large and statistically significant effects were found for the role of political and financial centers and for elite universities, even after bringing the population of the largest city into the equation. When the analysis is replicated separately for each inventory, no interpretably distinctive patterns emerge.

THE REGRESSION ANALYSES: FREEDOM OF ACTION

As the discussion of freedom of action in the first half of the chapter indicated (page 361), I focus on the de facto political state of affairs, not on the formal structure. I came to this position because the more conventional ways of categorizing polities proved to be useless in understanding where accomplishment flourishes. I begin with that exercise.

An Analysis Using a Conventional Political Typology

The conventional typology of political systems uses the following categories:[22]

Absolute monarchy. I follow S. E. Finer's definition of absolute monarchy as "a regularly constituted and conferred office whose holder is legally (procedurally) unconstrained, but not necessarily unconstrained by powerful conventional understandings on matters of substance."[23] This label is used for the type of monarchy that prevailed in most of Europe until the French Revolution and in some countries into 20C.

Parliamentary monarchy. This category includes political entities that were not yet democratic in a formal sense but in which the powers of the head of state were limited, especially in the creation of new laws. England from the Glorious Revolution in 1688 to 1832 falls in this category, for example. I also used this code for what John Adams called "aristocratical republics" such as Zurich or Venice, in which oligarchs exercised the same power as monarchs.[24]

Republics. As I noted earlier (page 361), European republics varied so widely that they don't really belong in the same category. The difficulties of coding them are compounded because they were usually small and seldom coincided with modern national borders. I restricted the code of *republic* to Switzerland and the Netherlands during the appropriate years of their history.

Liberal democracy. This code was reserved for countries in which all effective legislative and executive power is wielded by an elected legislative body or bodies and an elected head of government.

Totalitarian states. An invention of 20C, the totalitarian state concentrates all power in the hands of a ruling group, not subject to recall or restraint by the public. The code was used for the Soviet Union, Germany under Nazi rule, and countries under their occupation or domination.

Each country was coded by individual year, with the code for the two-decade generation representing the modal code.[25] The table below shows the results.

POLITICAL SYSTEM AS A PREDICTOR OF THE NUMBER OF SIGNIFICANT FIGURES

Dependent variable: Total no. of significant figures in a generation
Observations: 422
Exposure: Country population

	Beta	p value	Percent increase if "yes"*	Percent change per SD[†]
Dummy variables for characterizing the political system				
Liberal democracy	−.179	.198	−16	
Parliamentary monarchy	−.011	.925	+1	
Republic	+.382	.134	+46	
Absolute monarchy	(Reference group. Beta=0)			
Totalitarian	−.146	.447	−4	
Control variables				
Population density (logged)	−.066	.551		−6
Time dummy variables (results not shown separately)				

Bold italics indicate results statistically significant at or beyond the .05 level.

Results are based on a random-effects negative binomial model.

* Percent change in the expected number of significant figures if a dummy variable is coded "yes," holding all the other independent variables constant.

[†] Percent change in the expected number of significant figures for a standard deviation increase in the independent variable on that line, holding all the other independent variables constant.

The results show no pattern—liberal democracy, parliamentary democracy, and totalitarian states all do worse than the reference group, absolute monarchy. Only the category for republics had a positive coefficient and, like the coefficients for the other categories, it did not reach statistical significance. In sum: A conventional typology of political systems explains little.[26]

An Analysis Coding for De Facto Freedom of Action

After finding so little relationship of significant figures to a conventional typology, I recoded the countries for the freedom of action they provided. The objective was to regroup the observations into just four ordered categories going from high to low on this continuum. These codes obviously involve judgments, described below.

Category 1. This category, intended to designate the countries with the greatest freedom of action, was limited to liberal democracies.

Category 2. This category included all the parliamentary monarchies and the Netherlands and Switzerland in their republican phases. I also coded pre-unification Italy and Germany in this category. This coding is problematic for 18C Germany, when Prussia became a significant state on its own and qualified as a large autocracy. But throughout 18C, Prussia represented well under half the geographic area of Germany and was the origin of just 20 percent of German significant figures, so I left the coding for Germany as a whole unchanged. Similarly, the southern part of Italy was ruled more like a large autocracy than the north, but the Naples region (roughly, Italy south of Rome) and Sicily accounted for only eight percent of all the Italian significant figures before unification of the country in 19C.

Category 3. This category, *tolerant autocracy,* was the default coding for both true autocracies and strong monarchies. To be excluded from category 3, an absolute monarchy had to be notably repressive.

Category 4. This category, *despotic government,* intended to capture the countries that were unusually repressive of human freedom of action, includes all the totalitarian states of 20C plus the Balkans under the Ottoman Empire, Russia, Poland when it was under Russian rule, and Spain during its long imposition of an active, state-run Inquisition.

When these categories of freedom of action are treated as dummy variables, the results are as shown in the table on the following page.

How can category 4, despotic government, fail to show a large negative effect, given the dismal records of the Balkans and Russia, which make up the bulk of the despotic codings? The answer goes to the nature of regression models, and offers an object lesson in the ways in which results can be decisively affected by judgments that have no clear right or wrong answer. The model used to compute the results in the table takes the effects of the country into account. Suppose, for example, that I did not use either the random-effects or fixed-effects model, but simply entered a vector of dummy variables

FREEDOM OF ACTION AS A PREDICTOR OF THE
NUMBER OF SIGNIFICANT FIGURES

Dependent variable: Total no. of significant figures in a generation

Observations: 446

Exposure: Country population

	Beta	p value	Percent increase if "yes"*	Percent change per SD†
Dummy variables for characterizing de facto freedom of action				
Category 1 (liberal democracy)	+.232	.100	+26	
Category 2 (parliamentary monarchy)	**_+.368_**	**_.002_**	**_+44_**	
Category 3 (tolerant autocracy)	(Reference group. Beta=0)			
Category 4 (despotic government)	−.241	.227	−21	
Control variables				
Population density (logged)	+.047	.627		+5
Time dummy variables (results not shown separately)				

Bold italics indicate results statistically significant at or beyond the .05 level.

Results are based on a random-effects negative binomial model.

* Percent change in the expected number of significant figures if a dummy variable is coded "yes," holding all the other independent variables constant.

† Percent change in the expected number of significant figures for a standard deviation increase in the independent variable on that line, holding all the other independent variables constant.

for *country* and had a list of beta coefficients associated with each country. In that case, Russia and the Balkans (coded as a single "country" for the analysis) would have large negative coefficients which, in effect, are soaking up some of the variance that would otherwise be explained by the variable for despotic government. If I then rerun that equation without a vector of dummy variables for country, the negative coefficient for the despotic government variable becomes very large and highly significant.

Which model is correct? It is a question with no unequivocally right answer. If I were to translate these results into narrative explanations, it might be argued that something about Russian culture and Balkan culture (or Russian and Balkan people—any unmeasured characteristic will do) is the real cause of the disproportionately small number of significant figures from those countries, and that to leave out the dummy variables for country falsely inflates the negative effect of despotic government. Conversely, it could be argued that the real cause of the lower accomplishment is the despotic governments that afflicted both regions throughout their histories. But there is no way to tell which argument is correct, because despotic governments existed throughout the whole time period. All we can be sure of is that two places with despotic governments throughout the period 1400–1950 did poorly, given their populations, in producing great accomplishment in the arts and sciences. The quantitative analysis cannot tell us for sure that their form of government was to blame.

Interpreting the significantly positive effect of category 2 governments (parliamentary monarchy) is also problematic. Even though the dummy variables to control for time are in the equation, it remains the case that category 1 (liberal democracy) prevailed during the last half of 19C and the first half of 20C, while category 2 prevailed predominantly during 18C and early 19C. If the accomplishment rate were declining for other reasons after mid-19C (as the graphs in Chapter 14 suggest), then the smaller coefficient for liberal democracy could be reflecting that larger trend. The modest but safe interpretation of the results in the table above is that the coefficients for type of government move in the same direction as freedom of action, with the two freest forms of government (categories 1 and 2) both showing positive effects on accomplishment. These results survive when I replicate the model without the problematic coding judgments for 18C Germany and for Spain during the Inquisition.

EPILOGUE: THE FULL MODEL

At the outset of the regression analyses in Chapter 15, I described my reasons for presenting the results in chunks, with a few basic control variables serving as a first check on whether the variables for explaining accomplishment that we were examining had an important independent role to play, before putting all the variables into the hopper together.

The table below illustrates the reason for this cautious approach. It includes the most important variables from all the sections in the last two chapters, combined into a single regression equation. The columns show the results when two options are used: the random-effects option, which takes the role of the individual country into account under the assumption that countries are different in ways that are unrelated to the independent variables, and the fixed-effects option, which sacrifices some efficiency but does not require an assumption that the unmeasured characteristics of the country are unrelated to the independent variables in the model.[27]

THE FULL MODEL, COMPARING RESULTS FOR RANDOM EFFECTS AND FIXED EFFECT

Dependent variable: Total no. of significant figures in a generation
Observations: 312
Exposure: Country population

	Random Effects		Fixed Effects	
	Beta	*p* value	Beta	*p* value
War and Civil Unrest				
War index	***+.055***	***.009***	***+.066***	***.001***
Unrest Index	+.011	.387	+.011	.328
Economic Wealth				
GDP per capita (constant dollars, logged)	***+.501***	***.006***	+.259	.135
Models				
Significant figures, first lag	***+.407***	***.000***	***+.402***	***.000***
Significant figures, second lag	***+.158***	***.004***	***+.150***	***.003***
Elite Cities				
Population of the largest city (logged)	***−.295***	***.003***	−.132	.236
Number of political & financial centers	+.045	.445	***+.122***	***.019***
Number of cities with an elite university	+.084	.306	***+.168***	***.025***
Freedom of Action				
Category 1 (liberal democracy)	+.042	.743	+.003	.978
Category 2 (parliamentary monarchy)	+.082	.411	+.086	.354
Category 3 (tolerant autocracy)	(Reference group. Beta=0)			
Category 4 (despotic government)	***−.398***	***.021***	***−.325***	***.037***
Control variables				
Population density (logged)	−.151	.261	***−.512***	***.006***
Time dummy variables (results not shown separately)				

Bold italics indicate results statistically significant at or beyond the .05 level.

Both models use exactly the same data, and differ only in the way that they take the effects of the individual country into account. For all the analyses you have seen so far, the differences produced by the two versions have been trivial. But when many variables are assembled in the one equation, the results diverge. If we believe the random-effects model, per capita GDP is significant; the fixed-effects model says not. The fixed-effects model yields highly significant results for political/financial centers and elite universities; the random-effects model says no, it is the size of the largest city that counts.

Both methods contradict the earlier finding that war is not related to accomplishment. If we believe the full model, we must conclude that war has a statistically significant effect after all on accomplishment in the arts and sciences—but a positive effect, encouraging the emergence of significant figures, not a negative effect.

I prefer the random-effects model for conceptual reasons, and the relevant test for the full model indicates that it is statistically appropriate as well. But the choice is not so one-sided that it is safe to take all the random-effects results at face value and ignore the conflicts with the fixed-effect results.[28] Nor is it appropriate to throw out the findings from the piece-by-piece analyses and assume that the one-equation full model gives us a more accurate understanding of how these variables go together. In one instance—the important negative role assigned to despotic government—the results of the full model correspond to my reading of the narrative record, and I am predisposed to think that controlling for the additional variables in the full model has exposed an authentic relationship that was obscured when the freedom of action variables were analyzed alone. But in another instance—the positive relationship of war to accomplishment—it seems just as likely that the relationship in the full model is spurious.

At this point different analysts will choose different ways to proceed. Some will argue that if one conducts sufficiently sophisticated diagnostic tests and continues to refine the variables and re-specify the model, eventually an iron-clad interpretation of the results is possible. I do not agree, believing that such efforts as often produce false confidence as they produce more accurate results. My own interpretation of the findings in the last two chapters is to assume that large and statistically significant effects that emerged in the separate pieces are plausibly important in explaining trajectories of human accomplishment in the arts and sciences. The ways in which the importance of those variables shifted when put into a full model are interesting, and ought to be kept in mind in subsequent work, but should not be treated as decisive.

WHAT'S LEFT TO EXPLAIN?

The story line for Part 3 began with the steep upward climb of significant figures from the Renaissance onward. The last two chapters have introduced five topics—peace, prosperity, models, elite cities, and freedom of action—to try to explain why the timeline has that particular shape. How much has been explained, and what's left to explain?

At the level of the individual country and specific generation, the fit between the variables we have examined and the actual production of significant figures is good enough to be informative, but not good enough to answer all the important questions. You can get a visual sense of the amount left unexplained from the figure on the next page. It shows the difference between the actual and expected values for each of the countries for each of the generations after entering the explanatory variables of the last two chapters.[1] A difference of zero means that the number of significant figures has been perfectly "predicted." A plus figure indicates that the equation underpredicted the actual number of significant figures; a minus figure indicates overprediction.[2]

The predictiveness of the regression model is better than the figure indicates, insofar as many of those dots close to the zero line represent several observations stacked on top of each other. I cannot offer you the standard statistic for expressing how much has been explained (R^2), because the regression model for these data doesn't produce it. I can report the square of the correlation between the actual and predicted values of the dependent variable, which is .84, but it is no substitute for R^2.[3] Even without a precise measure, however, it is clear that the model's ability to predict how many significant figures any country produces in any generation is limited. This does not mean that the relationships discussed in the last two chapters are

For individual countries and time periods,
the difference between the actual and expected number
of significant figures is often substantial

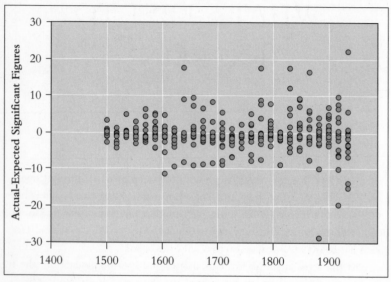

Note: Data represent Europe, the United States, and Canada, 1400–1950.

meaningless after all; just that many other factors, not part of the equation, are feeding into the process of producing significant figures. Such results are the rule, not the exception, in analyzing social and cultural phenomena. Adding more data of the same type—measures of education, health, equality, or urbanization for example—are unlikely to add much explanatory power. The variables already in the equation have already captured much of the information contained in those more detailed variables.

Three issues remain that lend themselves to investigation. First, the regression results do not explain the falling accomplishment rate observed after mid-19C in several inventories (Chapter 14). Nothing in the analyses of the last two chapters would lead us to conclude that the conditions for accomplishment deteriorated after mid-19C, and much would suggest that they improved.[4] Wealth, cities and their cultural resources, and political freedom of action all increased markedly during 19C and 20C—in their quantitative expressions, more than keeping pace with than the increase in population—and yet the production of significant figures per unit population declined.

The second issue involves non-European streams of accomplishment. The variables I introduced in the last two chapters are informative for Europe from 1400–1950, but even a casual scan of the histories of East Asia, India, and the Arab world tells us that GDP, population of the largest city, national population, and the other economic and political variables that helped explain the European trajectory are unlikely to work as well for those other centers of accomplishment. China's cities and wealth did not decline after the end of the Song dynasty, for example, but its great artistic and scientific accomplishments were mostly behind it by that time.

For West and non-West alike, there remains the final and great remaining question: Why do streams of accomplishment begin and end? So far, the variable we have examined that has the most explanatory power is the number of significant figures in the preceding generation. The relationship is important in itself. It bears directly on the question that puzzled Velleius from his vantage point two thousand years ago, that Alfred Kroeber tried to attack with the limited tools available to him the 1930s, and that Dean Simonton subsequently answered for both Western civilization and for China.[5] The processes that lead to human accomplishment in the arts and sciences are self-reinforcing, involving the emulation of models and the availability of a growing creative edifice that the new generation can build upon.

But valuable as it is, this finding does not tell us what generates a major stream of accomplishment in the first place. We face a more pedestrian version of the problem that faces cosmologists trying to understand the history of the universe. They know a great deal about what happened nanoseconds after the Big Bang began. They just don't know how it got started. The variables in the last two chapters tell us much about the dynamics governing streams of accomplishment once they are underway. They don't tell us what ignites the blaze or why it dies out. Those are the questions to which I now turn.

PART FOUR

ON THE ORIGINS AND DECLINE OF ACCOMPLISHMENT

F aced with the story of human accomplishment across time and
cultures, what is a parsimonious set of elements that helps to
explain what causes streams of accomplishment to begin and decline?
At this point I am no longer dealing with ideas and hypotheses that lend
themselves to clear-cut tests, though quantitative data can inform them.

Chapter 18 states the case for what I see as the mainspring for human
accomplishment, the inborn impulse of humans toward excellence.

Chapter 19 discusses two personal stances toward life, purpose and
autonomy, that cultures can foster or discourage, and that affect
the likelihood the people capable of excellence will devote their lives
to achieving it.

Chapter 20 takes up what I see as the elements that shape the nature
of human accomplishment: a rich organizing structure and a coherent
understanding of, and use of, transcendental goods.

Chapter 21 presents the case that the declines in the rate of
accomplishment from the mid-1800s onward reflect real changes in the
streams of Western accomplishment.

Chapter 22 brings together threads from throughout the book and
speculates about their meaning for accomplishment after 1950
and into 21C.

EIGHTEEN

THE ARISTOTELIAN PRINCIPLE

In Chapter 5, as this attempt to inventory excellence in the arts and sciences began, I took up a question that must be answered before such an endeavor makes sense: Is there such a thing as excellence in human accomplishment that exists independently of subjective tastes and contemporary intellectual fashion? Now, as I begin my attempt to explain the origin and decline of bursts of excellence, the starting point must be another elemental question: Is it in the nature of human beings to be drawn to excellence and, given the chance, to pursue it, or is excellence something that must be elicited from human beings who are naturally indifferent to it?

THE PRINCIPLE STATED

I proceed from the view that accomplishment in the arts and sciences is one manifestation of a characteristic of human nature discussed at length by Aristotle in books seven and ten of the *Nicomachean Ethics*. A leading topic in those books is the meaning of pleasure in human life. The core sentence for our purposes: "Life is an activity, and each man actively exercises his favorite faculties upon the objects he loves most."[1] Philosopher John Rawls distilled the sense of Aristotle's discussion into what he labeled *the Aristotelian principle*, which Rawls stated as follows:

> *Other things equal, human beings enjoy the exercise of their realized capacities (their innate or trained abilities), and this enjoyment increases the more the capacity is realized, or the greater its complexity.*

I add the italics to signify the importance of this statement. If it is not true, little of the rest of my explanation of what ignites excellence in human accomplishment hangs together. If it is true, elements of the explanation approach the self evident. Rawls continues:

> The intuitive idea here is that human beings take more pleasure in doing something as they become more proficient at it, and of two activities they do equally well, they prefer the one calling on a larger repertoire of more intricate and subtle discriminations. For example, chess is a more complicated and subtle game than checkers, and algebra is more intricate than elementary arithmetic. Thus the principle says that someone who can do both generally prefers playing chess to playing checkers, and that he would rather study algebra than arithmetic.[2]

Rawls's explanation speaks for itself, so I will add just a few comments. Mainly, I want to emphasize that neither Aristotle nor Rawls is talking about abstruse philosophical satisfactions but about the nature of pleasure. Exercising our realized capacities is, in the truest sense of the word, *enjoyable*.

We see the truth of the Aristotelian principle in our own lives, I assert, and I invite you to test that assertion against your own experience. The things we enjoy the most deeply are the things at which we are most expert. In Chapter 5, I discussed the ways in which the expert and the novice experience the same event differently. Then, I was careful not to argue that the expert *enjoyed* the same event more than the novice—it would have confused the issue—but I will say it now. Let me add a qualification that, in a sense, proves the principle: When a person is expert at something and does *not* find his greatest enjoyment in its exercise, it is usually because he feels that he became expert at something that does not draw upon his full capacities.

We see the truth of the Aristotelian principle from observations of others. Teachers trying to interest students in classical music know that Tchaikovsky's *1812 Overture* is a good way to begin, because children are more likely to respond to it than to a Bach fugue. The children who respond and go on to learn more about classical music begin to find that the Bach fugue gets more interesting, while the cannons booming in the *1812 Overture* lose their charm. The beginning photographer takes one shot each of many different scenes, and the pleasure comes from having pictures of lots of different things. The more deeply involved he becomes in photography, the more shots he takes of the same thing, and the pleasure begins to come from solving subtle problems of lighting and composition. The pre-adolescent chess prodigy revels in the flashy sacrificial attack. As he learns more about the game, he begins to relish subtle positional strategies. The talented mechanic who learns how to fix any car that someone brings into the shop dreams of working on the more complicated problems posed by high-performance racing engines.

EVIDENCE FOR THE PRINCIPLE'S REALITY

Until the 1960s, any psychologist who claimed that the Aristotelian principle says something true about the behavior of human beings faced ridicule. From its infancy through the first two-thirds of 20C, the new science of psychology was dominated by the behaviorist position, championed first by John Watson in 1914 and later made famous by B. F. Skinner.[3] The human mind and personality are driven by positive and negative reinforcements, the behaviorists said. A concept such as "enjoyment" is illusory—human beings will enjoy whatever they are trained to enjoy. All that is necessary to elicit any behavioral response is the appropriate set of reinforcement schedules.

During the height of the behaviorists' influence, psychologist Abraham Maslow published an article entitled "A Theory of Human Motivation" (1943) that introduced the initial version of what would become his famous needs hierarchy. His lowest level of human needs were primitive: food, water, shelter, sex. But once those needs were satisfied, Maslow argued, the human animal tried to satisfy a sequence of other inborn needs. The need for longer-term safety followed the need for day-to-day survival, then came a need for intimacy with other people, then the need for recognition and respect from others, and finally what Maslow called self-actualization.[4] His statement of the nature of self-actualization links the Aristotelian principle to the psychology of great accomplishment in the arts and sciences:

> A musician must make music, an artist must paint, a poet must write, if he is to be ultimately happy. What a man *can* be, he *must* be. . . . This tendency might be phrased as the desire to become more and more what one is, to become everything one is capable of becoming.[5]

Maslow may have been a lonely voice in 1943, but even as he wrote, experimental psychologists were beginning to come across bits and pieces of data that were hard to fit within the behaviorists' model, and these anomalies accumulated. Humans persistently exhibited tendencies to enjoy the stimulation of new things, complexity, surprises, even in the absence of any perceptible external reinforcement. People insisted on developing their skills, extending themselves, in patterned ways that did not fit easily into the view that humans are governed by a few primitive drives.[6] In the late 1950s, psychologist Robert White used the accumulated evidence to propose that humans take satisfaction from dealing with the environment around them. The reward (for all behavior must have a reward) is a feeling of "effectance," which in itself is sufficient to stimulate behavior. In the title of his article, he managed to say it in plain language: "Motivation Reconsidered: The Concept of Competence."[7] Here and there on the bleak plains of behaviorism, the possibility that man might be human in the Aristotelian sense was putting up shoots.

In the years that followed, the evidence accumulated that humans enjoy not just competence but excellence. Of the many strands that bear on the Aristotelian principle, the one that comes closest to operationalizing it has been the work of psychologist Mihaly Csikszentmihalyi. In the early 1970s, Csikszentmihalyi began studying the nature of enjoyment by interviewing people who spent long hours and intense effort on activities that had little monetary reward—in his initial study, rock climbers, chess players, composers of modern music, amateur modern dancers, and high school basketball players. Why did they invest so much of themselves in this activity? What did they get out of it? In the subsequent quarter-century, Csikszentmihalyi published a series of books elaborating the data and the theory that now goes under the label of *flow*, his word for what happens when one is fully engaged in an activity—the kind of absorption that leads you to lose track of time and of everything else that is going on around you.[8] Flow is human enjoyment in its most meaningful form. You are not saying to yourself, "How enjoyable this is," but are completely involved in the actual experience of enjoyment.

As Csikszentmihalyi and his colleagues analyzed the conditions that give rise to flow, they arrived at a model that has been has expressed in different ways over the years, but its essentials can be conveyed in a simple plot, as illustrated on the facing page.

When you are faced with a challenge that is far beyond your skills, the result is anxiety. When your skills are high but the challenges are low, you are bored. If you have low skills and the challenge is also low, you are able to do the job but are unlikely to become absorbed in it—apathy is the characteristic response. But when the skills are high and in balance with a stiff challenge, flow occurs. It is the Aristotelian principle on a two-dimensional plot.

Other developments in psychology, especially those dealing with the nature of intrinsic rewards, are coordinate with Csikszentmihalyi's research

The Aristotelian Principle in Graphic Form

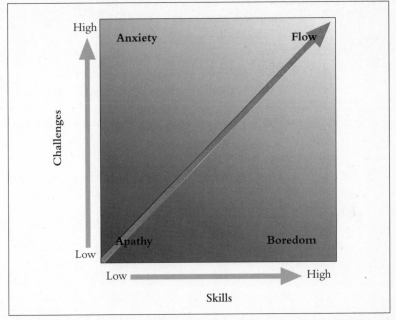

Sources: Adapted from Csikszentmihalyi 1975: 181 and Csikszentmihalyi 1997: 31.

and with the Aristotelian principle. The note provides some sources.[9] The Aristotelian principle is not just something that philosophers wish were true about human beings but corresponds to more systematic evidence about the way humans behave. Human beings enjoy the exercise of their realized capacities, with the enjoyment increasing the more the capacity is realized. Those with the capacity for excellence do not need to be cajoled into wanting to realize it. The pursuit of excellence is as natural as the pursuit of happiness.

NINETEEN

SOURCES OF ENERGY: PURPOSE AND AUTONOMY

The Aristotelian principle means that human beings with the potential for excellence will usually try to realize that potential, given the chance. But how hard they try, and how they go about it, are decisively affected by how they see their places in the universe at one extreme, and their places in their own families and communities at the other. Culture in turn affects these ways of seeing, and in doing so affects the likelihood that the people with the capacity for excellence will achieve it. I label two important ways of seeing one's place in the world *purpose* and *autonomy*. In this chapter I first describe what goes into the two sets of qualities I have in mind, then consider how they have corresponded with the history of accomplishment.

PURPOSE

A major stream of human accomplishment is fostered by a culture in which the most talented people believe that life has a purpose and that the function of life is to fulfill that purpose.

If the Aristotelian principle is valid, talented people of all personal convictions enjoy the exercise of their realized capacities. Why should it make any difference whether someone thinks life has a purpose? Why shouldn't people who don't think life has a purpose—I will use *nihilists* to label them—accomplish as much as anyone else? My position is that they *can* accomplish a lot, but if we are talking about means and distributions, nihilists as a group have a built-in disadvantage. The first reason for this has to do with the intense and unremitting level of effort that is typically required to do great things. The second reason goes to the nature of the goals that creative people set for themselves.

Work

One of the most overlooked aspects of excellence is how much work it takes. Fame can come easily and overnight, but excellence is almost always accompanied by a crushing workload, pursued with single-minded intensity. Strenuous effort over long periods of time is a repetitive theme in the biographies of the giants, sometimes taking on mythic proportions (Michelangelo painting the ceiling of the Sistine Chapel). Even the most famous supposed exception, Mozart, illustrates the rule. He was one of the lighter spirits among the giants, but his reputation for composing effortlessly was overstated—Mozart himself complained on more than one occasion that it wasn't as easy as it looked[1]—and his devotion to his work was as single-minded as Beethoven's, who struggled with his compositions more visibly. Consider the summer of 1788. Mozart was living in a city that experienced bread riots that summer and in a country that was mobilizing for war. He was financially desperate, forced to pawn his belongings to move to cheaper rooms. He even tried to sell the pawnbroker's tickets to get more loans. Most devastating of all, his beloved six-month old daughter died in June. And yet in June, July, and August, he completed two piano trios, a piano sonata, a violin sonata, and three symphonies, two of them among his most famous.[2] It could not have been done except by someone who, as Mozart himself once put it, is "soaked in music, . . . immersed in it all day long."[3]

Psychologists have put specific dimensions to this aspect of accomplishment. One thread of this literature, inaugurated in the early 1970s by Herbert Simon, argues that expertise in a subject requires a person to assimilate about 50,000 "chunks" of information about the subject over about 10 years of experience—simple expertise, not the mastery that is associated with great accomplishment.[4] Once expertise is achieved, it is followed by thousands of hours of practice, study, labor.[5] Nor is all of this work productive. What we see of the significant figures' work is typically shadowed by an immense amount of wasted effort—most successful creators produce clunkers, sometimes far more clunkers than gems.[6]

As one reviewer of the literature on creative people concluded, "Not only every sample, but every individual within each sample appears to be characterized by persistent dedication to work."[7] The accounts that he surveyed reveal not a few hours a week beyond 40, or a somewhat more focused attitude at work than the average, but levels of effort and focus that are standard deviations above the mean. Whether Edison's estimate of the ratio of perspiration to inspiration (99:1) is correct is open to argument, but his words echo the anonymous poet from ancient Greece who wrote that "before the gates of excellence the high gods have placed sweat."[8]

The willingness to engage in such monomaniacal levels of effort in the sciences and creative arts is related to a sense of vocation. By *vocation*, I have in mind the dictionary definition of "a function or station in life to which one is called by God."[9] I hedge on the necessity of God as the source. Many scientists see themselves as having a vocation in the service of Truth. Many other achievers see themselves as having a vocation without thinking about where it came from. My point is that a person with a strong sense of *this is what I have been put on earth to do* is more likely to accomplish great things than someone who doesn't. Ennui, anomie, alienation, and other forms of belief that life is futile and purposeless are at odds with the zest and life-affirming energy needed to produce great art or great science. Cultures vary in the degree to which they promote or discourage these alternative ways of looking at the world.

The Choice of Content

Nihilists are also at a disadvantage when it comes to their choice of content. Once again, I am talking about means and distributions for which there are individual exceptions, but most of those exceptions come at the beginning of a nihilistic period. Friedrich Nietzsche wrote about the great themes of philosophy, as did Jean-Paul Sartre. They had to, because they were struggling to bring down an edifice of thinking about the great themes that they thought was wrong. But once the edifice is down, whether in philosophy, literature, art, or music, the choice of content becomes more problematic. If life is purposeless, no one kind of project is intrinsically more important than any other kind. At the extreme, this can produce perversely capricious and trivial choices that represent, as Ronald Sukenick put it with regard to the plight of the novelist, ". . . ways of maintaining a considered boredom in the face of the abyss."[10] But even short of the extreme, this broader generalization applies: Without a sense of purpose, the creative personality has no template that constantly forces an assessment of whether he is making the best possible use of his talents.

People who see a purpose in their lives have a better chance of creating enduring work than people who don't, because the kind of project they work on *does* make a difference to them. The general statement here is that to believe life has a purpose carries with it a predisposition to put one's talents in the service of whatever is the best—not the most lucrative, not the most glamorous, but that which represents the highest expression of the object of one's vocation.

The link is to some degree a tautology. We use the phrase *life has a purpose* only when that purpose has a transcendental element, something more important than the here and now. Thus when someone says something like "Sure, my life has a purpose: to make as much money as I can," we recognize that as mocking the word *purpose*. To have a purpose in life is to be compelled to try to live up to that transcendental element. The composition and role of the potential transcendental elements are discussed in Chapter 20. For now, this simple proposition: Purpose in life shapes a life's work, and for the better.

PURPOSE, NOT SAINTLINESS

People who see purpose in their lives are not necessarily indifferent to motives based on money, power, or fame. Some of the giants spent a great deal of effort trying to get higher fees and complained profanely at being underpaid. Some were vain about their celebrity or bitter about their obscurity. Some sought power and relished the exercise of it. But a common theme in the biographies of the giants (and in the analyses of creative people in general) is that their work expresses the purpose they saw in their lives, a purpose that they usually had felt before they had achieved anything.[11]

AUTONOMY

A major stream of human accomplishment is fostered by a culture that encourages the belief that individuals can act efficaciously as individuals, and enables them to do so.

Purpose refers to a person's belief that life has a meaning. *Autonomy* refers to a person's belief that it is in his power to fulfill that meaning through his own acts. *Own acts* is a crucial element, for the creative act is both audacious and individual by nature. This is not equivalent to saying that great accomplishment always occurs among people acting alone. Scientific knowledge is advanced by sharing ideas with colleagues, and there is the occasional example of a great collaboration in the arts. But creativity ultimately comes down to small, solitary acts in which an individual conceives of something new and gives it a try, without knowing for sure how it will turn out. Streams of accomplishment are more common and more extensive in cultures where doing new things and acting autonomously are encouraged than in cultures that disapprove.

Whether people believe they have the power to fulfill their felt destiny depends in part on their psychological makeup. Within any culture, audaciousness is a trait that has a distribution from *none* to *a lot*, and any culture will produce some people who will do things on their own whatever anyone else might say. But cultural norms foster or discourage autonomy among the great middle of the distribution. In a familistic culture where the child's paramount obligation is to his parents and the adult's paramount obligations are to the extended family, the proportion of actively creative people will be smaller than in a culture where the obligations of family are less onerous. In a culture that disapproves of open argument, taking a stand against the consensus not only requires more courage than in a culture that accepts argument, it is also less likely to succeed. In a culture that dreads innovation, originality is suspect.

AUTONOMY, NOT WILLFULNESS

Lest there be any confusion: Autonomy as I am using the word has nothing to do with simple willfulness ("I'll do whatever I want"). A sense of efficacy is crucial to the construct I am trying to convey, which can seldom be sustained by people who are not genuinely efficacious. In its turn, efficacy requires personal qualities—self-discipline, especially—that are inconsistent with willfulness.

There is no vector of good-to-bad on this dimension, merely different ways of structuring a society. The extreme of familism may stifle individual initiative but nurture lives rich in human relationships. The other extreme of autonomy may be liberating but lonely. The point is not which system is better in the abstract, but what is the relationship of familism to autonomy. The proposition is that highly familistic cultures and ones that revere the past will limit both autonomy and creativity and hence will be ones in which streams of accomplishment are constrained.

THE HISTORICAL RECORD: EAST ASIA

Differences in purpose and autonomy help explain some of the differences in patterns of accomplishment between East Asia and Europe. The cultural differences in outlook are unmistakable, and their relationship to behavior is persuasive, though I must make that case by painting in broad strokes indeed. I begin with East Asia.

Purpose

The principal religious sources for both China and Japan were Daoism and Buddhism. They borrowed from each other in both countries and produced a variety of offshoots, with Zen being the best known in the West. Both taught that purposeful action in one's life on this earth is a snare and delusion. Buddhism went the farthest, explicitly urging that the path to wisdom lies in detaching oneself from the world. The life anyone lives right now is merely one out of thousands. The quest for any earthly good is bound to be a cycle of frustration. Life is painful, the origin of pain is desire, the cessation of pain comes with the cessation of desire, and the way to the cessation of pain is through an ascetic life of meditation. Daoism too taught the virtues of serene acceptance, humility, gentleness, and passivity, with *passivity* conceived not as weakness but as the way toward understanding the nature of the universe and the individual's role in it. Sometimes, the relationship between Daoist teachings and accomplishment as I have been talking about it in this book is startlingly explicit. This is from Laozi's *Dao-de Jing*:

> *To seek learning one gains day by day;*
> *To seek the Dao one loses day by day,*
> > *Losing and yet losing some more,*
> > *Till one has reached doing nothing*
> *Do nothing and yet there is nothing that is not done.*
> *To win the world one must attend to nothing.*
> *When one attends to this and that,*
> > *He will not win the world.*[12]

It is safe to say that neither Buddhism nor Daoism was a religion calculated to energize people to fulfill a purpose embodied in this life on this earth. Theology isn't the same as practice, however, and the fact that Buddhism and Daoism were the primary religious doctrines of East Asia doesn't mean that everybody behaved as theology prescribed. Buddhism in particular had little influence in China after about 1000. Even in the times of the greatest national religiosity, the educated classes of China and Japan were not known for religious fanaticism. Thus Buddhist and Daoist teachings, despite their dismissive view of the workaday world, could inspire artistic and poetic masterpieces and did not stop a curious Chinese scholar from making observations about sunspots or calculating the value of π. It is best to think of Buddhism and Daoism not as a day to day actuator of behavior among East Asian scholars and artists, but as a cultural backdrop. Buddhism and Daoism did not prevent the talented from realizing individual excellence. They stood aside, as it were. The *absence* of a tradition that put fulfillment of one's purpose now, in this life, at center stage, lowered the creative energy that the human capital in East Asia was capable of generating.

Autonomy

Familial constraints on personal autonomy have been the norm in human history, and for understandable reasons. The more precarious the existence of a community, the more important it is that a culture socialize children to care for their parents and siblings. But if East Asia did not originate such constraints, Confucianism articulated them at a new level of intellectual sophistication (see page 41), reinforcing a mélange of cultural and historical influences that have given East Asians ways of looking at the relationship of the individual to family and society that differ profoundly from the West's. Psychologist Richard Nisbett's *The Geography of Thought* (2003) has recently brought together the growing literature on how these differences manifest themselves. For our purposes, the chief point is that, throughout the histories of their cultures, properly raised Chinese or Japanese children have made their crucial life decisions with the wishes and welfare of their parents, then of their extended family, and then of their community, in the forefront of their minds. Nothing in either Chinese or Japanese culture encouraged the maturing child to focus on his own ideas and ambitions and seek out ways to fulfill them no matter what.

It is easy for Westerners to confuse deference with being intimidated, perhaps because intimidation often lies behind deferential behavior in the West. The East Asian understanding of deference is importantly different. The roots of the deference lie in an internalized sense of what is seemly and unseemly, virtuous and disgraceful. This internalized sense spills over into behavior that affects accomplishment in the arts and sciences. It makes sense, given a Confucian outlook, that the aesthetic authority of revered early painters and poets could remain nearly intact for centuries. Chinese artists were not necessarily afraid to try new things, but cultural cues made them less motivated to try new things for the sake of originality and more motivated to become a valued part of a high tradition.

In the sciences, the disapproval of open dispute took a toll on the abil-

---

A CAVEAT ABOUT UNCHANGING CHINESE ART

Generalizations about the unchanging nature of Chinese painting and literature irritate specialists, for whom later Chinese artists can be "as innovative as Cézanne or Picasso," as one Chinese art scholar said of Ming landscapist Dong Qichang, urging us "not to take too literally the claims of Chinese artists that they are imitating the past."[13] I would add that the continuity of Chinese language and customs indirectly affects the way we perceive changes in Chinese art and literature. If Shakespeare had been writing in Latin and living in a London still Roman in its manners, political organization, and architecture, it would have been harder for him to do new things with the story of Julius Caesar. Or, imagine that Michelangelo had not approached classic Greek sculpture with the excitement of rediscovering work that had been forgotten for more than a millennium, but instead had been born into a world in which master craftsmen had been turning out fine sculpture in the same style in an unbroken line since Phidias. Michelangelo enjoyed the advantage of a discontinuity in the West's history that was not available to Chinese and Japanese artists.

So let it be clear that I am not claiming that the low value put on personal autonomy in East Asia explains everything directly. On the other hand, Chinese artists did say they were imitating the past, as Western artists seldom felt constrained to do, and many of them really did imitate it. Combining both the direct effects (the need to justify one's work in terms of the past) and the indirect ones (the centuries of continuity engendered by the Chinese system), the role of autonomy clarifies much about the different routes taken in East and West.

ity of East Asian science to build an edifice of cumulative knowledge. As I have noted elsewhere (see pages 38, 235), the history of Chinese science is episodic, with the occasional brilliant scholarly discovery but no follow-up. Progress in science in the West has been fostered by enthusiastic, nonstop, competitive argument in which the goal is to come out on top. East Asia did not have the cultural wherewithal to support enthusiastic, nonstop, competitive arguments. Even in today's Japan, a century and a half after that nation began Westernizing, it is commonly observed that Japan's technological feats far outweigh its slender body of original discoveries. One ready explanation for this discrepancy is the difference between progress that can be made consensually and hierarchically versus progress that requires individuals who insist that they alone are right.

THE HISTORICAL RECORD: ISLAM'S GOLDEN AGE

For a few centuries at the turn of the first millennium, Islam presided over a burst of exuberant scientific and philosophical inquiry. It began with the translation of the treasure of Greek and Roman manuscripts that had lain forgotten for centuries. It then went beyond translation, producing a large body of original work in mathematics, chemistry, astronomy, optics, and philosophy, among other fields. Then this burst of activity died away. Summarizing and simplifying the argument that follows: Islam provided a sense of purpose and vitality that helped power the achievements of its golden age, but Islam could not accommodate itself to the degree of autonomy required to sustain it.

The extraordinarily rapid rise of the Arabic empire provides a number of reasons for the ignition of the burst of activity.[14] First, the empire brought the neglected raw materials of the ancient world under one roof. In the words of historian Thomas Goldstein, "A Muslim could study, from records preserved on his own soil, the astronomies of India, Babylon, and Egypt; Indian and Persian mathematics; the philosophical concepts of the Greeks; the medicine, geography, astronomy, and mathematics of the Hellenistic age; the botanical, pharmacological, zoological, geological, and geographic lore amassed by the ancient world as a whole."[15] The trade routes and commercial centers—the elite cities—of the Arab world made these materials accessible to scholars across the empire and encouraged cross-fertilization of ideas. Second, the Arabs brought the energy of a new and vibrant culture to these raw materials, as one might expect of a people who had conquered a land mass stretching from northeast India to the Atlantic in little more than a hundred years. The galvanizing effects of the new Islamic faith on its followers must be given credit for this energy. *Purpose* Islam had in abundance, centering on service to the Faith. Initially, the Islamic elites engaged the cultures they conquered undefensively, flexibly, and curiously.

Why did the burst of activity fade so rapidly? The specific explanations diverge in their particulars, but they agree on the central point that, as H. Floris Cohen, put it, "the root cause of its decline is to be found in the Faith, and in the ability of its orthodox upholders to stifle once-flowering science."[16] To Islamic scholar G. E. von Grunebaum, Islam was never able to accept that scientific research is a means of glorifying God.

> Those accomplishments of Islamic mathematical and medical science which continue to compel our admiration were developed in areas and in periods where the elites were willing to go beyond and possibly against the basic strains of orthodox thought and feeling. For the sciences never did shed the suspicion of bordering on the impious. . . . This is why the pursuit of the natural sciences as that of philosophy tended to become located in relatively small and esoteric circles and why but few of their representatives would escape an occasional uneasiness which not infrequently did result in some kind of apology for their work.[17]

When the religious leadership began to oppose scientific inquiry, Grunebaum continues, the internalized misgivings of the scientific elites led them to acquiesce.

For Turkish historian of science Aydin Sayili, Islam was unable to achieve the reconciliation with the Greek philosophical heritage that Christianity achieved.[18] Islam looked upon that heritage with suspicion from the beginning. When the Islamic religious reaction set in, it was directed primarily against Greek philosophy, not science, but the linkage was strong, and science was dragged down as well. For Arabist J. J. Saunders, the decisive blows came during the waves of barbarian invasion and economic decline starting in 11C, when the free, tolerant, and inquiring society of Omayyad, Abbasid, and Fatimid days gave place under the pressure of invasions to "a narrow, rigid, and 'closed' society in which the progress of secular knowledge was slowly stifled."[19] What all three scholars agree upon is that the tenets of Islam itself did not change. During the golden age, the orthodox did not aggressively enforce those aspects of the Faith that discouraged free-flowing inquiry and debate; once they began to do so, Islamic contributions to the sciences effectively ended.

Put in terms of autonomy, Islam bore similarities to medieval Christianity, seeing life on this earth as important primarily as a preparation for eternal life, and harboring deep suspicions about the piety of inquiring too closely into the nature of God's creation. But Islam, more than Christianity at any point in its history, also saw God as sustaining the universe on a continuing basis, and as a deity who is not bound by immutable laws. To proclaim scientific truths that applied throughout the universe and throughout time could easily become blasphemy, implying limits to what God could and could not do.[20] Islamic piety consisted in obedience to God's rules and submission to his will, not presuming to analyze his works or glorify him with flights of one's personal fancies and curiosities. Indeed, expressing one's fancies through representational art or most fictional literature ran directly against Islamic teaching. Islam was (and is) not a religion that encourages autonomy. Seen in the framework I have been using, it is no surprise that the burst of accomplishment in the golden age was aberrational, not characteristic, of Islamic culture.

Arabic culture in general was also highly familistic and hierarchical, like Chinese, Japanese, and Indian cultures, and this too worked against sustained accomplishment. But the same may be said of less advanced cultures throughout the rest of Asia and elsewhere. Highly familistic, consensual cultures have been the norm throughout history and the world. Modern Europe has been the oddball.

THE HISTORICAL RECORD: EUROPE

Purpose and *autonomy* are intertwined with the defining cultural characteristic of European civilization, *individualism*. Without getting pulled into historical and philosophical points of contention about the origins and nature of individualism, the following are some of the basics as they impinge on purpose and autonomy:[21]

The Athenian Formulation

The Aristotelian principle says that human beings delight in the exercise of their realized capacities. Implied in that statement is an understanding of what it means to be human that was the basis for Greek accomplishment—mainly Athenian accomplishment—and laid the foundation for subsequent Western thought. Classicist Bruce Thornton nicely sums up the Greek view of the human being as "the unique, free person whose rational powers of observation and critical inquiry, whose self-consciousness and perception define him as a human being and give his life value."[22] In the Greek view, acting as a rational individual *is* the essence of living a human life.

Ancient Greece was not an individualistic culture in the same way that the West would later become, however. Acting rationally was not considered to be the same as being self-sufficient. For Plato and Aristotle, self-sufficiency was still a characteristic of the *polis*, not the individual (part of the reason Athens could rationalize killing Socrates), and the Hellenistic schools that subsequently recognized the self-sufficiency of the individual (e.g., the Stoics) required that the self-sufficient individual remain detached from the things of this world. In this detachment, Stoic moral individualism echoed Hinduism and Buddhism, which allowed for liberation from this world only for individuals who renounced the things of this world.[23]

The Christian Transmutation

This brings us to role of Christianity in modern Europe. Mine is far from an original conclusion, but in recent decades it has not been fashionable, so I should state the argument explicitly: The Greeks laid the foundation, but it was the transmutation of that foundation by Christianity that gave modern Europe its impetus and differentiated European accomplishment from that of all other cultures around the world.[24]

Christianity did not bestow that impetus immediately. It took more than a thousand years. Through its early centuries, Christianity as practiced was not individualistic. On the contrary, early Christianity was absorbed in the collective Christian community to which individuals routinely subordinated their own interests. It was Christian theology itself that was potentially revolutionary, teaching that all human beings are invited into a personal relationship with God, and that all individuals are equal in God's sight regardless of their earthly station. Furthermore, eternal salvation is not reserved for those who renounce the world but is available to all who believe and act accordingly. It was a theology that empowered the individual acting as an individual as no other philosophy or religion had ever done before.[25]

The potentially revolutionary message was realized more completely in one part of Christendom, the Catholic West, than in the Orthodox East. The crucial difference was that Roman Catholicism developed a philosophical and artistic humanism typified, and to a great degree engendered, by

Thomas Aquinas (1226–1274). Aquinas made the case, eventually adopted by the Church, that human intelligence is a gift from God, and that to apply human intelligence to understanding the world is not an affront to God but is pleasing to him. Aquinas taught that human autonomy is also a gift from God, and that the only way in which humans can realize the relationship with God that God intends is by exercising that autonomy. Aquinas taught that faith and reason are not in opposition, but complementary.

In sum, Aquinas grafted a humanistic strain onto Christianity that joined an inspirational message of God's love and his promise of immortality with an injunction to serve God by using all of one's human capacities of intellect and will—and to have a good time doing it. In Fernand Braudel's words, "The Renaissance distanced itself from medieval Christianity much less in the realm of ideas than in that of life itself. It could perhaps be called a cultural, not a philosophical betrayal. Its atmosphere was one of lively enjoyment, relishing the many pleasures of the eye, the mind and the body, as if the West were emerging from a centuries-long period of Lent." [26]

This power of religious belief and a rediscovered humanism was a potent combination. Eastern Orthodoxy never experienced a comparable evolution. On the contrary, Orthodoxy resembles Islam in its stance toward autonomy, making obedience the primary criterion for judging man's relationship with God. It seems more than coincidence that Orthodox Russia never developed individualism of the kind known in Western Europe. [27]

Western individualism had another step to take, initiated when Martin Luther nailed his Ninety-five Theses to the door of the Schlosskirche in Wittenberg in 1517. The exact importance of that additional step is a subject of continuing dispute. A unique role for Protestantism has been most famously advocated by Max Weber in "The Protestant Ethic and the Spirit of Capitalism." [28] Weber proposed that specific features of Protestantism encouraged thrift, industriousness, and the accumulation of wealth, and underwrote the promethean growth of the European economy in 17C and thereafter. That degree of specificity pushes the limits, and Weber's thesis has attracted criticism. [29] But putting economic growth aside, is there reason to think that Protestantism added anything to Catholicism in promoting accomplishment in the arts and sciences?

Historian Robert Merton, in his study of the growth of science in 17C England, says yes, arguing for a direct link between Protestant characteristics of methodical, persistent action, empirical utilitarianism, and anti-traditionalism and the development of the scientific method in England. [30] An indirect link is also possible. As a matter of theology, Aquinas's Catholicism is more enthusiastic about the human exercise of autonomy and intellect than Lutheranism or Calvinism. As a matter of psychology, however, Protestantism pervasively affected the day-to-day practice of Christianity in ways that

JEWS AS A COMPARISON GROUP

The role that some historians have assigned to Christianity and that I have just endorsed raises the issue of Judaism. Judaism was not only the first great monotheistic religion. It also taught, long before Christianity came along, that individuals have a personal relationship with God, and the Judaic Bible represents one of the earliest characterizations of the individual as a moral agent. If individualism is so central to human accomplishment, why single out Christian individualism instead of grouping it with Judaic individualism?

Perhaps they should not be differentiated. The differing paths of Christian and Judaic achievements can easily be explained by specific historic circumstances, starting with the Diaspora. One may go back to the account of Jewish accomplishment in Chapter 12 and review the evidence that Jews have produced great accomplishment wherever they've been given a chance. But it has also been noted that Jews have made their greatest contributions to the arts and sciences when they were not isolated but in direct contact with another culture—first in the Middle East and Spain during the golden age of the Arab empire, and then in Christian Europe after emancipation.[31] One way of looking at this phenomenon is that traditional Jewish culture is not all that different from Confucianism or Islamic culture in the way that it embeds individual moral agency in family and community. Orthodox Jewish culture is effective in fostering human capital directly through its emphasis on education and indirectly through its effects on mating patterns, but duty takes precedence over vocation, and the interests of the family and community takes precedence over self-fulfillment. The implication is that the culture fostered by Christianity was as instrumental in unleashing accomplishment among Jews as among Christians— once that same Christian culture got around to relieving the suppression it had imposed on Jews in the first place.

cut its adherents loose from a powerful institution and its attendant rituals. While good Catholics confessed to the priest, did penance under the priest's instruction, and turned to the Church to tell them what the Bible meant, good Protestants read the Bible for themselves, confessed directly to God, received absolution directly from God, and didn't do penance at all. In this practical sense, Protestants were more on their own than Catholics were, and it is plausible to see this as an extension of individualism and of a sense of autonomy.

As history moved forward from 17C, the continuing effects of Protestantism divided into two currents, one involving true believers and the other spawning more and more nonbelievers. For true believers—and in this secular age it is important to remember that *true believers* encompassed most of the greatest writers and scientists of the Protestant countries until well into the Enlightenment—the act of Protestant prayer had effects, incalculable but surely significant, upon that stubborn confidence in one's own beliefs that is so valuable in creativity. Protestantism made prayer directly to God the focal point of communication with God.[32] Prayer usually produced a sense of the right thing to do, after which the believer was no longer doing something that he *hoped* was right, but something that he *knew* was right, backed by the ultimate Authority. There is nothing abstract about this source of individualism or its effects on human behavior. It is reflected in obdurate Protestant resistance to secular authority during 16C and 17C. It was a mindset that led some to the stake but, perhaps more indicative of its ramifications for science and the arts, led Quakers to refuse to doff their hats to their social superiors. Protestantism produced mavericks.

Protestantism also contributed to the secularization of Europe. It was a classic case of unintended consequences. Martin Luther and the other dissidents "were working for the desecularization of the Church, and the restoration of Christianity to its primitive purity," writes Christopher Dawson. "They did not realize that the attempt to purify and separate religion from its cultural accretions might find its counterpart in the separation of culture from religion."[33] But that's what happened. As court life became ever more dominant on the Continent, the hold of religion over intellectual elites slipped away, to be replaced in 18C with the Enlightenment, which for a time served as a kind of secular religion.

SUMMING UP

I cannot supply quantitative measures of purpose and autonomy, but at least I can visually specify the points made in the foregoing presentation. The figure below locates the times and places I have discussed on the dimensions of purpose and autonomy.

Where Places and Times Fit on Purpose and Autonomy

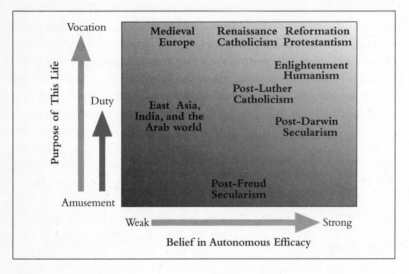

To keep this visual aid in two dimensions, I have collapsed different strands of the argument. The horizontal dimension labeled *belief in autonomous efficacy* combines two thoughts: The sense that one is *free* to act as an individual, and the sense that individual action can be *efficacious*. I treat this combined concept as a simple continuum from *weak* to *strong*.

The vertical dimension labeled *purpose of this life* also combines two thoughts: The sense that life in general has a purpose, as opposed to being pointless, and the sense that *this* life is uniquely important, and is not just one of an ongoing sequence of lives. You may also conceive of this as a continuum directly from a *weak* to a *strong* sense of purpose. I inserted *duty* in the middle, to indicate another way of thinking about this dimension. It is possible to take life very seriously indeed and to believe one has a purpose in life, but still without believing that one has a personal destiny that must be fulfilled come what may. *Duty* indicates that way of thinking about life. Duty is in the middle not because it is between *amusement* and *vocation* in seriousness, but because it is in the middle in its effects on accomplishment. Creative elites in a culture with a strong sense of duty are more likely to work hard, and be better able to carry on an existing stream of accomplishment, than in a culture where the creative elites see life as a matter of amusement. But for the ignition of creativity, an additional sense of *vocation* is required. That is the nature of my argument, reflected in the graphic.

Renaissance Italy and Protestant Europe are both at the far right-hand corner of the graphic. Both were cultures in which the creative elites saw themselves as having vocations and held strong beliefs in autonomous efficacy (Renaissance Catholicism is to the left of Reformation Protestantism on *autonomous efficacy* mostly because they can't both go in the same spot[34]). It goes without saying that both were also centers of accomplishment. I place the Enlightenment just below Protestantism on *Purpose*—the Enlightenment's passionate commitment to reason was close to religious.

My argument also holds that Europe after Darwin remained a dutiful culture, filled with virtuous and hard-working creative elites, but that their sense of vocation had diminished. I use Darwin partly as a cause of secularization, and partly as a label for a secularization that had been occurring since the beginning of the Enlightenment.

Finally, the graphic indicates my view of the post-Freud West as a place where purpose and autonomous efficacy among the creative elites have eroded. I am not arguing that the general populations of Europe and America necessarily changed in their morality, industriousness, or any other quality from late 19C through 20C. Rather, I propose that the creative elites changed. After Freud, Nietzsche, and others with similar messages, the belief in man as rational and volitional took a body blow. It became fashionable in the Europe of early 20C to see humans as unwittingly acting out neuroses and subconscious drives. God was mostly dead among the European creative elites; morality became relative. These and allied beliefs substantially undermined the belief of creative elites that their lives had purpose or that their talents could be efficacious.

At the opening of 21C, religion is an especially fraught topic in American life, with predominantly religious middle and working classes alongside creative elites that are not only overwhelmingly secular but often aggressively so. Introducing Christianity as an important causal variable into an account of human accomplishment will engender more misunderstandings than I can possibly forestall, but let me try anyway.

With regard to purpose, my position does not require that the secular life be a life without purpose.[35] Rather, I argue that it is *harder* to find that purpose if one is an atheist or agnostic than if one is a believer. It is harder still to maintain attention to that purpose over years of effort. Devotion to a human cause, whether social justice, the environment, the search for truth, or an abstract humanism, is by its nature less compelling than devotion to God. Here, Christianity has its most potent advantage. The incentives of forgiveness of sin and eternal life are just about as powerful as incentives get. The nonbeliever has to make do with comparatively tepid alternatives.

With regard to autonomy, I do not see Christianity as its only source. It is easily possible to believe in one's efficacy as an autonomous actor by holding to the secular Greek ideal of the human as "the unique, free person whose rational powers of observation and critical inquiry, whose self-consciousness and perception define him as a human being and give his life value," as Thornton put it. Possible—but, as in the case of purpose, *harder* if one is not a believing Christian. For evidence, look around at today's intellectual climate in both Europe and the United States. "Unique," "free," "rational," "powers of observation," "critical inquiry"—every one of those words and phrases is problematic in today's postmodernist intellectual milieu. It is much easier to use them with confidence if one is a Christian, or still clings to the Christian/humanistic synthesis of early modernity.

Finally, my position is not at odds with the obvious fact that great human accomplishment has been produced outside Christian cultures and, for that matter, in cultures where the creative elites are secular. I am treating Christian religious belief as one of the variables that help to explain how human accomplishment in the arts and sciences has been ignited. I am arguing that Christianity is an important variable, one of the most important in the story of modern accomplishment. I am not arguing that it explains everything—just as, for that matter, purpose and autonomy do not explain everything. But they do explain a lot.

TWENTY

SOURCES OF CONTENT: THE ORGANIZING STRUCTURE AND TRANSCENDENTAL GOODS

Suppose now that everything else is in place. We have a culture with wealth, elite cities, models, and freedom of action. People with the potential for excellence have a sense of purpose and autonomy. But take a musical prodigy, put him in different cultures that each enjoy those assets, and his pursuit of musical excellence can lead him to compose a motet, an atonal academic work, or heavy metal rock. The brilliant writer might produce an epic poem, a social novel, or a fictionalized account of his psychotherapy. The potential scientist might try to understand the world through experimentation, observation, or pure logic. What are the variables that help explain what kind of work is produced in a given era and place? The two variables I use are labeled *organizing structure* and *transcendental goods*.

THE ORGANIZING STRUCTURE

The magnitude and content of a stream of accomplishment in a given domain varies according to the richness and age of the organizing structure.

By *organizing structure*, I mean the framework for the conduct of science or the arts and the criteria according to which a society evaluates achievement.

In the sciences, the structure from the Renaissance onward has been an evolving scientific method. In the arts, structure not only takes different forms in the visual arts, literature, and music, but has also taken different forms across time and cultures. The rules of *haiku* are a structure, as are the rules of the sonnet. Pointillism is a structure. Structures can be nested: the movement in a symphony has a structure, the symphony of which it is part also has a structure, and the tonal harmony that the symphony employs has yet another structure.

One key characteristic of structure is its *richness*. To illustrate, recall the comparison that John Rawls drew between checkers and chess when he was describing the Aristotelian principle (see page 386). Both games are played on a board with 64 squares, but they have different structures. Checkers has one kind of piece, while chess has six different kinds of pieces. The movement of any checker piece is restricted to a single square per turn unless it is capturing, while movement in chess is different for each piece. In checkers, the goal is to capture all the opponents' pieces. In chess, the goal is to trap one particular piece. The structure of chess is objectively richer than the structure of checkers. It is no coincidence that chess has thousands of books written about tactics and strategy for every aspect of the game while checkers has a fraction of that number. The nature of accomplishment in checkers and chess is also objectively different, as reflected in their relative places in Western culture.[1]

I measure the richness of a structure by three aspects: *principles*, *craft*, and *tools*. The scientific method offers convenient examples. Conceptually, a scientific experiment proceeds according to principles such as replicability, falsifiability, and the role of the hypothesis that apply across different scientific disciplines. The actual conduct of a classic scientific experiment involves craft—the generation of a hypothesis to be tested or a topic to be explored, the creation of the methods for doing so, and meticulous observance of protocols and procedures during the actual work. The details of craft differ not only across disciplines but within disciplines. They also have a family resemblance, in the sense that a meticulous scientist behaves in ways that are recognizable to scientists in every field—"meticulous" being one of the defining characteristics of craft practiced at a high level.

Tools play a double role. Sometimes they are created in direct response to needs generated by principles and craft—accurate thermometers are an example—but at least as often, a tool turns out to have unanticipated uses that alter both principles and craft, independently expanding the realm of things a discipline can achieve. An example is the invention of the diffraction grating to study spectra of light, which 40 years later turned out to enable astronomers to study the composition of the stars.

Structure in the arts also can be characterized according to principles, craft, and tools. In the visual arts, the theory of linear perspective involves a set of principles, the techniques of painting are the craft, and oil paint is a tool. Similar distinctions apply to the principles of character development in a novel, the craft of writing, and the tool of the quill pen; or to the principles of sonata form, the craft of musical composition, and the tool of the pianoforte.

A structure that produces great accomplishment must foster two qualities in tension with each other: freedom and order. The scientific method is again the exemplar, holding the scientist to rigorous standards while at the same time giving him a framework within which he can attack any question he can think of.[2] In the arts, reconciling freedom and order is inherently problematic, "a remarkable *coincidentia oppositorum*," in the words of Paul Lang, "a self-discipline, a conquest of autonomy such as only the truly great can achieve."[3] The larger and more flexible the structure, the more room for freedom and order to coexist. (The novel offers more room for innovation than *haiku*.)

The other dimension by which I characterize structures is *age*. No structure is so large and flexible that it can offer room for innovation indefinitely, a problem that has plagued the arts more than science. The longer a structure has existed, the more it has been filled up with the best work that can be done within its confines, and the greater the incentives for artists to seek new structures.[4]

Matching the richness and age of organizing structures with changes in accomplishment has potential that I cannot realize in this presentation. At the extremes, it should be easy to reach consensus. Few would deny that drama is a richer structure for literary expression than the sonnet, though exquisite work can be produced in both. But in painting, how does one compare as structures the Renaissance's "window on the world" with the "patches of color on a canvas" that Manet and his colleagues introduced in mid 19C? In music, how does one compare the richness of the operatic form with that of the string quartet? Comparisons on specific dimensions are presumably possible, but such tasks are for experts.[5] I can, however, demonstrate a simpler relationship between structure and bursts of accomplishment, using the bursts in the graphs in Chapter 14. In each case, the explosion was preceded by and associated with events that enriched an organizing structure. I restrict myself to the Western inventories.

Changes in Structure and Bursts of Accomplishment in the Arts

The Visual Arts, 1420 (see page 317). The increase in accomplishment after 1420 is explained mainly by the appearance of painters, and is the archetypal case of response to a newly enriched structure. Two major changes occurred at about the same time, and the explosion followed right on schedule. The first was the introduction of a new principle on a grand scale: the meta-invention of linear perspective (see page 212). Brunelleschi had unveiled his mastery of linear perspective about a decade before the trendline shifts upward. Masaccio's *Trinity* at the church of Santa Maria Novella was painted in the mid-1420s, and Alberti published *Della Pittura* in 1436. The less obvious event was the invention that suddenly expanded the effects a painter could achieve: the use of oil in paints, developed by Jan van Eyck in the 1420s.

Literature, 1460 and 1700 (see page 318). The initial upward turn in the trendline in 1460 started from a low base, but it was certainly the beginning of a burst. The credit for the timing goes to the invention of a tool that transformed the relationship of writer to audience, the printing press. The Gutenberg Bible was printed in 1454. But another underlying change in structure had occurred as well: good literature was being written not just in Latin, but in the vernacular. Dante had been the standard-bearer for the idea with *De Vulgari Eloquentia* as far back as 1306, at about the same time that works in vernacular French began to appear. Dante had then shown what could be done with the vernacular when he wrote the *Commedia* in Tuscan a decade later. Boccaccio and Chaucer were the most famous of those who began writing in the vernacular, but the reach of their work was limited by the laborious process of manual copying. The printing press gave the author rapid access to a large audience.

The upward turn in literature in 1700 begins the run-up to the first full-fledged modern novels, *Pamela* and *Tom Jones*, in the 1740s (see page 221). It was not marked by any landmark change—precursors to the novel had been appearing sporadically since 1500—but by the spread of the idea that fiction as well as drama could expound upon social and political themes. Daniel Defoe, William Congreve, Jonathan Swift, Jean-Jacques Rousseau, and Alain Lesage were the early exemplars of 18C. Once the idea took hold, it provided such a wealth of possibilities that the production of significant figures continued to outstrip increases in population until the middle of 19C.

Music, 1470 (see page 319). The meta-invention of polyphony is an example of a new principle that evolved gradually into an ever more complex structure, and the nature of the burst in music is accordingly ambiguous. The timeline on page 319 actually shows an upward trend beginning in 1400, and would have shown increases further back if the graph had started earlier, all reflecting the elaboration of the new forms that polyphony had made possible. But a conspicuously steeper increase began in the last half of 15C that may be ascribed in part to the invention of tools. In the middle of the 1400s, the main instruments a composer had to work with were the organ and the human voice. Stringed instruments were still limited in their range and power. The trumpet was a long, clumsy instrument with a narrow range and indifferent sound quality. The clavichord and harpsichord were still in primitive forms. The last half of the 1400s saw major improvements in the organ and the harpsichord. The viol, a bowed stringed instrument, appeared in the second half of 15C, and we know from paintings that a three-string violin was in use by the end of the century. New methods of metalworking transformed the trumpet. In addition, the printing press was as important for disseminating written music as it was for disseminating prose and poetry. By 1476 a complete liturgical folio had been printed using a double printing process in which first the lines were printed in red and then the notes in black. The expansion of tools in 15C continued into 16C, along with the continued development of tonal harmony and new ideas for expressing text musically and combining instruments into ensembles.

Changes in Structure and Bursts of Accomplishment in the Scientific Inventories

The hard sciences (astronomy, biology, chemistry, earth sciences, and physics) (see page 312). The unrivaled example of a new organizing structure is the development of the scientific method itself, with the major developments occurring in the 1600s. The uptick that begins the major burst in the hard sciences as a whole begins shortly thereafter, in 1720. But different pieces of the scientific method emerged at different times for different sciences, and the bursts of activity in the sciences, not shown separately in the graphs in Chapter 14, vary as well. Often, the triggering event was the invention of new tools or a major augmentation in the theory available to that discipline, usually with a lag time of a few decades.

Astronomy began a major burst in the last half of 16C, following on the heels of the publication of Copernicus's *De Revolutionibus* (new principle) and augmented by the invention of the telescope (new tool) in early 17C. Biology's initial burst began in the second third of the 1500s, employing a tool that Leonardo had developed a few decades earlier: the precise drawing of three-dimensional objects applied to natural objects such as plants, animals, and the dissected human body. Chemistry took off in early 18C, a few decades after Robert Boyle's *Skeptical Chymist* had laid out principles of modern chemistry, defining elements and chemical analysis, distinguishing chemistry from medicine and alchemy, and urging the experimental method upon his colleagues. The earth sciences began their upward movement at about the same time, the antecedent events being the discovery that strata could be used to analyze geologic history (a combination of principle and tool) and the invention of the geologic map (tool) for analyzing the evolution of landforms. Physics offers a fascinating case of a rich set of principles, bequeathed by Newton, that had to wait upon the invention of tools. Between the *Principia* and the beginning of the burst in physics around 1800 came the invention of an accurate thermometer, devices for producing an electrical charge, devices for storing an electrical charge, the aneroid barometer, an accurate chronometer, the achromatic lens, methods of measuring electrical conduction, a method of measuring gravitational force at a given latitude, the electroscope, artificial magnets, the electrometer, the torsion balance, the accelerometer, the pressure gauge, and methods to measure the rate of flow of a fluid—not glamorous advances, but indispensable for giving physicists of 19C the tools without which the scientific method itself was limited.

Mathematics, 1560 (see page 313). Mathematicians already had the principles of the organizing structure in the form of the mathematical proof and a meta-tool in the form of the 10 Arabic (that is, Indian) numerals. The burst in the last half of 16C followed the development in the preceding half century of basic tools: the invention of $+, -, =, \times, \sqrt{}$, the use of letters to stand for unknowns, and the rest of a set of mathematical notation. They seem prosaic now, but try doing advanced mathematics without them. As the burst gathered energy, more tools were introduced: the first tables of trigonometric functions, the introduction of mathematical induction, and decimal fractions.

Technology, 1770 (see page 315). The stuff of technology *is* tools, to a large degree, and it is appropriate that the burst in technology began in the decade after James Watt's improvements made the steam engine into the great tool of the industrial revolution. But the steam engine was more than a tool. It also precipitated so deep a change in the organizing structure of technology that it was tantamount to a change in principles. Prior to the invention of an efficient, multi-purpose steam engine, technology could augment human and animal muscle power, but could *replace* muscle power only by using wind and water, each of which was limited to a few applications. With the steam engine, most of those limitations disappeared and the actual level of power produced by the steam engine was orders of magnitude greater than anything muscles could do. The possibilities for applying technology expanded by orders of magnitude as well.

Medicine, 1520 (see page 314). Medicine moved up in incremental fashion after an early burst that began in the 1500s when medical study was given a structure that could be filled in with truths. Until then, humans had been observing diseases and trying remedies for thousands of years, with some ad hoc successes, but medicine was riddled with fundamentally incorrect notions about the nature of disease. When structures were proposed, such as Galen's, they were so misleading that they inhibited rather than facilitated subsequent progress. The signal accomplishment of the first half of the 1500s was a (largely) correct framework for thinking about disease based on the principles that the body is a chemical system and diseases are specific ailments caused by specific agents, not an imbalance of the humors. It took centuries for the framework to be filled in with actual cures for diseases, but, with reasonably accurate principles established, accumulation of knowledge that could lead to cures and to prevention was under way.

• • •

In summary: To explain the onset of a prolonged increase in the rate of accomplishment, a first place to look is changes in the organizing structure. In virtually every instance, it is possible to identify substantial ways in which the principles, craft, or tools associated with a given field had changed, or were in the process of changing, when the burst began.

TRANSCENDENTAL GOODS

A major stream of accomplishment in any domain requires a well-articulated vision of, and use of, the transcendental goods relevant to that domain.

"Platonic ideal" is a figure of speech still in use 2,300 years after Plato died because the concept itself resonates so powerfully. We need not accept Plato's entire epistemological argument to think that the world is filled with objects imperfectly embodying ideal qualities. We know they imperfectly embody those qualities because we can envision perfection even if we never encounter it. They are transcendental in that they refer to perfect qualities that lie beyond direct, complete experience, even though they have referents in everyday experience.

In the classic Western tradition, the worth of something that exists in our world can be characterized by the three dimensions known as the true, the beautiful, and the good. The triad did not become iconic in other intellectual traditions as it did in the West, but the same three qualities have been recognized and treated as central in all of the great civilizations represented in the inventories. I hereafter refer to the true, the beautiful, and the good as transcendental goods.

THE TRANSCENDENTALS

In metaphysics, the term *transcendentals* is rigorously defined in a way that should not be confused with my more informal use of *transcendental goods*. The tradition began with Aristotle's discussion of the nature of existence—the nature of being—and the group of properties that belong to being *qua* being. In Thomas Aquinas's elaboration, those properties are one, true, good, and beautiful.[6]

The true and the beautiful are familiar phrases, even if we argue over what they mean. *The good* is not a term in common use these days, and I should spell out how I am using it. The ultimate Good, capitalized when used in that sense, is a way of thinking about and naming God. But I will be focusing on the good without the capitalization, explained by Aristotle in the opening sentence of the *Nicomachean Ethics*: "Every art and every inquiry, and similarly every action and pursuit, is thought to aim at some good; and for this reason the good has rightly been declared to be that at which all things aim."[7] Aristotle was evoking the concept, common to Plato and other Greek thinkers, that every object and creature has an end and an excellence. The end of the eye is sight, and excellence in the eye consists of clear vision. The end of the pruning hook is cutting the branches of a vine, and excellence in a pruning hook consists in being better able to cut off branches than other tools not designed for that purpose.[8] For human beings, the focus of my use of *the good*, the question then becomes, what is the end of human beings and in what lies excellence in achieving that end? The discussion of the Aristotelian principle in Chapter 18 has already given you a hint of Aristotle's answer, but a specific answer is not important for understanding my use of *the good*. If a culture has a coherent, well-articulated sense of what constitutes excellence in human-ness—what constitutes the ideal of human flourishing —it has a conception of the good as I am using the term.

The good in this sense is distinct from moral codes, but to hold a conception of the good is also to worry about right and wrong. In the preceding chapter, I noted that the word *purpose* rules out certain understandings of the meaning of the phrase *the purpose of life* (see page 394). Similarly, the word *good* rules out certain understandings of excellence in human flourishing. To say, for example, that the end of human beings is to enslave other human beings and excellence consists of enslaving them most ruthlessly makes a mockery of language. But though a conception of the good gives rise to moral codes, it should be remembered that the essence of *the good* is not rules that one struggles to follow, but a vision of the best that humans can be that attracts and draws one onward.

The inherent attractiveness of the good creates a second constraint on understandings of it: whatever is the good for humans must be grounded in an understanding of what is unique about humans. For example, to say that excellence in human flourishing consists exclusively of having enough to eat is to say that humans have no unique excellence. A culture that holds such a view does not have a sense of the good.

My proposition is that great accomplishment in the arts and sciences is anchored in one or more of these three transcendental goods. Art and science can rise to the highest rungs of craft without them, wonderful entertainments can be produced without them, amazing intellectual gymnastics can be performed without them. But, in the same way that a goldsmith needs gold, a culture that fosters great accomplishment needs a coherent sense of the transcendental goods. *Coherent sense* means that the goods are a live presence in the culture, and that great artists and thinkers compete to come closer to the ideal that captivates them. A conception of the beautiful was a live presence among artists of the Italian Renaissance and among composers of the Baroque. A conception of the truth remains a live presence in the scientific world of today's West. To the extent that you can think of an era and culture for which such statements are not true, I hypothesize that accomplishment in that era will have suffered thereby.

In discussing these issues during the preparation of *Human Accomplishment*, I have become aware that introducing words such as *true*, *beautiful*, and *good* into a discussion of historical issues is as problematic as introducing religion. Three misconceptions seem difficult to avoid, so let me begin by stating them explicitly. I will allude to them subsequently as well.

I am not using the good, true, and beautiful in a poetic sense. Their role is not just "inspiration" in the abstract, though it can be that as well. Conceptions of the good, true, and beautiful prevailing at any given time concretely affect how excellence manifests itself.

I am not using the good, the true, and the beautiful in a saccharine sense. Great paintings can portray brutality and ugliness. Great literature can depict human depravity. Truths need not be uplifting.

The effects of a culture's prevailing conceptions of transcendental goods are not limited to believers. When I said a moment ago that a conception of the beautiful was a live presence among artists in the Italian Renaissance, I didn't mean that every single artist spent his days thinking about what the beautiful meant, nor that all artists consciously held such a view. Rather, a culture's prevailing view provides a resource that suffuses the practice of that domain independently of the variation in beliefs among specific people.

The Role of Transcendental Goods in the Sciences

The good. The profession of scientist is an embodiment of what Aristotle had in mind as the excellence of human beings, the exercise of human capacity for rational thought. Other aspects of excellence which involve the capacity of humans to discern right behavior have less direct relationship to the conduct of science. The whole point of science is not to determine what *should* be, but what *is*. From a cold-blooded perspective, worries about the moral dimension of the good only get in the way—vivisection may be a terrible thing to do to animals, for example, but banning vivisection makes certain kinds of scientific knowledge more difficult to acquire. The contemporary debate about cloning and other forms of genetic research is another case in point. Should cloning be banned? Should stem cell research be permitted? The debate is being conducted in terms of ethics. But no matter who is right, restrictions will slow scientific accomplishment in that domain. This does not mean that ethics should not be brought to bear on science, but that these considerations come from outside the domain.

The beautiful. Beauty can be an integral part of the satisfaction that scientists take in their discoveries. Mathematicians are often attracted to mathematics because of qualities they consciously see as beautiful. Scientists in every field have been known to fall in love with their work because of aspects of order and harmony that fall within the realm of the beautiful. Physicists have been known to doubt their results because they were not elegant. But beauty is not intrinsic to the enterprise itself. The work and words of theoretical physicist Ludwig Boltzmann encapsulate the role of the beautiful in the sciences. At his inaugural lecture upon assuming a chair at the University of Leipzig, he reflected upon the sense of the beautiful as it must have arisen through human evolution, arguing that it was advantageous for survival "to construct in our minds the most accurate pictures possible of our surroundings and strictly to keep apart the true ones, those which correspond with experience, from the false, which do not. We can therefore explain the genesis of an apprehension of the beautiful as well as of the true in our mechanics."[9] The beautiful *is* the true, in a way, as the poet Keats observed. Boltzmann also created scientific beauty. His most famous achievement, inscribed on his gravestone, is among the most elegantly simple of any of the physical laws: $S = k \log W$.[10] And yet it was also Boltzmann, aesthetically so sensitive to the beautiful and elegant in science, who was the actual author of the famous *bon mot* often attributed to Einstein, "Elegance is for tailors."[11] When push comes to shove in the sciences, the ugly but correct equation wins and the beautiful but wrong one loses.

The true. Ultimately, the transcendental good that matters in the conduct of science is truth, and truth alone. Scientists can win acclaim for an insight that has not yet been verified but the acclaim is ruthlessly provisional. If the ingenious idea doesn't pan out (remember cold fusion?), its authors disappear from history. The discovery of truth is the coin of scientific eminence.

In trying to predict where streams of scientific accomplishment will be found, I am in part stating a tautology: In cultures where no group of people see themselves as engaged in understanding the truth in how the world works, we will find no stream of scientific accomplishment. The relationship of the true as a transcendental good to scientific accomplishment becomes less tautological when a continuum is invoked: The intensity of scientific activity is positively related to the clarity of a culture's articulation of the nature of scientific truth and to the strength of a culture's commitment to the search for truth.

The Role of Transcendental Goods in the Arts

In the arts, all three of the transcendental goods have played different roles at different times, interacting in ways that make it difficult to say which is which.

The beautiful. It goes without saying that beauty has often been the explicit measure of excellence in art. Artists in some eras have denied that any other consideration is even relevant. In Chapter 5, I backed away from using beauty as the standard of excellence in the arts, substituting *high aesthetic quality* instead, because criteria that do not fit the everyday meaning of beauty may be used to judge a work of art. Now, however, we are talking about those conditions that cause fine works of art to be created, not the standards for judging them. I propose that one of those conditions is artists' embrace of a transcendental standard of the beautiful as a good-in-itself.

Exactly what that conception of the beautiful might be is less important than that a coherent conception exists. By way of illustration, suppose you were able to talk to painters from the Tang dynasty, the Italian Renaissance, and France in the 1860s, three different eras and cultures with different conceptions of the beautiful. What links them is that they each *had* a well-articulated conception of the beautiful that the artists of the age saw themselves as trying to realize in their work independent of other considerations. Contrast that with a conversation you would have had with painters in two other eras, medieval Europe and Europe between the World Wars. Two more radically different sets of painters are hard to imagine, but they would have this in common: they would both resist the idea of a well-articulated conception of the beautiful as an *independent* goal in their work. The medieval painters would not have been hostile to the concept of beauty, because they would see beauty as pleasing to God. But, for most, pleasing God and glorifying God would have been the point, not the creation of beauty in itself. Most 20C inter-war artists would have turned the conversation to the nature of the creative act, the imperative of self-expression, and the ways in which the concept of the beautiful had become an impediment to the progress of art, not a framework for it.[12] That a work might turn out to be beautiful by classical definitions would be coincidental.

The true. Truth has also played an explicit role in the arts, with as many different roles for the true as there have been conceptions of the beautiful. In the visual arts, the centuries-long quest to perfect techniques for depicting people and objects was linked to the service of truth; so was the quest to capture the inner truth of a face or event, a quest that led some artists in 19C to abandon literally accurate depictions. Shakespeare attained his unique stature because of his unmatched ability to use drama to convey deep truths about human personality and the human condition. The novel was expressly seen as a vehicle for truth—in Stendhal's famous words from *Le Rouge et le Noir*, "A novel is a mirror that strolls along a highway. Now it reflects the blue of the skies, now the mud puddles underfoot." In music, the role of the true in the form of compositional logic—often logic of mathematical precision— is popularly associated with the works of J. S. Bach, but has characterized serious musical composition more broadly.

The good. The roles of the true and the beautiful in the arts have been leitmotifs in some of the preceding chapters, but I have not had much to say about the good. It is at least as important as the beautiful in shaping the nature of accomplishment in the visual arts and literature. Sometimes the shaping is a direct product of a moral vision, whether religious or secular. In Giotto's *The Lamentation* and Hugo's *Les Misérables*, completely different as these works are, the role of the moral vision that the artist brought to the work is palpable. The translation of the moral vision onto the canvas or into the written word is often what separates enduring art from entertainment. Extract its moral vision, and Goya's *The Third of May, 1808* becomes a violent cartoon. Extract its moral vision, and *Huckleberry Finn* becomes *Tom Sawyer.*

But the expression of the artist's moral vision is only one way—even a minor way—in which conceptions of the good shape the content of the arts. An artist's conception of the purpose of a human life and the measure of excellence in a human life provides a frame within which the varieties of the human experience are translated into art. Good art often explores the edges of the frame, revealing to us the depths to which human beings can fall as well as the heights to which they can climb. But the exploration of the edges of the frame is given structure by the nature of the frame. The depiction of violence in the absence of a conception of the good in human life is mere sensationalism; in its extreme form, a type of pornography. The depiction of violence in the presence of such a conception can be profound and clarifying; in its extreme form, a *Macbeth.*

Thus I hold that a stream of great accomplishment in the arts depends upon a culture's enjoying a well-articulated, widely held conception of the good. I suggest as well that art created in the absence of a well-articulated conception of the good is likely to be arid and ephemeral. To exclude a conception of the good from artistic creations withdraws one of the major dimensions through which great art speaks to us. For an artist to have no understanding of or commitment to the good is a handicap.

Changes in the Role of Transcendental Goods

If the question is what changes occurred in the conceptions of the true, the beautiful, and the good in the arts from 1400–1950, I refer you to the histories of the arts, which are in large degree descriptions of such changes. But if the question is *whether* artists and scholars saw themselves as employing the transcendental goods relevant to their respective fields, the answer is simpler: From 1400 until about 1900, yes. In the sciences, allegiance to truth as the guiding transcendental good remained unchanged thereafter. But for the arts, over a period starting in the late 1800s and extending through World War I, many of those who saw themselves engaged in high art consciously turned away from the idea that their function was to realize the beautiful, and then rejected the relevance of the true or the good as valid criteria for judging their work.

The change was least drastic in literature. An avant-garde—James Joyce is the exemplar—rejected the traditional conventions of narrative and tried to do for literature what their contemporaries were doing in the visual arts, but a large number of the best writers continued to write novels and poetry in familiar forms that were underwritten by more or less coherent conceptions of the true and the beautiful. For writers, the main casualty of 20C was a unifying conception of the good in the Aristotelian sense and of goodness in a moral sense. Exceptions existed, but the community of European and American writers from World War I to 1950 was for the most part secularized and disillusioned with Western culture. Many had substituted politics for religion as the source of their beliefs about right and wrong. With notable exceptions—Eliot, Yeats, Faulkner, Pound—they came from the left, caught up in the widespread enthusiasm among intellectuals for the young Soviet Union.

The moral vision that came with allegiance to Communist socialism lent itself to two tracks, neither of which had much to do with a transcendental conception of the good. The idealistic objectives of Communism were equality, liberation of the proletariat from grinding poverty and inhuman working conditions, and other admirable goals, but that same Communism held that man has no soul, that there is no God, and that you have to break eggs—meaning kill innocent people for social ends—if you want to make an omelet.[13] There's only so much a writer can do with a moral vision that excludes the soul and rationalizes the slaughter of innocents. Émile Zola, Maxim Gorky, and a few others had earlier shown that good literature is possible with that moral vision, at least until the Revolutionaries actually take power, but the range of themes is restricted and the logic of ideology pushes literature toward what came to be known as Socialist Realism—simplistic morality tales.

The other track for the left of the 1920s and 1930s was the kind of nihilistic, situational morality that by the end of the first half of 20C had become known as existentialism, fostered primarily by French intellectuals. This option consisted of an explicit denial that the classic conception of *the good* has any meaning. Human beings have no end; having no end, there is no definition of what constitutes excellence in a human life. Nihilist writers could still have their characters struggle with moral decisions, but if there's no real right or wrong out there, objective and regnant, what's the point of the struggle? Their characters could aspire to happiness, but the denial of the good means that whatever happiness they find is likely to be ephemeral. Not surprisingly, the pointlessness of life became a pervasive theme among the serious writers of this era. The portrayal of repugnant acts no longer aimed to clarify the vision of the good, but was used to deny the existence of any such thing, or, more depressingly, was inserted merely for the sake of sensationalism.

The effects of withdrawing the good from serious literature were substantial. I would enter most of the serious novels from 1920–1950 as evidence for my earlier statement that art in the absence of a well-articulated conception of the good is likely to be arid and ephemeral. But *most* is not the same as *all*—in America, the single exception of Faulkner is of huge consequence, and other countries have their own examples.

The more drastic revolution occurred in the visual arts and music. That painters, sculptors, and composers rejected the traditional ideals that had ruled their arts during early 20C is not a new or controversial proposition.[14] The artists and composers themselves said so, long and loudly. What happened was not merely one more turn in the endless cycle in which artists try to do something different from that which has gone before, but a wholesale throwing off of a legacy that had become unendurably burdensome. "The great geniuses of the past still rule over us from their graves," painter and author Wyndham Lewis lamented. "[T]hey still stalk or scurry about in the present, tripping up the living . . . a brilliant cohort of mortals determined not to die, in possession of the land."[15] And so the artists of 20C did something about it. They killed off the geniuses from the past as best they could. Jacques Barzun describes their three strategies:

> One, to take the past and present and make fun of everything in it by parody, pastiche, ridicule, and desecration, to signify rejection. Two, return to the bare elements of the art and, excluding ideas and ulterior purpose, play variations on those elements simply to show their sensuous power and the pleasure afforded by bare technique. Three, remain serious but find ways to get rid of the past by destroying the very idea of art itself.[16]

Barzun's reference to "excluding ideas and ulterior purposes" is what I have in mind by eliminating transcendental goods. Sometimes, the new way of thinking was expressed bluntly and cynically. "To be able to think freely," Andre Gide wrote, "one must be certain that what one writes will be of no consequence," adding that "The artist is expected to appear after dinner. His function is not to provide food, but intoxication."[17] Sometimes the proponents of the new art used the old language, but in a way that involved an Orwellian redefinition of words. Here, for example, is Guillaume Apollinaire's use of the word *beauty* in an essay extolling Cubism: "The modern school of painting seems to me the most audacious that has ever appeared. It has posed the question of what is beautiful in itself. It wants to visualize beauty disengaged from whatever charm man has for man."[18]

The idea that beauty can have meaning "disengaged from whatever charm man has for man" is audacious, but audacity was not in short supply among the new wave of artists in 20C—nor was contempt for their audiences. Painters and composers not only discarded their role as realizers of the beautiful, they put themselves and their own needs on the loftiest of pedestals. Arnold Schoenberg, who announced the death of tonality and then did all he could to make his prediction come true, wrote that

> . . . those who compose because they want to please others, and have audiences in mind, are not real artists. They are not the kind of men who are driven to say something whether or not there exists one person who likes it, even if they themselves dislike it. . . . They are more or less skillful entertainers who would renounce composing if they did not find listeners.[19]

Contempt for the audience could not be plainer, nor the godlike role in which Schoenberg placed the artist.

This is not the place to go into the reasons why artists and composers working in the high culture became so alienated from the legacy of Western culture and from their audiences in early 20C, but merely to note that they did. In this sense, the mainstream of the visual arts and of concert music in 20C was qualitatively different from the mainstreams of the preceding five centuries. I say *mainstream* to acknowledge that each of the arts in the first half of 20C had a channel that was a lineal descendent of pre-20C traditions —men such as Stravinsky and Kandinsky, who were aware of the legacy and valued it, but sought, as artists had sought before, to use the raw materials of great art in new ways for their own time. But they and other artists in this channel tended to come early in 20C, and their numbers dwindled as time went on. The generalization remains: In large part, the visual art and concert music of 20C is what visual art and concert music become when their creators do not tap transcendental goods.

SUMMING UP

I have argued in this chapter that great accomplishment in the arts and sciences is fed by both a rich organizing structure—and one that is still vital— and a coherent sense of transcendental goods. These two shapers of content need not vary together. In 18C Europe, the visual arts still had a strong sense of beauty and the good, but the organizing structure was aging and had lost vitality—a problem not unlike that facing Chinese artists at the same time. In 20C, which I have taken to task for its rejection of transcendental goods, concert music got a whole new organizing structure in the form of atonality and serialism, and the visual arts concocted one new organizing structure after another.

In the shaping of great accomplishment, structure and transcendental goods interact. In terms of its principles, tools, and craft, an organizing structure can be intricate and complex but nonetheless arid if it does not tap into transcendental goods. Conversely, artists may want to express their understanding of the true, the beautiful, and the good but, in the absence of a rich organizing structure, those expressions are likely to be trite or sentimental. Only a few eras in human history have had the fortune to possess the resources of both rich, vital structures and transcendental goods at the same time—the eras that we look back upon as golden ages.

TWENTY-ONE

IS ACCOMPLISHMENT DECLINING?

We arrive at this penultimate chapter with two ways of looking at the trajectory of human accomplishment. One perspective focuses on the count of significant figures, presented at the outset of Chapter 11. That count increased rapidly from 1700–1950. The other perspective, presented for the separate inventories in Chapter 14, focuses on the rate of accomplishment after taking population into account, and specifically on the rate of accomplishment in the West. Though the results vary among the inventories, the overall story is one of recent decline, usually starting sometime in 19C. The figure on the following page shows the aggregates across inventories.

The time has come to try to make sense of these competing story lines. I begin this endeavor assuming that I face a skeptical reader, which is as it should be. It is one thing to see a graph of the Chinese accomplishment rate in literature that shows the great ages occurring more than a thousand years ago, followed by decline (see page 323). The trajectory does not clash with the accepted reading of the history of Chinese literature by either Chinese or Western scholars. It is quite another thing to see a graph of the Western accomplishment rate in literature that shows a decline from the mid 1800s to 1950 (see page 318), a century that produced some of the greatest novelists and many important poets.

The key to reading these graphs, and the others in Chapter 14, is to take the rate for exactly what it measures, neither more nor less. "More" means confusing the rate with a measure of magnitude. The Western literature rate declined steeply in the decades when Flaubert, Hardy, Twain, Zola, Conrad, and James were publishing their greatest works, for example. The fact that the rate was declining doesn't mean these works aren't just as important as they are usually seen to be. A rate does not measure the quantity of fine work.

The conflicting stories told by the count of significant
figures and the rate of accomplishment

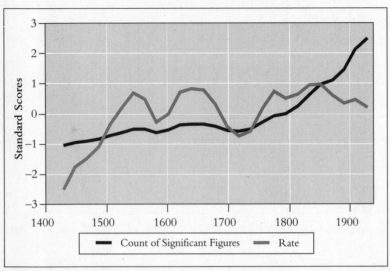

Note: Lines are two-generation moving averages for total significant figures from Europe,
USA, and Canada, expressed in standard scores (see page 463).

"Less" means assuming that the rate means nothing at all. It *may* mean
nothing at all, fully explained by artifacts, but that is an empirical issue to
be tested, not assumed. In the course of this chapter, I consider three such
artifacts:

- The supply of human capital for the arts and sciences cannot be
  expected to keep up with population.
- The markets for the arts and sciences are subject to market
  saturation.
- The procedures for assembling the inventories undercounted the
  significant figures in the most recent decades.

The three possibilities are discussed separately for the arts and sciences
in subsequent sections of this chapter, but they draw upon common ways of
thinking about what a decline in a *rate* means, and share two additional artifacts that *understate* the decline, so I begin with those issues.

THINKING ABOUT WHAT A RATE MEANS
FOR THE ARTS AND SCIENCES

When the accomplishment rate in, say, literature goes down, it means that there are fewer significant authors per unit of population, but the numerators for the ratios are small. For example, the United States in 1900 had a population of 76 million people, of whom 22 were adults who would end up as significant figures in the literature inventory. That's fewer than 3 authors per 10 million people. What difference can it make to the state of a culture if that raw number increases or decreases by a few people?

The answer goes back to the nature of the sample that significant figures represents. For every author, composer, painter, or scientist whose work survives into the history books and makes him a significant figure by the definition I have used, there are thousands of other people engaged in those occupations. Millions more are engaged in consuming the products of their work. The totality of all those people make up the environment for literature, music, art, and science. I used a stringent criterion for significant figures—being mentioned in 50 percent of the sources—for technical reasonsdescribed elsewhere (see page 110), but the number of significant figures is highly correlated (in excess of .9) with the results produced by less stringent criteria. So when the number of significant figures (by my definition) goes down, there is reason to be confident that the numbers of these larger groups of people are moving down as well.[1]

Thus the changes in the rate of significant figures in a given field can indicate a change in the Zeitgeist. When the ratio of significant figures to the total population goes down in literature, to continue with that example, one of two changes (or possibly both in tandem) must have occurred: the proportion of the total population involved with good literature as producers, critics, and audience, has gone down, or the proportion of people who write lasting work has gone down. The former is likely to signify a reduction in the value that the culture places on good literature. The latter is likely to signify a degradation in the quality of contemporary literature itself. I say "likely" because other causal mechanisms could be at work, but these are explanations that must be considered.

The explanations for a falling accomplishment rate can be benign. The first half of 20C offers an obvious possibility for the case of literature: among all the new talents who might have been engaged in novels and plays, a large portion became engaged in film and, later, television. The total cultural inter-

HOW CHANGES IN RARE EVENTS CAN CHANGE THE ATMOSPHERE

If you doubt that changes in the rates of rare events can affect daily life, consider the crime rate. Unless you live in a high-crime area, your chances of being the victim of a violent crime (murder, rape, aggravated assault, robbery) within, say, a year, are so small that they require several decimal places to express. They have always been small, even when American crime was at its highest. And yet changes in the violent crime rate have large effects on the national milieu, and even larger effects in our major cities. It is a truism among New Yorkers that the city in 2000, after a decade of falling violent crime, felt like a different place than it did in 1990. Daily life had materially changed—and yet the chances that any given New Yorker would be mugged over the course of a year had changed only infinitesimally.[2] Like changes in the accomplishment rate, a change in the violent crime rate is an indirect indicator of broader phenomena. In the New York of 2000, graffiti no longer covered public spaces. Beggars had become rarer. The squeegee men had disappeared. People behaved less fearfully and took fewer elaborate precautions against being mugged. The collateral aspects of a high-crime city had faded as part of the anti-crime policy.[3] New York was a more inviting city not just because crime had gone down, but because of a variety of changes that are reflected in changes in the crime rate.

est in drama and story-telling did not diminish, but it found new outlets. This same explanation can be seen as pessimistic: Yes, the new outlets account for the diminished rate of fine literature, but the new uses to which that talent was put did not generate films or television that many people will care about a hundred years from now. To summarize the rest of the chapter: My explanation for the recent decline in the scientific inventories is that it has been largely benign, while my explanation for the decline in the rates for the arts inventories is more pessimistic.

TWO WAYS IN WHICH THE DECLINES
ARE UNDERSTATED

A pessimistic statement that applies to all of the inventories: The declines you see in the graphs in Chapter 14 are all understated. Two well documented phenomena make it so: (1) more recent events and people get attention just because they are recent, and (2) the de facto population available for great accomplishment in the arts and sciences has been increasing more than the raw population that I have been using as the denominator.

Epochcentrism

At the end of 1899, the editor of London's *Daily Telegraph,* with the assistance of learned consultants, selected the "100 Best Novels in the World" from all the novels written in any language.[4] In all, 61 authors were represented in the list of 100 best novels. Only 27 of them—fewer than half—qualified as significant figures in *Human Accomplishment*'s inventory of Western literature. Seventeen of the 61—28 percent—were not mentioned even once by any of the 20 sources used to compile that inventory; not even by the most encyclopedic ones. And yet each of those 17 who are now ignored had written one of the supposedly 100 best novels of all time as judged in 1899. *Sic transit gloria mundi.*

    Recent lists have not been more judicious. In 2002, the editors of the Norwegian Book Clubs in Oslo published a list of the 100 best books of all time, based on their survey of about 100 well-known authors (e.g., Doris Lessing, Salman Rushdie, Seamus Heaney, Norman Mailer) from 54 countries.[5] The last 100 years monopolized almost half of the titles. The winners— supposedly the 100 best books in *any* genre written in *any* language since the dawn of civilization—included Nikos Kazantzakis's *Zorba the Greek,* Doris Lessing's *The Golden Notebook,* Toni Morrison's *Beloved,* Salmon Rushdie's *Midnight's Children,* and Astrid Lindgren's *Pippi Longstocking.* Franz Kafka got three titles on the list, the same number as Shakespeare. The list will appear as ludicrous to observers a century from now as the list of 1899 does today.

    Such lists exhibit the same bias that plagues more sophisticated histories and chronologies, found whenever historiometricians have looked for it: The recent past gets more attention than it will prove in the long run to have deserved. Dean Simonton, one of the first scholars to document this effect, named it *epochcentric bias.*[6] The magnitude of the bias for general histories is large. Two scholars who measured it for a news almanac published in 1978 found the decay in attention given to preceding eras to be exponential. Applying their findings, the implication is that (for example), the half century from 1800–1850 gets only 35 percent as much coverage as 1900–1950, for reasons having nothing to do with the potential amount of material that might have been included, but simply because those events were a century further back in time.[7]

The epochcentric bias for inventories of accomplishment in the arts and sciences is less extreme in histories of the arts and sciences than in general histories. The relevance of a political or military event seldom lasts more than a few years, and general histories focus on the few events that have had reverberations down the decades and centuries. A fine painting or musical composition has an importance to experts on art and music that is independent of its historical influence on subsequent work. I have been able to document the lesser impact of epochcentric bias in the arts through exploratory analyses described in the note.[8] But this is not to say that it disappears. The minimal assumption is that the numbers of significant figures in the inventories are inflated in 19C and 20C. Without this inflation, the decline in the accomplishment rate in 19C and 20C would be larger.

The Growth of the De Facto Population Available to Become Significant Figures

At any moment in history, people with the potential for great accomplishment exist in every society we have been examining, and in roughly similar proportions over time. The overwhelming majority of these people have gone to their graves without realizing that potential. We know this to be true just because of what we know about the distribution of opportunity. If 90 percent of a country's population lives by farming at a near-subsistence level, without education, isolated from contact with the outside world, something approaching 90 percent of all the potential Faradays and Cézannes remain subsistence farmers and their wives.[9]

Such conditions prevailed in Europe until a few centuries ago. To put it another way: If we wish to estimate the accomplishment rate *relative to the number of people who have a realistic chance of realizing their talents*, then the proper denominator for computing the accomplishment rate is not the population, but a shadow number that I will call the *de facto population*, consisting of people who have that realistic chance, whether through education, exposure to the larger culture, the lowering of barriers against one's ethnicity, race, class, or sex, or simply by growing up in a family that is prosperous enough to help their children do something with their lives. From this perspective, the accomplishment rate in Tuscany in 1500 should be computed by dividing the number of significant figures by the total number of craftsman, merchants, and aristocrats in Florence, Siena, and a few other important Tuscan towns—a fraction of the total Tuscan population.

Calculating a precise value for the de facto population across the centuries is impossible, but I can convey the shape of the trends. Suppose that we define *realistic chance* relative to the urbanization of Europe and simple exposure to the rudiments of education and the possibilities offered by the larger culture. From 1400–1800, centuries in which urbanization and the growth of the middle class still touched small proportions of the total European population, changes in the de facto population tracked closely with changes in the raw population. Then sometime in the 1800s, the de facto population began to increase more rapidly than the population as a whole, a change caused by the accelerating growth of the middle class, the spread of primary education, accelerating urbanization, and the development of a railroad system that transformed access to cities from the countryside.

To see just how rapidly, consider one fragment of the de facto population, those who obtained a university education. In Belgium and the Netherlands, the number of university students rose 3.5 times faster than the population from 1850–1900 and 8.6 times faster from 1900–1950. In Austro-Hungary, the number of university students rose 3.1 times faster than the population in 1850–1900 and 23.4 times faster than population in 1900–1950.[10] The numbers for France and Germany do not go back to 1850, but, from 1900–1950, the university population in France rose 48 times faster than the increase in population. In Germany, it rose 9.2 times faster.[11]

For the United States, which saw a disproportionate increase in its worldwide share of significant scientific figures in 20C, I can be more specific about the changes in professional training. In 1870, the first year for which official statistics are available, one Ph.D. was conferred in the entire United States. In 1880, that number had risen to 53; in 1900, 382. The percentage increases during this period were ridiculously high because of the low base. But consider 1900–1950, after the base had gotten higher: The number of Ph.D.s in scientific, medical, and technological fields increased 16.2 times faster than the population.[12]

The effect of the growing de facto population on the accomplishment rate is direct and substantial. Suppose we assume that the de facto populations in 1400, 1800, and 1950 consisted of 10 percent, 25 percent, and 75 percent of the total European population respectively. These are estimates, and should be given no more weight than that, but enough is known about the size of the European urban populations (where almost all opportunity was concentrated) from 1400 onward, and the proportion of those urban populations who had access to skills and education, to put these estimates within a reasonably narrow range.[13] The figure below shows the magnitude of the effect on the accomplishment rate when the estimated de facto population is substituted for the total population in computing the accomplishment rate.

Any plausible estimate of the de facto population must be expected to increase the estimated decline in the accomplishment rate

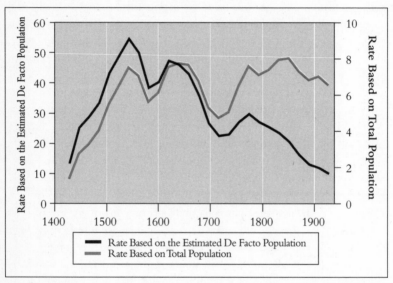

Note: Lines are two-generation moving averages for total significant figures from Europe, USA, and Canada.

If the question is how much art and science has been produced relative to the people who had a chance to produce it, the West has been on a downhill slide since the end of the Renaissance. And the graphic above makes no correction for epochcentrism in 19C and 20C.

In the rest of the chapter, I will not try to incorporate actual estimates of the effects of epochcentrism and the growth of the de facto population. But as I go through the various arguments trying to explain away the decline as an artifact, keep in mind that the size of the decline I am working with is already understated in these respects.

THE NATURE OF THE DECLINE IN SCIENCE AND TECHNOLOGY

It may seem absurd to argue that science and technology declined in any sense during any part of 19C or 20C. Those two centuries saw more progress in the well-being of mankind, by orders of magnitude, than any other two centuries in the history of mankind, and it was made possible by unprecedented strides in science and technology.[14] If the scientific inventories were designed to measure the impact of events on daily life, the rate of accomplishment unquestionably would have gone through the roof.

But that's not what the inventories purport to measure. Rather, they are designed to capture significant advances in knowledge. The impact of an invention such as the internal combustion engine was so far-reaching that it is hard to imagine a metric that could express it. But as an increment in human understanding of how the world works, it was similar to many other contemporaneous developments. The question at issue here is whether the inventories fairly represent such increments across time.

Potential Artifacts That Don't Seem to Apply

The supply of human capital devoted to science and technology could not keep up with population. I have already presented the data responding to this hypothesis (see page 433). The number of scientists has increased more rapidly than population during the same century that declines in the rate of accomplishment occurred. If we do not observe proportional increases in significant figures in the sciences, something more complicated than a failure of human capital devoted to science and technology must be at work.

The market for science and technology becomes saturated after a certain point, and the West passed that point in mid 19C. Market saturation is a complicated issue for the arts, and is discussed at length in the following section of this chapter. The same arguments do not apply to the sciences. If the question is the marketplace for publication of scientific findings, the same hundred years that saw a decline in the accomplishment rate for science saw a proliferation of technical journals and informal systems for exchanging work across the world. If the question is the economic marketplace for science, corporate investment in science and technology—basic science as well as applied science—is a product of the century from 1850–1950. I know of no evidence for the notion that it became harder to get scientific discoveries noticed during 20C, that journals were more likely to turn down articles about significant advances, or that corporations were less willing to look at the possibilities for making a profit out of a scientific discovery. On all of these dimensions, it would appear that that support for good basic science and useful technology was open-ended. The more the scientists could produce, the more the system was ready to absorb.

The use of significant figures as the measure systematically underestimates scientific accomplishment in 19C and 20C. Despite the general applicability of epochcentrism that inflates attention to recent occurrences, a special case could be argued for science that goes like this: From the mid 1800s onward, the larger-than-life scientist or inventor, working in his laboratory with a few assistants, exemplified by people like Lavoisier and Faraday, gave way to the scientist as member of a large team. The number of significant figures who show up in the inventories from mid 19C onward is radically reduced by including just the team leaders.

In one sense, this argument is surely true. If I were to list as significant figures all the people who substantively contributed to the achievement of the scientific events over the period 1400–1950, then I would expand the number of significant figures many-fold, and almost all that increase would come in the last century. But remember the underlying phenomenon that the inventories are trying to capture: *what* has been done, not who did it. It turned out for reasons discussed in Chapter 9 that focusing on people was a better way to calibrate what has been done in the arts than focusing on works of art. But in the sciences, I also assembled inventories of events, so we are in a position to ask whether the inventories of people and events tell different stories.[15] Additionally, I have weighted measures for both persons (the index scores) and events (percentage of sources including the event), so we are in a position to ask whether the weighted and unweighted measures tell different stories. The figure on the facing page shows four measures: the accomplishment rates based on significant figures and on events, weighted and unweighted.

We can reject the hypothesis that declines in the measure based on significant figures are attributable to changes in the number of people involved in making scientific discoveries. Measures based on events that

Significant events for the combined scientific inventories show
as much decline from 19C onward as significant figures

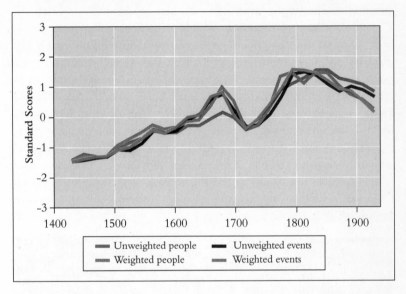

are quite different conceptually and mathematically tell indistinguishable stories.[16]

Scientific and technological discoveries after the mid 1800s were more complex than in earlier days, and therefore the increments in knowledge they represent could be undercounted. This is another plausible hypothesis that would work against the ordinary epochcentric inflation of recent events. Consider, for example, the radio—an invention of incalculable importance, but one that depended on many scientific and technological advances. If the inventory of events had *invention of the radio* as just one entry, it would be vulnerable to charges that it undercounts complex technological accomplishments. But the inventory actually has 19 different events associated with the invention of the radio, including the separate inventions of the rectifier, the amplifier vacuum tube, amplitude modulation, and the superheterodyne receiver. The invention of the airplane has 16 events associated with it. Even though the inventory stops at 1950, it includes 13 events associated with the invention of the computer. The inventory has 26 separate events relating to the biochemical basis of heredity, and 100 separate events involving discoveries about the structure of the atom. Scientific and technological discoveries were often more complex after the mid 1800s than in earlier centuries, but they also generated correspondingly more detailed accounts in the chronologies, duly reflected in the inventory.

As these examples indicate, the real problem with the inventories is likely to be in the direction of epochcentrism, inflating the number of events in 20C. It seems unlikely, for example, that chronologies of scientific events written a few centuries from now will still include 100 events about the unfolding understanding of the structure of the atom between 1897 and 1950, and more likely that historians will have condensed that number to a handful. The inventions of the radio and the airplane are more likely to be represented by a few entries than by 16 and 19 respectively. The inventories are not perfect—in the box, I describe the most glaring problem I have found—but it is not as easy as one might think to specify ways in which scientific accomplishment since mid 19C is understated, and easy to think of ways in which it may have been inflated.

WHEN AN INVENTORY MISLEADS

In reviewing the individual inventories, the one case in which the contents of the scientific inventories seems to under-weight the importance of recent discoveries is astronomy. Chronologies of scientific events customarily list many discoveries of individual celestial objects—the moons of the planets, comets, asteroids, and the like. About two dozen such events qualified for the astronomy inventory. Except for a few of them, such as the discovery that some planets have moons, these events have little substantive importance for understanding the solar system or universe. Many of them occurred in the early 1600s, shortly after the invention of the telescope, when population was still relatively low, thereby inflating the rate of accomplishment for those decades.

The Case That the Rate of Accomplishment in the Sciences Really Did Decline

It is time to consider the possibility that the rate of accomplishment in the sciences really did fall after the mid 1800s.

In 1969, Gunther Stent, a molecular biologist at the University of California's Berkeley campus, published *The Coming of the Golden Age: A View of the End of Progress.*[17] Stent's position had been voiced quietly by scientists before him, but he was the first to present a fully developed argument that progress in science and technology, along with all other enterprises based on accumulative knowledge, must soon come to an end—perhaps in Stent's lifetime, perhaps in another generation or two.

Stent acknowledged that his readers would resist the idea, but he asked them to consider the proposition in its component parts. No one would argue that anatomy or geography were subjects without limits, for example. But anatomy and geography differed from disciplines such as physics or chemistry only in their expanse, not in their ultimate bounded-ness. Everything there is to know about chemical reactions, for example, can be known. Once known, that field will be as closed to new discoveries as anatomy is now. Furthermore, it is a mistake to think that just because much is still undone in a given field means that much that is *significant* is still undone. Consider the thousands of chemical reactions, for example, that have not yet had papers written specifically about them. No matter; the goal of chemistry is to understand the principles that govern the behavior of molecules during reactions—a goal that was effectively reached in 1931 when Linus Pauling published "The nature of the chemical bond."[18] The same logic applies to the huge numbers of varieties of insect and plant life still undiscovered. Few of those undiscovered varieties will add substantively to our knowledge of biology. The catalogue of life will be more completely enumerated, not more completely understood.

Stent's argument, widely derided at the time, has been taken more seriously by his colleagues in recent years, as described in John Horgan's *The End of Science* (1997).[19] We may also apply his argument (which focused on the post-1950 situation) retrospectively to the declines in the scientific inventories.

Take as an analogy a large, complex jigsaw puzzle of an unusual kind. Unlike most jigsaw puzzles, it has no picture on the box. Also unlike most jigsaw puzzles, the pieces are of different sizes. Some are larger than others, large enough to give a sense of what that part of the puzzle is about, especially if just a few of the large pieces can be linked.

As the puzzle is assembled, the larger pieces serve as the focal points around which other pieces are tested. When those are exhausted, the next pieces to be worked on are ones with patterns or unusual colors on them, because those are easier to match up with other pieces than, say, pieces of a cloudless sky. At some point, the entire picture will be understood, even though most of the sky is left undone.

The history of science has been something like assembling that jigsaw puzzle. Long before the puzzle was complete, places had been found for the largest and most revealing pieces. As more and more people began to work on the puzzle in 19C and 20C, more pieces were linked up than ever before, but many of them were filling in blanks for parts of the picture that were already clear. The skills of the newly arrived puzzle assemblers can be just as high as ever, they can work just as hard, they can put together as many or even more pieces, but they will not be given nearly as large a place in the chronicle of how the jigsaw puzzle was assembled.

Life is no fairer for scientists than for anyone else. Physicist Richard Feynman had a strong sense of how lucky he was to have come along when he did. "It is like the discovery of America—you only discover it once," he wrote. "The age in which we live is the age in which we are discovering the fundamental laws of nature, and that day will never come again. It is very exciting, it is marvelous, but this excitement will have to go."[20] What Feynman didn't mention was that his specialty, particle physics, was among the most recent to hit its golden age, along with astrophysics, genetics, and neuroscience. For many specialties within astronomy, biology, chemistry, geology, physics, and mathematics, the fundamental laws had been found decades or centuries earlier. In philosophy, some of the fundamental truths had been discovered not decades, not even centuries, but millennia earlier.

THE NATURE OF DECLINE IN THE ARTS

The next graphic parallels the plot given for the scientific inventories on page 437, showing both the rates for the unweighted and weighted number of significant figures.

In the visual arts, the decline begins in the last half of the 1600s. Western literature shows a steep drop beginning in the second half of 19C. In music the number of significant figures drops from the mid 1700s into the early 1800s, and remains near the bottom thereafter. What can be going on?

Potential Artifacts That Don't Seem to Apply

The supply of human capital devoted to the arts could not keep up with population. On the contrary, the human capital devoted to the arts has increased far more than population. As a case in point, consider that the population of the United States as I write is on the order of 65 times greater

Declines in the arts

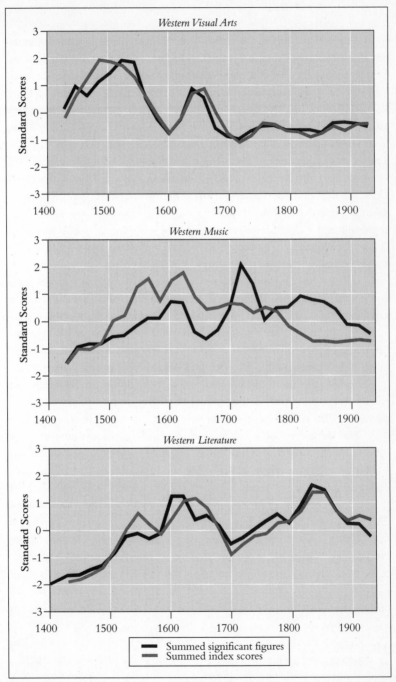

Note: Lines are two–generation moving averages for significant figures from Europe, USA, and Canada.

than the population of England under Elizabeth I. At first glance, it may not seem reasonable to expect the United States to have 65 playwrights for every one that Elizabethan England had. But this intuitive reaction is conditioned by our knowledge that the Elizabethan playwrights included Marlowe and Shakespeare, so we tend to think in terms of 65 playwrights of their caliber. But if I were to ask the question another way—is it reasonable to expect today's United States to have 65 times as many people who make their living from writing dramas as Elizabethan England?—the answer is of course yes. The half century from 1570–1620 had only 20 English playwrights mentioned in any of the sources, 13 of whom were significant figures.[21] Compare this with the single year of 2000 in the United States, when the Writers Guild that supplies writers for unionized television and screen projects numbered 12,735 members, about half of whom were employed during 2000.[22] This figure does not count all the non-unionized people who make a living writing for television, the screen, and the stage.

Elizabethan England probably did not have as many as a dozen playwrights making a living at their craft in any one year. If we say 20, which is surely too high, and say that 5,000 Americans made a living writing dramas in 2000, which is probably too low, the ratio is 250:1. Making the case that the United States today produces more than 65 times as many people who make their living writing drama than did Elizabethan England is easy. So the question becomes more complicated, and hinges not just on the number of people producing work, but the capacity of a society to recognize work at any one time. What is the saturation point for great accomplishment?

The market for great art becomes saturated after a certain point, and increases in the number of artists can no longer be expected to produce a larger number of important artists. It is plausible that the market for great accomplishment in the arts is limited. A society has a certain number of slots for great poets or painters at any one time, and the number of those slots is about the same for societies of widely differing size.

That a saturation point for stars exists in the *performing* arts is evident in everyday life. When you go to your local music store, the racks of CDs for sale in the classical music section do not allow you to select among the recordings of the top 50 solo violinists in the world, but, for practical purposes, the top dozen—and this does not represent the top dozen violinists playing today, but the top dozen spread out since high fidelity recording began in mid 20C.[23] The number of choices has nothing to do with the number of fine violinists. The racks of long-playing records for sale in the 1950s probably also featured a top dozen. A hundred years from now, it is safe to predict that a top dozen will still dominate.[24] The same phenomenon characterizes the salaries of star athletes, CEOs, and artistic performers. Why? In 1995, economists Robert Frank and Philip Cook published a book called *The Winner-Take-All Society* explaining the answer.

Frank and Cook list 11 conditions that give rise to winner-take-all markets.[25] The one most pertinent to the case of the violinists is "cloning," the capacity to reproduce the best performance cheaply. If you are the music company and can burn another 10,000 copies of Fritz Kreisler's performance of a particular violin concerto for pennies a CD, what's the point in hiring a lesser violinist to make a fresh recording of the same work? If you are the consumer, what's the point in buying the performance of a lesser violinist if you can buy Kreisler at the same price—or even if Kreisler should cost a buck or two more?

Winner-take-all markets can also occur under special conditions when familiarity breeds contentment. We become accustomed to a particular brand of scotch or coffee and continue to buy it even when alternatives we might like just as much are available. Similarly, we get used to artistic products. If you are already a Sue Grafton fan, you may well buy her latest mystery without looking at the dozens of other newly published mysteries that might be just as good. If you are producing a television news segment about the Palestinian problem, you don't go to the obscure professor who has just published a brilliant essay on the subject; you go to the tried-and-true talking heads whom your audience has come to expect. Thus do winner-take-all markets arise even if there is no difference between the quality of alternatives, or even if the rejected alternative is superior.[26] A closely related condition is what is known in politics as the advantage of incumbency. It is another version of the Matthew Effect that we have encountered more than once already (see pages 93, 353). Still another variant is limited mental shelf space—even if we wanted to, we don't have time to read a sample of every new mystery writer that publishes, so we tailor our lists to fit the space available.

Another condition leading to winner-take-all markets is the desire to have the best. If one surgeon has a 95 percent success rate and another has a 100 percent success rate in a life-and-death operation to be performed on your child, how much extra are you willing to pay for the slightly better surgeon? The answer is astronomically more than a slightly higher fee, and reasonably so. In other cases, the desire for the best leads people to pay more than most of us would think reasonable, but *reasonable* is a highly personal decision and takes us into questions of expertise and devotion to a subject that were discussed earlier (see page 65). The end result is the same: in products and celebrities alike, a few that get a reputation as the best, deserved or not, enjoy a huge advantage.

To what extent might these conditions limit the number of significant figures in the arts despite growth in the population?

Cloning and the Impulse to Buy the Best. These two conditions for winner-take-all markets, so clearly an issue for contemporary musicians and actors, do not apply with anything like the same force to the producers of works of art. What separates the producers from performers is the degree and nature of their product differentiation.

Return to the example of the 50 top violinists. They have their own nuances and styles that an expert may be able to detect and evaluate, but all 50 will have superb technique, and the differences among them will only occasionally be apparent to the average purchaser of classical music CDs. In contrast, the works of the top 50, or the top 500, composers, painters, or novelists are immediately, obviously, unique, and that uniqueness separates the producer of art from the performer of it. Johann Sebastian Bach was a better composer in historical perspective than Johann Strauss, Jr., but you can't use a Bach fugue to satisfy an urge to hear a Strauss waltz. That a publisher can produce an extra 10 thousand copies of *War and Peace* for pennies a copy does not cut into sales of *Moby Dick*.

Mental Shelf Space and Habit Formation. As my use of the Sue Grafton example suggests, winner-take-all markets can apply to producers of art as well as to performers. We have a limited amount of time to read, listen to music, and watch drama (live or on film), and so we economize on our search costs, as the economists say, and go with what we know we like. But while these dynamics are not a bad explanation of the stupendous sales of a handful of popular novelists, they do not help in explaining the production of significant figures. On the contrary, it backfires. Every new sensation spawns a school of smaller fish that swim in the same pool—or perhaps it is more accurate to say that new sensations can create new pools along with new fish. Arthur Conan Doyle opened the way for a long line of mystery writers who purloined his formula of brainy, eccentric hero and genial sidekick. Agatha Christie and the country house murder, Taylor Caldwell and the multi-generation family epic, Tom Clancy and the techno-thriller: Success in each new subgenre of novel has opened up markets that have inspired publishers to look eagerly for other authors who can be successful. New entry of producers of artistic works tends to resemble a win/win game. It can be hard to get the reader who is comfortable with Sue Grafton to try the new mystery writer, but if the publisher succeeds, the reader is likely to end up buying the novels of both.

The use of significant figures as the measure systematically underestimates artistic accomplishment in 19C and 20C. For the sciences, it is possible to devise plausible hypotheses explaining why the usual epochcentric bias does not apply and why scientific significant figures are undercounted for the most recent decades. Those hypotheses don't work, but at least they are plausible. For the arts, I can think of only one such hypothesis. Call it *greatness fatigue.* The logic is that we, the audience, have an elastic capacity for new mystery writers or new pop songs, whereas our capacity to absorb great novels or great music is less elastic. An audience of 400 million people cannot focus on and recognize for posterity 10 times as many fine artists as an audience of 40 million people.

The problem with this hypothesis is to find a way to falsify it. The best place to look is the most recent period of observation, 1900–1950, with its greatly enlarged population compared to the preceding 50 years. Can we see in retrospect any signs that the amount of great work outstripped the capacity of the audience to give it the reputation it deserved and that, if the audience had been up to its responsibilities, the number of people qualifying as significant figures from that era would be higher, and also their eminence? But where to look? The only way we could test this hypothesis is if two conditions were met: (1) An unrecognized great work got sufficiently into the public eye (the book or musical score was published, the painting or sculpture was exhibited) so that posterity could know about it, and (2) posterity has a better perspective on the quality of these works than contemporaries did.

Begin by assuming that both these conditions apply. I can find no evidence that today's critics have elevated their opinion of authors, composers, or artists from the first half of 20C. It is easy to find examples of people whose reputations are falling—compare Hemingway's literary standing in 1950 with his standing today, for example—but that is appropriate. Time is supposed to erode the reputation of all but the greatest work, peeling off the effects of epochcentrism. Proving a negative is notoriously difficult, so I will leave it to you to think of examples I have missed whereby a case could be made that the audience of 1900–1950 suffered greatness fatigue.

A subtler form of greatness fatigue could have been experienced not by the public, but by publishers, impresarios, and art galleries, who in 1900–1950 had great work shown to them that they uniformly rejected, thereby preventing the public from ever getting a chance to read, hear, or see it. This possibility is beyond empirical test. It is most plausible for genres that were commercially unattractive. One can easily imagine that worthy poetry went unpublished in 20C, for example. But did 1900–1950 really have an invisible *oeuvre* of beautiful symphonies or exquisite representational art created but never exposed to the world? It is hard to imagine. Isolated cases of competent work, yes; a substantial body of fine work, no. It is more plausible to believe that people who *could* have created beautiful symphonies in the classical style or exquisite representational art didn't, because those genres had fallen out of critical favor. But that would represent authentic decline in accomplishment, not greatness fatigue.

The Case That the Rate of Accomplishment in the Arts Really Did Decline

To argue that the rate of accomplishment in the arts really did begin to decline in 19C or earlier is to cast one's lot to some degree with the argument that Western civilization itself is in decline, a persistent theme of intellectual life from mid 19C onward. In his survey of the idea of decline, historian Arthur Herman dates its beginning to Arthur de Gobineau's *Essai sur L'Iné-galité des Races Humaines*, published in 1853 on the heels of the 1848 revolutionary movements. When its apocalyptic view of the disintegration of European culture was attacked, Gobineau shrugged it off. "I never supposed that I can tell people today, 'you are in a state of complete decadence, your civilization is a swamp, your intelligence a smoldering lamp, you are already halfway to the grave,' without expecting some opposition."[27] And this was in 1853, when the raw counts of significant figures in all the arts and sciences were shooting up, and the rate of accomplishment in the sciences and literature was at its peak.

Thinkers in both Europe (e.g., Nietzsche, Burckhardt, Berdyaev, Spengler, Sorokin) and in America (Henry and Brooks Adams, W. E. B. Du Bois) developed variants of this pessimistic vision in works that culminated in Arnold Toynbee's 10-volume *A Study of History* (1933–1954).[28]

As I read the works of the declinists—or in some cases the excellent summaries in the two sources in the note—I have three reactions.[29] One is skepticism about laws of history. One may acknowledge the erudition of a Spengler or a Toynbee, admire their attempts to make a coherent whole from a breadth of knowledge that few individuals have ever possessed, and nonetheless, with the advantage of several decades of hindsight, see ways in which they got things wrong. My second reaction is the occasional shock of recognition when a declinist forecasts future trends that apply with painful accuracy to today's society. My third reaction is that the best of the declinists are correct in this broad sense: Western European culture had a coherence in its values and institutions that did in fact begin to come apart during 18C, prompted by the Enlightenment and the Industrial Revolution. The political and economic aspects of the change represented not disintegration but great progress. The cliché is true, however: Progress has prices, and the declinists successfully identified those prices.

I described some of the ways in which I believe Western European culture came apart under the headings of purpose and autonomy in Chapter 19 and of transcendental goods in Chapter 20. Those discussions taken together provide the material for an argument—a strong argument, in my opinion—that the environment for producing great art in any field became progressively less favorable over the course of 19C, and that the environment deteriorated even more rapidly after the turn of 20C.

The declinists blame the decline on the failure of the elites, who in their view have lost the élan, self-confidence, and vitality of an earlier age.[30] But 19C also saw a phenomenon born not of cultural decay but of economic vitality: the growth of the middle class into the dominant social force in 19C and, in 20C, the spread of prosperity to blue collar workers and farmers. An inevitable result of these transforming social trends was a huge increase in the audience for popular plays, books, and music. The size of that new and growing market was bound to have attracted talent that in another age would have been monopolized by the aristocratic patrons of fine music and art. A science fiction story written some decades ago had as its premise that the dying Mozart is whisked by a time machine to the future, where modern medicine cures him of the disease that was about to kill him in 1791. His patrons send him into the modern world to continue composing ever greater symphonies and operas. Within a few months he is caught up in the rock 'n' roll world and, as I recall, dies soon thereafter of a drug overdose.[31]   The outcome of the story is not so implausible: If Mozart were alive today, he might well be writing rock 'n' roll—superb rock 'n' roll, presumably, but not another *Don Giovanni*.

I have no way of disentangling the relative importance of all these elements. But I see no reason to conclude that the declines in the accomplishment rates in the arts are artifacts that understate recent accomplishment. I see far more reason to suspect that the artifacts of epochcentrism and a growing de facto population mean that the declines are understated.

TWENTY-TWO

SUMMATION

Having explored data that sprawl over as much territory as these do, I come to the end with an urge to insert more equivocations into the conclusions than any reader can be asked to put up with. I will suppress that impulse and state as simply as I can my best reading of the data.

THE REALITY OF EXCELLENCE

A colleague whom I asked to look at my treatment of mathematical accomplishment wrote back with a list of corrections. He added that although Carl Gauss was ranked fourth in the mathematics inventory, a high ranking for an ordinary mortal,

> . . . it's a wee bit uncharitable not to point out that Gauss, as well as being a Grade A++ mathematician, was also a first-rank astronomer (found the first asteroid after Piazzi lost it, e.g.) and physicist (co-invented electric telegraph, invented heliotrope, etc, etc.). If you asked a surveyor, his work on surveying the Kingdom of Bavaria would probably put him in the first rank of THEM, too. In the large sphere of pure and applied math, I doubt there is anything Gauss wasn't first rank in. He even, via his descendants, helped to populate the state of Missouri. . . . Before the Eulers, Gausses and Newtons, we are worms, worms.[1]

I would not go so far as to say that the rest of us are worms, worms, but if the last several hundred pages can be said to have a principal message, it is this: Excellence exists, and it is time to acknowledge and celebrate the magnificent inequality that has enabled some of our fellow humans to have so enriched the lives of the rest of us.

The book's secondary message, more implicit than explicit, is this: It is also time to render unto equality that which is appropriate to equality, and unto excellence that which is appropriate to excellence. Equality is a fine ideal, and should have an honored place. To have understood that each person is unique, that each person must be treated as an end and not a means, that each person should be free to live his life as he sees fit, so long as he accords others the same freedom, that each person should be equal before the law and is equal in God's sight, and to incorporate these principles into the governance of nations—these are among the greatest of all human accomplishments. But equality has nothing to do with the abilities, persistence, zeal, and vision that produce excellence. Equality and excellence inhabit different domains, and allegiance to one need not compete with allegiance to the other.

Excellence is not simply a matter of opinion, though judgment enters into its identification. Excellence has attributes that can be identified, evaluated, and compared across works. The judgments reached by those who are most expert in their fields, and who work from standards of excellence that they are willing to specify and subject to the inspection of logic, are highly consistent—so consistent that eminence in the various domains of accomplishment can be gradated with higher reliability than is achieved by almost any other measure in the social and behavioral sciences. When the rating of eminence is scrutinized against the reasons for that eminence, it also becomes apparent that those who rank highest are those who have achieved at the highest levels of their field.

Different readers will have had different reactions to the presentation of those arguments in Part 2. To those who disagree, I ask only this: You have been presented with a case, here and in the extensive literature that informed it. A reply requires more than another assertion that we are prisoners of canons that unjustly privilege some works over others, that the achievements of those who have been ignored are just as good as the work of those who are celebrated. What are the alternative standards of excellence? The logic behind the standards? The methods for applying those standards to works of art and science? Spelling out the answers to those questions will probably do no more than clarify where the disagreement lies, but that would be a step in the right direction.

THE FOUNDATIONS OF ACCOMPLISHMENT

The state of knowledge about the forces that produce bursts of human accomplishment is bifurcated. On one set of questions, those addressed in Part 3, the empirical record can be specified precisely, alternative views of the data can be tested, and the resulting conclusions are subject to only a limited degree of data-based debate. For example, I consider the data about the dominance of Europe and of white males in Chapters 11 and 12 to be among the least problematic in the book. Public controversy about these issues is heated, but the data are knowable and straightforward. The analyses for explaining the patterns and trajectories presented in Chapters 15 and 16 are subject to more argument. With regard to the most important single variable in those chapters, the effect of preceding generations on accomplishment in succeeding generations, my analyses confirm what others have already demonstrated, and the likelihood of finding contrary results is small. But it is quite possible that better data or more sophisticated analyses of such issues as economic growth will reveal relationships that I have missed. The role of what I call elite cities may be confounded with the role of other variables such as the degree of political and cultural diversity.

Part 4 represents another kind of analysis altogether: less quantitative, more speculative, and definitely more opinionated. That does not mean my arguments should be exempt from systematic quantitative investigation. But my purpose in *Human Accomplishment* has been to get the arguments on the table, saying to others who are exploring human accomplishment and to those who might be drawn to the topic that it is time to take another look at some old-fashioned explanations. Trying to convert those propositions into hypotheses employing quantitative measures suitable for multivariate analysis seemed a step too far for this book.

But serious propositions they are, and about a deeply serious question: What are the conditions that ignite great accomplishment? For the rest of this section, I will be especially ruthless about suppressing equivocations as I recapitulate the claims I advanced in Part 4:

The nature of accomplishment in a given time and place can be predicted with reasonable accuracy given information about that culture's status with regard to the four dimensions of purpose, autonomy, organizing structure, and transcendental goods.

The predictions will vary by field, because the richness of structure and the vitality of transcendental resources can be different for different fields. At the same moment in history, the reigning structure can simultaneously be depleted in painting and vital in literature. At the same moment in history, authors (for example) can be tapping into transcendental goods while composers are not.

A culture can produce a stream of accomplishment while being strong on only some of the four dimensions. The East Asian, South Asian, and Arabic civilizations are examples. All were at a disadvantage (in terms of accomplishment in the arts and sciences) throughout their histories, in the sense that all were cultures in which duty trumped vocation, familism trumped individualism, and consensus trumped debate. Nonetheless, each of those civilizations produced great work in every field in which they developed rich structures and sought to realize transcendental goods.

The limits facing civilizations where duty, family, and consensus are primary values differ for the arts and sciences. In the arts, respect for tradition means that artistic structures are not periodically rebuilt from scratch, but elaborated slowly and incrementally. Respect for tradition does not diminish the technical excellence of the work at its best, but it does militate against variety and innovation. In the sciences, the constraints are more severe. The fuel of the scientific method—nonstop debate and fierce competition to put the next brick of the edifice in place—seems to demand individualism on the Western model. Improvements in the state of knowledge can be made without it, but individualism is valuable for achieving breakthroughs.

Some specific propositions about the roles of the shapers of accomplishment:

In the arts, the richness of the structure has most of its effect on the *amount* of work that is produced within a field; access to transcendental goods has most of its effect on the enduring *quality* of that work.

Where artists do not have coherent ideals of beauty, the work tends to be sterile. Where they do not have coherent ideals of the good, the work tends to be vulgar. Lacking access to either beauty or the good, the work tends to be shallow.

In the sciences (and humanities and the social sciences): Where scholars do not have allegiance to ideals of truth, the work tends to be false.

Accomplishment in the arts and sciences that is sterile, vulgar, shallow, or false does not endure.

PAST 1950

In many ways, we live in the best of times. As I wrote in the Introduction, we at the outset of 21C would be foolish to choose any earlier time to be born. We enjoy unprecedented wealth, health, and security. We have unprecedented access to the best that survives of everything humans in every culture have achieved over the past ten thousand years.

We retain the conditions for continued great accomplishment in the sciences. I see no important ways in which the allegiance to truth has been compromised in the hard sciences. The structure of the scientific method is self-renewing—certainly in its constant creation of important new tools and crafts, but also in its refinement and relentless reexamination of its principles. If the measure of the rate of accomplishment is to be the one I have used, calibrating the number of bricks added to the edifice, then the accomplishment rate may continue to fall. But if the measure is the magnitude of the changes in human life that new discoveries produce, there is no reason to think that scientific accomplishment will falter, and many reasons to think that it will increase. And who knows? Perhaps the Einsteinian universe is as far from the final answer as the Newtonian universe was, and basic science will find vast new *terrae incognitae* to explore.

The arts are another story. On three of the four dimensions—purpose, autonomy, and transcendental goods—I believe it can be demonstrated that the conditions for great accomplishment in the arts moved toward the unfavorable end of the spectrum in the first half of 20C. It does not seem possible to make a case that any of those conditions improved in the second half of 20C, and it is easy to make a case that some of them got worse.

If the conditions for accomplishment got worse in the second half of 20C, the implication is that accomplishment did too—that the accomplishment rate in the arts continued to go down, in terms of the measure I have used. Whether that happened in fact will require more distance from 1950–2000 to establish. But one may speculate. What play, novel, painting, sculpture, film, or musical composition produced during 1950–2000 are you confident will still be considered important as a work of art two hundred years from now? I can think of only a handful, and my confidence even in them is shaky.

Perhaps I am too unfamiliar with fine work that has been done. I am told that superb concert music, still almost unheard in the United States, has been produced in the last few decades by composers in Eastern Europe, and that some of the poetry of the last half-century, though not famous, reaches the highest artistic level. Perhaps I am simply too pessimistic. The auction prices for post-1950 art are high and still climbing. The world's film industries produce hundreds of major productions each year that draw hundreds of millions of ticket-buyers. The music industry turns out thousands of songs, more books are being published than ever before, and new possibilities for artistic expression are being generated by new technology. Why not entertain the possibility that the last half of 20C has seen a small-*r* Renaissance; that the arts are robust and thriving but don't happen to fit my tastes?

My pessimism goes back to themes I discussed in Chapter 5. The reason that some works of art endure is because people who know the most about that art continue to be attracted to them, and thus continue to talk and to write about them. For a work of art to continue to be compelling in this way requires substance—things for the expert to ponder, to discover beneath the surface, to be excited about anew upon reacquaintance.

I specify experts because they are the people who write the histories that carry the names forward into time. But my point applies to a broader audience. Indulge me in one more thought experiment, a familiar one: You will be stranded on a desert island, and you can take just 10 books and 10 music CDs. What do you choose? My prediction is that even people who don't listen to classical music regularly will take Bach, Mozart, and Beethoven. Even people who haven't picked up Shakespeare in years will take the collected works of Shakespeare. When we want something we can go back to again and again, we choose the same giants that the experts choose. My proposition about the literature, music, and visual arts of the last half century is that hardly any of it has enough substance to satisfy, over time.

The post-1950 West has unquestionably produced some wonderful entertainments, and I do not mean *wonderful* slightingly. *The Simpsons* is wickedly smart, *Saving Private Ryan* is gripping, *Groundhog Day* is a brilliant moral fable. The West's popular culture is for my money the only contemporary culture worth patronizing, with its best stories more compelling and revealing than the ones written by authors who purport to write serious novels, and its best popular music with more energy and charm than anything the academic composers turn out. It is a mixed bag, with the irredeemably vulgar side by side, sometimes intermingled, with the wittiest and most thoughtful work. But the quality is often first-rate—as well it might be. The people producing the best work include some who in another age could have been a Caravaggio or Brahms or Racine, and perhaps dozens of others good enough to have made their way onto the roster of significant figures.

Why not be satisfied with wonderful entertainments?

THE ARISTOTELIAN PRINCIPLE RECAST

Realized capacities are pleasing not only when they are exercised, but also when they are seen to be exercised. Or to recast the first two-thirds of the Aristotelian principle: *Human beings enjoy watching the exercise of the realized capacities of their species, and this enjoyment increases the more the capacity is realized.*

To be in the presence of greatness is exciting, even when we are not capable of appreciating all the nuances of the achievement. *The best* has a magic about it, whether we are eating a meal cooked by a great chef, watching a great athlete perform under pressure, or witnessing anything done superbly well, far beyond our own reach.

Now comes the last clause of the Aristotelian principle: "... *or the greater its complexity.*" The depth of gratification we get from watching people perform at the pinnacle increases as the difficulty and importance of what they are doing increases. Danger and self-sacrifice are part of this calculation, which explains why no sporting achievement has the same grip on our imaginations as heroism in war. In the sciences, Einstein's $E=mc^2$ became an icon not only because it represented such a dazzling mental leap, but because it illuminated our understanding of the very universe. In the arts, writers and painters and composers are engaged in another kind of complex and difficult endeavor, explaining ourselves to ourselves. When they succeed at the highest level, they transcend what we ordinarily believe to be within the capacity of our kind. Many chapters ago, I used the question, "How can a human being have done that?" as a device for conveying our response to the highest accomplishments in the arts. There is another aspect to the reaction, not a question but a declaration of pride: "A human being did that!"

That's why we cannot be satisfied with a culture that turns out nothing but shiny, craftsmanlike entertainments. We may outstrip our forebears in wealth, creature comforts, health, and lifespan. We may outstrip them in the breadth of political freedom and equality our governments provide. But a culture that is unable to compete with the past's greatest expressions of the human spirit is in some sense a backward culture—the kind of backwardness that led Edward Gibbon to call the Romans at the apex of their empire "a race of pygmies."[2] It is dispiriting to know that the greatest accomplishments are monopolized by past cultures whose heights we are unable to match. Being part of a culture that produces new giants would be inspiriting.

It is not at all clear to me how a culture gets from here to there, however, because I come to the end of this book convinced that religion is indispensable in igniting great accomplishment in the arts. I use *religion* at once loosely and stringently. Going to church every Sunday is not the definition I have in mind, nor even a theology in its traditional sense. Confucianism and classical Greek thought were both essentially secular, and look at the cultures they produced. But both schools of thought were tantamount to religion in that they articulated a human place in the cosmos, laid out a clear understanding of the end—the good—toward which humans aim, and set exalted standards of human behavior. And that brings me to the sense in which I use *religion* stringently. Confucianism and Aristotelianism, along with the great religions of the world, are for grownups, requiring mature contemplation of truth, beauty, and the good. Cultures in which the creative elites are not engaged in that kind of mature contemplation don't produce great art.

Suppose that this reading of history is correct. Today's creative elites are not just overwhelmingly secular but often hostile to the idea that transcendental goods have any meaning. Such is the reason to fear that well-made entertainments are as much as we can hope for. Great art requires a source of inspiration that the people who produce those entertainments are not tapping.

But what has been true for the last few decades need not be true perpetually. Gloomy prognoses sell short the regenerating power of certain truths.

The first of these truths is that the hold of great art on the human imagination is so binding that the present intellectual nihilism cannot survive. Not too many years from now, it seems safe to predict, people who love literature, music, and painting for their power to express beauty, truth, and the good will once again dominate the faculties of the world's leading universities and set the tone for public conversation about artistic excellence. It is bizarre that people who do *not* love literature, music, or painting for their transcendental power came to have any sort of influential role at all. It is a situation that was the product of specific historical circumstances, easily understandable in retrospect. Those historical circumstances are ephemeral. Signs that they are already coming to an end can be discerned. When the change is complete, children with the potential to create great art will once again grow up having worthy conceptions of what *great* means.

Gloomy prognoses also sell short the way in which thoughtful human beings are drawn to fundamental questions of existence. "Why is there something rather than nothing?" is a question that none of us can avoid completely, even in times when such questions are least fashionable. "What does it mean to live a good life?" is another. It is difficult to think about these things outside spiritual frameworks. The successive blows to traditional religion thought to have been struck by Darwin, Freud, and Einstein made some intellectuals give up the option of thinking about such questions within such frameworks, but there are good reasons for thinking that this too will prove to be ephemeral. It may well be that the period from the Enlightenment through 20C will eventually be seen as a kind of adolescence of the species— a time when humans were deprived of the comforting simplicities of childhood and exposed to more complex knowledge about the world. In the manner of adolescents, humans reacted injudiciously, thinking that they possessed wisdom that invalidated all that had gone before—if Darwin was right, then Aquinas was no longer worth reading; if Freud was right, the *Nicomachean Ethics* must be wrong. But adolescence is temporary, and when it passes young adults discover that their parents have gotten smarter. That may be happening with the advent of the new century, as glib answers to solemn questions start to wear thin.

I hope the underlying question posed by the foregoing chapters can play a modest role in that process. If it is a statement of fact, as I believe can be demonstrated, that human beings with the potential for excellence generally have done best in cultures where people believe the universe to have transcendental meaning, one must ask why. The easy answer is that the giants of the past were deluded. They imagined that what they were doing had some transcendental significance, and, lo and behold, their foolishness inspired them to compose better music or paint better pictures. But this line of thought can become embarrassing when one confronts just what those self-deluded people accomplished. Is it not implausible that those individuals who accomplished things so beyond the rest of us just happened to be uniformly stupid about the great questions? Another possibility is that they understood things we don't.

This is not the prelude to a revelation of what those understandings are, but a suggestion that when human beings are functioning at the heights of human capacity, it is a good idea to begin by assuming that they are doing something right. Johann Sebastian Bach does not need to explain himself; he made a prima facie case that his way of looking at the universe needs to be taken seriously. It behooves us to do so.

I first encountered this injunction as a college undergraduate, many years ago, in one of those rare moments that stand out from otherwise forgotten classes. It happened near the close of an introductory philosophy course taught by a grand old Platonist named Raphael Demos. He had spent two or three lectures on free will, reviewing the positions that philosophers have taken on that fraught issue. At the end, he said something like, "Now you know what the great philosophers have said about free will. Maybe you're wondering what I think." He paused for effect. "Well," he said briskly, "I think that since we all act every day as if we have free will, why not believe it?" We laughed, as he had expected. It was only later, thinking about it, that I realized he had not given us just a laugh line. He had asked us a *koan* of a question, one to meditate upon. Human beings cannot help acting as if they had free will. What does that tell us?

I will put my question again: Human beings have been most magnificently productive and reached their highest cultural peaks in the times and places where humans have thought most deeply about their place in the universe and been most convinced they have one. What does that tell us?

It is not a question to be answered with a quip. We strive to answer it knowing that human limits force us to look through a glass darkly. But persistent seeking is, after all, at the heart of the spirit that enables people to achieve great things. The rest of us may not be able to paint like Titian or compose like Debussy, but all of us who feel impelled to try to live the best possible human life are engaged in the same larger enterprise.

That larger enterprise has little triumphalism or hubris about it. The enduring impression I carry away from this exploration of human accomplishment is not so much what the people who built the human résumé did as how they did it. Some fit the image of the genius in their public personae (though more did not), but, in the way they did their work, they more commonly resembled a craftsman at his bench, struggling to get it right, agonizing over mistakes, doing it over again, with a vision of perfection insistently pulling him onward.

A story is told about the medieval stone masons who carved the gargoyles that adorn the great Gothic cathedrals. Sometimes their creations were positioned high upon the cathedral, hidden behind cornices or otherwise blocked from view, invisible from any vantage point on the ground. They sculpted these gargoyles as carefully as any of the others, even knowing that once the cathedral was completed and the scaffolding was taken down, their work would remain forever unseen by any human eye. It was said that they carved for the eye of God. That, written in a thousand variations, is the story of human accomplishment.

APPENDICES

STATISTICS FOR PEOPLE WHO ARE SURE THEY CAN'T LEARN STATISTICS*

The following is aimed at the liberal arts graduate who has not taken a math course since high school and knows nothing whatsoever about statistics but wants to understand the statistical terms in the text.

DISTRIBUTIONS AND STANDARD DEVIATIONS

Why Do We Need "Standard Deviation"?

Every day, formally or informally, people make comparisons—among people, among apples and oranges, among dairy cows or egg-laying hens, among the screws being coughed out by a screw machine. The standard deviation is a measure of how spread out the things being compared are. "This egg is a lot bigger than average," a chicken farmer might say. The standard deviation gives him a way of saying precisely what he means by "a lot."

---

* Adapted from *The Bell Curve: Intelligence and Class Structure in American Life* by Richard J. Herrnstein and Charles Murray. Copyright © 1994 by Richard J. Herrnstein and Charles Murray. Reprinted with permission of The Free Press, a Division of Simon & Schuster Trade Publishing Group. I have made a few minor changes to the original text, eliminating some material specific to issues in *The Bell Curve* and rewording a few sentences to fit the context of *Human Accomplishment*.

What Is a Frequency Distribution?

To get a clear idea of what a frequency distribution is, imagine yourself back in your high school gym, with all the boys in the senior class assembled before you (including both sexes would complicate matters, and the main point of this discussion is to keep things simple). Line up these boys from left to right in order of height.

Now you have a long line going from shortest to tallest. As you look along the line you will see that only a few boys are conspicuously short and tall. Most are in the middle, and a lot of them seem identical in height. Is there any way to get a better idea of how this pattern looks?

Tape a series of cards to the floor in a straight line from left to right, with "60 inches and shorter" written on the one at the far left, "80 inches and taller" on the card at the far right, and cards in one-inch increments in between. Tell everyone to stand behind the card that corresponds to his height.

Someone loops a rope over the rafters and pulls you up in the air so you can look straight down on the tops of the heads of your classmates standing in their single files behind the height labels. The figure below shows what you see: a frequency distribution.

The raw material of a frequency distribution

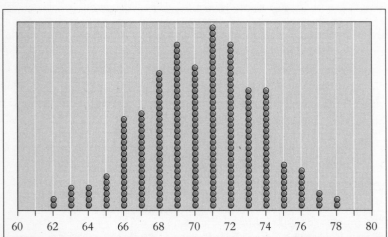

This a frequency distribution. What good is it? Looking at your high school classmates standing around in a mob, you can tell very little about their height. Looking at those same classmates arranged into a frequency distribution, you can tell a lot, quickly and memorably.

How Is the Distribution Related to the Standard Deviation?

We still lack a convenient way of expressing where people are in that distribution. What does it mean to say that two different students are, say, 6 inches different in height? How "big" is a 6-inch difference? That brings us back to the standard deviation.

When it comes to high school students, you have a good idea of how "big" a 6-inch difference is. But what does a 6-inch difference mean if you are talking about the height of elephants? About the height of cats? It depends. And the things it depends on are the average height and how much height varies among the things you are measuring. *A standard deviation gives you a way of taking both the average and that variability into account, so that "6 inches" can be expressed in a way that means the same thing for high school students relative to other high school students, elephants relative to other elephants, and cats relative to other cats.*

How Do You Compute a Standard Deviation?

Suppose that your high school class consisted of just two people who were 66 inches and 70 inches. Obviously, the average is 68 inches. Just as obviously, one person is 2 inches shorter than average, one person is 2 inches taller than average. The standard deviation is a kind of average of the differences from the mean—2 inches, in this example. Suppose you add two more people to the class, one who is 64 inches and the other who is 72 inches. The mean hasn't changed (the two new people balance each other off exactly). But the newcomers are each 4 inches different from the average height of 68 inches. So the standard deviation, which measures the spread, has gotten bigger as well. Now two people are 4 inches different from the average and two people are 2 inches different from the average. That adds up to a total of 12 inches, divided among four persons. The simple average of these differences from the mean is three inches (12÷4), which is almost (but not quite) what the standard deviation is. To be precise, the standard deviation is calculated by squaring the deviations from the mean, then summing them, then finding their average, then taking the square root of the result. In this example, two people are 4 inches from the mean and two are 2 inches from the mean. The sum of the squared deviations is 40 (i.e., 16+16+4+4). Their average is 10 (40÷4).

The square root of 10 is 3.16, which is the standard deviation for this example. The technical reasons for using the standard deviation instead of the simple average of the deviations from the mean are not necessary to go into, except that, in normal distributions, the standard deviation has wonderfully convenient properties. If you are looking for a short, easy way to think of a standard deviation, view it as the average difference from the mean.

As an example of how a standard deviation can be used to compare apples and oranges, suppose we are looking at the Olympic women's gymnastics team and men's NBA basketball teams. You notice a woman who is 5 feet 6 inches and a man who is 7 feet. You know from watching gymnastics on television that 5 feet 6 inches is tall for a woman gymnast, and 7 feet is tall even for a basketball player. But you want to do better than a general impression. Just *how* unusual is the woman, compared to the average gymnast on the U. S. women's team, and how unusual is the man, compared to the average basketball player on the U. S. men's team?

We gather data on height among all the women gymnasts, and determine that the mean is 5 feet 1 inch with a standard deviation (SD) of 2 inches. For the men basketball players, we find that the mean is 6 feet 6 inches and the SD is 4 inches. Thus the woman who is 5 feet 6 inches is 2.5 standard deviations taller than the average; the seven-foot man is only 1.5 standard deviations taller than the average. These numbers—2.5 for the woman and 1.5 for the man—are called *standard scores* in statistical jargon. Now we have an explicit numerical way to compare how different the two people are from their respective averages, and we have a basis for concluding that the woman who is 5 feet 6 inches is a lot taller relative to other female Olympic gymnasts than a 7-foot man is relative to other NBA basketball players.

How Much More Different? Enter the Normal Distribution

Everyone has heard the phrase *normal distribution* or *bell-shaped curve*, or, as in the title of a controversial book, *bell curve*. They all refer to a common way that natural phenomena arrange themselves approximately. (The true normal distribution is a mathematical abstraction, never perfectly observed in nature.) If you look again at the distribution of high school boys that opened the discussion, you will see the makings of a bell curve. If we added several thousand more boys to it, the kinks and irregularities would smooth out, and it would actually get very close to a normal distribution. A perfect one looks like the one in the figure below.

It makes sense that most things will be arranged in bell-shaped curves.

Extremes tend to be rarer than the average. If that sounds like a tautology, it is only because bell curves are so common. Consider height again. Seven feet is "extreme" for humans. But if human height were distributed so that equal proportions of people were 5 feet, 6 feet, and 7 feet tall, the extreme would not be rarer than the average. It just so happens that the world hardly ever works that way.

Bell curves (or close approximations to them) are not only common in nature, they have a close mathematical affinity to the meaning of the standard deviation. In any true normal distribution, no matter whether the elements are the heights of basketball players, the diameters of screw heads, or the milk production of cows, 68.3 percent of all the cases fall in the interval between one standard deviation above the mean and one standard deviation below it.

In its mathematical form, the normal distribution extends to infinity in both directions, never quite reaching the horizontal axis. But for all practical purposes, when we are talking about populations of people, a normal distribution is about 6 standard deviations wide. The numbers below the axis in the figure below designate the number of standard deviations above and below the mean. As you can see, the line has virtually touched the surface at ±3 standard deviations.

Furthermore, there are some simple characteristics about these scores that make them especially valuable. As you can see by looking at the figure below, it makes intuitive sense to think of a 1 standard deviation difference as

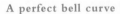

A perfect bell curve

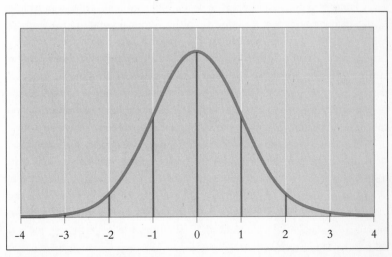

"large," a 2 standard deviation difference as "very large," and a 3 standard deviation difference as "huge." This is an easy metric to remember. Specifically: a person who is one standard deviation above the mean in IQ is at the 84th percentile. Two standard deviations above the mean puts him at the 98th percentile. Three standard deviations above the mean puts him at the 99.9th percentile. A person who is one standard deviation below the mean is at the 16th percentile. Two standard deviations below the mean puts him at the 2nd percentile. Three standard deviations below the mean puts him at the 0.1th percentile.

Why Not Just Use Percentiles to Begin With?

Why go to all the trouble of computing standard scores? Most people understand percentiles already. Tell them that someone is at the 84th percentile, and they know right away what you mean. Tell them that he's at the 99th percentile, and they know what that means. Aren't we just introducing an unnecessary complication by talking about "standard scores"?

Thinking in terms of percentiles is convenient, and has its legitimate uses. We often speak in terms of percentiles—or centiles, an almost identical term. But they can also be highly misleading, because they are artificially compressed at the "tails" of the distributions. It is a longer way from, say, the 98th centile to the 99th than from the 50th to the 51st. In a true normal distribution, the distance from the 99th centile to the 100th (or, similarly, from the 1st to the 0th) is infinite.

Consider two people who are at the 50th and 55th centiles in height. Using a large representative sample from the National Longitudinal Study of Youth (NLSY) as our estimate of the national American distribution of height, their actual height difference is only half an inch. Consider another two people who are at the 94th and 99th centiles on height—the identical gap in terms of centiles. Their height difference is 3.1 inches, six times the height difference of those at the 50th and 55th centiles. The farther out on the tail of the distribution you move, the more misleading centiles become.

Standard scores reflect these real differences much more accurately than do centiles. The people at the 50th and 55th centiles, only half an inch apart in real height, have standard scores of 0 and .13. Compare that difference of .13 standard deviation units to the standard scores of those at the 94th and 99th centiles: 1.55 and 2.33 respectively. In standard scores, their difference—which is .78 standard deviation units—is six times as large, reflecting the sixfold difference in inches.

CORRELATION AND REGRESSION

So much for describing a distribution of measurements. We now need to consider dealing with the relationships between two or more distributions— which is, after all, what scientists usually want to do. How, for example, is the pressure of a gas related to its volume? The answer is the Boyle's Law you learned in high school science. In social science, the relationships between variables are less clear cut and harder to unearth. We may, for example, be interested in wealth as a variable, but how shall wealth be measured? Is it yearly income, yearly income averaged over a period of years, the value of one's savings or possessions? And wealth, compared to many of the other things social science would like to understand, is easy, reducible as it is to dollars and cents.

But, beyond the problem of measurement, social science must cope with sheer complexity. Our physical scientist colleagues may not agree, but we believe it is harder to do science on human affairs than on inanimate objects—so hard, in fact, that many people consider it impossible. We do not believe it is impossible, but we recognize that it is rare that any human or social relationship can be fully captured in terms of a single pair of variables, such as that between the pressure and volume of a gas. In social science, multiple relationships are the rule, not the exception.

For both of these reasons, the relations between social science variables are typically less than perfect. They are often weak and uncertain. But they are nevertheless real, and, with the right methods, they can be rigorously examined.

Correlation and regression are the primary ways to quantify weak, uncertain relationships. For that reason, the advances in correlational and regression analysis since late 19C have provided the impetus to social science. To understand what this kind of analysis is, we need to introduce the idea of a scatter diagram.

A Scatter Diagram

We left your male high school classmates lined up by height, with you looking down from the rafters. Now imagine another row of cards, laid out along the floor at a right angle to the ones for height. This set of cards has weights in pounds on them. Start with 90 pounds for the class shrimp, and in 10-pound increments, continue to add cards until you reach 250 pounds to make room for the class giant. Now ask your classmates to find the point on the floor that corresponds to both their height and weight (perhaps they'll insist on a grid of intersecting lines extending from the two rows of cards). When the traffic on the gym floor ceases, you will see something like the figure below.

A scatter diagram

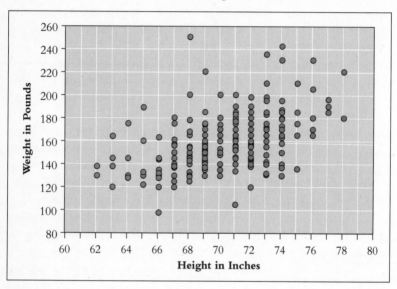

Some sort of relationship between height and weight is immediately obvious. The heaviest boys tend to be the tallest; the lightest ones the shortest, and most of them are intermediate in both height and weight. Equally obvious are the deviations from the trend that link height and weight. The stocky boys appear as points above the mass; the skinny ones as points below it. What we need now is some way to quantify both the trend and the exceptions.

Correlations and *regressions* accomplish this in different ways. But before we go on to discuss these terms, be assured that they are simple. Look at the scatter diagram. You can see just by looking at the dots that as height increases, so does weight, in an irregular way. Take a pencil (literally or imaginarily) and draw a straight, sloping line through the dots in a way that seems to you to best reflect this upward-sloping trend. Now continue to read, and see how well you have intuitively produced the basis for a correlation coefficient and a regression coefficient.

The Correlation Coefficient

Modern statistics provide more than one method for measuring correlation, but we confine ourselves to the one that is most important in both use and generality: the Pearson product-moment correlation coefficient (named after Karl Pearson, the English mathematician and biometrician). To get at this coefficient, let us first re-plot the graph of the class, replacing inches and pounds with standard scores. The variables are now expressed in general terms. Remember: *Any* set of measurements can be transformed similarly.

The next step on our way to the correlation coefficient is to apply a formula (here dispensed with) that, in effect, finds the best possible straight line passing through the cloud of points—the mathematically "best" version of the line you just drew by intuition.

What makes it the "best"? Any line is going to be "wrong" for most of the points. Take, for example, the boys who are 64 inches tall, and look at their weights. Any sloping straight line is going to cross somewhere in the middle of those weights, and will probably not cross any of the dots exactly. For boys 64 inches tall, you want the line to cross at the point where the total amount of the error is as small as possible. Taken over all the boys at all the heights, you want a straight line that makes the sum of all the errors for all the heights as small as possible. This "best-fit" is shown in the new version of the scatter diagram shown on page 470, where both height and weight are expressed in standard scores and the mathematical best-fitting line has been superimposed.

This scatter diagram has (partly by serendipity) many lessons to teach about how statistics relate to the real world. Here are a few of the main ones:

1. *Notice the many exceptions.* There is a statistically substantial relationship between height and weight, but, visually, the exceptions seem to dominate. So too with virtually all statistical relationships in the social sciences, most of which are much weaker than this one.

2. *Linear relationships don't always seem to fit very well.* The best-fit line looks as if it is too shallow—notice the tall boys, and see how consistently the line underpredicts how much they weigh. Given the information in the diagram, this might be an optical illusion—many of the dots in the dense part of the range are on top of each other, as it were, and thus it is impossible to grasp visually how the errors are adding up—but it could also be that the relationship between height and weight is not linear.

3. *Small samples have individual anomalies.* Before we jump to the conclusion that the straight line is not a good representation of the relation-

The "best-fit" line for a scatter diagram

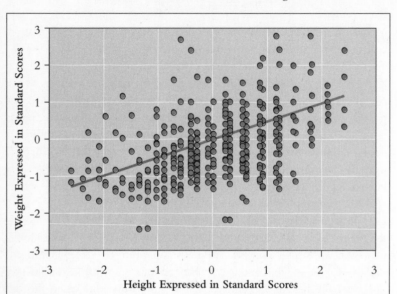

ship, we must remember that the sample consists of only 250 boys. An anomaly of this particular small sample is that one of the boys in the sample of 250 weighed 250 pounds. Eighteen-year-old boys are very rarely that heavy, judging from the entire NLSY sample, only one or two per 10,000. And yet one of those rarities happened to be picked up in a sample of 250. That's the way samples work.

4. *But small samples are also surprisingly accurate, despite their individual anomalies.* The relationship between height and weight shown by the sample of 250 18-year-old males is identical to the third decimal place with the relationship among all 6,068 males in the NLSY sample (the correlation coefficient is .501 in both cases). This is closer than we have any right to expect, but other random samples of only 250 generally produce correlations that are within a few hundredths of the one produced by the larger sample. (There are mathematics for figuring out what "generally" and "within a few hundredths" mean, but we needn't worry about them here.)

Bearing these basics in mind, let us go back to the sloping line in the figure above. Out of mathematical necessity, we know several things about it. First of all, it must pass through the intersection of the zeros (which, in standard scores, correspond to the averages) for both height and weight. Secondly, the line would have had exactly the same slope had height been the vertical axis and weight the horizontal one.

Finally, and most significant, the slope of the best-fitting line cannot be steeper than 1.0. The steepest possible best-fitting line, in other words, is one along which one unit of change in height is exactly matched by one unit of change in weight, clearly not the case in these data. Real data in the social sciences never yield a slope that steep. Note that while the line in the graph above goes uphill to the right, it would go downhill for pairs of variables that are negatively correlated.

We focus on the slope of the best-fitting line because it *is* the correlation coefficient—in this case, equal to .50, which is quite large by the standards of variables used by social scientists. The closer it gets to ±1.0, the stronger is the linear relationship between the standardized variables (the variables expressed as standard scores). When the two variables are mutually independent, the best-fitting line is horizontal; hence its slope is 0. Anything other than 0 signifies a relationship, albeit possibly a very weak one.

Whatever the correlation coefficient of a pair of variables is, squaring it yields another notable number. Squaring .50, for example, gives .25. The significance of the squared correlation is that it tells us how much the variation in weight would decrease if we could make everyone the same height, or vice versa. If all the boys in the class were the same height, the variation in their weights would decline by 25 percent. Perhaps, if you have been compelled to be around social scientists, you have heard the phrase "explains the variance," as in, for example, "Education explains 20 percent of the variance in income." That figure comes from the squared correlation.

In general, the squared correlation is a measure of the mutual redundancy in a pair of variables. If they are highly correlated, they are highly redundant in the sense that knowing the value of one of them places a narrow range of possibilities for the value of the other. If they are uncorrelated or only slightly correlated, knowing the value of one tells us nothing or little about the value of the other.

Regression Coefficients

Correlation assesses the strength of a relationship between variables. But we may want to know more about a relationship than merely its strength. We may want to know what it is. We may want to know how much of an increase in weight, for example, we should anticipate if we compare 66-inch boys with 73-inch boys. Such questions arise naturally if we are trying to explain a particular variable (e.g., annual income) in terms of the effects of another variable (e.g., educational level). How much income is another year of schooling worth? is just the sort of question that social scientists are always trying to answer.

The standard method for answering it is regression analysis, which has an intimate mathematical association with correlational analysis. If we had left the scatter diagram with its original axes—inches and pounds—instead of standardizing them, the slope of the best-fitting line would have been a regression coefficient, rather than a correlation coefficient. For example, the regression coefficient for weight regressed on height tells us that for each additional inch in height, we can expect an increase of 3.9 pounds. Or we could regress height on weight, and discover that each additional pound of weight is associated with an increase of .065 inches in height.

Multiple Regression

Multiple regression analysis is the main way that social science deals with the multiple relationships which are the rule in social science. To get a fix on multiple regression, let us return to the high school gym for the last time. Your classmates are still scattered about the floor. Now imagine a pole, erected at the intersection of 60 inches and 90 pounds, marked in inches from 18 inches to 50 inches. For some inscrutable reason, you would like to know the impact of both height and weight on a boy's waist size. Since imagination can defy gravity, you ask each boy to levitate until the soles of his shoes are at the elevation that reads on the pole at the waist size of his trousers. In general, the taller and heavier boys must rise the most, the shorter and slighter ones the least, and most boys, middling in height and weight, will have middling waist sizes as well. Multiple regression is a mathematical procedure for finding that plane, slicing through the space in the gym, that minimizes the aggregated distances (in this instance, along the waist size axis) between the bottoms of the boys' shoes and the plane.

The best-fitting plane will tilt upward toward heavy weights and tall heights. But it may tilt more along the pounds axis than along the inches axis or vice versa. It may tilt equally for each. The slope of the tilt along each of these axes is again a regression coefficient. With two variables predicting a third, as in this example, there are two coefficients. One of them tells us how much of an increase in trouser waist size is associated with a given increase in weight, holding height constant; the other, how much of an increase in trouser waist size is associated with a given increase in height, holding weight constant.

With two variables predicting a third, we reach the limit of visual imagination. But the principle of multiple regression can be extended to any number of variables. Income, for example, may be related, not just to education, but also to age, family background, IQ, personality, business conditions, region of the country, and so on. The mathematical procedures will yield coefficients for each of them, indicating again how much of a change in income can be anticipated for a given change in any particular variable, with all the others held constant.

CONSTRUCTION OF THE INVENTORIES AND THE EMINENCE INDEX

Here as in the main text, I use the word *inventory* to refer to a collection of persons who qualified as significant figures. This appendix describes how and why those collections were determined. To avoid confusion, I will use the word *roster* to refer to the entire list of persons mentioned by any source. *Category* refers to the twenty types of accomplishment (e.g., chemistry, literature) for which inventories were prepared.

TIME FRAME

The period covered by the rosters of persons is −800 to 1950. The cutoff at 1950 included all persons who had reached the age of 40 by 1950. Persons born after 1910 were included if their biographies included a major accomplishment that occurred prior to 1950.

ELIGIBILITY FOR AN INVENTORY

The rosters were compiled by listing everyone mentioned in a set of sources selected for each category. The table on the next page shows the total numbers of sources used to compile the inventories and the total number of persons who were identified in any of the sources.

Total Sources and Persons by Category

Inventory	Sources	Persons
The Sciences		
Astronomy	22	767
Biology	22	1,638
Chemistry	22	812
Earth Sciences	22	597
Physics	22	700
Mathematics	28	906
Medicine	20	1,080
Technology	19	1,139
Other*	22	137
Philosophy		
China	13	136
India	13	313
The West	14	885
Music (Western since 1200)	17	2,508
Visual Arts		
China	20	421
Japan	16	318
The West	13	2,248
Literature		
Arab world	15	209
China	15	548
India	12	353
Japan	12	258
The West	20	3,821
Total	**183†**	**19,794**

* Persons classified as "other" in the scientific categories could qualify as a significant figures, with an index score, for use in analyses where the scientific categories were aggregated.

† Some sources were used for more than one category.

The roster includes many people whose contributions were peripheral. Further, such people tended to be concentrated in the country of the source's author. For example, a history of literature prepared by an American is likely to mention more peripheral American writers than, say, peripheral German writers. The task was to develop selection rules for establishing a subset of persons who plausibly belonged in the analysis and had roughly equal probability of being identified regardless of their nationality.

An *encyclopedic source* was defined as one containing more than 50 percent of all the names in the roster. The *parent population* was defined as all persons in the roster who were mentioned in at least two sources, one of which had to be a non-encyclopedic source. The parent population was used to determine *qualifying sources,* defined as sources that (1) purported to contain broad and representative coverage of the field in question, and (2) contained a large enough number of names so that it would not artificially constrict the number of persons who might qualify as significant figures.

An examination of the distribution of coverage in the sources revealed that the lower end for well-regarded histories of a field had a cluster of sources that contained 18–20 percent of the parent population. A qualifying source was defined as one that contained 18 percent of all the persons in the parent population. The next table shows the number of qualifying sources and the size of the parent populations in each inventory.

Qualified Sources and Parent Populations

Inventory	No. of Qualified Sources	No. in Parent Population
The Sciences		
Astronomy	15	340
Biology	14	683
Chemistry	14	478
Earth Sciences	9	270
Physics	16	421
Mathematics	16	626
Medicine	13	540
Technology	15	848
Philosophy		
China	13	88
India	13	181
The West	14	473
Music (Western since 1200)	13	1,571
Visual Arts		
China	10	280
Japan	11	182
The West	12	1,232
Literature		
Arab world	15	91
China	12	304
India	12	115
Japan	11	182
The West	13	1,918
Total		**10,823**

The minimum number of qualifying sources for any inventory was 9, the maximum was 16, and the median was 13.

CLASSIFYING SIGNIFICANT
AND MAJOR FIGURES

The set of qualifying sources was then used to determine whether a person was classified as a significant or major figure.

The phrase *significant figures* is intended to denote those who are important enough to the development of a field that a well-versed student of that field is likely to be familiar with them. Significant figures are operationally defined as those mentioned in at least 50 percent of the qualified sources for which a given person was eligible (i.e., the source in question covered the period during which, and geographical area in which, the person in question was active).

Major figures is intended to capture the subset of people who are crucial to understanding the development of a field. The initial guideline for designating someone as a major figure was that he be mentioned in virtually any comprehensive history or biographical dictionary about a field. The operational definition of "virtually all" was at least 90 percent of the eligible sources.

Before implementing these criteria, another choice had to be made: Should all the qualifying sources be used, or a subset of them? The question arises because the coverage in the sources varied widely. The encyclopedic sources included 75 percent and upwards of the population of names, while even a large and comprehensive history might contain as few as 18 percent of the population. This variation was in itself useful—the encyclopedic sources were valuable in identifying the universe, while the more selective sources were valuable for providing the basis to discriminate between central and peripheral figures. But while the sources for every inventory represented a mix, the precise distribution of the mix was unavoidably different across inventories. Some inventories had several sources bunched in comprehensiveness of their coverage while others had sources that were more evenly distributed across the range.

It was clear that the persons identified as significant and major could vary depending on the distribution of the sources, but it was not obvious a priori how sensitive the results would be to differences in distributions. I therefore calculated the sets of significant and major figures that would be produced according to three alternative rules for including sources. The first alternative was to use all the qualified sources, which in effect meant sources with coverage of 18–96 percent of the population. The second alternative restricted the sources to those with coverage of 18–70 percent of the population, in effect eliminating discrepancies in the distributions caused by differences in the number of encyclopedic sources. The third alternative restricted the sources to ones with coverage of 18–50 percent of the population, thereby excluding the most encyclopedic histories and focusing on "normal" histories with extensive but by no means exhaustive coverage of the persons in a given field.

The next table shows the results of the exercise. Note that some of the inventories were augmented with additional sources after the exercise was conducted, hence the lack of correspondence with final totals of significant figures presented elsewhere.

Alternative Decision Rules for Selecting Significant Figures

| | Qualified Sources Used in the Selection | | |
| | All (18% to 96% Coverage) | Those with 18% to 70% Coverage | Those with 18% to 50% Coverage |
Inventory			
Science, Worldwide	701	714	653
Mathematics, Worldwide	196	216	164
Medicine, Worldwide	148	160	145
Technology, Worldwide	195	182	182
Philosophy, Chinese and Indian	76	55	49
Philosophy, Western	149	133	118
Literature, Chinese and Indian	107	106	88
Literature, Western	817	664	598
Art, Chinese	100	106	81
Art, Western	482	439	360
Music, Western	523	650	508
Total	3,672	3,365	2,946

A comparison of the first two columns of results shows that the elimination of the encyclopedic sources usually had little effect on the estimate of significant figures. The table does show a good reason not to use a highly restricted selection of sources (18–50 percent coverage): as the number of sources drops, an artifact increases—the artifact being a consequence of requiring that someone be mentioned in 50 percent of the sources. With, say, 15 sources versus 16 sources, the artifact is small. In the 15-source case, the de facto requirement for being designated a significant figure is not 50 percent but 53 percent. But if it is a difference between 7 and 8 sources, the de facto requirement in the 7-source case is 57 percent.

The next table shows the parallel results for the selection of major figures.

Alternative Decision Rules for Selecting Major Figures

Inventory	Qualified Sources Used in the Selection		
	All (18% to 96% Coverage)	Those with 18% to 70% Coverage	Those with 18% to 50% Coverage
Science, Worldwide	227	227	241
Mathematics, Worldwide	57	57	59
Medicine, Worldwide	32	32	33
Technology, Worldwide	29	29	29
Philosophy, Chinese and Indian	26	29	37
Philosophy, Western	40	40	41
Literature, Chinese and Indian	26	14	29
Literature, Western	250	251	255
Art, Chinese	59	60	81
Art, Western	156	188	192
Music, Western	180	271	274
Total	1,183	1,198	1,271

For the "major figures" category, the differences produced by the three decision rules are small, with the total of 1,183 for all qualified sources being fractionally smaller than the largest number (1,271) produced by the most restrictive decision rule. It is to be expected that the rule using the largest number of sources would produce the smallest number, given the criterion (at least all but one). The noteworthy feature of these results is how small the difference is. The statistical advantages of additional sources meant that, absent a reason not to, all qualified sources should be included.

CREATING THE INDEX SCORES

The categorizations of *significant* and *major* are based on whether a person is mentioned in a given source. The *index scores* are based on a quantitative measure of the amount of attention accorded to a person in a given source. Index scores were computed only for significant figures.

SUPPLEMENTAL SOURCES FOR COMPUTING THE INDEX SCORES

After the initial round of data collection, an inspection of the inventories revealed the desirability of augmenting the sources to provide better national or linguistic balance, or simply to permit finer discrimination within smaller subsets (e.g., computing index scores for the separate scientific disciplines instead of lumping them together). At this point, however, analysis of the existing datasets had revealed that they followed the Lotka phenomenon, and that ample data had already been collected for the basic task of discriminating significant figures from non-significant ones. It was further clear that when data for all the names in a major source were entered, most of that effort was wasted on people who would never enter into the analysis of significant figures. These later supplemental sources, as I shall term them, were therefore used to obtain data only on the persons classified as significant from the initial set of sources. The supplemental sources were not used to define the parent population or for any purpose other than to provide additional data for the computation of index scores.

Index Scores for the Inventories

The metric for scores from individual sources. Three methods were used to score the attention given to a person, with minor modifications to accommodate the peculiarities of a particular source. For a standard history, the measure usually consisted of the number of unique pages after a person's name in the index. For a chronology of events, the measure consisted of the total number of events involving that person. For biographical dictionaries, which are typically laid out in double columns, the measure was the amount of space devoted to a person's entry, expressed as the number of columns to the nearest tenth.

These different scores needed to be converted to a common metric that fairly represented their relative weights. "Relative weights" raises complicated issues. To be mentioned in 5 pages of a 400-page history has a different meaning from being mentioned in 5 pages in a multi-volume history totaling 3,000 pages. The first criterion for a scoring metric was therefore that it express the unusualness of a score relative to the coverage represented by a given source.

The most straightforward way to deal with this problem is to treat each source as a distribution that adds up to 1. Suppose, for example, that we are counting the number of page mentions in the index of a history of science, and that index includes 200 scientists with a total of 650 page references. The score of any one of those scientists is his number of mentions divided by 650. Scientists who are part of the inventory because they are mentioned in other sources, but not mentioned in this one, get a score of zero.

This procedure provides a natural weight within each source; however, it also gives a natural way of interpreting the overall index. The summed scores for the qualified sources used in computing the index scores for, say, mathematics, may be thought of as the total attention given to the world's qualifying mathematicians in that set of sources. Insofar as it may be demonstrated that those sources provide a representative estimate of the underlying "real" distribution of attention in the world's histories and chronologies for mathematics, it is easy to compute an endless variety of aggregations—the percentage of the distribution devoted to women mathematicians for example, or Scandinavian mathematicians, or mathematicians born from 1700 to 1750.

Treatment of missing data. Operationalizing the concept behind the index scores with a real set of sources means dealing with the problem of missing data. Data from any given source could be missing if that source covered a limited time period—1200 to 1930 in one case, nothing after 1900 in another, to take two examples. One option was to throw out all the sources that did not provide comprehensive coverage, but this would have meant discarding a great deal of valuable data. The *Dictionary of Scientific Biography*, for example, is probably the most authoritative single source of its kind, but it does not include anyone who was still living when it was compiled in the latter half of 20C, meaning that dozens of scientists who did important work in the first half of 20C have no entry in the *DoSB*. But to throw out the data for the 5,000+ scientists who were in the *DoSB* would be extravagant indeed.

I therefore chose to use sources with truncated chronological coverage, through the following procedures.

Establishing comparable denominators. The basis of the score for any person is a ratio: a measure of the attention given to that person divided by the total attention given to all persons in that volume. For any pair of sources with comprehensive chronological coverage (i.e., from −800 to 1950), the fact that the two sources went into different levels of detail, and thus had different denominators, is not a problem. On the contrary, it provides a natural weighting scheme, as discussed earlier: 5 pages devoted to a person in a history 400 pages long appropriately results a higher score (5/400=.0125) than five pages out of 3,000 (5/3,000=.0017).

In contrast, sources with different chronological scope create incomparable scores. Now suppose we are considering two science histories, Source *A* and Source *B*, each exactly 500 pages long. Source *A* is restricted to the period from 1885–1950 while Source *B* covers 1200–1930. Marie Curie is mentioned on 7 pages in each volume. This time, the fact that the two sources yield the same score (7/500=.014) is an artifact—one history covered 730 years of science, the other covered only 60. But, further complicating matters, the level of scientific activity in that particular 60 years was much higher than the level during the 730 years. How are the two scores to be made comparable?

In both cases, the objective is to calculate the best estimate of the denominator that the source would have had if it had covered the entire period from −800 to 1950. The method I used was first to conduct an analysis of events limited to sources that did have such comprehensive coverage. That analysis yielded the distribution of the activity in any given span of years. If, for example, the sources with comprehensive coverage from −800 to 1950 devoted 40 percent of their attention to the period from 1885–1950, the best estimate is that the 500 pages in Source *A* equal 40 percent of the total pages Source *A* would have had if it had covered the entire period. The imputed denominator for Source *A* is thus

$$\frac{500}{.4} = 1,250.$$

Imputed scores. Even after comparable denominators have been calculated, a problem remains. For example, Ptolemy had scores from all of the sources that covered his time period, but was missing data for one source that covered events from 1200–1930. This time, the task is to ask of the missing data, "What is the best estimate of the total score person *X* would have received if he had no missing scores?" The methods for imputing scores to missing data can be complex, but after experimenting with alternatives I chose a simple procedure that is intuitively understandable: Assume that Ptolemy's score from the missing source would be equal to the median of the observed scores (median rather than mean, to minimize the effect of an aberrant very high or very low score). Imputed scores were computed only for sources that covered a period including more than 75 percent of the total activity in that field, as determined from sources with universal coverage.

The metric for the index score. A raw score was computed by summing the comparable scores from the individual sources, then discarding the lowest and highest score, and taking the mean of the remaining scores. To be easily interpretable, the raw score needed to be transformed to a familiar range.

One useful conversion is to express the raw score as a percentage of the total content of that inventory. Thus, for example Nietzsche's raw score of .014 may be interpreted as meaning that in the set of sources used for the Western philosophy inventory, Nietzsche accounted for 1.4 percent of the discussion of significant figures in Western philosophy. This interpretation is only roughly accurate, because it is made up of a combination of measures of actual length of text devoted to a person (in sources such as biographical dictionaries) and index page citations (in histories), or numbers of events (in chronologies), which are not based on length of text, but it is a useful rough approximation for thinking about the results.

While useful for drawing some kinds of comparisons among figures, the raw score is not a good metric for comparing people across inventories, however. Philosophy happens to be a field that has been dominated by a few names. Literature, at the other extreme, is a field in which expert attention has been much more diffuse. Also, expressing the index score as a percentage of total expert attention is not directly interpretable. Is 1.4 percent a big number or a small one? We cannot tell without more information about the distribution.

In seeking a metric that is comparable across inventories, one consideration is that the raw scores are hyperbolically distributed (see Chapter 6). Thus metrics based on a normal distribution, such as IQ or SAT scales, are not appropriate. A second consideration is that any transformation of the raw scores must express the individual score relative to its distribution within the inventory, to preserve comparability across inventories. To satisfy both considerations, I chose a 100-point scale in which the upper bound is the raw index score of the top-rated person within that inventory, and a score represents the proportion of an individual's score to that top score. The algorithm for computing what I will subsequently refer to simply as the *index scores* is thus simply

$$\left[\frac{a_i}{A} \right] \cdot 100$$

where a_i is the raw index score of the ith subject, and A is the largest raw index score in the inventory.

Inventory-Specific Issues

For a few of the indexes, peculiarities specific to the nature of the inventory indicated modifications to the procedures described above.

Combining source types for the science and technology inventories. The science and technology sources consisted of three kinds: chronologies of important events, histories, and biographical dictionaries. The virtue of the chronologies is that they generally gave more complete enumerations of an individual's accomplishments; the virtue of the histories and biographical dictionaries was that they gave more space to the most important accomplishments. To prevent one type of source from dominating in the calculation of the index score, the sources were grouped—the chronological sources in one set and the history/biographical dictionary sources in the other—and given equal weight in the calculation of the index scores.

Index scores for the categories within science and technology. When computing index scores for the categories within the hard sciences (astronomy, biology, chemistry, earth sciences, and physics), it was necessary to add three steps to the normal procedures. First, sources had to be evaluated according to their coverage of the category. Thus a source eligible to determine significant figures for biology had to contain references to at least 18 percent of the people in the parent population for biology. Second, it was necessary to subdivide the events used to compute scores for the event-based sources. Thus, for example, Christiaan Huygens is represented by 18 events in the events-based sources. These consisted of 8 under the heading of physics, 2 under mathematics, 5 under engineering, and 3 under astronomy. In computing index scores for the physics inventory, only the events classified under physics were used. Third, the results from the events-based sources were used to weight the results from the biographical and historical sources. Continuing with the example of Huygens: Given his many interests, the measures of space devoted to him in the histories and biographical dictionaries were split as well, with part of it devoted to his achievements in astronomy, part to his achievements in physics, and so on. It was impractical to estimate the division of this textual discussion directly, given the number of sources and persons involved. To obtain a proxy measure, it was assumed that the division of textual discussion in the histories and biographical dictionaries was comparable to the division of attention in the six event-based sources with comprehensive coverage across time (Hellemans and Bunch 1988, Asimov 1994, Bruno 1997, Mount and List 1994, Adlington 1999, and Ochoa and Corey 1997). For Huygens, these six sources contained a total of 45 citations spread among the 18 events. Seventeen of these 45, or 38 percent, involved the events classified under physics. The scores for the histories and biographical dictionaries were thus multiplied by .38 for purposes of calculating their contribution to the physics index.

For the categories of mathematics, medicine, and technology, additional sources were added dealing specifically with those subjects. Procedures for computing index scores otherwise paralleled those for the categories in the hard sciences.

Western literature. Histories and biographical dictionaries of Western literature are much more affected by the language of the author than are sources for Western music art and visual art, and for an obvious reason. To repeat the point made in Chapter 5: A German can listen to a work by Vivaldi as easily as he can listen to one by Bach, and an Englishman can look at a painting by Monet as easily as one by Constable. The same cannot be said of literature, because of the language barrier. German historians of literature give markedly more attention to German authors than others, English historians to English authors, and so on. It is not just a matter of national chauvinism. Spanish historians of literature give more attention to New World literature written in Spanish than do historians of other nationalities.

Even if the sources consisted of one source per language group, a problem would remain: if none of the sources are from, say, Hungary, Hungarian literature is at a disadvantage compared to literatures written in French, German, Italian, Spanish, and English, each of which does have its own "advocate." The solution was to base the selection of significant figures and computation of the index scores on sources *not* written in the language of the literary figure. Thus Jane Austen's selection and index score are based exclusively on the attention paid to her in non-English sources, Racine's in non-French sources, and so on.

HOW MUCH CAN BE MADE OF THE INDEX SCORES?

Any time that social scientists start to attach numbers to qualitative concepts like *eminence*, three questions are bound to arise. Could someone assemble other data that would tell a different story? Couldn't another scoring system, apparently just as plausible, produce indexes that would tell a different story? Is there reason to think that these indexes reflect something important in the real world? The third question is discussed at length in Chapter 5. Some comments about the first two follow.

Could someone assemble other data that would tell a different story?

Underlying the question is the statistical concept of *reliability*. Applying it to the case of the indexes, think of each individual source as providing an imperfect measure of the construct called eminence. If it is true that any two of these sources really are imperfect measures of the same construct, they should be statistically correlated.

Now suppose we have not just two sources, but a dozen, all of which are tapping imperfectly into the same construct of eminence and all of which are intercorrelated. At this point we have achieved some safety in numbers—the average of all dozen of these sources is not much affected by any one of them, so any particular anomalous datum has little effect on the overall index score. But this still does not tell us the extent to which the index score is internally consistent—that it will look pretty much the same even if we had not happened to pick that exact set of sources.

The statistical measure of reliability that applies to this case is known as *Cronbach's alpha* (α) after its creator, psychometrician Lee Cronbach (Cronbach, 1951). It is technically defined as the square of the correlation between the index scores and the underlying factor, with *factor* referring to the statistical construct employed in factor analysis. To understand the sense of the statistic, supposing that we randomly select just half of our sources and compute an index based just on them. Suppose we then compute an index based on the other half of the sources. Then we compute the correlation coefficient between the two. The higher the correlation, the more confidence we can have that our index is reliable. But what if the way we chanced to split the sources into two just happened to be the split that produced a high correlation? It would be even better if we computed the correlation between every possible combination of split halves, then took the average of all those correlations. That number is roughly what is represented by α.

The table below shows α for the inventories in *Human Accomplishment*.

Reliability Coefficients by Inventory

Inventory	Cronbach's α
The Sciences	
Astronomy	.92
Biology	.88
Chemistry	.93
Earth Sciences	.81
Physics	.95
Mathematics	.93
Medicine	.87
Technology	.84
Philosophy	
China	.96
India	.93
The West	.96
Music (Western since 1200)	.97
Visual Arts	
China	.91
Japan	.93
The West	.95
Literature	
Arab world	.88
China	.89
India	.91
Japan	.86
The West	.95
Median	**.93**

A technical complication arises in computing α for the inventories in which imputed scores are used: the reliability coefficients are based in part not on the actual correlations among the sources, but the correlations after imputed data have been substituted for missing values. This would create a problem of interpretation if the use of imputed data inflated the correlations. Any such effect is so small as to be immaterial, however. Consider the inventory for which imputed data is by far the greatest potential problem, Western literature. Each source in the Western literature index uses imputed data for all the authors who wrote in the language of that source. This creates a situation in which hundreds of the 835 cases used to compute the bivariate correlations use imputed data.

The effects of this may be checked by computing pairwise correlations based only on cases for which both sources have valid scores (for example, the pairwise correlation between a French and English source omits all the cases involving French and English authors). When the pairwise correlation matrix is prepared for the Western literature sources, the mean correlation is .61. The mean correlation in the matrix used to calculate the reliability coefficient (which includes imputed data) is .63. In the other inventories, where imputed data are involved in many fewer cases than in the Western literature inventory, the differences (both plus and minus) are even smaller. The reliability coefficients presented in the table on page 448 are not exact for the inventories that employ imputed data, but there is no reason to think they are more than fractionally different from reliabilities that would have been obtained from sources with uniformly complete coverage.

The lowest reliability is for the earth sciences inventory (.81). Overall, 13 of the 20 inventories have reliabilities of .90 or higher, with a median reliability of .93. These very high reliabilities imply that similar results would be produced by any other set of histories, chronologies, and biographical dictionaries that meet basic criteria of representativeness and comprehensiveness.

Could another scoring system produce indexes that would tell a different story?

The choices to be made when creating an index make only a limited amount of difference in the outcomes. This is not to say that the right choices aren't important, but that the data used for these inventories' analysis are remarkably robust. The table below illustrates this point by showing what happens when we take the nine sources for the Western art index that had comprehensive coverage from −800 to 1950 and create index scores using five different methods. One (*percentage of source total*) is the procedure selected for use in the book. The second (*z scores*) is based on standard scores computed directly from the mean and standard deviation of a given source, a procedure that gives large weights to extreme scores. The third (*percentiles*) is based on percentiles, a procedure that gives no extra weight to extreme scores. The fourth (*binary*) throws away all the interval data within each measure and assigns "1" if a source mentions a given person, "0" if it does not, and adds up the eight 1s or 0s to reach a total. The fifth is the most unrealistic of all. It simply adds up the raw scores in their original metrics. The table shows two correlation matrixes: The correlations of the scores produced by the five methods, and the correlations of the rank orders produced by the five methods.

Correlations Among Five Different Scoring Methods for the Western Art Inventory

Correlation matrix for the interval scores (Pearson's *r*)

	1	2	3	4	5
1 Percentage of source total	1.00	1.00	0.81	0.72	1.00
2 z score	1.00	1.00	0.83	0.74	0.99
3 Percentile	0.81	0.83	1.00	0.97	0.81
4 Binary sum	0.72	0.74	0.97	1.00	0.72
5 Raw sum	1.00	0.99	0.81	0.72	1.00

Correlation matrix for the rank-ordered scores (Spearman's *Rho*)

	1	2	3	4	5
1 Percentage of source total	1.00	0.99	0.98	0.93	0.99
2 z score	0.99	1.00	0.98	0.93	0.98
3 Percentile	0.98	0.98	1.00	0.96	0.97
4 Binary sum	0.93	0.93	0.96	1.00	0.93
5 Raw sum	0.99	0.98	0.97	0.93	1.00

These five scoring methods, which are extremely different in their assumptions and in their arithmetic, produced correlations often approaching unity. Even the binary sum, a method that allows for only nine scores (0 through 8), had a correlation of at least .72 with the other four methods. Perhaps the most striking results come for the method that simply summed the raw scores. It had a correlation of .995 (rounding to 1.00 at two decimal places) with the 100-point score actually used in the book, and a correlation of .993 with the z-score method. Turning to the rank-order correlations, the lowest correlation in the matrix (between binary sum and raw sum) is .93. These results do not mean that all the effort to produce comparable scores across sources was a waste of time. But if the issue is the overall statistical results that would be yielded from the different scoring methods, the relevant observation is that almost any scoring system will produce similar results.

INVENTORY
SOURCES

The first requirement for any source used in an inventory was that it purport to be a balanced and comprehensive account of the category in question. Sources that were explicitly selective in their treatment of the subject were not used.

Sources were sought in the form of histories, chronologies of events, anthologies, encyclopedias, and biographical dictionaries. Ideally, a source would be used both to identify significant figures and to compute index scores, but often a source would be suitable for one of those uses but not both. For example, an anthology of literature could often be used to identify significant figures, because it purported to include selections from a comprehensive selection of authors, but it could not be used to compute index scores, because the length of a passage has no relationship to the eminence of the author (e.g., representative samples of a poet's poems tend to take up a lot less space than a representative sample of a novelist's prose). Other sources, often comparatively short histories of a field, were suitable for computing index scores, but contained such a small proportion of all the potentially significant figures that using them to identify significant figures would unduly restrict the population. After the significant figures had been identified, additional sources were used to expand the data for the computation of index scores. In such cases, data was entered only on those persons who were already in the inventories.

In the following lists, sources used to identify significant figures have a Q (for *qualifying source*) after their entry. Sources used to compute index scores have an I (for *index source*) after their entry.

PHILOSOPHY

Separate philosophy inventories were prepared for China, India, and the West. The Western philosophy inventory included thinkers from the Arab world. The philosophy inventories include persons who are described in the sources as philosophers or theologians. In the Chinese and Indian inventories, these categories include Confucian, Daoist, Hindu, and Buddhist thinkers. In the Western inventory, they include Christian and Islamic thinkers. People who were religious leaders, notably Jesus and Muhammad, were excluded, as were persons who were primarily ecclesiastics rather than theologians. The exception to this rule is Buddha, whose teachings I judge to be primarily philosophical rather than religious in content.

It should be remembered that the sources used to compile the inventory were exclusively ones about philosophy. Thus the attention paid to religious thinkers largely reflects the degree to which their work had impact on philosophical issues, not their importance to their respective religions.

The philosophy inventory excludes persons whose writings primarily involve economics, political science (as opposed to political philosophy), sociology, or psychology. Figures such as Adam Smith and Karl Marx are thus not part of the philosophy inventory. Political figures are part of the inventory only insofar as they also had impact on political philosophy. Thus Thomas Jefferson is part of the philosophy inventory while George Washington is not.

Philosophy sources with worldwide coverage

Encyclopedia Britannica. (China and India: I. Not used for the West)

T. Hayashi. 1971. *Tetsugaku Jiten (Encyclopedia of Philosophy)*. Tokyo: Heibon-sha. (India and the West: QI. Not used for China)

A. L. Kroeber. 1944. *Configurations of Culture Growth*. Berkeley, CA: University of California Press. (India and the West: QI. China: Q)

J.-F. Mattei, ed. 1998. *Les Oeuvres Philosophiques Dictionnaire*. 3 vols. Paris: Presses Universitaires de France. (India and the West: QI. China: Q)

J. C. Plott. 1989. *Global History of Philosophy*. 5 vols. Delhi: Motilal Banarsidass. (India and the West: QI. China: Q)

S. Radhakrishnan. 1953. *History of Philosophy Western and Eastern*. 2 vols. London: George Allen and Unwin. (QI)

B.-A. Scharfstein. 1998. *A Comparative History of World Philosophy: From the Upanishads to Kant*. Albany, NY: State University of New York Press. (QI)

N. Smart. 1999. *World Philosophies*. London: Routledge. (QI)

Philosophy sources specific to China

W. T. de Bary, W.-T. Chan, and B. Watson, eds. 1963. *Sources of Chinese Tradition*. New York: Columbia University Press. (QI)

W.-T. Chan. 1963. *A Source Book in Chinese Philosophy*. Princeton, NJ: Princeton University Press. (QI)

C. B. Day. 1962. *The Philosophers of China: Classical and Contemporary*. New York: Philosophical Library. (QI)

J. M. Koller. 1985. *Oriental Philosophies*. New York: Charles Scribner's Sons. (QI)

K. S. Murty. 1976. *Far Eastern Philosophies*. Mysore: Prasaranga. (QI)

L. C. Wu. 1986. *Fundamentals of Chinese Philosophy*. New York: University Press of America. (QI)

F. Yu-Lan. 1952–1953. *A History of Chinese Philosophy*. Princeton, NJ: Princeton University Press. (QI)

Philosophy sources specific to India

S. Chatterjee and D. Datta. 1968. *An Introduction to Indian Philosophy*. Calcutta: University of Calcutta. (QI)

D. Chattopadhyaya. 1964. *Indian Philosophy: A Popular Introduction*. New Delhi: People's Publishing House. (QI)

E. Frauwallner. 1974. *History of Indian Philosophy*. Delhi: Motilal Banarsidass. (Q)

R. King. 1999. *Indian Philosophy: An Introduction to Hindu and Buddhist Thought*. New York: Georgetown University Press. (QI)

J. M. Koller. 1985. *Oriental Philosophies*. New York: Charles Scribner's Sons. (QI)

K. H. Potter. 1970. *The Encyclopedia of Indian Philosophy*. 8 vols. New Delhi: American Institute of Indian Studies. (QI)

R. Puligandla. 1975. *Fundamentals of Indian Philosophy*. New York: Abingdon. (QI)

C. Sharma. 1960. *A Critical Survey of Indian Philosophy*. London: Rider & Company. (Q)

Philosophy sources specific to the West

M. Buhr and G. Klaus. 1970. *Philosophisches Wörterbuch*. 2 vols. Berlin. (QI)

F. Copleston. 1975. *A History of Philosophy*. 8 vols. Westminster, MD: Newman Press. (QI)

K. Jaspers. 1995. *The Great Philosophers*. 4 vols. New York: Harcourt, Brace & World. (Q)

A. Kenny. 1994. *The Oxford History of Western Philosophy*. Oxford: Oxford University Press. (QI)

W. I. Matson. 1987. *A New History of Philosophy*. 2 vols. New York: Harcourt Brace Jovanovich. (QI)

B. Russell. 1945. *A History of Western Philosophy*. New York: Simon & Schuster. (QI)

R. Tarnas. 1991. *The Passion of the Western Mind: Understanding the Ideas that Have Shaped Our World View*. New York: Ballantine Books. (QI)

THE LITERATURE INVENTORIES

Separate inventories were prepared for the Arab world, China, India, Japan, and the West. All the inventories include writers of fiction, drama, poetry, and nonfiction other than philosophy. Persons could qualify for both the philosophy and literature inventories if their writings included important work outside philosophy.

In the Arab world, China, and India, genres and styles of literature exhibited a sharp break between the traditional and modern eras. Many of the best sources covered only one period or the other. Even among those sources that covered the entire history, it was dubious that equal weight was given to both. It was feasible to identify significant figures on both sides of the break (when the criterion for qualification is based on the mention of an individual, regardless of length), but not to compute index scores across the break. Index scores for the Arab world and China are thus limited to significant figures who were active prior to 1800. For India, index scores are computed only for significant figures who were active prior to 1600. Because sources that covered literatures written in both Arabic and Persian seemed to indicate a tilt toward the former that was likely to be artifactual (i.e., the authors were treating Persian literature as secondary for reasons other than literary merit), I decided to limit index scores to authors who wrote in Arabic, although significant figures who wrote in Persian are identified.

Literature sources with worldwide coverage

Encyclopedia Britannica. (QI for the Arab world and India, I for China and Japan. Not used for the West.)

P. Gioan. 1961. *Histoire Générale des Littératures*. 3 vols. Paris: Librairie Aristide Quillet. (Q for the Arab world; QI for the others)

R. Goring. 1994. *Larousse Dictionary of Writers*. Edinburgh: Larousse. (QI for India and the West; Q for the Arab world and Japan. Not used for China)

F. J. B. Jansen, H. Stangerup, and O.P.H. Traustedt. 1974. *Verdens Litteratur Historie.* 12 vols. Copenhagen: Politikens Forlag. (QI for all)

A. L. Kroeber. 1944. *Configurations of Culture Growth.* Berkeley, CA: University of California Press. (Q for the West. QI for all the others)

R. Queneau. 1958. *Histoire des Littératures.* 3 vols. Paris: Gallimard. (Q for the Arab world, I for China and the West, QI for India)

M. de Riquer and J.M. Valverde. 1984. *Historia de la Literatura Universal.* 10 vols. (Q for the Arab world. QI for all the others.)

Literature sources specific to the Arab world

J.-M. Abd-el-Jalil. 1943. *Histoire de la Littérature Arabe.* St.-Germain: G.-P. Maisonneuve. (QI)

R. Allen. 2000. *An Introduction to Arabic Literature.* Cambridge, U.K.: Cambridge University Press. (QI)

F. F. Arbuthnot. 1890. *Arabic Authors: A Manual of Arabian History and Literature.* London: Darf Publishers. (Q)

H. A. R. Gibb. 1963. *Arabic Literature: An Introduction.* London: Oxford University Press. (QI)

C. Huart. 1903. *A History of Arab Literature.* London: William Heinemann. (QI)

R. A. Nicholson. 1941. *A Literary History of the Arabs.* Cambridge, U.K.: Cambridge University Press. (QI)

J. Vernet. 1967. *Literatura Árabe.* Barcelona: Editorial Labor, SA. (QI)

G. Wiet. 1966. *Introduction a la Littérature Arabe.* Paris: G.-P. Maissonneuve et Larose. (QI)

Literature sources specific to China

C. Birch. 1972. *Anthology of Chinese Literature.* 2 vols. New York: Grove Press. (Q)

W. Idema and L. Haft. 1997. *A Guide to Chinese Literature.* Ann Arbor: Center for Chinese Studies, University of Michigan. (QI)

O. Kaltenmark. 1948. *La Littérature Chinoise.* Paris: Presses Universitaires de France.

W. McNaughton. 1974. *Chinese Literature: An Anthology from the Earliest Times to the Present Day.* Rutland, VT: Charles E. Tuttle Co. (Q)

L. Ming. 1964. *A History of Chinese Literature.* New York: John Day Co. (QI)

S. Owen. 1996. *An Anthology of Chinese Literature: Beginnings to 1911.* New York: W. W. Norton & Co. (Q)

C. Shou-Yi. 1961. *Chinese Literature: A Historical Introduction.* New York: Ronald Press Co. (QI)

L. Wu-Chi. 1966. *An Introduction to Chinese Literature*. Bloomington: Indiana University Press. (QI)

Literature sources specific to India

S. C. Banerji. 1989. *A Companion to Sanskrit Literature*. Delhi: Motilal Banarsidass. (QI)

K. Chaitanya. 1975. *A New History of Sanskrit Literature*. Westport, CT: Greenwood Press. (QI)

H. H. Gowen. 1968. *A History of Indian Literature*. New York: Greenwood Press. (QI)

L. Renou. 1951. *Les Littératures de l'Inde*. Paris: Presses Universitaires de France. (QI)

M. Winternitz. 1933. *A History of Indian Literature*. 2 vols. New York: Russell & Russell. (QI)

Literature sources specific to Japan

J. I. Bryan. 1970. *The Literature of Japan*. Port Washington, NY: Kennikat Press.

S. Kato. 1997. *A History of Japanese Literature from the Man'yoshu to Modern Times*. Richmond, UK: Japan Library.

D. Keene. 1993. *Seeds in the Heart: Japanese Literature from Earliest Times to the Late Sixteenth Century*. New York: Henry Holt & Co.

D. Keene. 1976. *World Within Walls: Japanese Literature of the Pre-Modern Era, 1600–1867*. New York: Grove Press.

D. Keene. 1984. *Dawn to the West: Japanese Literature of the Modern Era*. New York: Holt, Rinehart and Winston.

J. Konishi. 1991. *A History of Japanese Literature*. 3 vols. Princeton, NJ: Princeton University Press.

H. Sen'ichi. *Japanese Literature: A Historical Outline*. Tucson: University of Arizona Press.

Literature sources specific to the West

W. R. Benét, ed. *The Reader's Encyclopedia*. 2nd edition. New York: Thomas Y. Crowell. (I)

H. Bloom. 1994. *The Western Canon: The Books and School of the Ages*. New York: Harcourt Brace & Company. (Q)

A. Burgio. 1963. *Storia della Litteratura*. 2 vols. Milan: Vallerdi. (QI)

O. M. Carpeaux. 1982. *História da Literatura Ocidental.* 8 vols. Rio de Janeiro: Ediçöes o Cruzeiro. (QI)

G. Díaz-Plaja. 1965. *La Litteratura Universal.* Barcelona: Editiones Danae. (I)

A. Eggebrecht. 1964. *Epochen der Weltliteratur.* Gütersloh: C. Bertelsmann Verlag. (Q)

E. Laaths. 1953. *Geschichte der Weltliteratur.* Deutscher Bucherbund. (QI)

J. Paxton and S. Fairfield. 1980. *Calendar of Creative Man.* New York: Facts on File. (Q)

G. Wilpert. 1963. *Lexikon der Weltliteratur.* 2 vols. Stuttgart: Alfred Kröner Verlag. (QI)

THE ART INVENTORIES

The Western art inventory is limited to painters and sculptors. The Chinese art inventory is limited to painters. The Japanese art inventory includes painters, sculptors, and potters. As in the case of literature, index scores could not be computed across the entire time span for some inventories. In the case of the West, the lack of surviving work artificially limited the attention given to artists in ancient Greece and Rome. Index scores are limited to artists active from 1200–1950. In the case of China, the shift in genres and styles after the decline of classical China made comparisons between traditional and modern Chinese artists problematic. Index scores are limited to artists active prior to 1800.

Art sources with worldwide coverage

Encyclopedia Britannica. (QI for Japan, Q for China, not used for the West.)

M. Akiyama. 1985. *Shincho Sekai Bijutsu Jiten (Shincho World Art Dictionary).* Tokyo: Shincho-sha. (Q for all three arts inventories.)

H. de la Croix and R.G. Tansey. 1975. *Gardner's Art Through the Ages.* New York: Harcourt Brace Jovanovich. Original edition, 1926. (QI for the West. I for China and Japan.)

L. Gowing. 1995. *Biographical Dictionary of Artists.* London: Andromeda Oxford Ltd. (QI for the West, I for China, Q for Japan)

A. L. Kroeber. 1944. *Configurations of Culture Growth.* Berkeley, CA: University of California Press. (Q for Japan and the West. Not used for China.)

J. Turner. 1996. *Dictionary of Art.* 34 vols. New York: Grove. (QI for all three art inventories.)

Art sources specific to China

L. Ashton and B. Gray. 1953. *Chinese Art*. New York: Beechhurst Press. (I)

L. Binyon. 1959. *Painting in the Far East*. New York: Dover. (QI)

J. Burling and A.H. Burling. 1953. *Chinese Art*. New York: Studio Publications, Inc. (QI)

J. Cahill. 1960. *Chinese Painting*. Skira. (QI)

D. O. Carter. *Four Thousand Years of China's Art*. New York: Ronald Press Co. (I)

C. Clunas. 1997. *Art in China*. Oxford: Oxford University Press. (QI)

W. Cohn. 1950. *Chinese Painting*. New York: Phaidon. (QI)

T. Froncek. 1969. *Arts of China*. New York: American Heritage Publishers (QI)

M. Loehr. 1980. *The Great Painters of China*. New York: Harper & Row. (QI)

W. Speiser. 1959. *China: Geist und Gesellschaft*. Baden-Baden: Holle & Co. (I)

M. Sullivan. 1999. *The Arts of China*. Berkeley, CA: University of California Press. (QI)

W. Willetts. 1965. *Foundations of Chinese Art from Neolithic Pottery to Modern Architecture*. New York: McGraw-Hill. (I)

Y. Xin et al., eds. 1997. *Three Thousand Years of Chinese Painting*. New Haven, CT: Yale University Press. (QI)

Art sources specific to Japan

R. Bird. 1980. *General Index*. 31 vols. Tokyo: Heibonsha. (QI)

D. Elisseeff and V. Elisseeff. 1985. *Art of Japan*. New York: Harry N. Abrams. (QI)

M. Ishizawa et al. 1982. *The Heritage of Japanese Art*. Tokyo: Kodansha International Ltd. (QI)

J. E. Kidder. 1981. *The Art of Japan*. New York: Park Lane. (QI)

P. Mason. 1993. *History of Japanese Art*. Englewood Cliffs, NJ: Harry N. Abrams. (QI)

H. Munsterberg. 1957. *The Arts of Japan: An Illustrated History*. Rutland, VT: Charles E. Tuttle Co. (QI)

S. Noma. 1966. *The Arts of Japan*. 2 vols. Tokyo: Kodansha International Ltd. (QI)

R. T. Paine and A. Soper. 1955. *The Art and Architecture of Japan*. New York: Penguin. (QI)

J. Stanley-Baker. 1984. *Japanese Art*. London: Thames and Hudson. (QI)

P. C. Swann. 1966. *The Art of Japan from the Jomon to the Tokugawa Period*. New York: Crown. (QI)

T. N. Museum. 1952. *Pageant of Japanese Art: Painting*. 2 vols. Tokyo: Toto Shuppan. (QI)

Art sources specific to the West

E. H. Gombrich. 1995. *The Story of Art*. London: Phaidon. (I)

H. Honour and J. Fleming. 1982. *The Visual Arts: A History*. Englewood Cliffs, NJ: Prentice-Hall. (QI)

Instituto Per La Collaborazione Culturale. 1959. *Enciclopedia Universale Dell'Arte (trans.)*. 17 vols. New York: McGraw Hill. (QI)

H. W. Janson and A. F. Janson. 1997. *History of Art*. New York: Harry N. Abrams, Inc. (QI)

J. Marceau. 1998. *Art: A World History*. New York: DK Publishing. (QI)

S. Sproccati. 1991. *A Guide to Art*. Milan: Arnoldo Mondadori. (QI)

W. Stadler. 1990. *Lexikon der Kunst*. 12 vols. Basel: Herder Freiburg. (QI)

M. Stokstad. 1999. *Art History*. 2 vols. New York: Harry N. Abrams, Inc. (QI)

J. Vinson. 1990. *International Dictionary of Art and Artists*. London: St. James Press. (Q)

THE MUSIC INDEX

The music index covers only the West. It includes both composers and musical theorists from 1200 to 1950. Performers who composed are included if the major portion of their reputation rests on their compositions. The sources were as follows:

G. Abraham. 1979. *The Concise Oxford History of Music*. Oxford: Oxford University Press. (QI)

L. Alberti. 1968. *Musica Nei Secoli*. Milan: CEAM. (I)

M.-C. Beltrando-Patier. 1998. *Histoire de la Musique*. Paris: Larousse. (QI)

E. Borroff. 1990. *Music in Europe and the United States*. New York: Ardsley House. (QI)

C. Dahlhaus and M. Eggebrecht. 1978. *Brockhaus Riemann Musiklexikon*. 2 vols. Mainz: F. A. Brockhaus. (QI)

D. J. Grout and C.V. Palisca. 1996. *A History of Western Music*. New York: W.W. Norton & Co. (QI)

P. Hamburger. 1966. *Musikens Historie*. Copenhagen: Aschehoug Dansk Forlag. (QI)

A. Harman and W. Mellers. 1962. *Man and His Music: The Story of Musical Experience in the West*. London: Barrie and Rockliff. (QI)

C. Headington. 1980. *The Bodley Head History of Western Music*. London: Bodley Head. (I)

K. Honolka et al. 1976. *Weltgeschichte der Musik*. Eltville am Rhein, Germany: Rheingauer Verlagsgesellschaft. (QI)

M. Kennedy. 1994. *The Oxford Dictionary of Music*. Oxford: Oxford University Press. (I)

A. L. Kroeber. 1944. *Configurations of Culture Growth*. Berkeley, CA: University of California Press. (Q)

P. H. Lang. 1997. *Music in Western Civilization*. New York: W.W. Norton & Co. Original edition, 1941. (QI)

D. M. Randel. 1996. *The Harvard Biographical Dictionary of Music*. Cambridge, MA: Belknap Press of Harvard University Press. (QI)

L. Rebatet. 1969. *Une Histoire de la Musique*. Paris: Robert Laffont & Raymond Bourgine. (QI)

O. Thompson and B. Bohle. 1938. *The International Cyclopedia of Music and Musicians*. New York: Dodd, Mead, and Co. (QI)

É. Vuillermoz. 1973. *Histoire de la Musique*. Paris: Fayard. (I)

THE SCIENTIFIC INVENTORIES

Separate inventories were prepared for astronomy, biology, chemistry, earth sciences, physics, mathematics, medicine, and technology. The division of individuals into these categories posed problems. Many physicists and astronomers also made important original contributions to mathematics; many scientists directly contributed to applied technology; many of the key medical discoveries were made by biologists.

Accordingly, a person was eligible for more than one inventory, but he had to qualify based on accomplishments specific to the field in question. To minimize double-counting of accomplishments, two steps were taken. For sources that enumerated events, the count of events was restricted to the field in question (e.g., only events classified as mathematics were used for the mathematics inventory). Sources that were scored on length of treatment (e.g., number of pages in an index, number of columns in a biographical dictionary) were restricted to those that dealt with the field in question (e.g., Isaac Newton's score in the mathematics index is based on references to his work in mathematics).

The following is a list of all the sources used in preparing the scientific inventories, listed under four headings: (1) general sources that could be used for several inventories, depending on the specifics of their coverage (a general source might meet the coverage requirement for physics but not for the earth sciences, for example), (2) mathematic sources, (3) medical sources, and (4) technology sources. These lists are followed by a table showing the use of each source for each inventory.

General sources

F. Adlington and C. Humphries. 1999. *Philip's Science and Technology: People, Dates, and Events.* London: George Philip Ltd.

I. Asimov. 1994. *Asimov's Chronology of Science and Discovery.* New York: HarperCollins.

L. C. Bruno. 1997. *Science and Technology Firsts.* Detroit: Gale.

C. C. Gillespie, ed. 1980–1990. *Dictionary of Scientific Biography.* 18 vols. New York: Charles Scribner's Sons.

B. Grun. 1991. *The Timetables of History* (based on Werner Stein's *Kulturfahrplan*). New York: Touchstone.

A. Hellemans and B. Bunch. 1988. *The Timetables of Science: A Chronology of the Most Important People and Events in the History of Science.* New York: Touchstone.

A. L. Kroeber. 1944. *Configurations of Culture Growth.* Berkeley, CA: University of California Press.

F. N. Magill. 1991. *Great Events from History II: Science and Technology Series.* 5 vols. Pasadena, CA: Salem Press.

E. Marcorini. 1975. *Scienza e tecnica.* 2 vols. Milan: Arnoldo Mondadori.

S. F. Mason. 1962. *A History of the Sciences.* New York: Macmillan.

J. E. I. McClellan and H. Dorn. 1999. *Science and Technology in World History: An Introduction.* Baltimore, MD: Johns Hopkins University Press.

E. Mount and B.A. List. 1994. *Milestones in Science and Technology: The Ready Reference Guide to Discoveries, Inventions, and Facts.* Phoenix, AZ: Oryx Press.

H. Muir. 1994. *Larousse Dictionary of Scientists.* Edinburgh: Larousse.

G. Ochoa and M. Corey. 1997. *The Wilson Chronology of Science and Technology.* New York: H. W. Wilson Company.

C. L. Parkinson. 1986. *Breakthroughs: A Chronology of Great Achievements in Science and Mathematics.* Boston: G. K. Hall & Co.

R. Porter and M. Ogilvie, eds. 2000. *The Biographical Dictionary of Scientists.* 2 vols. New York: Oxford University Press.

C. A. Ronan. 1983. *The Cambridge Illustrated History of the World's Science.* Cambridge, U.K.: Cambridge University Press.

M. Serres. 1989. *Élements d'Histoire des Science.* Paris: Bordas.

R. Taton. 1964. *Histoire Générale des Sciences.* 4 vols. Paris: Presses Universitaires de France.

P. Whitfield. 1999. *Landmarks in Western Science*. New York: Routledge.

H. Wussing. 1983. *Geschichte der Naturwissenschaften*. Cologne, Germany: Aulis Verlag Deubner & Co.

Mathematics

G. E. Owen. 1971. *The Universe of the Mind*. Baltimore, MD: Johns Hopkins Press.

H. Eves. 1990. *An Introduction to the History of Mathematics*. Philadelphia: Saunders College Publishing.

J. Gullberg. 1997. *Mathematics from the Birth of Numbers*. New York: WW Norton.

L. Hogben. 1960. *Mathematics in the Making*. London: Macdonald.

M. Kline. 1972. *Mathematical Thought from Ancient to Modern Times*. New York: Oxford University Press.

C. B. Boyer and U.C. Merzbach. 1989. *A History of Mathematics*. New York: John Wiley & Sons.

F. J. Swetz. 1994. *From Five Fingers to Infinity*. Chicago: Open Court.

Medicine

J. Bendiner and E. Bendiner. 1990. *Biographical Dictionary of Medicine*. New York: Facts on File.

R. Porter. 1996. *The Cambridge Illustrated History of Medicine*. Cambridge, U.K.: Cambridge University Press.

R. Porter. 1997. *The Greatest Benefit to Mankind*. New York: W. W. Norton.

L. N. Magner. 1992. *A History of Medicine*. New York: Marcel Dekker, Inc.

R. E. McGrew. 1985. *Encyclopedia of Medical History*. New York: McGraw-Hill.

Technology

T. I. Williams. 1987. *The History of Invention: From Stone Axes to Silicon Chips*. London: MacDonald.

D. Cardwell. 1995. *The Norton History of Technology*. New York: W. W. Norton & Company.

C. J. Singer et al. 1984. *A History of Technology*. 8 vols. Oxford: Clarendon Press.

B. Gille. 1978. *Histoire des Techniques*. 2 vols. Paris: Editions Gallimard.

Sources for the Scientific Inventories

	Astronomy	Biology	Chemistry	Earth Sciences	Physics	Mathematics	Medicine	Technology
Adlington	QI	QI	QI		QI		QI	QI
Asimov	QI	QI	QI		QI		I	QI
Bruno	QI	QI	QI	QI	QI	QI	QI	QI
Gillespie	QI	QI	QI	QI	QI	QI	QI	QI
Grun		Q	Q		Q	I	I	QI
Hellemans	QI	QI	QI	QI	QI	QI	QI	QI
Kroeber	Q				Q	Q		
Magill	Q	Q	Q		Q		Q	Q
Marcorini	QI	QI	QI	QI	QI	QI	QI	QI
Mason	I	I	I	I	I	I		
Mount	QI	QI	QI	QI	QI		QI	QI
Muir	Q	Q	Q	Q	Q	Q		
Ochoa	QI	QI	QI	QI	QI	QI	QI	QI
Parkinson	Q	Q	Q	Q	Q	QI	I	I
Porter 2000	QI	QI	QI	QI	QI	QI	I	QI
Ronan	QI	I	I		QI	I		
Serres		I	I		QI	QI		
Taton	I	I	I	I	I	I	I	I
Whitfield	I	I			I			
Wussing	QI	QI	QI	I	QI	QI		I
Boyer						QI		
Eves						QI		
Gullberg						QI		
Kline						Q		
Swetz						QI		
Bendiner							QI	
Porter 1996							QI	
Porter 1997							QI	
Magner							QI	
McGrew							QI	
Cardwell								QI
Gille								QI
Singer								QI
Williams								QI

Note: Sources used to identify significant figures have a Q (for qualifying source) after their entry. Sources used to compute index scores have an I (for index source) after their entry.

GEOGRAPHIC AND POPULATION DATA

A number of issues in the text depend on locating the significant figures geographically and on the estimation of population in various geographic units during the period 1400–1950. This appendix describes the procedures used for collecting and coding those data.

LOCATING THE SIGNIFICANT FIGURES
GEOGRAPHICALLY

The first problem is to establish rules for coding geographic location. Chopin's father was French, his mother was Polish. He was raised in Warsaw but spent his professional life in Paris. Shall we assign Chopin to Warsaw or Paris? A more prosaic example of a type common among the significant figures is Louis Pasteur, who was born and raised in Dôle, a town in eastern France, grew up in an even smaller town nearby, and spent his professional career in Strasbourg, Lille, and Paris, with occasional sojourns elsewhere. Where shall we place Pasteur?

I dealt with this confusion by recording two locations for each significant figure: *origin*, defined as the place where he spent his childhood (or the greater part of it, if he moved), and *workplace*, defined as the region in which he spent the most productive part of his career.

Both choices sometimes involved judgment calls. In the case of Pasteur, his workplace had to be chosen on the basis of both the time that Pasteur spent in his various homes and the importance of the work done at various places, with Paris ultimately winning out. In a few cases, a specific origin could not be assigned, either because data were not available for the more obscure significant figures, or because they had been born abroad to diplomats or soldiers. In such cases, significant figures were assigned the nationality of their parents.

In the case of immigration, the choice of workplace was based on a judgment of where the significant figure came to prominence. Thus the workplace of many of the Jews who fled Nazi Germany remains the German region where their careers took shape, even if they continued to make major contributions after emigrating to another country. In contrast, a young scientist who completed his training in Germany and worked there for a few years, but who made his mark after immigrating, is assigned a workplace in his adopted country.

Unassignable workplaces arose more frequently than unassignable origins. A substantial number of significant figures moved around so much during the course of their careers that it was impossible to assign just one place to them. A few, mostly composers, were so peripatetic that it was impossible to assign even a country to their workplace, let alone a region, and their workplace was defined simply as *Europe*.

When data were missing (as opposed to unassignable), regions were imputed based on the observed distribution within a country. For example, if data were missing for six significant figures of French origin and 31.7 percent of French significant figures with known origin came from Paris, then the algorithm for imputing origins would give each of those six figures a probability of .317 of being assigned to Paris, and correspondingly appropriate probabilities would be given for all other places of origin of the significant figures with known origins. Imputed codes are (obviously) to be used only for purposes of statistical analysis, not for discussions of specific cases.

The next consideration was how precisely to define *location*. Data were entered using the name of the exact city, town, or village (or nearest one in the case of significant figures who grew up on farms). After the inventories of significant figures had been established, I recoded these raw entries into a more manageable set on the basis of the following guidelines:

If the location was a major city or a well-known place (e.g., Bruges, Heidelberg), even if small, the precise location was retained.

If the location was an anonymous village, town, or small city, the location was replaced with the name of the region.

European regions were defined on a country-by-country basis—134 of them in all. The choices attempted to conform to units that have well-established historical identities. This left many arbitrary choices to be made. Italy and Germany could have been divided into still smaller pieces based on the old principalities, for example, but the point of the exercise was to break Europe into units that enable us to see variation within countries. For Germany, I used the borders of the current German states and then divided the lands that are now part of Poland into a reconstruction of the former Silesia, Posen/Pomerania, West Prussia, and East Prussia. For Italy, I followed the regions shown for preunification Italy in Barraclough 1993: 213. When small well-established regions had no nontrivial statistical role to play, there was no point in going to the smallest possible unit. Thus I combined the traditional Austrian regions of Upper Austria and Styria into a region called Mid-Austria while the Tyrol, Carinthia, and Salzburg were combined into a region called Southwest Austria. The regions in Hungary, Norway, Sweden, and Finland are similarly ad hoc.

The map on the following page shows the approximate boundaries (they were drawn by hand) for the regions in Western Europe. Inaccuracies in the boundaries on the map had no effect on the accuracy of the coding of place names into regions, which was based on their location as shown in standard world atlases. Russia is not shown on the map. The regions used to code Russian significant figures were Archangel, the Don region, Estonia, Georgia, Kazan, Kharkov, Kiev region, Kostroma, Latvia, Lithuania, Minsk, Moscow region, Nizhni Novgorod, Novgorod, Odessa, Orel, Orenbur, Podolia, Poltava, Pskov, Ryazan, Saratov, Siberia, Smolensk region, Tambov, Tula, Vitebsk, Vladimir, and Voronezh. Other regions not shown on the map are North Norway, North Sweden, North and South Finland, Bulgaria, Greece, Macedonia, and Romania. Luxemburg was coded with Belgium.

EUROPEAN CITIES AND REGIONS
USED FOR CODING ORIGINS AND WORKPLACE

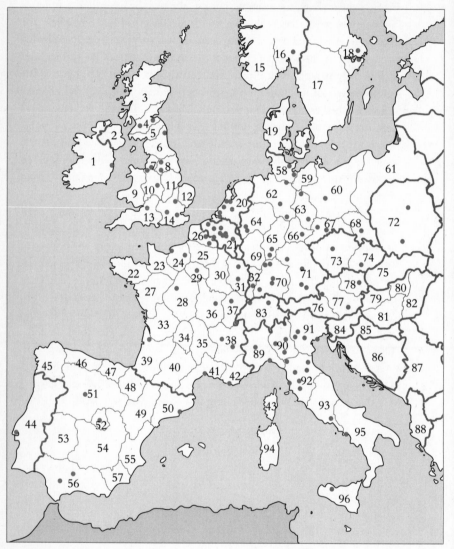

1. S Ireland
2. N Ireland
3. Scottish Highlands
4. Scottish Lowlands
5. S Uplands
6. N England
7. NW England
8. Humber
9. Wales
10. W Midlands
11. E Midlands
12. E Anglia
13. SW England
14. SE England
15. SW Norway
16. SE Norway
17. S Sweden
18. E Sweden
19. Denmark
20. Netherlands
21. Belgium
22. Bretagne
23. Basse-Normandie
24. Haute-Normandie
25. Picardie
26. Nord-Pas-de-Calais
27. Pays de la Loire
28. Centre
29. Île-de-France
30. Champagne-
    Ardenne
31. Lorraine
32. Alsace
33. Poitou-Charentes

34. Limousin
35. Auvergne
36. Bourgogne
37. Franche-Comté
38. Rhône-Alpes
39. Aquitaine
40. Midi-Pyrénées
41. Languedoc-
    Roussillon
42. Provence-Alpes-
    Côte d'Azur
43. Corsica
44. Portugal
45. Galicia
46. Asturias-Cantabria
47. Basque Country
48. Navarra
49. Aragon
51. Catalonia
51. Castilla y León
52. Madrid
53. Extremadura
54. Castilla-La Mancha
55. Valencia
56. Andalusia
57. Murcia
58. Schleswig-Holstein
59. Mecklenburg
60. Brandenburg
61. East Prussia
62. Lower Saxony
63. Saxony-Anhalt
64. N Rhine Westphalia
65. Hesse

66. Thuringia
67. Saxony
68. Silesia
69. Rhineland-Palatinate
70. Baden-Württemberg
71. Bavaria
72. Poland
73. Bohemia
74. Moravia
75. Slovakia
76. SW Austria
77. Mid Austria
78. Lower Austria
79. NW Hungary
80. SW Hungary
81. N Central Hungary
82. E Hungary
83. Switzerland
84. Slovenia
85. Croatia
86. Bosnia-Herzegovina
87. Yugoslavia
88. Albania
89. Piedmont
90. Lombardy
91. Venetia
92. Tuscany
93. Papal States
94. Sardinia
95. Naples
96. Sicily
97. Albania

The dots on the map indicate the 121 European cities and towns that qualified for their own code. They were as follow:

* *Austria*: Graz, Salzburg, Vienna.

* *Belgium*: Antwerp, Bruges, Brussels, Ghent, Ixelles, Jehay-Bodegnee, Liège, Louvain, Namur, St.-Amand, Tournai.

* *Britain*: Birmingham, Bradford, Bristol, Cambridge, Durham, Leeds, Liverpool, London, Manchester, Newcastle-upon-Tyne, Edinburgh, Glasgow, Belfast, Dublin.

* *Czech Republic*: Prague, Brno.

* *Denmark*: Copenhagen, Åarhus.

* *France*: Besançon, Bordeaux, Grenoble, Le Havre, Lille, Lyon, Marseilles, Metz, Montpellier, Nancy, Paris, Rouen, Strasbourg , Tours, Valenciennes.

* *Finland*: Helsinki.

* *Germany*: Augsburg, Berlin, Bonn, Breslau, Cologne, Danzig, Darmstadt, Dresden, Düsseldorf, Frankfurt, Freiberg, Göttingen, Halle, Hamburg, Königsberg, Leipzig, Lübeck, Magdeburg, Mannheim, Munich, Nuremburg, Stuttgart, Tübingen, Wittenberg, Wurzburg.

* *Greece*: Athens.

* *Hungary*: Budapest.

* *Italy*: Bologna, Brescia, Cremona, Ferrara, Naples, Padua, Palermo, Parma, Piacenza, Pisa, Rome, Siena, Turin, Venice, Verona, Vicenza.

* *Norway*: Bergen, Oslo.

* *Netherlands*: Amsterdam, Delft, Haarlem, Hague, Leiden, Rotterdam, Utrecht.

* *Poland*: Krakow, Warsaw.

* *Portugal*: Lisbon.

* *Russia*: Kiev, Moscow, Riga, St. Petersburg, Tallinn, Vilnius, Smolensk.

* *Sweden*: Stockholm, Uppsala.

* *Spain*: Barcelona, Cordoba, Granada, Madrid, Seville, Valladolid.

* *Switzerland*: Basel, Geneva, Zurich.

For the United States, the individual state was the equivalent of the European region. I also coded 14 cities separately: Baltimore, Boston, Buffalo, Chicago, Cleveland, Los Angeles, New York, New Orleans, Philadelphia, Pittsburgh, Princeton, San Francisco, St. Louis, Washington, D.C. Major American cities that came to prominence after World War II (and hence mainly after 1950) such as Houston and Phoenix are not given separate codes because they were not major cities during the period covered by the analysis.

DETERMINING AND ESTIMATING POPULATIONS

For national populations prior to 19C I relied chiefly on McEvedy and Jones 1978, picking up with national census data as reported in Mitchell 1992: Table A1 as they became available for late 18C and early 19C.

The two base sources for population data on cities were DeVries 1984: 270–77, which contains population data on the 31 largest European cities from 1500 to 1800, and Mitchell 1992: Table A4, which contains data on 100 major European cities from 1750 to 1950. Three other sources with a variety of city population data were Hall 1998 and Trager 1994 and the online version of the *Encyclopedia Britannica*. Other data were added from histories of the countries and cities in question, including historical information provided by the web sites of the cities in question.

For taking the data back to 1400 when no other information was available, I first determined the founding date of the city. If the city began as a village after 1400, I stipulated that the population in the founding year was 1,000 and extrapolated linearly to the first available data. For cities founded before 1400, I used McEvedy 1992, which categorizes the population of cities in 1346 (just before the black death) and 1483 under three categories: 15,000–23,000, 23,000–49,000, and 50,000–125,000. If I could locate qualitative historical descriptions of the city's size, role, and importance at those times, I assigned an estimated population within the range. In making these estimates, I was also often able to make use of known inequalities (e.g., that Paris was larger than London) in reducing the uncertainty.

THE ROSTER
OF SIGNIFICANT
FIGURES

The pages that follow begin with summary information about each inventory and the correlation matrix for the sources used to prepare the index scores. For a key to the sources, see Appendix 3. This material is followed by an alphabetical listing of all the significant figures in each inventory, showing the period in which they were active (fl), national origin, and index score. Names are repeated for those entered in more than one inventory. For a person with a known birth year, fl is based on the year in which he turned 40 or the year in which he died, whichever came first. National origin refers to the country in which the person lived as a child.

Names include only the first name, even for persons (e.g., Wolfgang Amadeus Mozart) who are ordinarily known by their full name, and just the first element in hyphenated given names (e.g., "Jean" for "Jean-Baptiste-Pierre-François"). Middle initials are included when they are necessary to distinguish between otherwise identical names. The purpose is to give enough information for unique identification, not provide definitive names. In the case of pseudonyms, I tried to list the person under the name by which he is best known (e.g., Twain instead of Clemens), showing the other last name in parentheses if it was a close call. Chinese and Japanese names are shown in their spoken order. For Japanese persons known primarily by a single name, I list that name alone. When Arabic figures are best known in the West by their Latinized name, I list them accordingly, with the basics of the Arabic version in parentheses. Western figures of the medieval period and early Renaissance are listed by their first name if that is the way their name was listed in the *Encyclopedia Britannica* or the most authoritative source in which they were mentioned. I have not tried to list variant spellings, which are legion.

THE ASTRONOMY INVENTORY

SUMMARY STATISTICS

Total number of entries	767
Parent population	340
Significant figures	124
Major figures	28
Index reliability (Cronbach's α)	.92

CORRELATION MATRIX FOR THE INDEX SOURCES ($n=124$)

		1	2	3	4	5	6	7	8	9	10	11	12	13	14
1	Adlington	1.00	.73	.71	.31	.71	.32	.18	.56	.70	.40	.22	.27	.24	.18
2	Asimov	.73	1.00	.64	.36	.71	.42	.29	.72	.77	.42	.33	.39	.33	.33
3	Bruno	.71	.64	1.00	.26	.68	.33	.26	.45	.67	.34	.28	.31	.24	.24
4	Gillespie	.31	.36	.26	1.00	.62	.78	.52	.52	.57	.45	.55	.70	.47	.65
5	Hellemans	.71	.71	.68	.62	1.00	.55	.42	.58	.81	.53	.36	.48	.34	.38
6	Marcorini	.32	.42	.33	.78	.55	1.00	.58	.55	.52	.46	.72	.86	.65	.86
7	Mason	.18	.29	.26	.52	.42	.58	1.00	.47	.36	.31	.49	.59	.44	.61
8	Mount	.56	.72	.45	.52	.58	.55	.47	1.00	.69	.43	.34	.54	.37	.53
9	Ochoa	.70	.77	.67	.57	.81	.52	.36	.69	1.00	.49	.36	.46	.35	.38
10	Porter(c)	.40	.42	.34	.45	.53	.46	.31	.43	.49	1.00	.42	.44	.53	.38
11	Ronan	.22	.33	.28	.55	.36	.72	.49	.34	.36	.42	1.00	.72	.82	.75
12	Taton	.27	.39	.31	.70	.48	.86	.59	.54	.46	.44	.72	1.00	.67	.91
13	Whitfield	.24	.33	.24	.47	.34	.65	.44	.37	.35	.53	.82	.67	1.00	.71
14	Wussing	.18	.33	.24	.65	.38	.86	.61	.53	.38	.38	.75	.91	.71	1.00

Note: The index scores for the scientific inventories combined separate subscores from the chronologies and the history/biographical dictionary sources. The reliability refers to Cronbach's α based on the correlations in the above matrix.

THE ROSTER OF SIGNIFICANT FIGURES

Name	fl	Nat'l orgin	Index	Name	fl	Nat'l orgin	Index
Adams, John	1859	England	16	Goodricke, John	1786	Netherlands	10
Adams, Walter	1916	USA	27	Hale, George	1908	USA	37
Airy, George	1841	England	1	Hall, Asaph	1869	USA	13
Ambartsumian, Viktor	1948	Russia	5	Halley, Edmond	1696	England	57
Anaximander the Elder	−571	Greece	9	Helmholtz, Hermann	1861	Germany	12
Apian, Peter				Henderson, Thomas	1838	Scotland	12
(Bennewitz)	1535	Germany	9	Heraclides Ponticus	−350	Greece	14
Argelander, Friedrich	1839	Germany	8	Herschel, Caroline	1790	Germany	6
Aristarchus of Samos	−270	Greece	28	Herschel, John	1832	England	27
Baade, Walter	1933	Germany	47	Herschel, William	1778	Germany	88
Baily, Francis	1814	England	6	Hertzsprung, Ejnar	1913	Denmark	35
Barnard, Edward	1897	USA	26	Hevelius, Johannes	1651	Poland	30
Bayer, Johann	1612	Germany	6	Hipparchus of Nicaea	−140	Greece	49
Bessel, Friedrich	1824	Germany	39	Hooke, Robert	1675	England	17
Biermann, Ludwig	1947	Germany	6	Horrocks, Jeremiah	1641	England	8
Bode, Johann	1787	Germany	12	Hubble, Edwin	1929	USA	45
Bond, George	1865	USA	12	Huggins, William	1864	England	37
Bond, William	1829	USA	9	Janssen, Pierre	1864	France	5
Bradley, James	1733	England	14	Jeans, James	1917	England	13
Brahe, Tycho	1586	Denmark	68	Kant, Immanuel	1764	Germany	20
Campbell, William	1902	USA	8	Kapteyn, Jacobus	1891	Netherlands	9
Cannon, Annie	1903	USA	6	Kepler, Johannes	1611	Germany	93
Carrington, Richard	1866	England	11	Kirkwood, Daniel	1854	USA	5
Cassini, Giovanni	1665	Italy	53	Kuiper, Gerard Peter	1945	Netherlands	32
Celsius, Anders	1741	Sweden	4	Lambert, Johann	1768	Germany	10
Chandrasekhar,				Laplace, Pierre	1789	France	79
Subrahmaryan	1950	India	9	Lassell, William	1839	England	21
Chang Heng	110	China	4	Le Verrier, Urbain	1851	France	22
Chapman, Sydney	1928	England	6	Leavitt, Henrietta	1908	USA	12
Clairaut, Alexis	1753	France	10	Lemaître, Georges	1934	Belgium	17
Copernicus, Nicolaus	1513	Poland	75	Lindblad, Bertil	1935	Sweden	7
Curtis, Heber	1912	USA	8	Lockyer, Joseph	1876	England	15
De La Rue, Warren	1855	England	11	Lomonosov, Mikhail	1751	Russia	13
Draper, Henry	1877	USA	13	Lowell, Percival	1895	USA	4
Dreyer, John	1892	Denmark	6	Maskelyne, Nevil	1772	England	2
Eddington, Arthur	1922	England	37	Maury, Antonia	1906	USA	10
Encke, Johann	1831	Germany	10	Mayr, Simon	1610	Germany	19
Eudoxus	−360	Greece	20	Messier, Charles	1770	France	11
Fabricius, David	1604	Germany	9	Meton of Athens	−440	Greece	5
Flamsteed, John	1686	England	23	Michell, John	1764	England	2
Galilei Galileo	1604	Italy	100	Milne, Edward	1936	England	11
Galle, Johann	1852	Germany	14	Mitchell, Maria	1858	USA	6
Gassendi, Pierre	1632	France	17	Moulton, Forest	1912	USA	9

Name	fl	Nat'l orgin	Index	Name	fl	Nat'l orgin	Index
Newcomb, Simon	1875	Canada	2	Scheiner, Christoph	1613	Germany	18
Olbers, Heinrich	1798	Germany	33	Schiaparelli, Giovanni	1875	Italy	21
Oort, Jan Hendrik	1940	Netherlands	22	Schwabe, Samuel	1829	Germany	12
Parsons, William	1840	Ireland	14	Schwarzschild, Karl	1913	Germany	19
Perrine, Charles	1907	USA	9	Secchi, Pietro	1858	Italy	19
Peurbach, Georg	1461	Austria	13	Shapley, Harlow	1925	USA	22
Philolaus of Crotona	−450	Greece	8	Sitter, Willem de	1912	Netherlands	6
Piazzi, Guiseppe	1786	Switzerland	16	Sosigenes	50	Rome	9
Pickering, Edward	1886	USA	17	Struve, Wilhelm von	1833	Germany	7
Pickering, William	1898	USA	9	Titius, Johann	1769	Germany	9
Plaskett, John	1905	Canada	5	Tombaugh, Clyde	1946	USA	11
Pons, Jean	1801	France	6	Trumpler, Robert	1926	Switzerland	6
Ptolemy	140	Egypt	73	Ulugh-Beg	1434	Central Asia	11
Regiomantus	1476	Germany	27	Vogel, Hermann	1882	Germany	12
Reinhold, Erasmus	1551	Germany	9	Whipple, Fred	1946	USA	11
Rheticus, Georg	1554	Austria	1	Wolf, Maximilian	1903	Germany	11
Riccioli, Giambattista	1637	Italy	11	Wright, Thomas	1751	England	4
Roche, Edouard	1860	France	8	Zwicky, Fritz	1938	Bulgaria	24
Russell, Henry	1917	USA	25	al-Zarqali (Arzachel)	1070	Spain	7
Rømer, Ole	1684	Denmark	12	ibn Yunus	1009	Egypt	8

THE BIOLOGY INVENTORY

SUMMARY STATISTICS

Total number of entries	1,638
Parent population	683
Significant figures	193
Major figures	34
Index reliability (Cronbach's α)	.88

CORRELATION MATRIX FOR THE INDEX SOURCES (n=193)

	1	2	3	4	5	6	7	8	9	10	11	12	13	14	15
1 Adlington	1.00	.45	.39	.17	.37	.09	.13	.42	.29	.01	.22	.21	.11	.12	.02
2 Asimov	.45	1.00	.39	.20	.46	.14	.26	.54	.47	.16	.22	.34	.11	.15	.08
3 Bruno	.39	.39	1.00	.29	.54	.28	.35	.42	.45	.16	.47	.31	.35	.31	.26
4 Gillespie	.17	.20	.29	1.00	.40	.51	.38	.30	.37	.39	.47	.23	.44	.51	.50
5 Hellemans	.37	.46	.54	.40	1.00	.45	.55	.50	.62	.25	.55	.41	.50	.49	.40
6 Marcorini	.09	.14	.28	.51	.45	1.00	.50	.33	.29	.32	.52	.16	.69	.50	.81
7 Mason	.13	.26	.35	.38	.55	.50	1.00	.28	.56	.30	.55	.39	.54	.59	.47
8 Mount	.42	.54	.42	.30	.50	.33	.28	1.00	.41	.11	.29	.30	.27	.19	.33
9 Ochoa	.29	.47	.45	.37	.62	.29	.56	.41	1.00	.28	.53	.42	.38	.40	.25
10 Porter(c)	.01	.16	.16	.39	.25	.32	.30	.11	.28	1.00	.29	.17	.25	.36	.26
11 Ronan	.22	.22	.47	.47	.55	.52	.55	.29	.53	.29	1.00	.31	.60	.65	.59
12 Serres	.21	.34	.31	.23	.41	.16	.39	.30	.42	.17	.31	1.00	.25	.37	.19
13 Taton	.11	.11	.35	.44	.50	.69	.54	.27	.38	.25	.60	.25	1.00	.56	.71
14 Whitfield	.12	.15	.31	.51	.49	.50	.59	.19	.40	.36	.65	.37	.56	1.00	.53
15 Wussing	.02	.08	.26	.50	.40	.81	.47	.33	.25	.26	.59	.19	.71	.53	1.00

Note: The index scores for the scientific inventories combined separate subscores from the chronologies and the history/biographical dictionary sources. The reliability refers to Cronbach's α based on the correlations in the above matrix.

ROSTER OF THE SIGNIFICANT FIGURES

Name	fl	Nat'l orgin	Index	Name	fl	Nat'l orgin	Index
Abel, John	1897	USA	27	Amici, Giovanni	1826	Italy	3
Alpini, Prospero	1593	Italy	7	Aristotle	−344	Greece	93
Audubon, James	1825	USA	8	Dart, Raymond	1933	Australia	7
Avery, Oswald	1917	Canada	22	Darwin, Charles	1849	England	100
Baer, Karl von	1832	Germany	44	Delbrück, Max	1946	Germany	12
Bateson, William	1901	England	24	Descartes, René	1636	France	26
Bauhin, Gaspard	1600	Switzerland	5	Dobzhansky,			
Bawden, Frederick	1948	England	9	Theodosius	1940	Ukraine	14
Bayliss, William	1900	England	17	Doisy, Edward	1933	USA	15
Beadle, George	1943	USA	15	Du Bois-Reymond,			
Beaumont, William	1825	USA	11	Emil	1858	Germany	12
Beijerinck, Martinus	1891	Netherlands	17	Dubos, René	1941	France	1
Belon, Pierre	1557	France	16	Duggar, Benjamin	1912	USA	1
Beneden, Edouard	1886	Belgium	21	Dutrochet, René	1816	France	10
Bernard, Claude	1853	France	46	Eberth, Karl	1875	Germany	1
Bichat, Marie	1802	France	15	Egas Moniz, Antonio	1914	Portugal	1
Bonnet, Charles	1760	Switzerland	19	Einthoven, Willem	1900	Netherlands	1
Bordet, Jules	1910	Belgium	2	Empedocles	−452	Greece	32
Borelli, Giovanni	1648	Italy	18	Erasistratus	−280	Greece	20
Boveri, Theodor	1902	Germany	17	Eustachio, Bartolomeo	1560	Italy	11
Bridges, Calvin	1929	USA	23	Evans, Herbert	1922	USA	18
Brown, Robert	1813	Scotland	23	Fabrici, Girolamo	1573	Italy	15
Brunfels, Otto	1529	Germany	9	Fabricius, Johan	1785	Denmark	3
Buckland, William	1824	England	11	Falloppio, Gabriele	1562	Italy	14
Buffon	1747	France	20	Fisher, Ronald	1930	England	3
Burdach, Karl	1816	Germany	12	Flemming, Walther	1883	Germany	29
Butenandt, Adolf	1943	Germany	37	Forbes, Edward Jr.	1854	England	18
Bèkèsy, Georg von	1939	Hungary	3	Francis, Thomas Jr.	1940	USA	1
Calmette, Albert	1903	France	1	Frisch, Karl von	1926	Austria	18
Camerarius, Rudolph	1705	Germany	13	Fuchs, Leonhart	1541	Germany	16
Candolle, Augustin de	1818	Switzerland	10	Gall, Franz	1798	Germany	9
Cannon, Walter	1911	USA	4	Galton, Francis	1862	England	27
Carlisle, Anthony	1808	England	16	Galvani, Luigi	1777	Italy	25
Carson, Rachel	1947	USA	1	Gesner, Konrad	1556	Switzerland	32
Cesalpino, Andrea	1559	Italy	14	Goethe, Johann von	1789	Germany	18
Claude, Albert	1938	Belgium	9	Golgi, Camillo	1883	Italy	25
Cohn, Ferdinand	1868	Germany	15	Gram, Hans	1893	Denmark	12
Colombo, Realdo	1550	Italy	14	Gray, Asa	1850	USA	5
Cope, Edward	1880	USA	11	Grew, Nehemiah	1681	England	29
Cori, Gerty	1936	Bohemia	1	Haeckel, Ernst	1874	Germany	41
Correns, Karl	1904	Germany	15	Haldane, John	1900	Scotland	1
Cuvier, Georges	1809	France	85	Hales, Stephen	1717	England	49
Dam, Peter	1935	Denmark	1	Haller, Albrecht von	1747	Switzerland	37

Name	fl	Nat'l orgin	Index	Name	fl	Nat'l orgin	Index
Harden, Arthur	1905	England	12	Mohl, Hugo von	1845	Germany	9
Harrison, Ross	1910	USA	15	Monod, Jacques	1950	France	15
Harvey, William	1618	England	51	Morgan, Thomas	1906	USA	78
Helmholtz, Hermann	1861	Germany	27	Müller, Hermann	1930	USA	34
Herophilus				Müller, Johannes	1841	Germany	13
of Alexandria	−315	Greece	26	Müller, Otto	1770	Denmark	8
Hershey, Alfred Day	1948	USA	13	Northrop, John	1931	USA	13
Hertwig, Wilhelm	1889	Germany	15	Ochoa, Severo	1945	Spain	7
Hopkins, Frederick	1901	England	21	Oparin, Alexander	1934	Russia	8
Humboldt,				Owen, Richard	1844	England	23
Alexander von	1809	Germany	23	Papanicolaou, George	1923	Greece	1
Huxley, Thomas	1865	England	22	Pfeffer, Wilhelm	1885	Germany	11
Hérelle, Felix d'	1913	Canada	12	Pincus, Gregory	1943	USA	1
Ingenhousz, Jan	1770	Netherlands	16	Pirie, Norman	1948	Britain	9
Ivanovsky, Dmitri	1904	Russia	12	Pliny the Elder	63	Rome	37
Johannsen, Wilhelm	1897	Denmark	23	Prout, William	1825	England	16
Jussieu, Antoine de	1788	France	11	Purkyne, Johannes	1827	Bohemia	16
Jussieu, Bernard de	1739	France	2	Ray, John	1667	England	43
Keilin, David	1927	Poland	18	Redi, Francesco	1666	Italy	1
Kendall, Edward Calvin	1926	USA	27	Remak, Robert	1855	Poland	9
Krebs, Hans	1940	Germany	22	Richet, Charles	1890	France	13
Kölliker, Rudolf von	1857	Switzerland	23	Rudbeck, Olof	1670	Sweden	10
Kölreuter, Joseph	1773	Germany	9	Sabin, Albert	1946	Poland	1
Lamarck, Jean	1784	France	90	Sachs, Julius von	1872	Germany	25
Landsteiner, Karl	1908	Austria	26	Saussure, Nicholas de	1807	Switzerland	6
Lartet, Edouard	1841	France	10	Schleiden, Matthias	1844	Germany	36
Laveran, Charles	1885	France	1	Schoenheimer, Rudolf	1938	Germany	10
Leonardo da Vinci	1492	Italy	34	Schwann, Theodor	1850	Germany	49
Levene, Phoebus	1909	Russia	17	Servetus, Michael	1551	Spain	26
Levi-Montalcini, Rita	1949	Italy	9	Sherrington, Charles	1897	England	18
Levine, Philip	1940	Russia	1	Spallanzani	1769	Italy	39
Linnaeus, Carolus	1747	Sweden	59	Spemann, Hans	1909	Germany	18
Lipmann, Fritz	1939	Germany	15	Sprengel, Conrad	1790	Germany	6
Lister, Joseph J.	1826	England	1	Spurzheim, Johann	1816	Germany	6
Lorenz, Konrad	1943	Austria	13	Stanley, Wendell	1944	USA	17
Ludwig, Karl	1856	Germany	3	Starling, Ernest	1906	England	21
Lwoff, André	1942	France	5	Steenbock, Harry	1926	USA	7
MacLeod, Colin	1949	Canada	15	Stensen, Niels (Steno)	1678	Denmark	29
MacLeod, John	1916	Scotland	1	Stevens, Nettie	1901	USA	7
Malpighi, Marcello	1668	Italy	46	Strasburger, Eduard	1884	Germany	12
Martin, Archer	1950	England	14	Sturtevant, Alfred	1931	USA	34
McClintock, Barbara	1942	USA	1	Sumner, James	1927	USA	14
Mendel, Johann	1862	Bohemia	38	Sutton, Walter	1916	USA	12
Meyerhof, Otto	1924	Germany	6	Swammerdam, Jan	1677	Netherlands	49

Name	fl	Nat'l orgin	Index	Name	fl	Nat'l orgin	Index
Szent-Györgyi, Albert	1933	Hungary	1	Vries, Hugo de	1888	Netherlands	44
Tatum, Edward	1949	USA	17	Waldeyer-Hartz,			
Theophrastus	-331	Greece	26	Wilhelm von	1876	Germany	15
Tiselius, Arne	1942	Sweden	12	Wallace, Alfred	1863	England	34
Tournefort, Joseph de	1696	France	6	Warburg, Otto	1923	Germany	22
Trefouel, Jacques	1937	France	1	Wassermann,			
Trembley, Abraham	1740	Switzerland	22	August von	1906	Germany	1
Treviranus, Goffried	1816	Germany	13	Weiner, Alexander	1947	USA	1
Tschermak, Erich	1911	Austria	13	Weismann, August	1874	Germany	26
Tsvet, Mikhail	1912	Russia	15	Wilson, Edmund	1896	USA	10
Twort, Frederick	1917	England	13	Wolff, Caspar	1774	Germany	15
Tyndall, John	1860	Ireland	1	Yersin, Alexandre	1903	Switzerland	1
Vigneaud, Vincent du	1941	USA	1				

THE CHEMISTRY INVENTORY

SUMMARY STATISTICS

Total number of entries	812
Parent population	478
Significant figures	204
Major figures	48
Index reliability (Cronbach's α)	.93

CORRELATION MATRIX FOR THE INDEX SOURCES ($n=204$)

	1	2	3	4	5	6	7	8	9	10	11	12	13	14
1 Adlington	1.00	.56	.65	.23	.70	.24	.27	.59	.63	.32	.16	.35	.30	.27
2 Asimov	.56	1.00	.75	.37	.74	.37	.46	.83	.87	.41	.44	.57	.58	.41
3 Bruno	.65	.75	1.00	.37	.77	.33	.47	.74	.80	.32	.44	.55	.50	.41
4 Gillespie	.23	.37	.37	1.00	.47	.57	.52	.38	.43	.51	.59	.51	.67	.69
5 Hellemans	.70	.74	.77	.47	1.00	.46	.59	.77	.84	.41	.49	.64	.66	.52
6 Marcorini	.24	.37	.33	.57	.46	1.00	.45	.40	.37	.49	.54	.46	.68	.60
7 Mason	.27	.46	.47	.52	.59	.45	1.00	.52	.53	.39	.80	.67	.68	.62
8 Mount	.59	.83	.74	.38	.77	.40	.52	1.00	.83	.35	.51	.62	.57	.44
9 Ochoa	.63	.87	.80	.43	.84	.37	.53	.83	1.00	.41	.48	.62	.63	.45
10 Porter	.32	.41	.32	.51	.41	.49	.39	.35	.41	1.00	.36	.34	.49	.56
11 Ronan	.16	.44	.44	.59	.49	.54	.80	.51	.48	.36	1.00	.59	.66	.63
12 Serres	.35	.57	.55	.51	.64	.46	.67	.62	.62	.34	.59	1.00	.70	.59
13 Taton	.30	.58	.50	.67	.66	.68	.68	.57	.63	.49	.66	.70	1.00	.68
14 Wussing	.27	.41	.41	.69	.52	.60	.62	.44	.45	.56	.63	.59	.68	1.00

Note: The index scores for the scientific inventories combined separate subscores from the chronologies and the history/biographical dictionary sources. The reliability refers to Cronbach's α based on the correlations in the above matrix.

THE ROSTER OF SIGNIFICANT FIGURES

Name	fl	Nat'l orgin	Index	Name	fl	Nat'l orgin	Index
Abel, Frederic	1867	England	1	Daniell, John	1830	England	1
Albertus Magnus, St.	1240	Germany	17	Davy, Edmund	1825	England	1
Alder, Kurt	1942	Germany	6	Davy, Humphrey	1818	England	47
Andrews, Thomas	1853	Ireland	7	Debierne, André	1914	France	5
Arfvedson, Johann	1832	Sweden	5	Debye, Peter	1924	Netherlands	15
Arrhenius, Svante	1899	Sweden	14	Demarcay, Eugène	1892	France	5
Aston, Francis	1917	England	20	Derosne, Charles	1820	France	4
Auer, Karl	1898	Austria	8	Dewar, James	1882	Scotland	14
Baekeland, Leo	1903	Belgium	1	Diels, Otto	1916	Germany	7
Baeyer, Johann von	1875	Germany	8	Dorn, Friedrich	1888	Germany	4
Balard, Antoine	1842	France	6	Draper, John	1851	England	2
Becher, Johann	1675	Germany	11	Dulong, Pierre	1825	France	9
Beguin, Jean	1590	France	3	Dumas, Jean	1840	France	17
Bergius, Friedrich	1924	Germany	1	Döbereiner, Johann	1820	Germany	5
Bergmann, Torbern	1775	Sweden	15	Elhuyar, Fausto d'	1795	Spain	4
Bernal, John	1941	Ireland	5	Fahlberg, Constantin	1890	Germany	4
Berthelot, Pierre	1867	France	12	Fajans, Kasimir	1927	Poland	14
Berthollet, Claude	1788	France	29	Fischer, Emil	1892	Germany	16
Berzelius, Jöns	1819	Sweden	68	Fischer, Hans	1921	Germany	4
Biringuccio, Vanuccio	1520	Italy	1	Fleck, Alexander	1929	Scotland	3
Black, Joseph	1768	Scotland	32	Fourcroy, Antoine de	1795	France	12
Boisbaudran, Paul de	1878	France	13	Fox Talbot, William	1840	England	1
Boltwood, Bertram	1910	USA	6	Frankland, Edward	1865	England	3
Boussingault, Jean	1842	France	4	Gay-Lussac, Joseph	1818	France	38
Boyle, Robert	1667	Germany	41	Geber (Jabir ibn			
Brand, Hennig	1650	Germany	5	Hayyan)	800	Persia	14
Brønsted, Johannes	1919	Denmark	5	Giauque, William	1935	Canada	10
Bunn, C.W.	1944	England	3	Glauber, Johann	1644	Germany	10
Bunsen, Robert	1851	Germany	23	Goldschmidt, Victor	1928	Switzerland	5
Butlerov, Aleksandr	1868	Russia	3	Gomberg, Moses	1906	Ukraine	4
Büchner, Eduard	1900	Germany	10	Graham, Thomas	1845	Scotland	13
Cannizzaro, Stanislao	1866	Italy	15	Gregor, William	1801	England	4
Carothers, Wallace	1936	USA	1	Grignard, F.A.	1911	France	5
Chardonnet, Louis de	1879	France	1	Grove, William	1851	England	1
Chevreul, Michel	1826	France	6	Guldberg, Cato	1876	Norway	5
Couper, Archibald	1871	Scotland	5	Guthrie, Samuel	1822	USA	1
Courtois, Bernard	1817	France	5	Guyton de Morveau,			
Cranston, John	1917	Scotland	3	Louis	1777	France	12
Crawford, Adair	1788	Ireland	3	Haber, Fritz	1908	Germany	1
Crookes, William	1872	England	31	Hahn, Otto	1919	Germany	18
Cross, Charles	1895	England	1	Hall, Charles	1903	USA	1
Cullen, William	1750	Scotland	1	Hare, Robert	1821	USA	1
Dalton, John	1806	England	37	Hatchett, Charles	1805	England	5

Name	fl	Nat'l orgin	Index	Name	fl	Nat'l orgin	Index
Haworth, Walter	1923	England	8	Midgley, Thomas, Jr.	1929	USA	1
Haüy, Rene	1783	England	9	Miescher, Johann	1884	Switzerland	5
Helmont, Jan van	1619	Belgium	25	Mohr, Carl	1846	Germany	6
Henry, William	1814	England	5	Moissan, Ferdinand	1892	France	5
Hess, Germain	1842	Switzerland	3	Morley, Edward	1878	USA	13
Hevesy, György	1925	Hungary	14	Müller, Franz	1780	Romania	5
Heyrovsky, Jaroslav	1930	Bohemia	6	Müller, Paul	1939	Switzerland	1
Hisinger, Wilhelm	1806	Sweden	6	Natta, Giulio	1943	Italy	1
Hodgkin, Dorothy	1950	England	8	Nernst, Hermann	1904	Germany	20
Hoffmann, August von	1858	Germany	7	Newlands, John	1877	England	7
Hofmann, Albert	1946	Switzerland	5	Nieuwland, Julius			
Homberg, Wilhelm	1692	Germany	3	Arthur	1918	Belgium	1
Hoppe-Seyler, Felix	1865	Germany	7	Nilson, Lars Fredrik	1880	Sweden	5
Karrer, Paul	1929	Switzerland	12	Nobel, Alfred	1873	Sweden	1
Kekulé, Friedrich	1869	Germany	28	Noddack, Walter	1933	Germany	5
Kennedy, J.W.	1941	USA	4	Ostwald, Wilhelm	1893	Russia	14
Kipping, Frederic	1903	England	3	Paneth, Friedrich	1927	Austria	7
Klaproth, Martin	1783	Germany	24	Paulesco, Nicolas	1921	Romania	1
Kolbe, Adolf	1858	Germany	5	Pauling, Linus	1941	USA	26
Kossel, Karl	1893	Germany	4	Perkin, William	1878	England	7
Kuhn, Richard	1940	Austria	1	Perrin, Jean	1910	France	15
Kühne, Wilhelm	1877	Germany	5	Pregl, Fritz	1909	Slovenia	3
Langmuir, Irving	1921	USA	10	Priestley, Joseph	1773	England	49
Laurent, Auguste	1847	France	8	Proust, Joseph	1794	France	14
Lavoisier, Antoine	1783	France	100	Ramsay, William	1892	Scotland	32
Le Bel, Joseph	1887	Germany	8	Raoult, François	1870	France	4
Le Châtelier, Henri	1890	France	3	Reich, Ferdinand	1839	Germany	6
Leblanc, Nicolas	1782	France	4	Reichenbach, Karl	1828	Germany	2
Lehmann, Johann	1759	Germany	1	Reichstein, Tadeus	1937	Poland	11
Lewis, Gilbert	1915	USA	15	Remsen, Ira	1886	USA	5
Libavius, Andreas	1580	Germany	7	Richards, Theodore	1908	USA	5
Libby, Willard	1948	USA	7	Richter, Hieronymous	1864	Germany	5
Liebig, Justis von	1843	Germany	30	Ritter, Johann	1810	Germany	10
Loschmidt, Johann	1861	Bohemia	5	Robinson, Robert	1926	England	7
Löwig, Carl	1843	Germany	4	Roscoe, Henry	1873	England	2
Macintosh, Charles	1806	Scotland	1	Runge, Friedlieb	1834	Germany	4
Macquer, Pierre	1758	France	1	Rutherford, Daniel	1789	Scotland	5
Marggraf, Andreas	1749	Germany	6	Ruzicka, Leopold	1927	Croatia	8
Marignac, Jean de	1857	Switzerland	8	Sabatier, Paul	1894	France	1
Markovnikov, Vladimir	1878	Russia	3	Sainte-Claire Deville,			
Mayow, John	1679	England	12	Henri	1858	France	1
Mendeleyev, Dmitry	1874	Russia	25	Scheele, Carl	1782	Sweden	55
Meyer, Julius	1870	Germany	12	Schönbein, Christian	1839	Germany	5
Meyer, Viktor	1888	Germany	5	Sidgwick, Nevil	1913	England	3

Name	fl	Nat'l orgin	Index	Name	fl	Nat'l orgin	Index
Sobrero, Ascanio	1852	Italy	1	Urey, Harold	1933	USA	11
Soddy, Frederick	1917	England	25	Van't Hoff, Jacobus	1892	Netherlands	20
Solvay, Ernest	1878	Belgium	1	Vauquelin, Louis	1803	France	18
Soubeiran, Eugene	1831	France	1	Wallach, Otto	1887	Germany	2
Stas, Jean Servais	1853	Belgium	3	Waterston, John	1851	Scotland	2
Staudinger, Hermann	1921	Germany	7	Werner, Alfred	1906	Germany	7
Stoll, Arthur	1927	Switzerland	6	Wigner, Eugene	1942	Hungary	6
Stromeyer, Friedrich	1816	Germany	5	Williamson, Alexander	1864	England	3
Svedberg, The	1924	Sweden	10	Willstätter, Richard	1912	Germany	14
Swinburne, James	1898	Scotland	1	Windaus, Adolf	1916	Germany	8
Sørensen, Soren	1908	Denmark	3	Winkler, Clemens	1878	Germany	5
Takamine, Jokichi	1894	Japan	5	Wollaston, William	1806	England	22
Tennant, Smithson	1801	England	14	Wurtz, Charles	1857	France	4
Thénard, Louis	1817	France	14	Wöhler, Friedrich	1840	Germany	19
Travers, Morris	1912	England	14	Young, James	1862	Scotland	1
Turner-Jones, A.	1944	England	3	Ziegler, Karl	1938	Germany	1
Unverdorben, Otto	1846	Germany	2	Zsigmondy, Richard	1905	Austria	1

THE EARTH SCIENCES INVENTORY

SUMMARY STATISTICS

Total number of entries	597
Parent population	270
Significant figures	85
Major figures	14
Index reliability (Cronbach's α)	.81

CORRELATION MATRIX FOR THE INDEX SOURCES ($n=85$)

	1	2	3	4	5	6	7	8	9	10
1 Bruno	1.00	.24	.39	.11	.28	.27	.30	.08	.44	.24
2 Gillespie	.24	1.00	.47	.41	.64	.28	.30	.52	.51	.52
3 Hellemans	.39	.47	1.00	.20	.53	.46	.57	.40	.38	.21
4 Marcorini	.11	.41	.20	1.00	.19	.04	.26	.27	.39	.34
5 Mason	.28	.64	.53	.19	1.00	.37	.38	.28	.40	.43
6 Mount	.27	.28	.46	.04	.37	1.00	.35	.15	.07	.12
7 Ochoa	.30	.30	.57	.26	.38	.35	1.00	.24	.26	.14
8 Porter	.08	.52	.40	.27	.28	.15	.24	1.00	.36	.27
9 Taton	.44	.51	.38	.39	.40	.07	.26	.36	1.00	.61
10 Wussing	.24	.52	.21	.34	.43	.12	.14	.27	.61	1.00

Note: The index scores for the scientific inventories combined separate subscores from the chronologies and the history/biographical dictionary sources. The reliability refers to Cronbach's α based on the correlations in the above matrix.

THE ROSTER OF SIGNIFICANT FIGURES

Name	fl	Nat'l orgin	Index	Name	fl	Nat'l orgin	Index
Agassiz, Louis	1847	Switzerland	37	Lenz, Emil	1844	Russia	14
Agricola (Georg Bauer)	1534	Germany	51	Love, Augustus	1903	England	4
Alberti, Friedrich von	1835	Germany	8	Lyell, Charles	1837	Scotland	100
Beaufort, Francis	1814	Ireland	4	Maclure, William	1803	Scotland	6
Bjerknes, Jakob	1937	Norway	18	Mallet, Robert	1850	England	4
Bjerknes, Vilhelm	1902	Norway	29	Mantell, Gideon	1830	England	13
Blumenbach, Johann	1792	Germany	2	Maupertuis, Pierre de	1738	France	21
Bowen, Norman	1927	Canada	4	Maury, Matthew	1846	USA	41
Brandt, Georg	1734	Sweden	17	Méchain, Pierre	1784	France	9
Brongniart, Alexandre	1810	France	31	Milne, John	1899	England	14
Buch, Leopold von	1814	Germany	25	Mitscherlich, Eilhard	1834	Germany	29
Bullard, Edward	1947	England	4	Mohorovicic, Andrija	1897	Croatia	14
Bullen, Keith	1946	N. Zealand	9	Mohs, Friedrich	1813	Germany	6
Buys-Ballot, C.H.D.	1857	Netherlands	1	Moro, Anton	1727	Italy	12
Cabeo, Niccolo	1626	Italy	7	Mosander, Carl	1837	Sweden	36
Chamberlin, Thomas	1883	USA	29	Murchison, Roderick	1832	Scotland	40
Cleve, Per	1880	Sweden	29	Nicol, William	1808	Scotland	2
Cronstedt, Axel	1762	Sweden	24	Omalius d'Halloy, Jean	1823	Belgium	8
Dana, James	1853	USA	22	Palissy, Bernard	1554	France	12
Daubrée, Gabriel	1854	France	11	Penck, Albrecht	1898	Germany	7
Davis, W.	1890	USA	12	Powell, John	1874	USA	3
Desmarest, Nicolas	1765	France	33	Rennell, James	1782	England	4
Dutton, Clarence	1881	USA	25	Richter, Charles	1940	USA	20
Ekeberg, Anders	1807	Sweden	13	Rio, Andres del	1804	Spain	7
Ekman, Vagn	1914	Sweden	1	Rossby, Carl	1938	Sweden	5
Elie de Beaumont, Jean	1838	France	16	Sabine, Edward	1828	Ireland	19
Eskola	1923	Finland	19	Saussure, Horace de	1780	Switzerland	34
Ewing, James	1895	Scotland	8	Sedgwick, Adam	1825	England	30
Ewing, William	1946	USA	27	Smith, William	1809	England	55
Ferrel, William	1857	USA	1	Sorby, Henry	1866	England	4
Gadolin, Johan	1800	Finland	11	Strabo of Amasia	-24	Greece	18
Gahn, Johan	1785	Sweden	14	Suess, Eduard	1871	Germany	24
Guettard, Jean	1755	France	37	Taylor, Frank	1900	USA	14
Gutenberg, Beno	1929	Germany	14	Teisserenc de Bort, Léon	1895	France	12
Hall, James	1801	Scotland	16	Thomson, Charles	1870	Scotland	5
Hess, Harry	1946	USA	18	Urbain, Georges	1912	France	12
Holmes, Arthur	1930	England	7	Vening Meinesz	1927	Netherlands	15
Hooke, Robert	1675	England	17	Waage, Peter	1873	Norway	15
Hutton, James	1766	Scotland	78	Wegener, Alfred	1920	Germany	32
Jeffreys, Harold	1931	England	11	Werner, Abraham	1789	Germany	46
Kipfer, Paul	1931	Switzerland	12	Wilson, John Tuzo	1948	Canada	3
Lacaille, Nicolas de	1753	France	9	Woodward, John	1705	England	1
Leakey, Louis	1943	Kenya	3				

THE PHYSICS INVENTORY

SUMMARY STATISTICS

Total number of entries	700
Parent population	421
Significant figures	218
Major figures	66
Index reliability (Cronbach's α)	.95

CORRELATION MATRIX FOR THE INDEX SOURCES (*n*=218)

	1	2	3	4	5	6	7	8	9	10	11	12	13	14	15
1 Adlington	1.00	.65	.56	.36	.61	.34	.35	.64	.63	.39	.47	.56	.39	.42	.44
2 Asimov	.65	1.00	.61	.44	.72	.48	.40	.78	.85	.51	.51	.69	.43	.47	.55
3 Bruno	.56	.61	1.00	.44	.69	.51	.45	.63	.63	.47	.50	.63	.57	.52	.56
4 Gillespie	.36	.44	.44	1.00	.51	.72	.55	.51	.54	.55	.62	.55	.69	.62	.70
5 Hellemans	.61	.72	.69	.51	1.00	.61	.54	.73	.84	.56	.58	.71	.64	.51	.63
6 Marcorini	.34	.48	.51	.72	.61	1.00	.59	.53	.56	.64	.63	.60	.74	.63	.76
7 Mason	.35	.40	.45	.55	.54	.59	1.00	.51	.50	.54	.63	.59	.72	.70	.71
8 Mount	.64	.78	.63	.51	.73	.53	.51	1.00	.77	.52	.56	.70	.56	.54	.62
9 Ochoa	.63	.85	.63	.54	.84	.56	.50	.77	1.00	.56	.58	.72	.60	.53	.61
10 Porter	.39	.51	.47	.55	.56	.64	.54	.52	.56	1.00	.51	.53	.56	.53	.63
11 Ronan	.47	.51	.50	.62	.58	.63	.63	.56	.58	.51	1.00	.64	.60	.77	.71
12 Serres	.56	.69	.63	.55	.71	.60	.59	.70	.72	.53	.64	1.00	.65	.63	.73
13 Taton	.39	.43	.57	.69	.64	.74	.72	.56	.60	.56	.60	.65	1.00	.61	.76
14 Whitfield	.42	.47	.52	.62	.51	.63	.70	.54	.53	.53	.77	.63	.61	1.00	.76
15 Wussing	.44	.55	.56	.70	.63	.76	.71	.62	.61	.63	.71	.73	.76	.76	1.00

Note: The index scores for the scientific inventories combined separate subscores from the chronologies and the history/biographical dictionary sources. The reliability refers to Cronbach's α based on the correlations in the above matrix.

THE ROSTER OF SIGNIFICANT FIGURES

Name	fl	Nat'l orgin	Index
Alfvén, Hannes Olof	1948	Sweden	1
Alhazen			
(ibn al-Haytham)	1005	Arab world	22
Amontons, Guillaume	1703	France	16
Ampère, André	1815	France	26
Anderson, Carl	1945	USA	23
Ångström, Anders	1854	Sweden	2
Appleton, Edward	1932	England	1
Arago, Dominique			
Archimedes	−247	Greece	20
Astbury, William	1939	England	1
Atanasoff, John	1943	USA	2
Avogadro, Amedeo	1816	Italy	23
Balmer, Johann	1865	Switzerland	9
Bardeen, John	1948	USA	17
Barkla, Charles	1917	England	11
Bartholin, Erasmus	1665	Denmark	12
Becquerel, Alexandre	1860	France	8
Becquerel, Antoine	1892	France	28
Berg, Otto	1925	Germany	8
Bethe, Hans	1946	Germany	3
Bhabha, Homi	1949	India	1
Biot, Jean	1814	France	14
Bloch, Felix	1945	Switzerland	15
Bohr, Niels	1925	Denmark	51
Boltzmann, Ludwig	1884	Austria	29
Born, Max	1922	Germany	20
Bose, Satyendranath	1934	India	1
Bothe, Walther	1931	Germany	8
Bragg, W. Henry	1902	England	16
Bragg, W. Lawrence	1930	Australia	17
Brattain, Walter	1942	USA	11
Braun, Karl	1890	Germany	10
Brewster, David	1821	Scotland	6
Bridgman, Percy	1922	USA	4
Broglie, Louis de	1932	France	20
Buridan, Jean	1335	France	13
Cagniard de la Tour, Charles	1817	France	8
Cailletet, Louis	1872	France	10
Canton, John	1758	England	1
Carnot, Nicolas	1832	France	21
Cavendish, Henry	1771	England	58
Chadwick, James	1931	England	19
Charles, Jacques	1786	France	11
Cherenkov, Pavel	1944	Russia	8
Chladni, Ernst	1796	Germany	2
Clausius, Rudolf	1862	Germany	33
Cockroft, John	1937	England	17
Compton, Arthur Holly	1932	USA	23
Coolidge, William	1913	USA	6
Coriolis, Gaspard de	1832	France	5
Coster, Dirk	1929	Netherlands	8
Coulomb	1776	France	17
Curie, Marie	1907	Poland	42
Curie, Pierre	1899	France	49
d'Alembert, Jean	1757	France	10
Davisson, Clinton	1921	USA	11
Democritus	−420	Greece	26
Descartes, René	1636	France	27
Dirac, Paul	1942	England	41
Doppler, Christian	1843	Austria	16
Dufay, Charles	1738	France	9
Edlefsen, Nils	1933	USA	8
Einstein, Albert	1919	Germany	100
Elster, Johann	1894	Germany	3
Eötvös, Roland	1888	Hungary	6
Fabry, Marie	1907	France	1
Fahrenheit, Daniel	1726	Germany	4
Faraday, Michael	1831	England	86
Fermi, Enrico	1941	Italy	43
Fitzgerald, George	1891	Ireland	13
Fizeau, Armand	1859	France	29
Foucault, Jean	1859	France	31
Franck, James	1922	Germany	5
Frank, Ilya	1948	Russia	8
Franklin, Benjamin	1750	USA	21
Fraunhofer, Joseph von	1826	Germany	12
Freiberg, Dietrich von	1290	Germany	2
Fresnel, Augustin	1827	France	16
Friedmann, Alexander			
Frisch, Otto	1944	Austria	3
Gabor, Dennis	1940	Hungary	11
Galileo Galilei	1604	Italy	84
Gamow, George	1944	Ukraine	5
Geiger, Johannes	1922	Germany	32

Name	fl	Nat'l orgin	Index	Name	fl	Nat'l orgin	Index
Geissler, Johann	1855	Germany	9	London, Heinz	1947	Germany	6
Geitel, Hans	1895	Germany	3	Lorentz, Hendrik	1893	Netherlands	26
Gibbs, Josiah	1879	USA	14	Lyot, Bernard	1937	France	1
Gilbert, William	1584	England	36	Mach, Ernst	1878	Bohemia	18
Goldstein, Eugen	1890	Germany	18	Malus, Etienne	1812	France	15
Goudsmit, Samuel	1942	Netherlands	2	Marsden, Ernst	1929	England	11
Gray, Stephen	1706	England	15	Maxwell, James	1871	Scotland	50
Grimaldi, Francesco	1658	Italy	14	Mayer, Johann	1762	Germany	2
Guericke, Otto von	1642	Germany	24	Mayer, Julius von	1854	Germany	18
Hall, Edwin	1895	USA	1	Mayer, Maria	1946	Poland	8
Hauksbee, Francis	1706	England	14	McMillan, Edwin	1947	USA	17
Heaviside, Oliver	1890	England	1	Meitner, Lise	1918	Austria	16
Heisenberg	1941	Germany	41	Melloni, Macedonio	1838	Italy	1
Heitler, Walter	1944	Germany	3	Michelson, Albert	1892	Germany	26
Helmholtz, Hermann	1861	Germany	16	Millikan, Robert	1908	USA	29
Henry, Joseph	1837	USA	19	Moseley, Henry	1915	England	16
Hero of Alexandria	62	Greece	12	Muller, Walther	1928	Germany	2
Hertz, Heinrich	1894	Germany	30	Musschenbroek,			
Hess, Victor	1923	Austria	10	Pieter van	1732	Netherlands	18
Hey, James	1949	England	1	Newton, Isaac	1682	England	100
Hooke, Robert	1675	England	36	Nobili, Leopoldo	1824	Italy	5
Hückel, Erich	1936	Germany	6	Nollet, Jean	1740	France	14
Hull, Albert	1920	USA	11	Ohm, Georg	1829	Germany	16
Huygens, Christiaan	1669	Netherlands	40	Oppenheimer, Robert	1944	USA	5
Jansen, Zacharias	1620	Netherlands	1	Ørsted, Hans	1817	Denmark	30
Jensen, Johannes	1947	Germany	5	Pauli, Wolfgang	1940	Austria	32
Joliot, Frédric	1940	France	17	Pearson, Gerald	1945	USA	1
Joliot-Curie, Irène	1937	France	15	Peltier, Jean	1825	France	6
Jordanus de Nemore				Perey, Marguerite	1949	France	8
(Nemorarius)	1220	France	2	Petit, Alexis	1820	France	12
Joule, James	1858	England	40	Piccard, Auguste	1924	Switzerland	1
Kamerlingh-Onnes,				Pictet, Raoul	1886	Switzerland	9
Heike	1893	Netherlands	19	Planck, Max	1898	Germany	33
Kapitsa, Pyotr	1934	Russia	5	Popov, Aleksandr	1899	Russia	1
Kirchhoff, Gustave	1864	Germany	45	Powell, Cecil	1943	England	7
Kleist, Ewald von	1740	Germany	10	Prandtl, Ludwig	1915	Germany	3
Laue, Max von	1919	Germany	14	Prevost, Pierre	1791	Switzerland	5
Lawrence, Ernest	1941	USA	13	Röntgen, Wilhelm	1885	Germany	22
Lebedev, Pyotr	1906	Russia	7	Rabi, Isidor Isaac	1938	Slovakia	7
Lenard, Philipp	1902	Germany	19	Raman, Chandrasekhara	1928	India	10
Leonardo da Vinci	1492	Italy	13	Rossi, Bruno	1945	Italy	1
Linde, Carl von	1882	Germany	3	Rowland, Henry	1888	USA	5
Lodge, Oliver	1891	England	1	Ruedenberg, Reinhold	1923	Germany	1
London, Fritz	1940	Germany	9	Rutherford, Ernest	1911	N. Zealand	89

Name	fl	Nat'l orgin	Index	Name	fl	Nat'l orgin	Index
Sabine, Wallace	1908	USA	1	Thompson, Benjamin	1793	USA	25
Saha, Meghnad	1934	India	1	Thomson, George	1932	England	11
Sauveur, Joseph	1693	France	6	Thomson, J.J.	1896	England	51
Schaefer, Vincent	1946	USA	1	Thomson, William	1864	Scotland	27
Schmidt, Bernhard	1919	Russia	1	Tomonaga, Sin-Itiro	1946	Japan	8
Schrödinger, Erwin	1927	Austria	27	Torricelli, Evangelista	1647	Italy	24
Schweigger, Johann	1819	Germany	1	Uhlenbeck, George	1940	Netherlands	1
Seebeck, Thomas				Van de Graaff, Robert	1941	USA	4
Segrè, Emilio	1945	Italy	23	Van der Waals,			
Shockley, William	1950	USA	10	Johannes	1877	Netherlands	15
Snell, Willebrord	1620	Netherlands	12	Veksler, Vladimir	1947	Ukraine	8
Sommerfeld, Arnold	1908	Germany	20	Villard, Paul	1900	France	10
Stark, Johannes	1914	Germany	9	Volta, Alessandro	1785	Italy	18
Stefan, Josef	1875	Slovenia	9	Walton, Ernest	1943	Ireland	12
Stern, Otto	1928	Germany	9	Watson, William	1755	England	1
Stokes, George	1859	Ireland	21	Weber, Wilhelm	1844	Germany	7
Stoney, George	1866	Ireland	11	Wheatstone, Charles	1842	England	10
Strassman, Friedrich	1942	Germany	9	Wien, Wilhelm	1904	Germany	11
Strutt, John William	1882	England	27	Wilcke, Johan	1772	Germany	2
Strutt, Robert John	1915	England	1	Wilson, Charles	1909	Scotland	14
Sturgeon, William	1823	England	8	Young, Thomas	1813	England	37
Szilard, Leo	1938	Hungary	7	Yukawa, Hideki	1947	Japan	14
Tacke, Ida (Noddack)	1936	Germany	8	Zeeman, Pieter	1905	Netherlands	13
Tamm, Igor	1935	Russia	10	Zernike, Frits	1928	Netherlands	1
Thales	−585	Greece	12	Zinn, Walter	1946	Canada	11

THE MATHEMATICS INVENTORY

SUMMARY STATISTICS

Total number of entries	906
Parent population	626
Significant figures	191
Major figures	48
Index reliability (Cronbach's α)	.93

CORRELATION MATRIX FOR THE INDEX SOURCES ($n=191$)

	1	2	3	4	5	6	7	8	9	10	11	12	13	14	15	16	17
1 Boyer	1.00	0.43	0.45	0.68	0.44	0.75	0.54	0.64	0.55	0.56	0.35	0.56	0.66	0.38	0.79	0.78	0.79
2 Bruno	0.43	1.00	0.35	0.24	0.36	0.41	0.46	0.26	0.29	0.47	0.12	0.33	0.27	0.22	0.50	0.41	0.38
3 Eves	0.45	0.35	1.00	0.29	0.41	0.54	0.52	0.22	0.31	0.55	0.18	0.49	0.29	0.33	0.47	0.43	0.43
4 Gilles.	0.68	0.24	0.29	1.00	0.44	0.46	0.38	0.61	0.32	0.42	0.42	0.49	0.62	0.27	0.51	0.62	0.68
5 Grun	0.44	0.36	0.41	0.44	1.00	0.50	0.43	0.28	0.32	0.50	0.23	0.40	0.40	0.33	0.47	0.44	0.49
6 Gull.	0.75	0.41	0.54	0.46	0.50	1.00	0.70	0.49	0.52	0.67	0.30	0.64	0.50	0.53	0.71	0.68	0.70
7 Hell.	0.54	0.46	0.52	0.38	0.43	0.70	1.00	0.45	0.32	0.69	0.40	0.75	0.23	0.61	0.57	0.60	0.55
8 Marc.	0.64	0.26	0.22	0.61	0.28	0.49	0.45	1.00	0.28	0.47	0.41	0.57	0.44	0.44	0.51	0.66	0.67
9 Mason	0.55	0.29	0.31	0.32	0.32	0.52	0.32	0.28	1.00	0.37	0.18	0.10	0.50	0.22	0.71	0.52	0.55
10 Ochoa	0.56	0.47	0.55	0.42	0.50	0.67	0.69	0.47	0.37	1.00	0.37	0.63	0.34	0.52	0.62	0.58	0.56
11 Porter	0.35	0.12	0.18	0.42	0.23	0.30	0.40	0.41	0.18	0.37	1.00	0.46	0.05	0.43	0.34	0.49	0.30
12 Park.	0.56	0.33	0.49	0.49	0.40	0.64	0.75	0.57	0.10	0.63	0.46	1.00	0.26	0.56	0.49	0.62	0.53
13 Ronan	0.66	0.27	0.29	0.62	0.40	0.50	0.23	0.44	0.50	0.34	0.05	0.26	1.00	0.12	0.59	0.50	0.66
14 Serres	0.38	0.22	0.33	0.27	0.33	0.53	0.61	0.44	0.22	0.52	0.43	0.56	0.12	1.00	0.37	0.44	0.34
15 Swetz	0.79	0.50	0.47	0.51	0.47	0.71	0.57	0.51	0.71	0.62	0.34	0.49	0.59	0.37	1.00	0.72	0.71
16 Taton	0.78	0.41	0.43	0.62	0.44	0.68	0.60	0.66	0.52	0.58	0.49	0.62	0.50	0.44	0.72	1.00	0.74
17 Wuss.	0.79	0.38	0.43	0.68	0.49	0.70	0.55	0.67	0.55	0.56	0.30	0.53	0.66	0.34	0.71	0.74	1.00

Note: The index scores for the scientific inventories combined separate subscores from the chronologies and the history/biographical dictionary sources. The reliability refers to Cronbach's α based on the correlations in the above matrix.

THE ROSTER OF SIGNIFICANT FIGURES

Name	fl	Nat'l orgin	Index
Abül Wafa (Qafa)	980	Persia	7
Abel, Niels	1829	Norway	24
Adelhard of Bath	1125	England	9
Albategnius (al-Battani)	898	Persia	4
al-Khwarizmi,			
Abu Ja'far	840	Arab world	23
Apollonius of Perga	−240	Greece	29
Archimedes	−247	Greece	33
Archytas of Tarentum	−390	Greece	8
Argand, Jean	1808	Switzerland	7
Artin, Emil	1938	Bohemia	2
Aryabhata I	500	India	16
Banach, Stefan	1932	Poland	8
Barrow, Isaac	1670	England	16
Beltrami, Eugenio	1875	Italy	6
Bernoulli, Daniel	1740	Switzerland	6
Bernoulli, Jakob I	1694	Switzerland	41
Bernoulli, Johann I	1707	Switzerland	19
Bernoulli, Nikolaus I	1727	Switzerland	5
Bhaskara II	1154	India	12
Birkhoff, George	1924	USA	6
Bolyai, János	1842	Slovakia	15
Bolzano, Bernardus	1821	Bohemia	14
Bombelli, Rafael	1566	Italy	12
Boole, George	1855	England	20
Borel, Felix	1911	France	8
Bourbaki,			
Nicolas (pseud.)	1950	France	6
Bradwardine, Thomas	1330	England	1
Brahmagupta	638	India	13
Briggs, Henry	1601	England	15
Brouncker, William	1660	England	3
Brouwer, Luitzen	1921	Netherlands	18
Bürgi, Justus	1592	Austria	13
Cantor, Georg	1885	Germany	50
Cardano, Girolamo	1541	Italy	37
Carnot, Lazare Nicolas	1793	France	17
Cataldi, Pietro	1592	Italy	8
Cauchy, Augustin	1829	France	34
Cavalieri, Francesco	1638	Italy	22
Cayley, Arthur	1861	England	32
Ceulen, Ludolf van	1580	Netherlands	6
Chasles, Michel	1833	France	8

Name	fl	Nat'l orgin	Index
Chuquet, Nicolas	1485	France	8
Clavius, Christoph	1577	Germany	5
Clifford, William	1879	England	2
Cotes, Roger	1716	England	8
Cramer, Gabriel	1744	Switzerland	6
d'Alembert, Jean	1757	France	8
De Morgan, Augustus	1846	England	7
Dedekind, Richard	1871	Germany	23
Desargues, Girard	1631	France	19
Descartes, René	1636	France	53
Dickson, Leonard	1914	USA	2
Dinostratos	−350	Greece	5
Diophantus			
of Alexandria	250	Rome	39
Dirichlet, Gustav	1845	Germany	13
Eratosthenes	−236	Greece	8
Euclid of Alexandria	−230	Greece	81
Euler, Leonhard	1747	Switzerland	100
Fermat, Pierre de	1641	France	72
Ferrari, Ludovico	1562	Italy	5
Ferro, Scipione	1505	Italy	6
Fibonacci, Leonardo	1210	Italy	33
Fourier, Jean	1808	France	24
Fréchet, Rene	1918	France	15
Frege, Friedrich	1888	Germany	7
Frobenius, Georg	1889	Germany	3
Galois, Evariste	1832	France	15
Gauss, Carl	1817	Germany	81
Gelfond, Aleksander	1946	Russia	7
Gergonne, Joseph	1811	France	14
Germain, Sophie	1816	France	4
Girard, Albert	1632	France	9
Gödel, Kurt	1946	Bohemia	18
Goldbach, Christian	1730	Germany	3
Grassmann, Hermann	1849	Germany	20
Green, George	1833	England	1
Gregory, James	1675	Scotland	23
Guldin, Paul	1617	Switzerland	6
Gunter, Edmund	1621	England	1
Hadamard, Jacques	1905	France	11
Hamilton, William	1845	Ireland	28
Hankel, Hermann	1873	Germany	3
Hardy, Godfrey	1917	England	7

Name	fl	Nat'l orgin	Index	Name	fl	Nat'l orgin	Index
Harriot, Thomas	1600	England	2	Mises, Richard von	1923	Austria	1
Hartmann, Georg	1529	Germany	1	Möbius, August	1830	Germany	10
Hausdorff, Felix	1908	Germany	6	Moivre, Abraham de	1707	France	18
Heine, Heinrich E.	1852	Germany	4	Monge, Gaspard	1786	France	27
Hermite, Charles	1862	France	7	Morgenstern, Oskar	1944	USA	7
Hero of Alexandria	62	Greece	17	Napier, John	1590	Scotland	19
Hilbert, David	1902	Germany	40	Newton, Isaac	1682	England	87
Hippias of Elis	−400	Greece	7	Nicomachus of Gerasa	100	Rome	5
Hippocrates of Chios	−430	Greece	10	Noether, Emmy	1922	Germany	10
Hudde, Jan	1668	Netherlands	5	Oresme, Nicole	1360	France	26
Huygens, Christiaan	1669	Netherlands	21	Oughtred, William	1615	England	13
Hypatia of Alexandria	410	Rome	3	Pacioli, Luca	1485	Italy	21
Jacobi, Carl	1844	Germany	17	Pappus of Alexandria	350	Greece	16
Jordan, Marie	1878	France	11	Pascal, Blaise	1662	France	47
Khayyam, Omar				Pasch, Moritz	1883	Germany	3
(al-Khayyami)	1088	Persia	13	Peacock, George	1831	England	8
Klein, Christian	1889	Germany	22	Peano, Giuseppe	1898	Italy	24
Kolmogorov, Andrey	1943	Russia	4	Pearson, Karl	1897	England	8
Kovalevskaya, Sonya	1890	Russia	8	Pitiscus, Bartholomew	1601	Germany	8
Kronecker, Leopold	1863	Germany	10	Plücker, Julius	1841	Germany	11
Kummer, Ernst	1850	Germany	7	Poincaré, Jules	1894	France	28
L'Hospital,				Poisson, Siméon	1821	France	12
Guillaume de	1701	France	9	Poncelet, Jean	1828	France	26
Lagrange, Joseph	1776	Italy	30	Ptolemy	140	Rome	28
Lambert, Johann	1768	Germany	15	Pythagoras of Samos	−520	Greece	23
Laplace, Pierre	1789	France	17	Quetelet, Adolphe	1836	Belgium	1
Lebesgue, Henri	1915	France	10	Ramanujan, Srinivasa	1920	India	7
Legendre, Adrien	1792	France	37	Recorde, Robert	1550	England	17
Leibniz, Gottfried	1686	Germany	70	Riemann, Bernhard	1866	Germany	47
Levi-Civita, Tullio	1913	Italy	4	Rolle, Michel	1692	France	3
Lie, Marius	1882	Norway	10	Rudolff, Christoff	1540	Germany	9
Lindemann, Carl von	1892	Germany	11	Ruffini, Paolo	1805	Italy	7
Liouville, Joseph	1849	France	13	Russell, Bertrand	1912	England	15
Liu Hui	250	China	5	Saccheri, Girolamo	1707	Italy	11
Lobachevsky, Nikolay	1832	Russia	19	Saint Vincent,			
Maclaurin, Colin	1738	Scotland	27	Gregorius	1624	Belgium	2
Markov, Andrei	1896	Russia	7	Simpson, Thomas	1750	England	3
Menaechmus	−350	Greece	11	Steiner, Jakob	1836	Switzerland	8
Menelaus				Stevin, Simon	1588	Belgium	20
of Alexandria	98	Rome	14	Stifel, Michael	1527	Germany	10
Meray, Hagues	1875	France	3	Stirling, James	1732	Scotland	3
Mercator, Nicolaus	1659	Belgium	6	Sylvester, James	1854	England	9
Mersenne, Marin	1628	France	6	Tartaglia (Fontana)	1539	Italy	32
Minkowski, Hermann	1904	Germany	11	Taylor, Brook	1725	England	16

Name	fl	Nat'l orgin	Index	Name	fl	Nat'l orgin	Index
Tchebycheff, Pafnuty	1861	Russia	4	Waerden, B.L. van der	1943	Netherlands	4
Theaetetus of Athens	−377	Greece	3	Wallis, John	1656	England	35
Theodorus of Cyrene	−425	Greece	5	Wedderburn, Joseph	1922	Scotland	1
Theon of Smyrna	130	Greece	5	Weierstrass, Karl	1855	Germany	20
Tschirnhaus, Ehrenfried	1691	Germany	2	Wessel, Caspar	1785	Norway	9
Vallée-Poussin,				Weyl, Hermann	1925	Germany	7
Charles de la	1906	Belgium	6	Whitehead, Alfred	1901	England	11
Vandermonde,				Widman, Johannes	1498	Bohemia	8
Alexandre	1775	France	1	Wiener, Norbert	1934	USA	1
Venn, John	1874	England	1	Zeno of Elea	−450	Greece	2
Viéte, Francois	1580	France	36	Zermelo, Ernst	1911	Germany	6
Volterra, Vito	1900	Italy	5	Zhu Shijie	1290	China	5
Von Neumann, John	1943	Hungary	19	Zu Chongzhi	479	China	5

THE MEDICINE INVENTORY

SUMMARY STATISTICS

Total number of entries	1,080
Parent population	540
Significant figures	160
Major figures	31
Index reliability (Cronbach's α)	.87

CORRELATION MATRIX FOR THE INDEX SOURCES ($n=160$)

	1	2	3	4	5	6	7	8	9	10	11	12	13	14	15	16	17
1 Adling.	1.00	.45	−.01	.33	.11	.29	.45	.19	.02	.11	.31	.33	.44	.04	.13	.16	−.02
2 Asimov	.45	1.00	.13	.39	.25	.34	.61	.19	.07	.05	.52	.29	.51	−.01	.18	.27	.07
3 Bendin.	−.01	.13	1.00	.08	.32	.16	.11	.41	.17	.39	.04	.17	.13	.47	.49	.29	.30
4 Bruno	.33	.39	.08	1.00	.35	.24	.37	.31	.08	.16	.34	.29	.43	.10	.21	.18	.13
5 Gilles.	.11	.25	.32	.35	1.00	.25	.37	.53	.29	.40	.30	.31	.30	.35	.44	.37	.42
6 Grun	.29	.34	.16	.24	.25	1.00	.40	.25	.07	.17	.35	.26	.30	.12	.28	.31	.11
7 Hellem.	.45	.61	.11	.37	.37	.40	1.00	.23	.06	.11	.43	.29	.51	.09	.23	.27	.15
8 Magner	.19	.19	.41	.31	.53	.25	.23	1.00	.31	.85	.21	.35	.29	.84	.74	.34	.35
9 Marc.	.02	.07	.17	.08	.29	.07	.06	.31	1.00	.37	.02	.03	−.01	.26	.32	.45	.52
10 McGr.	.11	.05	.39	.16	.40	.17	.11	.85	.37	1.00	.08	.37	.22	.83	.67	.29	.49
11 Mount	.31	.52	.04	.34	.30	.35	.43	.21	.02	.08	1.00	.39	.38	.03	.15	.20	.15
12 Ochoa	.33	.29	.17	.29	.31	.26	.29	.35	.03	.37	.39	1.00	.41	.24	.32	.24	.24
13 Park.	.44	.51	.13	.43	.30	.30	.51	.29	−.01	.22	.38	.41	1.00	.16	.19	.27	.18
14 Port(a)	.04	−.01	.47	.10	.35	.12	.09	.84	.26	.83	.03	.24	.16	1.00	.79	.25	.34
15 Port(b)	.13	.18	.49	.21	.44	.28	.23	.74	.32	.67	.15	.32	.19	.79	1.00	.47	.35
16 Port(c)	.16	.27	.29	.18	.37	.31	.27	.34	.45	.29	.20	.24	.27	.25	.47	1.00	.37
17 Taton	−.02	.07	.30	.13	.42	.11	.15	.35	.52	.49	.15	.24	.18	.34	.35	.37	1.00

Note: The index scores for the scientific inventories combined separate subscores from the chronologies and the history/biographical dictionary sources. The reliability refers to Cronbach's α based on the correlations in the above matrix.

THE ROSTER OF SIGNIFICANT FIGURES

Name	fl	Nat'l orgin	Index	Name	fl	Nat'l orgin	Index
Addison, Thomas	1833	England	22	Dick, Gladys	1921	USA	7
Alcmaeon	520	Greece	4	Dioskourides, Pedanius	80	Rome	32
Allbutt, Thomas	1876	Britain	10	Domagk, Gerhard	1935	Germany	36
Aselli, Gasparo	1621	Italy	2	Donders, Franciscus	1858	Netherlands	6
Auenbrugger, Leopold	1762	Austria	20	Drinker, Philip	1934	USA	8
Banting, Frederick	1931	Canada	27	Ehrlich, Paul	1894	Germany	59
Beddoes, Thomas	1800	England	17	Eijkman, Christiaan	1898	Netherlands	18
Behring, Emil von	1894	Germany	44	Einhorn, Alfred	1904	Germany	12
Bell, Charles	1814	Scotland	16	Enders, John	1937	USA	9
Bernard, Claude	1853	France	24	Euler, Ulf von	1945	Sweden	2
Best, Charles	1939	USA	19	Evans, Herbert	1922	USA	11
Billroth, Christian	1869	Germany	14	Fauchard, Pierre	1718	France	17
Blalock, Alfred	1939	USA	10	Fernel, François	1537	France	15
Böerhaave, Hermann	1708	Netherlands	29	Fibiger, Johannes	1907	Denmark	5
Bovet, Daniel	1947	Switzerland	21	Finlay, Carlos	1873	Cuba	9
Bretonneau, Pierre	1818	France	10	Finsen, Niels	1900	Denmark	6
Breuer, Josef	1882	Austria	25	Fleming, Alexander	1921	Scotland	47
Bright, Richard	1829	England	21	Flexner, Simon	1903	USA	3
Broca, Pierre	1864	France	3	Florey, Howard	1938	Australia	28
Brunschwig, Hieronymus	1490	Germany	1	Forssmann, Werner	1944	Germany	17
Burnet, Frank	1939	Australia	11	Fracastoro, Girolamo	1518	Italy	33
Cannon, Walter	1911	USA	16	Freud, Sigmund	1896	Bohemia	35
Carrel, Alexis	1913	France	37	Funk, Casimir	1924	Poland	23
Caventou, Joseph	1835	France	18	Galen of Pergamum	170	Greece	72
Celsus, Aulus	20	Rome	22	Garrod, Archibald	1897	England	3
Cerletti, Ugo	1917	Italy	5	Gibbon, John H.	1943	USA	14
Chain, Ernst	1946	Germany	27	Glisson, Francis	1637	England	8
Charcot, Jean	1865	France	25	Goldberger, Joseph	1914	Slovakia	17
Chauliac, Guy de	1330	France	16	Gorgas, William	1894	USA	5
Claus, Carl	1836	Russia	1	Graaf, Regnier de	1673	Netherlands	2
Cohnheim, Julius	1879	Germany	6	Hahnemann, Christian	1795	Germany	14
Collip, James	1932	Canada	19	Halsted, William	1892	USA	21
Constantine of Africa	1055	No Africa	5	Hata, Sahachiro	1912	Japan	15
Cordus, Valerius	1544	Germany	4	Hench, Philip	1936	USA	11
Cournand, André	1935	France	10	Henle, Friedrich	1849	Germany	15
Crile, George	1904	USA	4	Henry of Mondeville	1300	France	8
Cushing, Harvey	1909	USA	20	Hinshaw, Corwin	1942	USA	8
Dale, Henry	1915	England	6	Hippocrates of Cos	−420	Greece	83
Darwin, Erasmus	1771	England	6	Hodgkin, Thomas	1838	England	10
Davis, Marguerite	1914	USA	16	Holmes, Oliver	1849	USA	16
Denis, Jean	1680	France	11	Huggins, Charles	1941	Canada	5
Dick, George	1921	USA	7	Hunter, John	1768	Scotland	33

Name	fl	Nat'l orgin	Index	Name	fl	Nat'l orgin	Index
ibn an-Nafis				Ramazzini, Bernardino	1673	Italy	10
(al-Qarashi)	1250	Syria	4	Ramón y Cajal,			
Jackson, John	1875	England	13	Santiago	1892	Spain	4
Jenner, Edward	1789	England	32	Reed, Walter	1891	USA	14
King, Charles	1936	USA	16	Rhazes (al-Razi)	894	Persia	26
Kitasato, Shibasaburo	1892	Japan	42	Rice-Wray, Edris	1944	USA	1
Klebs, Edwin	1873	Germany	27	Richards, Dickinson	1935	USA	10
Koch, Robert	1883	Germany	89	Ricketts, Howard	1910	USA	19
Koller, Carl	1897	Austria	12	Riva-Rocci, Scipione	1903	Italy	10
Kuhn, Richard	1940	Austria	8	Rock, John	1930	USA	13
Laënnec, René	1821	France	54	Ross, Ronald	1897	England	20
Lind, James	1756	Scotland	23	Roux, Pierre	1893	France	25
Lister, Joseph	1867	England	43	Rush, Benjamin	1786	USA	15
Loewi, Otto	1913	Germany	2	Santorio, Santorio	1601	Italy	16
Löffler, Friedrich	1892	Germany	21	Semmelweiss, Ignaz	1858	Hungary	34
Lower, Richard	1671	England	18	Sertürner, Friedrich	1823	Bohemia	3
Magendie, François	1823	France	8	Sharpey-Schäfer,			
Manson, Patrick	1884	Scotland	14	Edward	1890	England	2
McCollum, Elmer	1919	USA	51	Shaw, Louis	1926	USA	8
Mellanby, Edward	1924	Scotland	15	Simpson, James	1851	Scotland	19
Minot, George	1925	USA	14	Snow, John	1853	England	28
Morgagni, Giovanni	1722	Italy	21	Soranus of Ephesus	120	Rome	13
Morton, William	1859	USA	23	Stahl, Georg	1700	Germany	11
Murphy, William	1932	USA	10	Sydenham, Thomas	1664	England	39
Neisser, Albert	1895	Germany	7	Szent-Györgyi, Albert	1933	Hungary	30
Nicolle, Charles	1906	France	11	Taussig, Helen	1938	USA	8
Oribasios of Pergamon	365	Greece	5	Theiler, Max	1939	So Africa	13
Paracelsus	1533	Switzerland	68	Vesalius, Andreas	1554	Belgium	19
Paré, Ambroise	1550	France	46	Virchow, Rudolph	1861	Germany	27
Parkinson, James	1795	England	10	Wagner von Jauregg,			
Pasteur, Louis	1862	France	100	Julius	1897	Austria	9
Pelletier, Pierre	1828	France	22	Waksman, Selman	1928	Russia	22
Petit, Jean	1714	France	7	Watson, Thomas	1832	England	2
Pettenkofer, Max von	1858	Germany	8	Wells, Horace	1848	USA	11
Pincus, Gregory	1943	USA	16	Whipple, George Hoyt	1918	USA	2
Pinel, Philippe	1785	France	22	Whytt, Robert	1754	Scotland	6
Pirquet, Clemens von	1914	Austria	7	Wilkins, Robert	1946	USA	10
Pott, Percival	1754	England	7	Willis, Thomas	1661	England	26
Praxagoras of Cos	−310	Greece	3	Withering, William	1781	England	22
Pringle, John	1747	Scotland	6	Wright, Almroth	1901	England	1

THE TECHNOLOGY INVENTORY

SUMMARY STATISTICS

Total number of entries	1,139
Parent population	848
Significant figures	239
Major figures	40
Index reliability (Cronbach's α)	.84

CORRELATION MATRIX FOR THE INDEX SOURCES ($n=239$)

	1	2	3	4	5	6	7	8	9	10	11	12	13	14	15	16	17
1 Adling.	1.00	.27	.50	.09	.08	.05	.41	.47	.15	.48	.26	.40	.16	.27	.16	.20	.02
2 Asimov	.27	1.00	.55	.20	−.01	.00	.34	.48	.13	.54	.58	.41	.25	.14	.10	.29	.05
3 Bruno	.50	.55	1.00	.25	.02	.01	.45	.55	.24	.58	.47	.42	.28	.22	.17	.37	.11
4 Card	.09	.20	.25	1.00	.26	.15	.18	.22	.32	.31	.05	.20	.35	.52	.19	.54	.25
5 Gille	.08	−.01	.02	.26	1.00	.56	.03	.27	.42	.20	−.03	.09	.09	.65	.47	.41	.49
6 Gilles.	.05	.00	.01	.15	.56	1.00	.07	.33	.47	.09	.00	.19	.04	.44	.66	.11	.51
7 Grun	.41	.34	.45	.18	.03	.07	1.00	.52	.12	.39	.31	.49	.25	.27	.15	.26	.06
8 Hellem..	.47	.48	.55	.22	.27	.33	.52	1.00	.32	.52	.35	.43	.18	.43	.34	.34	.22
9 Marc.	.15	.13	.24	.32	.42	.47	.12	.32	1.00	.28	.08	.16	.17	.44	.50	.28	.58
10 Mount	.48	.54	.58	.31	.20	.09	.39	.52	.28	1.00	.39	.42	.31	.35	.13	.32	.16
11 Ochoa	.26	.58	.47	.05	−.03	.00	.31	.35	.08	.39	1.00	.32	.23	.02	.05	.18	−.01
12 Park.	.40	.41	.42	.20	.09	.19	.49	.43	.16	.42	.32	1.00	.11	.26	.25	.24	.18
13 Porter	.16	.25	.28	.35	.09	.04	.25	.18	.17	.31	.23	.11	1.00	.28	.06	.45	.07
14 Singer	.27	.14	.22	.52	.65	.44	.27	.43	.44	.35	.02	.26	.28	1.00	.32	.55	.38
15 Taton	.16	.10	.17	.19	.47	.66	.15	.34	.50	.13	.05	.25	.06	.32	1.00	.18	.57
16 Will.	.20	.29	.37	.54	.41	.11	.26	.34	.28	.32	.18	.24	.45	.55	.18	1.00	.28
17 Wuss.	.02	.05	.11	.25	.49	.51	.06	.22	.58	.16	−.01	.18	.07	.38	.57	.28	1.00

Note: The index scores for the scientific inventories combined separate subscores from the chronologies and the history/biographical dictionary sources. The reliability refers to Cronbach's α based on the correlations in the above matrix.

ROSTER OF THE SIGNIFICANT FIGURES

Name	fl	Nat'l orgin	Index	Name	fl	Nat'l orgin	Index
Adams, Ansel	1942	USA	1	Chappe, Claude	1803	France	11
Aiken, Howard	1940	USA	12	Cierva, Juan de la	1935	Spain	8
Alberti, Leon Battista	1444	Italy	20	Claude, Georges	1910	France	10
Amici, Giovanni				Colt, Samuel	1854	USA	15
Battista	1826	Italy	1	Cooke, William	1846	England	13
Anschutz-Kämpfer,				Cort, Henry	1780	England	14
Hermann	1912	Germany	8	Crompton, Samuel	1793	England	7
Appert, Nicolas	1790	France	23	Crookes, William	1872	England	1
Archimedes	−247	Greece	50	Cross, Charles	1895	England	12
Arkwright, Richard	1772	England	27	Ctesibius	−270	Greece	20
Armstrong, Edwin	1930	USA	26	Cugnot, Nicholas	1768	France	12
Armstrong, William	1850	England	10	Daguerre, Louis	1827	France	16
Aspdin, Joseph	1839	England	11	Daimler, Gottlieb	1874	Germany	16
Auer, Karl	1898	Austria	9	Darby, Abraham	1717	England	18
Babbage, Charles	1832	England	32	Darby, Abraham III	1790	England	11
Baekeland, Leo	1903	Belgium	16	Davy, Humphrey	1818	England	18
Baird, John	1928	Scotland	13	De Forest, Lee	1913	USA	23
Beebe, Charles	1917	USA	1	Deslandres, Henri	1893	France	1
Bell, Alexander	1887	Scotland	25	Dewar, James	1882	Scotland	13
Bell, Patrick	1839	Scotland	11	Diesel, Rudolf	1898	Germany	28
Benz, Carl	1884	Germany	18	Dollond, John	1746	England	1
Bessemer, Henry	1853	England	33	Dornberger, Walter	1935	Germany	7
Birdseye, Clarence	1926	USA	8	Drake, Edwin	1859	USA	10
Biro Brothers	1938	Hungary	10	Drebbel, Cornelius	1612	Netherlands	10
Blanchard, Jean	1793	France	15	Duhamel du			
Blériot, Louis	1912	France	12	Monceau, Henri	1740	France	1
Booth, Herbert	1911	England	7	Dunlop, John	1880	England	10
Bosch, Carl	1914	Germany	14	Eastman, George	1894	USA	15
Boulton, Matthew	1768	England	17	Edison, Thomas	1887	USA	100
Boyle, Robert	1667	Germany	4	Eiffel, Alexandre	1872	France	6
Bramah, Joseph	1788	England	16	Ericsson, John	1843	Sweden	10
Branly, Edouard	1884	France	11	Evans, Oliver	1795	USA	23
Braun, Karl	1890	Germany	8	Fahrenheit, Daniel	1726	Germany	1
Brunel, Isambard	1846	England	23	Faraday, Michael	1831	England	31
Brunel, Marc	1809	France	11	Fessenden, Reginald	1906	Canada	14
Brunelleschi, Filippo	1417	Italy	1	Field, Cyrus	1859	USA	7
Bunsen, Robert	1851	Germany	13	Fitch, John	1783	USA	15
Bush, Vannevar	1930	USA	16	Fleming, John	1889	England	17
Böttger, Johann	1719	Germany	10	Ford, Henry	1903	USA	17
Cardano, Girolamo	1541	Italy	2	Fourneyron, Benoît	1842	France	9
Carlson, Chester	1946	USA	14	Fox Talbot, William	1840	England	16
Cartwright, Edmund	1783	England	10	Francis, James Bicheno	1855	England	8
Cayley, George	1813	England	24	Franklin, Benjamin	1750	USA	32

Name	fl	Nat'l orgin	Index
Fresnel, Augustin	1827	France	4
Fulton, Robert	1805	USA	21
Gagnan, Emile	1943	France	2
Galileo Galilei	1604	Italy	18
Gascoigne, William	1644	England	6
Gauss, Carl	1817	Germany	9
Gay-Lussac, Joseph	1818	France	15
Giffard, Henri	1865	France	9
Goddard, Robert	1922	USA	26
Goethals, George	1898	USA	10
Goldmark, Peter	1946	Hungary	15
Goodyear, Charles	1840	USA	18
Gramme, Zénobe	1866	Belgium	12
Gray, Elisha	1875	USA	14
Groves, Leslie	1936	USA	10
Gutenberg, Johannes	1430	Germany	23
Hadfield, Robert	1898	England	6
Hadley, John	1722	England	10
Hall, John	1805	USA	7
Hancock, Thomas	1826	England	9
Hargreaves, James	1760	England	10
Harrison, John	1733	England	18
Henlein, Peter	1502	Germany	2
Henry, Joseph	1837	USA	22
Hero of Alexandria	62	Greece	27
Hollerith, Herman	1900	USA	16
Hooke, Robert	1675	England	23
Hornblower, Jonathan	1793	England	12
Howe, Elias	1859	USA	11
Hughes, David	1871	England	14
Huntsman, Benjamin	1744	England	11
Hussey, Obed	1873	USA	11
Huygens, Christiaan	1669	Netherlands	50
Hyatt, John	1877	USA	15
Héroult, Paul	1903	France	19
Jacquard, Joseph	1792	France	15
Jansky, Karl	1945	USA	1
Kay, John	1744	England	15
Kelly, William	1853	USA	16
Kennelly, Arthur	1901	Ireland	12
Kettering, Charles	1916	USA	11
Korolev, Sergei	1947	Russia	1
Koster, Lauren	1410	Netherlands	11

Name	fl	Nat'l orgin	Index
Land, Edwin	1949	USA	19
Langley, Samuel	1874	USA	8
Laval, Carl de	1885	Sweden	9
Lawes, John	1854	England	16
Lebon, Philippe	1804	France	12
Leclanché, Georges	1879	France	8
Lee, William	1590	England	8
Leeuwenhoek, Antoni van	1672	Netherlands	1
Leibniz, Gottfried	1686	Germany	26
Lenoir, Jean	1862	Belgium	23
Lenormand, L.S.	1783	France	8
Leonardo da Vinci	1492	Italy	58
Lesseps, Ferdinand de	1845	France	9
Liebig, Justis von	1843	Germany	5
Lilienthal, Otto	1888	Germany	14
Lindbergh, Charles	1942	USA	10
Linde, Carl von	1882	Germany	10
Lippershey, Hans	1610	Netherlands	1
Lodge, Oliver	1891	England	10
Lumière Brothers	1902	France	14
Macmillan, Kirkpatrick	1839	Scotland	7
Marconi, Guglielmo	1914	Italy	50
Maskelyne, Nevil	1772	England	6
Mauchly, John	1947	USA	26
Maudslay, Henry	1811	England	15
Maybach, Wilhelm	1886	Germany	16
McAdam, John	1796	Scotland	12
McCormick, Cyrus	1849	USA	15
McCune, William	1942	USA	1
Meikle, Andrew	1783	Scotland	9
Mergenthaler, Ottmar	1894	Germany	10
Midgley, Thomas, Jr.	1929	USA	16
Moissan, Ferdinand	1892	France	7
Montgolfier Brothers	1785	France	19
Morse, Samuel	1831	USA	31
Murdock, William	1794	Scotland	24
Nasmyth, James	1848	Scotland	13
Neckam, Alexander	1125	Britain	7
Newcomen, Thomas	1703	England	32
Nicholson, William	1793	England	1
Niépce, Joseph	1805	France	21
Nobel, Alfred	1873	Sweden	32

Name	fl	Nat'l orgin	Index	Name	fl	Nat'l orgin	Index
Norman, Robert	1590	England	1	Sommeiller, Germain	1855	France	6
Otis, Elisha	1851	USA	10	Sostrastes of Cnidos	−270	Greece	8
Otto, Nikolaus	1872	Germany	20	Sperry, Elmer	1900	USA	12
Papin, Denis	1687	France	31	Sprague, Frank	1897	USA	11
Parkes, Alexander	1853	England	17	Steinmetz, Charles	1905	Germany	1
Parsons, Charles	1894	Ireland	21	Stephenson, George	1821	England	30
Pasteur, Louis	1862	France	25	Stevens, John	1893	USA	10
Pi Sheng	1045	China	8	Strutt, Jedediah	1764	England	8
Pixii, Hippolyte	1835	France	6	Swan, Joseph	1868	England	24
Planté, Gaston	1874	France	12	Tesla, Nikola	1896	Croatia	18
Platt, Hugh	1603	England	8	Thomson, James	1862	Scotland	4
Popov, Aleksandr	1899	Russia	19	Thomson, William	1864	Scotland	29
Porta, Giambattista				Trevithick, Richard	1811	England	29
della	1575	Italy	8	Tsiolkovsky,			
Poulsen, Valdemar	1909	Denmark	12	Konstantin	1897	Russia	5
Prony, Gaspard de	1795	France	6	Cai Lun	100	China	9
Pullman, George	1871	USA	6	Tull, Jethro	1714	England	17
Rankine, William	1860	Scotland	4	Vaucanson, Jacques de	1749	France	10
Reynolds, Osborne	1882	England	1	Vitruvius Pollio	−50	Rome	41
Riquet de Benrepos,				Von Neumann, John	1943	Hungary	26
Pierre	1664	France	6	Wankel, Felix	1942	Germany	13
Roebling, John	1846	Germany	9	Watson-Watt, Robert	1932	Scotland	16
Roebuck, John	1758	England	14	Watt, James	1776	Scotland	100
Ruhmkorff, Heinrich	1843	Germany	9	Weber, Wilhelm	1844	Germany	13
Ruska, Ernst	1946	Germany	1	Wedgwood, Josiah	1770	England	11
Réaumur, René de	1723	France	23	Westinghouse, George	1886	USA	24
Savery, Thomas	1690	England	28	Wheatstone, Charles	1842	England	31
Schmidt, Paul	1942	Germany	1	Whitney, Eli	1805	USA	24
Seguin, Marc	1826	France	13	Whittle, Frank	1947	England	15
Senefelder, Aloys	1811	Bohemia	9	Whitworth, Joseph	1843	England	14
Shockley, William	1950	USA	16	Wilkinson, John	1768	England	32
Sholes, Christopher	1859	USA	7	Winsor, Frederick	1803	Germany	5
Siemens, Charles	1863	Germany	32	Wren, Christopher	1672	England	1
Siemens, Ernst	1856	Germany	25	Wright Brothers	1911	USA	27
Sikorsky, Igor	1929	Ukraine	17	Young, James	1862	Scotland	10
Singer, Isaac	1851	USA	11	Zeppelin, Ferdinand von	1878	Germany	16
Smeaton, John	1764	England	36	Zworykin, Vladimir	1929	Russia	22

THE CHINESE ART INVENTORY

SUMMARY STATISTICS

Total number of entries	421
Parent population	280
Significant figures	111
Major figures	31
Index reliability (Cronbach's α)	.91

CORRELATION MATRIX FOR THE INDEX SOURCES ($n=104*$)

	1	2	3	4	5	6	7	8	9	10	11	12	13	14	15	16	17
1 Ashton	1.00	.46	.37	.30	.44	.39	.34	.44	.43	.24	.49	.33	.44	.38	.34	.19	.41
2 Binyon	.46	1.00	.39	.15	.55	.28	.49	.44	.27	.21	.42	.38	.41	.32	.18	.12	.23
3 Burling	.37	.39	1.00	.38	.43	.50	.47	.45	.31	.23	.43	.43	.49	.44	.41	.38	.39
4 Cahill	.30	.15	.38	1.00	.31	.51	.20	.45	.37	.42	.58	.57	.30	.58	.69	.33	.63
5 Carter	.44	.55	.43	.31	1.00	.32	.52	.56	.45	.36	.48	.47	.42	.55	.28	.30	.43
6 Clunas	.39	.28	.50	.51	.32	1.00	.26	.32	.27	.28	.54	.42	.34	.54	.48	.21	.63
7 Cohn	.34	.49	.47	.20	.52	.26	1.00	.30	.24	.13	.29	.46	.53	.40	.35	.23	.37
8 Croix	.44	.44	.45	.45	.56	.32	.30	1.00	.56	.37	.64	.54	.27	.50	.41	.44	.45
9 Enc. Brit	.43	.27	.31	.37	.45	.27	.24	.56	1.00	.31	.49	.44	.30	.37	.43	.41	.32
10 Froncek	.24	.21	.23	.42	.36	.28	.13	.37	.31	1.00	.48	.43	.36	.28	.36	.42	.37
11 Gowing	.49	.42	.43	.58	.48	.54	.29	.64	.49	.48	1.00	.64	.32	.65	.59	.39	.67
12 Loehr	.33	.38	.43	.57	.47	.42	.46	.54	.44	.43	.64	1.00	.43	.62	.68	.32	.63
13 Speiser	.44	.41	.49	.30	.42	.34	.53	.27	.30	.36	.32	.43	1.00	.39	.29	.30	.41
14 Sullivan	.38	.32	.44	.58	.55	.54	.40	.50	.37	.28	.65	.62	.39	1.00	.62	.39	.60
15 Turner	.34	.18	.41	.69	.28	.48	.35	.41	.43	.36	.59	.68	.29	.62	1.00	.28	.68
16 Willetts	.19	.12	.38	.33	.30	.21	.23	.44	.41	.42	.39	.32	.30	.39	.28	1.00	.39
17 Xin	.41	.23	.39	.63	.43	.63	.37	.45	.32	.37	.67	.63	.41	.60	.68	.39	1.00

* Index scores were not calculated for significant figures who were active after 1799.

THE ROSTER OF SIGNIFICANT FIGURES

Name	fl	Index	Name	fl	Index
Bada Shanren (Zhu Da)	1666	39	Li Zhaodao	715	6
Bian Wenjin	1420	5	Li Zhen	800	5
Cao Buxing	250	7	Liang Kai	1180	23
Cao Zhibai	1311	6	Lin Liang	1500	12
Chen Hongshou	1638	28	Liu Haisu	1936	
Chen Rong	1240	7	Liu Songnian	1190	7
Cui Bai (Cui Bo)	1060	10	Lu Ji	1517	6
Dai Jin	1428	30	Lu Tanwei	450	6
Dai Song	750	21	Ma Ben (Fen)	1110	3
Dong Qichang	1595	80	Ma Lin	1230	9
Dong Yuan	940	54	Ma Yuan	1200	78
Du Qiong	1436	2	Mi Fu (Mi Fei)	1091	70
Fan Kuan	1030	42	Mi Youren	1115	10
Fu Baoshi	1944		Muqi (Muxi)	1240	50
Gao Kegong	1288	13	Ni Zan	1341	68
Gao Qifeng	1929		Qi Baishi	1904	
Gao Qipei	1700	9	Qian Xuan	1275	36
Gong Xian	1658	10	Qiu Ying	1550	35
Gu Hongzhong	950	3	Ren Renfa	1295	11
Gu Kaizhi	385	100	Shen Zhou	1467	56
Guan Tong	910	13	Sheng Mao	1350	5
Guanxiu	872	9	Shi Ke	900	7
Guo Xi	1041	72	Shitao (Yuanji)	1682	50
Han Gan	760	34	Su Shi (Su Dongpo)	1076	54
Hongren (Jiang Tao)	1650	9	Tang Yin	1510	41
Hua Yan	1722	5	Wang Fu	1402	2
Huang Binhong	1905		Wang Hui	1672	28
Huang Gongwang	1309	76	Wang Jian	1638	16
Huang Jucai	973	5	Wang Meng	1349	48
Huang Quan	943	15	Wang Mo	790	2
Huang Shen	1727	5	Wang Shimin	1632	18
Huang Tingjian	1085	5	Wang Wei	739	63
Huizong	1122	59	Wang Xizhi	347	26
Jin Nong	1727	9	Wang Yuan	1320	2
Jing Hao	895	21	Wang Yuanqi	1682	28
Juran	970	26	Wei Xie	300	2
Kuncan (Shiqi)	1652	11	Wen Jia	1541	5
Li Cheng	959	30	Wen Shu	1634	3
Li Gonglin	1081	45	Wen Tong	1059	11
Li Kan	1285	7	Wen Zhengming	1510	46
Li Sixun	691	30	Wu Daoxuan (Wu Daozi)	720	83
Li Song	1210	3	Wu Li (Mojing Daoren)	1672	8
Li Tang	1090	17	Wu Wei	1499	17

Name	fl	Index	Name	fl	Index
Wu Zhen	1320	47	Zhang Sengyou	520	8
Xia Gui	1220	71	Zhang Xuan	730	16
Xiang Shengmou	1637	3	Zhang Zao	775	4
Xu Beihong	1935		Zhang Zeduan	1110	4
Xu Daoning	1010	11	Zhao Boju	1150	9
Xu Wei	1521	13	Zhao Chang	1000	9
Xu Xi	960	10	Zhao Lingrang (Zhao Danian)	1090	5
Yan Hui	1300	8	Zhao Mengfu	1294	100
Yan Liben	640	42	Zhou Chen	1512	7
Yan Lide	645	3	Zhou Fang	770	17
Yan Wengui	1007	7	Zhou Wenzhu	700	8
Yun Shouping	1673	17	Zou Fulei	1350	4
Zhang Daqian	1899				

THE JAPANESE ART INVENTORY

SUMMARY STATISTICS

Total number of entries	318
Parent population	182
Significant figures	81
Major figures	20
Index reliability (Cronbach's α)	.93

CORRELATION MATRIX FOR THE INDEX SOURCES (*n*=81)

	1	2	3	4	5	6	7	8	9	10	11	12	13	14
1 Bird	1.00	.44	.48	.37	.66	.40	.63	.49	.47	.55	.46	.54	.46	.62
2 Croix	.44	1.00	.43	.48	.51	.46	.49	.48	.44	.45	.33	.38	.45	.54
3 Elisseeff	.48	.43	1.00	.67	.68	.70	.41	.60	.51	.53	.43	.51	.69	.47
2 Enc. Brit	.37	.48	.67	1.00	.36	.72	.31	.57	.48	.31	.45	.34	.66	.54
3 Ishizawa	.66	.51	.68	.36	1.00	.56	.60	.54	.45	.81	.46	.67	.50	.60
6 Kidder	.40	.46	.70	.72	.56	1.00	.49	.62	.52	.50	.60	.50	.76	.50
7 Mason	.63	.49	.41	.31	.60	.49	1.00	.48	.55	.66	.56	.57	.48	.57
8 Munsterberg	.49	.48	.60	.57	.54	.62	.48	1.00	.52	.38	.54	.32	.64	.48
9 Museum	.47	.44	.51	.48	.45	.52	.55	.52	1.00	.48	.70	.45	.53	.61
9 Noma	.55	.45	.53	.31	.81	.50	.66	.38	.48	1.00	.52	.65	.43	.59
10 Paine	.46	.33	.43	.45	.46	.60	.56	.54	.70	.52	1.00	.43	.41	.57
11 Stanley-B.	.54	.38	.51	.34	.67	.50	.57	.32	.45	.65	.43	1.00	.37	.52
13 Swann	.46	.45	.69	.66	.50	.76	.48	.64	.53	.43	.41	.37	1.00	.47
14 Turner	.62	.54	.47	.54	.60	.50	.57	.48	.61	.59	.57	.52	.47	1.00

THE ROSTER OF SIGNIFICANT FIGURES

Name	fl	Index	Name	fl	Index
Ando Hiroshige (Ichiryusai)	1837	39	Nonomura Ninsei	1638	19
Aoki Mokubei	1807	11	Ogata Kenzan	1703	39
Asahi Chu	1896	5	Ogata Korin	1698	89
Fujiwara Nobuzane	1216	9	Okumara Masonobu	1731	11
Fujiwara Takanobu	1182	18	Sakai Hoitsu	1801	15
Fujiwara Takayoshi	1150	6	Sakaida Kakiemon	1636	10
Gei-ami (Shingei)	1432	12	Sasaki Chojiro (Tanaka)	1556	11
Goyo Hashiguchi	1920	3	Sesson Shukei	1544	17
Hamada Shoji	1934	15	Shiba Kokan	1787	12
Hasegawa Tohaku			Shimomura Kanzan	1913	9
(Kyuroku)	1579	63	Soami (Shinso)	1510	28
Hashimoto Gaho	1875	8	Soga Jasoku (Dasoku)	1470	6
Hishikawa Moronobu	1665	23	Sotan (Oguri Sukeshige)	1438	7
Hon'ami Koetsu	1598	56	Sotaro Yasui	1928	14
Ikeno Taiga (Taigado)	1763	33	Sumiyoshi Jokei	1639	7
Ito Jakuchu	1756	7	Suzuki Harunobu	1760	31
Iwasa Matabei (Shoi)	1608	10	Taiko Jocho	1050	44
Kaiho Yusho	1573	23	Taiko Josetsu	1415	21
Kaikei (Anamidabutsu)	1200	24	Taiso Yoshitoshi	1879	1
Kano Eitoku (Kuninobu)	1583	63	Tani Buncho	1803	18
Kano Masanobu	1474	16	Tankei	1213	10
Kano Motonobu	1516	36	Tanomura Chikuden	1811	8
Kano Naganobu	1617	7	Tawaraya Sotatsu (Nonomura Ietsu)	1620	96
Kano Sanraku Kimura Mitsuyori)	1599	32	Tensho Shubun (Ekkei, Soga)	1460	31
Kano Tan'yu (Morinobu)	1642	38	Toba Sojo (Kakayu)	1053	16
Katsukawa Shunsho	1766	11	Tomioka Tessai	1875	6
Katsushika Hokusai	1800	55	Tori Busshi	620	28
Kawase Hasui	1923	6	Torii Kiyomasu	1700	8
Kichisan Mincho (Cho Densu)	1392	19	Torii Kiyonaga	1792	22
Kitagawa Utamaro	1793	32	Torii Kiyonobu	1704	10
Kobayashi Kokei (Shigeru)	1923	16	Tosa Mitsunobu	1474	13
Kokei	1180	9	Toshusai Sharaku (Saito)	1795	22
Kukai (Kobo Daishi)	814	49	Toyo Sesshu	1460	100
Kusumi Morikage	1660	6	Umehara Ryusaburo	1928	14
Maeda Seison	1925	12	Unkei	1210	48
Maruyama Okyo	1773	32	Unkoku Togan	1587	11
Matsumara Goshun (Gekkei)	1792	10	Uragami Gyokudo	1785	20
Miyagawa Choshun	1723	7	Watanabe Kazan	1833	12
Mokuan Reien	1335	11	Yokoyama Taikan	1908	25
Nagasawa Rosetsu	1795	7	Yosa Buson	1756	35
Noami (Nakao Shinno)	1437	17	Yoshida Hiroshi	1916	6

THE WESTERN ART INVENTORY

SUMMARY STATISTICS

Total number of entries	2,248
Parent population	1,232
Significant figures	479
Major figures	154
Index reliability (Cronbach's α)	.95

CORRELATION MATRIX FOR THE INDEX SOURCES (n=455*)

	1	2	3	4	5	6	7	8	9	10	11
1 Croix	1.00	.73	.67	.75	.72	.82	.61	.58	.74	.74	.66
2 Gombrich	.73	1.00	.73	.74	.75	.78	.64	.55	.73	.72	.73
3 Gowing	.67	.73	1.00	.74	.65	.73	.70	.59	.72	.69	.69
4 Honour	.75	.74	.74	1.00	.70	.79	.76	.68	.79	.81	.71
5 Istituto	.72	.75	.65	.70	1.00	.74	.55	.56	.67	.62	.76
6 Jansen	.82	.78	.73	.79	.74	1.00	.64	.59	.74	.79	.69
7 Marceau	.61	.64	.70	.76	.55	.64	1.00	.65	.67	.70	.58
8 Sproccati	.58	.55	.59	.68	.56	.59	.65	1.00	.66	.61	.53
9 Stadler	.74	.73	.72	.79	.67	.74	.67	.66	1.00	.72	.67
10 Stokstadt	.74	.72	.69	.81	.62	.79	.70	.61	.72	1.00	.63
11 Turner	.66	.73	.69	.71	.76	.69	.58	.53	.67	.63	1.00

* Index scores were not computed for artists who were active prior to 1200.

THE ROSTER OF SIGNIFICANT FIGURES

Name	fl	Nat'l orgin	Index
Adam, Robert	1768	Scotland	9
Aertsen, Pieter	1548	Netherlands	2
Agesander	−50	Greece	
Albani, Francesco	1618	Italy	1
Albers, Joseph	1928	Germany	3
Algardi, Alessandro	1629	Italy	2
Altdorfer, Albrecht	1520	Germany	10
Altichiero da Zevio	1380	Italy	3
Ammanati, Bartolommeo	1551	Italy	3
Andrea del Castagno	1457	Italy	8
Andrea del Sarto	1526	Italy	6
Angelico (di Pietro)	1435	Italy	17
Antonello da Messina	1470	Italy	7
Apelles of Kos	−350	Greece	
Apollodorus of Athens	−450	Greece	
Archipenko, Alexander	1927	Russia	3
Arnolfo di Cambio	1300	Italy	8
Arp, Jean (Hans)	1927	Germany	5
Asam, Cosmas	1726	Germany	2
Athanodorus	−50	Greece	
Bacon, Francis	1949	England	8
Baldung, Hans (Grien)	1524	Germany	3
Balla, Giacomo	1911	Italy	4
Barlach, Ernst	1910	Germany	5
Bartolommeo, Fra	1512	Italy	3
Barye, Antoine	1836	France	3
Bassano, Jacopo	1557	Italy	4
Batoni, Pompeo	1748	Italy	2
Beardsley, Aubrey	1898	England	7
Beccafumi, Domenico	1526	Italy	1
Beckmann, Max	1924	Germany	5
Behrens, Peter	1908	Germany	5
Bellini, Gentile	1469	Italy	3
Bellini, Giovanni	1470	Italy	24
Bellini, Jacopo	1440	Italy	3
Bellotto, Bernardo	1760	Italy	2
Bellows, George	1922	USA	1
Benedetto da Maiano	1482	Italy	1
Benozzo (Gozzoli)	1460	Italy	3
Benton, Thomas	1929	USA	1
Berlinghieri, Berlinghiero	1240	Italy	3

Name	fl	Nat'l orgin	Index
Bernard, Emile	1908	France	4
Bernini, Gian Lorenzo	1638	Italy	46
Berruguete, Alonso	1528	Spain	1
Berruguete, Pedro	1490	Spain	2
Bertoldo di Giovanni	1460	Italy	1
Bingham, George	1851	USA	4
Blake, William	1797	England	9
Boccioni, Umberto	1916	Italy	12
Böcklin, Arnold	1867	Switzerland	3
Bonheur, Rosa	1862	France	1
Bonnard, Pierre	1907	France	6
Bosch, Hieronymus	1490	Netherlands	19
Botticelli (Filipepi)	1484	Italy	26
Boucher, François	1743	France	14
Boudin, Eugene	1864	France	2
Bouts, Diedric	1455	Netherlands	4
Bramantino (Suardi)	1500	Italy	1
Brancusi, Constantin	1916	Romania	13
Braque, Georges	1922	France	24
Broederlam, Melchior	1409	Belgium	6
Bronzino, Agnolo	1543	Italy	8
Brouwer, Adriaen	1638	Belgium	1
Brown, Ford Madox	1861	England	2
Brueghel, Jan	1608	Netherlands	1
Brueghel, Pieter the Elder	1565	Netherlands	24
Burgkmair, Hans the Elder	1513	Germany	1
Burne-Jones, Edward	1873	England	3
Calder, Alexander	1938	USA	6
Callot, Jacques	1633	France	2
Cambiasio, Luca	1567	Italy	1
Canaletto, Giovanni	1737	Italy	7
Cano, Alonso	1641	Spain	2
Canova, Antonio	1797	Italy	15
Caravaggio (Merisi)	1610	Italy	35
Carpaccio, Vittore	1500	Italy	3
Carpeaux, Jean	1867	France	4
Carra, Carlo	1921	Italy	4
Carracci, Agostino	1597	Italy	2
Carracci, Annibale	1600	Italy	23
Carracci, Ludovico	1595	Italy	4
Cassatt, Mary	1885	USA	3

Name	fl	Nat'l orgin	Index	Name	fl	Nat'l orgin	Index
Castiglione, Giuseppe	1656	Italy	2	Degas, Edgar	1874	France	26
Cavallini, Pietro	1280	Italy	7	De Kooning, Willem	1944	Netherlands	9
Cellini, Benvenuto	1540	Italy	9	Delacroix, Eugene	1838	France	30
Cézanne, Paul	1879	France	44	Delaroche, Paul	1837	France	2
Chagall, Marc	1929	Russia	10	Delaunay, Robert	1925	France	7
Champaigne,				Delaunay-Terk, Sonia	1925	Ukraine	3
Phillippe de	1642	Belgium	1	Demuth, Charles	1923	USA	1
Chardin, Jean	1739	France	11	Denis, Maurice	1910	France	5
Charonton, Enguerrand				Derain, André	1920	France	7
(Quarton)	1450	France	2	Desiderio da Settignano	1464	Italy	5
Chasseriau, Theodore	1856	West Indies	1	Dioskourides	−25	Greece	
Chirico, Giorgio de	1928	Greece	11	Dix, Otto	1931	Germany	3
Christus, Petrus	1450	Belgium	4	Doesburg, Theo van			
Cima da Conegliano	1499	Italy	1	(Kupper)	1923	Netherlands	5
Cimabue				Domenichino			
(Cenni di Pepo)	1280	Italy	13	(Zampieri)	1621	Italy	5
Claude Lorrain (Gelee)	1640	France	17	Domenico Veneziano	1450	Italy	4
Clodion				Donatello			
(Claude Michel)	1778	France	3	(di Betto Bardi)	1426	Italy	36
Clouet, Francois	1550	France	1	Doré, Gustave	1830	Germany	2
Clouet, Jean	1525	France	2	Dossi, Dosso	1530	Italy	1
Cole, Thomas	1841	England	4	Dubuffet, Jean	1941	France	7
Constable, John	1818	England	23	Duccio di Buoninsegna	1297	Italy	17
Copley, John	1778	USA	8	Duccio, Agostino di	1458	Italy	2
Cornelius, Peter	1823	Germany	1	Duchamp, Marcel	1927	France	24
Corot, Jean	1836	France	19	Duchamp-Villon,			
Correggio (Allegri)	1529	Italy	22	Raymond	1916	France	4
Cossa, Francesco del	1475	Italy	4	Dufy, Raoul	1917	France	2
Courbet, Gustave	1859	France	26	Duquesnoy, François	1637	Belgium	2
Couture, Thomas	1855	France	2	Dürer, Albrecht	1511	Germany	48
Coypel, Charles	1701	France	1	Dyck, Anthony van	1639	Netherlands	17
Coysevox, Antoine	1680	France	3	Eakins, Thomas	1884	USA	5
Cranach, Lucas	1512	Germany	11	Ensor, James	1900	Belgium	6
Crivelli, Carlo	1470	Italy	2	Epstein, Jacob	1920	USA	1
Cuyp, Aelbert	1660	Netherlands	3	Ernst, Max	1931	Germany	14
Daguerre, Louis	1827	France	3	Euphronios	−480	Greece	
Dali, Salvador	1944	Spain	12	Euthymides	−510	Greece	
Daubigny, Charles	1857	France	3	Exekias	−540	Greece	
Daumier, Honore	1850	France	18	Eyck, Hubert van	1406	Belgium	9
David, Gerard				Eyck, Jan van	1430	Belgium	37
(Gheeraert)	1500	Netherlands	1	Fabritius, Carel	1654	Netherlands	1
David, Jacques	1788	France	22	Falconer, Etienne			
Davis, Stuart	1934	USA	1	(Falconet)	1756	France	1

Name	fl	Nat'l orgin	Index	Name	fl	Nat'l orgin	Index
Fantin-Latour, Henri	1876	France	1	Goncharova, Natalia	1921	Russia	3
Fattori, Giovanni	1865	Italy	1	Gonzalez, Julio	1916	Spain	3
Feininger, Lyonel	1911	USA	4	Gorky, Arshile	1944	Turkey	5
Fetti, Domenico	1624	Italy	1	Gossaert, Jan (Mabuse)	1518	Belgium	5
Filarete				Gottlieb, Adolph	1943	USA	2
(Antonio Averlino)	1440	Italy	2	Goujon, Jean	1550	France	5
Flaxman, John	1795	England	3	Goya, Francisco	1786	Spain	34
Foppa, Vincenco	1467	Italy	3	Goyen, Jan van	1636	Netherlands	3
Fouquet, Jean	1465	France	10	Greco, El			
Fragonard, Jean	1772	France	12	(Theotokopoulos)	1581	Spain	20
Francia, Francesco	1490	Italy	1	Greuze, Jean-Baptiste	1765	France	5
Friedrich, Caspar	1814	Germany	13	Gris, Juan (Gonzalez)	1927	Spain	5
Fuseli, Henry	1781	Switzerland	7	Gros, Antoine Jean	1811	France	6
Gabo, Naum	1930	Russia	4	Grosz, George	1933	Germany	6
Gaddi, Agnolo	1390	Italy	1	Grünewald, Mathias	1500	Germany	23
Gaddi, Taddeo	1340	Italy	3	Guardi, Francesco	1752	Italy	7
Gainsborough, Thomas	1767	England	12	Guercino (Barbieri)	1631	Italy	7
Gauguin, Paul	1888	France	33	Hals, Frans	1621	Netherlands	18
Gaulli, Il				Hepworth, Barbara	1943	England	2
(Giovanni Baciccia)	1679	Italy	3	Hilliard, Nicholas	1587	England	4
Geertgen tot Sint Jans	1485	Netherlands	2	Hobbema, Meindert	1678	Netherlands	2
Gentile da Fabriano	1410	Italy	9	Hodler, Ferdinand	1893	Switzerland	5
Gentileschi, Artemisia	1637	Italy	3	Hofmann, Hans	1920	Germany	2
Gentileschi, Orazio	1603	Italy	1	Hogarth, William	1737	England	16
Géricault, Theodore	1824	France	17	Holbein,			
Gérôme, Jean	1864	France	3	Hans the Younger	1537	Germany	18
Ghiberti, Lorenzo	1418	Italy	20	Homer, Winslow	1876	USA	4
Ghirlandaio, Domenico	1489	Italy	16	Honthorst, Gerrit van	1630	Netherlands	3
Giacometti, Alberto	1941	Switzerland	7	Hooch, Pieter de	1669	Netherlands	4
Giordano, Luca	1672	Italy	2	Hopper, Edward	1922	USA	4
Giorgione				Houdon, Jean	1781	France	9
da Castelfranco	1510	Italy	21	Hugo, Victor	1842	France	2
Giotto di Bondone	1306	Italy	46	Hunt, William	1867	England	5
Giovanni da Bologna	1564	Belgium	11	Ingres, Jean	1820	France	23
Girardon, Francois	1668	France	3	Innes, George	1865	USA	1
Girodet-Trioson				Jongkind, Johan	1859	Netherlands	2
(de Roucy)	1807	France	3	Jordaens, Jacob	1633	Belgium	2
Girtin, Thomas	1802	England	1	Justus of Ghent	1460	Belgium	1
Gislebertus of Autun	1150	France		Kalf, Willem	1659	Netherlands	4
Giulio Romano	1539	Italy	13	Kandinsky, Vasily	1906	Russia	27
Goes, Hugo van der	1477	Belgium	11	Kauffmann, Angelica	1781	Switzerland	2
Gogh, Vincent van	1890	Netherlands	34	Kirchner, Ernst	1920	Germany	10
Goltzius, Hendrick	1598	Germany	1	Klee, Paul	1919	Switzerland	19

Name	fl	Nat'l orgin	Index	Name	fl	Nat'l orgin	Index
Klimt, Gustav	1902	Austria	8	Marc, Franz	1916	Germany	8
Kline, Franz	1950	USA	5	Marees, Hans von	1877	Germany	1
Klinger, Max	1897	Germany	2	Masaccio (Cassai)	1428	Italy	35
Kneller, Godfrey	1689	Germany	1	Masolino da Panicale	1423	Italy	5
Kokoschka, Oskar	1928	Austria	8	Masson, André	1936	France	3
Kollwitz, Kathe	1907	Germany	7	Massys, Quentin	1505	Netherlands	1
Kritios	−480	Greece		Master Bertram			
Kupka, Frank				of Minden	1385	Germany	1
(Frantisek)	1911	Bohemia	3	Master Francke	1420	Germany	1
La Tour, Georges de	1633	France	9	Master of Flemalle	1415	Belgium	9
Lancret, Nicolas	1730	France	1	Matisse, Henri	1909	France	33
Lanfranco, Giovanni	1622	Italy	2	Meidias Painter	−410	Greece	
Larionoff, Mikhail	1921	Ukraine	2	Melozzo da Forli	1478	Italy	2
Laurana, Francesco	1470	Croatia	1	Memling, Hans	1477	Germany	8
Lawrence, Thomas	1809	England	1	Mengs, Anton Raffael	1768	Bohemia	3
Le Nain Brothers	1635	France	6	Menzel, Adolf	1855	Germany	3
Lebrun, Charles	1659	France	13	Metsu, Gabriel	1667	Netherlands	1
Leger, Fernand	1921	France	13	Meunier, Constantin	1871	Belgium	2
Lehmbruck, Wilhelm	1919	Germany	3	Michelangelo			
Leibl, Wilhelm	1884	Germany	2	Buonarroti	1515	Italy	100
Lely, Peter				Millais, John	1869	England	3
(van der Faes)	1658	Belgium	1	Millet, Jean	1854	France	14
Leonardo da Vinci	1492	Italy	51	Minne, George	1906	Belgium	1
Limbourg Brothers	1500	France	15	Miro, Joan	1933	Spain	12
Lipchitz, Jacques	1931	Russia	6	Modersohn-Becker,			
Lippi, Filippino	1497	Italy	5	Paula	1907	Germany	1
Lippi, Fra Filippo	1446	Italy	6	Modigliani, Amedeo	1920	Italy	6
Lochner, Stephan	1450	Germany	6	Moholy-Nagy, Laszlo	1935	Hungary	6
Longhi, Pietro	1742	Italy	2	Mondrian, Piet	1912	Netherlands	20
Lorenzetti, Ambrogio	1348	Italy	13	Monet, Claude	1880	France	35
Lorenzetti, Pietro	1320	Italy	8	Moore, Henry	1938	England	9
Lotto, Lorenzo	1520	Italy	6	Mor van Dashorst,			
Lucas van Leyden	1533	Belgium	2	Anthonis	1560	Netherlands	1
Lysippos	−430	Greece		Morandi, Giorgio	1930	Italy	4
Maes, Nicolaes (Maas)	1674	Netherlands	1	Moreau, Gustave	1866	France	6
Magnasco, Alessandro	1707	Italy	2	Moretto (Bonvicino)	1538	Italy	2
Magritte, Rene	1938	Belgium	9	Morisot, Berthe	1881	France	4
Maillol, Aristide	1901	France	6	Moroni, Giambattista	1565	Italy	1
Maitani, Lorenzo	1315	Italy	4	Morris, William	1874	England	12
Malevich, Kasimir	1918	Ukraine	13	Moser, Lukas	1431	Germany	1
Malouel, Jean	1400	Netherlands	2	Munch, Edvard	1903	Norway	17
Manet, Edouard	1872	France	29	Murillo, Bartolome	1657	Spain	5
Mantegna, Andrea	1471	Italy	24	Muybridge, Eadweard	1870	England	4

Name	fl	Nat'l orgin	Index	Name	fl	Nat'l orgin	Index
Myron	−435	Greece		Praxiteles	−350	Greece	
Nanni di Banco	1415	Italy	4	Primaticcio, Francesco	1544	Italy	6
Newman, Barnett	1945	USA	6	Prud'hon, Pierre-Paul	1798	France	1
Nicholas of Verdun	1200	France		Puget, Pierre	1660	France	4
Nicholson, Ben	1934	England	3	Puvis de Chavannes,			
Nolde, Emil	1907	Germany	9	Pierre	1864	France	5
O'Keefe, Georgia	1927	USA	3	Quercia, Jacopo della	1407	Italy	7
Orcagna				Raeburn, Henry	1796	Scotland	1
(Andrea di Cione)	1348	Italy	2	Raimondi, Marc	1520	Italy	2
Orozco, Jose	1923	Mexico	2	Raphael (Sanzio)	1520	Italy	63
Overbeck, Johann	1829	Germany	3	Ray, Man	1930	USA	6
Ozenfant, Amedee	1926	France	1	Redon, Odilon	1880	France	5
Pacher, Michael	1475	Austria	6	Rembrandt van Rijn	1646	Netherlands	45
Palma il Vecchio	1520	Italy	1	Reni, Guido	1615	Italy	9
Pannini, Giovanni	1732	Italy	5	Renoir, Auguste	1881	France	25
Parmigianino, Francesco	1540	Italy	16	Repin, Ilya	1884	Ukraine	2
Parrhasios	−425	Greece		Reynolds, Joshua	1763	England	17
Patenier, Joachim	1520	Netherlands	2	Ribera, Jusepe de	1631	Spain	7
Pausias	−350	Greece		Riemenschneider,			
Perugino (Vannucci)	1488	Italy	12	Tilman	1500	Germany	6
Pevsner, Antoine	1926	Russia	3	Rigaud, Hyacinthe	1699	France	3
Phidias	−430	Greece		Rivera, Diego	1926	Mexico	3
Piazzetta, Giovanni	1723	Italy	2	Robbia, Luca della	1440	Italy	9
Picabia, Francis	1919	Switzerland	5	Roberti, Ercole de'	1490	Italy	3
Picasso, Pablo	1921	Spain	67	Rodchenko, Alexander	1931	Russia	4
Piero della Francesca	1457	Italy	24	Rodin, Auguste	1880	France	23
Piero di Cosimo	1501	Italy	3	Romney, George	1774	England	1
Pigalle, Jean	1754	France	2	Rossellino, Antonio	1467	Italy	3
Pilon, Germain	1565	France	2	Rossellino, Bernardo	1449	Italy	4
Pintoricchio (di Betto)	1494	Italy	2	Rossetti, Dante			
Pisanello (Pisano)	1435	Italy	6	Gabriel	1868	England	7
Pisano, Andrea				Rosso Fiorentino	1534	Italy	9
(Pontedera)	1330	Italy	7	Rosso, Medardo	1898	Italy	2
Pisano, Giovanni	1285	Italy	13	Rothko, Mark	1943	Russia	9
Pisano, Nicola	1270	Italy	12	Rouault, Georges	1911	France	8
Pissarro, Camille	1870	France	16	Rousseau, Henri	1884	France	10
Pollaiuolo, Antonio del	1471	Italy	15	Rousseau, Theodore	1852	France	6
Polydorus of Rhodes	−50	Greece		Rubens, Peter Paul	1617	Netherlands	41
Polygnotus	−410	Greece		Rude, François	1824	France	4
Polykleitos	−435	Greece		Ruisdael, Jacob van	1668	Netherlands	9
Pontormo, Jacopo	1534	Italy	9	Runge, Philipp	1810	Germany	4
Poussin, Nicolas	1634	France	27	Saenredam, Pieter	1637	Netherlands	1
Pozzo, Andrea	1682	Germany	3	Salviati (de' Rossi)	1550	Italy	1

Name	fl	Nat'l orgin	Index	Name	fl	Nat'l orgin	Index
Sansovino, Andrea	1507	Italy	2	Tiepolo, Giovanni	1736	Italy	17
Sansovino, Il (Tatti)	1526	Italy	5	Tino da Camaino	1335	Italy	2
Sargent, John	1896	USA	1	Tintoretto, Jacopo	1558	Italy	22
Sassetta (di Giovanni)	1432	Italy	2	Titian (Vecellio)	1530	Italy	51
Savoldo, Girolamo	1520	Italy	2	Tobey, Mark	1930	USA	1
Schiele, Egon	1918	Germany	4	Toulouse-Lautrec,			
Schlemmer, Oskar	1928	Germany	2	Henri de	1901	France	16
Schmidt-Rottluff, Karl	1924	Germany	3	Traini, Francesco	1361	Italy	3
Schongauer, Martin	1470	Germany	11	Tura, Cosimo	1470	Italy	5
Schwitters, Kurt	1927	Germany	7	Turner, J. M. W.	1815	England	21
Sebastiano del Piombo	1525	Italy	3	Uccello, Paolo	1437	Italy	14
Seghers, Hercules	1629	Netherlands	1	Valdés Leal, Juan de	1662	Spain	1
Seurat, Georges	1891	France	19	Valentin de Boulogne	1632	France	1
Severini, Gino	1923	Italy	3	Vantongerloo, Georges	1926	Belgium	3
Shahn, Ben	1938	Russia	2	Vasari, Giorgio	1551	Italy	14
Signac, Paul	1903	France	4	Velazquez, Diego y	1639	Spain	37
Signorelli, Luca	1481	Italy	6	Vermeer, Jan	1672	Netherlands	20
Simone Martini	1324	Italy	17	Veronese (Caliari)	1568	Italy	15
Siqueiros, David	1938	Mexico	3	Verrocchio (di Cione)	1475	Italy	19
Sisley, Alfred	1879	France	5	Vien, Joseph	1756	France	1
Skopas	−310	Greece		Vigee-Lebrun, Marie	1795	France	2
Sloan, John	1911	USA	2	Vitale da Bologna			
Sluter, Claus	1380	Netherlands	13	(Cavalli)	1369	Italy	3
Smith, David	1946	USA	6	Vivarini Brothers	1480	Italy	1
Snyders, Frans	1619	Belgium	1	Vlaminck, Maurice de	1916	France	4
Sodoma, Il	1517	Italy	1	Vouet, Simon	1630	France	3
Solimena, Francesco	1697	Italy	1	Vries, Adriaen de	1600	Netherlands	1
Soutine, Chaim	1933	Russia	4	Vuillard, Edouard	1908	France	4
Spranger,				Watteau, Jean-Antoine	1721	France	18
Bartholomeus	1586	Belgium	3	West, Benjamin	1778	USA	5
Steen, Jan	1666	Netherlands	7	Weyden,			
Still, Clyfford	1944	USA	2	Rogier van der	1440	Belgium	18
Stoss, Veit	1485	Germany	6	Whistler, James	1874	USA	16
Stuart, Gilbert	1795	USA	1	Wiligelmo of Modena	1120	Italy	
Stubbs, George	1764	England	3	Wilson, Richard	1754	England	1
Sutherland, Graham	1943	England	2	Witte, Emanuel de	1657	Netherlands	1
Tanguy, Yves	1940	France	1	Witz, Konrad	1440	Germany	7
Tatlin, Vladimir	1925	Ukraine	10	Wright of Derby,			
Teniers,				Joseph	1774	England	1
David the Younger	1650	Belgium	1	Zeuxis	−400	Greece	
Terbrugghen, Hendrick	1628	Netherlands	2	Zuccaro, Federico	1582	Italy	2
Thorvaldsen, Bertel	1810	Denmark	3	Zuccaro, Taddeo	1566	Italy	1
Tiepolo, Giandomenico	1767	Italy	3	Zurbaran, Francisco	1638	Spain	8

ARABIC LITERATURE

SUMMARY STATISTICS

Total number of entries	209
Parent population	91
Significant figures	82
Major figures	21
Index reliability (Cronbach's α)	.88

CORRELATION MATRIX FOR THE INDEX SOURCES ($n=48$*)

	1	2	3	4	5	6	7	8	9	10	11	12	13	14
1 Allen	1.00	.37	.58	.49	.31	.54	.46	.63	.33	.59	.20	.29	.74	.61
2 Arbuthnot	.37	1.00	.19	.04	.25	.27	.29	.34	.14	.33	.13	.39	.37	.35
3 Enc. Brit.	.58	.19	1.00	.40	.06	.54	.53	.54	.43	.65	.29	.35	.62	.49
4 Gibb	.49	.04	.40	1.00	.23	.58	.34	.42	.45	.37	.20	.16	.50	.56
5 Gioan	.31	.25	.06	.23	1.00	.19	.06	.27	.18	.14	.41	.07	.08	.22
6 Huart	.54	.27	.54	.58	.19	1.00	.36	.52	.44	.57	.04	.18	.54	.43
7 Jalil	.46	.29	.53	.34	.06	.36	1.00	.36	.24	.42	.20	.31	.54	.43
8 Jansen(b)	.63	.34	.54	.42	.27	.52	.36	1.00	.39	.47	.20	.41	.57	.59
9 Kroeber	.33	.14	.43	.45	.18	.44	.24	.39	1.00	.33	-.10	.00	.44	.23
10 Nicholson	.59	.33	.65	.37	.14	.57	.42	.47	.33	1.00	.39	.19	.58	.45
11 Queneau	.20	.13	.29	.20	.41	.04	.20	.20	-.10	.39	1.00	.25	.10	.36
12 Riquer	.29	.39	.35	.16	.07	.18	.31	.41	.00	.19	.25	1.00	.30	.38
13 Vernet	.74	.37	.62	.50	.08	.54	.54	.57	.44	.58	.10	.30	1.00	.69
14 Wiet	.61	.35	.49	.56	.22	.43	.43	.59	.23	.45	.36	.38	.69	1.00

* Index scores were computed only for writers in the Arabic language, omitting writers in Persian and Turkish.

THE ROSTER OF SIGNIFICANT FIGURES

Name	fl	Index	Name	fl	Index
'Adi ibn Zaid	630	21	Nasiri Khusrau	1044	
'Amr ibn Kulthum	560	14	Nasiru al-Din of Tus	1241	
'Antarah ibn Shaddad	550	29	Nezami	1200	
'Aqqad, 'Abbas Mahmud al-	1929		Nu'Aymah, Mikhail	1929	
'Umar ibn Abi Rabi'ah	683	31	Rudaki	899	
Abd al-Hamid	1720	9	Sa'di	1253	
Abd al-Rahman	1690	11	Sana'i	1130	
Abu Bakr al-Khwarismi	975	19	Shawqi, Ahmad	1908	
Abu Firas al-Hamdani	967	12	Ta'abbata Sharran	530	18
Abu Hayyan at-Tawhidi	1000	14	Taha Hussein	1929	
Abu Ishak (Bushak)	1410		Tarafah	550	20
Abu Nuwas	800	79	Tawfiq al-Hakim	1938	
Abu Shafar Ahmad ibn Said	1008		Usama ibn Munqidh	1135	13
Abu Tammam	847	54	Zaydan, Jurji	1901	
Abu al-'Atahiyah	788	34	Zuhayr	560	40
Akhtal	680	32	al-Balami	960	
Anwari	1150		al-Busiri	1252	16
Bashshar ibn Burd	780	19	al-Hutay'ah	665	11
Daqiqi (ibn Ahmad)	920		al-Khansa'	620	18
Dhu Al-Nun Ayybub	1948		al-Muwailihi	1898	
Farid od-Din 'Attar	1182		al-Rusafi	1915	
Ferdowsi	975		al-Shanfara	550	15
Gibran, Khalil	1923		al-Walid ibn Yazid [II]	730	15
Hafez	1365		al-A'sha	630	12
Hafiz Ibrahim	1911		al-Buhturi	861	43
Hassan ibn Thabit	603	19	al-Farazdaq	681	44
Haykal, Muhammed	1928		al-Hallaj, Husayn ibn Mansur	898	
Hedayat, Sadeq	1943		al-Hamadhani	1007	49
Ibrahim al-Mazini	1930		al-Hariri	1022	50
Imru' al-Qays	530	60	al-Ma'arri	1013	73
Jalal al-Din ar-Rumi (Mawlana)	1247		al-Mutanabbi	955	100
Jami	1454		ibn 'Abd Rabbihi	900	21
Jarir	693	42	ibn Abi ad-Dunya	863	7
Ka'b	580	16	ibn Battuta	1344	22
Khaqani	1146		ibn Ishaq	760	19
Khayyam, Omar (al-Khayyami)	1088		ibn Nubata al-Misri	983	12
Khwajah 'Abd Allah al-Ansari			ibn Quzman	1150	13
of Herat	1046		ibn Zaydun	1060	16
Kuthayir	710	15	ibn al-Farid	1222	30
Labid ibn Rabi	600	28	ibn al-Mu'tazz	901	19
Muhammed ibn Hani	972	12	ibn al-Muqaffa'	750	27
Nabighah Adh-Dhubyani	600	46			

THE CHINESE LITERATURE INVENTORY

SUMMARY STATISTICS

Total number of entries	548
Parent population	304
Significant figures	83
Major figures	19
Index reliability (Cronbach's α)	.89

CORRELATION MATRIX FOR THE INDEX SCORES ($n=70*$)

	1	2	3	4	5	6	7	8	9	10	11
1 Ch'en	1.00	.44	.48	.68	.65	.73	.35	.62	.63	.56	.34
2 Enc. Brit	.44	1.00	.13	.46	.48	.46	.25	.40	.26	.38	.08
3 Gioan	.48	.13	1.00	.32	.38	.45	.24	.46	.53	.62	.30
4 Idema	.68	.46	.32	1.00	.56	.63	.24	.41	.54	.41	.11
5 Jansen	.65	.48	.38	.56	1.00	.69	.42	.66	.60	.61	.18
6 Kaltenmark	.73	.46	.45	.63	.69	1.00	.29	.56	.50	.59	.23
7 Kroeber	.35	.25	.24	.24	.42	.29	1.00	.53	.29	.32	.29
8 Lai	.62	.40	.46	.41	.66	.56	.53	1.00	.59	.64	.15
9 Liu	.63	.26	.53	.54	.60	.50	.29	.59	1.00	.52	.23
10 Queneau	.56	.38	.62	.41	.61	.59	.32	.64	.52	1.00	.36
11 Riquer	.34	.08	.30	.11	.18	.23	.29	.15	.23	.36	1.00

* Index scores were not computed for figures active after 1800.

THE ROSTER OF SIGNIFICANT FIGURES

Name	fl	Index	Name	fl	Index
Ai Qing (Jiang Haicheng)	1949		Mei Sheng	−160	14
Ba Jin (Li Feigan)	1944		Meng Haoran	729	14
Ban Gu	79	37	Ouyang Xiu (Feng Yan-Si)	1047	61
Bao Zhao	454	5	Pu Songling	1680	30
Bing Xin (Xie Wanying)	1942		Qian Jianyi (Qian Qianyi)	1622	8
Bo Juyi (Bo Lotian)	812	86	Qu Yuan (Lingjun)	−295	78
Cao Pi	225	22	Ruan Ji	259	6
Cao Xueqin (Cao Zhan)	1755	32	Shen Jiji	780	7
Cao Yu (Wan Jiabao)	1945		Shen Yue (Shen Yo)	481	15
Cao Zhi	232	27	Shi Naian	1250	16
Chen Duxiu	1919		Sima Qian	−114	68
Ding Ling (Jiang Weiwen)	1944		Sima Xiangru	−139	41
Du Fu	752	100	Song Yu	−250	33
Du Guangting	890	6	Su Shi (Su Dongpo)	1076	83
Du Mu	843	9	Tang Xianzu	1590	20
Feng Menglong	1614	20	Tao Cian (Tao Yuanming)	405	68
Gao Ming	1350	25	Wang Anshi	1061	29
Gao Qi	1374	10	Wang Chong	67	15
Guan Hanqing	1281	45	Wang Shifu	1290	34
Guo Moruo	1932		Wang Shizhen	1566	19
Han Yu	808	80	Wang Wei	739	35
Hong Sheng	1685	14	Wei Zhuang	876	10
Jia Yi	−168	26	Wen Tingyun	858	18
Jiang Kui	1195	7	Wen Yiduo	1939	
Kong Shangren	1688	14	Wu Chengen	1546	30
Lao She (Shu Sheyu)	1939		Wu Jingzi (Xian Chai Lao Ren)	1741	25
Li Bo	741	87	Xie Lingyun	425	14
Li He	816	15	Xie Tiao	499	6
Li Qingzhao	1124	16	Xin Qiji	1180	22
Li Ruzhen	1803	13	Xu Zhimo	1931	
Li Shangyin (Li Yishan)	853	30	Yan Shu	1031	11
Li Yu (dramatist)	1651	26	Yang Xiong	−13	19
Li Yu (poet)	977	25	Yuan Ji	250	16
Liu Xiang	−37	18	Yuan Mei	1755	17
Liu Yong	1027	17	Yuan Zhen	819	49
Liu Zongyuan	813	40	Zhang Heng	400	8
Lu Xun (Zhao Shuren)	1921		Zhang Ji	768	13
Lu You	1165	19	Zhang Kejiu	1300	7
Lu Zhaolin	700	12	Zhao Bangyan	1096	17
Luo Guanzhong (Luo Ben)	1330	34	Zhao Shuli	1945	
Ma Zhiyuan	1266	34	Zuo Qiuming	−300	11
Mao Dun (Shen Yabing)	1936				

THE INDIAN LITERATURE INVENTORY

SUMMARY STATISTICS

Total number of entries	353
Parent population	115
Significant figures	43
Major figures	9
Index reliability (Cronbach's α)	.91

CORRELATION MATRIX FOR THE INDEX SOURCES ($n=35$*)

	1	2	3	4	5	6	7	8	9	10	11	12
1 Bamerji	1.00	.57	.72	.45	.28	.58	.51	.29	.65	.34	.76	.11
2 Chaitanya	.57	1.00	.66	.71	.42	.84	.54	.48	.54	.77	.73	.59
3 Enc. Brit.	.72	.66	1.00	.73	.53	.78	.57	.55	.81	.77	.71	.49
4 Gioan	.45	.71	.73	1.00	.31	.89	.68	.68	.68	.87	.58	.67
5 Goring	.28	.42	.53	.31	1.00	.36	.16	.37	.31	.42	.43	.24
6 Gowen	.58	.84	.78	.89	.36	1.00	.64	.58	.63	.84	.70	.74
7 Jansen	.51	.54	.57	.68	.16	.64	1.00	.62	.67	.61	.70	.42
8 Kroeber	.29	.48	.55	.68	.37	.58	.62	1.00	.56	.60	.50	.38
9 Queneau	.65	.54	.81	.68	.31	.63	.67	.56	1.00	.67	.62	.20
10 Renou	.34	.77	.77	.87	.42	.84	.61	.60	.67	1.00	.59	.78
11 Riquer	.76	.73	.71	.58	.43	.70	.70	.50	.62	.59	1.00	.39
12 Winternitz	.11	.59	.49	.67	.24	.74	.42	.38	.20	.78	.39	1.00

* Index scores were not computed for persons active after 1700.

THE ROSTER OF SIGNIFICANT FIGURES

Name	fl	Index	Name	fl	Index
Amaru	600	11	Kautilya	−300	11
Anand, Mulk Raj	1945		Kumaradasa	520	3
Asvaghosa	160	29	Madhusudana Dutt (Datta),		
Aurobindo, Sri (Ghose)	1912		Michael	1864	
Banabhatta	630	21	Magha	650	6
Banerji, Bibhutibushan	1934		Mira Bai	1538	13
Bharati, C. Subramania	1921		Naidu, Sarojini	1919	
Bharavi	600	8	Namdev	1310	14
Bhartrhari	460	27	Prem Chand	1920	
Bhasa	250	23	Rajasekhara	900	5
Bhatti	600	5	Ratnakara	850	3
Bhavabhuti	730	21	Somadeva	1070	14
Bhoja	1025	4	Subandhu	600	7
Bilhana	1080	8	Sudraka	300	11
Dandin	700	23	Surdas	1523	4
Gunadhya	200	6	Tagore, Rabindranath	1901	
Haricandra	990	6	Tulsidas	1572	26
Harsa	646	16	Valmiki	−300	72
Jayadeva	1200	19	Varahamihira	500	4
Kabir	1480	20	Vatsayana	250	4
Kalhana	1150	8	Visakhadatta	420	7
Kalidasa	490	100	Vyasa	−400	77

THE JAPANESE LITERATURE INVENTORY

SUMMARY STATISTICS

Total number of entries	258
Parent population	182
Significant figures	85
Major figures	16
Index reliability (Cronbach's α)	.86

CORRELATION MATRIX FOR THE INDEX SOURCES (n=85)

	1	2	3	4	5	6	7	8	9	10
1 Enc. Brit.	1.00	0.20	0.45	0.46	0.37	0.59	0.23	0.28	0.29	0.23
2 Gioan	0.20	1.00	0.49	0.60	0.31	0.45	0.40	0.14	0.21	0.44
3 Jansen	0.45	0.49	1.00	0.55	0.38	0.65	0.47	0.43	0.43	0.24
4 Kato	0.46	0.60	0.55	1.00	0.50	0.66	0.48	0.29	0.23	0.56
5 Keene	0.37	0.31	0.38	0.50	1.00	0.55	0.37	0.34	0.14	0.49
6 Konishi	0.59	0.45	0.65	0.66	0.55	1.00	0.43	0.55	0.48	0.49
7 Kroeber	0.23	0.40	0.47	0.48	0.37	0.43	1.00	0.41	0.34	0.37
8 Queneau	0.28	0.14	0.43	0.29	0.34	0.55	0.41	1.00	0.38	0.27
9 Riquer	0.29	0.21	0.43	0.23	0.14	0.48	0.34	0.38	1.00	0.34
10 Sen'ichi	0.23	0.44	0.24	0.56	0.49	0.49	0.37	0.27	0.34	1.00

THE ROSTER OF SIGNIFICANT FIGURES

Name	fl	Index	Name	fl	Index
Abutsu	1275	11	Nagatsuka Takashi	1915	13
Akiko	1918	29	Nakano Shigeharu	1942	15
Akutagawa Ryunosuke	1927	40	Namiki Sosuke (Senru)	1740	7
Arai Hakuseki	1697	9	Nijo Yoshimoto	1360	28
Arishima Takeo	1918	27	Nishiyama Soin	1645	21
Ariwara Narihira	866	43	Ogai	1902	75
Basho (Matsuo Munefusa)	1684	100	Ono no Komachi	850	38
Bin (Ueda Bin)	1914	13	Oshikochi Mitsune	950	6
Chikamatsu Hanji	1765	12	Otomo no Tabito	665	19
Chikamatsu Monzaemon	1693	94	Otomo no Yakamochi	775	22
Chomei	1193	37	Ozaki Koyo	1903	25
Dazai Osamu	1948	16	Ryutei Tanehiko	1823	6
Ejima Kiseki	1707	22	Saigyo (Sato Norikiyo)	1158	31
Fujiwara Kinto	1006	15	Saikaku	1682	79
Fujiwara Teika (Sadaie)	1202	44	Sakurada Jisuke	1774	10
Fujiwara Toshinari (Shunzei)	1154	28	Santo Kyoden	1801	56
Fukuzawa Yukichi	1875	31	Sei Shonagon	1005	52
Futabatei Shimei	1904	26	Shiga Naoya	1923	48
Hagiwara Sakutaro	1926	12	Shiki	1902	64
Hakucho	1919	24	Shikitei Samba (Kikuchi Hisanori)	1815	27
Hakushu	1925	17	Shoyo	1899	57
Hattori Ransetsu	1694	5	Sogi (Iio Sogi)	1461	29
Higuchi Ichiyo	1896	30	Soseki (Natsume Kinnosuke)	1907	60
Hino Ashihei	1947	3	Sugawara no Michizane	885	34
Horiguchi Daigaku	1932	6	Takeda Izume (Idzumo)	1731	23
Izumi Kyoka	1913	21	Takizawa Bakin (Kiokutei)	1807	42
Izumi Shikibu	1028	20	Takuboku	1912	16
Jippensha Ikku	1805	27	Tamenaga Shunsui	1830	10
Kafu (Nagai Kafu)	1919	44	Tanizaki Jun'ichiro	1926	54
Kakinomoto no Hitomaro	702	46	Tayama Katai	1911	27
Kamo no Mabuchi	1737	12	Tekkan (Yosano Hiroshi)	1913	24
Kawabata Yasunari	1939	57	Tokoku (Kitamura Tokoku)	1894	12
Kawatake Mokuami	1856	21	Toson (Shimazaki Toson)	1912	57
Kenko (Yoshida Kaneyoshi)	1323	30	Tsuruya Namboku	1795	18
Ki no Tsurayuki	908	67	Ueda Akinari (Wayaku Taro)	1774	26
Kobayashi Issa	1803	32	Yamabe Akahito	720	12
Kobayashi Takiji	1933	24	Yamada Bimyo	1908	3
Koda Rohan	1907	25	Yamanoue Okura	700	30
Kukai (Kobo Daishi)	814	30	Yamazaki Sokan	1485	14
Kunikida Doppo	1908	15	Yokomitsu Riichi	1938	27
Miyamoto Yuriko	1939	8	Yosa Buson	1756	41
Murasaki Shikibu	1010	86	Zeami Motokiyo	1403	32
Mushakoji Saneatsu	1925	22			

THE WESTERN LITERATURE INVENTORY

SUMMARY STATISTICS

Total number of entries	3,821
Parent population	1,918
Significant figures	835
Major figures	236
Index reliability (Cronbach's α)	.95

CORRELATION MATRIX FOR THE INDEX SOURCES ($n=835$)

		1	2	3	4	5	6	7	8	9	10	11
1	Benét	1.00	0.60	0.54	0.62	0.63	0.67	0.52	0.69	0.59	0.61	0.60
2	Carpeaux	0.60	1.00	0.63	0.64	0.61	0.76	0.61	0.74	0.67	0.56	0.57
3	Diaz	0.54	0.63	1.00	0.75	0.58	0.75	0.53	0.67	0.76	0.66	0.43
4	Gioan	0.62	0.64	0.75	1.00	0.63	0.83	0.59	0.79	0.78	0.77	0.47
5	Goring	0.63	0.61	0.58	0.63	1.00	0.74	0.48	0.65	0.65	0.55	0.53
6	Jansen	0.67	0.76	0.75	0.83	0.74	1.00	0.61	0.84	0.82	0.74	0.60
7	Laathes	0.52	0.61	0.53	0.59	0.48	0.61	1.00	0.64	0.57	0.55	0.46
8	Queneau	0.69	0.74	0.67	0.79	0.65	0.84	0.64	1.00	0.74	0.71	0.62
9	Riquer	0.59	0.67	0.76	0.78	0.65	0.82	0.57	0.74	1.00	0.70	0.44
10	Burgio	0.61	0.56	0.66	0.77	0.55	0.74	0.55	0.71	0.70	1.00	0.41
11	Wilpert	0.60	0.57	0.43	0.47	0.53	0.60	0.46	0.62	0.44	0.41	1.00

THE ROSTER OF SIGNIFICANT FIGURES

Name	fl	Nat'l orgin	Index	Name	fl	Nat'l orgin	Index
Abelard, Pierre	1119	France	3	Atterbom, Daniel	1830	Sweden	4
Adam of St. Victor	1140	France	2	Aubigné, Théodore d'	1591	Spain	2
Adams, Henry	1878	USA	2	Auden, W.H.	1947	Britain	7
Addison, Joseph	1712	Britain	10	Auerbach, Berthold	1852	Germany	2
Ady, Endre	1917	Hungary	3	Augustine, St.	394	Rome	13
Aeschylus	−485	Greece	26	Ausonius, Decius	349	Rome	3
Aesop	−550	Greece	6	Austen, Jane	1815	Britain	9
Akhmatova, Anna	1929	Russia	4	Babel, Isaak	1934	Russia	4
Aksakov, Sergey	1831	Russia	2	Bacchylides of Ceos	−484	Greece	3
Alain-Fournier				Bacon, Francis	1601	Britain	11
(Fournier)	1914	France	2	Baggesen, Jens	1804	Denmark	1
Alarcón, Pedro de	1873	Spain	5	Bahr, Hermann	1903	Austria	2
Alberti, Rafael	1942	Spain	2	Balmont, Konstantin	1907	Russia	2
Alcman of Sardes	−650	Greece	2	Balzac, Honoré de	1839	France	31
Alcuin	775	Britain	3	Bandello, Matteo	1525	Italy	4
Alemán, Mateo	1587	Spain	4	Bang, Hermann	1897	Denmark	5
Alfieri, Vittorio	1789	Italy	11	Baratynsky, Evgeny	1840	Russia	2
Almquist, Carl	1833	Sweden	4	Barbey d'Aurevilly,			
Ambrose of Milan, St.	379	Rome	3	Jules	1848	France	4
Anacreon of Teos	−540	Greece	8	Barbusse, Henri	1913	France	2
Andersen, Hans	1845	Denmark	9	Baroja y Nessi, Pio	1912	Spain	3
Anderson, Sherwood	1916	USA	2	Barres, Maurice	1902	France	5
Andrade, Mario de	1933	Latin Am	1	Basile, Giovanni	1615	Italy	3
Andréyev, Leonid	1911	Russia	4	Baudelaire, Charles	1861	France	30
Andric, Ivo	1932	Balkans	2	Beaumarchais,			
Andrzejewski, Jerzy	1949	Poland	2	Pierre de	1772	France	9
Angelus Silesius				Beaumont, Francis	1616	Britain	4
(Scheffler)	1664	Germany	3	Beauvoir, Simone de	1948	France	3
Anouilh, Jean	1949	France	6	Beckett, Samuel	1946	Britain	11
Anzengruber, Karl	1879	Austria	1	Beckford, William	1799	Britain	2
Apollinaire, Guillaume	1918	Poland	14	Becque, Henri	1877	France	3
Apollonius				Bécquer, Gustavo	1870	Spain	4
of Alexandria	−250	Greece	6	Bellay, Joachim du	1560	France	7
Apuleius	150	Rome	7	Bellman, Carl	1780	Sweden	6
Aragon, Louis	1937	France	5	Bely, Andréi (Bugayev)	1920	Russia	7
Archilochos of Paros	−700	Greece	6	Bembo, Pietro	1510	Italy	3
Aretino, Pietro	1532	Italy	6	Benavente y Martinez,			
Ariosto, Ludovico	1514	Italy	24	Jacinto	1906	Spain	3
Aristophanes	−408	Greece	18	Benn, Gottfried	1926	Germany	4
Arnaut Daniel	1180	France	3	Bennett, Arnold	1907	Britain	4
Arnim, Achim von	1821	Germany	6	Beranger, Pierre	1820	France	2
Arnold, Matthew	1862	Britain	8	Bergengruen, Werner	1932	Germany	2
Asturias, Miguel	1939	Latin Am	2	Bernanos, Georges	1928	France	8

Name	fl	Nat'l orgin	Index	Name	fl	Nat'l orgin	Index
Bernart de Ventadorn	1180	France	4	Byron, George	1824	Britain	42
Bertrand de Born	1180	France	3	Cabell, James	1919	USA	1
Bibbiena (Dovizi)	1510	Italy	1	Calderon de la Barca,			
Bilderdijk, Willem	1796	Netherlands	1	Pedro	1640	Spain	22
Bitzius, Albert	1837	Switzerland	6	Caldwell, Erskine	1943	USA	4
Bjørnson, Bjørnstjerne	1872	Norway	12	Callimachus	−265	Greece	7
Blake, William	1797	Britain	11	Camoens, Luis de	1564	Portugal	13
Blicher, Steen	1822	Denmark	2	Capek, Karel	1930	Czech	3
Blok, Aleksandr	1920	Russia	10	Carducci, Giosue	1875	Italy	7
Boccaccio, Giovanni	1353	Italy	35	Carlyle, Thomas	1835	Britain	14
Böhme, Jakob	1615	Germany	5	Carossa, Hans	1918	Germany	4
Boiardo, Matteo	1481	Italy	5	Carroll, Lewis	1872	Britain	1
Boileau-Despreaux,				Cary, Joyce	1928	Britain	1
Nicolas	1676	France	20	Castiglione, Baldassare	1518	Italy	8
Borges, Jorge	1940	Argentina	4	Cather, Willa	1913	USA	2
Boscán, Juan	1530	Spain	2	Cats, Jacob	1617	Netherlands	1
Bossuet, Jacques	1667	France	11	Catullus	−54	Rome	13
Bourget, Paul	1892	France	6	Cavafy, Constantine	1903	Balkans	4
Brant, Sebastian	1497	Germany	4	Cavalcanti, Guido	1280	Italy	4
Brantome, Pierre	1580	France	2	Céline, Louis	1934	France	4
Brecht, Bertolt	1938	Germany	17	Cellini, Benvenuto	1540	Italy	3
Brederode, Gerbrand	1618	Netherlands	3	Celsus, Aulus	20	Rome	2
Breitinger, Johann	1740	Switzerland	2	Cendrars, Blaise	1927	Switzerland	4
Brentano, Clemens	1818	Germany	13	Cervantes Saavedra,			
Breton, André	1936	France	8	Miguel de	1587	Spain	29
Brezina, Otokar	1908	Czech	2	Chamisso, Adelbert von	1821	France	3
Broch, Hermann	1926	Austria	3	Chapman, George	1599	Britain	3
Brod, Max	1924	Czech	2	Chateaubriand,			
Brontë, Charlotte	1855	Britain	5	François de	1808	France	17
Brontë, Emily	1848	Britain	5	Chatterton, Thomas	1770	Britain	2
Browne, Thomas	1645	Britain	3	Chaucer, Geoffrey	1380	Britain	18
Browning, Elizabeth	1846	Britain	4	Chekhov, Anton	1900	Russia	20
Browning, Robert	1852	Britain	11	Chénier, André	1794	France	10
Bryant, William	1834	USA	1	Chernyshevsky,			
Bryussov, Valery	1913	Russia	4	Nikolay	1868	Russia	4
Büchner, Georg	1837	Germany	6	Chesterton, Gilbert	1914	Britain	6
Bulwer-Lytton, Edward	1843	Britain	2	Chiabrera, Gabriello	1592	Italy	2
Bunin, Ivan	1910	Russia	4	Chrétien de Troyes	1184	France	15
Bunyan, John	1668	Britain	8	Cicero	−66	Rome	30
Bürger, Gottfried	1787	Germany	6	Claudel, Paul	1908	France	16
Burns, Robert	1796	Britain	7	Claudian	450	Rome	2
Burton, Robert	1616	Britain	3	Claudius, Matthias	1780	Germany	2
Butler, Samuel	1875	Britain	7	Cocteau, Jean	1929	France	5

Name	fl	Nat'l orgin	Index
Coleridge, Samuel	1812	Britain	19
Colette, Sidonie	1913	France	5
Collins, Wilkie	1864	Britain	2
Columella, Lucius	50	Rome	2
Commynes, Philippe de	1487	France	1
Congreve, William	1710	Britain	5
Conrad, Joseph	1897	Poland	11
Conscience, Hendrik	1852	Belgium	3
Constant de Rebecque, Henri	1807	Switzerland	6
Cooper, Anthony (Shaftesbury)	1711	Britain	4
Cooper, James	1829	USA	8
Coppée, François	1882	France	2
Corneille, Pierre	1646	France	29
Coster, Charles de	1867	Belgium	2
Cowper, William	1771	Britain	4
Crane, Hart	1932	USA	1
Crane, Stephen	1900	USA	3
Crashaw, Richard	1649	Britain	5
Cratinus of Athens	−444	Greece	1
Crebillon, Prosper de	1714	France	1
Cummings, e.e.	1934	USA	2
Cyrano de Bergerac, Savinien	1655	France	4
d'Alembert, Jean	1757	France	4
d'Annunzio, Gabriele	1903	Italy	12
d'Urfe, Honore	1607	France	6
Dalin, Olaf von	1748	Sweden	2
Dante Alighieri	1305	Italy	62
Dario, Rubén	1907	Latin Am	6
Daudet, Louis	1880	France	8
De la Mare, Walter	1913	Britain	2
De Quincey, Thomas	1825	Britain	5
Defoe, Daniel	1700	Britain	15
Dehmel, Richard	1903	Germany	4
Dekker, Thomas	1610	Britain	3
Deledda, Grazia	1911	Italy	3
Demosthenes	−344	Greece	9
Derzhavin, Gavril	1783	Russia	4
Dickens, Charles	1852	Britain	27
Dickinson, Emily	1870	USA	6

Name	fl	Nat'l orgin	Index
Diderot, Denis	1753	France	22
Dinesen, Isak	1925	Denmark	2
Dionysius of Halicarnassus	−50	Greece	2
Disraeli, Benjamin	1844	Britain	5
Döblin, Alfred	1918	Germany	6
Donne, John	1612	Britain	17
Dos Passos, John	1936	USA	8
Dostoyevsky, Fyodor	1861	Russia	41
Doyle, Arthur	1899	Britain	2
Drachmann, Holger	1886	Denmark	3
Dreiser, Theodore	1911	USA	10
Droste-Hulshoff, Annette	1837	Germany	2
Dryden, John	1671	Britain	15
Ducasse, Isidore (Lautreamont)	1870	France	6
Duhamel, Georges	1924	France	4
Dumas, Alexandre (père)	1842	France	11
Dumas, Alexandre (fils)	1864	France	7
Eça de Queiros, Jose	1885	Portugal	6
Echegaray y Eizaguirre, Jose	1873	Spain	3
Eckhart, Johannes	1300	Germany	3
Ehrenberg, Ilya	1931	Russia	4
Eich, Günter	1947	Germany	1
Eichendorff, Joseph von	1828	Germany	6
Eliot, George	1859	Britain	10
Eliot, T.S.	1928	USA	32
Éluard, Paul (Grindel)	1935	France	7
Emerson, Ralph	1843	USA	11
Eminescu, Mikhail	1889	Balkans	4
Ennius, Quintus	−199	Rome	5
Erasmus	1506	Netherlands	19
Espronceda, Jose de	1842	Portugal	3
Etherege, George	1675	Britain	2
Euripides	−444	Greece	35
Ewald, Johannes	1781	Denmark	2
Fallada, Hans (Ditzen)	1933	Germany	1
Farquhar, George	1707	Britain	1
Faulkner, William	1937	USA	16

Name	fl	Nat'l orgin	Index	Name	fl	Nat'l orgin	Index
Fedin, Konstantine	1932	Russia	2	George, Stefan	1908	Germany	11
Fenelon, François	1691	France	9	Gessner, Salomon	1770	Switzerland	4
Ferreira, Antonio	1568	Portugal	1	Gezelle, Guido	1870	Belgium	3
Fet, Afanasy	1860	Russia	2	Ghelderode, Michel de	1938	Belgium	2
Fielding, Henry	1747	Britain	14	Gibbon, Edward	1777	Britain	3
Fischart, Johann	1585	Germany	2	Gide, André	1909	France	23
Fitzgerald, Edward	1849	Britain	2	Giono, Jean	1935	France	5
Fitzgerald, F. Scott	1936	USA	3	Giraldi, Giambattista	1544	Italy	4
Flaubert, Gustave	1861	France	24	Giraudoux, Jean	1922	France	7
Fleming, Paul	1640	Germany	2	Gleim, Johann	1759	Germany	2
Fletcher, John	1619	Britain	4	Goethe, Johann	1789	Germany	81
Fogazzaro, Antonio	1882	Italy	6	Gogol, Nikolay	1849	Russia	26
Fontane, Theodor	1859	Germany	7	Goldoni, Carlo	1747	Italy	11
Fontenelle, Bernard de	1697	France	5	Goldsmith, Oliver	1768	Britain	12
Fonvizin, Denis	1785	Russia	3	Gombrowicz, Witold	1944	Poland	2
Ford, Ford Madox	1913	Britain	1	Goncharov, Ivan	1852	Russia	6
Ford, John	1626	Britain	2	Goncourt Brothers	1862	France	9
Forster, Edward	1919	Britain	5	Gondi, Paul (Retz)	1654	France	2
Foscolo, Ugo	1818	Balkans	8	Gongora y Argote,			
Fouque, Friedrich	1817	Germany	3	Luis de	1601	Spain	13
France, Anatole	1884	France	11	Gorky, Maxim	1908	Russia	15
Francis of Assisi, St.	1222	Italy	8	Görres, Johann	1816	Germany	3
Franklin, Benjamin	1750	USA	4	Gottfried			
Freud, Sigmund	1896	Austria	9	von Strassburg	1200	Germany	5
Freytag, Gustav	1856	Germany	3	Gozzi, Carlo	1760	Italy	6
Fröding, Gustav	1900	Sweden	5	Grabbe, Christian	1836	Germany	3
Froissart, Jean	1377	France	4	Gracian y Morales,			
Fromentin, Eugene	1860	France	2	Baltazar	1641	Spain	4
Frost, Robert	1914	USA	6	Gray, Thomas	1756	Britain	8
Fry, Christopher	1947	Britain	3	Greene, Graham	1944	Britain	5
Galsworthy, John	1907	Britain	8	Greene, Robert	1592	Britain	4
Garborg, Arne	1891	Norway	2	Griboyedov, Alexander	1829	Russia	4
Garcia Lorca, Frederico	1936	Spain	13	Grieg, Nordahl	1942	Norway	1
Garcilaso de la Vega	1536	Spain	6	Grillparzer, Franz	1831	Austria	6
Garnier, Robert	1574	France	1	Grimm, Brothers	1825	Germany	6
Garshin, Vsevolod	1888	Russia	2	Grimmelshausen,			
Gaskell, Elizabeth	1850	Britain	2	Johann von	1662	Germany	5
Gautier, Theophile	1851	France	12	Grundtvig, Nikolai	1823	Denmark	3
Gay, John	1725	Britain	2	Gryphius, Andréas	1656	Germany	5
Geijer, Erik	1823	Sweden	4	Guarini, Giovanni	1578	Italy	5
Gellert, Christian	1755	Germany	3	Guicciardini, Francesco	1523	Italy	2
Genet, Jean	1949	France	7	Guilhelm IX, Duke			
Geoffrey of Monmouth	1140	Britain	4	of Aquitaine	1111	France	1

Name	fl	Nat'l orgin	Index
Guillen, Nicolas	1942	Latin Am	1
Guinizelli, Guido	1270	Italy	2
Güiraldes, Ricardo	1926	Latin Am	2
Gundulic, Ivan	1629	Balkans	2
Gutzkow, Karl	1851	Germany	2
Hagedorn, Friedrich von	1748	Germany	2
Halevy, Ludovic	1874	France	2
Haller, Albrecht von	1747	Switzerland	3
Hamsun, Knut	1899	Norway	9
Hardy, Thomas	1880	Britain	13
Harte, Bret	1876	USA	4
Hartmann von Aue	1210	Germany	3
Hasek, Jaroslav	1923	Czech	2
Hasenclever, Walter	1930	Germany	1
Hauff, Wilhelm	1827	Germany	1
Hauptmann, Gerhart	1902	Germany	12
Hawthorne, Nathaniel	1844	USA	10
Hazlitt, William	1818	Britain	4
Hebbel, Friedrich	1853	Germany	7
Hebel, Johann	1800	Switzerland	1
Heiberg, Gunnar	1897	Norway	1
Heidenstam, Carl von	1899	Sweden	4
Heine, Heinrich	1837	Germany	22
Heinse, Johann	1786	Germany	1
Heliodorus	390	Greece	4
Hemingway, Ernest	1938	USA	15
Herbert, George	1633	Britain	5
Heredia, Jose de	1882	Latin Am	5
Herodotus	−445	Greece	15
Herrera, Fernando de	1574	Spain	3
Herzen, Aleksandr	1852	Russia	4
Hesiod	−700	Greece	11
Hesse, Hermann	1917	Germany	9
Heym, Georg	1912	Germany	2
Heyse, Paul	1870	Germany	1
Heyward, Dubose	1925	USA	1
Heywood, Thomas	1614	Britain	2
Hoffmann, E. T. A.	1816	Germany	12
Hofmann von Hofmannswaldau, Christian	1657	Germany	2
Hofmannsthal, Hugo von	1914	Austria	13
Holberg, Ludvig Baron	1724	Denmark	10
Hölderlin, Johann	1810	Germany	20
Hölty, Ludwig C.H.	1776	Germany	2
Homer	−700	Greece	54
Hooft, Pieter	1621	Netherlands	4
Hopkins, Gerard	1884	Britain	6
Horace	−25	Rome	35
Howard, Henry	1547	Britain	4
Howells, William	1877	USA	3
Hrostwitha of Gandersheim	970	Germany	2
Hugo, Victor	1842	France	40
Huidobro, Vicente	1933	Latin Am	2
Hutten, Ulrich von	1523	Germany	3
Huxley, Aldous	1934	Britain	8
Huygens, Constantijn	1636	Netherlands	1
Huysmans, Joris	1888	France	6
Ibsen, Henrik	1868	Norway	32
Immerman, Karl L.	1836	Germany	1
Ingemann, Bernhard	1829	Denmark	2
Irving, Washington	1823	USA	6
Isherwood, Christopher	1944	Britain	1
Jacopone da Todi	1270	Italy	3
Jacob, Max	1916	France	3
Jacobsen, Jens Peter	1885	Denmark	6
James, Henry	1883	USA	19
Jammes, Francis	1908	Belgium	5
Jarry, Alfred	1907	France	3
Jaufre Rudel	1175	France	2
Jean Paul (Richter)	1803	Germany	12
Jeffers, John Robinson	1927	USA	2
Jimenez, Juan	1921	Spain	7
Jodelle, Étienne	1572	France	2
Johnson, Samuel	1749	Britain	12
Joinville, Jean de	1264	France	3
Jonson, Ben	1612	Britain	15
Joyce, James	1922	Britain	30
Jozsef, Attila	1937	Hungary	1
Juan de la Cruz, San	1582	Spain	4
Juan Manuel	1322	Spain	1

Name	fl	Nat'l orgin	Index	Name	fl	Nat'l orgin	Index
Julius Caesar	−62	Rome	18	Leconte de Lisle,			
Jung-Stilling, Johann	1780	Germany	1	Charles	1858	France	6
Juvenal	95	Rome	10	Lenau, Nikolaus	1842	Austria	6
Kafka, Franz	1923	Czech	20	Lenz, Jakob	1791	Russia	4
Kaiser, Georg	1918	Germany	4	Leopardi, Giacomo	1837	Italy	14
Karamzin, Nikolai	1806	Russia	6	Lermontov, Mikhail	1841	Russia	12
Karlfeldt, Erik Axel	1904	Sweden	3	Lesage, Alain Rene	1708	France	10
Katayev, Valentin	1937	Russia	2	Leskov, Nikolay	1871	Russia	6
Kazantzakis, Nikos	1925	Balkans	4	Lessing, Gotthold	1769	Germany	20
Keats, John	1821	Britain	25	Lewis, Matthew	1815	Britain	2
Keller, Gottfried	1859	Switzerland	9	Lewis, Sinclair	1925	USA	6
Kellgren, Johann				Lie, Jonas Lauritz			
Henric	1791	Sweden	1	Idemil	1873	Norway	5
Kielland, Alexander	1886	Norway	4	Liliencron, Detlev von	1884	Germany	4
Kinck, Hans	1905	Norway	2	Lillo, George	1733	Britain	1
Kipling, Rudyard	1905	Britain	10	Lima, Jorge de	1933	Latin Am	1
Kleist, Heinrich von	1811	Germany	12	Livy (Titus Livius)	−19	Rome	10
Klinger, Freidrich von	1792	Germany	4	Lohenstein, Daniel von	1675	Germany	2
Klopstock, Friedrich	1764	Germany	17	Lomonosov, Mikhail	1751	Russia	3
Kochanowski, Jan	1570	Poland	3	London, Jack	1916	USA	4
Koltsov, Alexey	1842	Russia	3	Longfellow, Henry	1847	USA	6
Korolenko, Vladimir	1893	Russia	2	Longus of Lesbos	300	Greece	4
Kotzebue, August von	1801	Germany	2	Lönnrot, Elias	1842	Finland	3
Krasinski, Zygmunt	1852	Poland	4	Lope de Vega	1602	Spain	24
Krezla, Miroslav	1933	Balkans	3	Lorris, Guillaume de	1235	France	5
Krylov, Ivan	1808	Russia	4	Loti, Pierre (Viaud)	1890	France	5
Kyd, Thomas	1594	Britain	3	Lowell, James Russell	1859	USA	2
La Bruyere, Jean de	1685	France	10	Lucan	65	Rome	9
La Fontaine, Jean de	1661	France	16	Lucian of Samosata	157	Greece	9
La Rochefoucauld,				Lucilius	−140	Rome	4
Duc de	1653	France	8	Lucretius	−55	Rome	11
Labiche, Eugène	1855	France	2	Ludwig, Otto	1853	Germany	2
Laclos, Pierre de	1781	France	4	Luis de Leon, Fray	1568	Spain	3
Lafayette, Marie	1674	France	7	Lyly, John	1594	Britain	8
Laforgue, Jules	1887	France	6	Macaulay, Thomas	1840	Britain	4
Lagerkvist, Par	1931	Sweden	4	Machado, Antonio	1915	Spain	7
Lagerlöf, Selma	1899	Sweden	8	Machiavelli, Niccolo	1499	Italy	16
Lamartine, Alphonse de	1830	France	14	MacLeish, Archibald	1932	USA	1
Landor, Walter	1815	Britain	2	Macpherson, James	1776	Britain	9
Langland, William	1372	Britain	2	Maeterlinck, Maurice	1902	Belgium	12
Lavater, Johann	1781	Switzerland	2	Maffei, Scipione	1715	Italy	2
Lawrence, D.H.	1925	Britain	12	Malherbe, François de	1595	France	11
Laxness, Halldor	1942	Iceland	2	Mallarme, Stéphane	1882	France	23

Name	fl	Nat'l orgin	Index	Name	fl	Nat'l orgin	Index
Malory, Thomas	1470	Britain	3	Michaux, Henri	1938	Belgium	2
Malraux, André	1941	France	7	Michelangelo			
Mandelstam, Osip	1932	Russia	2	Buonarroti	1515	Italy	6
Mandeville, Bernard	1710	Netherlands	1	Michelet, Jules	1838	France	3
Mann, Heinrich	1911	Germany	4	Mickiewicz, Adam	1838	Poland	12
Mann, Thomas	1915	Germany	16	Middleton, Thomas	1620	Britain	2
Mansfield, Katherine	1923	New Zealand	3	Miller, Henry	1931	USA	3
Manzoni, Alessandro	1825	Italy	12	Milton, John	1648	Britain	31
Marcus Aurelius	161	Rome	8	Miranda, Francisco	1521	Portugal	3
Margaret				Mistral, Frederic	1870	France	5
of Angouleme	1532	Spain	6	Mistral, Gabriela			
Marie de France	1175	France	7	(Alcayaga)	1929	Latin Am	2
Marinetti, Filippo	1916	Italy	3	Moe, Jørgen	1853	Norway	1
Marino, Giovan	1609	Italy	8	Molière, Jean	1662	France	43
Marivaux, Pierre de	1728	France	14	Molina, Tirso de			
Marlowe, Christopher	1593	Britain	15	(Tellez)	1620	Spain	5
Marmontel, Jean	1763	France	3	Mombert, Alfred	1912	Germany	1
Marot, Clément	1536	France	5	Montaigne, Michel de	1573	France	17
Marquand, John	1933	USA	2	Montale, Eugenio	1936	Italy	4
Martial, Marcus	80	Rome	6	Montemayor, Jorge de	1555	Portugal	6
Martin du Gard, Roger	1921	France	6	Montesquieu, Baron de	1729	France	18
Marvell, Andréw	1661	Britain	4	Montherlant, Henri de	1936	France	5
Masefield, John	1918	Britain	2	Monti, Vincenzo	1794	Italy	3
Massinger, Philip	1623	Britain	2	Moore, Thomas	1819	Britain	3
Masters, Edgar	1908	USA	2	Moravia, Alberto			
Maturin, Charles	1822	Britain	2	(Pincherle)	1947	Italy	7
Maugham, Somerset	1914	Britain	5	More, Thomas	1518	Britain	7
Maupassant, Guy de	1890	France	14	Moreas, Jean	1896	Balkans	7
Mauriac, François	1925	France	8	Moreto y Cabana,			
Mayakovsky, Vladimir	1930	Russia	13	Augustin	1658	Spain	2
Mazzini, Giuseppe	1845	Italy	2	Morgenstern, Christian	1911	Germany	3
Meilhac, Henri	1871	France	2	Mörike, Eduard	1844	Germany	6
Meleager of Gadara	−100	Greece	2	Morris, William	1874	Britain	6
Melo, Francisco de	1648	Portugal	3	Moschus of Syracus	−150	Greece	1
Melville, Herman	1859	USA	14	Müller, Friedrich Max	1789	Germany	1
Menander of Athens	−303	Greece	9	Multatuli (Dekker)	1860	Netherlands	3
Meredith, George	1868	Britain	8	Murger, Henri	1861	France	2
Merezhkovski, Dmitri	1905	Russia	5	Murner, Thomas	1515	Germany	1
Mérimée Prosper	1843	France	6	Musaeus	500	Greece	2
Metastasio, Pietro				Musil, Robert	1920	Austria	4
(Trapassi)	1738	Italy	6	Musset, Louis de	1850	France	16
Meung, Jean de	1290	France	3	Nabokov, Vladimir	1939	Russia	3
Meyer, Conrad	1865	Switzerland	8	Nashe, Thomas	1601	Britain	2

Name	fl	Nat'l orgin	Index
Nekrasov, Nikolay	1861	Russia	5
Nemcova, Bozena	1860	Germany	3
Nemeth, Laszlo	1941	Hungary	1
Neruda, Jan	1874	Czech	3
Neruda, Pablo	1944	Latin Am	4
Nerval, Gerard de			
(Labrunie)	1848	France	7
Nestroy, Johann	1841	Austria	2
Newman, John Henry	1841	Britain	3
Nexø, Martin			
Anderson	1909	Denmark	3
Nievo, Ippolito	1861	Italy	2
Njegos, Peter	1851	Balkans	1
Norris, Frank	1902	USA	4
Novalis			
(von Hardenberg)	1801	Germany	13
O'Casey, Sean	1924	Britain	3
O'Neill, Eugene	1928	USA	8
Odets, Clifford	1946	USA	1
Oehlenschlaeger, Adam	1819	Denmark	6
Olesha, Yuri	1939	Russia	2
Opitz, Martin	1637	Germany	5
Orwell, George (Blair)	1943	Britain	3
Ostrovsky, Aleksandr	1863	Russia	5
Otway, Thomas	1685	Britain	2
Ovid	−3	Rome	29
Palamas, Kostis	1899	Balkans	2
Parini, Giuseppe	1769	Italy	4
Pascoli, Giovanni	1895	Italy	4
Pasternak, Boris	1930	Russia	10
Patmore, Coventry	1863	Britain	2
Pavese, Cesare	1948	Italy	4
Peacock, Thomas Love	1825	Britain	2
Péguy, Charles Pierre	1913	France	6
Pellico, Silvio	1829	Italy	3
Percy, Thomas	1769	Britain	3
Pereda, Jose Maria de	1873	Spain	3
Perez Galdos, Benito	1883	Spain	5
Perrault, Charles	1668	France	6
Persius	62	Rome	3
Pessoa, Fernando	1928	Portugal	3
Petöfi, Sandor	1849	Hungary	6
Petrarch	1344	Italy	40

Name	fl	Nat'l orgin	Index
Petronius Arbiter	50	Rome	9
Pindar			
of Cynoscephalae	−478	Greece	16
Pirandello, Luigi	1907	Italy	14
Pisemsky, Alexey	1860	Russia	2
Platen-Hallermünde,			
August von	1835	Germany	4
Plautus	−214	Rome	18
Pliny the Elder	63	Rome	5
Pliny the Younger	101	Rome	5
Plutarch (Boeotia)	86	Greece	15
Poe, Edgar	1849	USA	26
Poliziano, Angelo			
(Politien)	1494	Italy	7
Polybius	−160	Greece	6
Pontoppidan, Henrik	1897	Denmark	4
Pope, Alexander	1728	Britain	22
Porter, Katherine Anne	1934	USA	1
Pound, Ezra	1925	USA	12
Prévert, Jacques	1940	France	3
Prévost, Antoine	1737	France	8
Propertius, Sextus	−15	Rome	6
Proust, Marcel	1911	France	20
Prudentius, Aurelius	388	Rome	4
Przybyszewski,			
Stanislaw	1908	Poland	3
Pulci, Luigi	1472	Italy	5
Pushkin, Aleksander	1837	Russia	30
Quasimodo, Salvatore	1941	Italy	2
Quevedo y Vallegas,			
Francisco de	1620	Spain	12
Raabe, Wilhelm	1871	Germany	5
Rabelais, François	1534	France	23
Racine, Jean	1679	France	34
Radcliffe, Ann	1804	Britain	3
Radiguet, Raymond	1923	France	2
Radishchev, Alexander	1789	Russia	2
Raimund, Ferdinand	1830	Austria	2
Ramuz, Charles	1918	Switzerland	4
Regnard, Jean	1695	France	2
Regnier, Mathurin	1613	France	3
Rej, Mikolaj	1545	Poland	1
Remarque, Erich	1938	Germany	4

Name	fl	Nat'l orgin	Index	Name	fl	Nat'l orgin	Index
Renan, Joseph	1863	France	5	Sand, George			
Reuchlin, Johann	1495	Germany	2	(Dudevant)	1844	France	9
Reuter, Fritz	1850	Germany	1	Sandburg, Carl	1918	USA	3
Reverdy, Pierre	1929	France	3	Sannazzaro, Jacopo	1496	Italy	6
Reymont, Wladislaw	1907	Poland	5	Sappho of Lesbos	−600	Greece	10
Ribeiro, Bernardim	1522	Portugal	4	Sardou, Victorien	1871	France	2
Richardson, Samuel	1729	Britain	16	Saroyan, William	1948	USA	4
Rilke, Rainer	1915	Czech	25	Sartre, Jean-Paul	1945	France	11
Rimbaud, Jean	1891	France	19	Scarron, Paul	1650	France	5
Rodenbach, Georges	1895	Belgium	3	Scève, Maurice	1550	France	3
Rojas, Fernando de	1505	Spain	1	Schiller, Johann	1799	Switzerland	38
Rolland, Romain	1906	France	9	Schlegel, August von	1807	Germany	10
Romains, Jules				Schnitzler, Arthur	1902	Austria	3
(Farigoule)	1925	France	9	Schulz, Bruno	1932	Poland	1
Ronsard, Pierre de	1564	France	18	Scott, Walter	1811	Britain	33
Rossetti, Dante Gabriel	1868	Britain	6	Scribe, Eugene	1831	France	5
Rostand, Edmond	1908	France	5	Scudery, Madelaine de	1648	France	2
Roth, Joseph	1934	Austria	1	Seghers, Anna			
Rousseau, Jean-Jacques	1752	Switzerland	48	(Radvanyi)	1940	Germany	2
Rückert, Friedrich	1828	Germany	2	Seneca	43	Rome	23
Rueda, Lope de	1550	Spain	3	Sevigné, Marie de	1666	France	5
Ruiz de Alarcon				Shakespeare, William	1604	Britain	100
y Mendoza, Juan	1621	Latin Am	5	Shaw, George	1896	Britain	18
Ruiz, Juan				Shelley, Percy	1822	Britain	25
(Archpriest of Hita)	1323	Spain	3	Sheridan, Richard	1791	Britain	5
Runeberg, Johann				Sholokhov, Mikhail	1945	Russia	3
Ludvig	1844	Finland	3	Sidney, Philip	1586	Britain	11
Rutebeuf	1270	France	6	Sienkiewicz, Henryk	1886	Poland	6
Rydberg, Abraham	1868	Sweden	3	Sillanpää, Frans	1928	Finland	3
Sacchetti, Franco	1370	Italy	2	Silone, Ignazio			
Sachs, Hans	1534	Germany	4	(Tranquilli)	1940	Italy	3
Sade, Marquis de	1780	France	6	Simonides of Ceos	−516	Greece	4
Saint-Exupéry,				Sinclair, Upton	1918	USA	4
Antoine de	1940	France	4	Slowacki, Juliusz	1849	Poland	8
Saint-John Perse				Smollett, Tobias	1761	Britain	6
(Léger)	1927	France	5	Sologub, Fedor	1903	Russia	2
Saint-Pierre, Jacques de	1777	France	9	Solomos, Dionysus	1838	Balkans	3
Saint-Simon, Henri de	1800	France	1	Solon of Athens	−600	Greece	4
Saint-Simon, Louis	1715	France	2	Sophocles	−456	Greece	25
Salluste du Bartas,				Sorge, Reinhard	1916	Germany	2
Guillaume de	1584	France	3	Southey, Robert	1814	Britain	3
Saltykov, Mikhail				Spender, Stephen	1949	Britain	3
(N. Shchedrin)	1866	Russia	5	Spenser, Edmund	1592	Britain	14

Name	fl	Nat'l orgin	Index
Spielhagen, Friedrich	1869	Germany	1
Stadler, Ernst	1914	Germany	1
Staël, Madame de			
(Necker)	1806	France	11
Stampa, Gaspara	1554	Italy	2
Steele, Richard	1712	Britain	5
Stein, Gertrude	1914	USA	3
Steinbeck, John	1942	USA	6
Stendhal (Beyle)	1823	France	22
Sterne, Laurence	1753	Britain	15
Stevenson, Robert	1890	Britain	7
Stiernhielm, Georg	1638	Sweden	2
Stifter, Adalbert	1845	Czech	5
Storm, Theodor	1857	Germany	5
Stowe, Harriet	1851	USA	2
Strindberg August	1889	Sweden	22
Sturluson, Snorri	1219	Iceland	6
Sudermann, Hermann	1897	Germany	3
Suetonius, Gaius	109	Rome	5
Svevo, Italo (Schmitz)	1901	Italy	5
Swedenborg, Emanuel	1728	Sweden	8
Swift, Jonathan	1707	Britain	18
Swinburne, Algernon	1877	Britain	9
Synge, John	1909	Britain	5
Tacitus	95	Rome	13
Tasso, Torquato	1584	Italy	22
Tassoni, Alessandro	1605	Italy	2
Tegner, Esias	1822	Sweden	7
Tennyson, Alfred	1849	Britain	12
Terence, Publius	−159	Rome	18
Teresa de Jesus			
(Cepeda), Santa	1555	Spain	4
Tertullian	200	Rome	4
Thackeray, William	1851	Britain	12
Theocritus of Syracuse	−270	Greece	14
Theognis of Megara	−540	Greece	3
Theophrastus	−331	Greece	3
Thompson, Francis	1899	Britain	4
Thomson, James (poet)	1740	Britain	6
Thoreau, Henry	1857	USA	6
Thucydides	−420	Greece	15
Tibullus	−19	Rome	7
Tieck, Johann	1813	Germany	9

Name	fl	Nat'l orgin	Index
Toller, Ernst	1933	Germany	2
Tolstoy, Alexey K.	1857	Russia	2
Tolstoy, Alexey N.	1922	Russia	7
Tolstoy, Leo	1868	Russia	42
Tourneur, Cyril	1615	Britain	2
Trakl, Georg	1914	Austria	5
Trissino, Giovanni	1518	Italy	2
Trollope, Anthony	1855	Britain	6
Turgenev, Ivan	1853	Russia	24
Twain, Mark (Clemens)	1875	USA	12
Tyrtaeus of Sparta	−680	Greece	3
Tyutchev, Fedor	1843	Russia	3
Tzara, Tristan	1936	Balkans	4
Uhland, Johann	1827	Germany	5
Ulrich von			
Lichtenstein	1240	Austria	1
Unamuno, Miguel de	1904	Spain	12
Undset, Sigrid	1922	Norway	5
Ungaretti, Giuseppe	1928	Italy	4
Valery, Paul	1911	France	18
Vallejo, Cesar	1932	Latin Am	1
Vaughan, Henry	1661	Britain	2
Vauvenargues, Luc	1747	France	4
Veldeke, Hendrik van	1180	Belgium	2
Verga, Giovanni	1880	Italy	7
Verhaeren, Emile	1895	Belgium	7
Verlaine, Paul	1884	France	23
Vicente, Gil	1510	Portugal	7
Vigny, Alfred de	1837	France	10
Villehardouin,			
Geoffroy de	1205	France	1
Villiers de l'Isle			
Adam, Auguste	1878	France	4
Villon, François	1463	France	13
Virgil	−30	Rome	55
Vittorini, Elio	1948	Italy	4
Voiture, Vincent	1638	France	3
Voltaire, François			
(Arouet)	1734	France	47
Vondel, Joost van den	1627	Netherlands	7
Vörösmarty, Mihaly	1840		
Hungary	3		
Voss, Johann Heinrich	1791	Germany	3

Name	fl	Nat'l orgin	Index
Vrchlicky, Jaroslav (Frida)	1893	Czech	3
Wackenroder, Wilhelm	1798	Germany	3
Walpole, Horace	1757	Britain	4
Walser, Robert	1918	Switzerland	1
Walther von der Vogelweide	1210	Austria	5
Walton, Izaak	1633	Britain	1
Warren, Robert	1945	USA	2
Wassermann, Jakob	1913	Germany	2
Waugh, Evelyn	1943	Britain	3
Webster, John	1620	Britain	4
Wedekind, Frank	1904	Germany	5
Weinheber, Josef	1932	Austria	1
Wells, H.G.	1906	Britain	7
Werfel, Franz	1930	Czech	4
Wergeland, Henrik	1845	Norway	3
Werner, Zacharias	1808	Germany	2
West, Nathanael	1940	USA	1
Wharton, Edith	1902	USA	2
Whitman, Walt	1859	USA	23
Wiechert, Ernst	1927	Germany	4
Wieland, Christoph	1773	Germany	8
Wilde, Oscar	1894	Britain	20
Wilder, Thornton	1937	USA	5
Williams, William	1923	USA	1
Winckelmann, Johann	1757	Germany	8
Wolfe, Thomas	1938	USA	5
Wolfram von Eschenbach	1220	Switzerland	5
Wollstonecraft, Mary (Shelley)	1837	Britain	2
Woolf, Virginia	1922	Britain	12
Wordsworth, William	1810	Britain	21
Wright, Richard	1948	USA	1
Wyatt, Thomas	1542	Britain	3
Wycherley, William	1680	Britain	2
Wyspianski, Stanislaw	1907	Poland	5
Xenophanes of Colophon	-540	Greece	1
Xenophon of Athens	-395	Greece	7
Yeats, William	1905	Britain	19
Young, Edward	1723	Britain	10
Zamyatin, Yevgeny	1924	Russia	2
Zeromski, Stefan	1904	Poland	3
Zola, Emile	1880	France	33
Zorrilla y Moral, Jose	1857	Spain	5
Zoshchenko, Mikhail	1935	Russia	3
Zuckmayer, Carl	1936	Germany	2
Zweig, Stefan	1921	Austria	3

THE WESTERN MUSIC INVENTORY

SUMMARY STATISTICS

Total number of entries	2,508
Parent population	1,571
Significant figures	522
Major figures	182
Index reliability (Cronbach's α)	.97

CORRELATION MATRIX FOR THE INDEX SCORES ($n=522$)

	1	2	3	4	5	6	7	8	9	10	11	12	13	14	15	16
1 Abraham	1.00	.72	.79	.72	.75	.83	.69	.79	.76	.75	.54	.80	.69	.71	.52	.60
2 Alberti	.72	1.00	.74	.77	.86	.83	.60	.85	.86	.89	.69	.85	.83	.90	.69	.75
3 Beltrando	.79	.74	1.00	.75	.76	.83	.69	.80	.79	.75	.56	.81	.67	.76	.52	.69
4 Borroff	.72	.77	.75	1.00	.78	.83	.66	.78	.77	.77	.58	.79	.70	.75	.55	.60
5 Dahlhaus	.75	.86	.76	.78	1.00	.85	.66	.83	.85	.89	.78	.87	.85	.84	.75	.66
6 Grout	.83	.83	.83	.83	.85	1.00	.79	.90	.89	.87	.63	.93	.79	.85	.62	.69
7 Hamburg	.69	.60	.69	.66	.66	.79	1.00	.73	.71	.69	.42	.78	.53	.64	.40	.50
8 Harman	.79	.85	.80	.78	.83	.90	.73	1.00	.92	.90	.65	.92	.74	.87	.65	.71
9 Heading	.76	.86	.79	.77	.85	.89	.71	.92	1.00	.89	.69	.91	.76	.90	.69	.77
10 Honolka	.75	.89	.75	.77	.89	.87	.69	.90	.89	1.00	.67	.90	.76	.91	.69	.69
11 Kennedy	.54	.69	.56	.58	.78	.63	.42	.65	.69	.67	1.00	.64	.80	.64	.82	.52
12 Lang	.80	.85	.81	.79	.87	.93	.78	.92	.91	.90	.64	1.00	.77	.88	.64	.72
13 Randel	.69	.83	.67	.70	.85	.79	.53	.74	.76	.76	.80	.77	1.00	.76	.74	.64
14 Rebatet	.71	.90	.76	.75	.84	.85	.64	.87	.90	.91	.64	.88	.76	1.00	.68	.84
15 Thomps	.52	.69	.52	.55	.75	.62	.40	.65	.69	.69	.82	.64	.74	.68	1.00	.58
16 Vuiller	.60	.75	.69	.60	.66	.69	.50	.71	.77	.69	.52	.72	.64	.84	.58	1.00

THE ROSTER OF SIGNIFICANT FIGURES

Name	fl	Nat'l orgin	Index	Name	fl	Nat'l orgin	Index
Adam de la Halle	1284	France	4	Berwald, Franz Adolf	1836	Sweden	2
Adam von Fulda	1485	Germany	1	Besard, Jean	1607	France	1
Adam, Adolphe	1843	France	3	Biber, Heinrich von	1684	Bohemia	2
Agazzari, Agostino	1618	Italy	1	Binchois, Gilles	1440	Netherlands	6
Agricola, Alexander	1486	Belgium	2	Bizet, Georges	1875	France	10
Albéniz, Isaac	1900	Spain	4	Blacher, Boris	1943	Germany	2
Albert, Heinrich	1644	Germany	2	Bliss, Arthur			
Alberti, Domenico	1740	Italy	1	(Drummond)	1931	England	2
Albinoni, Tommaso	1711	Italy	3	Bloch, Ernest	1920	Switzerland	3
Alfano, Franco	1915	Italy	1	Blow, John	1689	England	4
Alfonso X of Castile	1261	Spain	1	Boccherini, Luigi	1783	Italy	4
Anerio, Felice	1600	Italy	2	Boësset, Antoine de	1626	France	1
Anerio, Giovanni	1607	Italy	2	Böhm, Georg	1701	Germany	2
Animuccia, Giovanni	1540	Italy	1	Boieldieu, Adrien	1815	France	5
Arcadelt, Jacques	1545	France	3	Boito, Arrigo	1882	Italy	3
Arensky, Anton	1901	Russia	1	Bononcini, Giovanni	1710	Italy	3
Ariosti, Attilio	1706	Italy	1	Borodin, Alexander	1873	Russia	8
Arne, Thomas	1750	England	3	Bortniansky, Dmitry	1791	Ukraine	1
Auber, Daniel	1822	France	5	Bourgeois, Loys	1550	France	1
Auric, Georges	1939	France	2	Boyce, William	1751	England	2
Bach, C.P.E.	1754	Germany	15	Brahms, Johannes	1873	Germany	35
Bach, J. Christian	1775	Germany	9	Bruch, Max	1878	Germany	2
Bach, J. Christoph	1682	Germany	2	Bruck, Arnold	1540	Belgium	1
Bach, Johann Sebastian	1725	Germany	87	Bruckner, Anton	1864	Austria	19
Bach, Wilhelm	1750	Germany	3	Brumel, Antoine	1500	Netherlands	3
Badings, Henk	1947	Netherlands	1	Bruneau, Alfred	1897	France	2
Balakirev, Mily	1877	Russia	6	Bull, John	1602	England	3
Banchieri, Adriano	1607	Italy	3	Burck, Joachim a	1586	Germany	1
Barber, Samuel	1950	USA	4	Burkhard, Willy	1940	Switzerland	1
Bartók, Béla	1921	Hungary	18	Burney, Charles	1766	England	4
Bax, Arnold (Trevor)	1923	England	3	Busnois, Antoine	1470	Belgium	3
Beck, Conrad	1941	Switzerland	1	Busoni, Ferruccio	1906	Italy	8
Beethoven,				Buus, Jacques	1540	Belgium	1
Ludwig van	1810	Germany	100	Buxtehude, Dietrich	1677	Denmark	7
Bellini, Vincenzo	1835	Italy	9	Byrd, William	1583	England	11
Benda, Georg	1762	Bohemia	2	Cabezón, Antonio de	1550	Spain	3
Benevoli, Orazio	1645	Italy	2	Caccini, Giulio	1591	Italy	8
Benoit, Peter	1874	Belgium	1	Caldara, Antonio	1710	Italy	5
Berg, Alban	1925	Austria	14	Cambert, Robert	1668	France	3
Berlin, Irving	1928	Russia	1	Campion, Thomas	1607	England	1
Berlioz, Hector	1843	France	41	Campra, André	1700	France	3
Bernhard, Christoph	1668	Germany	1	Cannabich, Christian	1771	Germany	2
Berton, Henri	1807	France	1	Cara, Marchetto	1510	Italy	1

Name	fl	Nat'l orgin	Index	Name	fl	Nat'l orgin	Index
Carissimi, Giacomo	1645	Italy	9	D'Anglebert, Jean	1675	France	1
Carpentras	1508	France	1	Dalayrac, Nicolas	1793	France	1
Carter, Elliott	1948	USA	4	Dall'Abaco, Evaristo	1715	Italy	1
Casella, Alfredo	1923	Italy	4	Dallapiccola, Luigi	1944	Italy	7
Catel, Charles	1813	France	1	Dandrieu, Jean	1722	France	1
Cavalieri, Emilio deí	1590	Italy	4	Daquin, Louis	1734	France	1
Cavalli, Francesco	1642	Italy	8	Dargomïzhsky,			
Cavazzoni, Girolamo	1560	Italy	1	Alexander	1853	Russia	3
Cavazzoni, Marco	1530	Italy	1	David, Félicien	1850	France	1
Cazzati, Maurizio	1660	Italy	1	Debussy, Claude	1902	France	45
Certon, Pierre	1550	France	2	Delibes, Clément	1876	France	2
Cesti, Antonio	1663	Italy	7	Delius, Frederick	1902	Germany	7
Chabrier, Alexis	1881	France	5	Demantius,			
Chambonniéres,				Christoph	1607	Bohemia	1
Jacques de	1641	France	3	Destouches, André	1712	France	1
Charpentier, Gustave	1900	France	2	Dietrich, Sixt	1533	Germany	1
Charpentier, Marc	1683	France	4	Dittersdorf, Karl von	1779	Austria	4
Chausson, Ernest	1895	France	3	Dohnányi, Ernö	1917	Slovakia	2
Chávez y Ramírez,				Donizetti, Gaetano	1837	Italy	9
Carlos	1939	Mexico	2	Dowland, John	1603	England	6
Cherubini, Luigi	1800	Italy	10	Draghi, Antonio	1674	Italy	2
Chopin, Fryderyk	1849	Poland	32	Du Caurroy, Eustache	1589	France	1
Ciconia, Johannes	1375	Belgium	2	Du Mont, Henri	1650	Belgium	1
Cimarosa, Domenico	1789	Italy	3	Ducis, Benedictus	1530	Belgium	1
Clemens, Jacobus	1550	Netherlands	4	Dufay, Guillaume	1440	Netherlands	13
Clementi, Muzio	1792	Italy	5	Dukas, Paul	1905	France	4
Clérambault, Louis	1716	France	1	Duni, Egidio	1749	Italy	1
Coclico, Adrianus	1539	Belgium	1	Dunstable, John	1430	England	7
Compère, Loyset	1490	France	2	Duparc, Henri	1888	France	3
Copland, Aaron	1940	USA	7	Durante, Francesco	1724	Italy	2
Coprario, John	1615	England	1	Durey, Louis	1928	France	1
Cordier, Baude	1420	France	1	Dussek, Jan	1800	Bohemia	2
Corelli, Arcangelo	1693	Italy	12	Dvorák, Antonin	1881	Bohemia	13
Cornelius, C. Peter	1864	Germany	2	Eberlin, Johann	1805	Germany	1
Corsi, Jacopo	1601	Italy	1	Eccard, Johannes	1593	Germany	1
Costelely, Guillaume	1570	France	2	Elgar, Edward	1897	England	8
Couperin, François	1708	France	13	Ellington, Duke	1939	USA	2
Couperin, Louis	1661	France	3	Enescu, George	1921	Romania	2
Cowell, Henry	1937	USA	4	Erlebach, Philipp	1697	Germany	1
Crécquillon, Thomas	1520	Belgium	2	Falla, Manuel de	1916	Spain	9
Croce, Giovanni	1597	Italy	1	Farnaby, Giles	1603	England	1
Crüger, Johannes	1638	Germany	1	Fauré, Gabriel	1885	France	13
Cui, César	1875	Russia	3	Fayrfax, Robert	1504	England	1

Name	fl	Nat'l orgin	Index	Name	fl	Nat'l orgin	Index
Ferrabosco,				Gluck, Christoph	1754	Bohemia	26
Alfonso the Elder	1583	Italy	1	Gombert, Nicolas	1545	Belgium	4
Ferrabosco,				Gossec, François	1774	Belgium	4
Alfonso the Younger	1618	England	1	Gottschalk, Louis	1869	USA	1
Ferrari, Benedetto	1637	Italy	1	Goudimel, Claude	1550	France	3
Festa, Costanzo	1530	Italy	2	Gounod, Charles	1858	France	13
Févin, Antoine de	1510	Netherlands	2	Granados, Enrique	1907	Spain	3
Fibich, Zdenek	1890	Bohemia	2	Grandi, Alessandro	1615	Italy	1
Field, John	1822	Ireland	3	Graun, Carl	1743	Germany	3
Fils, Anton	1760	Germany	1	Graupner, Christoph	1723	Germany	1
Finck, Heinrich	1484	Germany	2	Grenon, Nicolas	1420	France	2
Fischer, Johann	1705	Germany	3	Grétry, André	1781	Belgium	6
Flotow, Friedrich von	1852	Germany	2	Grieg, Edvard	1883	Norway	11
Forster, Georg	1550	Germany	1	Guerrero, Francisco	1567	Spain	1
Fortner, Wolfgang	1947	Germany	2	Hába, Alois	1933	Bohemia	2
Foster, Stephen	1864	USA	2	Halévy, Fromental	1839	France	4
Francesco da Milano	1537	Italy	2	Hammerschmidt,			
Franck, César	1862	Belgium	15	Andreas	1651	Bohemia	2
Franck, Johann	1679	Germany	1	Handel, George	1725	Germany	46
Franck, Melchior	1619	Germany	1	Harris, Roy	1938	USA	3
Franz, Robert	1855	Germany	1	Hartmann, Karl	1945	Germany	1
Frederick II of Prussia	1752	Germany	3	Hasse, Johann	1739	Germany	8
Fux, Johann Joseph	1700	Austria	6	Hassler, Hans	1604	Germany	4
Gabrieli, Giovanni	1593	Italy	11	Hauer, Josef	1923	Austria	1
Gade, Niels	1857	Denmark	3	Haydn, Franz	1772	Austria	56
Gaffurius, Franchinus	1491	Italy	1	Haydn, Michael	1777	Austria	4
Gagliano, Marco da	1622	Italy	2	Henry VIII of England	1531	England	2
Gallus, Joannes	1550	Belgium	1	Hérold, Louis	1831	France	2
Galuppi, Baldassare	1746	Italy	4	Hiller, Johann	1768	Germany	4
Gassmann, Florian	1769	Bohemia	2	Hindemith, Paul	1935	Germany	19
Gastoldi, Giovanni	1600	Italy	1	Hoffmann, E. T. A.	1816	Germany	6
Gaveaux, Pierre	1800	France	1	Hofhaimer, Paul	1499	Austria	3
Gerhard, Roberto	1936	Spain	1	Holst, Gustav	1914	England	5
Gershwin, George	1937	USA	6	Holzbauer, Ignaz	1751	Austria	2
Gesualdo of Venosa,				Honegger, Arthur	1932	France	9
Carlo	1600	Italy	5	Hothby, John	1450	England	1
Gherardello da Firenze	1360	Italy	1	Humfrey, Pelham	1674	England	1
Ghiselin, Johannes	1510	Netherlands	1	Hummel, Johann	1818	Austria	3
Gibbons, Orlando	1623	England	4	Humperdinck,			
Giovanni da Cascia	1340	Italy	2	Engelbert	1894	Germany	3
Glazunov, Alexander	1905	Russia	4	Ibert, Jacques	1930	France	2
Glier, Reinhold	1915	Ukraine	1	d'Indy, Vincent	1891	France	9
Glinka, Mikhail	1844	Russia	8	Ingegneri, Marc	1587	Italy	1

Name	fl	Nat'l orgin	Index	Name	fl	Nat'l orgin	Index
Isaac, Heinrich	1490	Belgium	8	Lesueur, Jean	1800	France	4
Isouard, Nicolas	1815	France	1	Liszt, Franz	1851	Hungary	45
Ives, Charles	1914	USA	8	Locatelli, Pietro	1735	Italy	2
Jacopo da Bologna	1350	Italy	2	Locke, Matthew	1670	England	3
Jacopo da Todi	1270	Italy	2	Loewe, Carl	1836	Germany	2
Janácek, Leos	1894	Bohemia	7	Loewe, Frederick	1941	Germany	1
Janequin, Clément	1515	France	5	Logroscino, Nicola	1738	Italy	1
Jenkins, John	1632	England	1	Lortzing, Albert	1841	Germany	4
Jolivet, André	1945	France	3	Lotti, Antonio	1707	Italy	2
Jommelli, Niccolò	1754	Italy	4	Lully, Jean	1672	Italy	24
Josquin des Prez	1480	France	17	Luther, Martin	1523	Germany	9
Kabalevsky, Dmitry	1944	Russia	2	Luzzaschi, Luzzasco	1585	Italy	2
Keiser, Reinhard	1714	Germany	5	MacDowell, Edward	1901	USA	3
Kerll, Johann von	1667	Germany	2	Machaut, Guillaume de	1340	France	12
Kern, Jerome	1925	USA	1	Mackenzie, Alexander	1887	Scotland	1
Kjerulf, Halfdan	1855	Norway	1	Mahler, Gustave	1900	Bohemia	23
Kodály, Zoltán	1922	Hungary	7	Malipiero, Gian	1922	Italy	5
Koechlin, Charles	1907	France	2	Manelli, Francesco	1634	Italy	1
Krenek, Ernst	1940	Austria	6	Marazzoli, Marco	1642	Italy	1
Krieger, Adam	1666	Germany	2	Marcello, Benedetto	1726	Italy	3
Krieger, Johann	1689	Germany	2	Marenzio, Luca	1593	Italy	6
Kuhlau, Friedrich	1826	Germany	1	Marini, Biagio	1627	Italy	2
Kuhnau, Johann	1700	Germany	4	Marschner, Heinrich	1835	Germany	4
Kusser, Johann	1700	Austria	2	Martin, Frank	1930	Switzerland	3
La Rue, Pierre de	1517	Netherlands	3	Martinu, Bohuslav	1930	Bohemia	3
Lalo, Edouard	1863	Belgium	3	Mascagni, Pietro	1903	Italy	3
Lambert, Michel	1650	France	1	Massenet, Jules	1882	France	9
Landi, Stefano	1626	Italy	3	Mattheson, Johann	1721	Germany	5
Landini, Francesco	1365	Italy	6	Mauduit, Jacques	1597	France	2
Lanier, Nicholas	1628	England	1	Mayr, Simon	1803	Germany	2
Lanner, Josef	1841	Austria	1	Mazzocchi, Domenico	1632	Italy	2
Lantins, Hugo de	1430	Italy	1	Mazzocchi, Virgilio	1637	Italy	1
Lassus, Orlando	1572	Belgiu	14	Méhul, Etienne	1803	France	5
Lawes, Henry	1636	England	2	Mendelssohn, Felix	1847	Germany	30
Le Jeune, Claude	1568	France	3	Mercadante, Saverio	1835	Italy	1
Le Maistre, Mattheus	1545	Netherlands	1	Merulo, Claudio	1573	Italy	3
Lechner, Leonhard	1573	Austria	2	Messiaen, Olivier	1948	France	13
Lecocq, Charles	1872	France	1	Meyerbeer, Giacomo	1831	Germany	14
Legrenzi, Giovanni	1666	Itay	4	Milán, Luis de	1540	Spain	2
Leo, Leonardo	1734	Italy	3	Milhaud, Darius	1932	France	13
Leoncavallo, Ruggerio	1898	Italy	3	Monn, Matthias	1750	Austria	1
Leoninus	1110	France	5	Monsigny, Pierre	1769	France	3
Leopold I	1680	Austria	1	Monte, Philipp de	1561	Belgium	3

Name	fl	Nat'l orgin	Index	Name	fl	Nat'l orgin	Index
Monteverdi, Claudio	1607	Italy	31	Piccinni, Niccolò	1768	Italy	7
Morales, Cristóbal de	1540	Spain	2	Pijper, Willem	1934	Netherlands	1
Morley, Thomas	1597	England	6	Pilkington, Francis	1610	England	1
Mouton, Jean	1499	France	3	Piston, Walter	1934	USA	2
Mozart, Leopold	1759	Germany	6	Pizzetti, Ildebrando	1920	Italy	4
Mozart, Wolfgang	1791	Austria	100	Pleyel, Ignace	1797	Austria	2
Mudarra, Alonso	1548	Spain	1	Pollarolo,			
Muffat, Georg	1693	Germany	2	Carlo Francesco	1693	Italy	1
Müller, Wenzel	1807	Bohemia	1	Porpora, Nicola	1726	Italy	4
Mussorgsky, Modest	1879	Russia	16	Poulenc, Francis	1939	France	8
Myaskovsky, Nikolay	1921	Russia	2	Power, Leonel	1430	England	2
Myslivecek, Josef	1777	Bohemia	1	Praetorius, Michael	1611	Germany	4
Nanino,				Prokofiev, Sergei	1931	Ukraine	12
Giovanni Maria	1583	Italy	1	Provenzale, Francesco	1666	Italy	2
Narváez, Luys de	1540	Spain	1	Puccini, Giacomo	1898	Italy	10
Neefe, Christian	1788	Germany	2	Pujol, Juan Pablo	1613	Spain	1
Neidhart von Reuental	1220	Germany	1	Purcell, Henry	1695	England	18
Neusidler, Hans	1548	Germany	1	Rachmaninov, Sergei	1913	Russia	7
Nicolai, Otto	1849	Germany	2	Rameau, Jean	1723	France	22
Nielsen, Carl August	1905	Denmark	3	Ravel, Maurice	1915	France	23
Novák, Vitezslav	1910	Bohemia	1	Reger, Max	1913	Germany	7
Obrecht, Jacob	1470	Netherlands	5	Regnart, Jacob	1580	Belgium	2
Ockeghem, Johannes	1450	Belgium	8	Reicha, Antoine	1810	Bohemia	2
Offenbach, Jacques	1859	Germany	6	Reichardt, Johann	1792	Germany	3
Orff, Carl	1925	Germany	5	Reincken, Johann	1663	Germany	2
Orto, Marbrianus	1500	Belgium	1	Respighi, Ottorino	1919	Italy	3
Osiander, Lucas	1574	Germany	1	Reutter, Georg von	1748	Austria	1
Pachelbel, Johann	1693	Germany	4	Reyer, Ernest	1863	France	1
Paër, Ferdinando	1811	Italy	2	Richter, Franz Xaver	1749	Bohemia	2
Paisiello, Giovanni	1780	Italy	4	Rimsky-Korsakov,			
Palestrina, Giovanni	1564	Italy	20	Nikolai	1884	Russia	15
Pallavicino, Carlo	1670	Italy	1	Rore, Cypriano de	1555	Belgium	6
Parker, Horatio	1903	USA	2	Rosenmüller, Johann	1659	Germany	2
Pasquini, Bernardo	1677	Italy	2	Rossi, Luigi	1637	Italy	4
Pepusch, Johann	1707	Germany	3	Rossi, Salamone	1610	Italy	1
Pergolesi, Giovanni	1736	Italy	11	Rossini, Gioachino	1832	Italy	22
Peri, Jacopo				Rousseau, Jean-Jacques	1752	Switzerland	8
(Zazzerino)	1601	Italy	6	Roussel, Albert	1909	France	5
Pérotin	1130	France	6	Ruggles, Carl	1916	USA	1
Petrassi, Goffredo	1944	Italy	2	Sacchini, Antonio	1770	Italy	2
Pfitzner, Hans	1909	Russia	4	Saint-Saëns, Camille	1875	France	13
Philidor, François	1766	France	3	Salieri, Antonio	1790	Italy	5
Philips, Peter	1600	England	1	Sammartini, Giovanni	1738	Italy	4

Name	fl	Nat'l orgin	Index	Name	fl	Nat'l orgin	Index
Sarti, Giuseppe	1769	Italy	2	Striggi, Alessandro	1580	Italy	1
Satie, Erik	1906	France	7	Sullivan,			
Scandello, Antonio	1557	Italy	1	Arthur Seymour	1882	England	5
Scarlatti, Alessandro	1700	Italy	16	Susato, Tylman	1540	Netherlands	1
Scarlatti, Domenico	1725	Italy	10	Sweelinck, Jan	1602	Netherlands	5
Schaeffer, Pierre	1950	France	2	Szymanowski, Karol	1922	Ukraine	4
Scheibe, Johann	1748	Germany	1	Tailleferre, Germaine	1932	France	2
Scheidemann, Heinrich	1635	Germany	1	Tallis, Thomas	1545	England	6
Scheidt, Samuel	1627	Germany	6	Taneyev, Sergei	1896	Russia	1
Schein, Johann	1626	Germany	4	Tartini, Giuseppe	1732	Italy	4
Schenk, Johann	1793	Austria	1	Tasso, Torquato	1584	Italy	3
Schmitt, Florent	1910	France	4	Taverner, John	1535	England	3
Schobert, Johann	1767	Germany	3	Tchaikovsky, Piotr	1880	Russia	20
Schoenberg, Arnold	1914	Hungary	39	Telemann, Georg	1721	Germany	11
Schreker, Franz	1918	Austria	2	Theile, Johann	1686	Germany	1
Schubert, Franz	1828	Austria	44	Thibaut			
Schulz, Johann	1787	Germany	2	de Champagne	1241	France	1
Schuman, William	1950	USA	2	Thomas, Ambroise	1851	France	3
Schumann, Robert	1850	Germany	42	Thomson, Virgil	1936	USA	3
Schütz, Heinrich	1625	Germany	13	Tinctoris, Johannes	1476	Belgium	3
Schweitzer, Anton	1775	Germany	1	Tippett, Michael	1945	England	5
Scriabin, Alexander	1912	Russia	8	Titelouze, Jean	1603	France	1
Senfl, Ludwig	1526	Switzerland	4	Tomkins, Thomas	1612	England	2
Sermisy, Claudin de	1530	France	3	Torelli, Giuseppe	1698	Italy	3
Sessions, Roger	1936	USA	4	Traëtta, Tommaso	1767	Italy	3
Shostakovich, Dmitri	1946	Russia	12	Tritonius, Petrus	1505	Austria	1
Sibelius, Jean	1905	Finland	10	Tromboncino,			
Simpson, Thomas	1622	England	1	Bartolomeo	1510	Italy	2
Sinding, Christian	1896	Norway	1	Tunder, Franz	1654	Germany	1
Smetana, Bedrich	1563	Bohemia	12	Tye, Christopher	1540	England	2
Soler, Antonio	1769	Spain	1	Varèse, Edgard	1923	France	8
Spohr, Louis	1824	Germany	7	Vaughan Williams,			
Spontini, Gaspare	1814	Italy	6	Ralph	1912	England	9
Staden, Sigmund	1647	Germany	1	Vecchi, Orazio	1590	Italy	3
Stamitz, Carl	1785	Germany	1	Veracini, Francesco	1730	Italy	1
Stamitz, Johann	1757	Bohemia	8	Verdelot, Philippe	1535	France	3
Stanford, Charles	1892	Ireland	3	Verdi, Giuseppe	1853	Italy	30
Steffani, Agostino	1694	Italy	4	Viadana, Ludovico	1600	Italy	2
Stoltzer, Thomas	1515	Germany	2	Vicentino, Nicola	1551	Italy	2
Stradella, Alessandro	1679	Italy	5	Victoria, Tomás de	1588	Spain	6
Strauss, Johann, Jr.	1865	Austria	5	Villa-Lobos, Heitor	1927	Brazil	4
Strauss, Richard	1904	Germany	26	Vinci, Leonardo	1730	Italy	2
Stravinsky, Igor	1922	Russia	45	Virdung, Sebastian	1505	Germany	1

Name	fl	Nat'l orgin	Index	Name	fl	Nat'l orgin	Index
Vitali, Giovanni	1672	Italy	2	Weerbeke, Gaspar van	1485	Belgium	1
Vivaldi, Antonio	1715	Italy	15	Weill, Kurt	1940	Germany	5
Vogel, Wladimir	1936	Russia	1	Wellesz, Egon	1925	Austria	2
Vogler, Georg Joseph	1789	Germany	2	Wert, Giaches de	1575	Belgium	2
Vulpius, Melchior	1610	Germany	1	Wilbye, John	1614	England	1
Wagenseil, Georg	1755	Austria	2	Willaert, Adrian	1525	Belgium	10
Wagner, Richard	1853	Germany	79	Wolf, Hugo	1900	Austria	11
Walter, Johann	1536	Germany	4	Wolf-Ferrari, Ermanno	1916	Italy	2
Walther				Zachow, Friedrich	1703	Germany	2
von der Vogelweide	1210	Germany	2	Zelter, Carl Friedrich	1798	Germany	3
Walton, William	1942	England	3	Zemlinsky,			
Weber, Carl von	1826	Germany	27	Alexander von	1911	Austria	1
Webern, Anton	1923	Austria	19	Zumsteeg, Johann	1800	Germany	2
Weckmann, Matthias	1659	Germany	2				

THE CHINESE PHILOSOPHY INVENTORY

SUMMARY STATISTICS

Total number of entries	136
Parent population	88
Significant figures	39
Major figures	16
Index reliability (Cronbach's α)	.96

CORRELATION MATRIX FOR THE INDEX SOURCES ($n=39$)

	1	2	3	4	5	6	7	8	9	10	11
1 Chan	1.00	.47	.72	.74	.86	.85	.74	.84	.46	.89	.42
2 Day	.47	1.00	.67	.72	.66	.68	.74	.61	.65	.73	.50
3 DeBary	.72	.67	1.00	.69	.65	.75	.82	.65	.48	.79	.50
4 Enc. Brit.	.74	.72	.69	1.00	.87	.84	.80	.82	.80	.84	.67
5 Fung	.86	.66	.65	.87	1.00	.84	.80	.87	.68	.85	.56
6 Koller	.85	.68	.75	.84	.84	1.00	.80	.92	.59	.93	.50
7 Murty	.74	.74	.82	.80	.80	.80	1.00	.74	.72	.84	.54
8 Radhakrishna	.84	.61	.65	.82	.87	.92	.74	1.00	.63	.87	.52
9 Scharfstein	.46	.65	.48	.80	.68	.59	.72	.63	1.00	.56	.55
10 Smart	.89	.73	.79	.84	.85	.93	.84	.87	.56	1.00	.48
11 Wu	.42	.50	.50	.67	.56	.50	.54	.52	.55	.48	1.00

THE ROSTER OF SIGNIFICANT FIGURES

Name	fl	Index	Name	fl	Index
Cheng Hao	1072	15	Mozi	−439	22
Chengi	1073	14	Sengzhao	414	4
Confucius	−511	100	Shaoyong	1051	6
Daizhen	1764	9	Shenhui	750	1
Dong Zhongshu	−139	16	Shenxiu	646	1
Fazang	683	4	Wang Bi	249	4
Feng Yulan	1935	13	Wang Chong	65	4
Gongsun Long	−270	5	Wang Yangming	1512	24
Gu Yanwu	1653	3	Xiong Shili	1925	5
Guoxiang	261	4	Xuan Zhuang	642	4
Hanfei	−240	9	Xunzi	−275	29
Hanyua	808	6	Yang Zhu	−310	3
Hu Shi	−340	3	Yen Si Chai	1675	4
Hui Yuan	373	2	Zhangzai	1060	8
Huineng	678	8	Zhiyi	578	1
Kang Yuwei	1898	10	Zhou Duni	1057	11
Laozi	−350	68	Zhuangzi	−329	39
Lisi	−200	4	Zhuxi	1170	50
Lu Xiangshan	1180	8	Zou Yan	−300	8
Mencius	−372	40			

THE INDIAN PHILOSOPHY INVENTORY

SUMMARY STATISTICS

Total number of entries	313
Parent population	181
Significant figures	45
Major figures	8
Index reliability (Cronbach's α)	.93

CORRELATION MATRIX FOR THE INDEX SOURCES (n=45)

	1	2	3	4	5	6	7	8	9	10	11
1 Chatterjee	1.00	0.70	0.61	0.46	0.59	0.37	0.32	0.67	0.75	0.72	0.62
2 Chattopadhyaya	0.70	1.00	0.35	0.41	0.64	0.32	0.41	0.43	0.50	0.48	0.34
3 Enc. Brit.	0.61	0.35	1.00	0.56	0.62	0.76	0.43	0.58	0.85	0.76	0.88
4 Hayashi	0.46	0.41	0.56	1.00	0.44	0.40	0.35	0.40	0.46	0.50	0.56
5 King	0.59	0.64	0.62	0.44	1.00	0.62	0.63	0.59	0.72	0.53	0.55
6 Koller	0.37	0.32	0.76	0.40	0.62	1.00	0.44	0.51	0.73	0.57	0.66
7 Mattei	0.32	0.41	0.43	0.35	0.63	0.44	1.00	0.64	0.59	0.45	0.44
8 Potter	0.67	0.43	0.58	0.40	0.59	0.51	0.64	1.00	0.80	0.77	0.64
9 Puligandla	0.75	0.50	0.85	0.46	0.72	0.73	0.59	0.80	1.00	0.85	0.82
10 Radhakrishnan	0.72	0.48	0.76	0.50	0.53	0.57	0.45	0.77	0.85	1.00	0.79
11 Smart	0.62	0.34	0.88	0.56	0.55	0.66	0.44	0.64	0.82	0.79	1.00

THE ROSTER OF SIGNIFICANT FIGURES

Name	fl	Index	Name	fl	Index
Aryadeva	200	5	Madhva (Anandatirtha)	1238	28
Asanga	310	5	Mandanamisra	40	3
Asvaghosa	160	6	Nagarjuna	150	56
Aurobindo, Sri (Ghose)	1912	13	Nimbarka	1200	9
Badarayana	390	6	Padmapada	750	1
Bhartrhari	460	10	Patanjali (Gonardiya)	−150	21
Bhavya	530	3	Prabhakara	690	5
Buddha	−520	47	Prasastapada	450	5
Buddhapalita	510	1	Ramanuja	1056	55
Candragomin	925	6	Sankara	820	100
Carvaka (Lokayata)	−600	16	Santaraksita	725	4
Dasgupta	1925	9	Sridhara	40	2
Dharmakirti	650	9	Suresvara	750	2
Dignaga	440	11	Udayana	1015	13
Gangesa	1325	6	Uddyotakara	640	4
Gaudapada	640	10	Vacaspatimitra	860	13
Gautama (Aksapada)	240	3	Vallabha	1481	12
Jaimini	190	3	Vasubandhu	350	14
Jayanta Bhatta	890	3	Vatsayana	390	9
Kamasila	755	2	Vijnana Bhiksu	1575	9
Kanada	140	6	Vivekananda	1902	15
Kapila	−600	9	Vyasa (the philosopher)	690	2
Kumarila	660	11			

THE WESTERN PHILOSOPHY INVENTORY

SUMMARY STATISTICS

Total number of entries	885
Parent population	473
Significant figures	154
Major figures	41
Index reliability (Cronbach's α)	.96

THE CORRELATION MATRIX FOR THE INDEX SOURCES (n=154)

	1	2	3	4	5	6	7	8	9	10	11	12
1 Buhr	1.00	.77	.80	.78	.69	.66	.78	.78	.62	.63	.65	.67
2 Copleston	.77	1.00	.73	.85	.70	.62	.78	.74	.63	.64	.73	.72
3 Hayashi	.80	.73	1.00	.82	.69	.77	.82	.81	.72	.60	.78	.77
4 Kenny	.78	.85	.82	1.00	.79	.68	.87	.80	.76	.69	.72	.81
5 Matson	.69	.70	.69	.79	1.00	.54	.76	.76	.78	.74	.66	.81
6 Mattei	.66	.62	.77	.68	.54	1.00	.71	.70	.60	.50	.68	.66
7 Plott	.78	.78	.82	.87	.76	.71	1.00	.87	.70	.70	.80	.76
8 Radhakrishnan	.78	.74	.81	.80	.76	.70	.87	1.00	.75	.71	.84	.76
9 Russell	.62	.63	.72	.76	.78	.60	.70	.75	1.00	.63	.68	.85
10 Scharfstein	.63	.64	.60	.69	.74	.50	.70	.71	.63	1.00	.65	.68
11 Smart	.65	.73	.78	.72	.66	.68	.80	.84	.68	.65	1.00	.74
12 Tarnas	.67	.72	.77	.81	.81	.66	.76	.76	.85	.68	.74	1.00

THE ROSTER OF SIGNIFICANT FIGURES

Name	fl	Nat'l orgin	Index	Name	fl	Nat'l orgin	Index
Abelard, Pierre	1119	France	4	Chrysippus of Soli	−242	Greece	2
Aenesidemos	−50	Greece	1	Clement of Alexandria	190	Greece	3
Albertus Magnus, St.	1240	Germany	5	Collingwood, Robin	1929	England	2
Alexander of Hales	1240	England	1	Comte, Isidore	1838	France	5
Ambrose of Milan, St.	379	Rome	3	Condorcet, Marie	1783	France	3
Ammonius Sakkas	215	Rome	2	Cooper, Anthony			
Anaxagoras				(Shaftesbury)	1711	England	3
of Clazomenae	−460	Greece	5	Critias	−415	Greece	1
Anaximander				Cudworth, Ralph	1657	England	1
of Miletus	−571	Greece	4	Democritus	−420	Greece	13
Anaximenes				Descartes, René	1636	France	51
of Miletus	−500	Greece	4	Dewey, John	1899	USA	10
Anselm of Canterbury	1073	Italy	6	Diderot, Denis ·	1753	France	6
Antiphon of Athens	−450	Greece	1	Dilthey, Wilhelm	1873	Germany	3
Antisthenes of Athens	−404	Greece	1	Diogenes	−372	Greece	2
Apollonius of Tyana	−80	Greece	1	Dionysius Areopagita	50	Greece	3
Aquinas, Thomas	1266	Italy	39	Duns Scotus, John	1308	Scotland	9
Arcesilaus of Pitane	−276	Greece	1	Eckhart, Johannes	1300	Germany	3
Aristippus of Cyrene	−435	Greece	1	Emerson, Ralph	1843	USA	2
Aristotle	−344	Greece	100	Empedocles	−452	Greece	6
Augustine, St.	394	Rome	30	Epictetus	90	Greece	5
Averroës (ibn Rushd)	1166	Spain	11	Epicurus of Samos	−301	Greece	11
Avicebron				Erigena, Johannes	850	Ireland	7
(ibn Gabirol)	1058	Spain	2	Feuerbach, Ludwig	1844	Germany	4
Avicenna (ibn Sina)	1020	Persia	15	Fichte, Johann	1802	Germany	17
Ayer, Alfred	1950	England	4	Gassendi, Pierre	1632	France	3
Bacon, Francis	1601	England	12	al-Ghazzali, Algazel	1098	Persia	4
Bacon, Roger	1254	England	4	Geulincx, Arnold	1665	Belgium	1
Bayle, Pierre	1687	France	2	Gorgias	−445	Greece	2
Bentham, Jeremy	1788	England	7	Gregory of Nyssa	371	Greece	1
Bergson, Henri	1899	France	9	Grosseteste, Robert	1208	England	2
Berkeley, George	1725	Ireland	21	Hegel, Georg	1810	Germany	47
Bernard of Clairvaux	1131	France	1	Heidegger, Martin	1929	Germany	12
Boehme, Jacob	1615	Germany	2	Helvetius, Claude	1755	France	2
Boethius, Anicius	520	Rome	4	Heraclitus of Ephesus	−500	Greece	11
Bonaventura, St.	1261	Italy	7	Herder, Johann	1784	Germany	4
Bradley, Francis	1886	England	4	Hobbes, Thomas	1628	England	18
Bruno, Giordano	1588	Italy	4	Holbach, Paul	1763	Germany	3
Buber, Martin	1918	Austria	2	Hume, David	1751	Scotland	36
Buridan, Jean	1335	France	2	Husserl, Edmund	1899	Bohemia	8
Calvin, John	1549	France	3	James, William	1882	USA	10
Carnap, Rudolf	1931	Germany	8	Kant, Immanuel	1764	Germany	75
Carneades of Cyrene	−174	Greece	2	Kierkegaard, Søren	1853	Denmark	10

Name	fl	Nat'l orgin	Index	Name	fl	Nat'l orgin	Index
al-Kindi	841	Persia	3	Pyrrho of Elis	−327	Greece	3
Leibniz, Gottfried	1686	Germany	27	Pythagoras of Samos	−520	Greece	15
Leucippus of Miletus	−440	Greece	3	Quine, Willard	1948	USA	2
Locke, John	1672	England	37	Reichenbach, Hans	1931	Germany	2
Lucretius	−55	Rome	6	Reid, Thomas	1750	Scotland	3
Luther, Martin	1523	Germany	4	Roscellinus	1090	France	1
Maimonides, Moses	1175	Spain	6	Rousseau, Jean-Jacques	1752	Switzerland	17
Manichaeus	256	Rome	5	Russell, Bertrand	1912	England	18
Marcus Aurelius	161	Rome	4	Saíadia ben Joseph			
Mendelssohn, Moses	1769	Germany	2	(Gaon)	932	Persia	1
Merleau-Ponty,				Santayana, George	1903	Spain	2
Maurice	1948	France	3	Sartre, Jean-Paul	1945	France	12
Mill, James	1813	Scotland	2	Schelling, Friedrich	1815	Germany	14
Mill, John	1846	England	13	Schiller, Ferdinand	1904	Switzerland	4
Montaigne, Michel de	1573	France	3	Schleiermacher,			
Montesquieu, Charles	1729	France	4	Friedrich	1808	Bohemia	4
Moore, George	1913	England	4	Schlick, Moritz	1922	Bohemia	4
More, Thomas	1518	England	3	Schopenhauer, Arthur	1828	Germany	24
Neurath, Otto	1922	Austria	2	Seneca	43	Rome	4
Nicholas				Sextus Empiricus	200	Greece	3
de Malebranche	1678	France	7	Socrates	−429	Greece	26
Nicholas of Cusa	1441	Germany	5	Spencer, Herbert	1860	England	5
Nicholas of Oresme	1365	France	2	Spinoza, Benedict	1672	Netherlands	27
Nietzsche, Friedrich	1884	Germany	20	Tertullian	200	Rome	2
Origen (Adamantius)	225	Greece	5	Thales	−585	Greece	6
Panaetius of Rhodes	−145	Greece	1	Vico, Giambattista	1708	Italy	2
Parmenides of Elea	−475	Greece	13	Voltaire, François	1734	France	9
Pascal, Blaise	1662	France	6	Wittgenstein, Lugwig	1929	Austria	13
Pelagius	400	Rome	2	Whitehead, Alfred	1901	England	6
Philo Judaeus	15	Greece	7	William of Champeaux	1110	France	1
Peirce, Charles	1879	USA	8	William of Occam	1325	England	14
Plato	−388	Greece	88	Wolff, Christian	1719	Germany	5
Plotinus of Lycopolis	244	Greece	18	Xenocrates			
Plutarch (Boeotia)	86	Rome	3	of Chalcedon	−355	Greece	1
Porphyrius of Phoenicia	272	Greece	4	Xenophanes			
Poseidoios of Apamea	−95	Greece	2	of Colophon	−540	Greece	3
Proclus	450	Greece	6	Zeno of Citium	−295	Greece	5
Protagoras of Abdera	−445	Greece	6	Zeno of Elea	−450	Greece	4

NOTES

CHAPTER 1: A SENSE OF TIME

1. Technically, we are known as *Homo sapiens sapiens*, to distinguish us from *Homo sapiens neanderthalensis*. The dates I give throughout these opening paragraphs will probably have been pushed backward by the time you read them, judging from past experience.

2. Wilson 1980.

3. McEvedy and Jones 1978.

4. I base this statement on the current understanding that the size and structure of the brain was fully evolved well before −8000. It goes without saying that the expression of wit and ribaldry might have been so different in −8000 that we wouldn't get the jokes, but there is no physiological reason to ascribe this to anything other than environment. See Mithen 1996 for a review of the evidence that what he calls *cognitive fluidity* had evolved by about 40,000 years ago, including not only fully modern language facility but comprehension of analogies and metaphors. An alternative viewpoint, contested when it was presented and still a renegade position, was famously expressed in Jaynes 1976, which argues that consciousness as we think of it didn't emerge until well after the invention of writing.

5. The statements about the state of progress as of −8000 in this paragraph are taken from Rudgley 1999: chapters 2, 11, and 12.

6. As I write, a site in Syria, Jerf el-Ahmar, dating back past −9000, is argued to have some of Çatal Hüyük's features. Even more controversially, a site in France, Viols-le-Fort, shows signs of being an agricultural town, but dating back to −10,000. These findings are still provisional, so I stick with −8000 in the text.

7. Rudgley 1999.

8. Rudgley 1999.

CHAPTER 2: A SENSE OF MYSTERY

1. Toynbee puts the artistic and technological peak of Egypt at the Fourth Dynasty (Toynbee and Somervell 1946: 30), while Quigley dates it a few centuries later, −2300, placing Sumer's peak at −1700 (Quigley 1961: 80).

2. The classification of civilizations follows Toynbee and Somervell 1946.

3. The account of the Antikythera Mechanism is drawn from Magill 1991: 1588–92.

4. A sidereal revolution is a lunar revolution with respect to the stars, while a lunation is a lunar revolution with respect to the sun.

5. The story popularized by Gibbon that the Muslims used the manuscripts as fuel to heat the baths of Alexandria is almost certainly a canard.

6. Petrie 1990 quoted in Hancock 1995: 350–51.

7. Petrie 1990 quoted in Hancock 1995: 351.

8. Lehner 1997: 210.

9. Lehner 1997: 214.

10. Edwards 1949: 220.

11. For a review of the alternative theories, see Lehner 1997: 215–17.

12. E.g., Hodges and Keable 1989.

13. R. Porter, discussed in James and Thorpe 1999: 201–12.

14. Lehner 1997: 209.

15. Vega 1961: 233.

16. Hemming 1993: 191.

17. For an example of such an explanation, see Protzen 1986.

18. Carl Jung and Mircea Eliade were among the first to broach the notion of universal myths, but it was Joseph Campbell who did the pioneering empirical work that established the reality of the monomyth. See for example Campbell 1949 and Campbell 1974.

19. De Santillana and von Dechend 1969. For any who pick up *Hamlet's Mill* with an eye to reading it, I recommend starting with what the authors call "Intermezzo: A Guide for the Perplexed," 56 pages into the text.

20. De Santillana and von Dechend 1969: 66, 340.

21. Schoch and McNally 1999: 40.

22. Dobecki and Schoch 1992.

23. Schoch 1992.

24. For the anti-Schoch case, see Harrell 1994b, Harrell 1994a, Gauri et al. 1995, and Lawton and Ogilvie-Herald 1999.

25. For a summary of Schoch's responses to the criticisms, see Schoch and McNally 1999. For an independent geological analysis supporting Schoch's position, see Coxill 1998.

26. Schoch 2000.

CHAPTER 3: A SENSE OF PLACE

1. Gibbon 1952: 27.
2. Balsdon 1969: 149.
3. Cowell 1961: 167.
4. Quoted in Honour and Fleming 1982: 114.
5. Quoted in Honour and Fleming 1982: 153.
6. Quoted in Honour and Fleming 1982: 139.
7. Honour and Fleming 1982: 153-4.
8. Honour and Fleming 1982: 139.
9. Gibbon 1952: 75.
10. Gibbon 1952: 76.
11. Cowell 1961: 145.
12. Cowell 1961: 161.
13. Balsdon 1969: 151.
14. Cowell 1961: 87.
15. Davis 1962: 161.
16. Casson 1975: 45–6.
17. Cowell 1961: 133.
18. Davis 1962: 160.
19. Balsdon 1969: 88.
20. Balsdon 1969: 139–40.
21. Quoted in Honour and Fleming 1982: 154.
22. Quoted in Honour and Fleming 1982: 154.
23. Gibbon 1952: 84.
24. Gibbon 1952: 64.
25. Gibbon 1952: 65.
26. Reischauer and Fairbank 1958: 321, Boorstin 1983: 190–7.
27. Laurence Binyon, quoted in Reischauer and Fairbank 1958: 183.
28. Gernet 1962: 23.
29. Reischauer and Fairbank 1958: 224.
30. Gernet 1962: 149.
31. Gernet 1962: 123.
32. Quoted in Gernet 1962: 49.
33. As identified by Jean-Anthelme Brillat-Savarin, this first luxury restaurant was La Grande Taverne de Londres—in his words "the first to combine the four essentials of an elegant room, smart waiters, a choice cellar, and superior cooking." Brillat-Savarin 1826.
34. Quoted in Gernet 1962: 50.
35. Shiba 1970: 6.

36. Shiba 1970: 92.

37. Shiba 1970: 109.

38. Hartwell 1966.

39. Shiba 1970: 190 ff.

40. The discussion of Chinese mathematics draws primarily from Ronan 1981: 1–66.

41. The discussion of Chinese astronomy draws primarily from Ronan 1981: 67–221.

42. The discussion of Chinese medicine draws primarily from Kaptchuk 1983.

43. Mair 1994 : 569.

44. Quoted in Gernet 1962: 152–3.

45. Quoted in Bary, Chan, and Watson 1963: 25.

46. Quoted in Bary, Chan, and Watson 1963: 33.

47. Quoted in Bary, Chan, and Watson 1963: 34.

48. Hough 1994: 59. Additional orders to seek out *Terra Australis Incognita* came only after the decision to make the voyage had already been taken.

49. Hough 1994: 37.

50. Quoted in Hough 1994: 56.

51. Brewer 1997: 28.

52. Bate 1975: 167.

53. Braudel 1979: 548.

54. Wain 1974: 79.

55. Brewer 1997: 30.

56. Bate 1975: 168.

57. Brewer 1997: 52.

58. Brewer 1997: 641.

59. Braudel 1979: 84.

60. Quoted in Cipolla 1980: 162.

61. Braudel 1979: 79.

62. Brewer 1997: 138.

63. Brewer 1997: 240.

64. Brewer 1997: 326.

65. Brewer 1997: 62, 398.

66. Brewer 1997: 211.

67. Brewer 1997: 399.

68. Barzun 2000: 361.

69. Gay 1966: 4.

CHAPTER 5: EXCELLENCE AND ITS IDENTIFICATION

1. James 1987: 572, 573.

2. The book in question was Berkeley's *Three Dialogues Between Hylas and Philonous* (1713).

3. Hume 1997: 77–78.

4. Hume 1997: 82.

5. Hume 1997: 80.

6. Hume 1997: 81.

7. The most accessible one-source review is the chapter on the arts in Pinker 2002: 400–420. Other sources outside the technical journals are Jourdain 1997, Benzon 2001, several articles in Barkow et al. 1992, and, from an anthropological perspective, Maquet 1986.

8. For some of the possibilities involving the double steal, see Will 1990: 68–70.

9. Kant 1997: 113.

10. This last example even lends itself to a quantitative test. Several published wine critics use numerical scales to rate wines. In the case of two of the best-known American critics, Robert Parker and Steven Tanzer, the correlation of their independent ratings of the 1995 vintage of the wines of Bordeaux is +.84—an extremely high correlation produced by two experts whose personal preferences (sentiments) are quite different, but who are drawing on common criteria for making judgments about excellence. Author's analysis.

11. If a large number of critics fairly represent the distribution of critics in a given field, then their individual sentiments will work out to random noise by definition. The only way that sentiments would be correlated is if the sample of critics is skewed toward one perspective. The samples of expert judges represented by the inventories in *Human Accomplishment* are drawn from a single (though broad) school, as described on page 69. Within that school, they are quite various in terms of nationality, backgrounds, and sex.

12. Twain himself attributed this famous line to humorist Bill Nye.

13. This and the following on pre-Platonic Western aesthetics draws from Beardsley's discussion in Beardsley 1966: 21–28.

14. For Chinese aesthetics, see Zehou 1981: 45–81 and Bush and Shih 1985.

15. Pandey 1950. For a more general discussion of Chinese, Indian, and Japanese aesthetics, see Munro 1965.

16. The best selling of the many indictments of late 20C academia is Bloom 1987. For an excellent recent analysis, see Ellis 1997.

17. Their landmark works were Croce 1902 and Dewey 1934.

18. Ogden and Richards 1923.

19. Bloom 1998.

20. On postmodernism and science, see Stove 1998; on postmodernism and art, see Munson 2000; on postmodernism and history, literature, culture, and academia, see Himmelfarb 1994, Kimball 2000, Windschuttle 1996, and the aforementioned Bloom 1987 and Ellis 1997.

21. The term *historiometry* was coined in Woods 1911.

22. Quoted in Forrest 1974: 92.

23. E.g., Candolle 1885.

24. Ellis 1904, Cattell 1903.

25. Quetelet 1834.

26. Eisenstadt 1978.

27. Goetzel and Goetzel 1962.

28. Simonton 1992.

29. Cattell 1903.

30. For anyone who is curious enough to check out this ordering and does not come up with the same result, note that not all of the works listed in the index are represented in the text (works represented in the text were basis for the totals).

31. Janson and Janson 1997.

32. See Simonton 1990 for an account of reliability in historiometry.

33. All but a handful of the sources were written in the last 30 years when postmodernism was in the ascendancy. But alongside postmodernism, which dominated the news, historians and critics in the classical tradition continued to write major works, and it is from this body of work that the inventories were prepared.

34. *Discount* originated with Taagepera and Colby 1979 and *epochcentric bias* with Simonton 1984.

35. Spengler 1926.

36. Simonton 1981, Taagepera and Colby 1979.

37. Beethoven used the phrase in letters regarding Bach's surviving daughter, Regina Susannah, whom Beethoven proposed to support financially through benefit concerts or by writing a composition for her (though he never actually got around to either). For an example, see Shedlock 1972: 29.

38. Lang 1997: 513–14, Grout and Palisca 1996: 515–16, 556.

39. Lang 1997: 514.

40. Greater uncertainty attaches to the precise level of development reached in Precolombian America, Oceania, and Subsaharan Africa, but that is not the topic of this book. For example, a body of African archaeological work, still the subject of debate within the profession, argues that traditional Subsaharan African cultures were more advanced than has been thought, but the technologies under debate were indisputably developed earlier elsewhere—which is the issue that concerns us.

CHAPTER 6: THE LOTKA CURVE

1. The index score is 100 times a ratio in which the numerator is the measure of attention given to a person divided by the measure of attention given to the highest scoring person. For the highest scoring person, the ratio equals one, and the score equals 100, by definition.

2. The number 455 refers to Western artists with index scores, which is limited to those active from 1200 onward.

3. Lotka 1926.

4. Lotka proposed that the number of authors who had published exactly n publications could be described by a power function (an exponent is involved) of the form C/n^a, in which C is a constant that varies by discipline and a is often close to two. Lotka then demonstrated that in the case when a is equal to two, the constant C must equal $6/\pi^2$, or slightly less than .61, almost exactly the percentage he had observed in his data.

5. For examples, see Murphy 1973, Voos 1974, Brookstein 1977, Potter 1981, Pao 1986, Furnham and Bonnett 1992.

6. Price 1963.

7. Price's Law works perfectly for the Moles' compilation of the performed classical music repertory (Moles 1958). For another example of an accurate prediction by Price's Law, see Zhao and Jiang 1985. For an attempt to derive Price's Law from Lotka's equation, see Allison et al. 1976.

8. Martindale 1995.

9. Simonton 1984a: 81. This view of the decisive nature of the data is endorsed by Eysenck 1995: 38.

10. In this chapter, I limit myself to explanations specifically directed at the Lotka curve. In Chapter 21, I take up the question of "winner-take-all" markets, whereby under some circumstances a few people can monopolize record sales or command huge salaries in the job market, even though their superiority over their competitors is small or even non-existent.

11. Dennis 1954. See also Nicholls 1972.

12. Simon 1972. See also Haitun 1983.

13. Galton 1869: 78.

14. Shockley 1957.

15. Merton 1968.

16. Herbert Simon, who refuted the view that scientific productivity is the right-hand tail of a normal distribution, was an early proponent of this explanation (Simon 1955). For later versions, see Price 1976 and Allison et al. 1982

17. Simonton has explicated his model in many publications. A complete early presentation may be found in Simonton 1988 and a recent version in Simonton 1999.

18. Huber 1998.

19. Martindale 1995: 231.

20. The normal distribution has a mathematical definition. If you know the mean and variance for any set of data, you can use an equation to generate the

perfect normal distribution implied by that mean and variance. The lines in the graphs were generated in this manner.

21. How is it possible for professional golfers to be on the right-hand tail of all golfers and yet have normal distributions within the population of professional golfers? Because the population of professional golfers is selected according to a combination of talents. Consider putting as an example. Some professionals who get onto the tour because they are five standard deviations above the mean for all golfers in their driving and iron play may be only one standard deviation above the mean in their putting. Another professional who can make a living on the tour because of his short game and putting may drive the ball only as far as a good amateur. Thus when the component skills of professional golfers are shown separately, normal distributions can emerge.

22. Position on the money list is an alternative measure of excellence, but a clearly inferior one for two reasons. The money prizes available in professional golf have increased at a rate that makes comparisons across time complicated (merely correcting for the Consumer Price Index doesn't do the job), and professional golfers themselves treat tournament victories, and especially victories in the most important tournaments, as their own measure of greatness.

23. Including men with unfinished careers would exaggerate the number of one-win or two-win players, because many top active players who have won only one or two Majors so far are likely to win more before their careers are finished. Tiger Woods is the obvious case of someone who is going to be way, way out on the tail of the curve by the end of his career. As I write, he already has eight Major championships at the age of 27.

24. The mathematics of the distribution of eminence are complex. It is one thing to present an explanation of why eminence is distributed in a way that generally resembles a Lotka curve; another to specify the equation you have in mind and mathematically link that explanation with the equation. The explanation presented here is more limited, saying merely that *difficulty* offers good reasons why the distribution of talents in normal curves shifts to a hyperbolic curve as the task to be accomplished gets harder. I will leave it to others to spell out what additional assumptions and factors need to be added to the explanation to produce a mathematically exact Lotka curve.

CHAPTER 7: THE PEOPLE WHO MATTER I: SIGNIFICANT FIGURES

1. Gillespie 1980.

2. Mattei 1998.

3. Grout and Palisca 1996. Claude Palisca began his collaboration on the book in its third edition.

4. The number of composers I list represents the number who qualified for inclusion in the inventories for *Human Accomplishment*, not the total number of composers mentioned in the source (the sources include composers who were primarily active after 1950, whereas the inventories do not.).

5. Rebatet 1969.

6. Music lovers who are familiar with the venerable *Grove's Dictionary of Music and Musicians* (the current version is Sadie 1980) may wonder why it is not among my sources. The answer is that the music inventory was one of the last to be assembled. By that time, I knew that the definition of significant figures would require that a person be mentioned by 50 percent of the sources, and that entering everyone in the 20-volume *Grove's* would entail a great deal of wasted effort. I therefore began with a very extensive but not quite so mammoth first source, the *Harvard Biographical Dictionary*. Had I used *Grove* as my first source, the aggregate number of persons added by subsequent sources would have been even fewer than 236.

CHAPTER 8: THE PEOPLE WHO MATTER II: THE GIANTS

1. This famous remark is translated in different ways by different sources; e.g., Grout and Palisca 1996: 566, Schonberg 1997: 298.

2. Note that these high positions in two inventories are not a function of the same aggregate score applied to both inventories. The scores are based on inventory-specific ratings (e.g., Galileo's astronomy score is based on the attention given to Galileo's work in astronomy).

3. Gombrich 1995: 308.

4. H. Bloom 1998: xvii–xviii.

5. Lang 1997: 775.

6. Occasionally he could still make out certain low frequencies, such as the rumble of thunder, and some reports have him able to hear words shouted into his ear.

7. Solomon 1998: 161–62.

8. Schonberg 1997: 116.

9. Quoted in Durant 1935: 577.

10. Quoted in Mayr 1982: 423.

11. More precisely, it was Copernicus's only major achievement. In 1497 he had observed and recorded the occultation of a star by the moon, his only other accomplishment to find its way into any of the sources for the scientific events inventory.

12. Note that a high score from the chronologies is not merely a count of the raw number of different accomplishments. Each mention in a chronology is also counted, so that a major accomplishment such as the discovery of Uranus, mentioned in all of the chronologies, counts for much more than an accomplishment mentioned in just one of the chronologies.

13. Quoted in Kanigel 1991: 281.

CHAPTER 9: THE EVENTS THAT MATTER I: SIGNIFICANT EVENTS

1. White 1962.

2. For the importance of the legume, see Eco 1999. For the machine-made screw, see Rybczynski 1999. The rest of the nominations come from an end-of-the-millennium poll of the members of an invitation-only Internet forum called *Edge* that includes many prominent scientists among its members.

3. Burke 1975. He followed it with a second volume, Burke 1985.

4. The stirrup controversy is recounted in detail in DeVries 1992.

5. The greater statistical utility of the inventory of persons compared to the inventory of events is a function of the method. If one were to extract from a set of histories of science a word count of all the material discussing the events in the scientific inventories, the resulting data set would probably be as reliable as the data for the inventory of persons. But it would have to be done through a detailed quantitative breakdown of the text, not by use of the indexes of those texts.

   Indexes just aren't good enough. The index entry under *electron* may tell you the pages on which all of the events involving electrons are located, but you are going to have to analyze the material on those pages to determine what the events are. In other cases, the index may not even include an entry to guide you to events that ought to be part of the inventory. In contrast, those same indexes are definitely going to include the names of the scientists involved in the crucial discoveries involving electrons, with numbers of page references commensurate (over many sources) with the importance of the discoveries made by those people. Thus my reliance on chronologies rather than histories to compile the inventory of events, and thus as well the reason that the data for assessing the importance of specific events is rougher, in a statistical sense, than the data for assessing the importance of specific people.

   Why not get the word counts for specific events? Practical considerations. The labor required to enter material from indexes is already daunting. To break down the text of a dozen long histories would require a team of researchers over a period of years, with the prospect of a small payoff. At the outset of the work on *Human Accomplishment*, I thought it possible that the number of anonymous events that would be missed in an inventory of persons was large enough that it could affect the interpretation, or that the importance of certain events might not be adequately reflected in the measures based on the people associated with those events. In the event, neither expectation was borne out.

6. I used more latitude in selecting central medical events than in selecting central events for any of the other indexes. Some chronologies had detailed coverage of medical events that involved advances in biology or chemistry but unmistakably sketchier coverage of medical events involving advances in medical procedures and instruments. I took this into account, but in doing so introduced more subjective judgment than was applied to choices for the other inventories.

7. In the text, I refer to the number of times a given work is shown in the nine sources. The more precise statement is that I counted the number of times a

work appeared in any form for eight of the nine sources, and appeared as a color plate in the 17-volume *Istituto:* 1959.

8. Lang 1997: 764.

9. Simonton 1998. For a comprehensive study of the cycles of artistic work, see Martindale 1990.

10. E.g., Farnsworth 1969, Simonton 1991.

11. Simonton 1998: 208.

CHAPTER 10: THE EVENTS THAT MATTER II: META-INVENTIONS

1. Abbott 1991: Section 18.

2. For the argument that language is in fact a sort of invention and of much more recent appearance (circa −40,000), see Klein and Blake 2002. As I write, it is still a distinctly minority view.

3. Dating the first known use of a symbol to stand for a number or word is still a matter of controversy among archaeologists, but the most conservative estimates put it at somewhere in the vicinity of −8000. The much more difficult task of assembling symbols into logograms or alphabets that can convey connected text is believed to have occurred in Sumer sometime between −3500 and −2800, with expert opinion currently favoring −3100. A minority argues that a writing system may go back to −4000 and may have originated in Europe rather than the Near East, throwing a large monkey wrench into the standard paradigm. For an account of the pre-cuneiform tablets and of the controversy over the timing of the first use of written language, see Rudgley 1999: chapters 3 and 4. For a concise account of the development of writing around the world, see Diamond 1997: chapter 12.

4. The nearest misses were monotheism, the personal god (along with heaven and hell), maps, and encoded information. Monotheism actually predates −800, so in that sense is not even eligible. But my larger reason for rejecting monotheism and the personal god is that their effects depend so fundamentally on felt belief, not merely on the idea itself. Thus in Chapter 19 I discuss what I consider to be the important effects of Christianity on European accomplishment—but what created that effect was the power of faith in the truth of Christian doctrine, not familiarity with the idea that a personal god exists. The invention of maps and similar abstract representations of geographic spaces (architectural drawings, plans, etc.) also predates −800. Most of what we know about their development postdates −800, but the concept of representation of geographic spaces seems to have already been a part of the human repertoire.

Encoded information—the concept that enables, among other things, the computer program—offers an interesting case of something that in retrospect we can call an addition to the cognitive repertoire, but that came about through a process so gradual that, to my mind, it doesn't fit the concept of invention. At first glance, it would seem to have a neatly specific starting point with the invention of the Jacquard loom in 1800 (borrowed from earlier versions by Bouchon and Vaucanson), which used punched cards to control the creation of patterns in woven cloth. This invention was known to Charles Babbage, who incorporated the idea into his design for the analytic engine, a mechanical computer. But Babbage's ideas were not realized for another hundred years, and then not because people still remembered anything about encoded information. By that time, they were working off other traditions. One of those was the use of punched cards in the American census of 1890—but it is not clear (stories vary) that Hollerith, the originator of the card-based tabulating machine, was aware of Jacquard's work. My interpretation of this story is that the idea of encoded information never energized progress in the same way that the 14 meta-inventions did. From our vantage point today, it looks like a meta-invention. At the time that different events were happening, it was a useful technical strategy that seems to have occurred to various people as the need arose, but not something seen as opening new, hitherto unknown possibilities for doing things.

The decision to leave the scientific method as a single meta-invention was pragmatic. In discussing the components of the scientific method—replicability, falsifiability, experiment, "blindness" in experimentation, and others that are individually so important that each could have been treated as a separate meta-invention—I would have had to write the text in ways that would constantly point out how each fit into a larger phenomenon called the invention of the scientific method. I decided to simplify the presentation by grouping them under that heading.

5. If we had more surviving works from China in the period surrounding –500, it might be appropriate to assign this invention jointly to China and Greece. Elements of artistic realism in painting have appeared on surviving objects dating to –316, and lifelike lacquer animals survive from –533 or earlier, but the record is still scattered. See Hung 1997.

6. Gombrich 1995: 81.

7. Kemp 1990: 9.

8. In these statements I rely on Kemp 1990, which incorporates a recently discovered letter that appears to place Brunelleschi's key discovery no later than 1413, compared to the previous dating of the mid 1420s. Dating Brunelleschi's demonstration from circa 1413 substantially changes our understanding of the speed with which perspective was adopted. Under the old dating, Masaccio painted the *Holy Trinity* later in the same year that Brunelleschi painted the baptistery. Under the new dating, about 15 years elapsed. See Edgerton 1975 and J. White 1987.

9. Quoted in Boorstin 1992: 396.

10. Boorstin 1992: 396.

11. See Abraham 1979: 563.

12. For a discussion of the development of Chinese musicology, see Ronan 1981: 371–87.

13. My primary sources for the discussion of the origins of polyphony are Lang 1997: 125–36 and Grout and Palisca 1996: chapter 3.

14. Aristotle credits Agathon (c. –445 to –400) with the first use of fictional characters in a drama, probably *The Flower*, but it seems prudent to assume that

stories with fictional characters predate Agathon by an unknown number of centuries.

15. Trilling 1951: 214.

16. Although usually classified as anonymous, *Lazarillo* is sometimes attributed to Fernando de Rojas. I follow Barzun 2000: 111 in naming *Lazarillo* rather than *Don Quixote* as the first true novel.

17. In Seldes 1985: 447.

18. Russell 1945: xiii.

19. Boorstin 1998.

20. Quoted in Kaplan 2000.

21. Quoted in Bernstein 1996: 44.

22. Quoted in Bernstein 1996: 43.

23. Quoted in Bernstein 1996: 17.

24. Stigler 1999: 213–14.

25. Ronan 1981: 224.

26. Needham 1981: 13.

27. Quoted in Ronan 1981: 292.

28. Ronan 1981: 293.

29. Needham 1981: 120.

30. Why didn't the Chinese discover the scientific method? I offer some general arguments about the role of purpose and autonomy in Chinese culture and their effects on accomplishment in Chapter 19. For explanations involving the scientific method specifically, see Joseph Needham's discussions, most easily accessible in Ronan 1978: vol. 1, and Needham 1981, especially chapter 5. See also Stark 2003: 50–51.

31. An excellent one-volume compilation of articles on the historiography of the scientific revolution is Cohen 1994.

32. The classic modern statement of the Principle of Falsification is Popper 1963: 33–39. In recent years, the principle has come under a variety of criticisms both technical and political. David Stove has led one aspect of the criticism, arguing that falsification is part of the attempt to undermine the concept of objective truth in science (e.g., in Stove 1998). As someone who has spent his career on issues of public policy in which most of the researchers have an emotional or political commitment to their favored policies, I continue to be an admirer of the principle. Invoking falsifiability is one of the ways to keep the discussion honest.

33. Ockham's name is sometimes Latinized as *Occam*.

34. The literal translation is "Plurality should not be posited without necessity." The more customary translation comes from "*Entia non sunt multiplicanda praeter necessitate*," a variant wrongly attributed to Ockham.

35. Settle 1983: 3–20.

36. Quoted in Shapin 1996: 57.

CHAPTER 11: COMING TO TERMS WITH THE ROLE OF MODERN EUROPE

1. I place the figures according to the decade in which they reached the age of 40, the average age at which the significant figures were at the height of their powers. Forty has consistently been found to be the peak of accomplishment. For an extensive review of the literature on this issue, see Simonton 1984a: 93–112.

2. To avoid confusing the issue, I omit philosophy. Adding it makes no difference to the results. More generally, the philosophy inventories get short shrift from here on out. The number of significant figures in Western philosophy after 1400 is too small (76) to be of much use in the quantitative analyses.

3. This is a conservative estimate. It is based on Hughes 1997, an art history of typical size and scope. The count of American authors I take from the index includes only the 77 U.S.-born artists that are mentioned in both *American Visions* and in at least one of the sources for the Western art index, thus under-counting the total number of U.S.-born artists mentioned in *American Visions*. I then estimated the number of significant figures that would be produced from a large set of American art histories that have 77 artists as the median value. This estimate draws from the very high correlation between the median number of persons mentioned in the sources and the number of significant figures (the sample was small, only 9 inventories, but the correlation was .99). The fitted value for a median of 77 is 91.

4. Comparing numbers of artists leaves open the possibility that the picture would change if only we paid attention to their quality rather than quantity. That is, suppose that Chinese histories of art are for some reason more selective than Western histories of art, readier to omit minor figures. I raise this because it is the only way I can imagine that the inflationary effect I invoke could be misleading, but I also cannot think of any reason why it should be true nor find any evidence in the sources used to compile the inventories that it is true. A reading of the histories of literature in China, India, Japan, and the Arab world and of histories of Chinese and Japanese art indicates that they are behaving just like historians everywhere as they describe some artists as major, others minor. The conclusions I draw in the text about the inflation of non-Western significant figures depend only on a few highly plausible assumptions about the nature of the qualitative distributions within the various inventories.

   The special case of China does raise additional issues, however. Chinese encyclopedic sources are known to list thousands of painters and poets—13,000 painters in one encyclopedia of art, for example (Clunas 1997: 13)—while the Chinese significant figures in art and literature number just 111 and 83 respectively. But encyclopedic rosters are useless as predictors of the number of significant figures. Imagine, for example, a compilation of all the people who have ever appeared in the *Who's Who* volumes for the arts, literature, music, business, and science that appear annually. Such works have now appeared in the United States for more than a century. Imagine that we had several centuries of such compilations to stitch together—that is the nature of China's endless lists. No matter how long they may be, they have little influence on who qualifies as a significant figure in any of the inventories, Western or non-Western, because, by design, most of the sources for all the inventories are histories. If it were indeed the case that China had many more important artists than emerge from the histories, one would expect to find some clues. For example, if a historian is faced with a hundred artists from a given era who, in his judgment, are all worthy of discussion, and he has space to discuss only a dozen of them, it seems likely that the text would say something to that effect. Nothing in the text of the histories of Chinese art used for the inventories conveys that impression. To the extent that historians of Chinese art must choose from a large pool of roughly equally wonderful artists, one would expect a wide degree of difference in the choices actually made by different historians. No evidence of that emerges from the inventories. The reliabilities for the Chinese art and literature indexes, .91 and .88, argue against that view. It seems plausible that a number of Chinese artists from the earliest centuries would be added if we still had full information on their work. On the other hand, the Chinese historical records are much better than comparable records from ancient Greece in recording the reputations of painters whose work has been lost. Taken as a whole, a prudent conclusion seems to be that the number of Chinese artists and writers may not be as inflated relative to all of Europe as other country-specific inventories are estimated to be; hence the extremely conservative conclusion stated in the text.

5. Sivin 1990 quoted in Landes 1998: 348.

6. Landes 1998: 348.

7. Pacey 1998: viii.

8. The Pacey and McClellan and Dorn books could not be used for constructing *Human Accomplishment*'s inventories. *Technology in World Civilization* is a concise work of just 207 pages of text and presents case histories illustrating Pacey's thesis, not a history of technology. *Science and Technology in World History*, with 373 pages of text, is intended as an introductory college textbook and was not sufficiently comprehensive to meet the 18 percent criterion for becoming a qualified source. Neither did McClellan and Dorn meet the 10 percent criterion for use as an index source. See Appendix 2 for a discussion of qualified sources and index sources.

9. Pacey 1998: 218–25.

10. Needham 1954. One obvious strategy for protecting against Eurocentrism is to use sources from non-European countries. I was able to do this for the arts and philosophy inventories, but not for science and technology. One problem is lack of translations for works in non-Roman alphabets. Such translations are common for works on the arts, because Europeans perceive that a book on Chinese art written by a Chinese fills a role that works on Chinese art by Europeans cannot fill. Works on science and technology are less likely to be translated because they are not perceived to fill a similar gap. The results when I attempted to find such sources in Japanese are instructive. A Japanese graduate student from the University of Chicago spent the better part of a summer canvassing Japanese library catalogs, over the Internet and with the help of friends in Japan, seeking histories, bibliographic dictionaries, and chronologies in the fields covered by the various inventories. His work is reflected in some of the Japanese sources used for the art, literature, and philosophy inventories. But for many weeks he was stymied in his search for sources for science

and technology, until he finally tracked down a biographical dictionary of scientists apparently prepared under the aegis of a committee of distinguished Japanese academicians. We had the book shipped to the United States, opened it with great anticipation—and it turned out to be a word-for-word translation of *Biographical Encyclopedia of Scientists* (1981) by J. Daintith, S. Mitchell, E. Tootill, and D. Gjertsen, a fine work, but a British one. The book was indeed introduced to its Japanese audience by the committee of distinguished Japanese academicians, but they had not felt it necessary to augment the text by adding material on Japanese scientists that the British had omitted.

11. If the focus is proportional differences within categories, the *DoSB* contains proportionally fewer entries from the Arab world than does the roster of people who would have been compiled without the *DoSB*, but more from South Asia. The raw numbers are small—e.g., the difference in the proportion from the Arab world comes from a raw difference of only 9 people in the two totals, out of samples that number 4,271 for the *DoSB* and 3,165 for the entries identified independently of the *DoSB*.

12. A few such events are in the inventory of accomplishments for European countries, such as Fibonacci's reintroduction of material from Euclid's *Elements* and the first European preparation of gunpowder. They amount to about one-tenth of one percent of the total accomplishments assigned to European countries. So a more precise statement of the challenge in the text would require that no more than one-tenth of one percent of the events added to non-European countries consist of accomplishments originally done elsewhere.

13. Kroeber 1944: 166.

CHAPTER 12: . . . AND OF DEAD WHITE MALES

1. My information on the pictures in the Columbia mathematics library was accurate as recently as January, 2003.

2. These percentages refer to significant figures in the hard sciences and mathematics, excluding technology and medicine, which were not comprehensively covered in the *DoSB*.

3. For the scientific sources, post-1950 data were collected for all the chronologies and for the *DoSB*, and the presentation in the text uses all the names mentioned by any of those sources. For the arts sources, post-1950 data were not as uniform, so I selected a recent encyclopedic source for each of the Western arts inventories and based the presentation on them. The sources were Gowing 1995 for the visual arts, Goring 1994 for literature, and Randel 1996 for music. These data cannot be used to estimate density of accomplishment in the post-1950 period without extensive compensating calculations, because of the uneven coverage of the sources. Some sources stop in the 1970s, others in the 1980s, still others in the 1990s. But we can use the raw data to estimate a ratio of men to women for the post-1950 data, because

whatever the differences in coverage across sources, the coverage of men and women within sources is presumably the same (e.g., no source stops covering men in 1970 but women in 1985, etc.).

4. Philosophy is omitted because of its usual problem with small sample size, plus the scant attention paid to philosophers in the last half of 20C (scant, for good reason). The most recent woman philosopher shown in my sources is Simone Weil (1909–1943).

5. Sarton 1927–48: vol. II, 323–29, 533–41, and 808–18. See also Patai 1977: 317.

6. Vital 1999: 6.

7. American Jewish Historical Society 1999: 5.

8. Patai 1977: 318.

9. Official accounts of parliamentary debate, quoted in Vital 1999: 179.

10. Examples are Jacobs 1886, Lombroso 1889, and Legoyt 1868.

11. The American Jewish population in 1900 is estimated at 938,000–1,058,000, which has a midpoint value of 998,000 (American Jewish Historical Society 1999: 35). In 1940, the same source puts the number at 4,770,000–4,975,000, with a midpoint value of 4,873,000. The best discussion of Jewish population in Europe at the turn of 20C, 9 million, is in Vital 1999: 297 ff. Vital assembled his data from a variety of statistical sources throughout Europe. The out-migration of Jews during the next 40 years meant that the European population of Jews actually fell, estimated as of 1940 to stand at about 9.24 million (Myron C. Taylor files in the Franklin Delano Roosevelt Library). I put the combined U.S./European Jewish population at 10.0 million for 1900 and 14.1 million for 1940.

12. I classified a significant figure as a Jew if either his mother or (departing from Jewish practice) father was identified as a Jew in the sources.

13. The Jewish ratio in the earth sciences would have been higher if anthropology had been classified within earth sciences. Franz Boas and Claude Lévi-Strauss were both Jews, for example.

14. The larger the denominator for figuring the Jewish contribution per million Jews in that country, the smaller the resulting ratio. By taking the average for 1900 and 1940, the entire period of 1870–1950 is represented, in effect, by the Jewish population as of around 1920, considerably larger than any figure based on the profile of population change over the entire period of 1870–1950. The available data on Jewish populations by country do not permit a finer-grained analysis. In any case, it is always best to allow for a margin of error when dealing with dramatic results, as in this instance.

15. For a recent history of the Jewish experience in Germany, see Elon 2002.

16. Persons were counted as Jewish if either parent was Jewish. Gustav Hertz and Maria Goeppert Mayer, Nobel laureates often identified as Jews, apparently had just one parent who was half-Jewish and are not included on this list of

Nobel winners, nor is Christian Anfinsen, born of Gentile parents and subsequently a convert to Orthodox Judaism. Three web sources give lists of Jewish nobel laureates: www.science.co.il, the Israel Science & Technology web site; www.us-israel.org, sponsored by the American-Israeli Cooperative Enterprise, and www.jinfo.com, a privately sponsored project established and maintained by an American physicist to document Jewish scientific and cultural achievements. Of these, jinfo.com is without doubt the best source, with excellent documentation of ambiguous cases, and I have relied on it. The most widely circulated list, from www.us-israel.org, has several errors of both inclusion and omission.

17. The discrepancy in proportional increase and raw increase reflects the substantially larger number of prizes awarded to more than one person in the second half of the century.

18. If anyone wonders why an analysis using post-1950 data like that conducted for women was not conducted for Jews, the answer is time. Using everyone, not just significant figures, born from 1830 onward, means augmenting the number of individuals by several thousand. For women from Western countries, names alone are a reliable basis for classifying sex in a large proportion of cases, and the ambiguous cases are a small enough set to be investigated one by one. In contrast, names are an unreliable basis for classifying Jewishness. Not only are some names often-but-not-always Jewish, every child of a Jewish mother married to a Gentile father would be missed if names were the only basis for classification. Identifying Jewishness for several thousand people, most of them obscure, would have required months, and still would have left a large proportion classified as "unknown" at the end of it.

19. Cuban poet Nicolas Guillen, Brazilian poet Jorge de Lima, American poet Vachel Lindsay, American novelist Richard Wright, and American composer Duke Ellington.

20. The *DoSB* contains an entry for just one African scientific figure throughout this period (Percy Julian, an African-American) that I was able to identify as such. The other Africans are mentioned exclusively by one source, Porter and Ogilvie 2000, which in its introduction openly states that it sought to represent minorities and women. Considering these factors plus the small numbers involved, the safest assumption is that the African trendline in the scientific domain from the latter part of 19C through about 1980 (when the information in the sources dwindles down) is flat.

21. Russell 1995.

22. Geary 1998 approaches the causes of male-female differences from the perspective of evolutionary biology, and in that sense is definitely on one side of the argument, but his treatment of the literature is so encyclopedic that you can use his book as a basis for exploring the literature on both sides for just about any specific aspect of male-female differences.

23. Geary 1998 once again offers the best single review of the literature, in chapter 8.

24. Rushton and Ankeny 1997, Kimura 1999.

25. Quoted in Vital 1999: 130.

26. The best summary of studies of Jewish IQ is Storfer 1990: 314–21. Lynn (in press), estimates American Jewish verbal IQ at 107–108.

27. For discussions of the Ashkenazi/Oriental (Sephardim and Mizrachim) difference, see Patai 1977: 306–14 and Storfer 1990: 504–7.

28. Modestly higher means have disproportionate effects on the tails of the distribution. It is a mathematical implication of a trait that has a normal distribution. The IQ test is normed for the entire population with a mean of 100 and a standard deviation of 15. A subgroup with a mean of 107 can be expected to have more than 4 times as many people with IQs of 145 or higher than a subgroup with a mean of 100. For a subgroup with a mean of 115, the disproportion rises to 16:1.

29. Sheldon 1954.

30. For a discussion of the logic behind these selection pressures, see Patai 1977: 304–6.

31. Reuters, 12/17/01, reporting the work of geneticist Ariel Darvasi and his colleagues at Jerusalem's Hebrew University.

CHAPTER 13: CONCENTRATIONS OF EUROPEAN AND AMERICAN ACCOMPLISHMENT

1. I inserted these pre-WWI borders on a map of modern Europe. The boundaries for the other countries are exact; my revisions are close, but approximate.

2. The locations of many of the small towns and rural areas were known and taken into account when plotting the data. For the rest, I distributed the dots randomly around the region except where mountainous or heavily forested areas are sparsely populated. In such instances, I gave preference to the most densely populated part of the region.

3. U. S. Bureau of the Census 1975: Series A 172–194.

4. Biographical data on some of the Jewish significant figures in question is lacking, hence the approximate figures. Note that the work country of people who had made their major contributions while in Germany is classified as Germany, even though they fled after the Nazis came to power.

5. A substantial number of significant figures who were raised in one place and spent their work life in another were moving within language and cultural settings and were not counted as emigrants. These included persons who moved within the Austro-Hungarian empire and between present-day Austria and present-day Germany. I also did not count as emigrants German-speaking Swiss who moved to Germany, Germans who moved to eastern Switzerland, French-speaking Swiss who moved to France, French who moved to western Switzerland, and French-speaking Belgians who moved to France.

CHAPTER 14: TAKING POPULATION INTO ACCOUNT: THE ACCOMPLISHMENT RATE

1. The variables are population in 1900 and the total number of scientific significant figures from 1900–1950 (scientific, because that inventory has worldwide coverage).

2. I use 10 million as the base even though many countries had fewer than 10 million people to make it easier to talk in terms of rounded whole numbers. Using one million as the base would produce many instances in which the accomplishment rate would have to be expressed as a fraction of one figure.

3. The Western rates shown in the graphs sum the rates calculated for the individual countries. I replicated the timelines for each inventory using an aggregated rate (sum of significant figures across countries divided by the sum of the population across countries). The shapes of the timelines were materially indistinguishable.

4. The baseline has no normative meaning, but merely expresses the empirical result when 1400–1950 is used for the calculation. The average would change markedly if I were to lop off a century at either end.

5. Specifically, I averaged the values of the two measures for each of those years, then computed the linear regression trendline.

CHAPTER 15: EXPLANATIONS I: PEACE AND PROSPERITY

1. Sorokin 1937: vol. 3, appendix to part three, 578–620.

2. Mee 1975: 25.

3. Hamilton 1934, reported in Clough 1968: 150, table 1.

4. Quoted in Landes 1998: 172.

5. Tawney 1958: 28.

6. Quoted in Cipolla 1980: 267.

7. Data involving money are always expressed in constant values based on the 1990 international dollar.

8. A fourth number of interest in the standard linear regression model is R^2, pronounced "r-squared," where the R refers to the multiple correlation of all the independent variables with the dependent variable. For mathematical reasons I won't go into, R^2 is equivalent to the proportion of variation in the dependent variable explained by all the independent variables combined. Go back to the example of predicting your child's height. If in a sample of children and their parents, the three independent variables (father's height, mother's height, sex of the child) were found to have an R^2 of .50, it would mean that we can explain 50 percent of the variation in children's height with those three independent variables. In the analyses conducted here, however, the standard linear model does not apply, because the dependent variables are count variables—counts of the number of times that a rare event occurs (see note 10 below). The regression model that does apply, the random-effects negative binomial model for panel data, is not suitable for computing the R^2 statistic. A "pseudo R^2"can be calculated for some types of negative binomial

models, but it does not have the same meaning (see Cameron and Trivedi 1998: 153–5; Long 1997: 102–8), and indeed does not lend itself to an easily expressed interpretation of any sort.

9. The choice makes no difference to the interpretation of the results. The betas associated with the democracy and autocracy dummy variables will be different depending on whether one chooses totalitarianism or limited monarchy as the reference group, for example, but the *difference* between the democracy beta and the autocracy one will be the same, as will all such pairwise differences, including the differences between the reference country and every other country.

10. The database consists of cross-sectional time-series data, also called panel data, of the form x_{it}, where x_{it} is a set of observations for unit i and time t. In this case, the units are countries and the times are two-decade periods from 1390–1410 to 1930–50. The basic analytic framework for the regression analysis is a negative binomial model using a vector of dummy variables for the two-decade periods and the random-effects option for the country units, implemented using the xtnbreg procedure in the computer program Stata, v.7. The reasons for these choices are as follows:

The dependent variable in the regression analyses in *Human Accomplishment* is always some variation on a count of significant figures. A count variable is by definition limited to zero or a positive number, which introduces a problem: the standard regression model, known as ordinary least squares (OLS), fits a straight regression line to the data. What does it mean if that straight line goes below zero? It is a nonsensical result, and symptomatic of ways in which the mathematics of the standard linear model can be misleading when count variables bounded from above, or as in the case of count variables, from below, are involved.

When the events being counted are common ones in which only a few observations will show numbers close to zero and the underlying distribution is plausibly close to normal, the standard linear model can often be used without problems. But as the events become rarer, the plausible underlying distribution is increasingly likely to be a Poisson distribution, not a normal one, and the defects of the standard linear model increase. When zeroes make up a large proportion of the values, as they do when we are measuring the appearance of significant figures over the course of a generation in a given country of Europe, the standard linear model must be discarded.

Since few count distributions fit all of the specifications of a Poisson distribution, the Poisson-based regression model comes in several variations. The one most appropriate to these data is the negative binomial model (chosen because the analyses uniformly showed highly significant evidence of over-dispersion). For discussions of the negative binomial model and other methods of analyzing count data, see Cameron and Trivedi 1998; Maddala 1983: 149–96, and Long 1997: 217–50.

Analyses of panel data raise a variety of issues. Subsequent notes take up special cases. The general framework requires decisions to be made about how to take into account the effects of the point in time t of an observation and the unmeasured country-specific effects of unit i.

In the case of time, the objective is to take out the effects of time altogether. If I enter the midpoint year of the two-decade period as a continuous independent variable, I constrain the ability of the regression model to do so. Suppose, for example, that the importance of the difference between the two time periods centered in 1440 and 1460 is far less than the importance of the difference between 1880 and 1900. When time is treated as a continuous variable, the regression model is forced to treat the two differences as the same. The alternative, and the choice used throughout the analyses, is to enter the two-decade periods as a vector of dummy variables, permitting the regression model to treat each value independently of the others. Thus an analysis from 1400–1950 includes 27 separate variables representing the two-decade periods from 1390–1410 to 1930–1950, plus one of the two-decade periods (it can be any of them) serving as the reference period and not entered in the equation.

In the case of the country units, one option would be to enter a set of dummy variables for countries. But because the dataset involves panel data, it is preferable to use software specifically designed for time-series data. The program used for these analyses, Stata v.7, provides such a version of the negative binomial model that offers two options for taking the unit into account: random-effects or fixed-effects over-dispersion models. For those who may be familiar with these terms as they are used for OLS, note that in a negative binomial analysis, *random-effects* and *fixed-effects* refer to the distribution of the dispersion parameter, not to a term associated with a dummy variable for a given country (see Hausman 1984 and Cameron and Trivedi: 280–92). In the case of the database for *Human Accomplishment*, the most plausible assumption about the countries is that they play different roles for reasons that are independent of the other variables I am using—Germans are different from the French, Swedes are different from Italians, and the British are different from the Spanish in cultural ways that are unrelated to variables such as GDP and population. In such a situation, the random-effects negative binomial model is the preferred choice. As a check, all of the analyses were replicated using the fixed-effects alternative. Hausman's specification test (Hausman 1978, Hausman 1984) was used to verify the statistical appropriateness of the random-effects assumption. The few cases in which the random-effects model failed that test are noted in the text, along with information about the results of the fixed-effects version.

11. Readers familiar with regression analysis may be wondering why lagged values of the dependent variable are not included among the control variables. They come later. See Chapter 16.

12. All the analyses were replicated with logged population entered as an independent variable in which its coefficient was not constrained. None of the results was materially different from those presented in the tables, with the single exception of an analysis in which another independent variable was population of the largest city. When national population was entered as the exposure variable, the coefficient of city population was small and insignificant; when national population entered as an unconstrained independent variable, the coefficient of city population dominated. An examination of multicollinearity suggests that entering national population as the exposure variable yielded the more interpretable result.

13. Variation in logged variables represents proportional variation and often better explains the dependent variable than movement in the raw values. Such

was the case with the variables used in these analyses. Logging a variable also has the virtue of suppressing extreme values—for example, when dealing with income distributions in which a comparative handful of people with multi-million-dollar incomes can distort the results.

When using logs, something must be done to accommodate values of zero, since the logged value of zero is undefined. The typical solution is either to rescale the entire variable, adding a constant between 0 and 1 to all values, or to leave all the nonzero values unchanged but assign some value between 0 and 1 to the zero values. I have chosen the latter option for all the analyses, assigning .25 to zero for purposes of computing logged values. This choice, a necessarily subjective attempt to preserve a difference between 0 and 1 that is neither unrealistically too big nor too small relative to the other logged values, produces a logged value for 0 (rescaled to .25) that is −1.4, while the logged values of 1, 2, and 3 are 0, .7, and 1.1 respectively. The analyses using such rescaled values were replicated using .1 and .5 to see if the results were affected.

14. For productive periods, see Dennis 1966 and Lehman 1953. For the choice of the 20 years in which an individual turns 40, see Simonton 1997d. The label assigned to the generation is in the middle—e.g., the label for the period 1630–1650 is 1640. Data on population and GDP are taken from the beginning of the period.

15. I eliminate philosophy from this calculation.

16. Sorokin 1937: vol. 3, appendix to part two and appendix to part three.

17. The source for this data, and for smaller European countries not covered by Sorokin, was Brownstone and Franck 1994.

18. The presentation of the methodology for the war and disturbance variables is given in Sorokin 1937: vol. 3, chapters 10 and 12.

19. For discussion and references, see Simonton 1997d: 7. See also the discussion of purpose and autonomy, Chapter 19.

20. For all the analyses, the results were also run using the number of significant figures in the separate inventories as the dependent variable. For all analyses using logged variables that had been rescaled to accommodate values of zero, I examined the results using three alternatives for rescaling zero: the one reported in the text, .25, plus .1 and .5. Another standard procedure was to check the results when the observation for the United States in 1940—an extreme outlier in most of the analyses—was omitted. A variety of other diagnostic tests for standard problems in regression analysis involving multicollinearity among the independent variables were also routinely conducted.

Additional analyses specific to the war and unrest variables included entering the war and unrest variables separately, and trying the different permutations of lagged values up to three generations back, including a version with no lagged values at all. The model was also run using unlogged values of the population and density variables. To check the possibility that the continuous variables were hiding relationships that might exist for very severe war but not for lesser levels of war, I also created categorical variables for both war and unrest, dividing war into categories of "no war during the generation," "minor war," "major war," and "very severe war," and dividing unrest into "no unrest during the generation," "minor unrest," and "severe unrest."

21. A few dozen different runs of a regression model employing several variables produces hundreds of betas, some of which are likely to be "statistically significant" just by chance. In this case, the number of significant figures in the visual arts had a statistically significant relationship with the war index in the preceding generation, but the effect was small. As soon as one toyed with the specification of the model (e.g., by dropping the lag for *t*–2), the effect disappeared.

22. Simonton 1997d found a significant relationship between his measures of creative activity and his political instability variable (similar to my civil unrest variable) in the first preceding 20-year period, in a dataset that extended from –700 to 1839. He did not find a significant relationship for his measure of war.

23. The framework is taken from the specific estimates of GDP for the benchmark years of 1500, 1600, 1700, 1820, 1870, 1913, and 1950, expressed in international 1990 dollars from Maddison 1998: Table B-18. To interpolate GDP for the decades within the period 1500–1800 (I did not try to estimate GDP for 1400–1500), the major sources were Barkhausen 1974, Van Dillen 1974, Romano 1974, and Clough 1968. For 1500–1700, I relied most heavily on Cipolla 1980: 249, fig. 10-1. For the period 1800–1950, I was able to increase the precision of the estimates considerably by combining Maddison's benchmark estimates (with their virtue of being expressed in a common metric) with the year-by-year estimates of GDP from another major compilation of historical economic data, Mitchell 1992: Table J1, expressed in the separate currencies of the countries involved.

24. I use per capita GDP instead of national GDP for the same reason I use population density rather than geographic area—it reduces high correlations with other independent variables. For example, the correlation of GDP with population is .84, while the correlation of per capita GDP with population is just .36.

25. Technological accomplishment (and, indirectly, accomplishment in the hard sciences) may be seen as a cause of wealth as well as its effect. A full analysis of the relationship of GDP and the emergence of significant figures would take this interactive causation into account, modeling the number of significant figures in technology and the sciences as causes of increased GDP, which in turn acts as a cause of accomplishment in the arts and further accomplishments in the sciences. Methods are available for modeling complex causation. I have chosen not to pursue them in this presentation, which focuses on making a simpler point about the relationship of wealth as a cause of accomplishment. I will note, however, that when logged GDP per capita is treated as the dependent variable and the measures of accomplishment (current and lagged) are entered as the independent variables, a large and highly significant relationship is found with the current and lagged values of the scientific significant figures, but much weaker relationships with the current and lagged values of significant figures in the arts.

26. There are 15 countries in each of the observations from 1400 to 1790. The USA, Finland, Norway, and Canada are added in 1790, 1810, 1820, and 1870 respectively.

CHAPTER 16: EXPLANATIONS II: MODELS, ELITE CITIES, AND FREEDOM OF ACTION

1. Quoted in Kroeber 1944: 17.

2. Quoted in Kroeber 1944: 18.

3. Simonton 1997d. The article was published in 1976.

4. Simonton 1997c. The article was published in 1988.

5. E.g., Simonton 1997a, Simonton 1997b.

6. The third era was chosen partly because the population data are the most accurate and the biographical data most complete for 19C and 20C, and also because the most recent era is the one in which the origins of the significant figures were most dispersed, thereby providing a conservative estimate of the dominant role of cities over the entire period from 1400–1950.

7. All computations are based on the place where the significant figures spent their childhoods. When more than one city is within the same comparison area, populations and significant figures from all the cities have been subtracted from the comparison area total. The computation divides the number of significant figures who were active over the course of a half-century by the relevant population at the midpoint of the half-century—a "per million" figure different from the one you might be thinking of, the number of significant figures who were active over the course of a half century divided by the number of people who lived in that country over the course of a half century.

   Note that the region within which Paris is located, Île de France, is almost coincident with greater Paris, hence it was not possible to get a clean comparison of the city of Paris with its immediately surrounding area. The lack of any other city/region comparison in France is explained by the remarkable fact that no other French region produced 25 significant figures from 1800–1950. The highest was 18. The same centralization of significant figures in the national centers explains the absence of city/region comparisons for Russia, Spain, and Italy.

   Some details about the mechanics of the calculations: For each half-century within the 1800–1950 period, I divided the number of significant figures from the city by the population of the city at the midpoint of the half-century, then repeated the calculation for significant figures coming from the rest of the region, divided by the population of the region (minus the city population, of course) at the midpoint. The numbers in the table represent the weighted average over the entire period. Unweighted averages were produced as well (the added ratio for the three half-centuries divided by three). Each option produces its own disadvantages. When a city had no significant figures in a half century, using the unweighted average tended to understate the real degree to which it out-produced the surrounding region. But a case such as Stuttgart's or Geneva's, which produced several significant figures while their populations were still extremely small, tend to overstate their roles. But those two cities are the only instances in which the weighted average created a problem, whereas the problems associated with the unweighted averages were much more common, hence the choice of measure to present in the table.

8. A map showing where the significant figures worked as adults makes the same point.

9. Almost all the generalizations about cities that follow in the text have changed in the last half century, altered by the growth of suburbs and, more recently, the ability of people to do work in rural areas that formerly had to be done in close physical proximity to colleagues, models, institutions, libraries, and audiences. But they held true until 1950.

10. Simonton 1997d: 5.

11. Simonton 1997d. As a proxy measure of cultural diversity, Simonton used a measure of political fragmentation across the Western world, counting the number of independent states. (His geographic unit of analysis embraced the entire West.) In effect, my measures of elite cities (see page 367) approximate political fragmentation within the countries I use as my geographic unit of analysis—e.g., Italy and Germany have the largest number of elite cities, and until 19C also had the greatest number of independent political units within their borders.

12. Finer 1997: vol. 2, 965.

13. Alexander Solzhenytsin and Boris Pasternak are not included in this list because their major works were not published until after 1950.

14. For a discussion of property rights in Russia and their relationship to freedom of action, see Pipes 1999: 159–208.

15. A. H. Lybyer, *The Government of the Ottoman Empire in the Time of Suleiman the Magnificent*, quoted in Toynbee and Somervell 1946: 176.

16. Lags can refer to any number of time periods. For example, if you have reason to believe that the causal role of a lagged variable is delayed, you might want to compute lags going back several time periods. For an extended discussion of the lagged analysis of creative figures and celebrities (which also uses Kroeber 1944 as a point of departure), see Simonton 1997c.

17. When the raw value of a first-order lag of a count variable, y_{t-1}, is entered as an additional regressor, it produces explosive results for values of beta greater than zero. Cameron and Trivedi recommend specifying a multiplicative role for y_{t-1}. This entails using a rescaled value of y_{t-1}, y^*_{t-1} in which a constant between 0 and 1 is added to the raw value, permitting logged values to be computed for $y_{t-1}=0$. Cameron and Trivedi 1998: 238–40. The constant used in these analyses was .25. The analyses were replicated using .1 and .5 as constants, to test for sensitivity to the choice of constant. The differences were minor. An alternative approach for dealing with the problem of explosive results is to use first differences as the regressands ($y-y_{t-1}$ for the first lagged period, $y_{t-1}-y_{t-2}$ for the second lagged period, etc.). The analyses were replicated using this approach. The results produced no important differences from those reported in the text.

18. Replication using the fixed-effects option showed no material differences from the results presented in the text. In the replication using equally weighted inventories, the beta for the second lag is only +.03 and is not statistically significant.

19. When the values of the dependent variable in successive time periods are

correlated, a condition known as *autocorrelation* may be present. Autocorrelation can affect the *p* values, deceiving us into thinking that a beta is statistically significant when it really isn't. Autocorrelation does not necessarily exist just because the values of the dependent variable are serially correlated. It exists when the error terms—the difference between the actual values of the dependent variable and the values predicted by the regression equation—are serially correlated. A standard method of identifying whether autocorrelation exists is the Durbin-Watson statistic, which can easily be computed when using OLS (ordinary least squares) regression models. The Durbin-Watson statistic cannot be calculated with the negative binomial model, the one we are using for the count data that constitute our dependent variable. The good news is that autocorrelation doesn't affect the beta coefficients themselves, so our estimates of the magnitude of the effect that an independent variable has remains interpretable. Also, autocorrelation biases the *p* values in just one direction. We don't need to worry that a statistically insignificant result has been falsely understated. I need only be cautious about placing too much weight on a marginally significant beta—and in fact, none of the substantive interpretations of these regression analyses is driven by close estimates of the statistical significance of the betas.

20. If a city had a population meeting one of the criteria, it was included throughout the database (e.g., a city that qualified by its 1900 population but not by its 1700 population was included for all half-centuries since its founding).

21. Classification was based on the position of the university relative to all of Europe, hence the leading universities in a given country may not be included. Universities that were on the cusp included the Universities of Bordeaux, Freiberg, Grenoble, Glasgow, Columbia, Princeton, and Chicago. Including them does not materially change the results presented in the text. With regard to American universities, it must be remembered that they are competing not just with other American universities, but with European ones, and not during the most recent decades when American universities have been dominant, but before 1950.

22. My chief source for the coding is S. E. Finer's magisterial three-volume study, Finer 1997. The categorizations of countries as democracies generally follows Vanhanen 1984, although I give democratic status to a few countries earlier than Vanhanen does (most conspicuously, I code Britain as a liberal democracy after the Reform Act of 1832).

23. Finer 1997: vol. 3, 1276.

24. Adams 1787.

25. In the very few instances when there was a tie, the code for the more authoritarian system was entered.

26. The replication using the fixed-effects option and the equally weighted transformation of the number of significant figures yielded comparable results.

27. Hausman 1984: 916.

28. The relevant statistical test for appropriateness of the random-effects model is the Hausman test (Hausman 1978). But whatever tests the random effects model passes, it requires the strong assumption that the unexplained between-

country differences are not functions of (or importantly correlated with) other variables already in the model. The fixed effects model does not require this assumption. I believe the assumption to be justified, but something like the Hausman test can demonstrate only that the assumption is not demonstrably false, not that it is unequivocally true. On that score, reasonable people can disagree. Showing the results from both models seems prudent.

CHAPTER 17: WHAT'S LEFT TO EXPLAIN?

1. The variables included in the regression that produced the figure are war, civil unrest, per capita GDP, wealth relative to other countries. the number of significant figures in each of the two preceding generations, the number of political and economic centers, the number of elite universities, the freedom of action categories, population of the nation's largest city, and population density. I omitted the dummy variables for time, and used a standard negative binomial procedure (Stata's nbreg procedure) rather than the version that takes the role of the individual country into account. The point of this exercise is not to obtain accurate estimates of the effects of the different independent variables (for which the time dummies and estimates of random or fixed effects are important), but to give you a sense of how much the variables operationalizing peace, prosperity, models, elite cities, and freedom of action explain, taken together. For this purpose, incorporating the time dummies is misleading. The time dummies improve the predictive power of the equation (the number of significant figures increased over time, and the time dummies take that into account), but they don't explain anything about why significant figures increased over time. Similarly, incorporating the country-specific effects doesn't explain anything except (to put it roughly) "Sweden is different from Italy in ways not measured by the other variables." We still don't know how they are different.

2. GDP data are not available for 1400–1500, hence there are no observations prior to 1500 for equations that include GDP data.

3. For readers who may be wondering if this correlation is inflated by the large number of zeroes in the values for the number of significant figures (the dependent variable), the correlation between the actual and predicted values for the subset of cases in which the number of significant figures was greater than zero (.910) was virtually identical to the correlation for the entire set of actual and predicted values (.917).

4. The only variable that might seem to help explain the drop in the accomplishment rate is the negative effect of despotic regimes, but that is illusory— Russia and the Balkans were despotic before the Communists took over, and the effects of Naziism are limited to the 1930–1950 generation.

5. Kroeber 1944, Simonton 1997b, Simonton 1997a.

CHAPTER 18: THE ARISTOTELIAN PRINCIPLE

1. Aristotle 1962: X,1175a, 12–14.
2. Rawls 1971: 426.
3. The seminal texts are Watson 1914 and Skinner 1938.
4. Maslow 1943.
5. Maslow 1943: 383. Italics in the original.
6. For a summary of the work over the course of the 1940s and 1950s that led away from behaviorism, see Murray 1988: 138–141.
7. R. L. White 1959.
8. Csikszentmihalyi 1996 is a recent discussion of flow that bears directly on human accomplishment in the arts and sciences.
9. For a review of work on intrinsic and extrinsic rewards, see Murray 1988: 148–54. For a review of the literature specifically focused on creative people, see Ochse 1990: 133–59.

CHAPTER 19: SOURCES OF ENERGY: PURPOSE AND AUTONOMY

1. For example, see Mozart's letter in Ghiselin 1952: 34–5.
2. Steptoe 1998: 153. The two famous symphonies were the G minor symphony (K550) and the "Jupiter" symphony (K551).
3. Quoted in Lang 1997: 646.
4. Simon 1972.
5. For the role of practice, see Ericcson and Tesch-Romer 1993.
6. For a summary and reference to other sources, see Simonton 1988: chapter 4.
7. Ochse 1990: 131, summarizing his review of the literature. For another review using other kinds of evidence, see Simonton 1994: chapter 5.
8. Quoted in Ochse 1990: 132.
9. This wording comes from the *Random House Dictionary of the American Language*, New York: Random House, 1981 edition.
10. Sukenick 1969: 41.
11. To get a sense of the evidence for this statement, a good single source is Cox 1926, because of the individual case studies she presents for each of the 300 geniuses in her sample. They are also characterized by a continuing reflection on the events of their lives. Howard Gardner sees this as one of the major lessons to emerge from his study of giants (Gardner 1997: 14).
12. Quoted in Bary et al. 1963: 61.
13. Xin et al. 1997: 6.
14. The following interpretation draws from Goldstein 1980: chapter 4.
15. Goldstein 1980: 98.

16. Cohen 1994: 389, which provides a summary of the work of von Grunebaum, Sayili, and Saunders (384–417).

17. Grunebaum 1969: 114.

18. Sayili 1960: 415 ff.

19. Saunders 1963: 716.

20. This point is elaborated in Stark 2003: 154–56.

21. Two primary sources that I have relied upon are Macfarlane 1979 and Dumont 1986. I was led to them by Deepak Lal's summary of the various positions on individualism and a guide to the references in Lal 1998: chapters 5 and 6.

22. Thornton 2000: 193.

23. For a discussion of views of Greek individualism, see Dumont 1986: 27–28. For a discussion of the reasons that the Athenian formulation did not produce continuing scientific progress, see Stark 2003: 151–54.

24. The positive role of Christianity may be on the verge of renewed intellectual respectability. Sociologist Rodney Stark's *For the Glory of God* (2003) appeared while this text was in final preparation for publication. Stark's long chapter on the role of Christianity in the scientific revolution (121–99) makes a number of points that are coordinate with my arguments regarding purpose and autonomy. It also has valuable quantitative data about the religious beliefs of leading scientists. Christianity's role also has a place in two recent and respected analyses of the sources of economic growth, Lal 1998 and Landes 1998.

25. The text paraphrases Dumont 1986: 29–31, who in turn is drawing on the work of Ernst Troeltsch, For another discussion of this common theme, see Tarnas 1991: 116-17.

26. Braudel 1993: 347–48.

27. Neither did the Balkans develop individualism, though the relative roles of the Muslim and Orthodox faiths are difficult to disentangle.

28. Weber 1958.

29. Weber's thesis is by no means dead, but it has taken a beating. For a recent assessment of Weber's standing among economists, see Landes 1998: 194–99 (who himself is inclined to be supportive). For an appraisal of Weber's characterization of Protestantism, see Novak 1993: 1–11. For an operationalization of Weber's thesis from a psychologist's perspective, see McClelland 1961: 47–57.

30. Merton 1970. For a discussion of scholarly reaction to what is known as the "Merton thesis," see Cohen 1994: 314–21. See also Stark 2003: 158–60.

31. These are the encounters that produced the greatest outpouring of accomplishment in the arts and sciences. Patai 1977 identifies six great historical encounters with Gentile cultures: the Canaanites, from the first patriarchs down to the Babylonian exile; Hellenism, late −4C to +2C; the Arab empire, beginning in 7C; Renaissance Italy from 14C; Christian sectarian movements in East Europe in 18C; and modern Western culture from 18C.

32. Catholics also could and did pray directly to God, but as one of several forms

of a relationship with God that was mediated by ritual, the priest, and by the distinctive roles of Mary and the saints as intercessors. My argument is that direct, unmediated prayer played a larger role in Protestantism than in Catholicism, and had a commensurately greater effect in producing mavericks.

33. Russello 1998: 175.

34. The phrase *Renaissance Catholicism* is short-hand for a moment in history when Aquinas's humanism was a new and vital part of Catholicism. I am not prepared to argue that Protestantism affirmed autonomous efficacy any more than Renaissance Catholicism did. Indeed, one could argue that the doctrine of the Calvinist doctrine of predestination should have had a depressing effect on autonomous efficacy, not an energizing one. Weber's original essay deals with this issue most effectively (Weber 1958: 98–128). Simplifying radically, insofar as predestination was a felt belief (it was not, for many Protestants), its practical effect was to inspire achievement as a visible proof, to oneself as well as to others, that one was among the elect.

35. Since I am arguing that the Christian religion is a primary force behind modern human accomplishment, readers may reasonably ask whether I am writing out of personal religious conviction. The answer is that I was raised as a mainstream Presbyterian, was drawn to Buddhism during the six years I lived in Asia (and still am), currently attend Quaker meetings, and can best be described as an agnostic.

CHAPTER 20: SOURCES OF CONTENT: THE ORGANIZING STRUCTURE AND TRANSCENDENTAL GOODS

1. I use chess as the example, but partisans of the Japanese game *go* could argue that *go* takes the prize for richness of structure combined with utter simplicity. *Go* is played with just one kind of piece (pebbles) and on a board consisting simply of a matrix of lines. The rules can be stated in a few paragraphs. And yet the game has such depth that, as I write, the same generation of computers that has completely solved checkers and that can play at the highest levels of grandmaster chess cannot play *go* better than does a middling amateur.

2. In practice, scientists who see themselves as faithful to the scientific method are often hostile to innovation, as witnessed by frequent episodes in the history of science when the pioneers of new theories were subjected to ferocious attacks and professional ostracism that went far beyond technical criticism of their findings. Such attacks continue to this day. But the strength of the scientific method is precisely that, by and large, it has successfully kept open a path whereby the pioneers (or their successors) could eventually be vindicated if their findings were sound.

3. Lang 1997: 623.

4. Martindale 1990 gives the most extensive treatment of the inherent need of artists to generate differences from those who have gone before.

5. In the visual arts, one can, for example, categorize the significant figures according to the school to which they are assigned in art histories—

Mannerism, Baroque, Impressionist, etc.—and then compare the relative space given to these schools. But the results are extremely sensitive to how the schools are defined. If Impressionism, Post-Impressionism, Expressionism, and Surrealism are all treated as separate schools but the Renaissance is treated as a single school, then the Renaissance is likely to look much more important. But the Renaissance can also be broken down by Florentine school, Venetian school, etc. Since there is no objective way (that I know of) to consistently define schools, I abandoned the attempt. Similar problems arise with categorizing music and literature.

6. This list comes from the opening of Gilson 1960: 137–63, which provides an excellent discussion of transcendentals in Catholic philosophy. I am indebted to Michael Novak for drawing this issue to my attention.

7. Trans. W. D. Ross, in Hutchins 1952: vol. 9, 339.

8. These examples are taken from Plato's *The Republic*, Book I, sections 352–53, in Hutchins 1952: vol. 7, 309.

9. Quoted in Lindley 2001: 226.

10. The equation describes the relationship between entropy and probability. S denotes the entropy of a system. k is Boltzmann's constant, which defines the relation between temperature and energy in each molecule of an ideal gas, expressed as joules per Kelvin. W is a probability that refers to the number of microstates for any given state of the system (given any gross distribution of particles, how many different ways could the particles individually be arranged to yield that gross distribution?). The equation thus describes entropy in a way that is inherently probabilistic—a common way for physicists to think today, but an epochal departure when Boltzmann did his work.

11. The full quote comes from Einstein in his book *Die Grundlage des Allgemeinen Relativitätstheorie* (1916): "I adhered scrupulously to the precept of that brilliant theoretical physicist L. Boltzmann, according to whom matters of elegance ought to be left to the tailor and the shoemaker." I have been unable to track down the occasion of Boltzmann's original remark.

12. The evolution of the role of beauty from the post-impressionists such as Cézanne and Van Gogh into the more radical forms of art in 20C is vividly conveyed by letters and essays written by the artists themselves, collected in Chipp 1968.

13. I use "kill innocent people" as shorthand for "kill people, directly or through imprisonment or starvation, including women and children, who are not fighting in an army, but are from classes that are a danger to the revolution." That the Soviet Union engaged in such policies was no secret in the 1920s and 1930s, even though Western intellectuals refused to confront the scale of those policies.

14. Among the many treatments of the ways in which artists and composers consciously saw themselves as overthrowing the Western tradition on a grand scale, two excellent recent ones are Watson 2000: chapter 4, and Barzun 2000: 713–71.

15. Quoted in Barzun 2000: 718.

16. Barzun 2000: 718.

17. Quoted in Maritain 1960: 21.

18. Apollinaire 1968: 228.
19. Quoted in Scruton 1997: 55–56.

CHAPTER 21: IS ACCOMPLISHMENT DECLINING?

1. Restrictions apply to that statement. Analyzing changes in the accomplishment rate by specific country becomes more problematic, especially for small countries with few significant figures to begin with. But the analyses throughout this chapter aggregate the significant figures across countries, and I analyze trends over several decades, not decade-by-decade changes. For these purposes, the correlations between significant figures as I have defined them and larger populations of artists and scientists are reliably interpretable.

2. For a discussion of the relationship between perceived danger and actual crime, see Murray 1988: 86–111.

3. I am referring to the "broken windows" theory of crime prevention originated by James Q. Wilson and George Kelling. See Wilson 1983: chapter 5.

4. London's *The Daily Telegraph* published an account of the 1899 list and listed the entries in its edition of 4 January 2000.

5. Chrisafis, Angelique, "Don Quixote is the World's Best Book Say the World's Top Authors," *The Guardian*, 8 May 2002.

6. Simonton 1984b.

7. Taagepera and Colby 1979. It should not be assumed that this exponential decay in attention is caused by lack of information about earlier events. The sources for 1700–1750 and 1800–1850 that I used in my example are so complete that they could easily support a level of detail comparable to 1900–1950 in an almanac of major news events of the type that Taagepera and Colby used. Dean Simonton notes that the same magnitude of epochcentric bias is seen in histories of China, for which the archival record is highly detailed well back into the pre-Christian era. Simonton 1990: 131.

8. I obtained histories of art, music, literature, and the sciences written in the first half of 20C or the latter decades of 19C and compared their treatment of a given half century with the treatment in the sources used for *Human Accomplishment*, almost all of which came from late 20C. Thus, for example, the half century from 1800–1850 is more than a century removed from the sources used for *Human Accomplishment*, but only half a century removed from sources written in early 20C. Did the source written in early 20C devote comparatively more space to 1800–1850 than the later sources did? Some such effects were observed, but they were much smaller than the effect reported by Taagepera and Colby 1979.

9. I must hedge the estimate of the percentage because, even in an era of low urbanization, the factors that produce concentrations of human capital in cities were at work (see page 355).

10. The figures for 1900–1950 combined the statistics for the countries that in 1950 were Austria, Hungary, and Czechoslovakia.

11. Mitchell 1992: Table I2. Britain is omitted because, strangely for a country that has some statistics stretching back to Elizabethan times, the numbers go back only to 1922. The number of British university students increased 6.1 times as fast as population during 1922–1950.

12. U. S. Bureau of the Census 1975: Tables A6–8, H751–765, H766–787.

13. My actual best estimates, based on the proportion of population that was urban and the proportion of the population that had more than a subsistence income and some rudimentary exposure to education, were 2 percent in 1400, 10 percent in 1800, and 80 percent in 1950. I decided to make the estimates conservative, hence the figures of 10 percent, 25 percent, and 75 percent in the text. Data include the United States and Canada after their foundings. The values for the de facto population in the intervening years are based on a geometric interpolation of values between the 1400, 1800, and 1950 estimates.

14. See Moore and Simon 2000 for a convenient summary of trends over 20C.

15. The subsequent statements about the inventory of events refer to the set of events that were mentioned by more than one source, amounting to 3,499 events.

16. The unweighted counts of people and events are conceptually and arithmetically independent. Whether someone qualified as a significant figure has no relationship to the number of events that a person might have in the events inventory. Whether an event qualified for the analysis above had no relationship to whether the scientist responsible for it is in the inventory of persons (e.g., the invention of the aerosol spray can gets into the inventory of events, while its inventor doesn't qualify as a significant figure). The count of significant figures and the summed index scores are not quite arithmetically independent (there is some degree of built-in correlation), but the strength of the link does not prevent the two measures from taking on very different values, as the results for the music inventory demonstrate (see page 319). Conceptually, the counts of significant figures and summed index scores are quite distinct. So much effort was expended creating the index scores for just that reason: It seemed unlikely that an undifferentiated count of significant figures would have nearly the explanatory power of a measure that captured the different eminence of people; a similar logic applied to events. But in fact the weighted measures, although more satisfactory aesthetically than the count of significant figures (it rubs against the grain to give Isaac Newton and the inventor of the ballpoint pen the same score of "1") tell the same story as the unweighted counts tell in every case except music. The explanation lies in the nature of the Lotka curve. The number of significant figures with high index

scores is tiny relative to the total number of significant figures, the great majority of whom have index scores ranging from 1 to 10, not 1 to 100.

17. Stent 1969. The discussion in the text is based on the account of Stent's views in Horgan 1997: 9–15.

18. Pauling 1931. This was his most famous single paper. The book laying out his full theory was published in 1939.

19. Horgan 1997.

20. Quoted in Horgan 1997: 90.

21. Most of what we think of as Elizabethan drama was written by men who turned 40 after she died in 1603, hence the use of the half-century ending in 1619.

22. Data are taken from the web pages of the Academy of Motion Picture Arts and Sciences and of the Writers Guild of America.

23. A search of violinists' CDs available from Barnes and Noble indicates that the top dozen violinists monopolize more than 80 percent of all the CDs featuring violinists. Fritz Kreisler, who died in 1962, appears as a performer on 250 CDs, more than twice as many as number 2, Isaac Stern, who died in 2001. The violinists with the third and fifth highest number of CDs, Yehudi Menuhin and Jascha Heifetz, died in 1999 and 1987 respectively. The only active performer among the top five is number 4, Itzhak Perlman.

24. The violinist example draws from Rosen 1981, who introduced some of the economic theory of winner-take-all markets.

25. Frank and Cook 1995: 32–44. The 11 conditions giving rise to winner-take-all markets are as follow: *Production cloning*, discussed in the text, refers to the ability of all consumers to get what they want, giving them the opportunity to converge on the best. *Network economies* refers to the advantage of being the prevalent choice (the reasons VHS won out over the Beta system in video recording despite its technical inferiority). *Lock-in through learning* parallels network economies except it comes from the supply side—the more that has been invested in a technology, the more research and development it gets in the next round. *Other self-reinforcing processes* includes qualities such as prestige—Harvard gets the best applicants partly because it has a reputation as the place with the best students. *Decision leverage* refers to situations in which small differences in the quality of a decision-maker become important because a single right or wrong decision can have huge consequences. *Natural limits on the size of the agenda* is discussed in the text under the heading of Frank and Cook's evocative phrase "mental shelf space." *Habit formation* is self-explanatory. *Purely positional concerns, gifts and special occasions,* and *avoidance of regret* are all different reasons why we search out the product or person that is considered number one, aside from their intrinsic merits. *Concentrated purchasing*

power refers to the effects of great wealth in bidding up the value of things desired by the very wealthy, whether individuals or corporations.

26. For the theory behind the cases when winner-take-all markets arise when the quality of products is equal, see Adler 1985.

27. Quoted in Herman 1997: 63.

28. Criticism of Western culture became even stronger in the 1960s and thereafter than it had been before, but the criticism came from a new direction. The earlier conservative declinists such as Spengler and Toynbee had valued Western civilization and saw its decay. In the 1960s and thereafter, a new generation of leftist scholars despised Western civilization, seeing it as a source of destruction throughout the world, whether of humane values (destroyed by multinational corporations and globalization) or the environment (destroyed by multinational corporations and the mindless consumerism of the West). Postmodernist critiques of the arts are another expression of the left's disdain for Western civilization. For thinkers on the right, cultural trends in the West were already worrisome before the new criticism came along. The ascendancy of the postmodernists compounded their gloom. The traditional repository for the best of Western civilization, the university, had been overrun by sophists and intellectual children heedless of the heritage they were destroying. Thus historian Gertrude Himmelfarb chose the title *On Looking into the Abyss* for her critique of postmodernism (Himmelfarb 1994).

29. I highly recommend both Brander 1998 and Herman 1997.

30. Toynbee has an especially persuasive account of this process in a long chapter entitled "Schism in the Soul." Toynbee and Somervell 1946: 429–532. For an essay describing what I see as one aspect of Toynbee's prescience, see Murray 2001.

31. Somehow the book containing this story has disappeared from my collection of science fiction. I may be misremembering some of the details—I recently heard someone else refer to the story, claiming that Pergolesi, who died at 26, was the protagonist. My memory says Mozart, and I'm sticking with him.

CHAPTER 22: SUMMATION

1. John Derbyshire (Derbyshire 2003), personal communication, 2002.

2. Gibbon 1952: 84.

BIBLIOGRAPHY

The sources used to create the inventories are listed in Appendix 3. The following includes only sources cited in the text.

Abbott, E. A. 1991. *Flatland: A Romance of Many Dimensions*. Princeton, NJ: Princeton University Press. Original edition, 1884.

Abraham, G. 1979. *The Concise Oxford History of Music*. Oxford: Oxford University Press.

Adams, J. 1787. *A Defence of the Constitutions of Government of the United States of America*. London: C. Dilly.

Adler, M. 1985. "Stardom and talent." *American Economics Review* 75: 208-212.

Allison, P. D., J. S. Long, and T. K. Krauze. 1982. "Cumulative advantage and inequality in science." *American Sociological Review* 47: 615-625.

American Jewish Historical Society. 1999. *American Jewish Desk Reference*: The Philip Leff Group, Inc.

Apollinaire, G. 1968. "The beginnings of Cubism." Pp. 216–28 in *Theories of Modern Art; A Source Book by Artists and Critics*, edited by H. B. Chipp. Berkeley: University of California Press.

Aristotle. 1962. *Nicomachean Ethics*. Translated by M. Ostwald. Indianapolis, IN: Library of Liberal Arts.

Balsdon, J. P. V. D. 1969. *Life and Leisure in Ancient Rome*. New York: McGraw Hill.

Barkhausen, M. 1974. "Government control and free enterprise in Western Germany and the Low Countries in the eighteenth century." Pp. 212–68 in *Essays in European Economic History 1500–1800*, edited by P. Earle. Oxford: Clarendon Press.

Barkow, J. H., L. Cosmides, and J. Tooby eds. 1992. *The Adapted Mind: Evolutionary Psychology and the Generation of Culture*. Oxford: Oxford University Press.

Barraclough, G. ed. 1993. *The Times Atlas of World History*. Maplewood, NJ: Hammond Inc.

Bary, W. T. de, W.-T. Chan, and B. Watson eds. 1963. *Sources of Chinese Tradition*. New York: Columbia University Press.

Barzun, J. 2000. *From Dawn to Decadence: 1500 to the Present*. New York: Harper-Collins.

Bate, W. J. 1975. *Samuel Johnson*. New York: Harcourt Brace Jovanovich.

Bauer, H. H. 1992. *Scientific Literacy and the Myth of the Scientific Method*. Urbana: University of Illinois Press.

Beardsley, M. C. 1966. *Aesthetics from Classical Greece to the Present: A Short History.* Tuscaloosa: University of Alabama Press.

Benzon, W. L. 2001. *Beethoven's Anvil: Music in Mind and Culture.* New York: Basic Books.

Bernstein, P. 1996. *Against the Gods: The Remarkable Story of Risk.* New York: John Wiley & Sons.

Bloom, A. 1987. *The Closing of the American Mind.* New York.

Bloom, H. 1998. *Shakespeare: The Invention of the Human.* New York: Riverhead Books.

Boorstin, D. J. 1983. *The Discoverers: A History of Man's Search to Know His World and Himself.* New York: Random House.

Boorstin, D. J. 1992. *The Creators: A History of Heroes of the Imagination.* New York: Random House.

Boorstin, D. J. 1998. *The Seekers: The Story of Man's Continuing Quest to Understand His World.* New York: Random House.

Brander, B. G. 1998. *Staring into Chaos: Explorations in the Decline of Western Civilization.* Dallas: Spence Publishing.

Braudel, F. 1979. *The Structures of Everyday Life: The Limits of the Possible.* Translated by S. Reynolds. New York: Harper & Row.

Braudel, F. 1993. *A History of Civilizations.* Translated by R. Mayne. New York: Penguin.

Brewer, J. 1997. *The Pleasures of the Imagination: English Culture in the Eighteenth Century.* London: HarperCollins.

Brillat-Savarin, J. A. 1826. *Physiologie du Goût, ou Meditations de Gastronomie Transcendante.* Paris: Sautelet et Cie.

Brookstein, A. 1977. "Patterns of scientific productivity and social change." *Journal of the American Society for Information Science*: 206–210.

Brownstone, D. M. and I. M. Franck. 1994. *Timelines of War.* Boston: Little, Brown.

Burke, J. 1975. *Connections.* Boston: Little Brown.

Burke, J. 1985. *The Day the Universe Changed.* Boston: Little, Brown.

Bush, S. and H.-y. Shih eds. 1985. *Early Chinese Texts on Painting.* Cambridge, MA: Harvard University Press.

Cameron, A. C. and P. K. Trivedi. 1998. *Regression Analysis of Count Data.* Cambridge, U.K.: Cambridge University Press.

Campbell, J. 1949. *Hero with a Thousand Faces.* New York: Pantheon.

Campbell, J. 1974. *The Mythic Image.* Princeton, NJ: Princeton University Press.

Candolle, A. d. 1885. *Histoire des Sciences and des Savants Depuis Deux Siècles.* Geneva: Georg.

Casson, L. 1975. *Daily Life in Ancient Rome.* New York: McGraw-Hill.

Cattell, J. M. 1903. "A statistical study of eminent men." *Popular Science Monthly*, February, pp. 359–377.

Chipp, H. B. ed. 1968. *Theories of Modern Art: A Source Book by Artists and Critics.* Berkeley: University of California Press.

Cipolla, C. M. 1980. *Before the Industrial Revolution: European Society and Economy 1000–1700.* New York: W. W. Norton.

Clough, S. B. 1968. *European Economic History: The Economic Development of Western Civilization.* New York: McGraw-Hill.

Clunas, C. 1997. *Art in China.* Oxford: Oxford University Press.

Cohen, H. F. ed. 1994. *The Scientific Revolution: A Historiographical Inquiry.* Chicago: University of Chicago Press.

Cowell, F. R. 1961. *Everyday Life in Ancient Rome.* London: B.T. Batsford.

Cox, C. M. 1926. *The Early Mental Traits of Three Hundred Geniuses.* Stanford, CA: Stanford University Press.

Coxill, D. 1998. "The riddle of the Sphinx." *InScription: Journal of Ancient Egypt*: 13–19.

Croce, B. 1902. *Estetica come scienze dell' espressione e linguistica generale.*

Cronbach, L. J. 1951. "Coefficient *alpha* and the internal structure of tests." *Psychometrika* 16: 297.

Csikszentmihalyi, M. 1975. *Beyond Boredom and Anxiety: The Experience of Play in Work and Games.* San Francisco: Jossey-Bass.

Csikszentmihalyi, M. 1996. *Creativity: Flow and the Psychology of Discovery and Invention.* New York: HarperPerennial.

Csikszentmihalyi, M. 1997. *Finding Flow: The Psychology of Engagement with Everyday Life.* New York: Basic.

Davis, W. S. 1962. *A Day in Old Rome: A Picture of Roman Life.* New York: Biblo and Tannen.

De Santillana, G. and H.v. Dechend. 1969. *Hamlet's Mill: An Essay on Myth and the Frame of Time.* Boston: Gambit.

Dennis, W. 1954. "Productivity among American psychologists." *American Psychologist* 9: 191–194.

Dennis, W. 1966. "Creative productivity between the ages of 20 and 80 years." *Journal of Gerontology* 21: 1–8.

Derbyshire, J. 2003. *Prime Obsession: Bernhard Riemann and the Greatest Unsolved Problem in Mathematics.* Washington, D.C.: John Henry Press.

DeVries, J. 1984. *European Urbanization 1500–1800.* London: Methuen.

DeVries, K. 1992. *Medieval Military Technology*: Broadview Press.

Dewey, J. 1934. *Art as Experience.* New York.

Diamond, J. 1997. *Guns, Germs, and Steel: The Fates of Human Societies.* New York: W. W. Norton.

Dobecki, T. L. and R. M. Schoch. 1992. "Seismic investigations in the vicinity of the Great Sphinx of Egypt." *Geoarchaeology* 10: 527–44.

Dumont, L. 1986. *Essays on Individualism: Modern Ideology in Anthropological Perspective.* Chicago: University of Chicago Press.

Durant, W. 1935. *Our Oriental Heritage.* New York: Simon & Schuster.

Eco, U. 1999. "How the bean saved civilization." *New York Times Magazine,* April 18, pp. 136–148.

Edgerton, S. Y. 1975. *The Renaissance Rediscovery of Linear Perspective.* New York: Basic Books.

Edwards, I. E. S. 1949. *The Pyramids of Egypt.* London: Penguin.

Eisenstadt, J. M. 1978. "Parental loss and genius." *American Psychologist* 33: 211–223.

Ellis, H. 1904. *A Study of British Genius.* London: Hurst.

Ellis, J. M. 1997. *Literature Lost: Social Agendas and the Corruption of the Humanities.* New Haven: Yale University Press.

Elon, A. 2002. *The Pity of It All: A History of the Jews in Germany, 1743–1933.* New York: Henry Holt & Co.

Ericcson, A. R. T. and C. Tesch-Romer. 1993. "The role of deliberate practice in the acquisition of expert performance." *Psychological Review* 100: 363–406.

Eysenck, H. 1995. *Genius: The Natural History of Creativity.* Cambridge: Cambridge University Press.

Farnsworth, P. R. 1969. *The Social Psychology of Music.* Ames, IA: Iowa State University Press.

Finer, S. E. 1997. *The History of Government.* Oxford: Oxford University Press.

Forrest, D. W. 1974. *Francis Galton: The Life and Work of a Victorian Genius.* New York: Taplinger.

Frank, R. H. and P. J. Cook. 1995. *The Winner-Take-All Society: Why the Few at the Top Get So Much More Than the Rest of Us.* New York: The Free Press.

Furnham, A. and C. Bonnett. 1992. "British research productivity in psychology 1980-1989. Does the Lotka-Price law apply to university departments as it does to individuals?" *Journal of Personality and Individual Differences* 13: 1333–1341.

Galton, F. 1869. *Hereditary Genius: An Inquiry into Its Laws and Consequences.* London: Macmillan.

Gardner, H. 1997. *Extraordinary Minds.* New York: Basic Books.

Gauri, K., J. J. Sanai, and Bandyopadhyay. 1995. "Geologic weathering and its implications on the age of the Sphinx." *Geoarchaeology* 10: 119–33.

Gay, P. 1966. *The Enlightenment: An Interpretation.* New York: Random House.

Geary, D. C. 1998. *Male, Female: The Evolution of Human Sex Differences.* Washington: American Psychological Association.

Gernet, J. 1962. *Daily Life in China on the Eve of the Mongol Invasion 1250–1276,* Translated by H. M. Wright. New York: Macmillan.

Ghiselin, B. ed. 1952. *The Creative Process: Reflections on Invention in the Arts and Sciences*. Berkeley: University of California Press.

Gibbon, E. 1952. *The Decline and Fall of the Roman Empire: A One-Volume Abridgement by Dero A. Saunders*. London: Penguin.

Gillespie, C. C. ed. 1980–1990. *Dictionary of Scientific Biography*. New York: Charles Scribner's Sons.

Gilson, E. 1960. *Elements of Christian Philosophy*. Garden City, NY: Doubleday & Co.

Goetzel, V. and M. G. Goetzel. 1962. *Cradles of Eminence*. Boston: Little, Brown.

Goldstein, T. 1980. *Dawn of Modern Science*. Boston: Houghton Mifflin.

Gombrich, E. H. 1995. *The Story of Art*. London: Phaidon.

Goring, R. 1994. *Larousse Dictionary of Writers*. Edinburgh: Larousse.

Gowing, L. ed. 1995. *Biographical Dictionary of Artists*. London: Andromeda Oxford Ltd.

Greenberg, M. H. 1979. *The Jewish Lists*. New York: Schocken Books.

Grout, D. J. and C. V. Palisca. 1996. *A History of Western Music*. New York: W. W. Norton & Co.

Grunebaum, G. E. v. 1969. *Islam: Essays in the Nature and Growth of a Cultural Tradition*. Cambridge, U.K.: Cambridge University Press.

Haitun, S. D. 1983. "The 'rank distortion' effect and non-Gaussian nature of scientific activities." *Scientometrics* 5: 375–395.

Hall, P. 1998. *Cities in Civilization*. New York: Pantheon.

Hamilton, E. J. 1934. *American Treasure and the Price Revolution in Spain*. Cambridge, MA: Harvard University Press.

Hancock, G. 1995. *Fingerprints of the Gods: A Quest for the Beginning and the End*. London: William Heinemann.

Harrell, J. A. 1994a. "More Sphinx debate: He said, I say . . ." *KMT* 5: 3–4.

Harrell, J. A. 1994b. "The Sphinx controversy: Another look at the geological evidence." *KMT* 5: 70–74.

Hartwell, R. 1966. "Markets, technology, and the structure of enterprise in the development of the eleventh century Chinese iron and steel industry." *Journal of Economic History* 26: 29–58.

Hausman, J. 1978. "Specification tests in econometrics." *Econometrica* 46: 1251–72.

Hausman, J., Bronwyn H. Hall, Zvi Griliches. 1984. "Econometric models for count data with an application to the patents-R&D Relationship." *Econometrica* 52: 909–38.

Hemming, J. 1993. *The Conquest of the Incas*. London: Macmillan.

Herman, A. 1997. *The Idea of Decline in Western History*. New York: Free Press.

Himmelfarb, G. 1994. *On Looking into the Abyss: Untimely Thoughts on Culture and Society*. New York: Alfred A. Knopf.

Hodges, P. and J. Keable. 1989. *How the Pyramids Were Built.* Shaftesbury: Element Books.

Honour, H. and J. Fleming. 1982. *The Visual Arts: A History.* Englewood Cliffs, NJ: Prentice-Hall.

Horgan, J. 1997. *The End of Science: Facing the Limits of Knowledge in the Twilight of the Scientific Age.* New York: Broadway Books.

Hough, R. 1994. *Captain James Cook.* New York: W. W. Norton.

Huber, J. C. 1998. "Invention and inventivity is a random, Poisson process: A potential guide to analysis of general creativity." *Creativity Research Journal* 11: 231–241.

Hughes, R. 1997. *American Visions: The Epic History of Art in America.* New York: Alfred A. Knopf.

Hume, D. 1997. "Of the standard of taste." Pp. 76–93 in *Aesthetics: The Classic Readings,* edited by D. E. Cooper. Oxford: Blackwell.

Hung, W. 1997. "The Origins of Chinese Painting." Pp. 15–86 in *Three Thousand Years of Chinese Painting,* edited by Y. Xin, R. M. Barnhart, et al. New Haven, CT: Yale University Press.

Hutchins, R. M. ed. 1952. *Great Books of the Western World.* London: Encyclopedia Britannica, Inc.

Istituto per la Collaborazione Culturale ed. 1959. *Enciclopedia Universale dell'Arte.* New York: McGraw Hill.

Jacobs, J. 1886. "The comparative distribution of Jewish ability." *Journal of the Anthropological Institute of Great Britain and Ireland* 15: 365.

James, P. and N. Thorpe. 1999. *Ancient Mysteries.* New York: Ballantine Books.

James, W. 1987. "Pragmatism: A New Name for Some Old Ways of Thinking." Pp. 479–624 in *William James: Writings 1902–1910.* New York: The Library of America.

Janson, H. W. and A. F. Janson. 1997. *History of Art.* New York: Harry N. Abrams, Inc.

Jaynes, J. 1976. *The Origin of Consciousness in the Breakdown of the Bicameral Mind.* Boston: Houghton Mifflin.

Jensen, A. R. 1980. *Bias in Mental Testing.* New York: Free Press.

Jensen, A. R. 1996. "Genius and giftedness: Crucial differences." in *Intellectual Talent,* edited by C. P. Benbow and D. Lubinski. Baltimore: Johns Hopkins.

Jourdain, R. 1997. *Music, the Brain, and Ecstasy: How Music Captures Our Imagination.* New York: Avon Books.

Kanigel, R. 1991. *The Man Who Knew Infinity: A Life of the Genius Ramanujan.* New York: Scribners.

Kant, I. 1997. "Critique of aesthetic judgment." Pp. 94–122 in *Aesthetics: The Classic Readings,* edited by D. E. Cooper. Oxford: Blackwell.

Kaplan, R. 2000. *The Nothing that Is: A Natural History of Zero*. Oxford: Oxford University Press.

Kaptchuk, T. J. 1983. *The Web that Has No Weaver: Understanding Chinese Medicine*. Chicago: Congdon and Weed.

Kemp, M. 1990. *The Science of Art: Optical Themes in Western Art from Brunelleschi to Seurat*. New Haven: Yale University Press.

Kimball, R. 2000. *Experiments Against Reality: The Fate of Culture in the Postmodern Age*. Chicago: Ivan R. Dee.

Kimura, D. 1999. *Sex and Cognition*. Cambridge, MA: MIT Press.

Klein, R. G. and E. Blake. 2002. *The Dawn of Human Culture*. New York: John Wiley & Sons.

Kroeber, A. L. 1944. *Configurations of Culture Growth*. Berkeley, CA: University of California Press.

Lal, D. 1998. *Unintended Consequences: The Impact of Factor Endowments, Culture, and Politics on Long-Run Economic Performance*. Cambridge, MA: MIT Press.

Landes, D. S. 1998. *The Wealth and Poverty of Nations*. New York: W.W. Norton.

Lang, P. H. 1997. *Music in Western Civilization*. New York: W.W. Norton.

Laozi. 1963. *Tao Te Ching*. Translated by D. C. Lau. Baltimore, MD: Penguin.

Lawton, I. and C. Ogilvie-Herald. 1999. *Giza: The Truth*. London: Virgin.

Legoyt, A. 1868. *De Certaines Immunités Biostatiques de la Race Juive*. Paris.

Lehman, H. C. 1953. *Age and Achievement*. Princeton, NJ: Princeton University Press.

Lehner, M. 1997. *The Complete Pyramids*. London: Thames & Hudson.

Lindley, D. 2001. *Boltzmann's Atom: The Great Debate that Launched a Revolution in Physics*. New York: Free Press.

Lombroso, C. 1910. *The Man of Genius*. London: W. Scott. Orig. ed., 1889.

Long, J. S. 1997. *Regression Models for Categorical and Limited Dependent Variables*. Thousand Oaks, CA: Sage.

Long, J. S. and J. Freese. 2001. *Regression Models for Categorical Dependent Variables Using Stata*. College Station, TX: Stata Press.

Lotka, A. J. 1926. "The frequency distribution of scientific productivity." *Journal of the Washington Academy of Sciences* 16: 317–323.

Lynn, R. In press. "The intelligence of American Jews." *Personality and Individual Differences*.

Lynn, R. and T. Vanhanen. 2002. *IQ and the Wealth of Nations*. Westport, CT: Praeger.

Macfarlane, A. 1979. *The Origins of English Individualism*. Oxford: Basil Blackwell.

Maddala, G. S. 1983. *Limited-Dependent and Qualitative Variables in Econometrics*. Cambridge, U.K.: Cambridge University Press.

Maddison, A. 1998. *The World Economy: A Millennial Perspective.* Paris: OECD Development Centre.

Magill, F. N. ed. 1991. *Great Events from History II: Science and Technology Series.* Pasadena, CA: Salem Press.

Mair, V. H. ed. 1994. *The Columbia Anthology of Traditional Chinese Literature.* New York: Columbia University Press.

Maquet, J. 1986. *The Aesthetic Experience: An Anthropologist Looks at the Visual Arts.* New Haven: Yale University Press.

Maritain, J. 1960. *The Responsibility of the Artist.* New York: Charles Scribner's Sons.

Martindale, C. 1990. *The Clockwork Muse: The Predictability of Artistic Change.* New York: Basic.

Martindale, C. 1995. "Fame more fickle than fortune: On the distribution of literary eminence." *Poetics* 23: 219–234.

Maslow, A. H. 1943. "A theory of human motivation." *Psychological Review* 50: 371–96.

Mattei, J.-F. ed. 1998. *Les Oeuvres Philosophiques Dictionnaire.* Paris: Presses Universitaires de France.

Mayr, E. 1982. *The Growth of Biological Thought: Diversity, Evolution, and Inheritance.* Cambridge, MA: Harvard University Press.

McClelland, D. C. 1961. *The Achieving Society.* New York: D. Van Nostrand.

McEvedy, C. 1992. *The New Penguin Atlas of Medieval History.* New York: Penguin.

McEvedy, C. and R. Jones. 1978. *Atlas of World Population History.* New York: Facts on File.

Mee, C. L. 1975. *Daily Life in Renaissance Italy.* New York: American Heritage Publishing.

Merton, R. K. 1968. "The Matthew effect in science." *Science* 159: 56–63.

Merton, R. K. 1970. *Science, Technology and Society in Seventeenth-Century England.* New York: Harper & Row.

Mitchell, B. R. 1992. *International Historical Statistics: Europe 1750–1988.* New York: Stockton Press.

Moles, A. 1958. *Information Theory and Esthetic Perception.* Translated by J. E. Cohen. Urbana, IL: University of Illinois Press.

Moore, S. and J. L. Simon. 2000. *It's Getting Better All the Time: 100 Greatest Trends of the Last 100 Years.* Washington, D.C.: Cato.

Munro, T. 1965. *Oriental Aesthetics.* Cleveland, OH: Press of Western Reserve University.

Munson, L. 2000. *Exhibitionism: Art in an Era of Intolerance.* Chicago: Ivan R. Dee.

Murphy, L. J. 1973. "Lotka's law in the humanities?" *Journal of the American Society for Information Science*: 461–462.

Murray, C. 1988. *In Pursuit: Of Happiness and Good Government*. New York: Simon & Schuster.

Murray, C. 2001. "Prole models: America's elites take their cues from the underclass." in *Wall Street Journal*. New York.

Needham, J. 1954. *Science and Civilisation in China*. Cambridge, U.K.: Cambridge University Press.

Needham, J. 1981. *Science in Traditional China*. Hong Kong: The Chinese University of Hong Kong.

Nicholls, J. G. 1972. "Creativity in the person who will never produce anything new and useful: The concept of creativity as a normally distributed trait." *American Psychologist* 27: 717-727.

Nisbett, R. E. 2003. *The Geography of Thought: How Asians and Westerners Think Differently . . . and Why*. New York: Free Press.

Novak, M. 1993. *The Catholic Ethic and the Spirit of Capitalism*. New York: Free Press.

Ochse, R. 1990. *Before the Gates of Excellence: The Determinants of Creative Genius*. Cambridge, U.K.: Cambridge University Press.

Ogden, C. K. and I. A. Richards. 1923. *The Meaning of Meaning: A Study of the Influence of Language upon Thought and of the Science of Symbolism*. New York: Harcourt, Brace.

Olby, R. C., G. N. Cantor, J. R. R. Christie, and M. J. S. Hodge, eds. 1990. *Companion to the History of Modern Science*. London: Routledge.

Pacey, A. 1998. *Technology in World Civilization*. Cambridge, MA: MIT Press.

Pandey, K. C. 1950. *Comparative Aesthetics.*, vol. 1, Indian Aesthetics. Banaras, India: Chowkhamba.

Pao, M. L. 1986. "An empirical examination of Lotka's Law." *Journal of the American Society for Information Science*: 26–33.

Patai, R. 1977. *The Jewish Mind*. New York: Charles Scribner's Sons.

Pauling, L. 1931. "The nature of the chemical bond: applications of results obtained from the quantum mechanics and from a theory of paramagnetic susceptibility to the structure of molecules." *Journal of the American Chemical Society*.

Petrie, W. M. F. 1990. *The Pyramids and Temples of Gizeh (Revised ed.)*. London.

Pinker, S. 2002. *The Blank Slate: The Modern Denial of Human Nature*. New York: Viking Penguin.

Pipes, R. 1999. *Property and Freedom*. New York: Alfred A. Knopf.

Popper, K. 1963. *Conjectures and Refutations*. London: Routledge and Keagan Paul.

Porter, R. and M. Ogilvie eds. 2000. *The Biographical Dictionary of Scientists*. New York: Oxford University Press.

Potter, W. G. 1981. "Lotka's law revisited." *Library Trends*: 21–39.

Price, D. 1963. *Little Science, Big Science*. New York: Columbia University Press.

Price, D. S. 1976. "A general theory of bibliometric and other cumulative advantage processes." *Journal of the American Society for Information Science* 27: 192–306.

Protzen, J.-P. 1986. "Inca stonemasonry." *Scientific American*, February, pp. 94–103.

Quetelet, A. 1834. *Sur l'Homme et le Developpement de ses Facultés*. Paris.

Quigley, C. 1961. *The Evolution of Civilizations: An Introduction to Historical Analysis*. New York: Macmillan Company.

Randel, D. M. ed. 1996. *The Harvard Biographical Dictionary of Music*. Cambridge, MA: Belknap Press of Harvard University Press.

Rawls, J. 1971. *A Theory of Justice*. Cambridge, MA: Harvard University Press.

Rebatet, L. 1969. *Une Histoire de la Musique*. Paris: Robert Laffont & Raymond Bourgine.

Reischauer, E.O. and J. K. Fairbank. 1958. *East Asia: The Great Tradition*. Boston: Houghton Mifflin.

Romano, R. 1974. "Italy in the crisis of the seventeenth century." in *Essays in European Economic History 1500–1800*, edited by P. Earle. Oxford: Clarendon Press.

Ronan, C. A. 1981. *The Shorter Science and Civilisation in China: An Abridgement of Joseph Needham's Original Text*, vol. 2. Cambridge, U.K.: Cambridge University Press.

Rosen, S. 1981. "The economics of superstars." *AER* 71: 845–858.

Rudgley, R. 1999. *The Lost Civilizations of the Stone Age*. New York: The Free Press.

Rushton, J. and C. Ankeny. 1997. "Race and sex differences in brain size and cognitive ability." *Advances in cognition and educational practice* 4: 24–77.

Russell, B. 1945. *A History of Western Philosophy*. New York: Simon & Schuster.

Russell, P. 1995. *The Gay 100: A Ranking of the Most Influential Gay Men and Lesbians, Past and Present*. Secaucus, NJ: Citadel Press.

Russello, G. J. ed. 1998. *Christianity and European Culture: Selections from the Work of Christopher Dawson*. Washington, D.C.: Catholic University of America Press.

Rybczynski, W. 1999. "One good turn: How machine-made screws brought the world together." *New York Times Magazine*, April 18, 133ff.

Sadie, S. ed. 1980. *The New Grove Dictionary of Music and Musicians*. London: Macmillan.

Sarton, G. 1927–48. *Introduction to the History of Science*. Washington, D.C.: Carnegie Institution of Washington.

Saunders, J. J. 1963. "The problem of Islamic decadence." *Journal of World History* 7: 701–20.

Sayili, A. 1960. "The causes of the decline of scientific work in Islam" in *The Observatory in Islam and Its Place in the General History of the Observatory*. Ankara, Turkey.

Schoch, R. M. 1992. "Redating the Great Sphinx of Giza." *KMT* 3: 53–59, 66–70.

Schoch, R. M. 2000. "Further evidence supporting a pre-2500 B.C. date for the Great Sphinx of Giza, Egypt." *Geological Society of America* 32: A276.

Schoch, R. M. and R. A. McNally. 1999. *Voices of the Rocks: A Scientist Looks at Catastrophes and Ancient Civilizations.* New York: Harmony Books.

Schonberg, H. C. 1997. *Lives of the Great Composers.* New York: W. W. Norton & Co.

Schuster, J. A. 1990. "The Scientific Revolution." *Companion to the History of Modern Science,* edited by R. C. Olby, G. N. Cantor, J. R. R. Christie, and M. J. S. Hodge. London: Routledge.

Scruton, R. 1997. "The eclipse of listening." *The Future of the European Past,* edited by H. Kramer and R. Kimball. Chicago: Ivan R. Dee.

Seldes, G. 1985. *The Great Thoughts.* New York: Ballantine Books.

Settle, T. B. 1983. "Galileo and early experimentation." *Springs of Scientific Creativity: Essays on Founders of Modern Science,* edited by R. Aris, H. T. Davis, and R. H. Steuwer. Minneapolis: University of Minnesota Press.

Shapin, S. 1996. *The Scientific Revolution.* Chicago: University of Chicago Press.

Shedlock, J. S. ed. 1972. *Beethoven's Letters.* New York: Dover Publications.

Sheldon, P. M. 1954. "The families of highly gifted children." *Marriage and Family Living* 16: 59–61.

Shiba, Y. 1970. *Commerce and Society in Sung China.* Translated by M. Elvin. Ann Arbor, MI: Center for Chinese Studies, University of Michigan.

Shockley, W. 1957. "On the statistics of individual variations of productivity in research laboratories." *Proceedings of the Institute of Radio Engineers* 45: 279–290.

Simon, H. A. 1955. "On a class of skew distribution functions." *Biometrika* 42: 425–440.

Simon, H. A. 1972. "Productivity among American psychologists: An explanation." *American Psychologist* 9.

Simonton, D. K. 1981. "Creativity in Western civilization: Intrinsic and extrinsic causes." *American Anthropologist* 83: 628–30.

Simonton, D. K. 1984a. *Genius, Creativity, and Leadership.* Cambridge, MA: Harvard University Press.

Simonton, D. K. 1984b. "Leaders as eponyms: Individual and situational determinants of monarchal eminence." *Journal of Personality* 52: 1–21.

Simonton, D. K. 1988. *Scientific Genius: A Psychology of Science.* Cambridge, U.K.: Cambridge University Press.

Simonton, D. K. 1990. *Psychology, Science, and History: An Introduction to Historiometry.* New Haven: Yale University Press.

Simonton, D. K. 1991. "Latent-variable models of posthumous reputation: A quest for Galton's G." *Journal of Personal and Social Psychology* 60: 607–619.

Simonton, D. K. 1992. "Social context of career success course for 2,026 scientists and inventors." *PSPB* 18: 452–463.

Simonton, D. K. 1994. *Greatness: Who Makes History and Why*. New York: Guilford Press.

Simonton, D. K. 1997a. "Artistic creativity and interpersonal relations." Pp. 29–53 in *Genius and Creativity: Selected Papers*. Greenwich, CT: Ablex Publishing.

Simonton, D. K. 1997b. "Foreign influence and national achievement: The impact of open milieus on Japanese civilization." *JPSP* 72: 86–94.

Simonton, D. K. 1997c. "Galtonian genius, Kroeberian configurations, and emulation: A generational time-series analysis of Chinese civilization." Pp. 55–76 in *Genius and Creativity: Selected Papers*. Greenwich, CT: Ablex Publishing.

Simonton, D. K. 1997d. "Sociocultural context of individual creativity: A transhistorical time-series analysis." Pp. 3–28 in *Genius and Creativity: Selected Papers*. Greenwich, CT: Ablex Publishing.

Simonton, D. K. 1998. "Fickle fashion versus immortal fame: Transhistorical assessments of creative products in the opera house." *JPSP* 75: 198–210.

Simonton, D. K. 1999. *Origins of Genius: Darwinian Perspectives on Creativity*. New York: Oxford University Press.

Sivin, N. 1990. "Science and medicine in Chinese history." Pp. 164–96 in *Heritage of China: Contemporary Perspectives on Chinese Civilization*, edited by P. S. Ropp. Berkeley, CA: University of California Press.

Skinner, B. F. 1938. *The Behavior of Organisms: An Experimental Analysis*. New York: Appleton-Century-Crofts.

Solomon, M. 1998. *Beethoven*. New York: Schirmer.

Sorokin, P. A. 1937. *Social and Cultural Dynamics*. New York: Bedminster Press.

Spengler, O. 1926. *The Decline of the West*, vol. 1. New York: Alfred A. Knopf.

Stark, R. 2003. *For the Glory of God: How Monotheism Led to Reformations, Science, Witch-Hunts, and the End of Slavery*. Princeton, NJ: Princeton University Press.

Stent, G. 1969. *The Coming of the Golden Age: A View of the End of Progress*. Garden City, NY: Natural History Press.

Steptoe, A. 1998. "Mozart: Resilience under stress." Pp. 141–64 in *Genius and the Mind: Studies of Creativity and Temperament*, edited by A. Steptoe. Oxford: Oxford University Press.

Stigler, S. S. 1999. *Statistics on the Table: The History of Statistical Concepts and Methods*. Cambridge, MA: Harvard University Press.

Storfer, M. D. 1990. *Intelligence and Giftedness: The Contributions of Heredity and Early Environment*. San Francisco: Jossey-Bass.

Stove, D. 1998. *Anything Goes: Origins of the Cult of Scientific Irrationalism*. Paddington NSW, Australia: Macleay Press.

Sukenick, R. 1969. "The death of the novel" in *The Death of the Novel and Other Stories*. New York: Dial.

Taagepera, R. and B. N. Colby. 1979. "Growth of Western civilization: Epicyclical or exponential?" *American Anthropologist* 81: 907–12.

Taine, H. A. 1889. *Philosophy of Art*. Translated by J. Durand. New York: H. Holt & Co.

Tarnas, R. 1991. *The Passion of the Western Mind: Understanding the Ideas that Have Shaped Our World View*. New York: Ballantine Books.

Tawney, R. H. 1958. *Business and Politics under James I*. Cambridge, U.K.: Cambridge University Press.

Terman, L. M. and M. H. Oden. 1947. *The Gifted Child Grows Up: Twenty-Five Years' Follow-Up of a Superior Group*, vol. 4. Stanford, CA: Stanford University Press.

Thornton, B. 2000. *Greek Ways: How the Greeks Created Western Civilization*. San Francisco: Encounter Books.

Toynbee, A. J. and D. C. Somervell. 1946. *A Study of History: Abridgment of Volumes I–VI*. Oxford: Oxford University Press.

Trager, J. 1994. *The People's Chronology: A Year-by-Year Record of Human Events from Prehistory to the Present*. New York: Henry Holt & Co.

Trilling, C. 1951. *The Liberal Imagination: Essays on Literature and Society*. London: Secker and Warburg.

U. S. Bureau of the Census. 1975. *Historical Statistics of the United States, Colonial Times to 1970*, vol. 1. Washington, D.C.: U. S. Bureau of the Census.

Van Dillen, J. G. 1974. "Economic fluctuations and trade in the Netherlands, 1650–1750." Pp. 198–211 in *Essays in European Economic History 1500–1800*, edited by P. Earle. Oxford: Clarendon Press.

Vanhanen, T. 1984. *The Emergence of Democracy: A Comparative Study of 119 States, 1850–1979*. Helsinki: The Finnish Society of Sciences and Letters.

Vega, G. de la. 1961. *The Royal Commentaries of the Incas*. New York: Orion Press.

Vital, D. 1999. *A People Apart: The Jews in Europe 1789–1939*. Oxford: Oxford University Press.

Voos, H. 1974. "Lotka and information science." *Journal of the American Society for Information Science*: 270–272.

Wain, J. 1974. *Samuel Johnson A Biography*. New York: Viking.

Watson, J. B. 1914. *Behavior: An Introduction to Comparative Psychology*. New York: H. Holt.

Watson, P. 2000. *A Terrible Beauty: A History of the People and Ideas That Shaped the Modern Mind*. London: Weidenfeld & Nicolson.

Weber, M. 1958. *The Protestant Ethic and the Spirit of Capitalism*. Translated by T. Parsons. New York: Scribner & Sons.

White, J. 1987. *The Birth and Rebirth of Pictorial Space*. Cambridge, MA: Belknap Press.

White, L., Jr. 1962. *Medieval Technology and Social Change*. New York: Oxford University Press.

White, R. L. 1959. "Motivation reconsidered: The concept of competence." *Psychological Review* 66: 297–333.

Will, G. F. 1990. *Men at Work: The Craft of Baseball.* New York: Macmillan.

Wilson, D. S. 2002. *Darwin's Cathedral: Evolution, Religion, and the Nature of Society.* Chicago: University of Chicago Press.

Wilson, E. O. 1980. *Sociobiology: The Abridged Edition.* Cambridge, MA: Harvard University Press.

Wilson, J. Q. 1983. *Thinking About Crime, rev. ed.* New York: Basic Books.

Windschuttle, K. 1996. *The Killing of History.* San Francisco: Encounter Books.

Woods, F. A. 1911. "Historiometry as an exact science." *Science* 33: 568–574.

Xin, Y., N. Chongzheng, J. Cahill, L. Shaojun, and W. Hung eds. 1997. *Three Thousand Years of Chinese Painting.* New Haven: Yale University Press.

Zehou, L. 1981. *The Path of Beauty: A Study of Chinese Aesthetics.* Translated by G. Lizeng. Hong Kong: Oxford University Press.

Zhao, H. and G. Jiang. 1985. "Shifting of world's scientific center and scientist's social ages." *Scientometrics* 8: 59–80.

INDEX

Page numbers in *italics* refer to charts, maps, and illustrations.
Page numbers 589 through 624 refer to notes.

Abbott, Edwin, 209
Abel, Niels, 313
Abraham, 132
absolute monarchy, 371, 372, 373
abstraction, 211, 215–16, 289, 290
Abu Nawas, 138
acceleration, 30
accomplishment:
   artistic vs. scientific, 205
   biology as factor in, 285
   blind spots about, 53–55
   categories of, 76
   Christianity and, 402–5
   delimiting of, 76
   environment in, 285
   foundations of, 451–52
   homosexuality and, 287
   in -800, *15*
   non-European, 258–61, 381
   outer boundaries of, 107, 108–9
   past 1950, 453–54
   popular lists of, 155
   population in, 309–29, *309*
accomplishment rate, 309–29, *312–28,* 427
   in the arts, 430, 453
   for Chinese literature, 323, *323,* 427
   decline in, *see* declining accomplishment
   de facto population and, 432–35, *434*
   meaning of, 429
   measuring of, 310–11
   population and, 427, 429
   in sciences, 430, 453
   significant figures vs., 427–28, *428,* 436–37,
     437, 445–46
   for Tuscany in 1500, 433
   for Western literature, 427, 429–30
accounting, 229
accumulative advantage, 93–94
achievements, inevitability and, 54
achromatic lens, 414
Ádám, Jeno, 108

Adams, Brooks, 446
Adams, Henry, 446
Adams, John, 371
Adler, Mortimer, 105
Advaita Vedanta school, 132, 144, 326
Advancement of Learning (Bacon), 299
Aeneid (Virgil), 26
aeronomy, 125
Aeschylus, 26, 220, 260, 333, 354
aesthesis, 69
aesthetics, 63–68, 69–70, 71, 224
Africa, Africans, 33, 265
   art forms of, 260
   decorative arts and crafts in, 261
   Nobel Prizes and, 282
   science in, 284
Agatharcus of Samos, 213
Agathon, 600
age, 411–12
agnosticism, 408
agriculture, 6, 7, 229, 315
   in China, 14, 73
air, composition of, 124
airplanes, 114, 159, 315, 437
air pressure, 240
Akhenaton, 212–13
al-Akhtal, 321
Alberti, Leon Battista, 215, 216, 412
alchemy, 414
Alexander the Great, 27, 220
Alexandria, 17, 275
al-Farazdaq, 321
algebra, Boolean, 228
al-Hamadhani, 321
al-Hariri, 321
al-Khwarizmi, 231–32
al-Ma'arri, 138, 321
Almagest (Ptolemy), 30, 162
al-Mansur, 231
al-Mutanabbi, 138, 143, 321
alphabets, 211, 599

America, pre-Columbian, 260, 261
American Association for the Advancement of Science, 23
American Council of Learned Societies, 257
American League, 104
American Revolution, 9, 50, 335
amusement, 406
Analects (Confucius), 42, 227
analytic geometry, 313
anatomy, 123, 439
Anaxagoras, 316, 333
Anaximander, 30
Anderson, Maxwell, 115
aneroid barometer, 414
anesthetics, 128
Anfinsen, Christian, 605
Angkor Wat, 264
Anglo-Dutch wars, 333
animals, domestication of, 229
Ankara, 6
anthrax, 128
anthropology, 77
antibiotics, 162
Antigone (Sophocles), 26
Antikythera Mechanism, 16–17
anti-Semitism, 276, 281, 286, 292
antisepsis, 162
Antonine Rome, 25, 26–32, 51, 235
    anatomy and physiology in, 29, 30
    architecture in, 27–28, 30
    arts in, 47
    governance of, 31–32
    history in, 26
    law in, 32
    life expectancy in, 29
    literature and drama in, 26, 31
    medical care in, 28–30, 46
    painting and sculpture in, 26–27, 30–31, 40
    parallels to 21st century life in, 28
    philosophy in, 26, 30, 31
    policing in, 45
    religion in, 31, 41
    roads in, 27
    science in, 30
    technology in, 27–28
    water supply and sewage in, 28
Antoninus Pius, 26, 30
Apelles, 27, 260
Apollinaire, Guillaume, 424
Apuleius, 220
Aquinas, Thomas, 223, 402–3, 404, 416, 457, 618
Arabic language, 138, 321

Arabic numerals, 161
    as meta-invention, 211, 230, 231–32, 244, 414
Arab literature inventory, 78, 84, *138,* 143
    accomplishment rate for, 312, *321*
Arabs, Arab world, 9, 33, 381, 452
    Arabic numerals in, 231–32
    arts inventories for, 250, 251
    as familistic and hierarchical, 401
    literature of, 138, 321
    mathematics in, 161, 230
    philosophy of, 78, 399–400
    scholar-scientists in, 256
    science in, 253, 254, 256, 257, 275, 284, 399–401
    see also Islam
archaeology, 219
Archimedes, 30, 129, 231, 241, 255
architecture, 77, 214, 215, 260–61
    in Antonine Rome, 27–28, 30
    of Michelangelo, 54
Argentina, 85
Aristophanes, 26, 220, 333
Aristotelian principle, 385–89, *389,* 391, 417, 422, 455–58
Aristotelians, Aristotelianism, 224, 240, 456
Aristotle, 7, 26, 54, 70, 71, 123, 133, 143, 144, 217, 224, 230, 236, 237, 240–41, 255, 260, 316, 332, 333, 385–86, 402, 416, 417, 418, 600
    ethics of, 227, 228
    logic established by, 225–26, 231
    mathematics and, 232
    as polymath, 114–15, 130
    as System Builder, 152, 153
Arkwright, Richard, 44
armillary, 38–39
Ars Amatoria (Ovid), 10
Ars Magna (Cardano), 242
art, *see* visual arts
artificial heating, 315
artificial lighting, 315
artists, undiscovered, 109
arts, 455
    accomplishment past 1950 in, 453–55
    accomplishment rate in, 430, 453
    artist as building block of, 207
    Catholic humanism in, 402–3
    craft in, 411
    declining accomplishment in, 440–47, *441*
    delayed recognition in, 82
    difficulty explanations for, 105–6
    enduring works in, 63, 453–54
    excellence in, 62–72

fashion and assessment of, 82, 83
genres in, 206
greatness fatigue in, 445–46
great works vs. great artists in, 206
human capital in, 428, 440–42
market saturation in, 428, 442–44
meta-inventions in, 211, 212–22
organizing structure in, 410
principles in, 411
religion and, 455–57
significant events in, 205–7
significant figures in, 445–46
tools in, 411
transcendental goods in, 420–25
see also specific arts
arts inventories, 84, 121, 144–47, 251, 497–99
accomplishment rate in, 311
Eurocentrism in, 248–51, 249
1950 cutoff for, 82
for non-European world, 250
for persons, 78
women in, 266, 271, 274, 289–90
see also specific inventories
Art Through the Ages (Gardner), 74–75
Ashkenazi Jews, 265, 291–93
Asia, Asians, 265
architecture of, 260
decorative arts and crafts of, 261
Nobel Prizes and, 282
Asia Minor, 230
Assayer, The (Galileo), 240
Assyria, 16, 213
asteroids, 438, 449
astrology, 31, 156
astronomy, 30, 60, 150, 153, 234, 266, 399, 411,
437, 440, 449
central events in, 160–61, 163–66
database for, 76
organizing structures in, 413–14
principles in, 413
astronomy inventory, 122, 143, 311
Jews in, 279
astrophysics, 440
Asvaghosa, 140
asymptotes, 110
As You Like It (Shakespeare), 8
atheism, 408
Athenian principle, 401–2
Athens, 223, 300
logic invented in, 225–26
Periclean Age in, 332–33
atomism, 30
atoms, 126, 437

Augustine, Saint, xviii, 70, 287
Austen, Jane, 71–72, 83
Australia, 43
Austria, 298, 307, 335
Austro-Hungary, 347
Jewish emancipation in, 276
university students in, 433
authors, significant vs. other, 429
autocorrelation, 614
autocracy, 343, 363, 373
autonomous efficacy, 407
autonomy, 391, 394–95, 403–5, 406, 409, 451,
453
in Christianity, 408
culture and, 395
in East Asia, 397–99
in Europe, 401
Islam and, 401
avant-garde, 422
Avicebron (Solomon ibn Gabirol), 275
axioms, 230
Ayrton, Herthe, 272
Aztecs, xvi, 337

Babbage, Charles, 599
Babel, Isaak, 362
Babst, Valentin, 108
Babylon, 399
number system in, 231
Bach, Johann Sebastian, 48, 66, 68, 83, 85, 120,
134, 146, 386, 421, 444, 454, 457
Bacon, Francis, 287, 299, 316
Bacon, Roger, 237
bacteria, 149
Baden-Württemberg, 298
Balkans, 298, 307, 349, 374
Ottoman Empire's rule of, 363–64, 373
wars in, 335
balloon flights, 114
ballpoint pens, 114
Baltic, 300
Balzac, Honoré de, 318
Banks, Joseph, 43, 49
Barcelona, 357
Baroque:
art in, 299
France in, 357
music in, 299, 417
tonal harmony in, 218
Barrow, Isaac, 313
Barzun, Jacques, 221, 424
baseball, 65, 66, 101, 102, 104
batting average in, 97, 101, 102

Basho, 121, 141, 143
Baths of Caracalla, 28
Baudelaire, Charles, 318
Baumgarten, Alexander, 69
Bavaria, 298
BBC, 156
Beagle, 148, 149
beauty, xx, 62, 69, 224, 416, 417, 418, 422, 452, 456
  in the arts, 420, 424
  in science, 418–19
Beethoven, Ludwig van, xix, 48, 54, 59, 64, 83, 119, 120, 134, 143, 144, 146–47, 153, 155, 207, 319, 392, 454, 597
behavioral sciences, 450
behaviorism, 387
Belgium, 298, 390, 433
Bell, Alexander Graham, 126, 148
bell curve, *87,* 88, 92–93, 101, 105, 464–66, *465,* 595
  in golf skills, 97–98, *98,* 99, 595–96
Bellows, George, 115
Bentham, Jeremy, 316
Benton, Thomas Hart, 115
Berenson, Bernard, 69
Berkeley, George, 61
Berkeley, University of California at, 438
Berlin, 305, 357, 368
Berlioz, Hector, 120
Bernini, Gian Lorenzo, 74, 75, 205, 317
Bernoulli, Jakob, 313
Berzelius, Jöns Jacob, 124, 130, 153
Beta coefficients, 341
bias, 84–86
Big Bang theory, 160–61, 381
biochemistry, 149
biographical dictionaries, 108, 151–52, *152*
  histories vs., 109, 157
biology, 60, 439, 440
  central events in, 160, 161, *167–70*
  classification in, 123
  database for, 76
  environment vs., 285
  as factor in achievement, 285
  organizing structures in, 414
  sex differences and, 289–91
  System Builders in, 152
  women in, 270–71
biology inventory, *123,* 128, 130, 143, 311
bipedality, 3
Birmingham, 44
Biro brothers, 114

Bismarck, Otto von, 276
Bjørnson, Bjørnstjerne, 121
Black Death, 299
black holes, 122
blitzkrieg, 289
blood, circulation of, 29
Bloom, Harold, 71, 145
Boccaccio, Giovanni, 147, 148, 412
Bohemia, 335
Bohr, Niels, 144
Boltzmann, Ludwig, 419
Bolyai, János, 228
books, 452, 454
Boolean algebra, 228
Boorstin, Daniel, 215
Boston marathon, 101, *102*
Boswell, James, 61
botany, 123, 399
Bourbaki, Nicolas, 114
Bow Street Runners, 45
Boyle, Robert, 240, 241, 243, 414
Boyle's Law, 241
Boylston, Zabdiel, 46–47
Brahma-sphuta-siddhanta (Brahmagupta), 230, 231
Brahms, Johannes, xix, 69, 119, 134, 153, 454
brain size, 289, 589
Braudel, Fernand, 403
Breakthroughs: A Chronology of Great Achievements in Science and Mathematics, 158
Brick Layers, 147, 151, 152–53
Britain, 73, 85, 251, 307, 309
  accomplishment in, 296–98, 338
  cities in, 357, *359*
  Georgian, *see* Georgian Britain
  Industrial Revolution in, 357
  Jews in, 276, 280–81
  Roman, *see* Roman Britain
  wars and civil unrest in, 335, 347
  writers from, 251
  see also England
British Open, 100, 101, 104
British Royal Society, 43
brothers, 114–15
Brunelleschi, Filippo, 214–15, 299, 412, 600
Buck, Pearl, 115
Buddha, 132, 133, 223, 224, 262, 326
Buddhism, 41, 223, 402
  ethics of, 227
  Madhvamika, 326
  Mahayana, 132
  purpose and, 396–97
bunraku, 141

buoyancy, 30
Burke, Edmund, 49
Burke, James, 156
Byron, George Gordon, Lord, 142, 287, 318

Cabezón, Antonio de, 338
cabinetry, 77
Cage, John, 69
calculation, 228
calculators, 159
calculus, 206, 228, 313
Calderon de la Barca, Pedro, 338
Caldwell, Taylor, 444
Calestani, Vinzenzo, 108
calibration of uncertainty, 211, 232–33
Caligula, 32
Calvinism, 404, 618
camera obscura, 215
Campbell, Joseph, 21, 590
Canada, 347, 349
canon, 59, 84, 101
Canon (Pachelbel), 207
Cao Zhan, 222
Cape Horn, 42
capitalism, 337
Capitol building, U.S., 28
Caravaggio (Merisi), 299, 317, 454
carbon, 124
Cardano, Girolamo, 232, 242
Caribbean, 33
Carracci, Annibale, 299
Cather, Willa, 115
Catholicism, 363, 364, 402–5, 407, 618
    meditation in, 225
Catlin, George, 250
Cattell, J. McKeen, 73
Cauchy, Augustin, 313
causation, 235–36
Cavalieri, Francesco, 313
CDs, 442–43, 444
celestial motion, 122
Cellini, Benvenuto, 261
Central America, 21
    architecture in, 260
    science in, 254
Central Europe, 260, 291, 363
central events, 159
    in astronomy, 160–61, *163–66*
    in biology, 160, 161, *167–70*
    in chemistry, 160, 161, *171–75*
    in earth sciences, 160, 161, *176–78*
    in mathematics, 160, 161, *188–93*

in medicine, 160, 161–62, *194–97*
in physics, 160, 161, *179–87*
in technology, 160, 162, *198–204*
Cervantes Saavedra, Miguel de, 221, 318, 338
Ceylon, 33
Cézanne, Paul, xix, 89, 206, 398, 432
chance-configuration theory, 94
Charlemagne, 9
Charles VIII, King of France, 333
Chaucer, Geoffrey, 412
chauvinism:
    cultural, 63
    national, 85–86
Chemical Abstracts, 90
chemical analysis, 414
chemical nomenclature, 124
chemical reactions, 439
chemical system, body as, 314
chemistry, 53–54, 60, 107, *124,* 149, 153, 267,
        399, 439, 440
    central events in, 160, 161, *171–75*
    database for, 76
    industrial, 315
    organizing structures in, 414
    quantitative, 124, 160
chemistry inventory, *124,* 143, 311
chess, 101, *102,* 104, 386–87
Chikamatsu Monzaemon, 141, 143
China, 10, 14, 16, 70, 600
    aesthetics in, 70, 90
    agriculture in, 14, 37
    anonymity in sculpture of, 78
    art in, 398, 425, 602
    arts inventories for, 250, 251, 262
    Communist, 362
    cultural activity shut down in, 131, 135, 139,
        140, 141
    Daoism in, 210
    ethics in, 226–28, 244
    experimentalism in, 235–37
    family in, 397, 401
    government in, 14
    Han dynasty of, 39
    Imperial, 34
    inventories for, 84
    literature in, 221–22, 328, 398, 602
    mathematics in, 228–30, 233
    Ming Dynasty of, 33, 34, 266, 398
    in -800, 16
    models in, 355, 381
    musical scales discovered in, 217
    music in, 217, 260

China (*continued*)
number system in, 228
paper money in, 229
philosophy in, 223, 224
poets of, 262
purpose in, 396–97
Qing dynasty in, 135
road system in, 37
science in, 253, 254, 255, 256, 262, 284, 398–99, 601
secular observation of nature in, 233, 234–35, 244
in Song Dynasty, *see* Song China
Tang dynasty of, 40, 135, 322, 323, 420
written language in, 211
Chinese art inventory, 78, 84, 120, 121, 131, *135,* 136, 139, 140, 143, 147, 260, 320
Chinese literature inventory, 78, 131, *139,* 140, 143, 147
accomplishment rate for, 323, *323,* 427
Chinese painting inventory, accomplishment rate for, 322, *322*
Chinese philosophy inventory, 78, 79, 121, *131,* 132, 133, 139, 143, 144, 320
accomplishment rate for, 324, *324*
cholera, 128
Chopin, Fryderyk, 79
Christianity, 31, 41, 275, 295, 338, 599, 617–18
in Arab world, 321
autonomy and, 408
divisions within, 364
and Greek philosophy, 400
humanism and, 402–3
individualism in, 210, 402–5
medieval, 401, 403
monotheism in, 226
purpose and, 407–8
in Renaissance, 403
Christie, Agatha, 444
chromosomes, 123
chronologies of events, 151–52, *152,* 157, 159
chronomoters, 414
Church, Frederic, 115, 250
Cicero, 31, 32, 133
cinematography, 114
cities, 380, 433–34
as accelerant, 358
dummy variables for, 368
elite, *see* elite cities
with elite universities, 368, 369, 370, 376
entrepôt, 368
human capital of, 358–60
industrial, 368, 369–70

maintenance of, 162
with non-elite universities, 368, 369
as political or financial centers, 367–68, 369, 370, 376
populations of, 367, 376, 381
significant figures and, *369, 370*
City of God (Augustine), xviii
Civil War, U.S., 8, 305
Clancy, Tom, 444
class, 25, 432, 447
Classical era, of music, 218
cloning, 418
close textual scrutiny, 254
Club, The, 48–49, 50
cognitive fluidity, 589
cognitive tools, 209, 210, 211, 213, 224, 227, 228, 243–44
Cohen, H. Floris, 400
coherent sense, 417
Coliseum, 27–28
Cologne, 305
Columbia University, 265–66
Columbus, Christopher, 33, 337, 363
combustion, 124
comedy, 354
comets, 438
Coming of the Golden Age: A View of the End of Progress, The (Stent), 438–39
commerce, 77
meta-inventions in, 229
commercial centers, 399
Communism, 422–23
comparative anatomy, 123
complexity, 360
composers:
significant vs. other, 429
unnamed, 259
composition, rules of, 64
compositional logic, 421
computers, 159, 599
"Concerning the System of the Earth" (Hutton), 160
concert music, 453
concreteness, 290
Condorcet, Marie, 316
Confederacy, 305
Configurations of Culture Growth (Kroeber), 261, 354
Confirmation of the Rule of St. Francis (Giotto), 214
Confucianism, 41–42, 131, 224, 228, 236, 324, 397, 398, 456
Confucius, 26, 42, 70, 71, 223, 260, 262, 324

ethics of, 227, 228
  as first in inventory, 120, 131, 132, 133, 139, 143, 144
Congreve, William, 48, 412
Connections, 156
Conrad, Joseph, 427
consciousness, 224
consensus, 68, 452
conservation of matter, law of, 124, 160
Constable, John, 85
construction, 162
Contagione et Contagiosis Morbis, De (Fracastoro), 314
content, choice of, 393–94
controlled data, 238–40
control variables, 344
Cook, James, 42–44
Cook, Philip, 443
Cooper, Anthony Ashley, 48
Copenhagen, 357
Copernican Revolution, 151, 155
Copernicus, 61, 62, 122, 150, 151, 161, 255, 413–14, 597
Copland, Aaron, 262
correlation coefficient, 75, 469–71
correlations, 75, 467–71
Cortez, Hernando, 337
cosmology, 381
Couperin, François, 48, 319
craft, 410, 411, 425
creative personalities, 360
creativity:
  predictors of, 354–55
  vocation and, 407
credit, 229
  assignment of, 242–43
Crete, 338
crime, 430
Critique of Judgment, The (Kant), 69
Croce, Benedetto, 70
Cromwell, Oliver, 9
Csikszentmihalyi, Mikhail, xvii, 388–89
Cubism, 216, 424
cultivated crops, 229
cultural attributes, meta-inventions vs., 210
cultural diversity, 360
culture, 433
  autonomy and, 395
cumulative advantage, 353
Curie, Marie, 159, 267, 290
Curie, Pierre, 159
Cush, 16
cutoff point, 111–13

Cuvier, George, 123
Cuzco, 20
Cybele, 31
cyclic quadrilaterals, 230
Czech Republic, 300

Daily Telegraph (London), 431
Dammonis, Innocentius, 108
dance, 77
  pre -800, 14
Dandin, 140, 325
Dante Alighieri, xvi, 142, 412
Dao-de Jing (Laozi), 223, 396
Daoism, 41, 210, 223, 236, 324
  purpose and, 396–97
Darby, Abraham, 44
Dark Ages, 9, 14, 32, 33, 262
Darwin, 123, 143, 148–49, 157, 255, 407, 457
Darwinian Revolution, 155
Davy, Edmund, 116
Davy, Humphrey, 116, 124
Dawson, Christopher, 405
dead white males, 25, 265
debate, 452
Debussy, Claude, 120, 458
De Caelo (Aristotle), 232
Decameron (Boccaccio), 147
Dechend, Hertha von, 21–22
decimal fractions, 414
Decline and Fall of the Roman Empire, The (Gibbon), 26
declining accomplishment, 14–16, 82, 329, 428–47
  in the arts, 440–47, *441*
  epochcentrism in, 431–32
  growing de facto population and, 432–35, *434*
  in science and technology, 435–40
declinists, 446–47
decorative arts and crafts, 77, 261
deductive reasoning, 226, 231
de facto population, 432–35, *434, 447*
deference, 397–99
Defoe, Daniel, 412
De Fu, 39–40
Delacroix, Eugene, 75
delayed recognition, 82
Della Pittura (Alberti), 215, 412
De Magnete (Gilbert), 239
democracy, 343, 361, 363
  liberal, 228, 361, 371, 372, 373, 375
Democritus, 30, 316, 333
demographics, 331

Demos, Raphael, 457–58
De Motu (Galileo), 237, 239, 299
Denmark, 85, 297
  polyphony in, 218
Dennis, Wayne, 93
dependent variables, 340, 345, 365
depth, 214
"De Ratioiniis in Ludo Alea" ("Of reasoning with random lots") (Huygens), 232–33
Derby, 44
de Santillana, Giorgio, 21–22
Descartes, René, 144, 255, 300, 313, 316, 339
  as polymath, 115, 130
despotic governments, 375, 377
detachment, 66
de Vries, Hugo, 339
De Vulgari Eloquentia (Dante), 412
Dewey, John, 70
Diamond, Jared, xvii
Diaspora, 292
diatonic scale, 217
Dickens, Charles, 318
Dictionary of Scientific Biography (*DoSB*), 108, 257–58, *258,* 268–71, 272, 273, 284–85, 603
Diderot, Denis, 316
difficulty explanation:
  for arts and sciences, 105–6
  for golf, 103–4
diffraction grating, 411
Dimanche Après-Midi à l'Île de la Grande Jatte, Un (Seurat), 206–7
discount effect, 82
disinterestedness, 65–66
dissection, 314
diversity, 360
divination, 234
Divine Comedy (Dante), 59, 412
diving, 97
division of labor, 229
DNA, 123, 292
Dobecki, Thomas, 23
Donatello (di Betto Bardi), 74
Dong Qichang, 398
Don Quixote (Cervantes), 221
Dorn, Harold, 254–55
Dos Passos, John, 116
Dostoyevsky, Fyodor, 318
Doyle, Arthur Conan, 444
drama, 138, 140, 412, 600
  as meta-invention, 211, 219–20, 244
  popular, 447
drawing of three-dimensional objects, 414

Dream of the Red Chamber (Cao Zhan), 222
Dream Pool Essays (Shen Gua), 39
Dreiser, Theodore, 116
Du Bois, W. E. B., 446
Duccio, Agostino, di, 214
Du Fu, 139, 143, 144, 323
dummy variables, 343
  for cities, 368
  for country, 373–75
  for time, 344, 375
Durandus of Saint Pourçain, 238
Durbin-Watson statistic, 614
Dürer, Albrecht, 74, 75, 89, 144, 317
duty, 406–7, 452
Dyck, Anthony van, 317, 339
dynamite, 315

earth sciences, 60, 153, 414
  central events in, 160, 161, *176–78*
  database for, 76
earth sciences inventory, 121, *125,* 143, 311
East Asia, 381, 452
  art forms of, 260
  autonomy in, 397–99
  purpose in, 396–97
  science in, 257, 275
Eastern Europe:
  Jews from, 281, 291
  totalitarian states in, 362
  wars in, 335
eclipses, 39, 234
economic conditions, 331
economics, statistical analysis in, 233
economy, 17C European, 403
Ecstasy of Saint Teresa (Bernini), 205
Edison, Thomas, 121, 126, 129, 143, 393
  as Brick Layer, 153
education, 432, 433
  university, 433
effectance, 388
Egypt, ancient, 10, 14, 16, 21, 23–24, 70, 222, 228
  artistic conventions in, 212–13
  astronomy in, 399
  climate in, 23
  gods in, 234
  government in, 14
  mathematics in, 228
  number system in, 228, 231
  technological puzzles of, 17–20
  written language in, 211
-800, accomplishment as of, 13–24
-800 to 1400, events during, 262–63, *263*

-8000, conditions in, 3–7
1848 revolutionary movements, 446
1812 Overture (Tchaikovsky), 386
eikos, 232
Eine Kleine Nachtmusik (Mozart) 72
Einstein, Albert, 7, 59, 126, 130, 143, 144, 254,
    419, 455, 457
Einsteinian Revolution, 155, 453
Eisenhower, Dwight D., 8
Eitoku, 327
Electra (Euripides), 26
electrical charge, 414
electrical conduction, 414
electric technology, 315
electromagnetic fields, 122
electron microscopy, 123
elements, 124, 414
Elements (Euclid), 231
Elert, Piotr, 108
Elgin marbles, 26
Eliade, Mircea, 21, 590
Eliot, George, 207
Eliot, T. S., 422
elite cities, 355–61, *356, 359,* 379, 399, 409,
    613
    regression analyses for, 367–70, *369, 370*
elites, 447
elitism, 86
Elizabethan drama, 48
Elizabeth I, 8, 44, 442
Ellington, Duke, 115
eminence, 59, 73, 450
    current fashion and, 81–83
    distribution of, 87–90, *88, 92, 94*
    giants in, 119–54
    index scores for, 79–80, 151–52, *152,* 475–93
    as measure, 249
    measurements of, 73–75
    significant figures as measure of, 78–79
emotion, 66
empiricism, 226
Enciclopedia Universale dell'Arte, 108
encyclopedic sources, 108–9, 110, 602–3
Encyclopédie Philosophique Universelle, 108
Endeavor, 42–44
End of Science, The (Horgan), 439
engineering, 228
    statistical analysis in, 233
    women in, 286
England, 27, 297, 335, 403
    Elizabethan, 440–42
    Enlightenment in, 49–50
    industrial cities of, 360

Jewish emancipation in, 276
    the novel in, 220–22
    as parliamentary monarchy, 371
    railroads in, 255
    Renaissance in, 71
    Southeast, 298, 375
    Southwest, 298
    see also Britain
English Historical Review, 156
enjoyment, 386, 388
Enlightenment, xviii, 142, 300, 316, 405, 407,
    447, 457
    in England, 49–50
    in France, 50, 357
    in Scotland, 50
environment:
    biology vs., 285
    women and, 286–87
Epicurus, 316
epistemology, 61, 224, 225
epochcentric bias, 82, 431–32, 434, 436,
    437–38, 445, 447
equality, excellence and, 450
equations, indeterminate, 230
equinox, 22, 39
Erasistratus, 29
erosion, 39
Essai sur L'Inégalité des Races Humaines
    (Gobineau), 446
Essay Concerning Human Understanding (Locke),
    49
ethics, 61, 224, 226–28, 418
    as meta-invention, 211
ethnicity, 432
ethnic minorities, 265
Euclid, 127, 130, 230, 231, 255
Eudoxus, 333
Euler, Leonhard, 127, 143, 449
Eurasia, 14
Euripides, 26, 220, 260, 333, 354
Eurocentric hypothesis, 247–48
Eurocentrism, 84–85, 603
    in arts inventories, 248–51, *249*
    meditation and, 225
    in scientific inventories, 251–58, *252*
Europe, 34, 299, 346, 451
    anonymous art in medieval, 260
    architecture in, 260–61
    autonomy in, 401
    calibration of uncertainty in, 232–33
    Christianity in, 275, 295, 338, 402–5
    cities in, 367–70, 433
    core area in, 295–99, *296, 297, 298*

Europe (*continued*)
  decline in dominance of, 264
  declinism in, 446–47
  decorative arts and crafts in, 261
  de facto population in, 432–35
  domination of inventories by, 143, 247–64, *248, 265*
  famines in, 47
  Jews in, 276, 278, 291
  major wars in, 334–35, 420
  medieval, 260, 420, 458
  the novel in, 220–22
  population and accomplishment in, 310
  post-Roman, 14
  Protestant, 407
  purpose in, 401
  science in, 275, 299–300
  scientific method in, 235–43
  secularization of, 405
  significant figures in, 299–300, *301–3*
  Western civilization as, 262
Euthymedes, 213
evolution, 30, 123, 148–49
  beauty in, 419
  of earth, 160
  gender and, 289, 290
  of landforms, 414
  Neptunist theory of, 53
evolutionary psychology, 64
excellence:
  in the arts, 62–72
  capacity for, 389, 391
  differences in, 95
  equality and, 450
  fame vs., 94, 95–96, 101, 106
  identification of, 59–86
  importance vs., 62
  operational measures of, 72–75
  opinion and, xvi, 59–60
  reality of, 449–50
  in science, 60–62
  in sports, 97–101, *98, 99, 100, 102*
  work involved in achieving, 392–93
excellent, direct vs. indirect measures of, 102–3
existentialism, 422
expected values, 342–43
experimental psychology, 387
experimentation, 237–39, 299, 414
expertise, judgment and, 66–68
explanatory variables, 379
Expressionism, 216
Eyck, Jan van, 75, 412

fables, 140
face validity, 80
  Lotka curve and, 95–96
factory system, 315
Fahrenheit, Daniel, 339
falsification, principle of, 238, 601
fame:
  excellence vs., 94, 95–96, 101, 106
  in literature, 95
families, accomplishment in, 114–15
familism, familial constraints, 395, 397, 452
famine, 47
Faraday, Michael, 126, 353, 432, 436
Faulkner, William, xix, 422, 423
Fauvism, 216
Federalist Papers, 228
Fedin, Konstantine, 362
Ferdinand, King of Spain, 364
Fermat, Pierre de, 232, 313
Feynman, Richard, 440
Fichte, Johann, 316
Fielding, Henry, 45, 48, 221, 412
Fifth Symphony (Beethoven), 54, 155, 207
film, 114, 221, 429–30, 442, 453, 454
findings, dissemination of, 242–43
Finer, S. E., 362, 371
Finland, 298
fire, 3, 4, 155
Fischer, Bobby, 104
Five Women Who Loved Love (Ihara), 222
fixed-effects model, 373, 610
fixed-effects option, 375–77
Flatland (Abbott), 209
Flaubert, Gustave, 318, 427
Fleming, Alexander, 149–50
Florence, 27, 215, 296, 305, 368, 433
  Renaissance, xix, 333, 337, 339, 350
  as republic, 362
Florence cathedral, 205, 214
flow, 388
folklore, 260
foreshortening, 213
form, 240
Fox, James, 49
Fracastoro, Girolamo, 314
fractions, decimal, 414
France, 73, 85, 251, 266, 307, 309, 317
  accomplishment in, 296–98, 310–11, 338
  autocracy in, 363
  Baroque, 357
  cities in, 357, 358, *359*
  Enlightenment in, 50, 357
  existentialism in, 423

famine in, 47
Florence invaded by, 333
Jews in, 276, 280–81
La Belle Époque in, 333
musical polyphony in, 217–18
population density of, 344
troubadors from, 260
university students in, 433
wars and civil unrest in, 335, 346–47
writers from, 251
Franco-Prussian war, 333
Frank, Robert, 443
Frederick the Great, 9
freedom, order vs., 411
freedom of action, 361–64, 379, 380, 409
de facto, 373–75, *374*
regression analysis for, 371–75, *372, 374,* 377
free will, 458
French Revolution, 9, 28, 50, 9, 28, 50, 312, 371
frequency distribution, 461–66, *462*
explanation of, 462–63
standard deviation and, 463
frescoes, 214, 215
Freud, Sigmund, 128, 149, 407, 457
Freudian Revolution, 155
Fujiwara Teika, 328
functional objects, 261

Gabbey, Alan, 241
Gabirol, Solomon ibn (Avicebron), 275
Gainsborough, Thomas, 48
galaxy, size of, 160
Galen, 29, 128, 415
Galileo, 122, 126, 143, 237, 239, 240–41, 255, 299, 312
telescope of, 242–43
Galois, Evariste, 313
Galton, Francis, 73, 93, 94
gambling, 232, 242
game, 59
Gansu, 37
gardening, 65, 66
Gardner, Helen, 74–75
Gardner, Howard, xvii
garment industry, 315
Garrick, David, 49
gas lighting, 315
Gates of Paradise (Ghiberti), 205
Gauss, Carl, 127, 231, 265, 313, 449
Gay, Peter, 50
Gay 100, The, 287
Gehrig, Lou, 104
genes, 123

genetics, 123, 130, 440
research in, 418
Geneva, 357
genius, 93
undiscovered, 109
geocentric solar system, 30, 161
geography, 399, 439, 505–11, *508*
Geography of Thought, The (Nisbett), 397
Geological Society of America, 23
geologic history, 414
geologic map, 414
geology, 53, 125, 399, 440
geometry, 127, 214, 230
analytic, 313
non-Euclidean, 228
Georgian Britain:
comfort in, 45–46
medicine in, 46–47
physics in, 45
transportation in, 45
Georgian London, xix, 25, 42–51
astronomy in, 42–43
as center of Western civilization, 44
drama in, 48
dynamism of, 51
illiteracy in, 51
intellectual life in, 48–49
literature in, 47
music in, 47, 48
painting in, 47–48
physical conditions of, 44–45
policing in, 45
right to vote in, 51
theater in, 47
wealth and poverty in, 45, 51
women's rights in, 51
Gericault, Theodore, 205
Germany, 73, 85, 251, 375
accomplishment in, 296–98, 300, 338
cities in, 357, 358, *359,* 613
earlier borders of, 300
Jews in, 275, 276, 280–81, 307
Nazi, 277, 281, 307, 371
pre-unification, 363, 373
university students in, 433
wars and civil unrest in, 332, 335, 336, 340, 357
World War II and, 332
writers from, 251
germs, 314
Ghiberti, Lorenzo, 205
giants, 119–54
Gibbon, Edward, 26, 31, 32, 49, 455

Gide, André, 424
Gilbert, William, 239, 312
Giotto di Bondone, 74, 89, 214, 421
Giza, 18–19, 20, 23–24
Glasgow, 44, 297
glasses, 129
Glorious Revolution (England), 50, 371
Gluck, Christoph, 48
go (game), 619
Gobineau, Arthur de, 446
God, as Clockmaker, 49
Goethe, Johann, 142, 147, 259, 318
Gogh, Vincent van, 89, 206
Gogol, Nikolay, 318
Goldberg, Steven, 289
Golden Ass (Apuleius), 220
Goldsmith, Oliver, 48, 49
Goldstein, Thomas, 399
golf, 97, 107
    bell curve in basic skills, 97–98, 98, 99,
        595–96
    component skills of, 97
    difficulty explanation in, 103–4
    Majors in, 100–101, 100, 103
    tournament wins in, 97–101, 99, 100
Gombrich, Ernst, 145, 213
Goncourt brothers, 114
Gongora y Argote, Luis de, 318, 338
goodness, 416, 417, 418, 422, 452, 456
    in the arts, 421–22
    existentialism vs., 423
    in science, 418
Gorky, Maxim, 423
Gothic cathedrals, 458
government, 14, 77
    consent of the governed, 229
    as contractual, 229
    despotic, 375
    limited, 361
    meta-inventions in, 229
    purpose of, 229
Goya, Francisco, 89, 338, 421
Grafton, Sue, 443, 444–45
gravity, 161, 414
Gray, Elisha, 148
greatness fatigue, 445–46
Great Pyramid, 17–19, 23
Great Revolution (Netherlands), 347
Great Sphinx of Giza, 23–24
Greco, El (Domenikos Theotokopoulos), 216,
    338
Greece, ancient, xvi, 16, 26, 30, 360, 399
    aesthetics in, 70

art in, 230
artistic realism in, 212–13, 600
drama in, 219–20, 354, 600
ethics in, 226–28, 244
individuality in, 210, 401–2
linear perspective in, 213–14
logic in, 54
mathematical proofs in, 228–31
mathematics in, 161
music in, 217
myths of, 260
number system in, 231
painting and sculpture in, 26, 27, 136, 137,
    213–14, 322
philosophy in, 78, 223–24, 354, 399, 400,
    416, 456
poetry in, 266, 393
sculpture of, 398
secular observation of nature in, 234–35,
    244
wars in, 335, 346
Greek chorus, 219
Grimm brothers, 114
Gross Domestic Product (GDP), 339, 346,
    349–51, 376, 381
Grosseteste, Robert, 237–38
Groundhog Day, 45
Grout, Donald, 109–10, 109
Grun, Bernard, 157
Grunebaum, G. E. von, 400
Gu Kaizhi, 135, 136, 143
Guldin, Paul, 275
Gulf War, 8
gunpowder, 155, 255
Gutenberg, Johannes, 157, 159
Gutenberg Bible, 412
gymnastics, 97

habit formation, 444–45, 623
haikai, 141
haiku, 141, 212, 410, 411
Hale, George Ellery, 122
Halley, Edmond, 43
Hals, Frans, 317, 339
Hamburg, 357
Hamilton, William, 313
Hamlet (Shakespeare), 155
Hamlet's Mill (de Santillana and von Dechend),
    21–22
Handel, George Frideric, 48, 63, 207, 319
Han Gan, 322
Hangzhou, in Song Dynasty, see Song Hangzhou
happiness, 224

hard sciences:
  fashion and assessment of, 82
  organizing structures in, 413–14
  statistical analysis in, 233
  statistical significance in, 342
  truth in, 60, 453
hard sciences inventories, 121, 130, 251
  accomplishment rate in, 311, 312, 312
  women in, 266, 270
Hardy, Thomas, 427
harmonic systems, 319
harmony, tonal, 217, 218, 410, 413
Harte, Bret, 116
Harvard Biographical Dictionary of Music, 109–10
Haydn, Joseph, 48, 134, 319
Heaney, Seamus, 431
heating, 45–46
Hegel, G. W. F., 70, 133
Heine, Heinrich, 318
heliocentrism, 62, 161
Hellenistic age, 399, 402
Helvetius, Claude, 316
Hemingway, Ernest, 116, 445
Heraclitus, 225, 316
Herder, Johann, 275, 316
Hereditary Genius (Galton), 73
heredity, 437
Herman, Arthur, 446
Herodotus, 19, 26, 333
Herschel, Caroline, 266
Herschel, William, 122, 150–51, 266
  as Brick Layer, 153
Hertz, Gustav, 605
high aesthetic quality, 62–63, 68, 420
high culture, alienation of, 424–25
high-value culture pattern, 354
Hinduism, 41, 132, 140, 144, 223, 230, 231,
    326, 402
  meditation in, 224–25
Hipparchus, 22
Hippocrates, 128, 143, 234, 333
  as System Builder, 152, 153
Hisab al-jabr w'al-musqabalah (al-Khwarizmi),
    231–32
Histoire de la Musique, Une (Rebatet), 109–10
histories, 112, 151–52, 152, 205
  of American art, 250
  biographical dictionaries vs., 109, 157
  literary vs. art and music, 142
historiography, 237
historiometry, 60, 73, 92
history:
  laws of, 446

  of science, 206
History of Art (Janson), 74–75
History of Western Music (Grout), 109–10, 109
Hitler, Adolf, 281
Hittite civilization, 16
Hobbes, Thomas, 133, 300, 316
Hogarth, William, 45, 48
Holocaust, 277
Homer, 10, 26, 63, 114, 140, 142, 219, 222
Homo erectus, 3
Homo sapiens, xix–xx, 3, 4, 5, 154, 224
homosexuality, 287
Hon'ami Koetsu, 136, 327
Honolka, Kurt, 109–10, 109
Hope, Bob, 155
Hopper, Edward, xvi
Horace, 31
Horgan, John, 439
Horner's method, 230
How Much Is that Doggy in the Window, 72
Huangzhou, 25, 32–42
Hubble, Edwin, 122
Hubble's Law, 122
Hubei, 37
Huckleberry Finn (Twain), 421
Hugo, Victor, 318, 421
human capital:
  in the arts, 428, 440–42
  in cities, 358–60
  population vs., 428, 435
  in science, 435
human condition, 421
Humani Corporis Fabrica, De (Vesalius), 314
humanism, 402–3
Hume, David, 63–64, 68, 70, 71, 72, 316
humors, 415
Hunan, 37
Hungary, 251, 298, 335
Hutton, James, 53, 125, 160, 236
Huygens, Christiaan, 129, 130, 232–33, 313,
    333, 339
Hypatia of Alexandria, 266
hyperbolic curve, 99, 103
  see also Lotka curve
Hypocrites (Answerer), 219
hypothesis, 237–38

Iberian peninsula, 363
Ibsen, Henrik, 121, 318
Ihara Saikaku, 222
Ikeno Taiga, 327
Île de France, 298
Iliad (Homer), 10, 26, 114, 219

immigration, 305–7
importance, 59
  excellence vs., 62
Impressionism, 206, 216, 317, 411
Imru' al-Qays, 321
Incas, 20, 337
independent variables, 340, 365, 375–76
  separate analysis of, 345–46
indeterminate equations, 230
indexes, 597–98
index scores, 79–80, 88–89, 95, 311, 312, 436
  creation of, 481–86
  distribution of, 89–90, 89
  for eminence, 79–80, 151–52, 152, 475–93
  face validity of, 80
  as not comparable across inventories, 120
  relativity of, 120–21
  same vicinity of, 120
  statistical reliability of, 80–81
  top 20, 119–21
  value of, 487–90
  of women, 267–68, 269
India, 9, 33, 381
  aesthetics in, 70
  anonymity in art of, 78, 260
  Arabic numerals invented in, 231–32
  arts inventories for, 250, 251, 262
  astronomy in, 399
  cultural activity hiatus in, 135, 140, 141
  drama in, 219–20, 244
  ethics in, 226–28, 244
  family in, 401
  inventories for, 84
  literature in, 221–22
  mathematics in, 161, 228, 256, 399
  meditation in, 224–25, 244
  Mughal empire in, 140
  music notation lacking in, 217
  number system in, 228, 231–32, 244
  philosophy in, 223, 224, 324
  science in, 253, 254, 255, 256, 257, 259, 284
Indian literature inventory, 78, 140, 143, 147, 320
  accomplishment rate for, 325, 325
Indian philosophy inventory, 78, 121, 132, 133, 143, 144, 320
  accomplishment rate of, 326, 326
Indic civilization, 14, 16
indirect proofs, 231
individualism, 401, 452
  Christianity and, 210, 402–5
  Greek, 210, 401–2

Jewish, 210, 404
  Stoic moral, 402
  Western, 210, 401–5
inductive proof, 231
Indus-Sarasvati civilization, 224–25
industrial chemistry, 315
industrial processes, statistical analysis in, 233
Industrial Revolution, xviii, 44, 300, 315, 357, 414, 447
Inevitability of Patriarchy, The (Goldberg), 289
infectious diseases, 128, 314, 415
inflation, 337
influenza, 46
information storage, punch cards in, 159, 599
innovation vs. tradition, 395, 397–99, 452
inoculation, 47
Inquisition, 363, 373, 375
intellect, 404
intellectual fashion, 67–68
intelligence, 93
interchangeable parts, 315
internal combustion engine, 315, 435
Introduction to the History of Science (Sarton), 256
inventories, 76–80
  construction of, 475–90
  sources of, 491–503
inventory-specific issues, 485–86
invertebrate zoology, 123
Invisible Hand, 50
IQ:
  Jews and, 291–92
  in men vs. women, 289
Iran hostage crisis, 8
Ireland, 298
iron, 38, 315
irrigation, 7, 162
Isabella, Queen of Spain, 364
Isis, 31
Islam, 41, 321
  autonomy and, 401
  golden age of, 399–401
  and Greek philosophy, 400
  Orthodox Christianity and, 402
  purpose in, 400
  see also Arabs, Arab world
Israelites, 16
Istituto per la Collaborazione Culturale, 108
Italy, 85, 307, 373
  accomplishment in, 296–98, 338
  cities in, 357, 358, 359, 613
  city-states in 12C, 34
  Jewish emancipation in, 276

linear perspective in, 213–15
Papal States in, 298
pre-unification, 373
Renaissance in, 299, 337, 357, 407, 417, 420
Spanish Hapsburg rule in, 357

Jacquard, Joseph-Marie, 159
Jacquard loom, 159, 599
James, Henry, 68, 69, 427
James, William, 60
Janson, H. W., 74, 75
Japan, 9, 85
    arts inventories for, 250, 251, 262
    family in, 397, 398
    inventories for, 84
    literature in, 221–22, 328
    philosophy in, 78
    purpose in, 396–97
    science in, 255, 284, 399
    technology in, 399
    World War II and, 332
Japanese art inventory, 78, 121, *136*, 143, 147, 320
    accomplishment rate in, 327, *327*
Japanese literature inventory, 78, *141*, 143, 147, 267
    accomplishment rate for, 328, *328*
Jarir, 321
Java, 33
Jenner, Edward, 47
Jerusalem, 27
Jesus, 10, 132, 223, 353
jewelry, 77
Jews, Judaism, 41, 275–83, 364, 605–6
    in Antonine Rome, 29
    Ashkenazi, 265, 291–93
    culture of, 292–93
    Diaspora of, 292
    disproportionate representation by, 278–82, *279, 280*, 285–86, 291–93
    emancipation of, 266, 276, 278
    emergence of achievement by, 276–77, *277*
    genetics and, 292
    immigration of, 281, 307
    individualism in, 210, 404
    IQ and, 291–92
    learning valued by, 291–93
    legal restrictions on, 276
    in literature inventory, 275
    at Masada, 32
    in mathematics inventory, 275
    monotheism in, 226

in music inventory, 275, 277
Nobel Prizes of, 281–82, *282, 283*
Oriental, 291
in philosophy inventory, 275, 277
population of, 278
since 1950, 281–82, *282, 283*
Jiangxi, 37
Jin Pingmei, 222
Jocho, 327
Johnson, Samuel, 44, 49, 51, 61
    London of, xix, 25, 42–51
Jones, William, 49
Jonson, Ben, 318
Joyce, James, 422
judgment, xvi, xviii, 64, 68–69
    consistency of, 72
    expertise and, 66–68
    knowledge and, 65–66
    objective aesthetic, 69–70
"judgmental," 60, 71
Juizhang Suanshu, 228
Julius Caesar, 10, 32, 398
Julius Caesar (Shakespeare), 8
Jung, Carl, 21, 590
Jupiter, 242–43

Kabalevsky, Dmitry, 362
Kac, Mark, 153–54
Kafka, Franz, 431
Kaifeng, 37
Kalf, Willem, 215–16
Kalidasa, 140, 143, 144, 147, 220, 325
Kandinsky, Vasily, 425
Kano school, 327
Kant, Immanuel, 61, 65–66, 69, 70, 71, 133, 316
Katayev, Valentin, 362
Kazantzakis, Nikos, 431
Keats, John, xx, 54, 318, 419
Kennedy, John F., 8
Kepler, Johannes, 143, 255
Kern, Jerome, 115
Khafre, 23
Khrushchev, Nikita, 8
Khufu, 17, 23
King, Helen Dean, 270, 272
King Lear (Shakespeare), 207
Ki no Tsurayuki, 328
Kinsay, *see* Song Hangzhou
Kleine Chirugia, Die (Paracelsus), 314
knowledge, judgment and, 65–66
known unknowns, 17–20
Koch, Robert, 128

Koch's postulates, 128
Kokei, 327
Kokinshu, 328
Korean War, 8
Kovalevskaya, Sonya, 265–66
Kreisler, Fritz, 443, 622
Kreutzer sonata (Beethoven), 76
Kroeber, A. L., 261, 354, 381
Kuhn, Thomas, 155
Kulturfahrplan (Stein), 157

labor, division of, 229
Lafayette, Madame de, 221
lagged variables, 365, 614
Lamarck, Jean, 123
Lamarckism, 123
Lamentation, The (Giotto), 421
Landes, David, 253
landscapes, 212
Lang, Paul, 83, 146, 207, 411
language:
    development of, 5
    written, 210–11
Laocoön, 26
Laozi, 131, 133, 139, 210, 223, 324, 396
Laplace, Pierre-Simon, 122
Last Judgment (Michelangelo), 54
Last Supper (Leonardo), 205, 333
Latin, 412
Latin America, Nobel Prizes and, 282
La Tour, 317
Lavoisier, Antoine, 53, 124, 130, 143, 159, 436
law, 14, 32
legends, 114–15
Lehner, Mark, 18, 19
Leibniz, Gottfried, 130, 206, 228, 313, 316
Leipzig, 305, 368, 419
Le Nain brothers, 114
Leonardo da Vinci, 74, 75, 129, 144, 155, 205,
    287, 315, 317, 333, 414
    as polymath, 114
    as System Builder, 152–53
Léonin (Leoninus), 218
Lesage, Alain, 412
Lessing, Doris, 431
Letters on the English (Voltaire), 50
Leucippus, 30, 234
lever, 30, 129
Lewis, Sinclair, 116
Lewis, Wyndham, 423
Lexikon der Kunst (Stadler), 74–75
liberal democracy, 228, 361, 371, 372, 373, 375
Li Bo, 259, 323

Libyans, 16
Life of an Amorous Man, The (Ihara), 222
light:
    shading of, 213
    spectra of, 411
Limbourg brothers, 114, 205
limited monarchy, 343
Limoges, France, 218
Lindgren, Astrid, 431
linear perspective, 211, 213–15, 299, 411, 412
Lippmann, Walter, 105
Li Qingzhao, 39–40
literary criticism, 254
literature, 44, 452, 455
    craft of, 411
    database for, 76
    delayed recognition in, 82
    environment for, 429
    fame in, 95
    as meta-invention, 219
    organizing structure in, 410
    other inventories and, 366–67, *367*
    polymaths in, 114
    popular, 447
    pre -800, 14
    principles of, 411
    structural changes and, 412
    television and film vs., 429–30, 442
    tools of, 411, 412
    transcendental goods in, 422–23
    truth in, 421
    Western vs. non-Western figures in, 259
    women in, 271, 274, *274,* 290
literature inventories, 494–97
    Jews in, 275, 282
    women in, 266
    see also specific inventories
Liu Jo, 236
Lobachevsky, Nikolay, 228, 313
Locke, John, 49–50, 133, 144, 229, 316
logarithms, 313
logic, 225–26, 450
    Aristotelian, 231
    Boolean algebra and, 228
    formal, 54
    mathematical, 230, 231
    as meta-invention, 211, 224
logical fallacies, 226
logograms, 211, 599
London, 35, 216, 299, 300, 305, 357, 360, 431
    Great Fire of 1666 in, 44
    Samuel Johnson's, *see* Georgian London
    in 12C, 34

London, Jack, 116
Lope de Vega, 318, 338
Lorenzetti, Ambrogio, 214
Lorrain, Claude, 317
Lotka, Alfred James, 90–91, 99, 105, 107
Lotka curve, 91–96, *92, 99, 100,* 101, 102–7,
    102, 112, 119, 158, 353
  bell curve vs., 93
  Top Five in, *96*
  women in, 267–68, *269*
Louis XIV, King of France, 9, 363
Low Countries, 317
Lucian, 30–31
Lumière brothers, 114
Luther, Martin, 403, 405
Lutheranism, 404
Lyell, Charles, 121, 125, 143, 148
Lysippos, 333
Lysistrata (Aristophanes), 26

Macbeth (Shakespeare), 207, 421
McClellan, James, 254–55
Machiavelli, 133
Machu Picchu, 264
Madhvamika, 326
Madonna of the Stairs (Michelangelo), 333
Madrid, 338, 357, 368
Magnete, De (Gilbert), 312
Mahabharata, 114, 140, 219, 325
Mahayana Buddhism, 132
Mailer, Norman, 431
Maimonides, Moses, 275
Maine, 304
major figures, classifying of, 478–80
Malacca, Straits of, 33
Mallarmé, Stéphane, 318
Manchester, 44
Manet, Édouard, 206, 216, 411
Mannerism, 299
Man'yoshu, 328
maps, 214, 599
Marconi, Guglielmo, 129
Marcus Aurelius, 26, 28
markets, winner-take-all, 443–44
market saturation, 428, 435–36, 442–44
Marlowe, Christopher, 95, 104, 106, 318, 442
Mars, 150
Marseilles, 46, 297
Martel, Charles, 156
Martindale, Colin, 92, 95, 104
Maruyama Okyo, 327
Masaccio (Cassai), 54, 74, 215, 412, 600
Maslow, Abraham, 387

mass production, 229
Masters tournament, 100, 101
mathematical induction, 414
mathematical notation, 414
mathematical proofs, 211, 414
mathematics, 60, 235, 399, 440
  beauty in, 419
  central events in, 160, 161, *188–93*
  database for, 76
  discovery of truth in, 60
  fashion and assessment of, 82
  golden age of, 313
  logic in, 230, 231
  meta-inventions in, 211, 228–33
  organizing structure of, 414
  principle of, 414
  as structure of nature, 241–42
  tools for, 414
mathematics inventory, 121, *127,* 130, 143, 251,
    449
  accomplishment rate for, 313, *313*
  Jews in, 275, 279
  women in, 265–66, 270
Mather, Cotton, 46–47
matter, 240
  law of conservation of, 124, 160
Matthew, Gospel of, 93
Matthew effect, 353, 443
Maxwell, James, 144
Maya, 21
  number system of, 228
Mayer, Maria Goeppert, 605
May Laws of 1882, 276
Meaning of Meaning, The (Ogden and Richards),
    70
measures, of excellence, 72–75
mechanics, 45, 387
Medea (Euripides), 26
medicine, 60, 399, 414
  application of truth in, 60–61
  central events in, 160, 161–62, *194–97*
  database for, 76
  empirical observation in, 234
  fashion and assessment of, 82
  organizing structure of, 415
  System Builders in, 152
medicine inventory, 121, 123, *128,* 130, 143,
    251, 314, *314*
  accomplishment rate for, 314, *314*
  women in, 266
Medici Venus, 27
Medieval Technology and Social Change (White),
    155

meditation, 211, 224–25, 244, 458
Mediterranean, 14, 33
  government in, 14
Mee, Charles, 337
melody, 217
Melville, Herman, 444
men:
  IQ and, 289
  mathematical and visual-spatial skills of,
    289
Mencius, 131, 139, 223, 324
Mendelssohn, Moses, 275, 316
Meninas, Las (Velazquez), 147–48, 205
mental illnesses, 128
mental shelf space, limited, 443–45
Merton, Robert, 403
Merton, S. K., 93
Mesolithic period, 6
Mesopotamia, 16, 70
meta-inventions, 157, 209–44, 412
  Arabic numerals as, 211, 231–32, 244, 414
  artistic abstraction as, 211, 215–16
  artistic realism as, 211, 212–13
  calculation of uncertainty as, 211, 232–33
  characteristics of, 210
  as cognitive tools, 209, 210, 211, 213, 224,
    227, 228, 243–44
  in commerce, 229
  cultural attributes vs., 210
  drama as, 211, 219–20, 244
  ethics as, 211, 226–28
  in government, 229
  linear perspective as, 211, 213–15, 412
  logic as, 211, 224, 225–26
  mathematical proofs as, 211, 228–31, 414
  meditation as, 211, 224–25, 244
  novel as, 211, 220–22, 244
  polyphony, 211, 217–18, 413
  scientific method as, 121, 233–43
  secular observation of nature as, 211, 233,
    234–35, 244
  Western prevalence in, 244
  written language as, 210–11
metaphysics, 61, 224, 416
Méthode de Traicter les Plaies (Paré), 314
Metonic cycle, 17
Mexico, written language in, 211
Michelangelo, 31, 54, 74, 75, 79, 88, 90, 135,
  145, 146, 149, 205, 230, 259, 287, 317,
  333, 392, 398
  as first in inventory, 120, 137, 143, 144
microbes, 314
microscope, 312

Middle Ages, medieval:
  anonymous arts in, 260
  Christianity in, 401, 403
  Europe in, 260, 420, 458
middle class, 447
Middle East, 275
Middlemarch (Eliot), 207
Milan, 305, 357
Miletus, 230
Milky Way, 151, 160
Minghuang, Emperor of China, 322
Minoan civilization, 14, 16
Misérables, Les (Hugo), 421
Mises, Ludwig von, 116
Mises, Richard von, 116
Missa Solemnis (Beethoven), 146
Mississippi, 304
Mithraism, 31
Moby Dick (Melville), 444
models, 353–55, 379, 409
  regression analyses of, 365–67, *365, 366, 367*
molecules, 439
Molière, 363
Mona Lisa (Leonardo), 155
monarchy, 363
  absolute, 371, 372, 373
  parliamentary, 371, 372, 373, 375
Monet, Claude, 85, 89, 206
money, 229
monomyth, 21–23
monotheism, 226, 599
Montagu, Mary, 46
Montaigne, Michel de, 275
Mont Blanc, 240
Montesquieu, Charles, 316
Monteverdi, Claudio, 299, 319
Montgolfier brothers, 114
Mont Puy-de-Dôme, 240
moons, planetary, 242–43, 438
Moorish Spain, 275
Moors, 364
Morgan, Augustus de, 231
Morgan, Thomas Hunt, 123
Morocco, 338
morphology, 123
Morrison, Toni, 431
Morse, Samuel F. B., 129
Mosaic Law, 226
Moscow, 357
Moses, Grandma, 90
Moses (Michelangelo), 54
motherhood, 287–88
motion, laws of, 161

"Motivation Reconsidered: The Concept of Competence" (White), 388
motor nerves, 29
Mount Wilson, 122
Mozart, Wolfgang Amadeus, 48, 54, 64, 83, 120, 134, 143, 146, 319, 392, 447, 454
Muhammad, 132, 223, 321
multiculturalism, xviii, 63, 244
multiple regression, 331, 472–73
multivariate time-series analysis, 354–55, 451
Munch, Edvard, 205
Murasaki Shikibu, 141, 220, 222, 259, 267, 328
music, 212, 386, 455
    academic, 454
    Baroque in, 299, 417
    beauty in, 417
    cities and, 360
    craft of, 411
    creation of, 55
    database for, 76
    delayed recognition in, 82
    diatonic scale in, 217
    environment for, 429
    instruments in, 413
    non-Western, unnamed composers in, 259
    notation in, 217
    organizing structure in, 410
    polyphony in, 211, 217–18
    popular, 261
    pre –800, 14
    principles of, 411
    scales in, 217
    structural changes and, 413
    tonal harmony in, 217
    tool of, 411
    transcendental goods in, 423, 424–25
    truth in, 421
    women in, 271, 274–75, 274, 290
musical compositions, 453–54
music inventories, 266, 499–500
    Jews in, 275, 277
    for the West, 78, 85
Music in Western Civilization (Lang), 207
Myron, 333
mysteries, 443, 444–45

Nabtian Pluvial, 23
Nagarjuna, 132, 223, 326
Naples, 297, 357, 373
Napoleonic Wars, 312, 357
narrative, conventions of, 422
National Gallery, London, 216
natural philosophy, 215, 239, 266

natural selection, 148–49
nature:
    mathematical structure of, 241–42
    secular observation of, 211, 233
Nature, 105
"nature of the chemical bond, The" (Pauling), 439
Near East, 6
nebulae, 150
Needham, Joseph, 236, 256, 259
needs hierarchy, 387
Nefertiti, 212
negative binomial model, 343
neo-Confucianism, 42, 324
Neolithic period, 6, 7
Neptunist theory, 53
Nero, 32
nerves, 29
Netherlands:
    accomplishment in, 296–98
    art in, 339, 365, 366
    golden age in, 333, 339
    Jewish emancipation in, 276
    philosophy in, 339
    as republic, 361, 371, 373
    science in, 339
    significant figures in, 365
    university students in, 433
    wars and civil unrest in, 347
neuroscience, 130, 440
Newcastle & London Post Coach, 45
Newcomen, Thomas, 129
New England, 305
New Jersey, 304, 305
New Testament, 49
Newton, Isaac, 7, 9, 49, 50, 126, 127, 143, 161, 206, 228, 230, 237, 241–42, 254, 255, 300, 313, 414, 449
Newtonian physics, 312
Newtonian Revolution, 155, 453
New World, 332, 337, 338, 364
New York, 305
New York, N.Y., 430
New Yorker, 7
New York marathon, 101, 102
Nicklaus, Jack, 100, 101, 104
Nicomachean Ethics (Aristotle), 227, 385, 416, 457
Nietzsche, Friedrich, 133, 393, 407, 446
Night Watch, The (Rembrandt), 54, 206
nihilists, nihilism, 391, 393, 423, 456
Nike of Samothrace, 26
Ninety-five Theses, 403

Ninth Symphony (Beethoven), 147
Nisbett, Richard, 397
Noah, 21
Nobel Prizes, 115, 129, 150, 282
   of Jews, 281–82, *282, 283*
   of non-whites, 283–84, *284*
   of women, 267, 273–74, *273,* 290
Noble Savage, xviii
Noether, Emmy, 265–66
non-Euclidean geometries, 228
non-European accomplishment, lack of, 258–61
nonjudgmental stance, 68–72
non-whites:
   Nobel Prizes of, 283–84, *284*
   recent trends for, 283–85
normal distribution, *see* bell curve
Norse sagas, 260
North Africa, 14
North America, science in, 253, 254, 259
Norway, 298
Norwegian Book Clubs, 431
notation:
   mathematical, 414
   musical, 217
novels, 318, 411, 412, 453
   as meta-invention, 211, 220–22, 244
Novum Organum (Bacon), 299
nuclear reaction, 126
number systems, 228, 244

objectivity, 65
observation, 236, 299
oceanography, 125
Ockham's Razor, 238
Odets, Clifford, 115
Odyssey (Homer), 10, 26, 114, 219
Oedipus plays (Sophocles), 26
"Of the Standard of Taste" (Hume), 63–64
Ogata Kenzan, 136
Ogata Korin, 136
Ogden, C. K., 70
Ogilvie, Marilyn, 272
oil paint, 411, 412
Old Testament, 10, 49, 226
Olesha, Yuri, 362
oligarchy, 371
"100 Best Novels in the World," 431
On the Construction of the Heavens (Herschel), 150–51
On the Origin of Species (Darwin), 157
opera, 299, 411
opinion, xvi, 59–60

optics, 399
order, freedom vs., 411
ordinary least squares (OLS), 609
Oresteia (Aeschylus), 26
organa, 218
organizing structure, 409–15, 425, 451–52
   age of, 411–12
   in hard sciences, 413–14
   in literature, 412
   in mathematics, 414
   in medicine, 415
   in music, 413
   richness of, 410–11
   in technology, 414–15
   in visual arts, 412
Organon (Aristotle), 226
Orthodox Christianity, 402, 403
Orwell, George, 424
Ostia, 27
Ottoman Empire, 335, 363–64, 373
Ovid, 10, 31

Paccioli, Luca, 232
Pacey, Arnold, 254–55, 256
Pachelbel, Johann, 207
painters, painting, 452, 453
   Greek, 214–15
   in Renaissance, 411
   significant vs. other, 429
   see also visual arts
Paleolithic era, 5, 6
Palmer, Arnold, 100
Palomar Observatory, 122
Pamela (Richardson), 221, 412
panel data, 608
Panini, 326
paper, 37–38
paper money, 229
Papin, Denis, 129
Paracelsus, 314
paradigm, truth vs., 155
parallax, 43
Paré, Ambroise, 314
Paris, xix, 44, 300, 305, 357, 358, 613
   art in, 366
   in 12C, 34
Parker, Dorothy, 115–16
parliamentary monarchy, 371, 372, 373, 375
Parmenides, 30, 225, 316, 333
Parrhasius, 27
parsimony, rule of, 102, 238, 289
particle physics, 440

Pascal, Blaise, 232–33, 240, 313, 316
Pascal's Triangle, 232, 233
passivity, 396
past:
    condescension towards, 25
    reverence for, 395
Pasteur, Louis, 123, 128, 143
Patai, Raphael, 276–77
Patanjali, 225, 326
pattern rupture, 354
Pauling, Linus, 439
Pausanias, 26
peace, 331–32, 333, 379
    see also war and civil unrest
Peale, Charles Wilson, 250
Peloponnesian Wars, 223, 332
pendulum, 129
penicillin, 149
Pennsylvania, 305
"Peony" (Xu Xi), 40
percentiles, 466
Percy, Bishop, 49
performing arts:
    market saturation in, 442–43
    product differentiation in, 444
Pergolesi, Giovanni, 48, 54
permutations and combinations, 230
Pérotin, 218
Persia:
    anonymous visual arts in, 260
    mathematics in, 399
Persian language, 138, 321
Peru, 20
Peter the Great, 9
Petrie, Flinders, 18
petroleum industry, 315
Petronius, 27, 30, 220
Petty, William, 46
PGA Championship, 98, 100, 101
PGA tour events, 100
pharmacology, 399
Phidias, 26, 27, 31, 260, 333, 398
Philistines, 16
Philo Judaeus, 275
philosophers, undiscovered, 109
philosophes, 50
philosophy, 61, 440, 457–58
    Arabic, 78, 399
    biographic sources in, 108
    Catholic humanism in, 402–3
    database for, 76
    definition of, 223

in Europe, 299–300
    Japanese, 78
    meta-inventions in, 211, 222–28
    nihilism in, 393
    polymaths in, 114
philosophy inventories, 84, 121, 492–94
    accomplishment rate in, 311
    for China, 78, 79
    for India, 78
    Jews in, 275, 277, 279
    for the West, 78, 85
    women absent from, 266
Phoenicia, 16
photography, 216, 315, 386
physics, 60, 66, 267, 439, 440, 449
    beauty in, 419
    central events in, 160, 161, 179–87
    database for, 76
    fundamental laws of, 61
    Newtonian, 312
    organizing principle of, 414
    particle, 440
    principles of, 414
    tools in, 414
    women in, 272
Physics (Aristotle), 237
physics inventory, 121, 126, 130, 143, 279, 311
physiology, 62, 123
Piazzi, Guiseppe, 449
Picasso, Pablo, xix, 74, 75, 89, 137, 144, 259, 398
pictographs, 228
pictorial images, 212
Pindar, 333
Pizarro, Francisco, 337
plagues, 46–47
planetaria, 39
planetary movements, 160, 234
planets, moons of, 438
plastics, 315
Plato, 26, 61, 70, 133, 144, 213, 217, 224, 225,
    241, 260, 316, 333, 402, 415–16
Platonic ideal, 415–16
Platonism, 457
plays, 453
pleasure, 385, 386
Pleistocene era, 3–4
Pliny the Elder, 27, 30
Plutarch, 26, 31
Poe, Edgar Allan, 318
poetry, 138, 140, 446, 453–54
pogroms, 276
Poincaré, Henri, 265–66

pointillism, 207, 410
Poland, 297, 298, 300, 349
    authors from, 251
    Jews in, 276, 291, 307
    under Russian rule, 373
polis, 402
political conditions, 331
political freedom, 361
political systems, significant figures and, 371–72, *372*
political theory, 227
Polo, Marco, 33, 34, 35, 39, 41
Polygnotus, 27, 260, 333
Polykleitos, 333
polymaths, 114–15, 129, 130, 232, 242
polyphony, 211, 217–18, 413
polyvinyl chloride, 156
Pompeii, 27, 29
Pompey, 32
popular culture, 447, 454
popular music, 261, 447
population, 367, 376, 381, 505
    accomplishment rate and, 427, 429
    of cities, 367, 376, 381
    of country, 344, 381
    cutoff point in, 111–13
    density of, 344
    determining and estimating of, 511
    human capital vs., 428, 435
    literature and, 429
    narrowing of, 109–10, *111*
    outer boundaries of, 107, 108–9
    significant figures vs., 111–13
Porter, Cole, 115
Portland, Maine, 304
Portugal, 298
Posterior Analytics (Aristotle), 237
posterity, 445
Post-Impressionism, 216, 317
postmodernism, 70–71, 623–24
Pound, Ezra, 422
Poussin, Nicolas, 317
Praxiteles, 333
prayer, 405
pre-Christian era, 161
"Precious Mirror of the Four Elements" (Zhu Shijie), 233
pre-Columbian America, art of, 260
predestination, 618
predictors of creativity, 354–55
preserved foods, 315
preventative medicine, 162
Price, Derek de Solla, 16, 91–92, 99

Price's law, 91–92
Pride and Prejudice (Austen), 71–72
primary qualities, 240
Princesse de Clèves, La (Lafayette), 221
Principia Mathematica (Newton), 49, 237, 414
principles, 410, 411, 414, 425
printing press, 155, 157, 159, 412, 413
probability theory, 232–33, 313
product differentiation, 444
production line, 156
Professional Golf Association (PGA), 97–101
Promissory Oaths Act of 1871, 276
proofs:
    indirect, 231
    inductive, 231
propositions, analysis of, 226
prosperity, 331–32, 379
    see also wealth
Protagoras, 316, 333
Protestant Christianity, 403–5, 407, 618
    meditation in, 225
"Protestant Ethic and the Spirit of Capitalism, The" (Weber), 403
proton, 126
Prussia, 298, 300, 373
    Jewish emancipation in, 276
psychoanalysis, 129
psychology, psychologists, 93, 129, 387–88, 392
    behavioral, 387
    experimental, 387–88
Ptolemy, Claudius, 30, 61, 162, 214, 236, 255
public health, 128, 162
punch cards, 159, 599
punctuated equilibrium, 81
Purcell, Henry, 48
purpose, 391–94, *406,* 407, 409, 417, 451, 453
    choice of content and, 393–94
    in Christianity, 407–8
    in East Asia, 396–97
    in Europe, 401
    in Islam, 400
    saintliness vs., 394
    work, 392–93
Pushkin, Aleksander, 318
p values, 341–42
Pynchon, Thomas, 81
Pythagoras, 228, 241
    musical scales discovered by, 217
Pythagorean Theorem, 85
Pythagorean triangle, 228

qasida, 321
Quakers, 405

qualified sources, 79
qualitative arguments, 331
quality, 452
quantitative arguments, 331, 451
quantitative chemistry, 124, 160
quantum theory, 233
Quetelet, Adolphe, 73
Quevedo y Vallegas, Francisco de, 338

race, 25, 295, 432
Racine, Jean, 454
racism, 86
radiation, 126
radio, 129, 315, 437
radium, 159
Raft of the Medusa (Gericault), 205
railroads, 255, 315
Ramanujan, 132, 153–54
Ramayana, 114, 140, 219, 325
Rameau, Jean, 48, 319
Ramses II, 11
random-effects model, 373, 610, 615
random-effects option, 375–77
Raphael (Sanzio), 74, 75, 89, 137, 144, 317, 333, 353
rare events, 430
rationality, 401–2
ratios, 310
Rawls, John, 385–86
raw scores, 79
realism, 138, 211, 212–13, 216, 327, 600
realistic change, 433
realized capacities, 389, 401
reason, 49
Rebatet, Lucien, 109–10, *109*
recession, 337
Redi, Francesco, 240
reductio ad absurdum, 231
Reformation, 299, 407
refraction, 237
refrigeration, 315
regression analysis, 340–43, 379, 608–9
    elite cities, 367–70, *369, 370*
    fixed-effects option in, 375–77
    freedom of action, 371–75, *372, 374*
    full model, 375–77, *376*
    interpreting results of, 341–42
    for models, 365–67, *365, 366, 367*
    random-effects option in, 375–77
    for war and civil unrest, 346–48, *348*
regression coefficients, 471–72
regression equations, 310
regression techniques, Poisson family of, 344

reinforcement, 387
relativism, 70, 360
relativity, theory of, 59, 148, 455
reliability, 81
religion, 6, 418
    arts and, 455–57
    in prehistoric era, 6
    see also specific religions
Rembrandt van Rijn, xvi, 54, 72, 75, 89, 206, 317, 333, 339
Remington, Frederic, 115, 250
ren, 41–42
Renaissance, 8, 29, 161, 232, 235, 305, 379, 410, 434
    architecture in, 260–61
    art of, 48, 317
    Christianity in, 403
    Copernicus' heliocentric model in, 62
    English, 71
    experiments in, 238
    in Florence, xix, 333, 337, 339, 350
    Italian, 299, 337, 357, 407, 417, 420
    painting in, 411
    physics in, 161
    tonal harmony in, 218
Renaissance Catholicism, 618
Renoir, Pierre Auguste, 206
republics, 361–62, 371, 372, 373
    oligarchical, 371
reputations, 73
    shifting, 83, 207, 445
Restoration, 9
résumé of human species, 76
Revolutionibus Orbium Coelestium, De (Copernicus), 150, 413–14
Reynolds, Joshua, 48, 49
rhythm, 218
Ribera, Jusepe de, 317
Richards, I. A., 70
Richardson, Samuel, 48, 221, 412
Richard the Lion-heart, 9
richness, 260, 452
    of structure, 410
rights, constitutional, 361
right triangles, 228
Rig Veda, 224–25
Rimpa school, 136
risk management, 229, 233
roads, 162
Robin Hood, 9
Rodgers, Richard, 115
Rojas, Fernando, 275
Roman Britain, 10

Roman Britain (*continued*)
  comfort in, 46
  transportation in, 45
Romanticism:
  in literature, xx, 48, 142
  in music, 218
Rome, xviii, 9–10, 14, 27, 29, 33–35, 357, 235, 399, 455
  Antonine, *see* Antonine Rome
  fall of, 34, 260
  law in, 30–31
  Republican, 30, 32
  slavery in, 32
Rossi, Salamone, 275
Rouge et le Noir, Le (Stendhal), 421
Rousseau, Jean-Jacques, 50, 133, 142, 316, 412
  as polymath, 115
rubber, 315
Rubens, Peter Paul, 74, 89, 317, 339
Ruisdael, Jacob van, 339
running, 101, *102*
Rushdie, Salman, 431
Ruskin, John, 69
Russell, Bertrand, 133, 223
Russia, 255, 362, 373, 374
  accomplishment in, 296–98
  as autocracy, 363
  Jews in, 276–77, 281, 291, 307
  Orthodox Christianity in, 403
  property rights in, 363
  war and civil unrest in, 33, 347
  see also Soviet Union
Russian Revolution, 281, 362
Rutherford, Ernest, 126, 130

Sachs, Hans, 275
Sacsayhuaman, walls at, 20
Sagan, Carl, 105
Saikaku, 141
St. Martial monastery, 218
St. Paul's Cathedral, 28
St. Petersburg, 357
Sandburg, Carl, xvi
Sankara, 132, 133, 143, 144, 326
Sanskrit literature, 325
Santa Maria, 33
Santa Maria Novello, 215
Sappho, 266, 290
Sarton, George, 256, 275
Sartre, Jean-Paul, 393
Satyricon (Petronius), 27, 220, 221
Saunders, J. J., 400
Saving Private Ryan, 454

Savonarola, Girolamo, 333
Saxony, 298, 363
Sayili, Aydin, 400
Scandinavia, 21
Scarlatti, Alessandro, 319
Scarlatti, Domenico, 48, 319
scatter diagrams, 467–68, *468, 470*
scatter plots, 299–300, *301–3*
Scheele, Carl, 124
  as Brick Layer, 153
Schiller, Johann, 70, 318
Schoch, Robert, 23
Schoenberg, Arnold, 64, 424
Scholasticism, 237
Schopenhauer, Arthur, 133
Schubert, Franz, 54
science:
  accomplishment past 1950 in, 453
  autonomy and, 394–95
  biographical sources in, 108
  chronologies of, 157–58, *158*
  cities and, 360
  collegiality of, 395–96
  complexity in, 437–38
  craft in, 410
  declining accomplishment in, 435–40
  difficulty explanation for, 105–6
  discovery as building block of, 207
  environment for, 429
  in Europe, 275, 299–300
  excellence in, 60–62
  history of, 85, 206, 440
  human capital in, 428, 435
  importance vs. excellence in, 61–62
  individuals vs. teams in, 436
  market saturation in, 428, 435–36
  meta-inventions in, 211, 233–43
  as natural philosophy, 215
  organizing structure in, 410
  principles in, 410
  System Builders vs. Brick Layers in, 147, 151, 152–53
  tools in, 410–11
  transcendental goods in, 418–29, 422
  truth in, 148, 419, 453
  women in, 268–71, 274, *274,* 275, 286, 290
  see also hard sciences; *specific sciences*
Science and Technology Firsts, 158
Science and Technology in World History (McClellan and Dorn), 254–55
sciences combined inventory, *130,* 143
scientific inventories, 121, 143, 147–53, 500–503

accomplishment rate in, 311
combined chart, 121
Eurocentrism and, 84–85, 251–58, *252, 258*
for events, 78
industrial cities and, 369–70
Jews in, 282
misleading, 438
1950 cutoff for, 81–82
non-whites in, 283–85, *284*
number of significant figures in, 345
organizing structures in, 413–15
of persons, 78
polymaths in, 114
purpose of, 435
significant events in, 157–62
women in, 266
scientific literature, 90–91, *92,* 105
scientific method, 403, 410, 413, 453, 601, 619
as meta-invention, 211, 233–34, 244, 599–600
as organizing method, 410
scientific reports, 242–43
scientific research, 400
scientific revolution, 226, 617
scientists, 107
Lotka's study of, 90–91
significant vs. other, 429
undiscovered, 109
Scotland, 44, 298
Enlightenment in, 50
Lowland, 298
Scott, Walter, 142, 318
Scream (Munch), 205
sculpture, 212, 333, 453
anonymity of Chinese, 78
see also visual arts
scurvy, 46
Sebokht, Severus, 231
secondary qualities, 240
Second Treatise of Government (Locke), 49
secularization, 405, 407, 422
secular observation of nature, 211, 233, 234–35, 244
sedimentation, 39
Sei Shonagon, 328
self-actualization, 387–89
self-expression, 420
self-sufficiency, 402
semiotics, 70
sensationalism, 421, 423
sensory nerves, 29
sentiment, 63–64, 68–69
September 11, 8
Sesshu, 136, 143, 260, 327

Seurat, Georges, 206–7
sex, 25, 289, 432
Shaftesbury, Lord Ashley, seventh earl of, 278
Shakespeare, William, 8, 9, 54, 59, 95, 104, 106, 114, 144, 145–46, 155, 259, 287, 299, 318, 399, 431, 442
as first in inventory, 120, 142, 143, 207, 421
postmodernist criticism of, 71
ups and downs in reputation of, 83
Shakuntala (Kalidasa), 147
Shanxi, 37
Shapin, Steven, 242
Shelley, Percy Bysshe, 318
Shen Gua, 39, 236
Sheridan, Richard Brinsley, 48, 49
Shockley, William, 93
Sholokhov, Mikhail, 362
Shostakovich, Dmitri, 362
Siberia, 363
Sicily, 373
Siemens, Charles, 129
Siena, 9, 433
significant events, 157–207, 259, 312
in the arts, 205–7
determination of, 158, *158*
roster of, 159–62
in scientific inventories, 157–62
significant figures vs., 159
significant figures, 79, 107–17, *113*
amount of recent, 428
classifying of, 478–80
decline in production of, 380
distribution of, *248*
in elite cities, 360–61
in Europe, 299–300, 301–3
freedom of action and, 374–75, *374*
lagged value of, 365, *365, 366*
least, 116–17, *117*
non-significant figures vs., 115–17
origins of, *301–3,* 355–58, *356*
in other domains, 365–67, *367*
political systems and, 371–72, *372*
ratio of, 429
roster of, 513–88
significant events vs., 159
upward climb of, 379
in U.S., 304–5, *304, 306*
variance in, 345, 379–80, *380*
war and, 332–36, 340–41, *348, 351*
wealth and, 349–51, *350*
women as, *267, 268, 269*
Silesia, 297, 300
Simon, Herbert, 93, 392

Simonton, Dean, xvii, 82, 92, 94, 207, 344, 354–55, 360, 381, 431
Simpsons, The, 454
Sinclair, Upton, 116
Sistine Chapel, 54, 59, 90, 145, 149, 205, 289, 392
Sivin, Nathan, 253, 254–55
Skeptical Chymist (Boyle), 414
Skinner, B. F., 387
Slovakia, 300
smallpox, 46–47
Smeaton, John, 129
Smith, Adam, 49, 50–51, 229
Smith, William, as Brick Layer, 153
Smollett, Tobias, 45
Social and Cultural Dynamics (Sorokin), 335, 346
social conditions, 331
social construction, 70
    sex differences and, 289
socialism, 422–23
social sciences, 77, 331, 450
    statistical analysis in, 233
    statistical significance in, 342
Socrates, 10, 223–24, 287, 316, 333, 354, 402
Socratic dialogues, 225
solar system, 30, 62, 150, 161
Solomon, Maynard, 146
solstices, 160
Song China, 25, 32–42, 235, 322, 324, 381
    art in, 39–40
    astronomy in, 38–39
    bureaucracy in, 40–41
    census in, 34
    earth science in, 39
    economic organization in, 38
    examination system in, 40–41
    experimentalism in, 235–37
    industrial, 37–38
    literature in, 40
    mathematics in, 38
    medicine in, 39, 46
    national economy in, 37
    philosophy in, 41–42
    religion in, 41
    tribute system of, 33
    water system and shipping in, 37
    see also Huangzhou
Song Hangzhou, 46, 51, 262
    administration in, 36
    arts in, 47
    cleanliness of, 34
    food and restaurants in, 36–37

peaceful character of, 41
    public amenities in, 35
    wealth and poverty in, 35
Sophism, 225
Sophocles, 26, 220, 260, 333, 354
Sorokin, Pitirim, 335, 346, 446
Sotatsu, 136, 143, 327
South America, 254
South Asia, 452
    art forms of, 260
    science in, 275
Southeast Asia, art forms of, 260
Soviet Union, 362, 422, 620
    literature in, 362
    music in, 362
    science in, 362–63
    as totalitarian, 371
    visual arts in, 362
Spain, 20, 85, 298, 307, 333, 337–39
    art from, 338
    Inquisition in, 364, 373, 375
    literature from, 338
    Moorish, 275
    music from, 338
    wealth of, 337–38, 339, 364
Spanish Armada, 335
spectroheliograph, 122
Spengler, Oswald, xvii, 82, 446, 623
Spenser, Edmund, 318
Spinoza, Baruch, 275, 316, 339
spontaneous generation, 240
sports, excellence in, 97–101, 98, 99, 100, 102
Sputnik, 8
stability, 81
Stadler, Wolf, 74–75
Stalin, Joseph, 281, 362
Stamitz, Johann, 48
standard deviations, 88, 366, 461–66
    computation of, 463–64
    frequency distribution and, 463
    need for, 461
    percentiles vs., 466
staphylococcus, 149
stars, 150
    binary, 150
    composition of, 411
    formation, 122
    maps of, 160
statistics, 68, 74, 120, 233
    explanation of, 461–73
    objectivity and, 65
    reliability of, 80

significance in, 341–42
see also specific terms
steam engine, 44, 50, 129, 315, 414–15
Steamer in a Snowstorm (Turner), 216
steamships, 315
steel, 315
Stein, Werner, 157
Steinbeck, John, 116
Steinberg, Saul, 7
stem cell research, 418
Stendhal, 318, 421
Stent, Gunther, 438–39
Stephenson, George, 129
sterilization, 128
still life paintings, 215–16
stirrup, 155–57
Stoics, 31, 402
Stove, David, 601
Strabo, 30
Strato, 30
Strauss, Johann, Jr., 444
Stravinsky, Igor, 425
string quartets, 411
string theory, 81
Structure of Scientific Revolutions (Kuhn), 155
Strutt, John, 116
Strutt, Robert, 116
Studies in Medieval and Renaissance History, 157
Study of History, A (Toynbee), 446
Sukenick, Ronald, 393
Sumatra, 33
Sumer, 10, 14, 16, 21, 222, 599
    artistic conventions in, 212
    mathematics in, 228
    money and credit in, 229
    number system in, 228
    written language in, 211
sunspots, 38, 122, 234
Surrealism, 216
surveying, 228
Swammerdam, Jan, 339
Sweden, 298
    authors from, 250–51
Swift, Jonathan, 412
Switzerland, 298, 357, 390
    Jewish emancipation in, 276
    as republic, 371, 373
syllogism, 226
symphonies, 212, 410, 446
Syria, 231
Syriac civilization, 16
systematic investigation, 236, 451

System Builders, 147, 151, 152–53

tabula rasa, 49
Tagore, Rabindranath, 140
Tahiti, 42, 43
Taiko Josetsu, 327
Tailleferre, Germaine, 266
Tale of Genji, The (Murasaki), 141,
    220, 221, 222, 267, 328
Talmud, 233, 276, 292
Tartaglia, Niccolò, 242
Tartuffe (Molière), 363
taste, 62, 63, 66, 69
Tate Gallery, 216
Tawney, Richard, 338
taxonomic systems, 61–62
Tchaikovsky, Piotr, 287, 386
technology, 60, 153, 300
    application of truth in, 60–61
    brothers in, 114
    central events in, 160, 162, *198–204*
    chronologies of, 157–58, *158*
    complexity in, 437–38
    database for, 76
    declining accomplishment in, 435–40
    fashion and assessment of, 82
    organizing structures for, 414–15
    principles of, 415
    System Builders in, 152–53
    tools for, 414
technology inventory, 121, *129,* 130, 143, 251,
    264, 315, *315*
    accomplishment rate for, 315, *315*
    women in, 266
Technology in World Civilization (Pacey), 254–55
telegraph, 315, 449
Telemann, Georg Philipp, 48, 319
telephone, 148
telescope, 122, 312, 414, 438
television, 429–30, 442
tennis, 97, 101, *102*
    Grand Slam in, 101, *102*
Terman study of gifted children, 291–92
testosterone, 289
textiles, 5, 315
Thackeray, William, 86
Thales, 230–31, 234–35
theaters, ancient, 219
Themistius, 219
Theophrastus, 333
"Theory of Human Motivation, A" (Maslow),
    387

Theory of the Earth, With Proofs and Illustrations (Hutton), 160
thermometer, 414
Thespis, 219
Third of May, 1808, The (Goya), 421
Thirty Years' War, 333, 335, 336, 340
Thomas Aquinas, 223, 402–3, 404, 416, 457, 618
Thornton, Bruce, 401–2
Thucydides, 26, 333
Thurber, James, 115–16
Tiberius, Emperor of Rome, 353
Tikhy Don (Sholokhov), 362
time, understanding scale of, 7–12
timekeeping, 129
time-series analysis, 354–55
Timetables of History, The (Grun), 157
Timetables of Science, The, 157–58
Tipitaka, 227
Titian (Vecellio), 63, 66–67, 69, 71, 72, 74, 89, 144, 317, 458
Tohaku, 327
tolerant autocracy, 373
Tolstoy, Leo, 155, 207, 318, 444
Tom Jones (Fielding), 221, 412
Tom Sawyer (Twain), 421
tonal harmony, 217, 218, 410, 413
tools, 3, 4–5, 410, 411, 412, 413, 414, 425
Torah, 226
totalitarian states, 343, 362–63, 371, 372, 373
Tour de France, 120
Toynbee, Arnold, xvii, 446, 623
trade routes, 399
tradition, innovation vs., 395, 397–99, 452
Traité Élémentaire de Chemie (Lavoisier), 159
transcendental goods, 409, 415–25, 451–52
    in the arts, 420–22, 453
    changes in role of, 422–25
    in science, 418–19
transcendentals, 416
transcontinental traffic, 315
transportation, 162
traumatic injuries, 314
Très Riches Heures du Duc de Berry, Les (Limbourg brothers), 205
trial and error, 235
triangles:
    Pythagorean, 228
    right, 228
trigonometry, 414
Trilling, Lionel, 220
Trinity (Masaccio), 412
Trojan War, 10
Trojan Women, The (Euripides), 260

truth, xix, 60–61, 416, 417, 418, 422, 452, 453, 456
    in the arts, 420–21, 453
    paradigm vs., 155
    in science, 419, 453
tuberculosis, 128
Turgenev, Ivan, 318
Turkey, 400
Turner, J. M. W., 85, 216
Tuscany, 298, 299, 433
Twain, Mark, 68, 116, 262, 421, 427
twenty-first century, 453
typhus, 46

Uffizi gallery, 27
uncertainty, calibration of, 211
Union of Soviet Writers, 362
United States, 73, 85, 307, 347
    artists from, 250, 261–62
    cities in, 367–70
    declinism in, 446–47
    figures significant only in, 116, 261–62
    Jews in, 276, 278, 280–81, 291
    Ph.D. rate in, 433
    population and accomplishment in, 310, 429
    religion in, 407
    science in, 261, 363, 433
    significant figures in, 304–5, *304, 306*
    South in, 304–5
    wealth of, 349, 350
universe, history of, 160–61
universities, 615, 623–24
    elite, 358, 368, 369, 370, 376
    growth in, 433
    non-elite, 368
Unkei, 327
unweighted accomplishment rate, 310–11
Upanishads, 132, 133, 223, 224
uplift, 39
Uranus, 150
U.S. Open, 100, 101

Valmiki, 114, 140
vase paintings, Greek, 213, 214
Veda, 132
Vega, Garcilaso de la, 20
Velazquez, Diego, 74, 147–48, 205, 317, 338
Velleius Paterculus, 353–54, 381
Venetia, 298
Venice, 9, 296, 339, 371
    as authoritarian republic, 361–62, 371
Venn diagrams, 109, *109,* 110
Venus, transit of, 42–43

Venus de Milo, 26, 155
Venus of Urbino (Titian), 63, 66–67, 71, 72
Verlaine, Paul, 318
Vermeer, Jan, 317, 333, 339
vernacular writing, 412
Vesalius, Andreas, 314
Vida de Lazarilla de Tormes, La, 221
Vietnam War, 8
Vikings, 21
violence, 421
Virgil, 10, 26, 31, 142
virtue, 224, 227
visual arts, 212, 260–61, 455
   achievement in, 54–55
   anonymity in, 78, 260
   auction prices for, 454
   Baroque in, 299
   cities and, 360
   craft, 411
   database for, 76
   delayed recognition in, 82
   environment for, 429
   organizing structure in, 410
   pre -800, 14
   principles in, 411
   structural change in, 412
   tools in, 411, 412
   transcendental goods in, 417, 420–21, 423–25
   Western vs. non-Western figures in, 259
visual arts inventory, 88
   for China, 78, 84
   for Japan, 78
   for West, 78, 79, 84, 85
   women in, 266, 274–75, *274,* 290
Vital, David, 275–76
Vivaldi, Antonio, 48, 85, 319
Vivarini family, 114
vocation, 393, 406–7, 452
volcanos, 30
Voltaire, 50, 142, 316
vulcanization, 315
Vyasa, 114, 140

Wagner, Richard, 68, 134
Wales, 298
   polyphony in, 218
Wallace, Alfred Russel, 148–49
Wallis, John, 313
Wang Wei, 322
war and civil unrest, 332–36
   major European, 334–35
   regression analysis for, 346–48, *348,* 351, 377
War and Peace (Tolstoy), 155, 207, 444

Warhol, Andy, 69, 81
Watergate, 8
Watson, John, 387
Watt, James, 44, 50, 129, 143, 414
wealth, 332, 336–40, 380, 409, 432–33, 612
   regression analyses of, 349–51, *350*
Wealth of Nations (Smith), 50–51
Weber, Max, 403
weighted accomplishment rate, 311
welfare state, 229
Weltgeschicte der Musik (Honolka), 109–10, *109*
Wen Shu, 266
West:
   aesthetics in, 70
   arts inventories for, 250
   mathematics in, 230
   meta-inventions of, 244
   philosophy in, 224, 324
   popular culture of, 454
   significant figures in, 259–61
Western accomplishment rate, decline in, 329
Western art, 299
   biographical sources for, 108
   borderline figures in, 115
   brothers and families in, 114
   calculating eminence in, 74–75, 88–90
   significant events in, 205–7
   women in, 274–75, *274*
Western art inventory, 78, 79, 84, 85, *89, 91,*
      120, 121, *137,* 143, 144, 320, 322
   accomplishment rate for, 311, 317, *317*
   American artists in, 250, 251
   number of significant figures in, 345
   people vs. works, 205–6
Western civilization, 262, 381
   decline in, 446
   models in, 354–55
Western Europe, 403
   cultural coherence in, 447
Western individualism, 210
Western literature:
   accomplishment rate in, 427, 429–30
   borderline figures in, 115
   brothers in, 114
   lost, 260
   women in, 274, *274*
Western literature inventory, 78, 85–86, *142,*
      143, 250–51
   accomplishment rate for, 311, 318, *318*
   number of significant figures in, 345
Western music:
   borderline figures in, 115
   lost, 260

Western music (*continued*)
women in, 274–75, *274*
Western music inventory, 78, 85, 110, 120, *134,* 143
accomplishment rate for, 311, 319, *319*
number of significant figures in, 345
Western philosophy inventory, 78, 85, 121, *133,* 143, 144, 262
accomplishment rate for, 311, 316, *316*
significant figures in, 345
wheel, 14, 155
Whistler, James McNeill, 262
White, Lynn, 155–57
White, Robert, 388
Whitehead, Alfred North, 144, 223
white males, 84, 451
dead, 25, 265
Whitman, Walt, 262, 287, 318
Why Men Rule (Goldberg), 289
Wilde, Oscar, 287
Will, George F., 105
willfulness, autonomy vs., 395
William of Ockham, 238
Williams, Ted, 104
Wilson Chronology of Science and Technology, The, 158
winner-take-all markets, 443–44, 623
Winner-Take-All Society, The (Frank and Cook), 443
Winter's Tale, A (Shakespeare), 54
Wolfe, Thomas, 116
women, 86, 265–75, 432
achievement since 1950, 273–75, *274*
biology and, 288–91
in *DoSB,* 268–71
environment and, 286–87
exclusion and emancipation of, 267
index scores of, 267–68, *269*
in inventories, *266,* 267–69
IQ and, 289
low numbers of, 143, 285–91
motherhood and, 287–88
Nobel Prizes won by, 273–74, *273*
rights of, 51

verbal skills of, 289
Women in Science: Antiquity through the Nineteenth Century (Ogilvie), 272
women's studies, 271–72
Wood, Grant, 250
Woods, Tiger, 596
Wordsworth, William, 318
work, in achieving excellence, 392–93
World War I, xviii, 281, 300, 357, 358, 420, 422
World War II, xviii, 300, 358, 360, 420
Wright brothers, 114, 159
Writers Guild, 442
written language, 210–11, 589, 598–99
Wu Daozi, *135,* 322
Wyndham, William, 49

Xerxes, 332
Xu Xi, 40

Yeats, William Butler, xix, 422
Yoga, 225, 326
Yoga-sutras, 326
Yongle, Emperor of China, 33–34
Yosa Buson, 327
Yule, George, 92

Zeitgeist, 429
Zeno of Elea, 225
zero, 9, 161, 231–32
Zeuxis, 27, 136, 260, 333
Zhang Xuan, 322
Zhao Mengfu, *135,* 143, 260
Zhejiang, 37
Zheng He, 33, 34, 262
Zhuangzi, 210, 223, 324
Zhu Shijie, 233
Zhu Xi, 42, 131, 324
Zola, Émile, 318, 423, 427
zoology, 123, 399
invertebrate, 123
Zoshchenko, Mikhail, 362
Zurbaran, Francisco de, 317, 338
Zurich, 371